Good Schools for Young Children

Who Am I?

I am a child.
I live in suburbia, the ghetto, Appalachia, on the Reservation—
   I live anywhere.
I go to nursery school, Head Start, day care center, kindergarten—
   This is my first day. I am new.
I don't know what my teacher says.
I don't understand her so I don't listen.
   I don't know what to do.
I do nothing.

I don't listen.
   I don't sit still. I bother children.
I am naughty. I am unhappy. . . .

Today the teacher smiled at me!
   "Hello—I'm glad to see you this morning!"
I see some trucks—I roll them and roll them—
I take blocks and make a garage for my trucks.
   I lie on the rug and look at it.
My teacher says, "You made a big garage.
   You used some red blocks.
Let's count together and see how many red blocks you used.
Let's see how many wheels are on that truck 1-2-3-4.
   You can count!"
I feel very, very good!

That child next to me—
She wanted to make a garage too—I helped her.
   We made a garage. We put a big truck in it.
We had two garages and two trucks.
We counted eight green blocks.
   I feel good. I am happy.
My teacher likes me.

That girl and I play together. She likes me.
   I feel good!
I'm glad I'm me!

Adapted from "Who Am I?" by Theron Jacobson. *Educ. Leadership,* **23**:2 (1965), pp. 121–123.

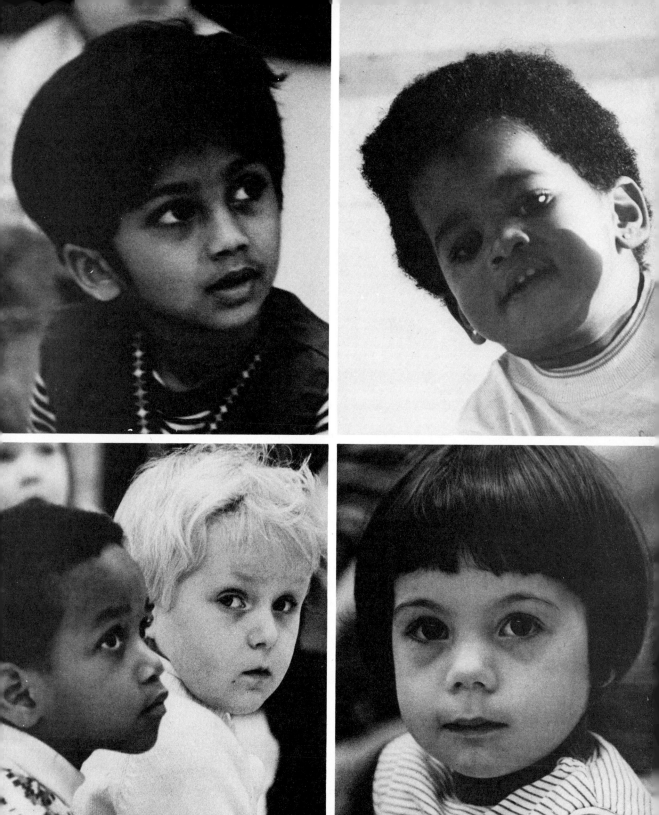

Good Schools for Young Children

Third Edition

A Guide for Working with Three-, Four-,
and Five-Year-Old Children

Sarah Hammond Leeper
University of Maryland

Ruth J. Dales
Florida State University

Dora Sikes Skipper
Florida State University

Ralph L. Witherspoon
University of South Carolina

MACMILLAN PUBLISHING CO., INC.
NEW YORK

COLLIER MACMILLAN PUBLISHERS
LONDON

Macmillan Publishing Co., Inc.
866 Third Avenue, New York, New York 10022

Collier-Macmillan Canada, Ltd.

Library of Congress Cataloging in Publication Data

Leeper, Sarah Hammond,
   Good schools for young children.

   Includes bibliographies.
   1. Education, Preschool. I. Title.
LB1140.L4   1974   372.21   72-13973
ISBN 0-02-369280-4

Printing: 6 7 8   Year: 7 8 9 80

Preface

The 1960's and early 1970's brought many changes in early childhood education. They include (1) operational changes in the schools and centers; (2) programs for disadvantaged children; (3) revision in curricula and facilities in the preparation of teachers; and (4) more parent involvement. These changes were in response to a growing concern for all children, resulting in an expansion of public kindergartens, day care services, and other programs for young children.

No longer are all centers planned alike. Instead they are planned according to the needs of the children who are now attending the school and their parents. Basic values and principles are retained and utilized but the operational procedures vary in different communities and even in centers in the same community.

All persons who guide the development of young children need an understanding of the child, his world, and the forces that influence him, as well as the basic principles on which decisions are made regarding instruction and practice. This third edition has been prepared to fulfill the need of the undergraduate students in early childhood education and teachers who are inexperienced or who have little training in working with young children. The graduate student should also find this book valuable for study and reference in regard to research and practice. Parents, volunteers, and aides who are interested in the development and education of young children will likewise find this book a helpful guide.

The interdisciplinary approach in this volume emphasizes the interrelationship of the culture, the research relating to children, the goals sought, and the practices employed. As a basis for planning the program for young children, the findings of research in biological, sociological, and psychological areas are utilized. Factors in the social scene that influence children, their homes, and family life, along with their implications for schools for young children, are included. Extensive lists of related readings and of suggested activities are to be found at the end of each chapter. The photographs, illustrations, and case records are of real persons in actual situations and activities. They are used to clarify and extend concepts.

The book is divided into three parts:

Part I, "Why Centers for Young Children?," considers the young child as a person and the importance of the early years of his life in relation to the effects of present-day society and culture upon the child, the goals of education for young children in a democracy, and the guidance and discipline which the child receives. The chapter on historical development of schools for young children provides a basis for understanding the importance of such schools. Two new chapters have been added. Current developments including innovations, Head Start and implementation of planned variations, and other intervention and compensatory programs are presented in light of today's complex and changing society.

Part II, "The Curriculum: Planning and Teaching," develops the school program within the framework of the concepts presented in Part I. Each subject area is planned to take these factors into account. The developmental sequence and suggested teaching strategies, activities, and learning encounters are discussed for each subject area. In planning and teaching, however, the subject areas are not isolated; they are interrelated in treating the concerns that young children have and wish to pursue.

Part III, "Organizing Centers for Young Children," concentrates on details essential to the organization of a good program for children, records and reports, physical facilities and equipment, working with children who have uniquely different needs, parental involvement, and the transition to the first grade.

S. H. L.
R. J. D.
D. S. S.
R. L. W.

Acknowledgments

The authors express sincere appreciation to their co-workers at the Florida State University, the University of Maryland, and the University of South Carolina. Special recognition is given to Mrs. Sarah Blackford, Dr. Nancy Douglas, Mrs. Geraldine Edwards, Mrs. Julia Fussell, Miss Harriet Harlan, Miss Lucy Harrison, Mrs. Anna Lane, Miss LaMattice Pearson, and Miss Susie Whitener at the Florida State University, who assisted with the first edition.

Grateful appreciation is expressed to the following persons who helped with the second edition: at the Florida State University, Dr. Myles Ritchie for photography, Mrs. Phyllis C. Smith for illustrative material, and Dr. Donald W. Rapp for material on acoustics; at the University of Maryland, Dr. Glenn O. Blough, Dr. Jo Graham, Dr. Joan E. Moyer, Miss Miriam E. Quigley, and Mrs. Tupper D. Webster.

In development of the third edition, the authors are deeply indebted to their families, friends, and professional associates. They wish to thank the following persons: Dr. Robert R. Leeper for editorial assistance; Mr. Colin K. Ducolon,

Mrs. Jean C. Findley, Mrs. Arlene Friedland, Mrs. April Garrard, Mrs. Cynthia Jones, Mrs. Elizabeth T. King, and Mrs. Helen Rubin for help with illustrative materials; co-workers at the University of Maryland, Mrs. Susan H. Akman, Dr. Louise M. Berman, Mr. Charles Bohn, Dr. Marilyn J. Church, Mrs. Rose Marie Dorn, Dr. Robert V. Duffey, Dr. Walter N. Gantt, Miss Nancy Goldsmith (Head Start Regional Training Officer), Mrs. Joan B. Kissinger, Mrs. Marion L. Leiserson, Dr. Carol Seefeldt, Mrs. Lynn E. Sherald, Mrs. Shirley Shelley, Mr. O. Eugene Smith, Dr. V. Phillips Weaver, Mrs. Tupper D. Webster, and Dr. David L. Williams; and Dean John C. Otts and the Early Childhood faculty of the College of Education, University of South Carolina.

Credits for photographs follow. Charles Bohn, Frontispiece, 1, 2b, 3, 5, 6, 8a, 9a, c, 10a, b, c, 11, 14a, b, 16a, 17a, b, c, d, 18a, b, 22, 23, 26, 27, 29, 30, 31a, b, c, d, 34, 35, 36, 40a, b, 41, 42a, b, c, 43, 46, 47, 51, 52, 53, 54; Fred Dickson, 9e, 38, 39; Rita Eisenberg, 24, 49a, b, c, d, e; April Garrard, 12, 19, 28, 45; Head Start, 2a (Esther Bubley, Children's Bureau), 8b, 9b, d, 13a, b, 15 (James Foote), 25, 32, 37, 48, 56; Helen Rubin, 57.

Contents

Why Centers
for Young
Children?

Part I

Figure 1. (OVERLEAF) The early years are important learning years.

The Early Years: Their Importance

Chapter 1

Each September witnesses a familiar American scene as thousands of young children—radiantly alive, anxious, trusting, hopeful—enter school for the first time. A tremendous responsibility is placed upon the schools and their teachers, for everyone believes that these youngsters are the hope of the future. Schools cannot afford to ignore the mistakes or gains of the past, for today's world is far more complicated than ever before, and there is a growing feeling that the demands on every life, if not properly met, can be disastrous. But what about the first half-decade of life? How prepared are these children for the reality and demands of school? Does it matter, educationally, what has gone before? In America, until recently, there has been little concern for the education of the young child.

Although parents today are better educated than ever before, our educational system has given little time to preparation for marriage, to studies of home and family life, or to a consideration of child-rearing practices. Most information of this type must be gained from one's own experience, from certain professional personnel such as the pediatrician or family doctor, and from the flood of conflicting views found in all types of popular books, magazines, and newspapers. Consequently, many children approach the school experience with fear and trepidation. Some, too, come with severe, unavoidable physical, mental, and emotional handicaps. Fortunately, such children constitute a small minority of the total child population.

As a result of the ever-increasing affluence of American economic life and of the demands of a complex technological society, those persons without special skills and without advanced education are greatly disadvantaged. The public school, with its relatively late entrance age, became less and less able to cope with the two to three years learning retardation present at school entrance in children from disadvantaged homes. Researchers had found that young children lacking the opportunity to experience the learning environment common to middle-class children had great difficulty in bridging the gap. They often became early school dropouts and later joined the ranks of the unemployed. In an effort to break the poverty cycle thus engendered, the federal government provided unprecedented funds for the education of children from disadvantaged homes—especially preschool-age children. Thus the value of early education quickly became accepted and the young child was "rediscovered" by educators, the public, and the parents.

Schools must be prepared to meet the needs of these disadvantaged children as well as those of the great majority for whom the conditions of nature and nurture have been more favorable.

During the 1960's, the realization that one fourth of the children entering first grade were from one to three years retarded academically called for a re-evaluation of the educational system. The public schools in the United States came under severe attack. Costs continued to rise, citizens revolted at rising taxes, and bonds issues were repeatedly voted down in many communities. Crime and delinquency were on the rise and high school dropouts increased. The federal government was called on to provide more funds to bolster the school system. Children primarily from low income families had been denied the early experiential opportunities so necessary for normal cognitive growth enjoyed by their counterparts from middle and upper income families. Early (preschool) education for the first time in the history of the nation became the priority educational concern of educators, communities, and government.

Recently, the mother of a five-year-old started a conversation in the following manner: "Is it true that the first few years of a child's life are the most important?" Without waiting for a reply, she added, "I feel so helpless now that Mary is five years old. I'm afraid I have made too many mistakes and that there is nothing I can do about them now!" Such concepts often stem from only partially understanding what is written in popular articles about the young child; and far too often from the rather perfunctory treatment given child psychology in many introductory textbooks on psychology and child development. Emphasis on the futility of aiding the child's personality after the age of five could easily arise as a result of reading some of the popular interpretations of Freudian psychology. On the other hand, until the impact of Freud's theories began to be felt in the early part of the present century, it was all too commonly believed that the early years were unimportant as long as the physical needs of the child were met.

The questions asked by Mary's mother and by many young mothers today reveal the fears mothers have of frustrating their children by disciplining them, or of developing overdependent children by not giving them enough attention. Many have developed guilt feelings about not being "good mothers." It is generally agreed that the present generation of parents is more concerned about the personality development of their children than any generation of parents has ever been. Parents' misconceptions of how personality is influenced, and the lack of understanding on the part of adults in general as to what to expect developmentally from children, point dramatically to the need for study and planning by all persons who teach or work with young children.

To some, education of young children means very little other than what the child happens to learn before starting school, usually at the age of six. To many, education begins with the entrance to a public school. Others realize that there are nursery schools and kindergartens for younger children, but to many it is not necessary that they be "real" schools. Most parents, however, are unaware that play schools, day care centers, nursery schools, and kindergartens are not just different names for the same services. They tend to think of them all as "schools." The importance of understanding these differences will be considered in detail in later chapters.

In recent years, many parents have come to feel that a good nursery school is a "must" for their children because they believe that what happens to a child's personality and his attitudes during the preschool years are very important to later development. They also recognize that the teacher has had, or they expect that she has had, special training for her work, a competency that most parents of young children feel they themselves sadly lack. Yet others feel that a child under six is "still a baby" and needs to be treated as one. These persons think that mothers can provide, at home, all the education that is necessary.

Research conducted during the late 1950's and the early 1960's (to be discussed in Chapter 4) had clearly demonstrated that at a very early age a child can master rather complex learnings such as the abilities to read and to master complex mathematical concepts. Concurrently, emphasis on the necessity of a college education was increasing and the demands for more and better education caused parents to become greatly concerned about the adequacy of their children's education. It was logical to assume that the more a child learned as early as possible, the better his chances would be to meet college entrance requirements. The proponents of a child-centered philosophy for nursery and kindergarten programs found themselves widely criticized by a new influx of researchers and scholars who held that the mastery of knowledge was not only possible and desirable at an early age, but necessary to later school success. It is small wonder that parents were worried if their children were not taught to read in kindergarten. (Throughout this text the authors have carefully evaluated research and implemented the findings in terms of programs of instruction without losing sight of the values inherent in earlier programs with their heavy emphasis on the needs of children at various maturation and developmental levels.)

HISTORICAL PERSPECTIVE

Interest in schools for young children is not a modern innovation. In 1657 Comenius, in *The Great Didactic*,[1] advocated the Mother School for the first six years of life. There was to be a Mother's School in every home for every child. He also advocated prenatal education for mothers. The course of study prescribed in his *School of Infancy*, first published in German in 1633, contained "Simple lessons in objects, taught to know stones, plants, and animals; the names and uses of the members of the body; to distinguish light and darkness and colors; the Geography of the cradle, the room, the farm, the street, and the field; trained in moderation, purity and obedience, and taught to say the Lord's Prayer."[2] Comenius wrote the first picture book for children in 1658, the famous *Orbis Pictus*.[3] This book has been widely used and translated into every major language in the world.

Published in 1762, Rousseau's *Emile* gave great impetus to the importance of beginning education early.[4] Rousseau felt education should commence at birth and be continued until twenty-five years of age. He stressed the need for allowing natural development rather than preparation for later life—"the first of all blessings is not authority, but liberty. This is my fundamental maxim. We have but to apply it to childhood, and all the rules of education will flow from it." His fundamental concept was that sense perception is the only true foundation of human knowledge.

During the early years of the nineteenth century, Frederick Froebel, influenced by the earlier work of Pestalozzi, became convinced that the most needed educational reform concerned the early childhood years.[5] He considered carefully planned play materials essential to the proper education of the young. His gifts and occupations were not mere materials used in play for the sake of play. Rather, proper use of the gifts or material objects and the occupations or play activities expressed spiritual principles of deep philosophic sig-

[1]J. A. Comenius (Komensky), *The Great Didactic*, de Geer Family, Amsterdam, 1657.

[2]W. S. Monroe, ed., *Comenius' School of Infancy* (Boston: D. C. Heath, 1908), p. ix.

[3]J. A. Comenius (Komensky), *Orbis Pictus*, Nuremberg, 1658. (C. W. Bardeen, Syracuse, N.Y.), 1887.

[4]J. J. Rousseau, *Emile*, trans. Barbara Foxley (London: J. M. Dent, 1911), p. 48.

[5]F. Froebel, *The Education of Man* (New York: Appleton-Century-Crofts, 1903).

nificance essential to the child's proper development. Society is indebted to him for the kindergarten idea, which recognized the educational value of play. The first kindergarten was established in Blackenberg in 1842, and the first kindergarten training college was founded by Baroness Bertha von Marenholtz Bülow-Wendhausen, a disciple of Froebel, in 1870 at Dresden. Mrs. Carl Schurz, a pupil of Froebel, established the first kindergarten in the United States at Watertown, Wisconsin, in 1855. This was a German-speaking kindergarten. The first English-speaking kindergarten in the United States was privately operated by Miss Elizabeth Peabody in Boston in 1860. A significant event in the history of education in the United States occurred in 1873 when Susan E. Blow (with William T. Harris) established the first public school kindergarten in St. Louis, Missouri. The following decade witnessed rapid developments in kindergarten education. Since the 1880's the kindergarten movement has had its ups and downs, often giving way to the pressures of the times for public education at other levels. Recent emphasis on quality education, higher education, and the sciences tended to de-emphasize the importance of kindergarten and nursery school education.

In the United States the early 1960's witnessed a revival of early childhood education for exactly the same reason that early education had been advocated so often in the past by such leaders as Froebel, Montessori, the McMillan sisters, and many others. Conditions of the times had created slum cultures that produced serious social problems. In each case it was recognized that the lack of experience in early cognitive manipulations resulted in later incompetence and lack of self-esteem which proved difficult to overcome. Children from better homes seemed to escape these problems; it was therefore thought that early education in the slum home was inadequate. Projects such as Head Start had the same goals as those sponsored by the followers of Froebel, by Montessori, and by the McMillans.

Between periods of social crises, nursery and kindergarten education continued in a limited way, usually without public support but for quite different reasons. Middle- and upper-class parents believed that early education was essential to later school success, or at least necessary to maintaining family status in the community. Although there is evidence that early childhood education found an acceptable place in the academic world during the 1960's, only time will tell the outcome.

In the search for panaceas and quick results, the Montessori approach promised an answer. Montessori schools quickly became popular and were glamorized by magazines, television, and the news media.

Maria Montessori began her work with slum children in Rome in 1907. A medical doctor by profession, she developed methods and accompanying materials that are used in today's schools exactly as she prescribed in the early 1900's. Her principal contributions lie in the emphasis on learning and the importance of the environment in the learning process. However, today's teacher of young children should be familiar enough with the total field of early child-

hood education to choose which of the Montessori concepts, materials, and procedures will best serve children in the context of today's individual and cultural needs. The pros and cons of Montessori are objectively set forth in
Montessori in Perspective.[6] Students of early childhood education should become thoroughly familiar with the history of education in the United States in
order to understand how the needs of society affect educational programs.

TODAY'S NEED

An analysis of census data reveals facts vital to those involved in planning
programs for young children. There were 55,000,000 children under fourteen
years of age in the United States in 1970. Of these, 18,013,000 were under five
years of age. By 1980 these figures are projected to be 52,736,000 for children
under fourteen years of age and 19,881,000 for children under five years of age.[7]
From April 1948 to March 1969 the labor participation rate of mothers of children under six had increased from 12.8 to 30.4.[8] By 1969 more than half of the
mothers who had children from ages 6 to 17 were working. The largest group
of employed mothers were from families where the husband's annual income
was under $7,000, and more of these families proportionately were black
rather than white.[9] Because these employed mothers were married, widowed,
or divorced, it becomes obvious that millions of preschool-age children have
mothers working outside the home and receive little or no education other than
that provided by maids, relatives, or the many day care centers and baby-
sitting services, some of which are inadequate.[10]

Few people realize that in 1970 children under five years of age accounted
for 8.7 per cent of the total population in the United States. The important ten-
year span from twenty-five through thirty-four only amounted to 12.3 per cent,
and 18.6 per cent of all citizens were fifty-five years of age and older. Only
9.3 per cent of the total population were in the adolescent years fifteen through
nineteen.[11] The latter group included the senior high school and lower college
age group where proportionately more dollars are spent for educational purposes.

Of the 9.8 million mothers in the work force in March 1969, 1.2 million were
nonwhite; 63.7 per cent of these nonwhites (compared to 47.3 per cent of whites)

---

[6]*Montessori in Perspective,* National Association for the Education of Young Children, Publication #406 (Washington, D.C., 1966).

[7]*Profiles,* White House Conference on Children, 1970 (Washington, D.C.: Superintendent of
Documents, U.S. Government Printing Office, 1970), p. 85.

[8]Ibid., p. 140.

[9]Ibid., pp. 61–62.

[10]Ibid., p. 85.

[11]Ibid.

had children six to seventeen years old; 44.3 to 26.8 per cent had children under six years of age.[12]

Next to the growing number of employed women, the second force in the increasing demand for making available supplementary child care to all citizens grows out of recent discoveries concerning the importance of early experience on human growth and development. Psychologists, pediatricians, psychiatrists, educators, nutritionists, anthropologists, and other investigators continue to document the critical significance of the first years of life.[13] Despite this increasing recognition of the importance of the early years of life, conditions indicated by the facts presented make difficult the adequate provision for young children's programs.

RESEARCH AND THE EARLY YEARS

The present century has witnessed a shift to intensive early childhood research because of many theoretical points of view concerning the importance of the early years to the later development and behavior of the individual.

The nation experienced a severe case of jitters during the late 1950's blamed on the "late start" in the Space Age race. During the same period practically nothing was spent on the education of preschool-age children. In view of the changed social, economic, and family life in the United States and the rapidly expanding scientific information relative to the importance of the education of the young child, could it be that lack of public concern for education before the age of six is another unfortunate "late start?" A detailed discussion of these factors is presented in the materials prepared for the deliberations of the 1960 White House Conference on Children and Youth.[14]

Noting the needs of young children in today's world, delegates to the 1960 White House Conference on Children and Youth stressed that nursery schools, kindergartens, day care centers and other children's groups be open to children of all socioeconomic levels, creeds, and national origins. They further recommended that every organized group of young children away from home be under the supervision of at least one person qualified in the field of early childhood education.[15]

It is of significance to note that the *Report to the President* issued by the 1970

---

[12]*Report to the President*, White House Conference on Children, 1970 (Washington, D.C.: Superintendent of Documents, U.S. Government Printing Office, 1970), p. 230.

[13]Ibid., p. 276.

[14]E. Ginzberg, ed., *The Nation's Children*, 3 vols., and *Children and Youth in the 1960's, Survey Papers* (Washington, D.C.: The Golden Anniversary White House Conference on Children and Youth, Inc., 1960).

[15]*Conference Proceedings* (Washington, D.C.: The Golden Anniversary White House Conference on Children and Youth, Inc., 1960).

White House Conference on Children made virtually the same recommendations.[16]

Much has been written and a great deal of research has been done about the early years of life. For example, one of the preschool child's greatest achievements is the basic mastery of a spoken language. While there are great individual differences, first grade children have an average vocabulary of 23,700 words and some first graders may know 48,800 words.[17] Typically a child acquires a mastery of the spoken language between the ages of one and five.[18]

When one considers the importance of language throughout life, education during the foundation years becomes increasingly important. Many fields of research and knowledge are required to correctly interpret the needs of this period of development. The science of child development attempts an integration of these various aspects of knowledge in an effort to understand the factors at work in the development of the whole child. Although a young science, great strides have been made that point to the importance of education in the early childhood years. While their suggested procedures are not always applicable to today's child, much that the early educational philosophers believed to be true of the nature of childhood has been found to be true by present scientific research.

With the rediscovery of the importance of the early years to later development, research productivity using infants and young children as subjects reached a new high during the late 1950's and during the 1960's. For this reason selected research as related to early childhood education is presented in Chapter 4 of this text.

The following chapter is a discussion of the young child in his world today and of the child as a person. It should help the reader develop an awareness and knowledge of the growth of children as a factor to be considered in planning for young children and as a basis for planning and evaluating educational practice.

Suggested Activities

1. Using the most recent census data, determine how many children in your home (or college) community are three through six years of age. Find out how many are in some kind of nursery school or kindergarten. What proportion of the children in the age group three to eighteen fall in the three to six year age group? In what proportion of homes in your community does a need exist for nursery schools, kindergartens, or all-day care centers? Plan a discussion on the need for nursery

---

[16]*Report to the President,* op. cit.

[17]Mary K. Smith, "Measurement of the Size of General English Vocabulary Through the Elementary Grades and High School," *Genet. Psychol. Monogr.,* 24:2 (1941), pp. 311–345.

[18]Dorothea McCarthy, "Language Development in Children," in *Manual of Child Psychology,* ed. L. Carmichael, 2nd ed. (New York: John Wiley and Sons, 1954), p. 494.

schools and/or kindergartens. Include persons from the community other than teachers in this discussion.

2. It has been said that most communities cannot afford education for children of nursery school and kindergarten age because the need is so great for better education for children in grades one through twelve. Gather facts and present arguments for or against the above statement.

3. Contact your state department of education for statistics concerning the number of new kindergartens and other preschool programs established during the past five years. Chart or graph your findings. Explain the change.

Related Readings

Aties, Phillippe. *Centuries of Childhood.* New York: Vintage Books, 1965.

Baylor, Ruth M. *Elizabeth Palmer Peabody.* Philadelphia: University of Pennsylvania Press, 1965.

Church, Joseph, ed. *Three Babies.* New York: Random House, 1966.

Frank, Lawrence K. *On the Importance of Infancy.* New York: Random House, 1966.

McCarthy, Dorothea. "Language Development in Children," in *Manual of Child Psychology,* ed. L. Carmichael, 2nd ed. New York: John Wiley and Sons, 1954.

Montessori in Perspective, NAEYC publication #406. Washington, D.C.: National Association for the Education of Young Children, 1966.

Profiles of Children, 1970 White House Conference on Children. Washington, D.C.: Superintendent of Documents, U.S. Government Printing Office, 1970 (Price $3.00).

Rasmussen, Margaret, ed. *Readings from Childhood Education.* Washington, D.C.: Association for Childhood Education International (ACEI), 1966.

Report to the President, Washington, D.C.: White House Conference on Children 1970, Superintendent of Documents, U.S. Printing Office. (Price $4.75).

U.S. Bureau of the Census, *Statistical Abstracts of the United States.* Washington, D.C.: U.S. Government Printing Office, 1966.

The Young Child's World

Although the young child's world today offers more opportunities for him, this same world may be both confining and restricting. A child in his world today is influenced by many outside forces, some of which are social, some economic, others philosophical. The child's individuality is molded by the pressures and changes in his society; his development is also influenced by those around him—his parents, other adults, his peers, and his siblings. The many pressures of the society in which the child lives are also reflected upon him as they affect the behavior of those rearing or teaching him. During their lifetime, the adults responsible for the child's care and guidance have seen many changes in society, but they may not recognize that the present is the only world known to the child.

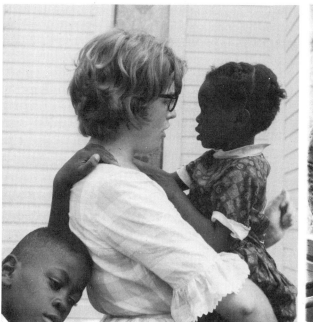

(Courtesy of Head Start)

Figure 2.   A young child is influenced by many forces in his world, especially by those around him—parents, other adults, peers, and siblings. An understanding adult communicates with the child.

SOCIAL FORCES

Improved Communication

Improvement in communication has been one of the greatest forces bringing about the change in adult understanding of children. Through years of study and research much has been learned regarding the child. Improved means of communication have made it possible to disseminate this information widely. While the research has been continuous, informing the public at large as to the interpretation of child growth had not taken place until recently. There are many organized groups and many individual experts interested in communicating to parents on "how to raise your child." In the same manner national and local groups are better organized to protect the health, education, and welfare of children. The opportunities provided to read or hear what is known about child development through books, radio, films, newspapers, professional publications, television, speakers, and discussion groups have all had their effect on the adult; and the adult's changed attitude has affected child rearing practices.

In today's child's world the trend toward shifting responsibility to persons other than the parents is significant. Both private and public day care facilities have increased at a very rapid rate. In many of these centers extensive use is made of maids, high school students, and untrained or partially trained adults or paraprofessionals to supplement the regular staff. These members of the staff are usually assigned duties other than instructional. Nevertheless, their presence undoubtedly has a profound effect on the development of the children in their care.

A listing on p. 461 gives some of the pertinent publications that are available from organizations. Some of these groups disseminate material as a function of their organization because of the heavy demand for information by the public. Parents and teachers are requesting up-to-date material; those working in the child development field have recognized the need to convey such knowledge; child development courses at the college and junior college level have continued to expand; and there is an increasing demand to incorporate more knowledge about children into the high school curriculum.

With the increasing use of television as a medium of communication, children as well as parents have been affected in the changing of attitudes and concepts. Studies seem to conclude that the cognitive effects are disappointing; although children may be better informed, what television could do has been limited as a result of commercialism. However, this medium has great potential in widening children's horizons.[1] There are many television programs designed especially for preschool children on both commercial and educational TV. Best known is "Sesame Street," which was developed to test the effectiveness of television as an instructional medium for preschool children, especially children living in the inner cities. "Sesame Street" is discussed in considerable detail elsewhere in this text.

Mobility of Population

Another important social change that is exerting pressure on the child is the increased mobility of our present population.

> Of the 190.2 million persons 1 year old and over living in the United States in March 1966, 36.7 million, or 19.3 percent, had been living at a different address in March 1965, according to estimates from the Current Population Survey conducted by the Bureau of the Census. . . . In the 19 annual surveys conducted since 1948, the proportion of movers has ranged from 18.6 to 21.0 percent.[2]

The over-all mobility rate has continued to be high. There is greater local mobility of nonwhites and higher mobility in general of the white population. Young adults aged eighteen to thirty-four had a higher mobility rate (34 per

---

[1] Wilber Schramm, J. Lyle, and E. B. Parker, *Television in the Lives of Our Children* (Stanford, Calif.: Stanford University Press, 1961), p. 173.

[2] U. S. Bureau of the Census, *Population Characteristics*, Series P-20, No. 156 (Washington, D.C.: U.S. Government Printing Office, December 1966).

cent) than persons thirty-five years old and over (12 per cent), and also a higher rate than children under eighteen (21 per cent).[3] This mobility factor causes persons interested in the child to ask, what does shifting from one place to another do to the children? Do children need the security that comes through establishing roots in one place or are they able to adjust to constant change? Is it more advantageous for them to know more of the outside world than to have prolonged contacts with one neighborhood?

More divisions within the family have arisen as families move about; each family member develops his own friends thus increasing the contacts each acquires as he shifts from place to place. Widening and broadening of acquaintances may shift both the adult's and the child's perspective as individuals in society. The concern is this: Does the individual thus acquire greater understanding of human relations or broader knowledge of regional differences? Does the family remain intact? What are the effects of shifting population upon the family with growing children? To date, the specific answers are not known. It is only surmised that changes do take place in personalities from more contacts with more people in the widening world.

Ease of Travel

Along with increased mobility and expanded means of communication, the world is known more easily and readily to children and adults through ease of travel, whether to nearby state parks or to far-away vacation spots. Families tend to take vacations; thus mobility in leisure time activities has increased. Advertising has tended to lure families to see the parts of the world known only in earlier times through a geography book. There has been an increased desire to become acquainted firsthand with other localities. State parks and camping facilities have expanded and "campers" of all types are available for families. "Package" family trips are advertised to entice parents at any season of the year. Young children travel with their families by plane great distances in brief spaces of time. Thus the world is better known to children today than it was to a previous generation.

Changes in Living Styles

Today's child lives in a "push-button age" surrounded by new gadgets and inventions represented to him as intricate plastic toys. Through the increasing influence of advertising, adults strive to make more money to purchase more goods to increase the ease of living and to have more leisure time. One can only surmise what effect this continuous circle of striving will have on the growing child. Consideration is also given to the type of value system the child is developing in this fast-changing world. Easy acquisition of toys and other possessions may tend to develop irresponsibility for their care and use. With the increased emphasis on new commodities, we need to be aware of the effect of

[3]Ibid.

the adult's constantly shifting values on those of the child. This problem is accentuated as children move from place to place. What is acceptable to children in one region may only seem cheap or unacceptable to children in another region.

Because of longevity there are more grandparents in the child's world today. Some grandparents are in their early forties or fifties and thus more people are assuming grandparental roles than ever before. The role may be warm and indulgent with grandchildren, since less direct responsibility is assumed.[4] A grandparent may give the child more possessions and more affection, which may be both important and meaningful to him as well as detrimental.

The elderly population (sixty-five and older) has increased from 4.1 per cent of the nation's total population in 1900 to 9.6 per cent in 1970 and is projected to 10.1 per cent by 1980. This means that there were nearly 20 million people in the United States aged 65 and over in 1970. Those aged 45 through 64 increased from 13.8 per cent in 1900 to 20.4 per cent in 1970. On the other hand those in the high productive ages 25 through 44 decreased from 28.1 per cent to 23.6 per cent during the same period of time. These shifts in proportions by age groups have important implications for planning for housing, schools, and social services.

The percentage of children under six years old living in poor families had dropped from 26 per cent in 1959 to 14 per cent by 1969. However, this still meant that at the start of the 1970's 10 million children were from families living in poverty.[5] The same source indicates that 30.4 per cent of mothers with children under six were working (employed) as of March 1969 as compared to 12.8 per cent as of April 1948. Of the working mothers of children under six, 44.3 per cent were Negro and other races, while 26.8 per cent were white in relation to the total married.

The incidence of physical child abuse in America is of considerable concern. In 1968, of the 6,617 abused children surveyed, 53.37 per cent were six years of age or under.[6]

During the 1969 school year, 6,934,000 or slightly over half of the 12,964,000 children aged three to six were enrolled in school. Of the total, 15.1 per cent of the three- and four-year-olds and 89.2 per cent of the five- and six-year-olds were in school.[7] Public school kindergarten enrollment increased 14.2 per cent

[4]B. L. Neugarten and K. Weinstein, "The Changing American Grandparents," *Marr. and Fam. Liv.,* 16 (May 1964).

[5]*Profiles,* White House Conference on Children, 1970 (Washington, D.C.: Superintendent of Documents, U.S. Government Printing Office, 1970), p. 20.

[6]Ibid., p. 112 (from the U.S. Department of Health, Education, and Welfare Survey funded by the Children's Bureau's study, *Physical Abuse of Children in the U.S.,* Dr. David Gil, Brandeis University, 1968).

[7]Ibid., p. 118 (U.S. Department of Commerce, Bureau of the Census).

from 1964 to 1969[8] and many states especially in the South had passed legislation to have public school kindergartens for all children desiring to attend by the early 1970's.

Because of the disparity between income levels, most innovations in the schools have occurred in programs for children of low-income families. Best known are the Title I programs under the Elementary and Secondary Education Act of 1965, Head Start, Follow Through, the Parent Child Centers, whose target children are under three years of age, and the Pilot Parent and Child Advocacy Center programs. These new programs will be discussed in Chapter 8, "Emerging School Programs for Young Children."

Population Trends

Another important factor to consider in today's world for children is the increase in population.

The population of the United States was 180,684,000 in 1960, 205,395,000 in 1970, and is projected to be 227,510,000 by 1980. Because of changing birth rates there were 20,162,000 children five years of age and under in 1960 but only 18,013,000 in 1970. The number is expected to rise to 19,881,000 by 1980.

Despite the slowing of the birth rate in the United States, the USSR, and Europe, the world population is expected to double between 1975 and the year 2010. The approximate doubling time was 1600 years to the year 1620, 130 years from 1800 to 1930, and 45 years from 1930 to 1975.[9]

With increase in population comes the need for more schools and more facilities to care for children. Also needed are such personnel as pediatricians, authors of children's literature, inventors of appropriate new toys for children, nutritionists, designers of suitable children's clothing, and writers of television programs for and about children. The concern is not only for increased numbers but for a high quality of service rendered by this personnel. Better health facilities as well as solutions to problems confronting welfare programs for children are a part of the needs created by this increase in population.

Mothers Working Outside Home

There has been a steady increase in the number of working mothers. In April 1948, 43.5 per cent of mothers of children under 18 were in the labor force, in 1960 the percentage was 62.7, and in March 1969 81.1 per cent. For the same years the percentage of mothers with children under six were 12.8, 20.2, and 30.4 respectively. Obviously the need for parent surrogates and/or day care has steadily increased since 1949.[10]

[8]Ibid., p. 117 (U.S. Department of Commerce, Bureau of the Census).

[9]Ibid., p. 85.

[10]Ibid., p. 40.

Husband-wife families with one or more children under eighteen years accounted for 84.7 per cent of all families with children. Although the remaining 15.3 per cent consisting of mothers or fathers raising children without the other parent is proportionately small, it is large in actual numbers of children growing up in a world with only one parent. Problems faced by the one-parent family are many with varying degrees of concern for the children.[11]

Economic need has been the primary reason that mothers work: one out of every seven working mothers in 1965 came from families in which the income of the husband was less than $3,000. More than 80 per cent of the working mothers have husbands living in the homes, but over 1.4 million women were heads of families with incomes of less than $3,000. The more schooling a woman has received, the more likely that she is employed. Among mothers of preschool children who have only eight years of schooling or who have completed high school, about 20 per cent are in the labor force. This percentage rises to 22 per cent for mothers who have four years of college, and to 33 per cent for mothers who have five or more years of college.[12]

Studies conducted on the effects of maternal deprivation resulting from mothers working outside the home show varying results.

An earlier study of maternal employment and development of children had revealed no detrimental effects. Orientation in maternal deprivation has leaned toward the assumption of its ill effects on young children, but studies do not bear this out. The authors of this study felt that in the research to date, "maternal employment by itself is too broad a concept to be used fruitfully in parent-child studies and that, in future work, test variables should be introduced to make this concept more psychologically meaningful."[13]

Housing

Housing is an important area to consider in relation to the activity of a child and his play space. The home may be crowded, small, and have poor sanitation or safety hazards. It may be too large, overly clean, and have no playmates accessible. There may be good sleeping arrangements and storage space for the child, or there may be noise, confusion, clutter, and no place a child can call his own for his possessions. Outdoor play areas may be adequate on a roof or in a yard, or nonexistent.

Lemkau feels that "the house does not have a constant relationship to the household which lives in it, but that the relationship changes according to economic ideals and philosophic ideals." As a psychiatrist he feels that a house

[11]Ibid., p. 141.

[12]M. P. Ilgenfritz, "Mothers on Their Own—Widows and Divorcees," *Marr. and Fam. Liv.*, 23(1961), p. 38.

[13]F. I. Nye and L. W. Hoffman, *The Employed Mother in America* (Chicago: Rand McNally, 1963), p. 210.

must offer a place for children to lead a satisfactory existence. Crowded conditions and too many adults lead to lack of independence and poor control in guiding children.[14]

Little research has been conducted on the effect of housing in rearing children, and yet recommendations have been made as to how children should be housed. Concern has been expressed that families have adequate housing and building programs have been expanded. In 1965, over one and one-half million housing units were started in the building process in the United States. "Proper balance between housing and income-supplementing programs will be important in achieving the goal of decent housing for every family. . . . The Department of Housing and Urban Development is intensifying its efforts to formulate and develop a balanced relationship between housing and income-supplementing programs."[15]

It seems clear that adequate housing for families is a prerequisite to adequate family life and learning experiences for young children. Schools and universities bulged with children and students during the 1950's and 1960's as a result of the World War II baby boom. The 1970's found these same babies, then young adults, forming families of their own. Housing was the neglected industry during the 1960's, during the same period rot and neglect, especially in the large inner cities, created acute housing problems for young families. Mobile homes, apartments, and government subsidized low-cost housing mushroomed because of the rapidly rising cost of new housing. This trend is indicated by the fact that "44 per cent of today's housing (1971) is multi-family row houses and apartments, vs. only 26 per cent back in 1961."[16] The same source indicated that mobile homes increased fourfold during the past decade. Even so, inadequate as these types of housing are for families with young children, most of the new housing was not built where the need was the greatest.[17]

What importance housing plays in the life of a child is an area that needs, and will continue to need, increased and intensive exploration.

Parents Today

The young child today may be reared in a home by parents who are both working or attending school. Young parents may be continuing their education, either in vocational school or college. These parents are likely to be in

[14]P. V. Lemkau, "A Psychiatrist's View of Housing," *Proceedings of Housing Conference*, Publication 180 (Philadelphia: Pennsylvania State University, College of Home Economics), p. 27. (Unpublished paper) n.d.

[15]U.S. Department of Agriculture, *Family Economics Review*, ARS 62-5 (Washington, D.C., December 1966), p. 12.

[16]"Home Building: Is the Boom Hollow?" *Forbes, 108*:9(1971), pp. 28–36.

[17]Ibid., pp. 30–33.

their early twenties. Census data show that the marriage rate among those in their teens is on the decline.[18]

These parents were born and reared during or after World War II. It is important to consider the world in which these young parents were growing up, for many of their childhood years continued to be war years. The present world in which these parents and their offspring live is different from that known by many of the earlier child development writers, researchers, or so-called "experts." Many of the earlier writings, still used and read by young parents, were written in a different kind of world. The child-rearing practices as prescribed for that day may have been suitable then, but some may be questioned now. Practices recommended were based on data collected during the 1920's and 1930's and later selected by other writers in the field. Senn feels that "the public, professional and nonprofessional alike, has been much more willing to accept as cause of emotional disturbance in children such factors as constitution, body build, physical disease, and single psychological determinants than the deep unconscious mechanisms within the child, or the multiple, mass influences of social forces."[19]

Young parents today have available a vast array of information regarding the child himself as well as advice to parents. At times they are confused by contradictory or conflicting points of view. They need guidance in distinguishing between recommendations based on reliable research and those made by biased individuals or groups.

Cultural and Class Differences

As an important factor in the continuation of the culture, the child is the connecting link between the cultures of succeeding generations. How a parent rears a child is dependent on the culture, the trends of the decade in which the parent is presently living, and on the past experience of the adult. Wolfenstein feels that "awareness of past trends in child rearing in our own culture is a prerequisite to the working through to real conviction of reasoned preferences."[20]

Variations in Methods of Child Rearing

Sears, Maccoby, and Levin conducted intensive research in the area of child rearing with 379 mothers of five-year-old children. They found wide variations in the different methods measured—from mothers who never under any circumstances allowed certain behavior to others who felt specific behavior should be ignored. Some mothers were quite uncertain in the strength of their con-

[18]U.S. Department of Agriculture, *Family Economics Review*, ARS 62-5 (Washington D.C., December 1966), p. 12.

[19]M. J. Senn, "Fads and Facts as the Bases of Child-Care Practices," *Children*, 4:2 (1957), p. 44.

[20]M. Mead and M. Wolfenstein, *Childhood in Contemporary Cultures* (Chicago: University of Chicago Press, 1955), p. 445.

victions. Some of the child-rearing practices reported placed emphasis on training children, others on caretaking only, and others on reactions of love, annoyance, pride, or concern. One of the most pervasive qualities measured was the warmth of the mother's feeling for her child.[21]

The present emphasis on early childhood education and day care is clearly an indication that today there is a lack in the traditional socializing influences of the family and school. Emphasis on the disadvantaged child has dominated the field of early childhood education since the early 1960's and most research since then has been concerned with that group of children and families. Studying the teaching styles of mothers from different social classes, Hess and Shipman found that mothers of culturally disadvantaged children controlled the child's behavior by imperatives. This method did not provide an opportunity for mediation of behavior by verbal cues nor the use of language to bring meaning to the experience encountered.[22]

Such a cognitive environment, they conclude, "produces a child who relates to authority rather than to rationale . . . and for whom the consequences of an act are largely considered in terms of immediate punishment or reward rather than future effects and long-range goals."[23] This, of course, is in *direct contrast to the future-oriented long-range planning goals of middle-class American families.* As a consequence, schools of middle-class value orientation have not provided for the needs of children from lower income families in such a way as to enable them to cope with the schools' expectations and demands.

Because of the time it takes to conduct research and to have it published and later interpreted for public consumption, there is a lag in adapting it to practice. Thus, if research finds it is "all right or better" to be less permissive in dealing with children, this concept may not be put into practice for seven or eight years. Therefore, we are likely to find some parents still being very permissive in rearing children because of something they read in the late 1940's, while other parents who have attended a study group and discussed various ways of raising children may be recognizing individual differences and comparing these differences of their own children to new research findings.

Social Class

Regional and class differences are apparent in the literature and in research on ways parents rear their children. Attitudes and values of families in lower, middle, and upper classes differ in regard to customs and aspirations; these differences are revealed in most communities.

Some researchers classify the social groups in American urban society as

---

[21]R. Sears, E. Maccoby, and H. Levin, *Patterns of Child Rearing* (Evanston, Ill.: Row Peterson, 1957), p. 482.

[22]R. D. Hess and Roberta M. Bear, "Maternal Influences upon Early Learning," in *Early Education* (Chicago: Aldine Publishing Company, 1968) p. 103.

[23]Ibid., p. 103.

upper, upper-middle, lower-middle, working, and lower class. Classification of variables that characterize these classes is dependent on value orientations as they form, integrate, and symbolize a certain way of life.[24] Hollingshead and Redlich have analyzed family patterns in lower and middle classes. They show contrasts in respect to aspirations, for middle-class children continue to strive upward and lower-class children show less striving for specific goals.[25]

There is need to carefully analyze class influences that young children acquire from parents, teachers, and other adults. In the study by Sears, Maccoby, and Levin, the authors analyzed their data by socioeconomic status. Their cases were analyzed and divided into two groups, namely, "middle class" and "working class." There were marked differences in the practices and attitudes of these two classes of mothers. Working-class mothers were more punitive and restrictive. They were less permissive with respect to sex behavior, aggression, and dependency, and they placed high restrictions and demands on their children in all major respects. Many other findings in respect to differences in child rearing can be found in these research studies.[26]

Studies to date are limited in regard to subcultures of the very poor; however, Chilman has presented research findings showing differences in child-rearing patterns. These summarize studies on various aspects of child rearing according to middle-class versus very low-income families. Since schools are basically middle-class institutions, lower-class children have trouble achieving in such centers. For example, some of the studies revealed that low-income families use inconsistent, harsh discipline and ridicule; the discipline is based on whether the child's behavior does or does not annoy the parent. Middle-class parents used verbal, mild, reasoning and consistent discipline with more emphasis on rewarding good behavior.[27]

Such studies, while helpful, merely describe differences and seldom produce an understanding of the differences and why they exist. The following quotations from the 1970 White House Conference on Children report will help bridge the gap:

> Many children, effectively isolated from their cultural heritage by poverty, home environment, racial discrimination, and geography, do not develop pride in their heritages, and their feelings of identity remain vague and confused. These children need help in finding out who they are and where they came from.[28]

[24]J. A. Kahl, *The American Class Structure* (New York: Holt, Rinehart and Winston, 1959).

[25]A. B. Hollingshead and F. C. Redlich, *Social Class and Mental Illness* (New York: John Wiley and Sons, 1958).

[26]Sears, Maccoby, and Levin, op. cit., p. 480.

[27]Catherine Chilman, "Child-Rearing and Family Relationship Patterns of the Very Poor," *Welfare in Review* (Washington, D.C.: U.S. Department of Health, Education, and Welfare, January 1965).

[28]*Report to the President.* White House Conference on Children 1970, (Washington D.C.: Superintendent of Documents, U.S. Government Printing Office, 20402, Price $4.50), p. 48.

Forum 6 reported,

The Forum on Creativity and the Learning Process states that it has been jolted by the realization that the Child of America is growing up in captivity. His prison is his communication.[29]

On the role of culture, the same Forum reported,

Cultural forces, like the forces of nature, are never fully under control. They are massive in comparison with the very limited power that man can exert through rational planning and design. Creativity depends upon the culture's emotional climate in its major institutions: the home, the church, the school, the mass media, and other forms of public communication, the town or city, the state or nation, and international relations.[30]

It would thus appear that social class and the influence of culture are powerful determinants of young children's behavior and must be taken into account when planning teaching and instructional strategies.

Recognition of Importance of Child's Sex Role

There is a growing awareness by those interested in child development of the importance of the child's sex role. How the parents think of the masculine or feminine role plays an important part in how they rear the child. Questions relative to this include: Are the father's and mother's concepts the same or does each parent have a different way of looking at masculinity or femininity? Is the child's time spent mainly with the mother; if so, does the child have more awareness of the feminine role than the masculine? If the child is only seen and cared for by the father at brief intervals daily, is that enough for the child to identify with a masculine figure?

A child learns early in life that boys and girls are treated differently, are dressed differently, and are expected to behave differently. Each culture defines the meaning of *male* or *female*, usually in terms of its social and economic needs. As these needs change so do the roles of each sex change. Nevertheless, early in life each child must find his sex role in his family and in the ethnic group to which he belongs if he is to be an accepted member.

Family Relationships

The number of brothers and sisters as well as the ordinal position of each sibling should be taken into account in each individual family. Another factor is the effect of the parents' newness to the situation with the first child versus the parent becoming more sure of himself with each successive child. Parents who rear only boys or only girls within their families have different ways of

[29]Ibid., p. 89.
[30]Ibid., pp. 90–91.

bringing up children. A child may find himself reared in a family where he is more than wanted because of the physical incapability of his parents of having other children, or he may be an unwanted child. He may be one of the large number of exceptional children who are physically or mentally handicapped, or he may be a superior or gifted child.

Many families are not aware that children identify closely with parents and others in the home. How the parents act with each other, how they treat those within the family group, constitute attitudes and values passed on to and acquired by the young child. Parents' reactions to various happenings locally or in the world and to the daily routines within the home are all part of how the child accepts and begins to acquire his own ways of conduct with others. Since today's world for the young child is brought into the home by many media, children in turn are influenced by how parents verbalize their reactions to this information. Early impressions of adults' concerns over the constantly changing world will continue to play an important part in their own attitudes as the world affairs shift or change.

Conflicting Educational Theories

Another factor in the child's world is the conflict of theories relative to educating the child. Parents have been advised to have the child ready for school at age six, "ready for school" meaning to them ability to read, write one's name, to know certain facts. Others have advised the parent to leave the child alone, that the school's job is to teach him everything he should know. Some children therefore arrive in first grade with certain taught skills, others with none.

The push to educate very young children has had growing impetus since the atomic age intensified the need for further education in all lines of endeavor. Parents may pressure young children to "know certain facts" where other parents have a "let well enough alone" attitude. Those working with or teaching young children in organized groups also may feel they should prepare the five-year-old to read and write in order that he be equipped to meet the standards of first grade. Pressure from society that all five- or six-year-olds should be able to measure up to certain prescribed standards may find school and parents in conflict.

Along with conflicting theories of child rearing and education, there are conflicting beliefs regarding the responsibilities of the home. Many young parents depend mainly on outside agencies—welfare organizations, family services, clinics, state and local societies—to handle their problems. One has yet to determine whether or not the agencies are so numerous that young parents are over-aided and do not develop necessary self-sufficiency. Are there too many day care groups so that mothers may go to work, feeling secure that children are cared for properly?

The recognition of the importance of the early years has given impetus to research in early learning. As a result, many different theories, methods, and types of instructional materials exist. Many of these will be discussed and evaluated elsewhere in this text.

IMPLICATIONS FOR THE TEACHER

Because there are many new pressures and continuing forces that bear on each child as he grows up in his world today, the teacher needs to consider what adults can do to help this growing individual. The teacher needs to consider the effects upon the child of such factors as mass media, family relationships, social patterns, and other forces discussed in this chapter. Adults must be aware that the child will continually be a changing individual because of these many forces acting upon him. Human relations will become a greater force as today's children become adults. The teacher will need to recognize the importance of such factors as: the child's mother working outside the home; whether the child is the oldest, middle, or youngest child; the community or region from which the child has come; the age of the child's parents; whether the child has had a wide range of experiences; what attitudes or values the parents have in their rearing of this child. It is a challenge for a teacher of young children to keep constantly in focus all the new literature, research, and materials that appear as she attempts to assimilate these in connection with each new youngster she teaches.

Suggested Activities

1. Note the variety of nursery schools, kindergartens, day care centers, and other programs for young children in your community. Determine sponsorship of these. Visit one and determine the goals of such a school.
2. Make a list of values or attitudes you feel you have acquired from your own family. Analyze one of these in detail as to how it originated.
3. Study two preschool children, one who has been given every advantage and one who has had very few advantages. Contrast the two types of environment and predict possible types of children they will become.
4. Discuss the pros and cons of sending "your" child to a nursery school or kindergarten.

Related Readings

Albrecht, R. "The Parental Responsibilities of Grandparents," *Marr. and Fam. Liv.*, 26:2 (1954)

Chilman, C. *Growing Up Poor*, Publication 13. Washington, D.C.: U.S. Department of Health, Education, and Welfare, May 1966.

Chilman, C., ed. "Poverty in the United States in the Mid-Sixties," *Marr. and Fam. Liv.*, 26:4 (1964).

Kremer, J., and S. Day. *Indoor Play Areas for Preschool Children in the Homes of Farm Owners*, Bulletin 410. Raleigh, N.C.: Agricultural Experiment Station, February 1959.

Prall, R. C. "Child Development and the Dwelling Unit," *Forum on Neighborhoods Today and Tomorrow*, No. 2. Philadelphia Housing Association, March 1958.

Profiles of Children, White House Conference on Children, 1970. (Washington D.C.: Superintendent of Documents, U.S. Government Printing Office, 1970).

Report to the President, White House Conference on Children, 1970 (Washington D.C.: Superintendent of Documents, U.S. Government Printing Office, 1970).

The Young Child
as a Person

Current literature in child development tends to stress the importance of the child's way of viewing himself.[1] Because of his own physical and mental characteristics, what adults do and say to him, his view of others, and his own inner feelings, the child develops a self-image or self-concept early. The way each child views himself may not be the way others see him, or may even be far from objective reality. Nevertheless, the view he holds is how he feels about himself and is all-important in determining what he says, does, and thinks.

This is in contrast to most child development writings of a decade or two ago which tended to be detailed descriptions of what the average child was like for a particular chronological age. These averages or norms had been obtained from observations of many children at each age level and were unrelated to the effects of particular teaching strategies, intervention techniques, or

[1]Interested readers see Kaoru Yamamoto, ed., *The Child and His Image* (Boston: Houghton Mifflin, 1972).

other than normal health care and family life patterns. It should not be inferred that information about normal growth and development is unnecessary for teachers (and parents). On the contrary, it is the base from which slow or fast, normal or deviate, behavior can be detected and is an invaluable aid in planning learning strategies for any group of children.

IMPORTANCE OF THE SELF-IMAGE

Although a child's awareness of differences because of social class does not become clearly evident until well along in the elementary school years,[2] self-awareness in its simplest form probably occurs during the first year of life. During the preschool years a child receives condemnation or support from other children. A child may receive approval, constant praise, and acceptance from his playmates, or he may be reminded of the disapproval of others by being "told that he is 'messy,' 'dumb,' a 'cry-baby,' or, a 'brat.'"[3] Often such designations are a reflection of the visible physical characteristics possessed by particular children. They may also be a reflection of how the child appears to behave as seen by his peers or by adults.

Taunts of "Fatty," "Shorty," "Clumsy Ox," "Dumbbell," "Smarty," and the like, are often heard as one listens to a group of children at play or work. Such designations may be fitting descriptions of particular children in particular situations but at the same time may cause emotional concern resulting in permanent psychological scars. Regardless of the beliefs one holds, it is almost impossible not to form impressions of others based on the image of their physical selves. As a result, a great deal of psychological suffering occurs even though no harm is intended or even perceived.

In recent years studies of body image, identification, motivation, self-control, self-actualization, selfhood, and similar concepts have occupied the attention of many researchers and theorists. For example, Jahoda categorizes the self-concept as (1) *accessibility to consciousness,* or the ability to achieve self-awareness; (2) *correctness,* or objectivity in being able to assess one's true characteristics; (3) *feeling about the self,* or acceptance including imperfections and faults; and (4) *sense of identity,* or clarity of the self image.[4] There is little research in this area during the early years because of the difficulty of objective control and measurement. It seems clear, however, that the self emerges only in the presence of other human beings for the comparison with others serves as a guide to behavior. One fashions his self-identification early in terms of cues from others, such as the reflected appraisals of parents, siblings, playmates, and other persons present in his environment.

Recognition of the importance of a healthy self-concept during the early

[2]Celia B. Stendler, *Children of Brasstown* (Urbana, Ill.: University of Illinois Press, 1949).

[3]A. T. Jersild, *Child Psychology,* 5th ed. (Englewood Cliffs, N.J.: Prentice-Hall, 1960), p. 174.

[4]M. Jahoda, *Current Concepts of Positive Mental Health* (New York: Basic Books, 1958), pp. 13–15.

years was recognized by the planners of Head Start programs for disadvantaged children. Included in the goals was: "To help children develop self-identity and a view of themselves as having competence and worth."[5]

The processes involved in the emergence of the self are varied and complex. In the early years, social and emotional factors are likely most important, although cognitive and intellectual development play an important role in both these areas. Demands of parents and of society in general include early learning. Young children must be provided varied and rich environments in order to develop feelings of competence in the world in which they find themselves. Fortunately, young children are curious and eager to learn and the rapidity with which they learn amazes adults. The important question for parents and teachers is, "What should be taught to children at each age level and why?" Choosing between required learning activities and the other essential activities of childhood can be a perplexing problem. Reported research has not been very helpful, for although complex and abstract concepts can be learned early, long-range effects have not been determined. It is doubtful that the time and effort expended on early reading or other academic pursuits make it a wise and efficient educational procedure.

EARLY DOCTRINES OF CHILD DEVELOPMENT

Although individual differences are the rule in growth and development, the teacher must have a thorough knowledge of normal development in order to know when growth or behavior deviates to the extent that special consideration and handling of a child or event is called for. It is commonly proclaimed by present-day educators that a knowledge of the characteristics of children at any age or developmental level will enable the teacher to select and pace activities suitable for any given child at any age. This is the central concept in the value of the child study movement and in child development research. That this concept is not without precedent may be found in the more philosophical doctrines of earlier great educators. A few examples might be enlightening before presenting a brief summary of the physical, mental, and personal-social characteristics of young children as found by researchers in the field.

Hinting at the concept of natural changes, Plato in the "Laws" states "up to the age of three years, whether of boy or girl, if a person strictly carries out our previous regulations and makes them a principal aim, he will do much for the advantages of the young creatures. But at three, four, five or even six years the childish nature will require sports. . . . Children of that age have certain natural modes of amusement which they find out for themselves when they meet . . . the age of thirteen is the proper time for him to handle the lyre."[6]

[5]Office of Economic Opportunity, *Project Head Start—Daily Program I* (Washington, D.C.: U.S. Government Printing Office, 1965), p. 11.

[6]B. Jowett, trans., *The Dialogues of Plato*, vol. 2 (New York: Random House, 1937), p. 549.

Representative of sixteenth-century English thinking, Elyot would exercise extreme care in the selection of the child's nurse.[7] Since knowledge of value was written in Greek and Latin at the time Elyot lived, he would begin instruction in these languages before the "age of seven." However, pupils were not to be forced to learn but rather were to be "sweetly allured thereto with praises and such pretty gifts as children delight in."[8] Recognizing the need for education in keeping with the child's maturation and regardless of his economic status, Comenius wrote "when boys are only six years old, it is too early to determine their vocation in life, or whether they are more suited for learning or for manual labor. At this age neither the mind nor the inclinations are sufficiently developed, while, later on, it will be easy to form a sound opinion of both. Nor should admission to the Latin School be reserved for the sons of rich men, nobles and magistrates, as if these were the only boys who would ever be able to fill similar positions. The wind blows where it will, and does not always begin to blow at a fixed time."[9]

An early proponent of child study, Locke, characteristic of modern thinking, stated in 1689, "Follow a child from its birth, and observe the alterations that time makes, and you shall find, as the mind by the senses comes more and more to be furnished with ideas, it comes to be more and more awake; thinks more, the more it has matter to think on. After some time, it begins to know the objects which, being most familiar with, have made lasting impressions."[10]

More explicitly, in regard to instruction, Pestalozzi states, "The elementary method limits itself to employ the impressions which nature puts at random before the child's senses, but extends the natural process along definite lines adapted to his capacities and requirements."[11] Foreshadowing modern readiness concepts, he wrote, "This principle [adapting instruction to intellectual capacity and mental development] necessitated the subject matter being presented at the psychological moment in order, on the one hand, not to hold him back if ready, and on the other, not to load him and confuse him with anything for which he is not ready."[12]

Froebel, also, was aware of developmental processes, for he affirmed, "It is highly important that man's development should proceed continuously from one point, and that this continuous progress be seen and even guarded."[13] He further adds, "Human education needs a guide which I think I have found

[7]Sir Thomas Elyot, *The Boke Named the Governour*, 1531 (London: J. M. Dent, 1907), p. 19.

[8]Ibid. Cited by R. R. Rusk, *The Doctrines of Great Educators* (London: Macmillan & Co., 1926), p. 55.

[9]A. Comenius (Komensky), *The Great Didactic*, 1657, Ch. 29; quoted in Rusk, op. cit., p. 101.

[10]John Locke, *An Essay Concerning Human Understanding*, Book 4.

[11]J. A. Green, ed., *Life and Work of Pestalozzi* (London: W. B. Clive, 1913); quoted in Rusk, op. cit., p. 179.

[12]J. H. Pestalozzi, *How Gertrude Teaches Her Children* (Syracuse, N.Y.: C. W. Bardeen, 1898), p. 26.

[13]F. Froebel, *Education of Man*; quoted in Rusk, op. cit., pp. 236–237.

in a general law of development that rules both in nature and in the intellectual world. Without law-abiding guidance, there is no free development."[14]

Montessori in a more modern vein asserted, "By education, must be understood the active help given to the normal expansion of the life of the child."[15] She goes on to state, "It is necessary then to offer those exercises which correspond to the need of development felt by an organism, and if the child's age has carried him past a certain need it is never possible to obtain, in its fullness, a development which missed its proper moment."[16] Although today considerable opposition can be found to the latter statement, Montessori implied the importance of pacing activities to psychological and developmental needs.

Early attempts at describing the characteristics of childhood, mostly biographical in nature, were made by Galton,[17] Preyer,[18] Taine,[19] Tiedemann,[20] and Darwin.[21]

This type of observation led to later adaptations such as the questionnaires of G. Stanley Hall[22] and the more recent extensive longitudinal observations as represented by the "ages and stages" development by Gesell and Ilg,[23] and by many others.

While many of the early writers projected their views from the standpoint of philosophy, they provided an excellent basis for extensive present-day research. The following statement by Olson is representative of present-day growth philosophy for education.[24]

> The general philosophy as applied to the growing child is a simple one . . . each child is to be assisted in growing according to his natural design, without deprivation or forcing, in an environment and by a process which also supply a social direction to his achievement. For the student of child development, education is a process by which children are assisted in growing; and the adequacy of administration, of the physical environment, of curriculum experiences, and of methods of teaching should be appraised in terms of the extent to which this function is realized.

There are infinite possibilities and challenges afforded the adult who, as he works with young children, attempts to see each child for what he is, to

[14]Baroness B. von Marenholz-Bülow, *Reminiscences of Frederick Froebel*, 1877; quoted in Rusk, op. cit., p. 238.

[15]Maria Montessori, *The Montessori Method* (New York: Frederick A. Stokes, 1912), p. 104.

[16]Ibid., p. 358.

[17]F. Galton, *Hereditary Genius*, 1869.

[18]W. Preyer, *Die Seele des Kindes*, 2 vols., 1888.

[19]H. Taine, "On the Acquisition of Language by Children," *Mind*, 2 (1877), pp. 252–259.

[20]C. Murchison and S. Langer, "Tiedemann's Observations on the Development of the Mental Faculties of Children," *J. Genet. Psychol.*, 34:2 ,1921), pp. 205–230.

[21]C. Darwin, "Biographical Sketch of an Infant," *Mind*, 2 (1877), pp. 285–294.

[22]G. S. Hall, "The Contents of Children's Minds," *Pedag. Sem.*, 1:2 (1891), pp. 139–173.

[23]A. Gesell and Frances Ilg, *Child Development* (New York: Harper, 1949).

[24]W. C. Olson, *Child Development*, 2nd ed. (Boston: D. C. Heath, 1959), p. 449.

see the influences of natural endowments and natural growth processes at work, and to discover and put into practice methods and use of materials which provide the best possible educational environment for the growing child.

GROWTH, LEARNING, MATURATION, AND DEVELOPMENT

It is all too easy to speak of growth, learning, maturation, and development as a single concept, although in reality each has a separate meaning that should be understood. Concepts of growth, borrowed from biology, deal basically with an increase of some dimension such as height, circumference of the head, and similar physical characteristics. Present-day educational literature sometimes uses the term to express change in function and includes such expressions as growth in vocabulary, growth in reading, or growth in social understanding. Often these and similar expressions are used in such a way as to imply development, a concept which will be dealt with presently.

Figure 3. Much has been written about the importance of individual differences. In no other area of growth and development are differences so obvious as in that of physical growth. These children all attend the same kindergarten. Their unique features and differences in height and body build illustrate the folly of the often-used description of "fiveness." Although a general description of a five-year-old may be helpful as a reference point, it is generally agreed that individual differences due to innate and experiential variations make the concept of "five" or "fiveness" misleading, and often suggest practices that do not enhance the opportunity for optimum development of each child.

It is helpful to think of maturation as a process, its characteristics and temporal patterns peculiar to the organism involved, that represents the innate forces producing growth and change in a fixed direction. When environmental forces such as the effects of food or exercise interact with the innate force responsible for maturation, development takes place. Development may then be thought of as the changing end-product resulting from the interaction of maturation and the environmental factors or nurture. Thus, there is the implication that development represents a "stage" that has been achieved at any particular point of time in the maturation process.

A great deal has been written about learning and psychologists devote much of their efforts to research on learning. In this frame of reference learning is usually thought of as any observable or inferred change in response behavior caused wholly or in part by experience. As a result, several theories of learning have been developed; much is known about the conditions of learning but the process itself still remains a mystery. In the context of education, learning is assumed to have occurred when a person has acquired relatively permanent knowledges and skills. It is generally assumed that such knowledges and skills happen as a result of practice, although learning certainly takes place as a result of single experiences. Because there is so much to learn, the young child, unhampered by a large number of previous experiences, finds the world a very fascinating place. As a result he learns easily and acquires knowledges and skills at a very rapid rate when his environment provides an opportunity for him to do so. While learning theory is outside the scope of this text, the student of early childhood education should become familiar with the various theories of learning and their implications for education. (See Chapter 8.)

Early compensatory education for disadvantaged children is an attempt through direct intervention to enable such children to "catch up" in school learning. Previous experience and child development research and theory would indicate a pessimistic outlook for much success. The availability of funds in the early 1960's for such programs spurred a vast amount of controlled research in this field. Notable is the work of Bereiter and Engelmann,[25] Bloom,[26] Deutsch,[27] and Hunt.[28] While early reports indicate a high level of achievement success by using direct methods and by eliminating other developmental areas common in most preschool programs, follow-up studies will be necessary to determine the effectiveness of such programs. A review of many studies done two to five years following intensive educational efforts would seem to cast doubt on the effectiveness of compensatory programs.

[25]C. Bereiter and S. Engelmann, *Teaching Disadvantaged Children in the Preschool* (Englewood Cliffs, N.J.: Prentice-Hall, 1966).

[26]B. S. Bloom, A. Davis, and R. Hess, *Compensatory Education for Cultural Deprivation* (New York: Holt, Rinehart and Winston, 1965).

[27]M. Deutsch, "Facilitating Development in the Preschool Child: Social and Psychological Perspectives," *Merrill-Palmer Quart.*, 10:3 (1964), pp. 249–263.

[28]J. McV. Hunt, "The Psychological Basis for Using Pre-School Enrichment as an Antidote for Cultural Deprivation," *Merrill-Palmer Quart.*, 10:3 (1964), pp. 209–248.

It must be kept in mind that most children involved in these efforts continue to live in the same environments which brought about the deprivation in the first place. It seems highly unrealistic to expect a child to maintain gains resulting from short intensive learning programs without rather drastically restructuring the home and community living conditions and bringing about greatly improved family life. Many emerging programs are attempting to do just that. (See Chapter 8.) It must also be kept in mind that these programs are designed for children with severe learning deprivation and not for the majority of American children.

The expression "normal development," when applied to an individual child, means that the nurture has been such that the child concerned has achieved whatever stage of development is under consideration at about the same time and with similar characteristics as has been achieved by most children his age. Developmental changes may be thought of as occurring because of the complex interaction of the forces of nature and nurture. The teacher and school have as a major purpose to provide many types of experiences which the child might not otherwise encounter, but which are designed to assist nature in the child's developmental process.

As adults work with preschool-age children and observe the numerous and varied movements, expressions, behavioral attitudes, and seemingly endless and often meaningless activities, they will have a better understanding of the needs of children if they are familiar with characteristics of growth, development, and maturation common to all children. For example, because movement and activity are essential to normal physical growth at this time, the wise teacher avoids experiences which require long periods of quiet attention to the tasks at hand.

Likewise, all young children possess varying degrees of curiosity. Yet, not all children confront new and novel situations with bubbling enthusiasm and excitement. Standing quietly and closely observing details by intently gazing at a new object or event may be one child's way of expressing curiosity while another child in the same situation may jump up and down screaming joyously. Most preschool children are functioning in what Piaget describes as the sensory-motor stage of cognitive development. The use of any one, or of several sensory modalities simultaneously, may be appropriate as children explore new experiences in ways that are unique to each. An observing adult soon learns and respects the mode of sensory-motor expression peculiar to each child in the group while at the same time encouraging new and different ways of discovering meaningful concepts. In each case the child grows in confidence as he learns more about the world by experiencing it through his available sensory-motor repertoire at any given point in time.

The following observations depict activities and behavior common to children of normal development for the ages described. A range of individual differences is included but these discussions are not intended to portray the characteristics of those who deviate widely from the expectancies of the respective age groups.

Observations in a Child Development Center

Early one morning, Dorothy, Robert, Mary, and Billy—all three years old—were happily playing in a large outdoor sand enclosure. To the casual observer nothing of importance was happening. Mary and Dorothy seemed to be piling and shaping the moist sand into separate, rather large, indescribable objects, while Robert and Billy were scooping up the sand with their hands, tossing it in the air, and letting it fall wherever it happened to go. All were talking constantly but not to each other. Billy's "ride-em cowboy" and Mary's "mother says, 'No! No!'" seemed to have no relationship to what they were doing. After a few minutes Robert, without warning, climbed out of the enclosure, falling on his hands as his feet did not quite clear the low wall which kept the sand inside. Without concern he got up, and ran to stand and watch another boy and girl simultaneously trying to claim a tricycle. Dorothy, Billy, and Mary appeared to be unaware that Robert had left their company. Suddenly, Billy's "whoopee" accompanied by a shower of sand from his rapidly rising arms attracted the attention of the teacher as Mary began to cry loudly, and Dorothy quietly rubbed the sand from her moist eyes with the convenient skirt of her dress. The teacher reassuringly put her arm about Mary's shoulders as Mary clung tightly to one of the teacher's legs, and then proceeded to remedy the situation by quietly asking Dorothy whether the sand got in her eyes and suggesting to Billy that he had not said "good morning" to the rabbit in the nearby hutch. Soon, with the teacher's guiding suggestions, all four children were engaged in new activities. Apparently, the unfortunate end of the sand play was over with and forgotten by all concerned.

What can be learned about the maturation, growth, learning, and development of normal three-year-olds from the above incident? Do these observations agree with summary findings of research intended to discover the characteristics of normal three-year-olds? Did the teacher act wisely in terms of the implications of established research findings?

Professional personnel working with the young child have long been concerned with the problem of physical growth and development for they have observed that behavior of the moment is often related to the physical make-up of the child. The observer of the sand incident noted the use of large, somewhat uncontrolled muscle movements such as the seemingly purposeless piling of sand and the upward swinging of the arms with an aimless release of sand from the hands. Large-muscle activity is the rule during the early years. Out of these large-muscle, aimless, and seemingly endless activities there gradually emerge patterns of coordination and control.

Physical growth has been so well charted that most events, like the eruption of a particular tooth, the start of walking, or a later growth spurt can be predicted with considerable accuracy. In fact, the helpless, uncoordinated, and unskilled infant is able to progress through a succession of predictable and orderly developmental tasks with advancing age. Of course, this progress assumes the prerequisite nurture supplied by the parent and the home.

Stages of development, as previously indicated, always follow in a particu-

Figure 4. Play may be just fun to the little girl coming down the slide from the barrel. Climbing up through the barrel and holding back as she comes down the incline head first provides unlimited opportunity for tensing and flexing numerous muscles and provides the much needed movements for normal growth of the young child. Physical activity and physical growth are major concerns in centers for young children.

lar order. The child does not stand before he sits, nor does he draw a square before he draws a circle. This orderly progression of events moves forward at different rates of speed, some children growing and developing at a faster rate than others. In general, girls pass through these periods of maturity more rapidly than boys. It was noted that Dorothy and Mary seemed to be making "something" from the moist sand, while Billy and Robert were just actively, and more or less purposelessly, playing with the sand. Robert's fall wasn't merely an accident, rather it was a result of body proportions in which the legs and lower body parts are not developed proportionately to the upper body region with the result that the center of gravity is high and falls occur at the slightest excuse. For the same reason, three-year-olds tend to run rather than walk in order to get where they want to go. Longer legs would mean longer steps!

The plan of physical growth is so well coordinated that the emergence of each stage seems to depend on the mastery of the previous one through activity and exercise. The result is a continuous orderly process. The motivation for this process is one of the marvels of life itself. There is a certain urgency about growth inherent in the child. The growing, developing child is the end product of meeting this urgency through interaction with his environment.

Physical disproportions at ages three and four as compared to later years dictate many of the expectancies adults should have for the three-year-old child. Eyes, for example, are a part of the body proportions that are "oversize." It is just so much easier for objects, such as sand, to get into them! Because of their peculiar shape and developmental status, farsightedness is the expectation. Large objects, long play runways, big sheets of paper, and lots of room for active play are essential partly because the eyes play an important role in eye-muscle coordination. Growth inconsistencies, improperly proportioned body parts, lack of fine control and of personal learning experiences add to the picture and account for many of the characteristics of the motor activities of the young child. Reading, work requiring fine muscle skills, or concentrated attention are wisely postponed until development catches up with the demands of these activities.

The teacher of young children should become familiar with what research has found to be true of the age group of children she is working with. Such books as those by Breckenridge and Vincent,[29] Landreth,[30] Stone and Church,[31] Merry and Merry,[32] Smart and Smart,[33] and Garrison and Jones[34] will enable the teacher to acquire an excellent grasp of research important to an understanding of the growth and development of the young child as well as what to expect later. (See also Chapter 4.)

But the child as a person is not just a physical being. While he is developing physically, his personal-social and mental development is moving forward at a pace that challenges the abilities of adults working with him. Through language the child expresses his very being as well as the outside world as he sees it. Mary's "mother says 'No! No!' " is a sure sign that socialization is taking place. Already she is learning that doing or saying what adults closest to her think is wrong will bring disapproval.

The importance of language to the child's early development cannot be over emphasized. Language development is treated in detail elsewhere in this text.

Unfortunately, science has not been able to determine such orderly laws for the personal-social and mental areas of development as it has for physical development. It is likely that the unique personality characteristics that are so treasured by all account for the fact that personality descriptions tend to defy

---

[29]Marian E. Breckenridge and E. Lee Vincent, *Child Development*, 4th ed. (Philadelphia: W. B. Saunders, 1960).

[30]Catherine Landreth, *The Psychology of Early Childhood* (New York: Alfred A. Knopf, 1958).

[31]L. Joseph Stone and Joseph Church, *Childhood and Adolescence*, 2nd ed. (New York: Random House, 1968).

[32]Frieda K. Merry and R. V. Merry, *The First Two Decades of Life*, 2nd ed. (New York: Harper & Row, 1958).

[33]Mollie S. Smart and Russell C. Smart, *Children: Development and Relationships*, 2nd ed. (New York: Macmillan, Inc., 1972).

[34]Karl C. Garrison and Franklin R. Jones, *The Psychology of Human Development* (Scranton, Pa.: International Textbook Co., 1969).

lawful prediction. However, great strides are being made in personality research. Such publications as *Child Development, Childhood Education, Your Today's Child,* and *Young Children* enable teachers to keep abreast of new research findings as they apply to young children.

The fact that the other children did not notice Robert's leaving is characteristic of three-year-old children. It is true that they are happier in the presence of a few other children their own age, yet seldom do they play together. This type of play in the presence of, but not with, others their own age is known as parallel play. While the three-year-old is less demanding than he will become later, he usually stays with others only a few minutes and then leaves for a new group or to explore new worlds.[35]

Murphy found that the ability to perceive the need to sympathize with another when in distress does not occur until four years of age. This could explain why no one except the teacher came to Dorothy's aid when sand got in her eyes.[36] At no time was there evidence of cooperative endeavor on the part of the children in the report observation. Again, this type of effort is seldom observed before four years of age.[37]

Even as early as three, sex roles are being learned, as evidenced by Billy's cowboy type expressions and actions. However, sex-role identification is at a minimum. Little boys and girls can play together, fight with each other, share the same toilet facilities, and are seemingly unaware of sex differences. Modesty played no part whatever when Dorothy used the skirt of her dress to wipe the sand from her eyes. However, using a picture-interview technique, Fauls and Smith found that five-year-olds had well-established sex-role perceptions in keeping with the expectations of the social group of which their parents were a part.[38] Obviously, much social learning occurs very rapidly during the preschool years. It is felt by many that the attitudes toward others and toward right and wrong developed during these years strongly persist throughout childhood and adolescence and even during the entire life span. The implications for the need of well-qualified teachers of irreproachable character for preschool children are clear.

The question might be raised as to whether the teacher handled the sand-throwing incident correctly. What were the characteristics of three-year-olds that the teacher took into account? It should be pointed out that although the children were playing alone, the teacher must have been supervising carefully for she was present when needed. She knew that in times of distress three-year-olds need the reassurance of adults. She knew that crying and running to

[35]Gesell and Ilg, op. cit., pp. 209–210.

[36]Lois Barclay Murphy, *Social Behavior and Child Personality: An Exploratory Study of Some Roots of Sympathy* (New York: Columbia University Press, 1937).

[37]M. B. Parten, "Social Participation Among Pre-school Children," *J. Abnorm. Soc. Psychol.,* 27:2 (1932), pp. 243–269.

[38]Lydia B. Fauls and W. D. Smith, "Sex-Role Learning of Five-Year-Olds," *J. Genet. Psychol., 89*:2 (1956), pp. 105–107.

cling to the nearest adult are ways in which children of limited language facility bring their immediate needs to the attention of those they have learned to trust. The teacher knew that Billy wasn't being naughty and intentionally throwing sand at the girls in order to be mean. She was aware of the fact that three-year-olds do not carry grudges, that they forget their hurts quickly, and that most hurts are more surprise than real injury. One of the surest ways to aid developmental processes is to quietly and immediately redirect children's activities in positive directions. The professionally informed will recognize the teacher's handling of the situation as a case of positive child discipline despite the complete absence of physical punishment, threats, or depriving of privileges. Each child was reassured by word or act and enabled to quickly return to normal and satisfying activities. It should be recognized that what was right to do for the discipline and guidance of three-year-olds might not necessarily be the proper management of children of other ages and in other situations.

In discussing the reported observation of three-year-olds, little has been said about two very important facets of development: language and learning other than social. Although accounts vary, three-year-olds are reported to have a vocabulary of approximately 1,000 words.[39] They chatter incessantly, as was observed by the recorder of the typical observation reported earlier. It is theorized that this continuous use of words is the young child's way of testing his new-found power— the ability to communicate. The rapid learning of language and its ability to make possible the control of environment, is one of the most challenging and important aspects of development during the preschool years. At this stage, language is, at least partly, an imitative process. The adults present must avoid baby talk and be conscious of the fact that their enunciation and pronunciation is always the model that the child is following.

Although there is no lack of communication among children and adults in low income families, it is more often nonverbal in nature, making more use of gestures, stares, foot stomping, or physical handling. When communication is verbal the adult model uses fewer words and often the enunciation and grammatical structure is limited as few adults in low income families have had the opportunity to learn what is commonly called standard English.

The mere repetition of sounds or words on the part of younger children represents the beginnings of verbal communication. The child soon learns that speech is useful in bringing approval or disapproval to himself. In this way language is a strong force in the socialization process. At the same time it is directly functional, for through it the child is learning to communicate first with and about himself, and then with and to others. Many studies refer to these patterns of speech as the egocentric and socialized functions of language. There seems to be a gradual replacement of the egocentric expressions so prevalent in the early stages of language development by those of a socialized

[39]Mary K. Smith, "Measurement of the Size of General English Vocabulary Through the Elementary Grades and High School," *Genet. Psychol. Monogr.*, 24:2 (1941), pp. 311–345.

nature so that egocentric speech practically disappears by the time the child is seven or eight years of age.[40]

It is probably more realistic to point out that language and other forms of learning develop together than it is to argue whether language is a product of learning or that learning results from language development. Whatever the genesis, it is generally agreed that language plays an essential role in the rapid acquisition of knowledge, attitudes, and other ways of responding during the early preschool years.

It is not within the scope of this book to report in a detailed fashion a summary of the voluminous research in child development on the characteristics of preschool-age children. The preceding observational report and discussion concerned itself with some of the major findings of importance to the teacher of young children. There follows a similar report of the findings of major importance to the kindergarten teacher.

Observations in a Kindergarten

A student observer arrived at the kindergarten shortly after the opening of school one morning late in the school year. The day before she had observed a group of 14 three-year-olds. She had noticed that at no time were the three-year-olds all together as a group, and she was rather surprised to find 25 five-year-olds grouped comfortably and quietly in a semicircle around the teacher intently making plans for the day. During the discussion the teacher wrote in large letters on newsprint on the easel "quiet corner," "wheel toys," "picture making," "clay," "science," "story time," "juice," "outdoors," "rest," and

Figure 5. Individual or group play takes many forms, and objects of every description take on new meaning as they are given fascinating roles by the unlimited imagination possessed by children between the ages of three and six. Such explorations and experiences provide the basic raw materials upon which formal school learning is built.

[40]R. I. Watson, *Psychology of the Child* (New York: John Wiley and Sons, 1959).

Figure 6. Colorful and interesting puzzles provide young children an opportunity to recognize contrast, shape, form, and generalizations so important in the early phases of mental development. This boy studies intently the remaining pieces of the puzzle as he tries to decide where they will go to complete the picture.

"lunch." Three girls chose an activity by pointing to the words, "quiet corner," and went to a special corner set aside for this purpose. Three boys and one girl chose "wheel toys" and immediately proceeded to walk leisurely to the large covered porch where the tricycles, wagons, and similar toys were kept. Soon all the others were actively taking part, knowing that the teacher would warn them in plenty of time when it was story time, outdoor play time, time to rest, and time for lunch.

Obviously, great developmental strides had been made since these children were three years old. They could now plan as a group; they could be given more responsibility; they were learning that words had meaning and that choices meant certain responsibilities. Boys often selected energetic activities and girls often chose quieter and more intellectual tasks.

During the course of the morning the observer made certain notes that agreed with what she had learned in her child development courses. The following discussion includes the major characteristics of five-year-olds most of which were recorded as a result of one morning's observation in a typical kindergarten setting. The observer was struck by the fact that kindergarten children appeared more grown-up and had lost their "baby" looks. There seemed to be little difference in the size of boys and girls, some of each were larger than others, "perhaps the boys are slightly taller and heavier." There was no question that the boys were noisier, more easily distracted, and more active physically than the girls.

During outdoor play, both boys and girls exhibited good large-muscle control. They could run easily without tripping, they seemed especially good at climbing, swinging, and performing acts of daring on parallel bars, jungle gyms, suspended planks, and rope ladders. Those who climbed the sturdy branches of the several large oak trees near the building exhibited great assurance. "At one time, they looked and sounded like a flock of birds in the trees, as they went through their well-practiced 'acts,' singing merrily as they did so," recorded the student. Another significant comment was "at no time during the morning did any of the children appear to miss mother or home. Once, a little girl picked herself up after getting in the way of two boys playing horse, looking shyly as if deciding whether to cry, ran to the teacher and held her hand momentarily, then hurried back to join her group at the outdoor easel."

The morning's observation produced some additional statistics. Two boys and one girl were left-handed; all the rest were obviously right-handed. No one seemed concerned about the fact that three of the children used their left hands predominantly. All of the children participated in preparing, serving, and drinking juice and eating crackers just before going out to play. All seemed to be ready for and to enjoy the "nap" just before lunch. The morning produced surprisingly few conflicts and squabbles, which were usually resolved quickly, often without the teacher's help.

In comparison to three-year-olds, most five-year-olds handle language well, using it to question, to answer, to suggest, and to get permission to do things. Both vocabulary and sentence structure have greatly improved. The five-year-old has become quite independent and responsible. He can run errands, follow directions and carry out rather complicated tasks. His conscience seems to be developing rapidly for he quickly judges and reports the small deeds of others as right or wrong.[41] Gesell and Ilg have provided a detailed account of the typical five-year-old.[42]

Emotional Development

Various studies of certain aspects of the emotional development of young children show that emotional control and generally more mature behavior gradually develop during the preschool years. For example, Goodenough's classic study of expressions of anger in young children showed a gradual decline with age of undirected general anger outbursts and a corresponding increase in anger resulting from conflicts or situations which might be described as a reasonable excuse for anger. Of interest to teachers was the finding that there were more anger expressions just before mealtime, when the

[41]Gladys G. Jenkins, Helen Schacter, and W. W. Bauer, *These Are Your Children*, 3rd ed. (Chicago: Scott, Foresman, 1966).

[42]Gesell and Ilg., op. cit., Ch. 20.

children were tired, were coming down with an illness, or when some atypical home condition, such as the presence of visitors, existed.[43]

Likewise, Jersild and Holmes found that most of the specific situations which evoked fear responses in two- and three-year-old children did not produce like responses from five-year-olds.[44] These developmental differences, like so many others, apparently are due to a combination of the effects of maturation and learning. At any rate, the five-year-old represents a rather well-organized, somewhat calm and delightful period of life as if in preparation for the demanding expectations of the more academic school years ahead.

Development of Motor Skills

Hicks studied the learning skills of young children involved in ball throwing at a moving target over a period of eight weeks. One group practiced ten throws each week while another group, which was matched with the experimental group on initial ball throwing ability, was not given the practice. When tested at the end of the experiment, both groups had made gains but the experimental (practice) group did not make significantly better gains than the second (control) group. Apparently, children not in the control group were practicing the same skills in the course of daily living. Of course, it could be questioned whether the practice periods were often enough or intensive enough over a period as short as eight weeks to produce measurable differences in learning a complex skill.[45] Psychologists speak of learning which goes on without specific intent to learn in keeping with the maturation process as autogenous learning. Much of the learning of preschool children falls into this category.

SUMMARY

Rather than list a set of characteristics of the young child at various age levels, it should prove more meaningful to illustrate some of the principles this chapter has developed. Young children are not alike; each has unique qualities and features that are evident early in life. Starting with innate differences, variations in growth and maturation processes interacting with the multiplicity of possible environmental differences, both physical and human, result in development which further differentiates, and thus accounts for the individuality of personality. An excellent example of this differentiation is found in the usually retarded language and achievement levels of children from severely disadvantaged homes. These basic components of individuality are well established during the preschool years. Because these processes take place very rapidly during the early years of life, major developmental dif-

[43]Florence L. Goodenough, "Anger in Young Children," *Univ. Minn. Inst. Child Welf. Monogr. Ser.*, 9 (1931).

[44]A. T. Jersild and Frances B. Holmes, "Children's Fears," *Child Develop. Monogr.*, 20 (1935).

[45]J. A. Hicks, "The Acquisition of Motor Skill in Young Children: A Study of the Effects of Practice in Throwing at a Moving Target," *Child Develop.*, 1:2 (1930), pp. 90–105.

ferences occur during this period at shorter intervals than at any later period of life, accounting for dramatic and challenging changes observed in young children.

Today much emphasis is placed on the importance of how a child views himself, that is, on the development of the concept of self. There are those who would build a young child's learning experiences entirely around this concept. However, it is becoming increasingly clear that a healthy self-concept is dependent on how well a child's behavior fits social and environmental expectancies for only such behavior receives the reinforcement provided by approval, praise, and acceptance. For example, "Sesame Street" has become a symbol of good child-rearing practice by middle-class families in America even though the program was not designed with this audience in mind. A young middle-class child who is not exposed to "Sesame Street" would be likely to feel somewhat inferior among his peers and their parents who are familiar with the program. It would seem realistic, therefore, to view each child's concept of himself in relation to all aspects of his development, including cognitive development, rather than as an isolated concept.

Students of child growth and development have found that development corresponds rather closely with maturational change and growth patterns. To the person who understands the processes of growth, maturation, and development, there are always little signs as to what will occur later. For example, not long ago a mother called who was very concerned because her child was not walking when other children of the same age were. The child was observed during the interview. Certain signs were noticed such as creeping and moving in a circular direction, attempting to pull himself up on every occasion, and a general effort to arrive in an upright position. These signs indicated that within a few weeks the child would be walking and that development was occurring as a result of maturation and growth. The mother was reassured and reported several weeks later that her child was walking. The important point here is that when one understands the developmental process and watches for the little signs that precede an actual act, anxieties can easily be relieved. It is also important to know that readiness is often primarily a biological function which cannot be hurried. Nevertheless, it is necessary to keep in mind that biological development does not proceed on its own without suitable environmental nurture. Unfortunately, in the past, lack of readiness has often been mistaken for an inherent biological lack rather than a lack of adequate environmental stimulation to enable maturation to occur on schedule. However, when the state or maturation point is arrived at and the act can be completed, the child will complete the act and do it with enthusiasm and with a high degree of motivation. Psychologists call this indigenous motivation which means that when one is able to do something because of maturation, he will do it, and with zest and vigor. Everyone has observed young children arriving at this stage.

Another important factor is that growth, although it occurs rather uniformly for an individual, may take place in one child at a speed or rate different from that of other children. So far as is known, this is an inherited characteristic and each growing child possesses an individual pattern and rate of growth. When he arrives at a certain place in this pattern he can "tune in" and achieve the goal just the same as a radio can be tuned in to get a program that was present all the time but was not coming in until the radio was tuned in to the proper wavelength. Similarly, certain activities and certain behavioral acts cannot be achieved until the proper "wavelength" represented by development can be tuned in to the circumstances provided in the environment. The teacher or parent can no more change this process than the color of one's hair can be changed. True, hair can be dyed and temporarily it will appear different but it will grow out to be the color it should be at a particular time; the change is only temporary. The same kind of thing often happens when youngsters are pushed and undue pressures put upon them, or when remedial work is carried on for long periods of time. Always, the individual functions in keeping with his stage of development.

Perhaps the best way to summarize is to indicate that there is likely to be no "static," or discipline problems, when the wavelength is right and the activities are tuned in to the child's stage of development. It is important to realize further that all behavior is caused and that undesirable behavior results when the individual is not properly "tuned in" in terms of his activities in relation to his stage of development and his ability "to do."

Some three-year-olds may be able to do the tasks normally expected of five-year-olds, and some five-year-olds can do only the tasks usually expected of three-year-olds. But in general, the expectancies adults have for each child should be in keeping with those suitable to his age group and his particular stage of development. The concept of "threeness," "fiveness," and so on, so common in the literature, has served a useful purpose by pointing out to teachers and parents the direction they can reasonably expect a child's development to take. However, educational programs for groups based on such concepts without provision for a wide range of individual differences in development, would most surely fail to provide for the optimal development of each child as a person.

Suggested Activities

1. Prepare a class report in detail on the development of children on specific topics such as "readiness to learn," "a typical four-year-old," "learning sex roles," "early speech development," "motor development of five-year-olds." Use the references given in the text and any other that you can find on the topic.

2. Discuss and decide on a specific topic such as some of those in 1 above, "readiness for the first day of school," "teeth and the preschooler," "children's diseases," "socialization," "motor development and materials and equipment," "sibling relationships," "development of creativity," "crying," and so on. Prepare and report

on one research study from the current periodicals related to the above topics. Discuss each report and use the study as a basis for continuing discussion.

3. Arrange with a nursery school or kindergarten teacher to observe for 15 minutes a planned activity with a group of young children. Immediately afterwards, write down what you learned about children and about yourself from the experience. If several members of the group do the same thing, such observations can provide the information for a lively class discussion.

4. Select a child to observe over a period of time. Evaluate his concept of self. Document with descriptive observations how you arrived at the conclusions of your evaluation.

Related Readings

Bandura, A., and R. H. Walters. *Social Learning and Personality Development.* New York: Holt, Rinehart and Winston, 1963.

Bereiter, C., and S. Englemann. *Teaching Disadvantaged Children in the Preschool.* Englewood Cliffs, N.J.: Prentice-Hall, 1966.

Bloom, B. S., A. Davis, and R. Hess. *Compensatory Education for Cultural Deprivation.* New York: Holt, Rinehart and Winston, 1965.

Bruner, J. S. *The Process of Education.* Cambridge, Mass.: Harvard University Press, 1960.

Deutsch, M. "Facilitating Development in the Pre-School Child: Social and Psychological Perspectives," *Merrill-Palmer Quart.,* 10 (1964), pp. 249–263.

Flavell, J. H. *The Developmental Psychology of Jean Piaget.* Princeton, N.J.: Van Nostrand, 1962.

Gardner, Bruce D. *Development in Early Childhood—The Pre-School Years.* New York: Harper & Row, 1964.

Hechinger, F. M., ed. *Pre-School Education Today.* Council for Public Schools, Inc., Boston, 1963.

Hunt, J. McV. *Intelligence and Experience.* New York: Ronald Press, 1961.

———. "The Psychological Basis for Using Pre-School Enrichment as an Antidote for Cultural Deprivation," *Merrill-Palmer Quart.,* 10:3 (1964), pp. 209–248.

Jahoda, M. *Current Concepts of Positive Mental Health.* New York: Basic Books, 1958.

Kagan, J. "A Developmental Approach to Conceptual Growth," in *The Analysis of Concept Learning,* ed. H. Klausmeier. New York: Academic Press, 1966.

Mednick, S. A. *Learning.* Englewood Cliffs, N.J.: Prentice-Hall, 1964.

Mowrer, O. H. *Learning Theory and Behavior.* New York: John Wiley and Sons, 1960.

Mussen, P. H., J. J. Conger, and J. Kagen, *Readings in Child Development and Personality,* 2nd ed. New York: Harper & Row, 1970.

Office of Economic Opportunity. *Head Start Child Development Programs—An Invitation to Help.* Washington, D.C.: U.S. Government Printing Office, 1965.

Piaget, J. "The General Problems of the Psychobiological Development of the Child," in *Discussions on Child Development,* ed. J. M. Tanner and B. Inhelder, Vol. 4. New York: International Universities Press, 1960.

———. *The Origins of Intelligence in Children,* trans. Margaret Cook. New York: International Universities Press, 1952.

Rasmussen, Margaret, ed. *Readings from Childhood Education.* Washington, D.C.: Association for Childhood Educational International, 1966. Section II, pp. 51–126.

Smart, Mollie S., and R. C. Smart. *Children: Development and Relationships,* 2nd ed. New York: Macmillan, Inc., 1972.

Torrance, E. Paul. *Constructive Behavior: Stress, Personality, and Mental Health.* Belmont, Calif.: Wadsworth, 1965.

Wann, K. D., Miriam S. Dorn, and Elizabeth Ann Liddle. *Fostering Intellectual Development in Young Children.* New York: Teachers College, Columbia University, 1960.

Yamamoto, Kaoru, ed. *The Child and His Image.* Boston: Houghton Mifflin, 1972.

The Young Child as a Research Subject

Chapter **4**

Behavioral scientists often use animals as subjects because custom and human values tend to discourage the use of human subjects in controlled experimentation. In many cases the information obtained from such research is likely to be as valid when interpreted in terms of human behavior; still, the question always remains: would humans react in the same way? College students provide a readily accessible source of subjects for research and have been used extensively as such. Preschool-age children as research subjects, except for hospital and institutional populations such as orphans, seriously ill, and physically disabled children, have been much more difficult to secure.

Today with thousands of young children in Child Development Centers, which usually require some participation on the part of parents, opportunities for research with children and their families are almost unlimited. It has been the experience of researchers in centers where parents participate that it is easier to secure their consent to have their children take part in research efforts. Such has not been the case where parents were only responsible for seeing that the children were delivered to the custody of the school or center. It enhances the self-concept of parents when they feel that they are actively participating in an effort that may produce new and better ways of providing a chance for their own children to have a richer, more rewarding life than they themselves have enjoyed.

Experimental Programs

Beginning in the 1920's, a few universities established nursery schools and kindergartens to provide preschool-age children for research. This practice has continued and many universities now have such laboratory groups of children. However, it was not until the advent of Head Start in 1965 that a large number of groups of preschool-age children became readily available for research purposes. Research sponsored by the Office of Economic Opportunity, other government agencies, and foundations during the present decade is providing a wealth of information about how young children, particularly disadvantaged children, learn and give clues to the improvement of educational practices for all young children. As would be expected, a rapid search for quick panaceas for the faults of the entire educational program took place at once and often extravagant claims were made on the basis of short-term, sometimes poorly designed, and small-sample research.

While innovation and experimentation are to be encouraged, the early childhood education teacher should carefully weigh the evidence presented before making radical departures from accepted procedures that have in the past enabled most preschool children to successfully make the transition to the more formal public school program.

Most experimental programs are conducted at a much greater cost than regular programs. Consequently, more and better equipment and materials and usually more faculty and helpers are involved. Often the teacher or experimenter is imbued with confidence and a missionary zeal. Without comparable conditions and support of existing programs, it is unfair to make comparisons and claim superior achievements. Many such research programs have deliberately excluded the stimulation of areas of development other than the one being studied, usually the cognitive or intellectual area. It is not surprising that children learn specific facts or skills more rapidly when they are formally taught rather than when expected to learn them incidentally. The important question is whether these specific facts and skills are the "right" ones and whether they will truly be effective in the later school and personal life of the child involved. When areas of development, earlier shown to be necessary correlates to learning and personality development, have been purposefully omitted or relegated to roles of secondary importance, will the end-product be in keeping with the goals of American education? Observations of the preschool programs in the early 1960's have indicated that the cognitive and intellectual

Figure 7. An observation booth with a one-way vision mirror lends itself to conducting research about children.

development of young children, in some instances at least, have received less attention than other areas such as social, physical, and emotional development.[1] Calling attention to this lack can well serve a useful purpose in helping bring a better balanced program of education for young children, provided that other areas of development are not neglected. It is a well-known fact that the medical profession soon discovered that the quick acceptance and widespread use of antibiotics and other miracle drugs had made it harder to cure the very diseases the drugs were developed to cure, because through overuse of these medications the organism tends to develop an immunity. Child development specialists caution that too intensive emphasis on academic learning, too early, might likewise make later learning more difficult to achieve.

Although it has been claimed that early research in child development neglected the cognitive areas, it can also be said with equal vindictiveness that much of the research in the last half of the 1960's tended to ignore areas of development other than the cognitive area. The futility of an either-or approach was becoming evident as research merged into the decade of the 1970's. It was becoming accepted that whatever the research orientation or focus, the ulti-

[1]F. M. Hechinger, ed., *Pre-School Education Today* (Garden City, N.Y.: Doubleday & Co., 1966). Also, C. Bereiter and S. Engelmann, *Teaching Disadvantaged Children in the Preschool* (Englewood Cliffs, N.J.: Prentice-Hall, 1966).

mate goal was the extension of knowledge that would enable children to have an opportunity for optimum personal development, assuring a "good" life for all.

Research, of necessity, cannot be global in nature. Rather, research must focus on specifics that can be defined and controlled but, at the same time, can be fitted into the larger stream of theory and ongoing practice. To expect the busy teacher or center worker to select helpful guidelines from thousands of research reports is expecting the impossible. Rather, it is the responsibility of scholars and professional organizations to digest and integrate research findings into useful terms for research to serve its function and to justify its cost. One such effort worthy of note is a volume editied by Hartup.[2] For an encyclopedic, up-to-date review of research in child psychology, see Mussen.[3]

REVIEW OF EARLIER RESEARCH

Although large sample research using young children was not extensive prior to the 1950's, important reviews have been made. Excellent analyses of research in all areas of development in young children can be found in *The Manual of Child Psychology*.[4] Descriptions and evaluations of the most common techniques and methods used in studying many aspects of child growth and behavior, as well as other valuable content, are included in the *Handbook of Research Methods in Child Development*.[5]

Prepared under the auspices of the Society for Research in Child Development, the *Review of Child Development Research* provides the student with a reference to important research studies in child development as well as an excellent source of additional readings.[6] Use should also be made of standard library resources such as the *Annual Review of Psychology*, the *Encyclopedia of Educational Research, The Handbook of Research on Teaching, The Review of Educational Research, Child Development Abstracts and Bibliography*, and *Psychological Abstracts*.

Sears and Dowley have traced the effect of research on teaching and procedures used in the nursery school.[7] They draw attention to the fact that nursery education in the United States has had as its primary objective the welfare of persons other than the children, with a resulting lack of emphasis on the child

---

[2]Willard W. Hartup, ed., *The Young Child, Reviews of Research*, Vol. 2., (Washington D.C.,: National Association for the Education of Young Children, 1972).

[3]Paul H. Mussen, ed., *Carmichael's Manual of Child Psychology*, 3rd ed., Vols. 1 and 2. (New York: John Wiley and Sons, 1970).

[4]Ibid.

[5]P. H. Mussen, ed. (New York: John Wiley and Sons, 1960).

[6]M. L. Hoffman and Lois Wladis Hoffman, *Review of Child Development Research*, Russell Sage Foundation, 2 vols., 1964 and 1967.

[7]Pauline S. Sears and Edith M. Dowley, "Research on Teaching in the Nursery School," in *Handbook of Research on Teaching*, ed. N. L. Gage, Chapter 15 (Chicago: Rand McNally, 1963).

as an individual. The results of the several longitudinal studies of the 1920's and 1930's caused teachers to change their emphasis to concern for the growth and development of children. Following World War II more concern for parent involvement developed, and the permissive, protective programs of small groups of children gave way to more structured programs of larger groups of children.

RECENT RESEARCH

It was not until the late 1950's and 1960's that a genuine need for, and interest in, research on the early learning and development of cognitive skills took place. Landmarks in this area were the publication of Piaget's *The Origins of Intelligence in Children*,[8] Hunt's *Intelligence and Experience*,[9] Bruner's *The Process of Education*,[10] and Bloom's *Stability and Change in Human Characteristics*.[11] As a result of these and similar publications, researchers and programmers turned their attention to the early years of development. There were numerous experimental programs concerned almost wholly with the concept of learning as being the acquisition of specific material. Such acquisition was, and still is, widely lauded as superior to the kind of learning that grows out of meaningful experience and results from the interests and needs of children. Proponents of the acquisition concept point out that such early acquisition is necessary because the materials taught are the basic elements of what the child is expected to learn on entering a regular elementary school program.

Students of the history of education are not surprised by these developments, for history shows that educational programs have always been sensitive to contemporary social and cultural conditions. In a like manner, the accompanying research always has as its objective finding more efficient means of achieving the desired outcomes. The Space Age has brought about a need for highly structured areas of knowledge and public concern for the quality of education in the schools. The best development of each child as an individual thus became secondary to the aim of having children acquire as much specific knowledge as possible in the shortest possible time. Because research had discovered that young children learn rapidly and acquire vast amounts of specific knowledge quickly, much attention was directed to the education of preschool children in the middle 1960's.

Concurrent with the increased Space Age needs, poverty and its attendant educational problems increased at an alarming rate. Children of poverty-stricken families have always suffered an acute educational disadvantage.

---

[8]J. Piaget, *The Origins of Intelligence in Children* (New York: International Universities Press, 1952).

[9]J. McV. Hunt, *Intelligence and Experience* (New York: Ronald Press, 1960).

[10]J. S. Bruner, *The Process of Education* (Cambridge, Mass.: Harvard University Press, 1961).

[11]B. Bloom, *Stability and Change in Human Characteristics* (New York: John Wiley and Sons, 1964).

However, it was not until the affluent 1960's that the disparities between the poor and the rest of society became critical enough to cause national concern. Educators applauded when the federal government took measures to attack poverty with educational programs, especially programs for very young children. This mammoth effort required not only educational programs but large-scale research concerning the effectiveness and improvement of these programs.

Language Research

Crucial to all education is the acquisition of language and communication skills. Typical of the all-out attack on language acquisition is the work of Bereiter and Engelmann. They conclude:[12]

> Evidence was cited which suggests that lack of concrete learning has relatively little to do with the intellectual and academic deficiences of disadvantaged children and that it is the lack of verbal learning, in particular the lack of those kinds of learning that can only be transmitted from adults to children through language, that is mainly responsible for these deficiencies. Thus there is justification for treating cultural deprivation as synonymous with language deprivation.

Bereiter and Engelmann have presented evidence that the exclusion of every possible opportunity to experience other than the specifics being taught results in a much greater rate of learning than is normally experienced by children. It is their thesis that by teaching the essential and fundamental content for school achievement that disadvantaged children will quickly catch up with their more privileged peers and, thus, be able to compete favorably with them in regular school. The experienced educator, while impressed with the valuable contributions of this work, will view with caution the authoritarian evangelism with which the authors present their program.

Because highly developed speech and language distinguish man from all other living organisms, the importance of these faculties has long held the attention of scholars and research workers. As both faculties are highly developed before American children are required to enter school, a knowledge of research findings in these areas can be of great value to the preschool teacher.

Language is not only a symbolic representation of objectives and ideas, it is also a means of expressing feelings and thoughts including facial expression and gestures. Piaget early believed that thought precedes language but that as language competency develops language directs thinking.[13] The earliest and most frequent use of language by the very young child is essentially emotional in nature and is used to express his desires and feelings.[14] The use of words and

---

[12]C. Bereiter and S. Engelmann, *Teaching Disadvantaged Children in the Preschool* (Englewood Cliffs, N.J.: Prentice-Hall, 1966), p. 42.

[13]J. Piaget, *Language and Thought of the Child* (New York: Humanities Press, 1951).

[14]Dorothea McCarthy, "Language Development in Children," in *Manual of Child Psychology*, ed. L. Carmichael, 2nd ed. (New York: John Wiley and Sons, 1954).

symbols for objects or events comes later. Thus, it would appear that teaching letters of the alphabet, parts of words representing sounds and sound combinations, and written symbols before meaningful experiences that result in feelings and thoughts on the part of the child, would not be the most efficient way of promoting language success.

Language development is indeed an exceedingly complex problem and much research attention is being given to it by psychologists, linguists, learning theorists, and grammarians. Reacting to papers presented at a conference on the acquisition of language, Deese comments:[15]

> The human being is able to transcend the effects of a reinforcement schedule through his ability to store and internalize environment behavior and intrabehavioral relations through the mediation of language; therefore, it is that aspect of language which makes it different from elements of behavior simply and entirely under the control of reinforcement contingencies, which makes language unique and worth studying in its own right.

It is the belief of the authors of this text that any program that ignores major areas of the growth and developmental needs of the child will not succeed in producing an individual who can function intelligently in a democratic society.

Cognitive Research

Cognition, or the process of knowing, has long been a subject for theory and research, especially by European scientists. Because cognition embraces thought and concept formation or meaningful understanding, an increasing number of American researchers and theorists have turned to studies of cognition in young children in an effort to determine more effective educational procedures. While the age-old battle concerning the effects of heredity and environment on intelligence and learning ability is far from resolved, much emphasis today is placed on environmental effects. The Russian scientist, Zaporozhets, summarizes thus:[16]

> At the beginning, a new way of becoming acquainted with an object is usually carried into practice by organs that are capable of performing both practical and cognitive functions, such as the hands' touching and manipulating an object or by the muscle apparatus of the larynx. . . . In reality, as we have tried to show in our paper, a given form of perception is the product of a continuous development that goes on in the child under the influences of practical experiences and learning.

---

[15]J. Deese, "Comments and Conclusions," in U. Bellugi and R. Brown, *The Acquisition of Language, Monogr. Soc. Res. Child Develpm.*, 29:1 (1964), p. 180.

[16]A. V. Zaporozhets, "The Development of Perception in the Preschool Child," in *European Research in Cognitive Development, Monogr. Soc. Res. Child Develpm.*, 30:2 (1965), pp. 98 and 100.

Flavell,[17] an American exponent of Piaget, Ojemann and Pritchett,[18] and Deutsch,[19] among others, have presented evidence to show that cognitive development can be modified and/or accelerated by manipulating the child's environment in specific ways. As a result, many preschool programs are becoming more structured than in the past. Considered modifications of the more permissive, relatively unstructured, programs of the past, placing more emphasis on learning and intellectual development, does result in better educational experiences for young children. It is only when undue stress is placed on learning, or on a single component of development, that the quality of a good school program is endangered. The early childhood teacher must have preparation to enable her to understand and interpret research if she is to provide the best possible educational experiences for young children.

To say that, since the first edition of this text, interest in the importance of early education to the child's later development had waned would be a gross misstatement. The National Society for the Study of Education devoted its four-hundred-page Seventy-first Yearbook to early childhood education.[20] While reading the Yearbook, one cannot help but be impressed by the documented dependence on research for the viewpoints expressed by the various authors. It would be highly premature to say that a theory of early childhood education had emerged at the time of the publication of this text. Indeed, it would be more accurate to say that the research of the 1960's and early 1970's, while clearly building on and adding to earlier findings was only a beginning, albeit, a fruitful and encouraging one. The Yearbook's chapter on research and evaluation[21] points the way toward more fruitful research strategies and methodology to provide information enabling the development of innovative and functional educational programs for young children. It is long past the time when research efforts solely to raise the IQ should be abandoned in favor of recording sophisticated observable change resulting from the implementation of clearly stated objectives, whether they be in the physical, affective, or cognitive domains.

Perhaps the concept *educational assessment* is more fitting than research per se in determining the effectiveness of specific educational and teaching strategies when dealing with programs for young children. This should in no way detract from the value of basic research as a means of providing assumptions and hypotheses for making decisions for change. However, assessment rather than research may well provide the most valuable data on which to make de-

[17]J. H. Flavell, *The Developmental Psychology of Jean Piaget* (New York: Van Nostrand, 1964).

[18]R. Ojemann and K. Pritchett, "Piaget and the Role of Guided Experience in Human Development," *Perceptual and Motor Skills*, 17 (1963).

[19]M. Deutsch, "Facilitating Development in the Pre-School Child: Social and Psychological Perspectives," *Merrill-Palmer Quart.*, 10:3 (1964), pp. 249–263.

[20]Ira J. Gordon, ed., *Early Childhood Education*, The Seventy-first Yearbook of the National Society for the Study of Education, Part II (Chicago: University of Chicago Press, 1972).

[21]Ibid., pp. 261–290.

cisions to continue, discontinue, or modify existing procedures and programs. For an elaboration of educational assessment see the ASCD publication edited by Beatty.[22]

For an excellent resource of research in process refer to current issues of *Research Relating to Children.*[23]

SUMMARY

The technological, economic, and social developments of recent decades have brought about a re-evaluation of the effectiveness of the American educational program. As a result, the importance of education during the early childhood years has become accepted. However, there is little accord as to the best methods and curriculum to be used.

Influenced by an abundance of sponsored research, many innovative and experimental schools for young children have come into being. Recent research has pointed particularly to the importance of language and cognitive development during the early years. Much of this effort has been aimed at enabling children who have been deprived of normal early experiences to catch up, or compensate, for the lack of learning competencies thus brought about.

Research on the early years of life is long overdue and should be welcomed and encouraged. However, as is true of all research, findings should be implemented only as they apply to conditions under which the research was conducted; they should not be generalized. Educators should not view all research efforts with alarm. Rather, with the present improved research technology and support, early childhood educators should view these developments as the frontier movement in education today and point the way to innovation and improvement in the entire educational system.

Suggested Activities

1. Ask child psychologists and research personnel to discuss with the class latest research findings in relation to early childhood education.
2. Have various members of the class report on research findings published in current journals.
3. Organize a discussion or debate on the pros and cons of the more structured programs for young children. Use research findings to support each view.
4. Select one instrument for assessing a teaching strategy. Use it with children and evaluate its effectiveness.

---

[22]Walcott H. Beatty, ed., *Improving Educational Assessment and an Inventory of Measures of Affective Behavior,* (Washington D.C.: Association for Supervision and Curriculum Development, NEA, 1969).

[23]*Research Relating to Children,* ERIC Clearing House on Early Childhood Education (For sale by the Superintendent of Documents, U.S. Government Printing Office, Washington D.C. 20402).

Related Readings

Bellugi, U., and R. Brown, eds. *The Acquisition of Language, Mono. Soc. for Res. in Child Develpm., 29* (1964).

Bereiter, C., and S. Engelmann. *Teaching Disadvantaged Children in the Preschool.* Englewood Cliffs, N.J.: Prentice-Hall, 1966.

Bloom, B. *Stability and Change in Human Characteristics.* New York: John Wiley and Sons, 1964.

Bruner, J. S. *The Process of Education.* Cambridge, Mass.: Harvard University Press, 1961.

Gage, N. L., ed. *Handbook of Research on Teaching.* Chicago: Rand McNally, 1963. Ch. 15.

Gordon, I. J. *Early Childhood Education* The Seventy-first Yearbook of the National Society for the Study of Education, Part II. Chicago: University of Chicago Press, 1972.

Hartup, W., ed. *The Young Child Review of Research,* Vol. 2. Washington, D.C.: The National Association for the Education of Young Children, 1972.

Harris, C. W., ed. *Encyclopedia of Educational Research,* 3rd ed. New York: Macmillan, Inc., 1960.

Hechinger, F. M., ed. *Pre-School Education Today.* Garden City, N.Y.: Doubleday & Co., 1966.

Hoffman, M. L., and Lois W. Hoffman, eds. *Review of Child Development Research,* 2 vols. New York: Russell Sage Foundation, 1964 and 1967.

Hunt, J. McV. *Intelligence and Experience.* New York: Ronald Press, 1960.

Johnson, O. G., and J. W. Bommarito. *Tests and Measurements in Child Development.* San Francisco: Jossey-Boss Inc., 1971.

Mills, Belen Collantes. *Understanding the Young Child and His Curriculum.* New York: Macmillan, Inc., 1972.

Mussen, P. H., ed. *Carmichael's Manual of Child Psychology,* Vols. I and II, 3rd ed. New York: John Wiley and Sons, Inc., 1970.

Mussen, P. H., ed. *Handbook of Research Methods in Child Development.* New York: John Wiley and Sons, 1960.

The Behavior
of Young Children:
Guidance and Discipline
Chapter **5** ━━━━━━━━━━━━━━━━━━━━━━

"You know . . . that the beginning is the most important part of any work, especially in the case of a young and tender thing; for that is the time at which the character is being formed." These words, as expressed by the philosopher Plato, have been emphasized by the findings of research in the areas of child growth and development. The early years are particularly important because habits and attitudes formed at this time may affect many aspects of a child's later life. The guidance given the child at the time that he has an experience may determine whether the resulting habits and attitudes are good or bad, even in adult life. Children learn, with or without instruction, and persons working closely with young children often are not aware that they offer guidance almost continuously. The effectiveness of this guidance depends on an understanding of the young child, his environment, and the goals and aspirations of the adults with whom he comes in contact.

Problems related to the guidance of behavior and to discipline do not solve

57

themselves. It is important, then, to consider related factors such as objectives and values, the environment, and the behavior that is considered normal and healthy for the age of the child.

Objectives and Values

Attitudes and habits are developed as children work and play together in an environment that provides opportunities for physical, mental, and social growth. "Understanding," "getting along," and "cooperating" are not taught during designated periods of the day but are experienced as the child participates in activites such as science experiments or getting ready for lunch. The concern is not only for the experiences that a child may have, but also for what happens to the child as he participates in these experiences. For example, as the child plays with other children, certain questions arise. Is he growing in his ability to "trust others," "get along," "take turns," or "have fun," and, as a result, learning to like people and to feel adequate as a person? Or, are the other children too much for him? Are they a threat? As a result, is he becoming bossy, aggressive, or withdrawn? What is happening to the child's concept of himself? Is he coming to think of himself as a person who can tackle hard jobs or one who says "I can't"; one who tries new activities, or one who hangs back; one who has friends, or one whom nobody likes?

If objectives and values are to be realized, there is need for consistency between purposes and actions both verbal and nonverbal. Adults who guide the behavior of children need to examine their values and goals in relation to practice. A thoughtful consideration of the following questions can help: What are the values which it is hoped the child will come to accept? Are they, for example, honesty, cooperation, or respect for the worth and dignity of the individual? What type of individual will the child become? Will he be understanding, adequate, cooperative, enthusiastic, aggressive, submissive, self-directing, or inquiring? Answers to questions such as these can serve as guides for the examination of practices. It is important that each teacher answer them for herself. Teachers of young children will find a basis for answering such questions on pp. 61–64. As each teacher answers the questions for herself, she may find that her procedures are not consistent with the desired ends or values. It is easy to say one thing and do something else. The following example illustrates how conflicts between purposes and practices may result in undesirable outcomes in the behavior of children.

In a meeting of kindergarten teachers, one member asked, "How do you make children sit still during story time?" There were several questions in reply. "What types of stories do you read?" "How long are the stories?" "When do you have story time?" The first teacher, impatient with the questions, replied, "It doesn't matter when or what I read. I intend to see that the children sit still and listen when I read a story." If one were to ask this teacher her purposes in reading the story, the following would probably be included:

(Courtesy of Head Start)

Figure 8. An atmosphere in which the self-concept may be enhanced is one in which the child can make an error and not lose face, one in which each child can help to purpose and plan.

(1) to develop an appreciation of good literature, (2) to stimulate interest in reading, and (3) to provide pleasure and information. Her actions, however, tended to defeat the purposes she was trying to accomplish. By giving little or no attention to the selection read, by insisting that children sit and hear material that might have little meaning for them, story time was becoming not only an ordeal for the teacher, but a very uninteresting activity for the children. Such emphasis could easily cancel the values of appreciation and pleasure.

Values, however, can reinforce one another. A story, carefully chosen and well read, can provide pleasure and information, as well as develop interest, appreciation, and listening skills. In recognizing the importance of consistency between goals, values, and practice in guiding behavior, it is necessary to examine the opportunities during the school day for learning values and the ways in which concepts are acquired.

At times children have not shown much ambition or enthusiasm for learning what has been expected of them. The "natural" learning capabilities and aspirations of each child must be considered.[1]

It is important to consider how the teacher develops goals for and with the

[1]D. Russell, "Goals for American Education: The Individual Focus," *Educ. Leadership, 28*:6 (1971), pp. 592–594.

children. Teaching objectives are related to broad educational goals and are planned for both the group and the individual. The teacher may be concerned with helping the group in setting standards for behavior as she and the children plan together for using the new tools. In helping an individual achieve the same goal, she may plan to support his attempts to make a decision, and to carry it out. For example, Emmie was having trouble in sawing the wood and started to leave. The teacher offered to hold the board and with this help Emmie was able to finish the job.

The teacher has the responsibility of helping the child to be aware of the goal currently being developed. For example, she may be trying to help the child gain confidence in his ability. When the child says, "I can't do this," the teacher may reply, "Do it in your own way. What can you do first?"

In selecting a goal for emphasis, the teacher might choose a focus because of the interest and readiness of the children or because there has been little opportunity to work toward achieving this goal. Attainment of goals may often involve teacher support and clarification as well as participation in selected activities.

The behavior of the child may tend to obscure his goals. The wise teacher understands. Kim picked up Jane's mitten and ran to the jungle gym. Jane told the teacher. The teacher said, "She was trying to play with you. I think she wanted to be your friend." The role of the adult in working with children involves observing, supporting, clarifying, enhancing, and sharing.[2]

Prescott identifies the opportunities and responsibilities that teachers and parents have in the education of children. These are as follows:[3]

1. To maintain conditions appropriate for each individual's growth and development.
2. To establish and to maintain supporting, security-giving relationships with each individual.
3. To supply informative and developmental experiences as they are needed.
4. To accept and to give scope for functioning to the individual "selves" that emerge as the result of the interaction between individuals with their developmental dynamic and the world with its physical and social forces.
5. To provide social situations and group experiences through which the individual may learn to plan and carry out self-actualization through socially responsible actions and with consideration for the rights and welfare of other human beings.

Van Til states that the fundamental difference between our American society and some other societies is "one of values." He points out that, "At our best, we in America prize the individual and cherish the worth and dignity of each person. At our best, we prize the importance of inquiry. At our best, we have a faith that, in the long run, life is better for all of us when free individuals

[2]Sandra B. Horowitz, *From Theory to Practice: A Personal Diary of a Teacher of Young Children* (College Park, Md.: University of Maryland, 1971), pp. 19–22.

[3]D. A. Prescott, *The Child in the Educative Process* (New York: McGraw-Hill Book Co., 1957), pp. 49–50.

exercise their right to agree and disagree. The difference may be as simple—and as complex—as that."[4]

The goal of good schools for young children is to provide a succession of situations, of activities, whereby the child may have the opportunity to develop at his own rate and in his own way in personal affective skills and values, academic learnings and cognitive skills, group values, and parental relationships. The following examples will illustrate behavior that can be observed and that seems to indicate progress in the realization of particular goals.

PERSONAL VALUES, SKILLS, AND AFFECTIVE RELATIONSHIPS

Learning to like and trust others. For example, In the house-keeping center Lynn said, "I made a cake like yours. You make good things to eat."

Expanding the concept of what it means to be human.

Gaining a positive image of self.

Accepting children of differing ethnic and cultural traits.

Learning to manage his feelings. For example:

Ron was building an elaborate structure with blocks. Roy ran up and knocked down one of the walls. Ron turned as if to give chase. He seemed to be angry. Suddenly he stopped short, paused a moment and said, "And I was making it for you."

Developing the ability to organize, to plan, and to follow through on simple tasks.

Increasing in ability to make wise choices and decisions in a consistent manner.

Developing a sense of the importance of and relationship between independence and dependence.

Developing the ability to set standards for personal behavior and to live by them.

Establishing routines and patterns of living.

Developing spiritual values.

Developing physical adequacy and mental health.

Finding both satisfactions and limitations in the field of make-believe.

Expecting failures as well as successes.

GROUP VALUES AND RELATIONSHIPS

Feeling wanted, valued, and cared for by his peers and the adults in his life.

Making voluntary contacts with other children without regard to sex, race, or class.

Understanding that a cultural trait which is different is not inferior or nonhuman. For example:

Harry took one of Gale's blocks. Gale asked, "Why doesn't he know how to play?" The teacher replied, "He is learning to speak English. He comes from another country. He may not know how to ask for the block."

Developing a willingness to share privilege with groups differing from themselves. For example:

Gloria said, "They *are* boys, but let's let them use the wagon."

[4]W. Van Til, "A Question of Values," *Educ. Leadership, 18*:8 (1961), p. 479.

Becoming a social person; developing ability to interact with age mates.

Developing the attitude toward and the ability for being a part of a social group.

Knowing what is acceptable socially for his development and having the desire to apply this knowledge consistently in functional situations.

Learning to distinguish between private or personal property and that which belongs to the group.

Learning the necessity of sharing and cooperating with others. For example:

> Debbie, wanting to play with the bear which Lisa was using, said, "Lisa, will you let me have the bear when you're finished?" Lisa said, "I'm not ever going to finish today." Debbie said, "Lisa, you are supposed to say 'yes' when I ask you like that." Lisa smiled and said, "Let's build a house for this bear."

Participating in the group while preserving his own distinct ethnic and cultural traits.

ACADEMIC LEARNINGS

Satisfying natural curiosity which results in creative learnings.

Pursuing an interest wholeheartedly to greater depth and breadth.

Developing new interests and building upon recent ones.

Bringing into consciousness those things in his environment that he does not perceive (physical and biological).

Developing the beginnings of good work-study habits; learning successes are earned through repeated effort.

Learning to think; learning how things are done.

Developing meaningful vocabularies basic to thinking; developing language as a satisfactory means of communication.

Applying mathematical and scientific information to the solution of a problem.

Expanding his knowledge through exploration, investigation, assimilation, and reflection.

Building new or expanding concepts and correcting misconceptions. For example:

> Sally, while examining the seed experiments, remarked that the formica table top was soft. Hearing her comment, the teacher asked her to tap the table with her fist, and then to tap the cotton used in the experiments. Sally tapped both the table and the cotton. She replied, "Oh, the cotton is soft, the table is hard." The teacher asked her what word could be used to tell how the table felt when she slid her hand across it. Sally slid her hand over it, thought for a moment and said, "Smooth. The table is hard and smooth." She then proceeded to touch and tap other materials and objects. She explained that the jar was hard and smooth, the wall was hard and rough. The egg carton was rough but not as hard as the jar.

Having experiences with many types of media and yet using them wisely.

Becoming interested in and appreciating books.

PARTNERSHIP WITH PARENTS

Learning to relate self to family and near associates.

Selecting clothing, toys, and activities (books, television, and radio programs) appropriate to his developmental level.

Developing an understanding of changes in himself as he progresses through his own developmental sequence.

Participating in educational experiences that cannot be offered through the home situation; extending these experiences through cooperative planning involving teacher, parent, and child.

Beginning to recognize his sex role through identification with family members and other age mates. For example:

> Mitchell rode up on his tricycle and said, "Well, goodbye. I have to go downtown to work. I'll see you tonight." Away he went on his tricycle. In a few minutes he was back. He got off his tricycle, dropped on a bench and said, "Boy, I'm tired. That garage work is mighty hard. Yeh, man, it sure is hard."

Although goals have been identified in the areas of personal and affective skills, cognitive and academic learnings, group values and parental relationships, this does not mean that each child must develop the same values, learnings, and skills in the same way or at the same time. One child may have feelings of fear while another may have feelings of impatience and anger. For example, the teacher observed that both Louise and Lester need help in managing their feelings. Lester seems to feel afraid of making a mistake or doing anything wrong. Each day he sits quietly looking at a book or builds carefully with blocks, activities in which he feels safe and in which he can succeed. He is not yet able to try new activities. Louise wants her turn to ride the tricycle and pushes Laney off the saddle. Although the overall goal for the two children is in the area of personal skills, the skill needed by each child is different.

These goals for each child are based upon belief in (1) the worth, value, and dignity of each individual, and (2) the recognition that group interaction and understanding are fundamental needs which are basic to our American society. When translated into practical application, this means that each child needs to develop in keeping with his potential so that he can, through critical and creative thinking, (1) select and set for himself worthwhile goals, (2) arrive at purposes that will give direction to his behavior, and (3) plan and carry out the necessary actions to realize these goals in terms of his own purposes.

Accepting these goals for children, the goal of the teacher then becomes one of determining:

1. How does the child feel about himself? What is happening to this child? What kind of picture of self is he building—self-confidence and respect or defeatism and failure?
2. How can she provide opportunities for experience so that the child will learn to set realistic goals for himself and select appropriate means for arriving at these goals?
3. How can she develop an atmosphere of mutual trust so that each child retains his right to be different as he thinks, discusses, and plans for his own experiences at the level of his ability and within clearly established limits?
4. How can she establish a climate of increasing freedom coupled with an acceptance of increasing responsibility?

5. How can a stable environment be built by means of consistent patterns of freedom to do and to explore the new? How does one avoid overstimulation? How does one adapt the program to the child's needs?
6. How can she develop within each child the habit of placing value on accomplishments? How can she help each child value his own achievement according to standards and criteria appropriate for his purpose at this time but which will eventually lead to broader purposes and higher standards and criteria for his own achievements?
7. How can she find new and better ways to work with each child?
8. How should she provide and interpret experiences so that the child achieves the desired goals of personal values and skills, academic learnings, group values and relationships, and partnership with parents?

The program developed in schools for young children provides for activities that will contribute to the physical, mental, and social development of children. The objectives both for the program and for the activities are the changes expected to take place in each child as a result of his experiences. Provision is made for continuous growth in social and emotional development through a balanced program that will meet the developmental needs of the preschool-age child. Since all children, however, do not develop at the same rate, do not come from the same backgrounds, do not have the same needs and aspirations, the program is flexible and varied. The learning environment is made up of many people and many factors. Every environment is a learning environment. As has been said, "No environment in itself is good or bad. It is good or bad, effective or ineffective, only in terms of response to it."[5] It is important, then, to examine the people, places, and things which surround the child in terms of his reactions to them.

THE ENVIRONMENT

The school environment can help or hinder the realization of goals for young children. The environment may be loving or frightening, stimulating or boring, conducive or inhibiting to the development of purposes and goals. What makes the difference? No one single factor can be identified for it is the interaction, the "cause and effect" relationship, of many elements that characterizes the total situation. One such element, group size, is considered here.

The effect of group size on the behavior of children is significant. McConkie and Hughes studied two groups, one with 37 and one with 26 children, each attending school for a half day, occupying the same room space, and taught by the same teacher. It was found that the larger group had less opportunity to work at its own problems and received less individual guidance. More aggressive behavior was also observed in the larger group. Its tempo revealed greater

[5]R. R. Leeper, ed., *Creating a Good Environment for Learning* (1954 Yearbook, ASCD) (Washington, D.C.: ASCD, 1954), p. 5.

excitement, more noise, and a less permissive atmosphere. Twenty per cent of the children in the larger group initiated no personal contact with the teacher, while only 4 per cent of the smaller group had no such contact. The smaller group utilized space and materials better and played more cooperatively.[6]

The size of the group, then, should be considered in relation to the realization of the goals desired. If children are to grow in self-direction, wise use of materials, and cooperative behavior, provision should be made for a group situation small enough in number to make such behavior possible.

Another factor concerns the availability of materials and equipment. If the child is to grow in decision-making, opportunities for choice are important. Interest or learning centers can offer the child possibilities for working at the easel, with blocks, or even with puzzles. To encourage independence and responsibility in the use and care of materials, storage space must be accessible to the child.

The extent of aggressive behavior may be influenced by the play material and space available. Two earlier studies report findings that are applicable today. Johnson reported her observation of nursery school children on the playground under different conditions. When only the stationary equipment (slides, climbing apparatus) was available, the children seemed to engage in more quarrels and required more teacher intervention and direction than when movable equipment and toys were also available.[7] Jersild and Markey found that where play space was most restricted, conflicts were greatest in number.[8]

The Influence of the Home

The home environment also has an influence upon the child and the realization of goals. Before the child comes to nursery school or kindergarten, he has experienced various types of behavior in response to parental guidance and expectations. Some children have become independent while others are unable to make decisions. Some have become submissive while others are rebellious. The teacher, then, should be alert to the fact that the children have experienced different types of parental guidance that may have been influenced by various factors and in several ways.

How the adult was reared as a child plays an important part in how he treats his own child. The adult may have come from a home where a strict father insisted that he obey instantly, or from a very lenient home where neither parent could actually agree as to what the child was permitted to do. Thus, the adult may carry over certain feelings from his own childhood that give direction in dealing with his children. The parent may have resented how he was treated

---

[6]Gwen W. McConkie and Marie M. Hughes, "Quality of Classroom Living Related to Size of Kindergarten Group," *Child. Educ., 32*:9 (1956), pp. 428–432.

[7]Marguerite W. Johnson, "The Effect on Behavior of Variation in the Amount of Play Equipment," *Child Develop., 6*:1 (1935), pp. 56–68.

[8]A. T. Jersild and F. V. Markey, "Conflicts Between Preschool Children," *Child Develop. Monogr., 21* (1935).

as a child and may now attempt to direct his child differently. He may be an outgoing person who yells at a child but quickly gets over his anger. Another parent may show no anger but demand that the child obey him without question.

The parent may have read much of the literature written during the years when permissiveness without limits was in vogue and may have been influenced by ideas of permitting the child to do exactly as he pleases. Feelings regarding the words *guidance* or *discipline* play an important part in dealing with children. The word *discipline* has different connotations. Some people feel that it means keeping order in a group, while to others it may mean the technique of maintaining order. To still others, discipline means punishment. Regardless of definition, both parents and teachers should realize that controls or limits are necessary for children to adjust to societal standards. Children feel more secure if they know what is expected of them and understand what conformity means.

The child may come from a home in which he has learned to expect physical punishment, threats, and abuse. This child may have difficulty in adjusting to a teacher if she does not shout, threaten, or hit him. This child may need help in learning to make his decisions, for he may have been told quite firmly how to behave at home. Since our society leans toward independent decision-making and choice of behavior, such a child may have ambivalent feelings and difficulty in adjusting to the expected behavior for his school and peers. Other children, having received much attention and constant direction, may have become overly dependent upon what the parents think is correct behavior. Still other children are insecure and appear shy and withdrawn. They need activities to help them develop a feeling of security and self-confidence.

There has been the tendency to equate certain modes of behavior with social classes. While the socioeconomic level of the family does limit or extend the opportunities of the child, it is the emotional and intellectual climate that determines the child's outlook. Home environment may be so harmful with regard to physical punishment that a family welfare agency may need to intervene. Today, child abuse has been openly recognized by the courts and the medical profession. There still are parents who are unable to restrain themselves physically and as a result there are some unfortunate instances of bodily injury to children.[9] Bain points out that "Gross physical abuse is only one segment of a much wider problem of parental neglect. The unloved child, the emotionally deprived child, becomes part of our group of neurotic, disturbed, retarded, or delinquent adults."[10]

Parents are entrusted by nature, society, and the child himself to care for the child and provide appropriate limits for his behavior. However, there are

[9]M. G. Paulsen, "Legal Protections Against Child Abuse," *Children, 13*:2 (1966), pp. 43–48.

[10]Katherine Bain, "Commentary: The Physically Abused Child," *Pediatrics, 31*:6 (1963), p. 897.

times when families cannot fulfill their responsibilities alone. When children's needs are unmet who takes responsibility?

Child advocacy is the term being used to describe the growing emphasis placed on identifying unmet needs of children, suggesting ways to meet these needs, and on stimulating public support for projects already in operation.[11] Child advocacy is a concept and a process designed to make the needs of children real to the public, to give us, at local and national levels, a structure with which to deal with these problems, and to insure needed services to children, youth, and their families.[12]

The ultimate goal for the child and all individuals is the acquiring of self-discipline. Gradually the child learns how to make his own decisions and to know whether his behavior is acceptable to others. At first the teacher or parent may help the child to make wise choices by offering him two definite alternatives where either one is acceptable. Gradually the child can move to more difficult decision-making where the alternatives are less clear. For example, it is raining and yet, with proper clothing, Charles may play out in the rain. The adult might say, "It is raining, but if you wear your boots and raincoat, you can go out to play in the rain, or you can stay inside and play with your trucks. You decide which you'd rather do."

A young child needs to move toward independent thinking, for as he matures, he moves away from the parental home to the school, to his peers, and to a larger society. He will no longer have an adult always beside him to make his choices for him. It will be easier for him to know which path to take as he approaches adolescence and adulthood if he has begun to make appropriate decisions in his early years.

LEVEL OF MATURITY

Time is an important dimension in a child's behavior, for a relationship exists between a child's behavior and his level of maturity. If the adult recognizes that each child develops at his own rate, he does not expect the same behavior of each child in the group; he plans opportunities for experiences appropriate to the child's level of maturity. There will be differences in many abilities. Examples follow.

1. The ability to share and wait for turns. One child may be able to take turns with four other children in riding a tricycle, but be unable to wait for 20 children to ride before he has another chance.
2. The ability to listen attentively. The length of time one can listen varies, as does the content one has the background to enjoy.

[11]Shelia B. Kamerman, A. J. Kahn, and Brenda G. McGowan, "Research and Advocacy," *Children Today*, 1:2 (1972), pp. 35–36.

[12]S. A. Ward, "Components of a Child Advocacy Program," *Children Today*, 1:2, (1972), pp. 38–40.

3. The ability to participate in a group. Some children are comfortable in small group activities, but are not yet ready to cope with the total group of 25 children. Refusal to come "to a group story" may not indicate lack of interest in stories on the part of a child, nor an inappropriate story, but could indicate fear of the large group.
4. Muscular coordination. Some children can skip, while others can only run; some can cut exactly on the line, while others can only tear paper.
5. Reaction time. Some children take longer to respond or react than others.

The good teacher provides opportunities for the child to engage in activities in terms of these differences. As she recognizes certain behavior such as negativism or inattention, she remembers that these are to be expected of children at certain developmental ages.

The very young child of two or three may be extremely negative to any and all requests. This negative "No, I don't want to!" or, "No, I won't" is expected at this age. The child is beginning to be self-assertive and may express this self-awareness in a negative way. The power of "no" as a word has been discovered by the child. He begins to realize that adults are disturbed by "no" and thus uses it constantly, even when he really would like to carry out the activity requested. The wise teacher either rephrases her request, ignores his negativism, or redirects his activity. The teacher makes no issue when she announces, "Time to eat lunch." She simply takes the child by the hand and together they go to eat. He is not indulged by being allowed not to eat; neither is he punished for saying "no" when in reality he may not mean "no" at all. He is helped to do what needs to be done.

Knowing that manners cannot always be counted on with four-year-olds does not mean that manners are ignored. It simply means, for example, that on leaving a party, the parent does not ask the child, "What do you say?" and risk a scene and embarrassment. Rather, the adult may say, "Jerry and I enjoyed the party. Thank you for inviting us." She sets the example which later the child will make a part of his own behavior.

Knowing that most five-year-olds can listen in a group for only 10 to 15 minutes, listening experiences with stories, in sharing, and with music are planned accordingly. To expect the child to sit attentively for a longer period is to expect more than he is capable of doing. One teacher kept five-year-olds in a circle for 45 minutes. After the first few minutes they were very restless, falling out of chairs, playing and wrestling with their neighbors. By insisting that they remain for that length of time, she was not only causing difficulties for herself in the form of discipline problems, but she was teaching children to be rude, impolite listeners rather than to listen attentively while others were speaking.

Hymes, however, warns that the teacher must be careful not to become too easygoing and content with too little on the one hand, or become too demanding and maintain unrealistic expectations on the other. For example, if the children are wiggling, it may be because of their age or their maturity level.

Yet the reason may be entirely different. The children may be bored. The teacher, then, must determine the cause of the behavior and take action that is consistent with the cause.[13]

The developmental point of view is based on knowledge and understanding of the growth and development of the child. According to Hymes, this approach does not mean that anything goes; nor does it call for lowering of standards. The teacher has the highest possible standards for the age group that she teaches. The child development approach means accepting the behavior that is normal and healthy for a specific age.[14] The teacher recognizes the maturity level of each child and lives with it.

GUIDANCE AND DISCIPLINE

Although each teacher may have her own special strategies and techniques, it is important that she understand something of the philosophy of the approach she chooses as the basis for her guidance.

Butler reports that techniques advocated during the past several years come from two quite divergent sources.[15] One point of view, expressed by Maslow, Rogers, Kelley and Combs in *Perceiving, Behaving, Becoming,* is based on the following assumptions:

(a) that each person is worthy of respect; (b) that each grows continuously from birth to death, at all times merging the past and future into the now; (c) that each is a product of an inner core, developed and modified by experience; (d) that interaction with people is the strongest environmental determinant in the self concept; (e) that when the environment is basically unthreatening, the individual's own behavior toward elements in the environment is basically open, self-and-others trusting, interactive, sympathetic and constructive; and (f) that in this environment dignity and integrity emerge as characteristics of people.[16]

These authors believe that the attributes of dignity, integrity, and autonomy are concomitants of the environment which impinges positively on the individual. They hold that "situations where the conditions for social development are kept open and fluid are most favorable for the development of these characteristics."[17] An atmosphere in which the self-concept may be enhanced is one in which:

[13]J. L. Hymes, Jr., *Behavior and Misbehavior* (Englewood Cliffs, N.J.: Prentice-Hall, Inc., 1955), p. 53.

[14]Ibid., p. 52.

[15]Annie L. Butler, *Current Research in Early Childhood Education: A Compilation and Analysis for Program Planners* (Washington, D.C.: American Association of Elementary-Kindergarten-Nursery Educators, 1970), p. 117.

[16]A. W. Combs, chm., *Perceiving, Behaving, Becoming* (1962 Yearbook) (Washington, D.C.: ASCD, 1962), p. 214.

[17]Ibid., p. 221.

Human development in dignity and honesty is put first.

Each child's spiritual integrity—his right to be—is recognized.

Individuality is considered an asset rather than a liability.

Genetic growth patterns are respected and used as a basis for teaching.

Each child helps to purpose and plan.

Each can act freely, knowing those around him accept him as he is.

Each can make an error—or even do wrong, and not lose face thereby.

Each child can grow each day and know that he is growing.

Each can hold his head up high and meet the other's gaze.

Each can make friends, enjoy other people, learn how to extend a hand to help.

Each can learn the warm flood of gratitude that comes from being regarded with warmth.

Each can venture into unknown worlds and stretch his wings to find new truths.

Above all where each child can experience success in subject matter, human relationships and the discovery of self as a person of worth and dignity.[18]

"From a quite different point of view the theory of operant conditioning sees a preschool as essentially a behavior-modifying environment in which the teacher plays an important role in choosing behavior that will be systematically reinforced," says Butler.[19] Operant conditioning is usually based on the use of consequences to strengthen or weaken behavior in areas such as decreasing aggressive responses and threatening or violent behavior, increasing social skills, and learning to take responsibility for simple tasks. The behavior that is compatible with desired ends is reinforced.[20]

Katz points out, however, that the application of these techniques must be thought through carefully. She says, "Stop, look, and listen before you condition."[21] Limitations of this approach are seen in the example described by Katz. Three children manifest disruptive behavior for which behavior modification is likely to work. When used without concern for the origins of the behavior, however, the positive results may be questioned.

Child 1 learned to be disruptive because such behavior resulted in attention or some other reinforcement. For this child operant conditioning seems appropriate. The reinforcement which usually followed his disruptive behavior could be consciously withheld.

Child 2's disruptive behavior may express some kind of emotional injury, some kind of internal stress. Although behavior modification may work and the undesirable behavior disappear, the injury could remain. A new manifestation of the stress may appear. A therapeutic response seems indicated in this case.

[18]Ibid., pp. 232–233.

[19]Butler, op. cit., p. 120.

[20]W. C. Becker, D. R. Thomas, and D. Carnine, *Reducing Behavior Problems: An Operant Conditioning Guide for Teachers* (Urbana: ERIC Clearinghouse University of Illinois, 1969), pp. 4–5.

[21]Lillian G. Katz, "Stop, Look, and Listen Before You Condition," *ERIC/ECE Newsletter* 5:6 (1971), pp. 1–2.

Child 3 may lack the social skills or alternative ways of responding to the situation. This child can be helped by clarifying or explaining alternative solutions for solving the problem at hand. The teaching strategy appears to be appropriate.

Katz does not reject the principles of behavior modification but warns against the indiscriminate application of conditioning techniques. She emphasizes the fact that before applying the principles the teacher should know the child.[22]

"In the final analysis," says Butler, "these two approaches . . . arise from very different systems of beliefs."

The important question is how one goes about building satisfying interpersonal relationships: whether one chooses to develop the relationships that encourage the child to want to change his behavior and give the guidance and support necessary to do this, or whether steps must be taken to urge him forward in the desired direction; whether the child should be motivated by some real desire to change, or whether he responds to tangible rewards for desired behavior until the behavior becomes a habit.[23]

Helping the Child Become a Group Member

The transfer from home to school may bring many new or different activities for the child. Being a part of a group is definitely one of them. A child new to the group may withdraw and watch the others, or become aggressive and push and grab toys. Too often the teacher may not realize that children new to the group need more individual help as well as introduction to various group activities. Some children require a longer time to become a part of the group while others feel at home in the group almost immediately.

Some of the difficulties that teachers encounter with young children are related to different behavior expectations of the home and the school. At home the child may have been encouraged or at least permitted to fight; use the language he hears; take whatever he wants without asking. The teacher, then, accepts the child and begins at his level in helping him learn to take turns, to share toys, and to become an active participant in a group. The child may use words for which he does not know the meaning:

Tip, a four-year-old boy, called out happily to the teacher, "You look like a bastard!" The teacher, somewhat taken aback, responded by asking, "What do you mean when you say that I look like a bastard?" Tip replied, "You look funny." "Tip," said the teacher, "You need to explain what you mean when you say 'bastard.' People don't know that you mean *funny*." Tip said, "O.K. I'll just say, 'You have a funny face.'"

[22]Ibid.
[23]Butler, op. cit., p. 121.

Other difficulties that teachers encounter with young children are related to assisting the child in learning to take turns, to share toys, to become an active participant in a group. Children need this kind of help for most of them have been the center of attention at home. They have lived in a family setting where the other members were not of the same age as themselves. Thus, we find some three- and four-year-olds grabbing toys from others and hitting, pinching, biting, or using physical force to obtain what they want. Others stand back, watching, or withdrawing, or appealing to an adult for help. Comments frequently heard are "Tommy won't let me ride the tricycle," "Nancy doesn't want me to be the daddy." The teacher can help the children by suggesting, "Tommy, you've had the tricycle quite a while; two more trips around the circle, then it's Billy's turn." In other activities the teacher can often guide a child by merely saying, "You could do it this way." So often the manner in which the teacher suggests new ideas to a child will encourage him to tackle a project or stick to one on which he is now working.

Establishing Routines

When entering one of the many programs, children who are unaccustomed to group activities, may find it hard to engage in the expected routines such as washing, toileting, going out or coming indoors, resting, and eating at lunch time. Many of the children will imitate the others, yet usually there are a few who need help in adjusting to a daily schedule.

Furthermore, some children come from homes where there are few, if any, routines other than doing whatever they find to do at whatever time is convenient for the parents. They are not accustomed to washing their hands before eating. Meals have not been served according to a schedule. Resting is unimportant. These boys and girls must first have help in understanding the "why" of doing things. The child needs encouragement and support while he is in the process of acquiring the desired behavior. In helping the child, it is important for the teacher to consider the possible effect of her guidance on the child's concept of himself and his home.

Children often become confused when an activity is shifted because of weather conditions, a field trip, or special event. Explaining the necessity for a shift in plans or letting children know ahead that a routine will be shifted does avoid confusion.

Younger children who have never had a chance to engage in water play may enjoy spending a longer time washing hands and face than the teacher has counted on. The teacher may need to give such a child a special "water play" time. Some children may be hesitant about going to the toilet when others are in the bathroom, or may refuse to go at all. A teacher may need to supervise such a child slowly and carefully until he becomes accustomed to groups in a bathroom. Some schools are equipped with child-size lavatories that may be a novelty to a child, and thus he may spend a longer time in the bathroom. The teacher must be aware of the home training in regard to toileting, as some parents have probably stressed modesty and others may have been rather free. New children are likely to have more frequent need to use the toilet facilities, because of the newness of the situation, nervousness, or when the weather becomes colder. Thus, in planning a daily schedule the teacher would need to include more frequent toileting with new or younger children.

The routine of the rest period can provide a relaxing time or it may produce only a group of squirming, restless children. The length and number of rest periods should be determined by the length of time children are in school, how much sleep they get at home, when they go to bed, and when they get up in the morning. For children who are in the center for only two or three hours, the 15–20 minute period may be considered a quiet time. Some children may need or want to lie down on mats while others may choose a quiet activity such as listening to music or looking at a book.

It is important for the teacher to remember that such a period provides not only physical relaxation but also a time for the child to be by himself: in the group, yes, but not an active part of it. Rhodes found that when children in a morning kindergarten were provided with a rest period, there were less evidences of fatigue.[24]

For children who are in the center all day, nap time is usually arranged just after lunch. Some children may sleep for an hour, while others may not nap. They may spend the time relaxing on their cots and engaging in a quiet activity. The teacher's attitude about rest makes a difference as to whether the children do relax. Some teachers feel that soft music and darkened rooms are helpful for rest, whereas in other schools the quiet attitude of the teacher with her expectation of relaxation may provide a better atmosphere.

The routine of eating should be considered in relation to both the midmorning snack and the noon lunch. Some children have not been used to sitting down with a group their own age to eat, nor to a variety of foods, nor to conversation with other children while eating. The lunch hour can be a pleasant experience instead of a nagging time. Small portions and the teacher's expectancy that each child will feed himself and complete his meal without undue urging will be conducive in helping those children who are having difficulty at meal time.

Throughout the school day children become engrossed in their work and play and are not conscious of time. Many teachers encounter difficulty with children who are not ready to put blocks away, to stop their activity at the work bench, or to return indoors for a story. Some children have become accustomed to what comes next in the daily routine and yet rebel at moving on to the next activity. Teachers can help children by warning them a few minutes prior to change of activity by quietly commenting, "It is almost juice time; we will

---

[24]Frances Rhodes, *A Study of the Effects of Various Types of Rest Periods in a Morning Kindergarten on the Behavior Characteristics of Five-Year-Olds,* Unpublished Graduate Paper, Florida State University, Tallahassee, August 1954.

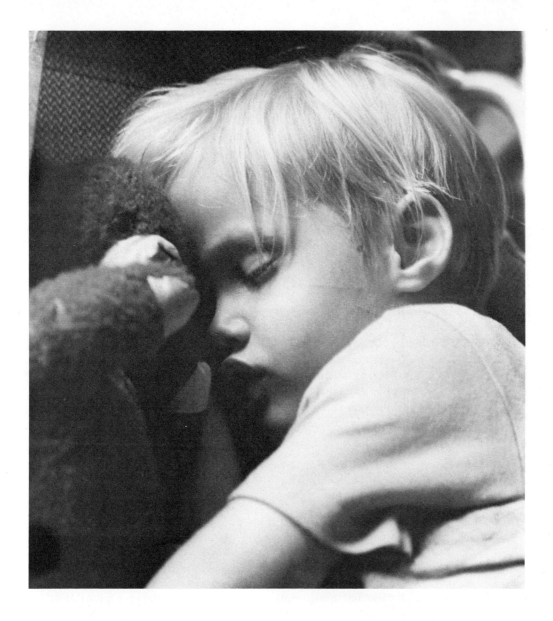

Figure 9. Teachers of young children consider it a part of their function to help children establish routines and habits dealing with dressing, cleanliness, elimination, eating, and rest.

The rigid conformance once required in nursery school or kindergarten routines has given way to a more relaxed and informal pattern that permits children to establish these requirements at their own pace, consistent with the demands of maturation attained at the time. Like most learned activities, changes occur gradually in keeping with the stage of development. It is, therefore, undesirable to expect the same level of conformity and perfection from all children.

These pictures illustrate activities characteristic of those in centers with a well-planned program designed to help children establish basic routines.

need to start putting the blocks away very soon now." Sometimes there are too many blocks and the job is too big for the child. The teacher can help by gaining the cooperation of other children as well as assisting in the putting away. Recognizing that each child may be accustomed at home to a variety of differences in routines is important in helping children know what is expected in a school group.

Teaching Techniques

Diverting the child by redirecting his unfavorable behavior into more constructive channels is a challenge to every adult, whether parent or teacher. It sometimes takes foresight or ingenuity for the adult to use favorable diversion as he suggests to the child other ways of handling situations. Sometimes a reminder may be used, such as "Remember we said the shovel is used to dig with. How about getting the wagon and filling it with dirt?"

Sometimes children who are overstimulated need quiet time to look at books or to play alone. The difficult child who disturbs the entire group may need to be removed from the group for a short period of time. This removal should not be in the form of a threat such as "If you don't behave I'll have to put you in another room." Rather, the teacher should suggest, "You seem to be having trouble playing with Bob. Perhaps you should play by yourself for a while." If a child is extremely difficult or disturbing to a group, the teacher may need to isolate him in another room in order to calm the entire situation.

If the child is removed from the group, there are several factors to be considered:

1. Length of time. Briefness of isolation is extremely important, because of the child's short span of attention. Five minutes can be a long time for a child.
2. Child's understanding of purpose. It is important that the child knows why he was removed, because many times he does not understand. Learning reasons for removal from the group can be helpful in preventing further behavior difficulties.
3. Safety. The safety and supervision of the child while he is outside the group should be assured.
4. The child's reaction. If the child is alone in a room or hall, is his security threatened? Is he frightened? Does the child enjoy the experience?
5. Provision for learning. If frequently excluded, does the child ever learn that the activity from which he was excluded can be an interesting and happy one? Is he being helped to learn "what to do" and "how to behave" in order to remain in the group?
6. Reinstatement in the group. When does the child return to the group? Does the child or the teacher decide? Is the child told, "Come back when you can behave," or does the teacher reinstate the child within the group by saying, "Jim is ready to hear the story now"?

One of the most important traits in a teacher of young children is sensitivity to each child's needs and how these needs relate to the group as a whole. Knowing the developmental characteristics of children at each age level will assist the teacher in becoming aware of these needs. When guiding the behavior of children under six in group situations, the teacher needs to be aware that:

1. The tone of voice used should be positive yet not demanding, pleasant yet firm, calm yet forceful and matter-of-fact.
2. The teacher should give a feeling of expectancy that the request needs to be carried to completion. If she has to leave the group because of an unexpected situation, the children will know that the teacher will return and follow through with the activity.
3. The nonverbal behavior of the teacher should be consistent with her verbal behavior. The effects of a positive comment may be minimized if the teacher does not look directly at the child, while the effects may be reinforced if she places a hand on the child's shoulder.
4. The teacher places herself so that she can see the entire group at all times to know where they are and what they are doing. In giving directions, she may find it helpful to stand near the child who has difficulty in listening.
5. The teacher gives suggestions rather than commands; for example, "How about trying to do it this way," or "You might ask Larry to help you."
6. The teacher avoids favoritism by not giving too much attention to an attractive, a talented, a handicapped, or a disturbing child because doing so may result in neglect of others in the group.

It is expected that in a school situation teachers will not use threats with young children, nor will they use physical punishment. Parents may feel that these are necessary types of punishment but they should not be used by teachers. The teacher who understands children is aware of other methods of guiding the child and does not have to rely on physical punishment.

Giving young children special privileges or attention may be legitimate if such practices do not become crutches on which teachers lean to gain cooperation from youngsters. Older children in elementary school are more likely to be helped in the area of discipline by the withdrawing of privileges than are preschool children. Praise, too, is an effective method of control. However, some teachers tend to use it too frequently, especially with the so-called "good children." Too often praise is withheld from a difficult child who needs more attention and would profit by having his efforts accepted.

For some children in the group, the activities may be too difficult, either because the child does not know what is expected of him or because he may be slower in some aspects of development. Insight may be gained through study of the home situation, or it may be necessary to secure outside assistance from a child guidance clinic in cooperation with the parents. Too often teachers are afraid to admit failure with a child; in reality, however, the admission of the need for help is an indication of a professional teacher. Recognition of serious behavior difficulties and prompt referral can insure early treatment for the child.

Through careful analysis of the child's feelings, attitudes, and reactions, appropriate steps in guiding his behavior can be evolved. In the following paragraphs, two different types of school situations involving the behavior of children are described as illustrations of the application of guidance principles. No attempt is made to answer all questions but rather to suggest a process which may be used by the teacher in answering questions.

TOTAL GROUP SITUATION. The teacher determines the goals for behavior in a group situation such as music or story time. For example:

> Each child will be a good listener; participate in group activity; share turns; show consideration for others in group.

In working to achieve these goals, the teacher plans and provides for:

1. The activities to be within the attention span of the group.
2. A balance of types of activities within the period—active with quiet, listening with participating.
3. Physical arrangements that are comfortable; seating arrangements so that children can see the leader and are not directly facing the light; proper temperature.
4. Content of the group activity appropriate for maturity level of the children.

Even with all the planning, there still may be need for guidance on the part of the teacher. For example:

> It is story time. Fred, a five-year-old, is wiggling and squirming. He annoys the children next to him by an occasional kick, a slap on the back, a whisper, or a pinch. Should the teacher reprimand, ignore, or send Fred from the group? To do any one of the three is to disrupt the listening climate for the group. Yet, something needs to be done for the sake of the group as well as for Fred.

Before making the decision, it will be well to remember that Fred's behavior may be due to any number of causes and that it is important to ask "why?" If he needs to be excused from the group, the way in which it is done and the follow-up will vary according to the cause of the behavior. The teacher considers, Is Fred tired? He was listening to a recording during the free activity period. This is much the same type of activity. Perhaps he has done enough listening for now. The teacher might say, "Fred, you have listened to the story on the record and you may find something else to do now. Remember, the rest of us are listening to the story. If you want to listen with us, you are welcome; but if not, choose something that will not disturb us."

Is Fred insecure in total group situations? Is such behavior an evidence of his inadequacy to cope with the group? It is important that the treatment of this behavior not create more insecure feelings. Fred may be excused in much the same manner as described above. It is important, however, that Fred not be deprived of hearing stories and that he be helped to grow in his ability to participate within the group. The teacher may accomplish this by (1) finding time to read to Fred alone or with one or two other children, helping him to make "friends" with one of these children, (2) helping him to participate in an activity—in block building or in the doll corner with a few other children, and (3) gradually increasing the size of the group in which Fred participates.

Is the content of the activity too difficult or perhaps boring for Fred? Does the vocabulary of the story relate to concepts and experiences which are not yet Fred's? If so, perhaps using pictures, a model, or giving an explanation might help.

THE ACTIVITY PERIOD. The teacher determines goals for behavior during work time or the activity period. For example, each child will:

1. Find a job to do.
2. Gain satisfaction from his job or activities.
3. Take turns.
4. Put away materials.
5. Show consideration for others in the group.

There is much that the teacher can do in advance to set up an environment conducive to the desired behavior, such as the following:

1. Set up several centers of interest or activities in which the children can participate. For the youngest, these will be set up on arrival. The child simply goes to the activity of his choice. The five-year-olds may participate in group planning and choose a job for which materials are available and accessible.
2. Balance activities to provide several that require a minimum of teacher supervision, thus enabling the teacher to give guidance in new activities or in those requiring more supervision.
3. Plan activities that are interesting and challenging but not too difficult or frustrating. Provide a variety of activities of varying difficulty so that each child can find something satisfying to do.
4. Provide materials in amounts that encourage sharing. For example, there need not be a pair of scissors for every child, but neither will the child's capacity to wait and take turns be strained by insisting that he wait while five other children cut. Perhaps he begins sharing most easily by using the scissors with one or two other children. To share, then, does not mean waiting indefinitely or losing one's turn completely.

Despite this planning, Paul, age four, knocks down the block structure which three other boys have built. The teacher questions, Was it an accident? If not, was it an attempt to play with the others? Is Paul's aggressiveness perhaps due to a change in routines at home? Is his place in the family threatened by the new baby? Did a visit from relatives keep him up late last night? Has Daddy lost his job? Was there food for breakfast? Is there money for the rent? To scold or exclude Paul may cause him to think, "Not even the teacher cares any more." Certainly, Paul cannot be permitted to annoy the other boys but the treatment should not make him more aggressive. A quiet comment such as, "Paul, you were angry and knocked down the blocks. Pat and Hugh worked hard to build the house. They will build it again. You can work over here." Thus Paul is directed to an activity such as painting at the easel, pounding clay, or using hammer and nails. The teacher recognized that Paul felt aggressive but did not condone his behavior. She set the limits with positive guidance. "They will build it again. You can work over here."

Could Paul's aggressiveness be a way of saying, "I want to play with you"? If so, he needs help in learning acceptable ways of getting into a group. The teacher may say, "Boys, Paul wants to play with you. He will help you build the house again." In this instance, the teacher did not ask Paul, "What do you say when you want to play with the boys?" If he had been able to say it, he would not have resorted to the behavior he used. Rather, the teacher will supply the verbal request, "Boys, Paul really wants to play with you, but he had a strange way of showing it, didn't he?" Paul has experience, then, in another way of joining in play with the boys.

Summary

Guiding the behavior of children, helping them develop a core of values, fostering good human relationships, and building healthy personalities are important yet exacting tasks for the teacher. Suggestions for this task, which have been presented, include the following:

1. Know the children. Review the general characteristics of children at this age level. For each child, study his home environment, health status, goals, and interests.
2. Determine goals and values.
3. Plan a school environment and a program conducive to the understandings, attitudes, and habits which it is hoped the children will develop. As Hymes has said, "A program in school that is dull and dreary, uninteresting and boring, makes it harder for children to be good."[25]
4. Establish positive, friendly relationships between the teacher and the children. Keep verbal and nonverbal behavior consistent.
5. When an incident does arise, remember the following steps in guiding the child:
   a. Realistically accept the child's feelings through the use of verbalizations.
   b. Set up the necessary limits for the child, so he does not and cannot continue to build up unacceptable behavior patterns.
   c. Provide the necessary release for unacceptable feelings at the moment they occur through the use of materials appropriate for release of tense and difficult feelings.
   d. Encourage and support the child while he is in the process of getting release.[26]
6. Try to find the cause of the child's behavior difficulty.
7. Plan a course of action which is appropriate for the cause of the behavior and consistent with the goals sought for the child.

[25]J. Hymes, "They Act Their Age," *Discipline* (Washington, D.C.: ACEI, 1957), p. 22.

[26]Eleanor Evans, "Vents for Children's Feelings," *Discipline* (Washington, D.C.: ACEI, 1957), p. 26.

Today, the child development point of view emphasizes the importance of helping the child become a self-directing individual. Both inner urges and outer pressures need to be considered.

Suggested Activities

1. Observe teacher-child contacts in a nursery school, day care center, or kindergarten. Note the number of ways the teacher insists the child carry through on requests, when the teacher gives choices, when the child refuses, and the outcome of such.

2. Observe teacher-child contacts. Note the tone of voice used by the teacher when speaking to a child, the wording of requests, the teacher's poise, the children's behavior in terms of requests completed, requests refused. Analyze why the children behaved as they did during such contacts.

3. Select one child to observe, either in a home or at a preschool. Note the number of "don'ts" used, the number of "would you like to's" or direct commands given the child by an adult. Analyze how this child behaved as a result of the way the teacher or parent communicated with the child.

4. Observe children who are having difficulty belonging to or getting into groups. Note leadership qualities of certain children, shyness of others, aggressiveness, and the general outcome of "groupness" among the children. Did adults interfere or assist children or did the children handle the situations without adult help?

5. Observe a child who manifests aggressive behavior. Seek to determine the cause. Does the application of behavior modification techniques seem appropriate? Why? Discuss your reasons with the class.

6. Observe one child in a center for young children. Identify ways in which his self concept was enhanced. Share your observations with the class.

Related Readings

Abel, H., and R. Gingles. "Life Goals of Parents for Children," *J. Home Economics, 57*:9 (1965), pp. 734–735.

Ausubel, D. P. "How Reversible Are the Cognitive and Motivational Effects of Cultural Deprivation?" H. Passow, ed. *Education of the Disadvantaged.* New York: Holt, Rinehart and Winston, 1965.

Axline, Virginia. *Dibs in Search of Self.* Boston: Houghton Mifflin Company, 1964.

Baker, Katherine Read, and Xenia F. Fane. *Understanding and Guiding Young Children.* Englewood Cliffs, N.J.: Prentice-Hall, Inc., 1970.

Baumrind, D. "Parental Control and Parental Love," *Children, 12*:6 (1965), pp. 230–234.

Becker, W. C., D. R. Thomas, and D. Carmine. *Reducing Behavior Problems: An Operant Conditioning Guide for Teachers.* Urbana, Ill.: ERIC Clearinghouse, University of Illinois, 1969.

Cohen, M. D., ed. *When Children Move from School to School.* Washington, D.C.: ACEI, 1972.

Galambos, Jeannette W. *A Guide to Discipline.* Washington, D.C.: NAEYC, 1969.

Hildebrand, Verna. *Introduction to Early Childhood Education.* New York: Macmillan, Inc. 1971, pp. 14–19; 58–64.

Hughes, Marie M. "Teacher Behavior and Concept of Self," *Child. Educ.*, *41*:1 (1964), pp. 29–33.

Katz, Lillian G. "Condition with Caution," *Young Children*, *27*:5 (1972), pp. 277–280.

Krumboltz, J., and Helen Krumboltz. *Changing Children's Behavior.* Englewood Cliffs, N.J.: Prentice-Hall, Inc., 1972.

Leiserson, Marion Laurence. *Creating a "Loving" Environment for Young Children.* College Park, Md.: University of Maryland, 1971.

Lipton, A. "Classroom Behavior: Messages from Children," *Elem. Sch. J.*, *71*:5 (1971), pp. 254–261.

MacMillan, D. L. *Behavior Modification in Education.* New York: Macmillan Publishing Co., Inc., 1973.

Madsen, C. K., and Madsen, C. H., Jr. "What Is Behavior Modification?" *Instructor*, *81*:2 (1971), pp. 47–56.

———. *Teaching Discipline*: *Behavioral Principles Toward a Positive Approach.* Boston: Allyn and Bacon, 1970.

Maslinoff, L. "Identifying Classroom Boundaries," *TIP* (June 1969).

Mead, Margaret. "Rearing Children to Live in a Changing World," *Parents Magazine*, *41*:1 (1966), pp. 33–35.

Morris, M. G., et al. "Toward Prevention of Child Abuse," *Children* 11:2 (1964), pp. 55–60.

Oettinger, Katherine B. "The Abused Child," *Child. Educ.*, *41*:5 (1965), pp. 235–237.

Parke, R. D. "Some Effects of Punishment on Children's Behavior," *Young Children*, *24*:4 (1969), pp. 225–238.

Sheviakov, G. *Anger in Children.* Washington, D.C.: EKNE, 1969.

Schools and Centers for Young Children

Chapter **6**

Recognition of educational programs for young children as an essential part of continuous education has developed gradually in the United States. Today parents and educators know the significance of the child's early experiences for his educational foundation. Recent research has confirmed what many people have believed regarding the importance of a good program in early childhood education for all children. Recognition of growing needs of disadvantaged children has brought a tremendous increase in government-sponsored programs. It is believed that sound education during the early years will enable children to function more effectively when entering elementary schools.

DEVELOPMENT OF SCHOOLS IN THE UNITED STATES

Kindergartens have been a part of American education for over a century. The first kindergarten was established in the United States in 1855 at Watertown, Wisconsin. The first public kindergarten was established in 1873 in St. Louis. Prior to this date, kindergartens were established and maintained largely from private funds. Since 1950, as the percentage of children enrolled in all schools has been greater than ever before, there has been a proportionate increase in the number of children attending public kindergartens as well as an increase in the number of children attending private or church-related kindergartens.

Nursery schools were first introduced into the United States at Teachers College, Columbia University, and at the Merrill Palmer School of Motherhood and Home Training in Detroit, as experimental centers where children could be thoughtfully cared for and observed.[1] They emphasized educational guidance of parents and children, in contrast to programs of custodial care hitherto considered adequate for children of working mothers. The Iowa Child Welfare Research Station was established under a state legislative grant in 1917. Through a trust fund left by Lizzie Pitts Merrill Palmer of Detroit, the Merrill Palmer School was established in 1920. In 1922 a nursery school demonstration-center for student study and practice was opened at the Merrill Palmer School. Through the Laura Spelman Rockefeller Memorial, grants were made available in 1923 whereby child study centers were developed or expanded at various universities. These, and many other centers established soon after, have given stimulus to the growing interest in child development research, and education has assumed much larger significance in the programs for young children.

During the period from 1920 to 1932 the number of nursery schools reported to the United States Office of Education increased from three to 203. There were many more nursery schools that did not report. During this same decade the evidence supporting the need for schools for young children centered around the needs of the only child, limited play space for children at home, women seeking employment outside the home and needing care for their children, and parents seeking the best environment for the development of their children.

Federally Supported Programs

The provision in 1933 for children's centers as a part of the Federal Emergency Relief Administration was the first time schools for young children became an integral part of a federally supported program. Even though this program was designed to relieve unemployment and to supplement existing educational programs, the increasing concern for the welfare of the young child gave direction to the development of children's centers. Many and varied laws and regulations resulted from the study of the programs in these centers for underprivileged children.

Since 1930 two national emergencies—the financial depression and the war period—have greatly expanded the demand for schools for young children. The war-created emergency schools were developed in 1942 through the

---

[1]Mary Dabney Davis, *Nursery Schools, Their Development and Current Practices in the United States*, Bull. 9 (Washington, D.C.: U.S. Office of Education, 1932).

cooperative endeavor of the Federal Emergency Relief Administration and the United States Office of Education, assisted by the three professional organizations concerned with the education of young children—the National Association for Nursery Education, the Association for Childhood Education, and the National Council of Parent Education—to provide adequate care for children of working mothers. This program was later administered by the Work Projects Administration and the Federal Works Agency.[2]

THE LANHAM ACT.   A rapid expansion of programs for young children resulted from this movement. As women were mobilized for war emergency work and to replace men in service, attention was focused on the need for legislation to insure that schools for young children provided an educational experience in a satisfactory environment. This was made possible through funds made available by the Lanham Act:[3]

> In August, 1942, the War Manpower Commission issued a directive instructing the Office of Defense Health and Welfare Services to present plans for the development and coordination of federal programs for the care of children of working mothers. Very soon thereafter the President made $400,000 of emergency funds available for transmittal to the U.S. Office of Education and the U.S. Children's Bureau to assist the states in establishing needed services. By June, 1943, thirty-nine states had developed plans for extended school services to be developed under state and local educational agencies, and thirty states had similar plans for child-welfare programs to be administered by welfare agencies. These state allotments provided 222 positions in state governments, among them state supervisors for extended school services, which included both nursery schools for young children and before- and after-school programs for children of school age. One of the supervisor's functions was the stimulation of state and local committees for the study of community needs and the development of program plans.

At the 1960 National Day Care Conference, Study Group 7 "affirmed the spirit of the White House Conference recommendation on training that every group care center for young children be supervised by at least one person qualified in early childhood education. This was considered as a minimum rather than a goal."[4] Dean stated that:[5]

> In a 1959 U.S. Office of Education study, it was reported that there were 102,000 public elementary schools in the nation. Of this number, 70 percent maintained kindergartens, 5 percent maintained nursery schools. Public kindergartens derive 81 per-

[2]Bess Goodykoontz, Mary Dabney Davis, and Hazel F. Gabbard, "Recent History and Present Status of Education for Young Children," *Early Childhood Education* (46th Yearbk.), Part II, NSSE (Chicago: Univ. Chicago Press, 1947), p. 60.

[3]Ibid., p. 61.

[4]Recommendations of Study Groups at National Day Care Conference, Washington, D.C., Nov. 18, 1960, mimeographed.

[5]S. E. Dean, *Elementary School Administration and Organization*, U.S. Office of Education, Bull. No. 11, Super. Documents (Washington, D.C.: U.S. Government Printing Office, 1960), p. 19.

cent of their maintenance from public funds, 6 percent from private funds, and 3 percent from a combination of public and private support. Information was not reported from 10 percent of the schools. In the same study it was shown that public nursery schools derive 45 percent of their support from a combination of public and private funds; 34 percent entirely from private funds; 17 percent from public tax monies; 4 percent did not furnish information on this question.

HEAD START CHILD DEVELOPMENT PROGRAM

In a democracy the right of every child to have an equal opportunity is recognized. Therefore, it is essential to provide a good environment for each child; this means that an inadequate home environment must be compensated for by a rich and varied preschool curriculum.[6]

The 1960's have become known as the decade of the disadvantaged. A brief but inclusive definition of the culturally disadvantaged (the low-income deprived) is that these are individuals or a group of people who lack social amenities and cultural graces associated with middle-class society. Historically, overwhelming numbers of the culturally deprived began to appear around 1860 when the population changed largely to rural-urban with the rural living in urbanized communities for which they were not vocationally equipped. Large groups of culturally deprived children are today found in the slums of large cities, certain rural areas, Indian reservations, and migrant workers camps.

Great progress has been made in recent years in legislation for the assistance of the culturally deprived child. It is now recognized that deprived children and their parents have a positive attitude toward education but are alienated from the regular public school situation because of frustrations and failure.

There is a coming together of forces in a concerted effort to develop programs to help the underprivileged child. Many aspects of the social environment contribute to a child's behavior, but the most crucial is his interaction with his parents. The focal point is moving steadily downward and is now pointed to early childhood. Programs are being developed for the child of the low-income group in city slums, the child from a minority group, the child who is physically remote from more modal society, and the child of migrant workers. Because cultural deprivation goes with economic dependency, it is anticipated that these special programs will not only assist in giving these children a knowledge of the culture and its values but also encourage and motivate them to develop skills that will make them vocationally independent.

The Economic Opportunity Act of 1964 provided for varied ways through which these children may derive the best from child development, social

[6]M. L. Goldschmidt. "Early Cognitive Development and Preschool Education." *Internatl. J. of Early Child. Educ.*, 3:1 (1971), pp. 5–6.

welfare, teaching methods, and motivational techniques.[7] It authorized the establishment of programs for economically deprived children of preschool age, designed to prepare them to enter public school. These programs are called Head Start Child Development Programs, a part of the Federal government's War on Poverty.

The Head Start Program is an attempt to reach children of low-income families between the ages of three and five through a preschool education program. It provides language opportunities (speaking and listening), a wide variety of experiences, and adequate behavior models for the children. It is an attempt to break the poverty cycle in early ages since evidence indicates that the early years of childhood are the most crucial in educational development. Bloom has pointed out that environment can mean as much as 20 IQ points in the developing child and is most critical in preschool years because the child goes 50 per cent of the way in organizing his thinking patterns by the time he is four years of age and the next 30 percent by the time he is eight.[8]

Head Start is a total program to meet the child's mental and emotional needs in preparing him to find success in his first school experience. It has many component parts—medical and dental examinations and corrections, immunizations, social services, nutritional care, and phychological services. The parents are involved in all aspects of the program, filling many nonprofessional positions. Other interested people in the community are encouraged to work as volunteers. Activities are planned by the center to help parents deal with general and specific problems of making a home and bringing up a family.

The planning for Head Start programs was based on first looking at the needs of children and then setting up appropriate goals. It was found that many children were lacking in language development and often have difficulty in expressing themselves because of limited vocabulary and inability to speak so as to be heard. Because of limited experiences they did not fit into social groups and were often unable to use simple toys or scissors, crayons, paper, pencils, and such, which are readily accessible to privileged children. The program which emerged placed emphasis on improving language, healthful living, developing curiosity, building self-image, and respecting authority as a means to self-discipline.

The 1965 summer program of Head Start began at 13,344 centers in 2,000 communities with an attendance of approximately 500,000 children.[9] One of every two economically deprived children eligible to enter public school in the fall of 1965 was helped. Forty thousand teachers and 500,000 volunteers were involved in the eight-week program. Local communities paid 10 per cent (either cash or in kind). The Federal Government paid up to 90 per cent of the cost.

[7]D. Brieland, "Cultural and Social Change," *Young Children, 20:*4 (1965), pp. 223–229.

[8]B. S. Bloom, *Stability and Change in Human Characteristics* (New York: John Wiley and Sons, 1964), p. 88.

[9]Irwin Ross, "Head Start Is a Banner Project." *The PTA Magazine, 60:*7 (1966), p. 3.

This 1965 summer program was so successful that in August of that year it was announced that Project Head Start would become a year-round program. There were the following three types of programs:[10]

1. Programs, including health, education, social service, and parent activities, during the school year for the children who participated in summer Head Start.
2. Full-year programs for preschool children who would enter school in the fall of the year.
3. Short-term summer programs for children who would enter school in the fall of the year.

The local programs were conducted by the Community Action Agency or delegated to a group that has the capacity to organize and operate the program, such as the public schools, other public agencies, private nonprofit organizations, or institutions of higher education. In communities without a Community Action Agency other provisions were made for sponsorship of a Head Start program. Children were selected on the basis of an index of whether a family was earning a minimum-standard income, where the family lived (farm or nonfarm family), and number of children in the family. At least 90 per cent of the children came from families that fell below the poverty "line." The other 10 per cent could come from the community at large but could not share in the medical benefits.

Groups were limited to 15–20 children per teacher. The Office of Economic Opportunity financed an eight-week teacher training course for a limited number of local people who were to teach in the program. Short-term courses were planned for other teachers.

Such programs as *Institutional Development Studies*,[11] the program in New Rochelle, New York,[12] the Early School Admission Project in Baltimore,[13] Early Training Project at Murfreesboro, Tennessee,[14] and the New York Housing Authority Project,[15] had given direction to the development of preschool programs before the need for compensatory education had attained such national scope.

Some educators questioned whether an eight-week program or even a

[10]Keith Osborn, "Project Head Start—An Assessment," *Educ. Leadership*, 23:98 (1965), pp. 18–103.

[11]M. Deutsch, "Early Social Environment: Its Influence on School Adaptation," *Pre-School Education Today* (Garden City, N.Y.: Doubleday & Co., 1966).

[12]Thelma G. Wolman, "A Preschool Program for Disadvantaged Children—The New Rochelle Story," *Young Children*, 21:2 (1965), pp. 98–111.

[13]Catherine Brunner, "Deprivation—Its Effects, Its Remedies," *Educ. Leadership*, 23:2 (1965), pp. 103–107.

[14]R. A. Klaus and Susan W. Gray, "Murfreesboro Preschool Program for Culturally Deprived Children," *Child Educ.*, 42:2 (1965), p. 92.

[15]Alice M. Brophy, "Children's Centers—Three Decades of Progress," *J. of Nursery Educ.*, 13:3 (1964), pp. 173–177.

year-round program could make up for four years of deprivation. Some leaders in the field suggested that emphasis in these programs be placed only upon academic learning. Others believed that the broader program would insure greater achievement in academic learning and contribute more to the cultural development of the child.[16] Spodek raised the questions of the value of "massive intervention" and quality control of programs for such large groups of disadvantaged children.[17]

The Head Start Statistical Fact Sheet for the 1971 Fiscal Year showed that $360 million were budgeted in 1971 for 1,663 programs composed of 415,800 children. There were 275,586 children in year-round programs in 1971 with an average cost per child of $1,109.

A total of 4,183,400 children have participated in Head Start since its beginning in 1965. In addition, in 1971 the 50 states had full year programs including 88 Indian and migrant projects. These data, however, did not include five programs in Puerto Rico and three each in the Virgin Islands and Pacific Island Trust Territories.

Sixty per cent of the programs were located in urban sites and 40 per cent in rural sites. In the thirty-three Parent and Child Center Programs, the Federal contribution to the operating cost was 80 per cent. The Head Start Summer Programs in 1971 included 503 centers serving 118,125 children with 8,595 educational professionals, 14,719 nonprofessionals, and 27,301 volunteers. Head Start publishes a newssheet and issues fact sheets each fiscal year.[18]

In the six years Head Start has contributed to all educational programs by (1) enrolling more employees in training programs; (2) inspiring the nation to focus attention on preschool education, especially that of the deprived child; (3) having a dramatic impact upon education in philosophy, materials, and facilities; (4) providing lower pupil-teacher ratios and making use of volunteers as well as health and welfare agencies; (5) keeping better records and passing such records to teachers of primary grades; (6) proving that young children learn more, faster, and at an earlier age than was previously thought to be true.

The Follow Through programs of Head Start show that two thirds of the children received medical and dental services they required through Head Start. The Parent and Child Centers emphasize the re-enforcement of parental skills because the staff works with the entire family.[19]

The objectives of Planned Variations are twofold: comparing short-term and long-term effects of well-defined approaches to early childhood education and

[16]"Project Head Start," *NEA J., 54*:7 (1965), p. 58.

[17]B. Spodek, "Is Massive Intervention the Answer?" *Educ. Leadership, 23*:2 (1965), p. 109.

[18]*Project Head Start Statistical Fact Sheet Fiscal Year 1971.* (Washington, D.C.: U.S. Department of Health, Education, and Welfare, Office of Child Development).

[19]*Head Start, a Child Development Program.* Washington, D.C.: U.S. Department of Health, Education, and Welfare.

assessing the cumulative impact of a continuous, systematically different program from preschool to primary grades. During the first year, the evaluation of the program was devoted to the extent and nature of its implementation and its effects on children and their families. A review describing three case studies showed the values of the program not only to children and their families but also to their aides and others who work with the groups.[20]

The Evaluative Studies of Project Head Start are divided into census surveys, research, educational testing service, longitudinal studies, and national evaluation studies. The studies showed a need for more careful instrumentation particularly in research designs, the need to study long-term interventions, and the need to avoid quick judgments on the basis of data or the art of early childhood education.[21]

Jenny W. Klein states that it took almost one hundred years before a comprehensive, federally sponsored intervention program emerged for preschoolers. Experimental and pilot programs, planned variations of Head Start, and other models provide information to show that early intervention may raise the quality of children's lives before the effects of poverty are established into a self-perpetuating cycle.[22]

NATIONAL WHITE HOUSE CONFERENCES

At the 1950 White House Conference, the citizens attending expressed their approval of education for young children by this recommendation: "As a desirable supplement to home life, nursery schools and kindergartens, provided they meet high professional standards, should be included as a part of public opportunities for all children."[23]

At the 1960 Conference, three forums recommended that free public education be extended downward to include kindergartens as a part of the school system. It was further recommended that every organized group of young children away from home be under the supervision of at least one person qualified in the field of early childhood education.[24]

The 1970 Conference had certain unique features, namely: (1) the division into two groups, one conferring on children and another on youth so that the problems of children not become secondary to the problems of youth; (2)

---

[20]*Implementation of Planned Variations in Head Start, 1969–70.* (Washington, D.C.: Institute of Child Study, College of Education, University of Maryland, College Park, and Office of Child Development, Department of Health, Education, and Welfare).

[21]Lois-Ellen Datta. "A Report on Evaluation Studies of Project Head Start." *International Journal of Early Childhood Education,* 3:2 (1971), pp. 58–68.

[22]Jenny W. Klein. "Head Start: Intervention for What?" *Educ. Leadership,* 29:1 (1971), pp. 16–19.

[23]*Conference Proceedings* (Washington, D.C.: Midcentury White House Conference on Children and Youth, 1950).

[24]*Conference Proceedings* (Washington, D.C.: The Golden Anniversary White House Conference on Children and Youth, 1960).

the multi-disciplinary approach, by bringing together groups from both inside and outside educational circles so that clergymen, scientists, health practitioners, lawyers, parents, media representatives, and businessmen as well as children could work together; (3) selection of delegates to represent all sections of the country.[25]

A series of meetings were developed prior to the conference for young children. After three months of sharing, the conference itself was planned. The 1970 Conference generated many recommendations to be implemented at the local level. (Typical examples may be found in the Illinois and Kentucky models.) The recommendations also included (1) establishing in each state a strong statutory mandated committee with backing from the governor's office; (2) including both lay and professional representatives, enlightened citizens, children, and members of minority groups; (3) providing a full-time paid staff of workers, employed to take care of organizational plans; and (4) holding an annual committee meeting in a workshop situation to discuss local problems and to make recommendations for the decennial White House Conference on Children.[26]

In addition to State Committees, the conference participants further recommended that each state set up community-coordinated child care committees (4C).[27] These committees were to be composed of parents and professionals (both public and private) who serve in the field of child development. There were already ten such committees when the White House Conference on Children met in 1970.

Public Support of Schools and Centers for Young Children

In 1953 only 43 per cent of the children in the five-year age group had the opportunity to attend kindergarten. In 1959, over 64 per cent of five-year-olds were in school. Although all but one of the states had some type of legislation relating to the education of children under six, only nineteen had authorized the use of state funds for this age group. The legislative provisions seem to give considerable status to nursery schools and kindergartens. In October 1964, there were 3,187,000 children aged three to five years enrolled in public or private nursery schools or kindergartens. This was approximately one-fourth of the children in the United States of this age. Of this group 2,716,000 enrolled in kindergartens were five years old.[28]

The Economic Opportunity Act of 1964 and the Elementary and Secondary

[25]*Report to the President,* White House Conference on Children (Washington, D.C.: U.S. Government Printing Office, 1970), pp. 5–15.

[26]Ibid., pp. 14–15.

[27]Office of Child Development. *Interim Policy Guide for the 4C Program, Pilot Phase.* (Washington, D.C.: U.S. Department of Health, Education, and Welfare, 1969).

[28]Samuel Schloss, *Enrollment of 3- 4- and 5-Year-Olds in Nursery Schools and Kindergartens,* (Washington, D.C.: U.S. Department of Health, Education, and Welfare, 1965), pp. 1, 16.

Act of 1965 brought the Federal government increasingly into the educational scene. For the first time, funds in unprecedented amounts were made available to every community in the nation. Both of these Acts and their subsequent implementation placed major emphasis on early education, particularly for children of disadvantaged families. The tremendous and immediate public response to Head Start Programs pointed up the urgent need for such a program.

The influence of this Federal legislation during the mid 1960's has given impetus to the changing trends in early childhood education and should prove beneficial to all children of all socio-economic levels. The prospects for kindergartens in all public school systems are brightened. In addition, the child care centers are rapidly changing to carefully planned educational programs under the direction of trained teachers.

Schloss analyzed the data collected by the Bureau of Census in 1964 and found that of all the children enrolled in kindergarten 83 per cent were in public schools. Over 80 per cent of the Head Start Centers for the summer of 1965 were sponsored by local school systems. Only one-half of the states in 1965 provided for kindergarten on the same basis as other grades in public schools, and seven states had no public kindergartens.[29] By 1969 state aid for kindergartens was available in 29 states.[30]

In crowded situations, however, there has been a tendency for the teacher to teach two groups, one in the morning and one in the afternoon, and to increase the size of the group to as high as 45 to 50 pupils. Inability to meet the cost involved may prevent many children from attending a private school, thereby depriving them of the opportunity to attend preschool or kindergarten unless schools are made available through public funds.

As a result of the growing need and the inadequate provision made by public schools, the private preschools have experienced rapid growth. This rapid expansion raises questions as to the types of schools, quality of programs, and preparation of the teachers. While many private schools maintain excellent facilities, have a good teacher-pupil ratio, and employ well-trained teachers, there are many centers that do not maintain standards necessary for the well-being of children. Some of these services may be educationally detrimental, although they may seem to fill a need in the care of young children.

In order to safeguard all children who are enrolled in schools or centers, some states have enacted legislation requiring state registration. The number of states providing such safeguards is small, while the need for this protection is great. In several states, committees composed of private-school directors, as well as representatives of state agencies and public schools, are at work to

[29]Anne Peet, "Why Not Enough Public School Kindergartens?" *Young Children,* 21:2 (1965), p. 114.

[30]*Kindergarten Education in Public Schools, 1967-68.* (Washington, D.C.: National Education Association, 1969), p. 52.

have protective legislation passed. The plan is one of cooperative action rather than coercion.

Types of Schools and Centers for Young Children

Many types of children's centers and schools are in operation today. The centers vary as to purpose and program. Yet each type of school or center has a place in our society and has a contribution to make to the development of young children. Leaders from all groups, organizations, agencies, and institutions interested in the welfare of the young child are working cooperatively at the local, state, and national level in initiating research to clarify the role of each type of center. These groups are also investigating ways in which the purpose and program of each may be improved and to determine what shall be the criteria by which each type can be evaluated.

Parents of young children need help in selecting the school that is best for their child. Although the name of a school may not appear important, it should provide some guidance to parents in their selection. Frequently, however, the name of the school is misleading and this creates a problem. Selecting challenging and interesting names for children's centers is a common practice; however, leaders in public and nonpublic programs are giving this situation careful study because of the implication the name has for programs for young children. Although the purpose and program may be consistent with the best educational philosophy and practice, the name may be such that it implies the opposite. An examination of any local or state directory will show such names as "Finishing School for Tots" or "Kountry Klub for Kiddies," which do not interpret to the parents what type of center is available or the purpose and program as related to the child's continuous educational experience. Names such as "Community Play School" or "School for Young Children" present a clearer indication of what one might expect to find in the center.

In any center organized for a group of young children, whether desirable or undesirable, learning takes place. Without some basic criteria to use in selecting a center, parents and lay citizens find it difficult to distinguish between a program designed primarily for physical care of children and one that accepts the responsibility for a sound educational program providing for the development of the whole child emotionally, socially, and mentally as well as physically. Thus it becomes important to define each type of center in terms of purpose and program.

The following classifications of schools and centers for young children are generally agreed upon by national leaders:

Nursery School

Nursery schools are of many types and forms. The term is often confused with day care centers, day nurseries, or nurseries. A nursery school is the first of the series of units that compose elementary education. In public schools it usually is planned for the four-year-olds, when operated under non-public auspices it generally includes children of three and four years of age. Whether operated on a basis of one- or two-year periods, it provides for a continuous educational program under qualified teachers and in close cooperation with parents.

In addition to the public and nonpublic nursery schools, there are many nursery schools that may be classified according to the purposes they serve. These include cooperative nursery schools, nursery schools that serve as laboratory or research centers for an institution or agency, sponsored nursery schools, and nursery schools for children with special needs that cannot be provided in the regular program provided for all children.

Kindergarten

The unit of the school which enrolls five-year-olds on a regular basis for a year prior to entrance to the first grade is designated as a kindergarten. The purpose of the kindergarten program is to further the developmental growth of the children through experiences that are of interest and help to them. This unit provides for a continuous educational experience under the direction of a qualified teacher in close cooperation with the parents. A few kindergartens admit four-year-olds and provide for two years of continuous educational experience. Many of these units are a part of the public school systems; others operate as church-related, privately owned, or sponsored groups. Some public and private and/or church-related kindergartens are on two half-day sessions— one in the morning, the other in the afternoon.

Child Development Center

The center is organized around a classroom and a play area and provides a program for early diagnosis of problems not recognized by parents, including dental, medical, and emotional. This type of program is both a concept and a community facility. It is a drawing together of all the resources in a community—both family and professional—which can contribute to the child's total development. The skills of professional workers in the fields of education, health, welfare and related areas are utilized in building a program for each child. In planning, it is recognized that both professionals and nonprofessionals can make a meaningful contribution; therefore, it emphasizes the family as fundamental to the child's total development. The parents have an important role in developing policies and participating in the program. The concept of the child development center was used as a model for Head Start centers for disadvantaged children.

School for Disadvantaged Children

Obviously all disadvantaged children are not alike. As with all good pre-school programs, the program needs to be tailored to fit the special needs of each child enrolled; however, the disadvantaged child has special needs not found in groups of other children. Such a center should provide many opportunities to widen the child's horizons, to assist him to express himself orally, to succeed in a climate of confidence, and to develop within him and his family a responsible attitude toward society and a feeling of belonging to a community. Notable among such preschools are the Head Start Programs just discussed. The teacher ratio, which needs to be lower since these children require additional attention, is usually one teacher for 15–20 children with additional aides and/or teachers. Time schedules are adapted to needs of individual children and their parents. A well-planned follow-through program with parents and children is a functional part of the activities. Special training for teachers and courses and clinics for parents are included. The parents are actively involved in planning and following through the activities.

Guided Observation Nursery School / Kindergarten

The purpose of these schools is to provide for parent guidance and education under the leadership of a trained teacher. Many of the other types of schools for young children incorporate this feature. A large number of these schools also serve as laboratories for the study of human growth and development, either by high school or college students.

School for Exceptional Children

This type of school is developed to meet the needs of an atypical child. Frequently, the entrance age is younger than three years and special provisions are made for early diagnosis, treatment, and guidance of the atypical child. Teachers in these specialized schools require additional training, and clinical services are provided for teacher and parents as they work closely together in meeting specific mental, physical, or social needs of the child.

Cooperative Nursery School and/or Kindergarten

These schools serve a real purpose in our present-day life. Through this program many children have opportunities to participate in an educational program within the limits of the family's income. Often they serve a twofold purpose, providing an intensive program of parent education as well as worthwhile educational experiences for the children. Some cooperatives are operated by parents under church sponsorship; others are neighborhood or community ventures sponsored by parents only. Most of these schools provide for a director qualified in early childhood education who is assisted by the parents. As they work with the children, these parents receive guidance and close supervision from the director. The term "cooperative" itself implies that each parent contributes services and/or time to the on-going program.

Child Day Care Center and Day Nursery

Many of these centers have the qualities desired for a good nursery school or kindergarten; many others place the greater emphasis on custodial care and offer a very limited educational program. A number of these centers provide for care of children while mothers are working; some are organized to provide for care of children from less privileged homes.

At times the necessity to be self-sustaining and/or to provide an income in some centers makes it difficult to offer the most desirable situation. Often center administrators think it necessary to operate with inadequate facilities and personnel. Training programs are being developed throughout the nation to assist personnel in providing educationally sound programs for young children.

In many areas legislation and inspections of centers by health and welfare groups have provided protection for children physically. In some areas addition of new, carefully planned facilities, training programs for personnel and development of policies relating to employment of personnel have greatly improved the quality of this type of program.

The Play School

These centers are usually operated in a neighborhood or a church under the sponsorship of a church, an organized group of parents, a civic club, or as a part of a program of recreation for all children or for care of underprivileged children. Many are called schools; however, emphasis is placed upon group play, which is not usually interpreted as being a part of the continuous educational plan for young children. A large number of play schools have expanded facilities and programs and have incorporated activities formerly considered as those provided in a nursery school and/or kindergarten.[31]

A description of recent developments in program may be found in Chapter 8.

GUIDES FOR PARENTS IN THE SELECTION OF A SCHOOL

A parent's selection of a school for his child under six should be regarded as an important decision in terms of what will contribute most effectively to the mental, physical, and emotional health of the child. However, directors of some of the centers for preschool children report that many parents are careless in choosing a school for their child.

The following is a list of generally accepted information for parents to consider in identifying good schools for young children.

PURPOSE

Is the primary purpose to provide a program that fosters the total development of the child?

PROGRAM

Is the primary purpose of the program to provide an organized, continuous experience suited to the maturity level and growth pattern of the children attending?

[31]Hazel F. Gabbard, "Status and Trends in Early Childhood Education," *Those First School Years*, vol. 40 (Washington, D.C.: NEA, 1960), pp. 219-221.

Is the program so designed that regular continuous attendance is expected of each child?

Does the program provide for continuous uninterrupted growth of the child as he progresses to other units within the center and to units outside the center?

Are the records of each child systematically kept and available as he progresses to the next unit?

Is the period scheduled for operation adequate for such a program?

Does the daily period of operation require additional plans for child care? If so, are these planned to be developmental, and are additional staff and facilities provided for this service?

Are there adequate provisions for the planned educational program? Health program? Nutritional program? Social services?

PERSONNEL

Are the teachers professionally competent?

Do the teachers meet the certification requirements for specialization in early childhood education?

Are associates, aides, and volunteers utilized?

Is the adult-child ratio adequate so that individual and group experiences are provided for young children under proper guidance?

FACILITIES

Is the center easily accessible?

Is adequate space indoors and outdoors provided?

Are facilities carefully maintained according to best practices for health and sanitation?

Are adequate and appropriate equipment and materials provided?

HEALTH AND SAFETY

Are there adequate provisions for health and safety?

Are food services available, adequately supervised, and sanitary?

Is the food nutritious?

Are health records kept of employees and children?

What plans are made for children who are ill at school?

SPECIAL SERVICES

What types of special services are provided?

How are these offered?

Are persons rendering this service fully qualified and certified?

Parents and teachers will find discussions of these questions in Parts II and III of this book.

LEGISLATION PERTAINING TO SCHOOLS FOR YOUNG CHILDREN

A real concern is developing today about the quality of the experiences that are provided for young children. In the early days a very limited number of schools were available for a select group. The socioeconomic conditions did not create a great demand for child care away from the home; the importance of experiences in schools for young children was not generally accepted. Today, many centers for children have developed to meet a social demand for child care while the mother is working outside the home.

This trend toward provision of educational opportunities for greater numbers of children under six has focused attention on the need to insure that schools and centers for young children meet acceptable standards. Parents have faith in the term *school*; therefore, they frequently place their child in a center called a school without further investigation.

As early as 1879 state legislators began to enact laws permitting local school authorities to establish kindergartens. In a 1928 survey, Davis found that children's centers were expanding in number and enrollment at a rapid rate. This survey indicated that parents were seeking the best possible environment for their children; in addition it also indicated that parents desired guidance and cooperation in the supervision of the child's development.[32]

However, the strongest demand for provision and protection of schools for young children has come since 1940. Many states have taken legislative action regarding standards for schools for young children. This legislation has been related to the following five areas:

1. Authority to establish and administer such a school.
2. Age of children in attendance.
3. Financial support.
4. Teacher certification and evaluation centers.
5. State and Federal leadership.

Legislative and Federal action that pertains only to schools supported through public funds is not adequate. Many of the leaders of nonpublicly financed programs are giving aggressive leadership toward securing legislative action related to supervision and control of all schools for young children. Practically all states now provide for some authority vested either in the state or local officials to exercise some leadership function and to provide, in some instances, more or less limited supervision over nonpublic schools, either through directly expressed or implied legislative action.

Gabbard states that in 1960 many state departments of education were interested in the growing movement of nonpublic schools for young children and that there was a trend toward providing consultants for these programs who would evaluate and register the schools.[33]

Administering the programs for early childhood education is either permissive or mandatory, depending on the type of legislative enactment. Legal authorization usually provides for some or all of the following: (1) registration and approval of schools; (2) authorization to develop rules and regulations for approval of nonpublic schools; (3) establishment of standards for schools; and

---

[32]Davis, op. cit., pp. 1–15.

[33]Gabbard, op. cit., p. 222.

(4) regulatory, administrative, supervisory, and leadership powers for the State Departments of Health, Education, and Welfare.

Since the 1960's, as federal legislation relating to education of young children has been enacted, state legislation has followed in many areas. In addition, nonpublic funds have been made available for experimental and special programs.

TRENDS IN EARLY CHILDHOOD EDUCATION

In an effort to note trends in any area of our rapidly changing life today, it appears significant to identify landmarks by which the degree of change can be measured. In identifying trends in education for the young child, the following landmarks will indicate the changes that have developed both in beliefs and practice:

1. *The acceptance of the Froebelian philosophy and program for kindergartens.* For a time, the European philosophy of the kindergarten was transplanted with little change in relation to the needs of American life. The emphasis was on following Froebel and using his program and gifts for all children. Froebel's philosophy, rather than the child, was the center of study.
2. *The beginning of the child study movement.* Dewey and Hall found leaders in the kindergarten field eager to apply their findings and philosophy to the education of young children. But it was not easy. For, only a century ago, the study of children was frowned upon by many. G. Stanley Hall has told how difficult it was in the middle of the last century to measure the height and weight of school children because parents objected to the invasion of the child's rights.[34]

   Studies today are far reaching and have great implications for what happens to young children. For example, in the recent survey of "400 Famous People and How Their Childhood Affected Them," it was found that none of them had an easy time in their home but that certain common elements were in the backgrounds of these leaders. As children, these famous people had more opportunity for traveling, reading, thinking, and initiating and conducting original experiments. Many children do not have these opportunities at home; therefore, they need to have experiences provided under guidance to assist them in developing qualities of leadership and creativity. Such studies substantiate the value of and give direction to the content of desirable programs in early childhood education.[35]

[34]J. E. Anderson, "Principles of Child Development," *Early Education* (Washington, D.C.: NEA, 1956), p. 14.

[35]Mildred G. Goertzel and V. Goertzel, *Cradles of Eminence* (New York: Little, Brown & Co., 1962).

3. *Expansion of interest in child development and research to include children under six, soon after World War I.* The research in this period was concerned with establishing the value of the kindergarten in relation to later school adjustment and progress. In the 1930's and early 1940's there was concern for establishing tests and norms of development. In the light of these research findings, kindergarten teachers have tried to better understand and meet the needs of individuals in their groups—to relate findings of child development to practice. Headley reported that:[36]

The findings of the research of this period seemed to indicate:

Children with kindergarten experience tend to make relatively more rapid progress in the first five grades than children who have not attended kindergarten.

The proportion of first-grade repeaters in cities without kindergarten programs is much greater than in cities with programs.

Children in grades one through three with kindergarten background show a marked advantage in both reading rate and comprehension over children who have not attended kindergarten.

They excel others in the rate and quality of their handwriting in the first grades.

In grades one through three, they tend to establish better person-to-person and person-to-group contacts.

They tend to receive higher teacher ratings on oral language and such traits as industry and initiative.

4. *Progressive Education.* Although the era of the Progressive Education Movement is usually associated with the years between 1896 and the late 1930's, extensions of the movement are found today in many programs such as the British Infant Schools and other examples of open education for children, as well as in various alternative forms of schooling.

The common principles that Dewey felt existed in progressive schools included the following: expression and cultivation of individuality; free activity; learning through experience; acquiring meaningful and needed skills; making the most of each day of school because school is life; developing acquaintances with the social and physical world. Progressive education combined the psychological principles of child growth with the moral principles of democracy.[37]

5. *Federal interest in early childhood centers.* The federal government has not only appropriated money for childhood centers but it has developed materials, established supervisory programs, and assisted parents and whole communities in developing a changed concept of early education. Many types of experimental programs have been established.

---

[36]Neith Headley, "The Kindergarten Comes of Age," *NEA J.,* 43:3 (1954), p. 153.

[37]James M. Squire, ed. *A New Look at Progressive Education,* 1972 Yearbook (Washington, D.C.: ASCD, 1972), pp. 1–13.

6. *The influence of Montessori.* The influence of Montessori may be found in special Montessori schools and also to some extent in many pre-schools in the United States. The Montessori method provides for a personal space for each child, allowing him freedom to learn at a rate suitable for him, but supervised by a teacher as he moves about and talks. However, the first movement for exploration must come from the child. Each task is broken down into a series of smaller tasks. All the learning tasks, guided by the teacher, lead the child into the mastery of reading, writing, and mathematics as well as related skills. This program provides a variety of models for imitation as well as providing for older children to help and to teach younger children. The materials have been modernized, the use of equipment is more permissive, and the methods are used to insure greater academic achievement.[38]

7. *The Influence of Piaget.* Piaget's theory is concerned with the development of thinking or intelligence from infancy to adulthood. The theory consists of three interdependent aspects, namely structural, stage, and functional aspects.[39] Although Piaget's work has identified four major stages, two are especially important in early childhood: the sensori-motor period and the preoperational period. One of the preschool's basic functions is to facilitate the transition from one stage to another. By consolidating knowledge of objects, time, and space, the child builds a foundation upon which at a later date he can build other structures. (See Chapter 13.)

SOME AREAS NEEDING SPECIAL CONSIDERATION IN THE 1970's

The rapid expansion of early education evident in the 1960's is even more apparent in the 1970's. With this expansion came some significant changes in points of emphasis. Among these are

1. *Changes in philosophy and practice.* The confusion in early childhood education today "is as though a bombshell exploded with the pieces going in every direction."[40] In this period changes of points of view or of greater emphasis are significant in the areas of interrelated learnings and learning by inference; the place and importance of expectancy in the learning process; greater emphasis on learning of the child from the peer group, especially in terms of hobbies and interests; the child's need for love from the teacher and his peers; the application of science to the child's development; and the positive interrelation between pre-school attendance and behavior in adolescent years.

[38]Evelyn Beyer et al., eds. *Montessori in Perspective.* Washington, D.C.: NAEYC (1971), pp. 25–35.

[39]*A New Look at Progressive Education,* op. cit., pp. 88–114.

[40]Edythe Margolin, "Critical Issues in Contemporary Childhood Education," *Child. Educ.,* 45:8 (1969), p. 503.

2. *Environmental influences.* The environment exerts a powerful influence on the preschool child. Children need space to play in large and small groups, to work, to discuss, to be alone, to listen, to think, and to create. They do need clean air, freedom from excessive noise, and a well-planned attractive environment indoors and outdoors that has adequate space. The emotional climate should provide security, develop positive self-image, and encourage good health.

3. *Acceptance of individuals who are culturally or racially different.* To meet the objective of accepting into our society individuals who are culturally or racially different, teachers must be sensitive to all children. Although she may place little emphasis on direct teaching, the teacher places great emphasis on the daily living within the center. Each child, rich, poor, or handicapped, racially or culturally different, makes his own contribution. The child needs to learn each other child for his own worth.

4. *The need for day care services.* Whether they are to serve the children of working mothers or the children of disadvantaged families, day care services for the preschool child should provide adequate care and educational guidance. Not all children needing preschool care are from indigent families; many families can provide financially for the care of their children. In well-established day care centers, at least two adults are available at all times. In addition, they have professional help and volunteer workers to assist as scheduled. In one study, the mothers of young children expressed dissatisfaction with the care their children were receiving as follows: not being with their child, 18 per cent; behavior, 27 per cent; and general dissatisfaction, 20 per cent. On the whole, though, the working mothers believed that it was better for children to attend a full-time or part-time preschool than to remain at home with relatives or maids.[41]

Importance of Cooperative Effort

There are many organizations interested in the educational welfare of children at the local, state, regional, and national levels. Representatives from these organizations are working closely together to provide educational opportunities that allow the child to reach his highest potential as he enters the continuous program of education from childhood through adulthood. Their cooperative efforts have greatly aided in securing better legislation, improved facilities and staff, and additional funds for programs for young children.

Through the years this willingness of leaders to work together for the

[41]Seth Low and Pearl G. Spindler, *Child Care Arrangements in the United States.* Washington, D.C.: U.S. Department of Health, Education, and Welfare and U.S. Department of Labor, Women's Bureau (1968), pp. 6–12.

development of the programs of good schools for young children has been evident. This cooperative effort in searching for better ways to provide educational opportunities for the young child has resulted in the present-day recognition of the implications of these experiences for the continued education of the child. Through analyzing the strengths and weaknesses of the present programs, a basis for improved educational opportunities can be established. America has faith in education and holds to the belief that all children should have access to the best possible educational opportunities according to each child's potential. This faith and belief should continue to give direction to the expansion of the present-day schools and to the development of new schools for young children in the world of today and of tomorrow.

SUMMARY

The trends and issues in preschool programs which have been discussed include the following:

1. Extending public schools downward to include kindergarten, nursery school, child development centers, and programs for infants.
2. Changing patterns of school organization and adapting programs for specific purposes, such as those for the culturally deprived or for exceptional children.
3. Changing emphasis in day care programs to educational programs as well as day care.
4. Changing curriculum for preschool children by differentiating goals, activities, and materials to provide for individual differences within the group.
5. Changing role of the teacher to that of a guide of child development as opposed to a director of activities.
6. Increasing number of church-related schools for preschool children.
7. Expanding cooperative programs for preschool children.
8. Changing parent participation to parent involvement and replacing formal parent education with a cooperative teacher-parent team approach, which utilizes parents in the instructional programs of their children in both home and center.
9. Replacing nursery schools and kindergartens with child development centers that provide the comprehensive programs made possible by available funds from the Federal government and various foundations.
10. Recognizing the importance of process in education.

In analyzing these trends, it will be noted that some are positive and good for children; others indicate situations which contradict all that is known about how children grow and learn. Shortened sessions and large groups of children are being accepted as emergency measures. Too frequently there has been a tendency to rationalize and accept these make-shift arrangements, rather than to evaluate the services in terms of the effect on children. The present confusion regarding what is good for children must be cleared up and, in order to do this, there must be some guidelines by which to evaluate trends.

Suggested Activities

1. Make a survey of nursery schools and kindergartens in your community. Trace the historical development of a selected number according to types. List requirements for admission, length of day, and types of services offered.

2. Compile a directory of these schools with an annotation showing services offered and so forth.

3. Compile a report of laws pertaining to schools for young children in your state and in your community. Discuss the historical development of these laws and what provisions are made for enforcing them in your local community.

4. Have a panel discussion on present strengths and improvements needed in schools for young children in your area. Present statistical data to support this discussion.

5. Investigate the Head Start Program, defining provisions made by federal government and the realtionship to state and local community. Describe programs in operation in your community, listing strengths and weaknesses. Describe follow-through activities.

6. Discuss pending legislation relative to schools for young children (at the national level, the state level, and the local level).

Related Readings

Almy, Millie. "New Views on Intellectual Development in Early Childhood," *Intellectual Development: Another Look*. Washington, D.C.: ASCD, 1964.

ASCD. "Federal Funds to Assist or to Control?" *Educ. Leadership*, 24:1 (1966).

——. "The Young Child: Today's Pawn?" *Educ. Leadership*, 23:2 (1965).

Bissell, Joan S. *Implementation of Planned Variation in Head Start*, First Year Report, I, Review and Summary. Washington, D.C.: Office of Child Development, April 1971.

Children's Bureau Research. *Prelude to School, An Evaluation of an Inner-City Program*, Report No. 3. Washington, D.C.: U.S. Department of Health, Education, and Welfare, 1968.

Chilman, C. S. *Growing Up Poor*. U.S. Department of Health, Education, and Welfare, Welfare Administration, Division of Research, Publication No. 13. Washington, D.C.: U.S. Government Printing Office, 1966.

Compilation of Legislation on Title I Financial Assistance to Local Educational Agencies for the Education of Children of Low Income Families (reflecting 1966, 1967, and 1970 amendments). Washington, D.C.: U.S. Department of Health, Education, and Welfare, 1971.

Concept of a Child Development Center, Relationship to Preschool and Day Care. Washington, D.C.: Office of Economic Opportunity, March 18, 1965.

Curtis, Hazen A., and Joseph A. Klock. *Florida Pre-Kindergarten Migrant Compensatory Program: An Evaluation*. Florida State University, Tallahassee, Fla., 1972. (Mimeographed)

Dittman, Laura, ed. *Early Child Care: The New Perspectives*. New York: Atherton Press, 1968.

Forest, I. *Preschool Education, A Historical and Critical Study*. New York: Macmillan, Inc., 1927.

Frazier, Alexander, ed. *Early Childhood Education Today*. Washington, D.C.: ASCD, 1968.

Frost, J. L., ed. *Early Childhood Education Rediscovered: Readings*. New York: Holt, Rinehart and Winston, 1968.

Goldschmidt, M. L. "Early Cognitive Development and Preschool Education." *International Journal of Early Childhood Education*, 3:1 (1971), pp. 1–7.

Hechinger, F. M., ed. *Pre-School Education Today*. Garden City, N.Y.: Doubleday & Co., 1966.

Hurd, G. E. *Preprimary Enrollment*. Washington, D.C.: U.S. Department of Health, Education, and Welfare, 1969.

Leeper, R. R. "A Time for Reevaluation." *Educ. Leadership*, 29:1 (1971), p. 3.

Light, N. S., chairman, *Early Childhood Education*, Part II, 46th Yearbook, Bloomington, Ill.: Public School Publishing Co., 1929.

Loving, A. D. "Intervention for What?" *Educ. Leadership*, 29:1 (1971), p. 7.

Malone, Margaret. *Congressional Research Service, Summary of Selected Proposals Related to Child Care*. Washington, D.C.: Library of Congress, June 24, 1971.

Meek, Lois M., chairman. *Pre-School and Parental Education*, Part I, *Organization and Development*, and Part II, *Research and Method*, 28th Yearbook, NSSE. Bloomington, Ill.: Public School Publishing Co., 1929.

Rambusch, Nancy McCormick. *Learning How to Learn—An American Approach to Montessori*. Baltimore, Md.: Helicon Press, 1962.

Snyder, Agnes, et al. *Dauntless Women in Childhood Education 1856–1931*. Washington, D.C.: ACEI, 1972.

Taylor, Katherine Whiteside. *History of the Parent Cooperative Movement, 1916–1966*. Indianapolis, Ind.: Parent Cooperative Preschools International, 1966.

Weber, Evelyn. *Early Childhood Education: Perspectives on Change*. Worthington, Ohio: Charles A. Jones Publishing Co., 1970.

———. *The Kindergarten: Its Encounter with Educational Thought in America*. New York: Teachers College Press, 1969.

Providing Qualified Teachers and Maintaining Standards in Preschool Programs

Chapter **7**

Insuring good teachers for young children is one of today's greatest challenges. Laymen and educators regard teachers as the most significant factor in determining the quality of experience that a child will have in school. Yet throughout the nation it is possible for individuals without the essential qualities of a good teacher to operate schools for young children. Certification based upon required training and experience is only one means whereby good teachers are assured. Regardless of the requirements, certification cannot assure the personal qualities required of a good teacher.

Throughout the years, love of children has been recognized as basic to successful work with them. However, love is not enough. The teacher must also enjoy working with children and the love of the teacher should be different from that of the mother or of other adults who work with the child. Patience and understanding not only of what is happening but why it is happening are essential to guiding the development of the young child. Only the teacher who is secure herself can build security within children. A warm, outgoing, but not dominating, individual can work well with children and parents. However, a teacher may have all the desirable personal qualities and not be a good teacher. Basic information, understanding, knowledge, skill, and appreciations can only be secured through training and experience. The teacher must apply this knowledge in her daily work with children. Many programs that prepare one for teaching in the field of early childhood education provide counseling and guidance in the development of these essential qualities while the training and experience are secured.

In the selection of teachers for preschool children, special attention is given to personal qualities such as warmth, openness, humor, efficiency, confidence, appearance, creativity, speech, voice, and the ability to communicate well by speaking clearly and choosing words carefully.

Credentialing teachers today, however, places emphasis on the demonstration of professional competencies as well as personal qualities.[1,2] The competencies may be acquired in a variety of settings including teacher education institutions, on the job training, and in the community through the utilization of human resources.

The new direction is away from inflexible adherence to regulatory functions and toward constructive dynamic leadership at the local level. Widespread exploration and change is indicated. Among the changes are earlier exposure to teaching situations and a shifting in preparation from the campus to the school systems.[3]

Licensing standards for directors of child care center staff vary from state to state. The director or head teacher is usually a college graduate with professional study in early childhood education. Staff training is one of her responsibilities. The age for the director varies from sixteen years in four states to twenty-one years in the other states. The requirements also vary from high school graduation or its equivalent in sixteen states to four years of college in others. Two years of college are required in ten states. However, all states do require experience and also that the individual be equipped to do the work required.

The qualifications of the other staff members also vary from state to state. All of the states require high school graduation or its equivalent and a few require two years of college work in child development. The staff-in-training must be capable of doing work required and must have a sensitivity to children and their needs.[4]

[1]W. C. Allen, et al., "Performance Criteria for Education Personnel Development: A State Approach to Standards," *J. Teacher Educ., 20*:2 (1969), pp. 133–135.

[2]D. W. Allen and P. Wagschal, "New Look in Credentialing," *Clearing House, 44*:3 (1969), pp. 137–140.

[3]*A Manual on Certification Requirements for School Personnel in the United States,* 1970 edition (Washington, D.C.: National Commission on Teacher Education and Professional Standards, NEA, 1970).

[4]Child Care Data and Materials, Committee on Finance, U.S. Senate, June 16, 1971.

Suggested Certification Requirements

A number of reports concerning the preparation of teachers have been made.[5,6,7] In 1967 the Association for Childhood Education International identified the areas to be included in the preparation of teachers for children from three to eight years of age. The areas included: (1) liberal education, (2) foundations of early childhood education, (3) child growth and development, (4) nature of the learning process, (5) small group dynamics, (6) curriculum and method, and (7) professional laboratory experiences.[8]

The Ad Hoc Joint Committee on the Preparation of Nursery and Kindergarden Teachers of the National Commission on Teacher Education included desirable goals in their report for both preservice and inservice education.[9] These included: independence, positive self image, intellectual stimulation, creativity, socialization, physical development, emotional development, and staff collaboration and cooperation. The committee also sets forth proposals on personnel selection and programs for personnel at different levels.

A Pilot Study of Day Care Centers and Their Clientele gives a very factual description of day care facilities and the requirements for day care leaders and volunteers.[10]

Paraprofessionals

It has long been recognized that one teacher cannot do all that is needed for each child. Paraprofessionals render many services under the supervision and direction of the head teacher.[11,12] *Aides* can assist with clerical services, house-

[5]C. L. Rampton, ed., *Early Childhood Development, Alternatives for the Program Implementation in the States* (Denver, Col.: Education Commission of States, 1971), pp. 4, 6, 13.

[6]U.S. Office of Education, *Compilation on Legislation on Title I—Financial Assistance to Local Agencies for the Education of Children of Low-Income Families* (Washington, D.C.: Department of Health, Education, and Welfare, July, 1971).

[7]*State Agencies Administering Services Under Title V, Parts 1 and 2, and Title IV, Part B, of the Social Security Act* (Washington, D.C.: U.S. Department of Health, Education, and Welfare, Social and Rehabilitative Services, Children's Bureau, 1969).

[8]*Preparation Standards for Teachers in Early Childhood Education* (Washington, D.C.: ACEI, 1967).

[9]*Preliminary Report of Ad Hoc Joint Committee on the Preparation of Nursery and Kindergarten Teachers* (Washington, D.C.: National Commission on Teacher Education and Professional Standards, NEA, 1969).

[10]Elizabeth Prescott, *A Pilot Study of Day Care Centers and Their Clientele* (Washington, D.C.: Children's Bureau, Welfare Division, U.S. Department of Health, Education, and Welfare, 1965).

[11]D. Findley and K. T. Henson, "Teacher Aides: Should They Be Certified?" *Contemporary Education,* 42:4 (1971), pp. 177–180.

[12]A. J. Mauser, "The Paraprofessional: Panacea or Frankenstein?" *Contemporary Education,* 41:3 (1970), pp. 139–141.

keeping activities, group supervision, technical assistance, and some instructional activities as assigned by the teacher.[13]

Volunteers may or may not be trained personnel. They assist the trained teacher and also help with community service. They share what they can do best. The trend is to involve *parents* and *community groups* in the instruction and care of children.

All personnel must have an understanding of the objectives and concepts of early childhood education, a personality that children and adults respond to readily, and an intense interest in the development of the children.

The number of persons working in a center depends upon the number of children and the maturity of the children. The type of head teacher also affects the enrollment. However, all centers should have at least one qualified person.

Other personnel may include a career assistant, a career community assistant, career health specialist as well as trainees or aides, the volunteer worker, and paraprofessional personnel. Trainees or aides may assume office or administrative responsibilities as a part of their duties or they may have this type of work exclusively.[14] As the personnel gives evidence of continued interest in children every opportunity should be given them to have additional responsibilities and additional work in courses and experience. There also need to be opportunities for developing career ladders for paraprofessionals.[15]

CHILD DEVELOPMENT ASSOCIATE

A pilot program for the *Child Development Associate* (CDA) project was initiated in the Fall of 1972.[16]

The basic CDA program is to promote a system of training and to set up credentials for persons working with preschool children. It will not be based on courses or units required but on the individual's competency to assume primary responsibility for the development and education of children under his care. The program is based on competencies with children, and the training varies according to the individual.

The Child Development Associate will not work in isolation but will be in close contact with a staff member who has more training and experience. She will not have direct responsibility for extended educational service, but

---

[13]Sylvia Sunderlin and B. Willis, *Aides to Teachers and Children* (Washington, D.C.: ACEI, 1968).

[14]Project Head Start, *Career Planning and Progression for a Child Development Center* (Washington, D.C.: U. S. Department of Health, Education, and Welfare, 1970).

[15]Margaret Malone, *Summary of Selected Proposals Related to Child Care* (Washington, D.C.: Library of Congress, Congressional Research Service, Education and Welfare, June 1971).

[16]From material supplied by: Jenny W. Klein, Senior Education Specialist, Bureau of Head Start and Child Service Programs (Washington, D.C.: U.S. Department of Health, Education, and Welfare, April 24, 1972).

she will have the assistance of paraprofessional aides. The associate will be expected to carry out supplementary responsibilities related to the children's program.

School Standards and Licensing

Because of the importance of preschool to the child's development, standards and licensing for these schools and centers are vital. Furthermore, facts uncovered by Forbes on how and why parents select schools reveal the need for standards. She found that (1) most parents selected centers because of friends' recommendations; (2) some parents selected centers because of enrichment activities; others, however, considered the convenience of the location; (3) although most parents talked by telephone or personally with the director of the center before enrolling their child, 19 per cent did not visit the center or meet the director before enrolling their child; and (4) most of the children were attending the center because parents were not home during the day.[17]

The procedure for insuring improved standards for schools for young children varies from state to state and within cities. Through programs of cooperative action, plans suitable for a given locality are developed and put into effect. Participants include leaders from public, private, and church-related schools, and federal programs, as well as social workers, doctors, psychologists, directors of educational programs for teachers, and other community leaders. Through educational and interpretive programs on television and radio, and through newspapers and magazine articles, the general public is being informed as to values and problems of good schools for young children. As a result, parents are becoming more and more discriminating toward the schools their young children attend. They are cooperating with leaders in the movement to insure that all schools for young children meet minimum standards.

Licensing is one form of insuring standards in preschool centers. Licensing does not guarantee optimum conditions, but rather indicates a level at which a center can operate safely and efficiently. Many persons consider the licensing of child care facilities as the responsibility of departments of welfare. In some situations, however, other agencies cooperate or assume the responsibility.[18]

Organizations Concerned with Schools for Young Children

Professional organizations can be of great assistance to teachers. A brief history of some of these organizations follows.

[17]Marcia Boyer Forbes, *Parental Selection of Schools for Pre-School Children.* Unpublished Master's Thesis, Florida State University, 1960.

[18]E. Class, *Licensing of Child Care Facilities by State Welfare Departments.* Washington, D.C.: U.S. Department of Health, Education, and Welfare, Social and Rehabilitation Service, Children's Bureau, 1968.

The organization of the Primary Department of the National Education Association in 1870 did much to stimulate interest in the kindergarten. Prior to this kindergartens were established and largely maintained by private funds. During the period of 1880 to 1889 the kindergarten movement was expanded through private and church kindergartens and centers for young children in social settlements. During this same period, as the number of these groups became larger, kindergarten associations were formed to provide leadership and guidance for all programs for young children. This concept of cooperative action stimulated the development of many organizations at local and state levels among groups interested in schools for young children.

Among the first of such organizations were the Golden Gate Kindergarten Association in San Francisco, the Sub-Primary Society of Philadelphia, the Des Moines Kindergarten Association, the Los Angeles Association, and the Louisville Kindergarten Association in Louisville, Kentucky. Immediately following the development of these organizations, kindergarten associations were rapidly formed in Albany, New Orleans, Detroit, Denver, Asheville, Grand Rapids, Chattanooga, Buffalo, and Minneapolis.

From 1890 to 1899 the public kindergarten movement spread rapidly and training departments for teachers of young children were established. Kindergarten associations were developed in many areas as the movement expanded. The International Kindergarten Union was formed at the National Education Association Conference in 1892 to unify and give direction to the many local associations. The influence of the expanding number of associations resulted in a Kindergarten Exhibit at Columbia Exposition in Chicago in 1893.

By 1895 it became evident that the crowded conditions of programs of the National Education Association made it necessary to appoint a separate time and place for meetings of the International Kindergarten Union. Therefore, this group had its first independent meeting at Columbia's Teachers College, New York. Interest in the child study movement stimulated by the International Kindergarten Union was a significant factor in the development of the National Congress of Mothers in 1897.

By 1910 three large groups—The National Kindergarten Association, The International Kindergarten Union, and The National Congress of Mothers—were working closely together for kindergartens for all children. At this time teachers of the primary groups and the kindergarten worked cooperatively in planning programs for children that would supplement and not overlap the work of each group. At a meeting of the Superintendents and the National Education Association in Cincinnati in 1915, 30 primary teachers formed a National Council of Primary Education. One of the stated purposes of this council was to unify the work of the kindergarten and the primary school.

During the year 1920 the nursery school at Teachers College, Columbia University, was introduced to America through a course taught by a specialist from Miss McMillan's School in London. At this time three nursery schools existed in America: one in a college, one private, and one philanthropic. The

Merrill-Palmer School and the Child Development Research Centers were established in 1920 and 1924. During the next decade nursery schools expanded until, in 1931, the National Association for Nursery Education was established. This same year the International Kindergarten Union appointed a committee to project plans for reorganization to include both nursery schools and primary schools; this resulted in the Association for Childhood Education, which includes all three groups. This association is a predominant influence on the development of programs for all children under twelve years of age.

Following is a description of the major organizations concerned with schools for young children:

Association for Childhood Education International

The purposes of the ACEI are as follows; to work for the education and well-being of children; to promote desirable conditions, programs, and practices in the schools—nursery through elementary; to raise the standard of preparation and to encourage continued professional growth of teachers and leaders in this field; to bring into active cooperation all groups concerned with children in the school, the home, and the community; and to inform the public of the needs of children and how the school program must be adjusted to fit those needs.

Individuals, local branches, state and province associations work together and with other organizations to support a unified movement for children through a plan of action developed at two-year intervals by analyzing existing conditions which affect children and suggesting appropriate action. The annual study conference is planned for members and others to discuss current developments and exchange ideas and experiences relating to children. ACEI offers an information service to which anyone may write for help on a subject related to education and well-being of children. Its publications include *Childhood Education*, the official journal, and bulletins on current problems in education.

The Childhood Education Center is maintained at ACEI headquarters in Washington, D.C. Members include nursery, kindergarten, and elementary teachers, parents, all community workers, and others concerned with the education and well-being of children.

National Association for the Education of Young Children

The purpose of the NAEYC is to provide a medium for the advancement, development, and assessment of sound group programs focussed on the education and well-being of young children under eight years of age. NAEYC cooperates actively with other organizations having compatible goals to extend, develop, and interpret sound standards and practices in services to young children. It was established in 1931 as the National Association for Nursery Education.

NAEYC offers its members an opportunity to become part of a national movement concerned with improving the education and the growth and development of young children across the country; to receive *Young Children,* the official journal; to participate in annual conferences devoted to exploration and appraisal of research: to have a resource for guidance and information about the field of early childhood education through the journal and other NAEYC publications; and to think and work with people in related professions, to deal with current problems, to consider helpful ways of working with parents, and to explore with others problems of improving and coordinating community services for young children.

Membership in the NAEYC is open to all who are professionally engaged or are otherwise concerned with the well-being of young children. Members may join through a recognized and approved affiliate group or as independent individual members, when such affiliation is not available.

American Association of Elementary-Kindergarten-Nursery Educators

This Association is an affiliate of the National Education Association.

In serving its central purpose, EKNE seeks to unite all elementary, kindergarten, and nursery educators so that they may have a more influential role in American education, and to support and work with other organizations interested in the educational well-being of young children.

The Association discusses pertinent topics in elementary education through publications and meetings. It reports research in areas where knowledge is needed. It seeks higher standards for those who work with children.

The Association issues a yearbook annually; four issues of *Educating Children: Early and Middle Years*; two 12-page study action publications; and three issues of *News Notes*, the Association's official newsletter.

Child Study Association of America

Founded in 1888 as the Society for the Study of Child Nature, it is the oldest organization having a continuous parent education program. In 1912 it published the first selected list of books for children and in 1921 began publishing *Outlines of Child Study*. The *Child Study Quarterly* was published until 1960. At present, publications consist of leaflets on parent-child topics, which may be obtained upon request.

World Organization for Early Childhood Education

The World Organization for Early Childhood Education, known as OMEP from the initials of the French translation, Organisation Mondial pour l'Education Prescolaire, was founded in 1948. OMEP is an educational organization that promotes the study and education of young children, fosters happy childhood and home life, and thus contributes to world peace. It strives to help all those who work with children to think clearly and wisely about the needs of young children and to provide opportunities for all professions and organizations to cooperate in serving those needs.

OMEP was initiated in 1946 by Mrs. Alva Myrdel (Sweden) and Lady Allen of Hurtwood (Great Britain), who met in Sweden to discuss how to create a greater understanding throughout the world of the educational needs of young children and how to unite all those working in this field. In July 1946, a group of interested people from different countries gathered together in London to prepare plans for an international organization in the field of early childhood education. National committees, the units of this world-wide organization, were then set up in a number of countries to work for a wider understanding of early childhood education.

These national committees bring together for discussion and action as many disciplines as possible that have a concern for the education and well-being of young children and their parents. Of importance in this respect are educators and teachers; medical doctors and others concerned with mental health; representatives from training colleges, universities, and parent-teacher organizations; architects; recreation directors; administrators at both national and local levels; religious bodies; and others. These committees also promote research on early childhood education; conduct surveys of nursery schools; encourage parent education; prepare and publish pamphlets for parents and the public on nursery schools and kindergartens; supply toys and books for children; foster the training of teachers for young children; hold national conferences; and publish a newsletter.

OMEP holds an international assembly biennially on aspects of preschool education. This is open to all members and to other interested persons. It has cooperated with UNESCO on projects of mutual concern, such as a seminar on the training of teachers, a world survey of nursery schools, a study of children's drawings, a seminar on parent education, and a bibliography on status and trends in preschool education. OMEP has consultative status with both UNICEF and UNESCO and sends a representative to the meetings of each. Cooperation is sought with other international organizations having similar aims. The *International Journal of Early Childhood* is published by OMEP.

Other Organizations

As need arises local or regional organizations become national in scope and influence.

Suggested Activities

1. Discuss requirements for teacher certification and plans for school accreditation in your area.
2. Have a panel discussion on relative merits of different organizations and contributions of each to teacher certification and standards for preschool children.
3. List and discuss local organizations interested in schools for young children in your area. Invite members of these organizations and groups to share their plan of action, problems encountered, and progress being made in their efforts to provide good preschools for all young children in your area.

4. Discuss how these preschools in your area are financed. List financial plans for full-time and part-time attendance in the preschools in the area.

5. List requirements for joining and participating in professional and community organizations in your area.

6. Select an instrument for the evaluation of teacher interaction with children. Analyze your interaction with a group of children using the instrument.

7. Examine a Career Ladder. Discuss the steps with your class or group.

Related Readings

Black, W. M. "A Look at Teacher Certification." *School and Community*, 57:1 (1970), pp. 36–38.

Cohen, M. D., ed. *That All Children May Learn We Must Learn*. Washington, D.C.: ACEI, 1970.

Daly, P. L. "Certification by Performance." *Changing Education*, 4:4 (1970), pp. 23–24.

Dittman, Laura, ed. *Children in Day Care with Focus on Health*. Washington, D.C.: U.S. Department of Health, Education, and Welfare, Children's Bureau, 1971.

Hartup, W. W., and Nancy L. Smothergill, eds. *The Young Child, Reviews of Research*. Washington, D.C.: NAEYC, 1970, pp. 262–291.

Hechinger, F. M., ed. *Pre-School Education Today*. Garden City, N.Y.: Doubleday & Co., 1966.

Howard, A. E. *Characteristics of Early Childhood Teacher Education*. Washington, D.C.: ACEI, 1967.

Low, S., and Pearl G. Spindler. *Child Care Arrangements of Working Mothers in the United States*. Washington, D.C.: U.S. Department of Health, Education, and Welfare and U.S. Department of Labor, Children's Bureau, 1968.

Merrill-Palmer School, Sixteenth Report for the Years 1945–47. Detroit: Merrill-Palmer School, 1947.

Morris, M. S. "California Credential Story: A New Specialization for Teachers of Young Children." *Young Children*, 25:5 (1970), pp. 268–281.

Naylor, Naomi Le B., and Bittner, Marguerite. *Curricular Development Program for Preschool Teacher Aides: Final Report*. Edwardsville, Illinois: Southern Illinois University, Center for the Study of Crime, Delinquency, and Correction, 1967.

NEA. *Research Bulletin*, 49:3 (1971), Washington, D.C.: Research Division, NEA.

Project Head Start. *The Staff*, #1. Washington, D.C.: Office of Economic Opportunity, 1965.

————. *Volunteers*, #5. Washington, D.C.: Office of Economic Opportunity, 1965.

————. *Social Services*, #8. Washington, D.C.: Office of Economic Opportunity, 1966.

————. *Volunteers in the Child Development Program*. Office of Economic Opportunity, 1968.

Report to The President, White House Conference on Children, 1970. Washington, D.C.: U.S. Government Printing Office, 1970.

Stinnett, T. M. "Trends in Teacher Certification," *The Science Teacher*, 38:2 (1971), pp. 24–25.

Tarney, Elizabeth Doak. *What Does the Nursery School Teacher Teach?* Washington, D.C.: NAEYC, 1965.

U.S. Office of Education. *Child Care and Guidance: A Suggested Post High School Curriculum*. Washington, D.C.: U.S. Department of Health, Education, and Welfare, 1967.

Emerging School Programs for Young Children

Chapter **8**

An assessment of developments in early childhood education during the early 1970's revealed clearly emerging trends. As a natural consequence of a decrease in birth rate in the United States, elementary school enrollments were generally lower than formerly, making once-scarce space available for kindergartens, federally sponsored early education programs, or Child Development Centers. This fact, coupled with a broader acceptance of the value of early educational experiences for later success in school, encouraged the establishment of more opportunities for kindergarten experiences in the public schools. Even more dramatic was the development of comprehensive child development programs for three- and four-year-old children. Pilot programs for even younger children, including infants, were appearing. Although most of the programs for pre-kindergarten children sponsored by various federal agencies were not administered by the public schools, many were found in public school facilities, often in close cooperation with school programs. At the same time, more and more schools were developing programs for children below the kindergarten

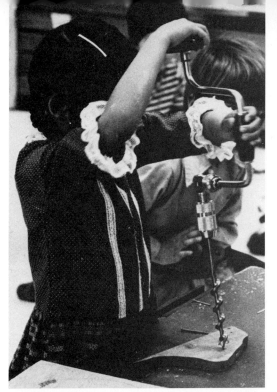

Figure 10. Planning the learning environment for and with young children calls for intelligence, imaginativeness, and flexibility on the part of the teacher rather than formulas. It is in the selection and guidance of experiences and activities for young children that the teacher's education and skill are evident.

level. The designation "Child Development Center" rather than "school" has gained popular acceptance for such programs.

Most Child Development Center personnel, especially for the educational component, were not trained or "certified" in early childhood education. However, many centers were adding qualified teachers, especially in supervisory roles, because earlier experience had shown a particular need for those in leadership positions. Clearly, at the time of the publication of this text, educational qualifications and standards had not been established except for kindergarten teachers employed in public schools.

Although most federally funded programs for young children were basically limited to children of low income families, there was a growing demand for early education for all children. States and local governments were responding by making provision for such programs, especially public school kindergartens. The education of young children was fast becoming the responsibility of the public and private sectors of society, including business and industry. The importance of health and nutrition, family and personal development, and agency cooperation in providing services for young children and their families had been established. Program staffing patterns included parents, aides, and volunteers from the community and were truly interdisciplinary in nature. A coordinated educational effort never before known in American education, making effective use of various levels and types of competencies was emerging. Most significant to teachers and educators was the development of pilot and model programs with built-in research components to determine the effect of various curriculum approaches, teaching strategies and newly developed materials of instruction on the immediate and long-range cognitive and learning abilities of young children.

Psychologists had long observed the value of continuous, consistent procedures to learning and therapy, regardless of the theoretical orientation employed. Continuous learning programs, best exemplified by the federally sponsored Follow Through programs, were developed to determine long range values of common strategies and approaches on the learning and achievement of children aged four or five through nine. The Parent and Child Center programs were designed for the same purpose, extending the program downward to birth or during pregnancy.

THEORIES OF LEARNING

Education in America has been heavily influenced by stimulus-response (S-R) psychology. This view (behaviorism) holds that the child is a purely reactive organism and reacts or responds rather than initiates; thus his behavior can be predicted from past experiences. Behaviorism as a psychological theory is represented by the well-known work of Ivan Pavlov, Edward Lee Thorndike, John B. Watson, Kenneth Spence, and Edwin Guthrie among many others, and culminating in the work of B. F. Skinner. In its simplest form, behaviorism teaches that all behavior is learned. The neurons automatically respond to incoming stimuli and when such responses are strengthened by reward (reinforcement), learning takes place. However, without further reward or later reinforcement at certain intervals such responses are extinguished. In this manner all responses (learning) can be shaped or modified by rewarding only predetermined desired responses. One of the strengths claimed by proponents of this approach is that "it works." The system is mechanistic and precise and resulting behavior is highly predictable. Accordingly, in this view, one's behavior is molded by outside forces and measurable only by observable overt responses. Current behavioristic terminology places stress on "operant" conditioning and "behavior modification." For a description of a utopian society based on behavioristic principles, see the novel *Walden Two*.[1] Hence, the need in programs for carefully planned structure and drill, and for programmed materials of instruction reduced to small bits of information, assuring success each step of the way. However, there have always been those who believe that the child is capable of actively participating in and influencing his own behavior as he interacts with his environment.

Most markedly opposed to behaviorism is a group of philosophies and theories which together are known as the humanistic approach to psychology. Proponents of humanism insist that the uniqueness of each individual is because of the fact that each human being has the inherent potential to actively and creatively become what he is by behaving in ways that are consistent with his view of self. One behaves as a total, dynamic unity, accepting, rejecting, or acting upon external stimuli in keeping with his own internalization of present and past events in terms of his developed goals for self-realization. Thus the child has inner motivations (as compared to outer stimuli) that trigger his response patterns. Under this view, learning environments are provided to enable the child to initiate and create rather than merely to respond to a fixed set of conditions.

A few of the many well-known leaders in the humanistic psychology movement are Gordon Allport, Arthur Combs, Abraham Maslow, Gardner Murphy, and Carl Rogers. Presently the emerging school programs are largely based on one or the other or some variation of these opposing psychological viewpoints.

The early work in child development as exemplified by the work of Gesell[2] would lead to the conclusion that behavior emerges in a fixed order or sequence according to a genetically determined timetable. Therefore, a child's development can be described in stages in relation to chronological time. The literature of the 1940's and 1950's described "typical two-year-olds," "typical five-year-olds," and so on. This approach led to the belief that innate forces peculiar to each child determined his "ability" to respond at any given time and that en-

---

[1] B. F. Skinner, *Walden Two* (New York: Macmillan, Inc., 1948).

[2] A. Gesell and Catherine S. Amatruda, *Developmental Diagnosis* (New York: Harper and Brothers, 2nd ed., 1952).

vironmental experiences, though necessary, played a minor role in the child's behavior and learning. Instructional activities were designed to fit the stage of development for each child or for groups of "normal" children at each particular stage of development. Little attention was given to the possibility that response patterns could be changed or speeded up by intervention at some earlier point in time. Traditionally, schools have waited until the child displayed "readiness" for certain learnings, or waited until a child fell behind his expected level of performance and then applied so-called remedial techniques in an effort to help him "catch up." This is basically the approach of present day "compensatory" programs.

It was not until the 1960's that the concept of intervention was used extensively to forestall expected deficiencies in learning. Placing major emphasis on intervention and compensatory techniques was the appropriately named Head Start program. It had been found that most children who didn't fit the expectations of the public school program were from lower-income families. Therefore, Head Start and similar programs were designed for children whose learning, physical, and social deficits were associated with problems faced by families with inadequate income. A new emphasis was also given to compensatory or remedial programs for children who were already behind in learning abilities when entering school. Both intervention and compensatory programs place more emphasis on environmental than maturational influences than was previously true.

In recent years the concept of critical periods in development has received much attention and has had a strong influence on programming experiences for young children. Biologists, who generally believe that the capacity to respond at any given time to specific aspects of the environment is originally genetically determined, were making breakthroughs of their own. Study of the genes, segments of the deoxyribonucleic acid (DNA) that fills the chromosomes in cell nuclei, suggested a master genetic code that provides a blue-print for life itself. Ribonucleic acid (RNA) is made in the nucleus of the cell by DNA and serves as the messenger to amino acids in the cell's cytoplasm, carrying out the genetic master plan. All the elements needed for any response an individual is capable of making are present in the DNA code at conception but do not go into operation until an appropriate environmental stimulus triggers the response. While all the possibilities of growth, development, and learning are inherent, environment at all times plays an important role.

It is environment that must always fit the unfolding of the code. Consequently, throughout life there are critical periods during which the presence or absence of appropriate environmental stimuli results in following or altering DNA's master plan. A dramatic example of critical periods in development was the sharply increased incidence about a decade ago of babies being born without or with deformed arms and legs. The cause was traced to the fact that the mothers of these children had taken the tranquilizing drug thalidomide during the first seven weeks of gestation. The effects of maternal rubella (German measles) on the offspring during the prenatal period are well known. For a more detailed account of the biological bases of behavior and the importance of critical periods see Beadle's lucid analysis.[3] There are also indications that chromosome aberrations may be directly responsible for certain behaviorial characteristics. For example, in the case of Down's Syndrome (Mongolism) the child inherits three chromosomes of a given kind instead of the usual two.[4]

New discoveries of this type as well as findings in the fields of biochemistry and nutrition offer strong evidence that behavior described as "good" or "bad" by parents and teachers may well bear no relationship to the connotations thus implied and is not subject to change by known instructional strategies. Emerging schools are now often staffed with professionals from many disciplines who can detect and advise on procedures for those children who show early developmental and/or learning deviations. It would be all too easy to make the same error made by researchers and practitioners of the 1920's to the 1950's and assume that growth, development, and learning, while sequential through time, are fixed at conception and "unfold" according to each individual's timetable. Rather, what the newer evidence indicates is that, though growth, development, and learning are sequential through time, the expression of the genetic potentialities is determined by environmental influences at any given time during the life span. Although behaviors in the learning sphere are much more difficult to pinpoint than in the area of physical development, it can reasonably be said that a child who doesn't progress from random vocalizing of vowels to consonants, to words within the first twenty-four months of life is likely to be severely handicapped in the use of language later.[5]

During the middle 1960's American education was badly in need of a panacea to remedy everything from poverty and unemployment to reaching the greatest potential of the gifted. There was an almost universal acceptance that early education could serve this purpose. Unanswerable questions arose immediately. How early should early education begin? Age five? Age four? Three or earlier? Who should receive early education? All children, or just those whose parents are poor and those who are "exceptional" in some way? What should be taught to young children? How should young children be taught and by whom? Which learning theory applies best to young children? Who should control schools for young children? The parents? The existing educational system? Or some other form of government or community organization? Because of these and similar questions, a wide variety of approaches and forms of control quickly emerged. They ranged from public or private Montessori schools to open classroom approaches and versions of the British Infant School.

As the nation approaches the middle 1970's, the evangelistic fervor of proponents of many various schools of thought has somewhat abated. For-

---

[3]Muriel Beadle, *A Child's Mind* (Garden City, N. Y.: Doubleday and Company, 1970), pp. 11–24, 61–71.

[4]Ibid., p. 19.

[5]Ibid., p. 61.

tunately, foundations and the federal and state governments insisted on re-search to validate or invalidate the effectiveness of sponsored innovations. At this writing the evidence is not all in but certain trends are emerging. Among them:

1. Because of the uniqueness of each individual child, both genetically and ex-perientially, no one approach is acceptable for all children.
2. Parents are important to the education of their young children and parent involve-ment in the program can be an essential ingredient for success.
3. Specific content itself is not as important as the use that is made of the content to establish positive attitudes toward learning and toward self.
4. Young children, including very young infants, can and do learn. Because many au-thorities now feel that the first five years of life, including infancy, represent a critical period with regard to basic attitudes and values about self and others, the development of language, and the establishment of basic interpersonal relation-ships, programs for young children should not be entered into lightly and without careful planning and judicious use of qualified personnel.
5. Although aides, volunteers, and other paraprofessionals are now accepted as necessary and valuable personnel, adequately trained teachers and supervisory leaders are the most promising avenue to successful programs.
6. Traditional teacher education programs have not adequately prepared teachers for the emerging new schools for young children. New and innovative practices in the preparation of teachers at both the pre-service and in-service levels are being developed to fill this need.
7. As the age for starting education has moved downward from the traditional first grade entrance at age six, there has been in each case mounting evidence that an earlier start was needed. Most prominent examples of programs designed to im-plement these findings are kindergartens for five-year-olds, Head Start, Home Start, a program to demonstrate alternate ways of providing Head Start type services, for three-, four-, and five year-old children where kindergartens were not available, and Parent Child Centers for children from birth to three years of age. All represent efforts to enable large numbers of children to make use of learning opportunities provided by the nation's schools.
8. All recent programs place a new emphasis on the importance of early cognitive development, at the same time giving recognition to the profound influence of good health and nutrition, healthy psychological and social development, and stable and accepting family relationships on successful learning.
9. Teachers and other staff personnel in these programs must be aware of the total needs of each child and be able to work with professionals in other fields to see that these needs are met. In fact, most programs now provide fully staffed compon-ents and consultative services in these areas to complement the educational process. Staffing of programs for young children is truly becoming interdiscipli-nary with differentiated but cooperative responsibilities.

TECHNOLOGY AND THE PRESCHOOL CHILD

It is commonly held that television, computers, teaching machines, tape recorders, and a host of other electronic devices, games, and kits of programmed materials offer hope of breaking the age-old boring procedures used in the public schools. In effect, it is claimed that modern technology has the potential of bringing about a "revolution" in education. Almost all of these devices offer the self-evaluation and immediate feedback features much sought by educators, parents, and taxpayers. Seizing an opportunity beginning in the early 1960's, and late 1950's, huge commercial firms, often conglomerates, sought to provide the necessary hardware and often the "software" or programs for the emerging revolution in education. As preschool programs gained priority, mainly because of federal and foundation funding, the availability of "complete" educational programs for young children greatly increased. Today, preschool teachers and administrators can choose from an almost endless variety of kits, pro- grammed and talking books, packaged learning materials, computer-assisted or computer-managed instructional materials, prepared television tapes, and the usual array of what were formerly known as audiovisual instructional materials. The list is almost endless. Yet after fifteen years the impact has been visible only where programs have been heavily funded and researched; these programs often stopped when outside funds were no longer available. The most common research finding is that children in these programs achieve as well as they would under less costly conventional methods.

There are two commonly recognized problems with the use of educational technology—excessive cost and the fact that technology lends itself best to instructional programming based on behavioristic theory. Many educators, however, especially classroom teachers, accept more readily procedures and materials based on humanistic approaches. This is especially true in relation to programs for young children. For a thought-provoking analysis of edu- cational technology see *The Myth of Educational Technology*.[6]

"Sesame Street"

Although there are many programs for young children on commercial and educational television, none have captured the imagination of audiences (of all ages) to the extent that "Sesame Street" has. The multi-million dollar program, funded by grants from the Carnegie Foundation, the Ford Foundation, the U. S. Office of Education, the Office of Economic Opportunity, and other federal agencies, went on the air on 163 public television stations on Novem- ber 10, 1969. Its purpose was to determine whether television could teach pre- school children via popular approaches used by commercial television. It is too early to assess long-term effectiveness of "Sesame Street" as a feasible means of teaching young children, especially children from low-income and slum homes. Berkman[7] suggests that "something just drastic" could happen to the generation of children, regardless of race or family income, who have watched "Sesame Street" regularly. He feels that schools, as they now exist, could "turn off" large numbers of children who are accustomed to the "Sesame Street"

---

[6]D. Berkman, "The Myth of Educational Technology," *The Educational Forum*, 36:14 (1972), pp. 451–460.

[7]Ibid., p. 460.

exposure, necessitating a profound effect on early grade education. Edward L. Palmer,[8] vice-president and director of research at The Children's Television Workshop, which created and produced "Sesame Street," has described the careful planning and research involved in this best-known effort to teach young children by television.

To the authors of this text, "Sesame Street" represents a pioneer experiment in early childhood education—an attempt to bring about social change as well as early cognitive learning. It is a well-known fact that children have different learning styles in keeping with their early family and cultural influences. There is evidence that certain children, especially children denied early exposure to cognitive experiences that best fit them for the demands made upon them when entering school, learn best when exposed to more structured, repetitive bits of information. "Sesame Street," with its deep roots in behaviorism, fits this requirement well. However, the authors feel that for most children real life experiences strongly buttressed in early sensory-motor experiences, as indicated in Piaget's theory,[9] are essential for later, more complex forms of *learning*.

Although television and other forms of technology are of immense importance in assisting learning, they should never be expected to replace the human element in the instructional process. Nor should behaviorally oriented programs exclude the values and creative initiative inherent in teaching strategies based on humanistic theory.

NATIONAL PROGRAM ON EARLY CHILDHOOD EDUCATION

The United States Office of Education (OE) did not come into the "big time" in education until the early 1960's with the passage of federal legislation involving substantial appropriations. The major purpose of most education legislation at that time was to enable the public schools to provide quality education for children of low-income families and to find and research innovative and alternative ways of improving the instructional process. One such effort was the establishment of the National Laboratory on Early Childhood Education, which became The National Program on Early Childhood Education (NPECE) under the administration of CEMREL (Central Midwestern Regional Laboratory, Inc.) on June 1, 1970. NPECE has headquarters at St. Louis, Missouri, and operates seven university-based early childhood education centers. Its purpose is to engage in activities to continuously bring about new knowledge, materials, and practices that can be appropriately used under a variety of conditions to improve early childhood education. The *Cemrel Newsletter*, a semiannual publication, is designed to disseminate news

[8]E. L. Palmer, "Television Instruction and the Preschool Child," *International Journal of Early Education*, 4:1 (OMEP, Dublin, Ireland: Irish University Press, 1972), pp. 11–17.

[9]B. J. Wadsworth, *Piaget's Theory of Cognitive Development* (New York: David McKay Co., Inc., 1971), p. 33.

of the activities of CEMREL and to aid readers in keeping abreast of new developments in education.

Another important source of information on current programs is known as ERIC, also sponsored by the United States Office of Education. ERIC (Educational Resources Information Center) has several clearinghouses on education, one of which is the ERIC Clearinghouse on Early Childhood Education. The various clearinghouses may change locations from time to time but current addresses and information on the Clearinghouse on Early Childhood Education can be obtained by contacting Central ERIC, U. S. Office of Education, 400 Maryland Avenue, S. W., Washington D. C. 20202. Each state's Department of Education can also supply information on current developments in early childhood education in the respective states.

CURRICULUM AND PROGRAM DEVELOPMENT

As mentioned previously, the emerging programs placed more emphasis on cognitive development than was formerly thought necessary in preschool education. When this need for effective curriculum development and programming in early childhood education arose, there was a paucity of thoroughly researched programs to provide guidance for the rapidly developing programs. As a result, large scale federal and foundation funds, usually in the form of research and development grants, were made available to universities, schools, individuals, and consulting and technical assistance firms (often hastily organized). Those conducting the programs were often without previous training or experience in early childhood education. The newly developing multimedia industry also quickly rose to the challenge. As a result, packaged programs complete with sponsors and consultative services soon dominated the early childhood education scene and continue to do so. Their goal was the development of exportable models and corresponding materials for sale or adoption by those conducting programs for young children.

An indication of the stress placed on certain areas is reported in the Spring 1972 *CEMREL Newsletter*. All forty-four children in CEMREL's experimental kindergartens received reading certificates at their graduation exercises as a result of participation in their Instructional Systems Program. Thirty of the children were awarded "special recognition" for having completed the entire series of fifty-two SWRL reading books. Some of the children read books considered "fourth grade level."[10]

It was the original intention of the writers to include descriptions of the models existing during the early 1970's. However, because of the unusually large number of models, packages, and systems increasingly available, it was decided not to carry out the original intent. Instead, a selected few models whose names and brief descriptive statements indicate the variety that exists

---

[10]"Kindergarten Children Demonstrate Reading Ability for Parents," *CEMREL Newsletter*, 6:2 (Spring 1972), p. 8.

on the continuum from behavioristic to humanistic are listed. This list will show the variation that exists among emerging programs. The examples listed fall roughly into four categories: (1) those stressing basic learning skills through the use of behavioristic techniques, (2) those stressing the importance of parents on the instructional team, (3) those employing individualized instruction, and (4) those based on humanistic approaches. Some, of course, do not fall clearly into any one of the above categories and are more eclectic in nature. The list follows.

Systematic Use of Behavioral Principles Program (Focuses strongly on objectives, presenting tasks in a rapid-fire order)

Behavioral Analysis Program (Uses the techniques of reinforcement to accelerate social and learning development during the early years)

Behavior-oriented Prescriptive Teaching Approach (Employs intensive individualized instruction for the attainment of specific behavior objectives)

Florida Parent Education Model (Emphasizes the use of "trained" mothers on the instructional team with the major thrust being in the home)

Home-School Partnership—A Motivational Approach (Enlists parents as partners in the education of their children)

Parent Implementation Approach (Strives to make use of parents and other community residents as significant people in the learning process)

Responsive Environment Approach (Makes individual problem solving the essence of learning by providing an environment responsive to each child's needs)

Hampton Institute Nongraded Model (Individualizes instruction in the classroom on a nongraded basis)

Learning Research and Development Center Model (Uses individually prescribed instruction, IPI)

Bank Street College of Education Approach (Designed to enable each child to build a positive self-image of himself as a learner)

Education Development Center Approach (Rooted in the philosophy of the British Primary Schools to provide a broad humanistic education)

New School Approach (Stresses self-directed learning through the use of learning centers in the classroom)

Mathemagenic Activities Program (Provides sequentially structured materials to stimulate learning as a coherent interpretation of reality)

Cognitively Oriented Curriculum Model (Provides home and school experiences with learning materials derived from the theories of Piaget)

Cultural Linquistic Approach (An oral language program building on the strengths of another language or nonstandard English)

In actual practice there are only a few programs using exported models such as the above. Most programs for young children continue to stress the importance of children's needs. An effort is usually made to stress the importance of learning environment based on an understanding of child development. These programs usually have less structure than the models listed above and permit children more freedom to explore their feelings and environment in imaginative and play type activities. The teacher serves as an observing guide, encouraging the children to participate in activities allowed by a prearranged environment. Such programs emphasize personal and social development with less emphasis on skills believed to be needed "later." Although difficult to evaluate because of the lack of specifics, to some extent all show more concern for preplanned activities to reach more specific objectives than was generally true of programs a decade ago.

SUMMARY

One of the encouraging signs of the early 1970's was the emergence of a large number and variety of innovative and experimental programs in early childhood education. The designation *Child Development Center* has become established for programs for children below the kindergarten level and pilot programs for infants and their families have flourished. Longitudinal programs such as Follow Through for children aged three to nine have offered an opportunity to study the effects of several well-defined and planned innovative approaches to the education of young children.

Philosophical and theoretical differences prevailed. Programs based on behavioristic and humanistic approaches, with many variations and combinations, have provided an opportunity to discover the most effective educational strategies for children with different learning styles from various socioeconomic backgrounds.

A significant characteristic of the emerging programs has been the greater involvement of parents in the education of their children. Equally important is the interdisciplinary nature of the training and experience of staff members and the extensive use of volunteers and paraprofessionals with differentiated responsibilities.

Because of the high cost of early childhood education, exportable models, programs using educational technology, and packaged instructional materials have been developed in an effort to make early learning experiences available to a larger number of young children. Changing social values and the rising number of mothers of young children in the labor market have created a need for more day care facilities. Public and professional demands have mandated an educational component in all such programs.

It can truthfully be said that although early childhood education was rediscovered in the 1960's, it is coming of age during the 1970's. These developments have placed unprecedented demands on training programs, stressing the need for consultative services, in-service training, and on-the-job training. Most colleges and universities have responded with greatly expanded, innovative approaches of staff members, both professional and paraprofessional, including parents and volunteers.

Suggested Activities

1. Visit a child development center, a nursery school, and a kindergarten in your community. Determine the philosophy or theory on which each program is based.

Write a comparison of the three giving examples of activities that are clearly a result of the theory or philosophy followed.

2. Watch Sesame Street and at least two other television programs for young children. Evaluate what you saw in terms of interest level, theory on which the program is based, and the goals of each, in terms of meeting the needs of young children.

3. Ask your librarian how to use the services of ERIC as a resource for your studies in early childhood education.

4. Talk with several first grade teachers and ask them what they would like children to be able to do when they enter first grade.

5. Consult the yellow pages of your local telephone directory to determine the types of schools for young children in your community. Visit at least three that appear to be different from the others such as Montessori, academically oriented, or co-operative nursery schools. Evaluate each.

6. Find out from your state department of education and state OEO offices how many children below kindergarten age are participating in programs. Determine the goals of these programs and the kind of activities used to meet these goals.

Related Readings

Baldwin, A. L. *Theories of Child Development.* New York: John Wiley and Sons, Inc., 1968.

Beadle, Muriel. *A Child's Mind.* Garden City, N.Y.: Doubleday & Co., 1970.

Berkman, D. "The Myth of Educational Technology," *The Educational Record, 36*:4 (1972), pp. 451–460.

Crary, R. W. *Humanizing the Schools.* New York: Alfred A. Knopf, 1969.

Gordon, I. J., ed. *Early Childhood Education,* The Seventy-first Yearbook of the National Society for the Study of Education, Part II. Chicago: University of Chicago Press, 1972.

Grotberg, Edith H. *Critical Issues in Research Relating to Disadvantaged Children.* Princeton, N.J.: Educational Testing Service, 1969.

———. *Day Care: Resources for Decisions.* Washington, D.C.: OEO, 1971.

Hess, R. D., and Roberta Meyer Bear. *Early Education.* Chicago: Aldine Publishing Co., 1968.

Hess, R. D., and Doreen J. Croft. *Teachers of Young Children.* Boston: Houghton Mifflin, 1972.

Mills, Belen Collantes, and R. A. Mills. *Designing Instructional Strategies For Young Children.* Dubuque, Iowa: Wm. C. Brown Co., 1972.

Palmer, E. L. "Television Instruction and the Preschool Child," *International Journal of Early Childhood,* OMEP, 4:1. Dublin, Ireland: Irish University Press, 1972, pp. 11–17.

Skinner, B. F. *Walden Two.* New York: Macmillan, Inc., 1948.

Tanner, D. *Using Behavioral Objectives in the Classroom.* New York: Macmillan, Inc., 1972.

Wadsworth, B. J. *Piaget's Theory of Cognitive Development.* New York: David McKay Co., Inc., 1971.

The Curriculum: Planning and Teaching

Part II

Figure 11. (OVERLEAF) Cooking activities are enjoyable and also provide opportunities for discussing and planning, taking turns, following directions, learning quantitative measurement, using desirable health habits, developing scientific concepts, and beginning reading experiences.

Chapter 9

Curriculum and Young Children

Ferment, experimentation and change are evident in early childhood education. There is much confusion about the purposes of programs for young children; the means for achieving the purposes are even more diffuse and uncertain.[1] The current period in early childhood education seems to be one of trial and error in program development, says Weber. There seems to be no consensus regarding the most valuable and worthwhile educational experiences for young children.[2]

Some proposals would introduce formal instruction in the academic areas to very young children, while others maintain that the program can continue to meet the needs of children and at the same time offer "content." Almy, in

[1]Louise M. Berman, *Toward New Programs for Young Children,* University Nursery-Kindergarten, Monograph 1, (College Park, Md: University of Maryland, 1970), p. 1.

[2]Evelyn Weber, *Early Childhood Education: Perspectives on Change* (Worthington, Ohio: Charles A. Jones Publishing Company, 1970), p. 5.

discussing the two positions, reviews research that suggests that acceleration in a particular subject area sometimes results in pseudoconcepts. The child knows the answers only under conditions similar to those in which he learned them. Concepts acquired when the child is more mature tend to be more stable and can be applied in different situations. According to Almy, "It seems doubtful, therefore, that early childhood education programs that are narrowly focused or designed primarily for acceleration in a particular area will have much beneficial effect on later intellectual development."[3] She points out, however, that new views on the nature of intellectual development offer new opportunities for guiding children in more effective learnings. She states:[4]

> Such views need not, as some educators have feared, mean so exclusive a preoccupation with the intellect that other aspects of the child's being are necessarily neglected. Rather to the extent that teaching of this sort is based on understanding of the developing child and his thinking and is able to free the child's intellect, it should also free him to be a more effective person.

Goodlad describes the current curriculum reform movement as an updating of content, a reorganization of subject matter, and some fresh approaches to methodology. He states, "It is not simply a return to the Three R's. . . . And many of the central concerns of progressive education—emphasis on principles rather than facts, on learning through problem solving rather than by precept, and on individual differences, for example—are stressed and extended by some of today's curriculum builders."[5]

INNOVATIONS

Changes have been proposed in the areas of curriculum, organization, and instruction. Experimentation is under way in mathematics, science, reading, and social studies. Children in some situations have been encouraged to inquire on their own and to learn through discovery. Team teaching and multiage grouping are beginning to appear.

Many of the proposals for program development have been motivated and influenced by the special problems and needs of children who come from environmental situations that are thought to handicap them severely in their later schooling. Goodlad and Klein point out, however, that the early education of all young children, whether environmentally disadvantaged or not, should be guided by sound principles of learning and development.[6]

[3]Millie Almy, "New Views on Intellectual Development in Early Childhood Education," *Intellectual Development: Another Look* (Washington, D.C.: ASCD, 1964), p. 24.

[4]Ibid., p. 25.

[5]J. I. Goodlad et al., *The Changing School Curriculum* (New York: Fund for the Advancement of Education, 1966), p. 15.

[6]J. I. Goodlad, M. Frances Klein, and associates, *Behind the Classroom Door* (Worthington, Ohio: Charles A. Jones Publishing Company, 1970), p. 7.

Some of the innovations, including curriculum, organization, and instruction are described here. No one innovation is the answer for every learner. Each must be studied and evaluated.

OPEN SPACE CENTERS.   Open space centers provide the setting for a new kind of learning experience planned in terms of the potentialities of children and the environment. "The open space concept in teaching is, as much as anything, a state of mind."[7] It is the structuring of a living situation with a wide range of educational alternatives.[8]

Facilities for such a center include large open spaces that can be used flexibly and in a number of ways. There are no separate, individual classrooms. The teacher does not work alone. Rather, a team of adults, including teachers, aides, and volunteers, is available.

Open education is considered by some as the legacy of the progressive education movement.

BRITISH INFANT SCHOOL.   The British primary school, although English in origin, is thought by some to reflect many of the characteristics of progressive education in America.[9] The infant stage of British education includes children from 4+ to 7+ years of age, and utilizes vertical or family grouping. Children of varying ages are placed together in the same class as a deliberate educational policy.[10] Lavatelli points out that play is more explicitly used for cognitive growth than in the American child-centered schools.[11]

Rogers lists the salient features of the British philosophy as follows:[12]

Children should live fully and richly now. Education is life, not preparation for life.
The curriculum is a series of jumping-off places and emerges through the mutual interests and explorations of children and teachers working together.
Studies are interrelated and cut across subject matter lines.
The teacher is "largely a stage setter," a stimulator who encourages and guides but who does not appear to direct.
Teachers are concerned with how the child learns, the significance of the process; the development of independence and responsibility in children. Teachers care deeply about children and respect children's ideas.

PIAGET'S THEORIES.   Lavatelli describes Piaget's theory as a developmental one, pointing out that, according to him, the thinking of all children tends to go through the same stages and usually when they are at about the same age.[13]

[7]AASA, *Open Space Schools* (Washington, D.C.: American Association of School Administrators, 1971), p. 20.

[8]J. Macdonald, "The Open School: Curriculum Concepts," *Open Education* (Washington, D.C.: NAEYC, 1970), p. 26.

[9]B. Spodek, "Introduction," *Open Education* (Washington, D.C.: NAEYC, 1970), p. 7.

[10]Mary A. Mycock, "Vertical Grouping," in V. R. Rogers, *Teaching in the British Primary School* (New York: Macmillan, Inc., 1970), pp. 34–35.

[11]Celia S. Lavatelli, *Piaget's Theory Applied to an Early Childhood Curriculum* (Boston: American Science and Engineering, Inc., 1970), p. 23.

[12]V. R. Rogers, *Teaching in the British Primary School* (New York: Macmillan, Inc., 1970), pp. 288–290.

[13]Lavatelli, op. cit., p. 27.

Using what Piaget has identified as the important cognitive developments for children, Lavatelli has planned a curriculum centered on *Classification, Space and Number,* and *Seriation,* based upon step-by-step development in these areas. Short, structured periods are utilized, along with periods of self-directed play. Directed learning activities are conducted by a teacher with a small group of children. The concepts acquired are reinforced during play. The children's observations are directed to phenomena that they might otherwise miss.[14]

A Developmental-Interaction Point of View. This theory has been developed by Biber et al. to promote cognitive growth. It emphasizes the identifiable patterns of growth, the child's interaction with the environment (people as well as material objects), and the interaction between the cognitive and affective spheres of development.[15] The Bank Street program for children, a model of developmental-interaction, is based on "a consistent philosophy of education comprising values, goals, and strategies congruent with a humanist approach. Central to this philosophy are concepts of competence, interpersonal relatedness, individuality, and creativity."[16] Cognitive categories for use in analyzing teaching techniques have been developed and illustrated.

Cognitively Oriented Curriculum. The academically oriented centers for children are primarily interested in the cognitive development of children and in speeding up the acquisition of academic skills. Weikart et al. have developed a cognitively oriented curriculum in which attention is not explicitly paid to the affective development of the child. Proponents feel that these needs are met through the style of classroom operation that the curriculum creates.[17] Bereiter and Engelmann developed a program for disadvantaged children with emphasis on the development of pre-academic skills in reading, language, and arithmetic.

Process Approach. Berman holds that any carefully designed conception of curriculum must be based on some basic assumptions about man, whom she considers to be "a process oriented being." Curriculum, therefore, is concerned with process and process skills that include Perceiving, Communicating, Loving, Decision Making, Knowing, Organizing, Creating, and Valuing.[18] Teachers at the University of Maryland Center for Young Children, using the process approach in developing a curriculum for young children, have focused on the process of *decision making.*

They developed suggestions for teacher statements, designed to focus the

---

[14]Ibid., p. 24.

[15]Barbara Biber et al., *Promoting Cognitive Growth; A Developmental-Interaction Point of View* (Washington, D.C.: NAEYC, 1971).

[16]Ibid., p. 7.

[17]D. P. Weikart, *The Cognitively Oriented Curriculum* (Washington, D.C.: NAEYC, 1971), p. x.

[18]Louise M. Berman, *New Priorities in the Curriculum* (Columbus, Ohio: Charles E. Merrill Publishing Company, 1968).

children's thinking on possibilities, outcomes, and awareness that choices have been made. Examples of the suggested statements follow:[19]

> Thinking of possibilities: "Where do you think you could work?" "What other way could you have . . . ?"
> Thinking of outcomes: "What else could you do to . . . avoid . . . ?" ". . . stop . . . ?" ". . . help . . . ?"

Summary. A summary of general trends has been developed by Weber who, after visiting many of the innovative programs, has identified the following features:[20]

Concern for the young child who is economically disadvantaged.
Use of smaller groups of children with more mixing of age levels.
Involvement of parents both at home and at school.
Reduction of the adult-child ratio, with expanding use of teacher aides.
Extension of the educational process to parents and infants.
Emphasis on cognitive development of the young child.

Curriculum Planning

According to Weber, "Education in the preschool years has always been responsive to prevailing assumptions about the nature of man and his development, the ways in which learning takes place, and sociological concerns."[21] Incorporating such factors into curriculum planning is indeed a complex operation. For example, while playing in the housekeeping center the child may use a variety of skills, such as language arts—conversation, asking questions, talking on the telephone, and listening; or mathematics—cooking, measuring a cup, quart, teaspoon, and reading numerals on radio or TV dials.

Table 9-1, based on a study of birds, emphasizes some of the conceptual learnings a child might acquire in a given subject area as he participates in a variety of activities. Opportunities for the practice of some of the process skills are also indicated. However, not all of the subject areas or the process skills have been included. (See p. 136.)

A good program is not totally organized into a rigid schedule with separate periods for language arts, number activities, and science. Neither are certain activities labeled as appropriate for a day care center, nursery school, or kindergarten, some for four-year-olds and some for five-year-olds. Rather, within the stream of each curriculum area, there is a developmental sequence of skills.

---

[19]Louise M. Berman, ed., *Decision Making in Young Children: Part 1*, Monograph 2 (College Park, Md.: University of Maryland, 1971), p. 48.

[20]Weber, op. cit., pp. 1–5.

[21]Ibid., p. 4.

TABLE 9-1
CONCEPTUAL LEARNINGS—THE BIRDS[22]

Conceptual Understandings	Experience, Activity, and Play Possibilities
1. There are many kinds, colors, and sizes of birds. 1,2,3,5.	1. Identifying and classifying local birds. 2,5 and A,B,C.
2. All birds have feathers for protection. 3,4,5.	2. Collecting feathers on a nature walk for use in making collages and in other activities. 1,5, and A,B.
3. Birds live in many different kinds of localities and homes as families. 4,5.	3. Making a bird house. 1,2,3,5. and A,B, C,D.
4. Birds depend on nature for their variety of food needs. 3,5.	4. Making a feeding station and observing birds at the station. 1,2,3,4,5. and A,B,D
5. Travel, communication, and self preservation vary with the species of the bird. 1,3,4,5.	5. Imitating the movement, habits, and sounds of a variety of birds. 1,2, and A,D.

Key: Subject Areas
    Music and the Arts   1   Process Skills
    Mathematics   2   Communicating   A
    Science   3   Decision Making   B
    Social Studies   4   Patterning   C
    Language   5   Creating   D

This sequence serves as a guide for the teacher. For example, when the child has developed enough control of his muscles to make more precise movements, as he becomes more interested in what he is making than in the manipulation of materials, he is indicating that he is moving out of the "scribbling" stage of art development into the presymbolic. For some children this occurs while they are in nursery school, but for others it may not take place until kindergarten or even first grade. Whether the child is four, five, or six, whether he is in a child development center, nursery school, or kindergarten, when the child is ready for the next step in the sequence, the alert teacher is ready to help him take it.

In the traditional sense there are no required subjects in the child development center, nursery school, and kindergarten and the program is usually not rigidly prescribed. There are, however, certain curriculum principles that are important in planning the program. These principles also apply to programs for the disadvantaged. For example, although the immediate environment of the children is different, a good program develops from the environment, whether it is slum or suburb. The following are a few of the most important of these principles:[23]

[22]Adapted from *A Guide: Early Childhood Education in Florida Schools,* Bull. 76 (Tallahassee: Florida State Department of Education, 1969), pp. 46–49.

[23]Adapted from *A Guide for Organizing and Developing a Kindergarten Program in Florida,* Bulletin 53A (rev.) (Tallahassee: Florida State Department of Education, 1955), pp. 31–33.

1. A good program provides many opportunities for social adjustment. Most young children are individualists, and one of their most important developmental tasks is to learn to play and work with other boys and girls. They must learn through experience to share toys and equipment, to take turns, and to plan and act with individuals and groups.
2. A good program develops from the immediate environment of the children. They are interested in all that goes on about them. Their immediate environment points up and emphasizes such interest.
3. A good program allows plenty of time and adequate opportunities for children to express themselves freely through many media. Young children like to work with things, to get their hands into water, to paint with their fingers or with brushes, to pound nails into wood, to "dress up" in the clothes of adults, to work with clay, and to build with blocks. Opportunities for talking are provided as children engage in these activities.
4. A good program allows a child to use his whole body and to develop wholesome attitudes toward it. The child development center, nursery, or kindergarten is a place for children to use their voices in talking and singing. It is a place for laughter and dramatizing. It is a good place to dance, to engage in rhythms, and to sing. The school day should also be arranged to help establish the rhythm of bodily functions in the taking of food, resting, sleeping, eliminating, and in the establishing of acceptable health habits.
5. A good program utilizes the experiences of children and attempts to meet their needs as three-, four-, and five-year-olds, and at the same time builds firmly for later experiences. The good program does not ignore so-called formal subject matter. On the contrary, it provides opportunities for experiences which build foundations for these fields. Cognitive development is a vital element.
6. A good program involves parents as well as children. When the program is planned, the teacher should take into account the fact that different families have special needs. Moreover, since young children are so closely identified with their parents, the teacher should make every effort to determine policies and plans with the parents. Provision should be made in the teachers' professional load for parents' meetings, conferences with parents, and for frequent home visits. Both the program and the school day should provide time for the work of teachers with parents. Parent involvement is an essential part of Head Start activities.

There is no one formula or method that can be used by the teacher to plan an effective program. This task calls for intelligence and understanding, imagination, and flexibility, rather than formulas. There is need for knowledge of research and the factors that influence the learning of children. These include (1) what the culture expects, (2) what the children are like and how they learn, and (3) academic content and skills. The first two factors are discussed in this chapter. The third factor is treated in subsequent chapters.

CULTURAL EXPECTATIONS

A child growing up in the American society is confronted with certain "tasks" to be mastered if he is to make normal progress. These "developmental tasks are those major common tasks that face all individuals within a given society."[24] These tasks are set by forces from two major areas; namely, the expectancies and pressures of society, and the changes which take place in the physical organism through the process of maturation. For each task there are certain stages of development which are appropriate to each age group—infancy, early childhood, adolescence, adulthood, and old age. These tasks are reflected in the goals on pages 61–63.

Some of the developmental tasks have been selected and the stages of development appropriate in early childhood have been summarized:

1. The task—achieving an appropriate dependence-independence pattern. The child needs to adjust to less private attention and to become more independent. This means that physically while he is learning to be independent in dressing, eating, and toileting, he is also learning to share the teacher's attention with others in the group. In order to help the child in this respect, the school needs to:
   a. Maintain a warm, accepting atmosphere in the group. The child cannot adjust to less personal attention unless he is secure and receives much private attention. The group must be small enough for the teacher to give this attention to each child.
   b. Provide facilities that enable the child to become independent. For example, child-size bathroom fixtures, accessible lockers for hanging clothing, table and eating implements of appropriate size.
   c. Provide time in the program and facilities suitable for the child to put away materials or to hang up his clothing. Explain to parents how important it is for the clothing to be such that the child can manage it independently.

2. The task—achieving an appropriate giving-receiving pattern of affection. The child needs to achieve an appropriate pattern of giving and receiving affection. At this stage, he learns to give as much love as he receives and to form friendships with other children of his own age. In order to help the child in this respect, the school program should:
   a. Provide opportunities for children to show affection for others in desirable ways —greetings, sharing toys, playing together.
   b. Avoid unfavorable comparison of one child with another. It is difficult for a child to share affection or love unless he himself feels secure and loved.

3. The task—relating to changing social groups. It is important that the child develop the ability to relate to changing social groups. At this stage of development he is learning to feel a part of the school group, beginning to interact with age-mates, and to adjust to the expectations of the group. In order to help with this task, the school program should:
   a. Provide opportunities for the child to be a part of the group in planning and sharing, such as news and possessions.
   b. Stress cooperative and voluntary effort rather than domination and force.
   c. Provide opportunities for learning to give and to receive helpful suggestions and criticisms.

---

[24]Caroline Tryon and J. W. Lilienthal, "Developmental Tasks: The Concept and Its Importance," *Fostering Mental Health in Our Schools*, 1950 Yearbook (Washington, D.C.: ASCD), p. 77.

4. The task—developing a conscience. In early childhood this task involves developing the ability to take directions, to be obedient in the presence of authority, and gradually becoming able to be obedient in the absence of parents or teachers when conscience substitutes for authority. This is usually the period in which, as the child identifies with adults, he identifies with their values and standards of behavior. In order to help with this task, the school should:

   a. Offer explanations of or reasons for actions in simple, direct terms which can be understood by the child.

   b. Avoid moralizing.

   c. Provide opportunities for choices within limits.

   d. Provide opportunities to respond to signals and directions, and to learn respect for authority.

5. The task—learning one's psycho-socio-biological sex role. In early childhood the child is learning to identify with adult male and female roles. As children enter this stage, at the age of two, three, or four years, boys and girls exchange roles freely. During this stage, however, a change usually commences. The boys usually begin to identify with their fathers, then with men in general, while the girls begin to identify with their mothers and then with other women in general. In order to help with the task, the school program should:

   a. Provide opportunities for dramatic play.

   b. Provide opportunities for the child to find out about the work that mothers and fathers do. Visit some parents at work, or invite them to visit the school.

6. The task—accepting and adjusting to a changing body. Still another task includes managing a growing body and learning new motor patterns. The child needs to develop muscular control and skill in coordinating his movements. At school, space, equipment, and opportunities are needed for climbing, running, sawing, painting, cutting, as well as opportunities for dressing, using buttons, and tying shoe laces.

7. The task—developing an appropriate symbol system and conceptual abilities. At this stage of development, the child is increasing his vocabulary and improving his sentence structure and pronunciation, so basic to his ability to communicate. He is gaining concepts, not only of values but of ideas and things. At school, help in achieving these specific tasks can be provided by experiences gained through trips, stories, books, and opportunities for conversation and speaking in the group.[25]

These tasks, expected of the young child in present-day culture, have implications for the teacher in planning the program.

WHAT THE CHILDREN ARE LIKE

The children, too, are an important consideration in planning. Each group is different just as the child differs from the other members of the group. The teacher opens the top file drawer in which the records of a group are

[25]Ibid., pp. 77–128.

kept. She examines the first folder—a boy, age four years, six months; height, 42 inches; weight, 38 pounds. The next folder is also a boy's—age, four years, five months; height, 41 inches; weight, 39¾ pounds. Now for a girl's record— age, four years, six months; height, 43 inches; weight, 44 pounds. The folders reveal that among 16 children there is variation in height, weight, and age. In Table 9-2 the range in heights, weights, and ages of four groups of children is given. These groups include children in a nursery school, a child development center, and a kindergarten. Note the overlap in height and weight among the groups and the variation within each group.

TABLE 9-2
VARIATIONS IN FOUR GROUPS

Group	Age Range	Height Variation	Weight Variation
Threes	2 years, 9 months	$36\frac{3}{4}$ inches	33 pounds
	3 years, 8 months	$39\frac{1}{2}$ inches	$45\frac{1}{2}$ pounds
Fours	3 years, 9 months	$36\frac{3}{4}$ inches	32 pounds
	4 years, 7 months	45 inches	48 pounds
Fours	4 years, 1 month	39 inches	35 pounds
	5 years, 1 month	47 inches	60 pounds
Fives	4 years, 11 months	$37\frac{1}{2}$ inches	35 pounds
	6 years, 1 month	48 inches	55 pounds

What do these heights, weights, and chronological ages mean for equipment, activities, and materials? Important as these factors are, there are still others to be considered. A closer examination of several folders reveals more details:

Karen and Kirsten are twins, five years old. They live in a six-room house with their parents and a sister who is three years older. The father attended college for two years, has no church affiliation, and is engaged in a business of his own—upholstering. The mother was born in Denmark and lived there until she married. She has no church affiliation and feels that for her civic and social activities can wait until the children are older. She speaks both English and Danish to the children.

In the testing situation both girls showed good discrimination in objects and forms and performed best on items requiring nonverbal responses. Test results, probably influenced by language, indicate that the girls are of low average intelligence. They are among the oldest children in the group, and above average in height and weight. Karen enjoys mealtime, while Kirsten often refuses food. The girls have had few trips in the community but spent last summer in Denmark with their grandparents.

The teacher notes: twins, mother of foreign background, limited language development, good muscular control, limited experiences in community.

Lisa, now four, is the older of two children. The walk to and from school each day with her mother serves as exercise for her mother who is expecting another baby soon. Once home, Lisa must remain in the apartment because her mother is not able to take her to a playground. Her father, a day laborer, is proud of Lisa, but has little time to spend with the children except during inclement weather when he can't work. Lisa is a bit larger than the other children in her group. She often takes leadership roles in small group activities and participates eagerly in school activities.

The teacher notes: mother pregnant, father can't work in bad weather, limited outdoor activity, assumes leadership roles, few experiences in the community.

Shaw knows that he is an adopted child. He lives with his foster parents and an older brother (also adopted) in a comfortable seven-room house. His father is a very successful businessman. Both father and mother are active in civic and church activities. Shaw accompanies his parents on trips to the beach and mountains. He is his father's hunting companion. He expresses himself well, enjoys books, likes school. Results of an individual intelligence test indicate that he is a gifted child. His height and weight are average but he is one of the youngest in the group. In situations which seem difficult, Shaw continues to try. His mother says, "He does not get hot and bothered. He has the patience of Job."

The teacher notes: adopted, gifted child, meets difficult situations confidently, good language facility, rich experience in immediate environment.

Gloria's oldest sister, a first grader, is responsible for bringing her and another sister, who is in kindergarten, to the center each day. Before the parents leave for work at 7:30 A.M. the mother gets the children up, dresses and feeds them. The girls stay in the apartment alone until a neighbor tells them that it is time to go to school. In the afternoon they are alone until the parents come in from work. The mother gives them money for candy and gum because they are left alone so much of the time. Gloria is a superior child and learns easily. She has difficulty in joining a group activity. At story time she sits on the lap of the adult assistant.

The teacher notes: both parents work, often left alone without an adult, given money as compensation, seeks adult attention, superior child, difficulty in group situations.

Jennie's father and mother are both students. The mother arranges her classes around the father's schedule so that one parent is free to care for the children, Jennie and a younger sister. The family lives in a small, dirty, cluttered apartment. The mother worked until the week before Jennie was born. Jennie is not permitted to cry at home. The father says, "Carsons do not cry." At school Jennie cries often and is afraid of children. An offer of friendship is greeted by, "He's bothering me." When she first entered the group, she became so excited by the children that she had a fever for several days. Her muscular coordination appears jerky. She tires easily. Mental test results indicate that she is a child of high average ability.

The teacher notes: preoccupation of both parents in their work—little time for children, cramped living space, normal emotional outlets denied, ill at ease with children, poor muscular coordination.

And there are others: Bob, whose father deserted the family; June, whose father is unemployed—only the "relief" money is available to feed and clothe six children; Roger, whose father makes a great deal of money—there is plenty of money to buy things but little time for shared family experiences; Jan, who seldom stops talking and is at home in any group; and Pete, who seldom utters a word—occasionally, there is a faint smile of communication.

These children face common developmental tasks, yet because of various factors in their own lives, they will achieve them in different ways. Wise is the teacher who understands this and is able to plan a program to provide for experiences that meet common needs of the group as well as individual needs. In planning such a program, the teacher, then, becomes familiar with various factors involved in the lives of the children in her group and the expectations of the culture in which they live. She reviews the research pertinent to these factors and determines the implications of these findings for the children she teaches. Within this framework of the child, the culture, and research findings, the teacher selects, plans, and organizes activities for the children in her particular group.

"At the very heart of curriculum planning," says Weber, "stands the problem designated by Hunt as the 'problem of the match.'"[26] The perfect match may mean boredom and little development. Differences that are too great may mean distress or negative motivation. Teachers must seek to find the match which will challenge the child to learn without undue stress.

> Young children have to have a balance between vigorous motor activities and quieter moments. They require individual and small-group situations. They depend upon significant adults working together—parents, teachers, aides, pediatricians. They need an expanse of space indoors and outdoors with adequate equipment and materials to challenge them and keep curiosity alive. They must have spontaneous and planned experiences which utilize their deep motivation to understand their world. They require a program that fosters intellectual growth. The need for integrating intellectual and affective growth is readily apparent.[27]

The authors of this text maintain their belief in the theories of child growth and development. The need for cognitive or intellectual development is recognized but emphasis is also placed on socialization, physical development, creativity, and the processes of learning. The task of translating these beliefs into daily activities and programs is not an easy one.

Suggested Activities

1. Visit a school for young children and evaluate the program in terms of the criteria presented on pages 96–97. Discuss findings with the class.
2. Select one developmental task which is characteristic of early childhood. Observe

[26]Weber, op. cit., p. 179.
[27]Ibid.

a group of children and note evidences in their behavior which indicate attempts to meet the task selected. Share observations in class discussion.

3. Visit a center that has developed an innovative program. Note the curriculum, organization, and teaching strategies used. Discuss observations with the class.

4. Visit a center for disadvantaged children and a nursery school. Compare the principles of learning and development, and teaching strategies operating in each situation.

5. View a film depicting one of the innovative programs. Compare the program you observed with the one presented in the film.

Related Readings

Anderson, Robert H. "Schools for Young Children: Organizational and Administrative Considerations," *Phi Delta Kappan*, 50:7 (1969), p. 381.

ASCD. "The Young Child—Today's Pawn?" *Educ. Leadership*, 23:2 (1965), entire issue.

———. "Early Childhood Education: A Perspective," *Educ. Leadership*, 28:8 (1971), entire issue.

Berson, Minnie P. "Individual Differences Among Preschool Children: Four-Year-Olds," *Individualizing Instruction*, 61st Yearbook, Part I. University of Chicago Press: NSSE, 1962, pp. 112–125.

Biber, Barbara. *Challenges Ahead in Early Childhood*. Washington, D.C.: NAEYC, 1968.

———. "Goals and Methods in a Preschool Program for Disadvantaged Children," *Children*, 17:1 (1970), pp.15–20.

Combs, A. W. *Educational Accountability: Beyond Behavioral Objectives*. Washington, D.C.: ASCD, 1972.

Elkind, D. "Preschool Education: Enrichment or Instruction?" *Child. Educ.*, 45:6 (1969), pp. 321–328.

Frank, L. K. "Evaluation of Educational Programs," *Young Children*, 24:3 (1969), pp. 164–174.

Frazier, Alexander. *Open Schools for Children*. Washington, D.C.: ASCD, 1972.

Heath, D. H. "The Education of Young Children: At the Crossroads?" *Young Children*, 25:2 (1969), pp. 73–84.

Featherstone, J. *Informal Schools in Britain Today*. New York: Citation Press, 1971.

NAEYC. *Curriculum Is What Happens*. Washington, D.C.: NAEYC, 1970.

Phi Delta Kappa. "Early Childhood Education—Special Issue," *Phi Delta Kappan*, 50:7, 1969.

Pines, Maya, and Catherine Brunner. "How and What to Teach the Very Young Child," *NEA J.*, 57:2 (1968), pp. 43–46. Also in *Elementary Education Today*. Washington, D.C.: EKNE, 1971, pp. 30–35.

Raths, J. D. "Teaching Without Specific Objectives," *Educ. Leadership*, 28:7 (1971), pp. 714–720. Also in *Curricular Concerns in a Revolutionary Era*. Washington, D.C.: ASCD, 1971, pp. 20–26.

Senn, M. J. E. "Early Childhood Education: For What Goals?" *Children*, 16:1 (1969), pp. 8–13.

Shane, H. "The Renaissance of Early Childhood Education," *Phi Delta Kappan*, 50:7, (1969), p. 369.

Smith, Marilyn, and Rosemary Giesy. "A Guide for Collecting and Organizing Information on Early Childhood Programs," *Young Children*, 27:5 (1972), pp. 264–271.

Spodek, B. "What Are the Sources of Early Childhood Curriculum?" *Young Children*, 26:1 (1970), pp. 48–58.

Weaver, Kitty. *Lenin's Grandchildren: Preschool Education in the Soviet Union*. New York: Simon & Schuster, 1971.

Weisdorf, Pearl S. "A Comparison of Two, Three and Five Days of Nursery School," *Young Children*, 21:1 (1965), pp. 24–29.

Planning for Learning

Chapter 10

A center for young children is a place where children are engaged in interesting, stimulating activities, relevant to their life styles, not a place where children just do "busy work."

Each center for young children is unique. The type of program and the schedule planned for various activities depend on such factors as the educational philosophy of the staff, the amount of time the children spend in school, the special needs of the children enrolled, the physical facilities available, and the location in terms of climate. However, all centers aim to provide a happy place with opportunities for worthwhile play and work experiences so that children will grow and learn under the guidance of well-qualified teachers.

The teacher knows that each day is important and that the child can live this day only once; therefore, she is acutely conscious of the fact that how he lives *this day* helps to determine how capable he will be to direct his own energies as he slips into the next day and on and on into adulthood. She asks herself how to plan so that this child can acquire skills and work habits, yet be flexible enough to live in a rapidly changing society with ever-changing occupations. How to plan for a child who will live in this world with the expanded community concept? How to plan so that the child will develop a pattern of work and play that will guide him in knowing how to work, how to use leisure time, and how to relax and rest?

In order for children to have such opportunities, the teacher utilizes her knowledge about each child, the level of the developmental tasks he faces, and the sequence of skills within the various subject areas in selecting learning activities and episodes and materials to be used. It is in the selection and guidance of activities for young children that the teacher's education and skill are evident.

As she plans, a teacher of a group of five-year-olds looks at her notes on each child. Examples of what she might read are: Gloria needs help in group situations; Karen and Kirsten, the twins, have limited language development; Jennie needs to develop muscular control; and so on until she considers the needs of each child in the group. (See page 140.) The teacher studies these notes and ponders: What is the role of the teacher as she works with these children? What shall be the teaching tasks, the children's activities? What materials will be needed? Which materials should be prepared or assembled in advance of the arrival of the group and which materials should be selected and collected by the children under teacher guidance? How can she tell if the children are developing according to their potential as they participate in the planned and the incidental activities?

Using the long-range goals already developed (see Chapter 5), the teacher must analyze each child's achievement and discover his needs, plan a daily schedule, and select learning opportunities and activities. Suggestions for the teacher in each of these areas follow.

Analyzing Pupil Achievement

The teacher's concern in analyzing the child's present level of development or achievement is in securing information to be used as the basis for curricular planning for each child. There are conflicting opinions among those who work with young children as to what should be included in the preschool program. Some introduce formal, abstract learning to very young children even though the children usually do not develop such concepts and generalizations at a high level of abstraction. Others maintain that if the learnings are paced for each child, he develops enthusiasm for learning as he participates in numerous yet diverse learning opportunities.

Within each curricular field and in the areas of physical, mental, and social growth there is a developmental sequence that can serve as a guide for the teacher. (See chapters 11–19.) She can identify the child's present level and when the child is ready for the next step in the sequence she is ready to help him take it. There is a need for instruments to help the teacher in analyzing the child's achievement. An analysis of each child can help the teacher in utilizing experiences and activities to facilitate learning. For example, if the teacher finds that a child does not recognize a dime or a quarter, she can include him when planning for a committee to buy bird food at the pet store so that he will have opportunities to become acquainted with and use money. This information—that he does not recognize certain coins—can be shared at a parent conference and parents can be encouraged to provide similar meaningful opportunities.

An analysis of the entire class may reveal that only 10 per cent recognize a dime and a quarter. Is this to be expected? In answering this question, the teacher can consult research and authorities in this area and then set her goals. If such competency is to be expected for children at this age, she will need to consider appropriate learning encounters for the group as well as for individuals within the group. Thus she can plan for each child in terms of his achievement. Results of periodic evaluation may be also used by the teacher to determine a child's achievement over a given period of time.

The following Achievement Checklist is planned to help in making an analysis of each child. It is not a test. No attempt was made to establish norms for different age groups. It consists of a list of items for assessing achievement that were selected from the literature and have been reviewed by specialists as being appropriate for the early childhood years. The checklist is intended to help the teacher gain a picture of the child's status that will serve as a basis for planning and guidance and as a means of assessing a child's progress.

TABLE 10-1

Child's Name _____ Date _____

ACHIEVEMENT CHECKLIST FOR
YOUNG CHILDREN

Directions for Using: Below is a list of items which may be achieved by some three-, four-, and five-year-old children. Put a check (✔) in the appropriate column to indicate how frequently, in your experience with this child, he has achieved in each item.

Section I	Always	Sometimes	Never	Does Not Apply
Eats with spoon				
Eats with fork				
Holds silver correctly				
Holds cup with one hand				
Spills food or drink only once during meal				
Spills food or drink more than once during meal				
Goes to toilet without help with clothing				

TABLE 10-1 (Cont.)

Section I	Always	Sometimes	Never	Does Not Apply
Flushes toilet				
Hangs clothing in locker				
Puts on sweater that opens down front alone				
Puts on coat alone				
Buttons sweater				
Buttons coat				
Puts on slip-on sweater alone				
Manages zipper				
Ties shoe laces				
Climbs jungle gym				
Jumps from 12-inch height				
Skips				
Catches ball				
Pedals tricycle				
Climbs steps with alternate feet				
Puts three-piece puzzle together				
Puts puzzle of five or more pieces together				
Holds scissors correctly				
Cuts on a line				
Knows full name				
Writes given name				

Section II				
Follows simple directions				
Sits and listens to story for at least 5 minutes				
Sits and listens to story for at least 10 minutes				
Puts away blocks or toys when finished				
Responds to own name				
Recognizes locker				
Leaves mother after one "good-bye"				
Rides to school in car with someone other than parent				
Chooses to look at picture books				
Looks at books from front to back				
Looks at page from top to bottom				

Section II	Always	Sometimes	Never	Does Not Apply
Recognizes name				
Recognizes name of at least one other child				
Contributes to experience story				
Reads experience story with group				
Identifies words in experience story				
Can identify rhyming words				
Can match beginning consonant sounds				
Counts by rote 1–5				
Counts by rote 1–10				
Counts rationally 1–5				
Counts rationally 1–10				
Uses ordinal numbers first through third				
Recognizes money—penny, nickel, dime				
Recognizes geometric shapes—circle, square, triangle, rectangle				
Solves problem without number				
Uses number in problem solving				
Writes numerals 1–5				
Speaks without baby talk				
Uses personal pronouns				
Speaks in sentences (uses sentences of at least five words)				
Tells events or story in sequence				
Engages in conversation with other children				
Engages in conversation with adults				
Speaks in group situation				
Section III				
Sings alone				
Sings songs of at least two phrases				
Recognizes songs sung or played by others				
Manipulates and experiments with instruments				
Uses instrument as accompaniment to his movements (beats drums as he marches, but not necessarily in time with his steps)				

TABLE 10-1 (Cont.)

Section III	Always	Sometimes	Never	Does Not Apply
Knows names of at least two better-known musical instruments				
Listens and identifies sounds of different instruments				
Matches tones				
Draws or paints lines and circles				
Draws or paints squares				
Shows ground line in painting or drawing				
Names his paintings or drawings				
Names (or recognizes) primary colors				
Names at least five colors				
Adjusts bodily movements to accompaniment of regular beat (can keep time to music)				
Adjusts bodily movements to accompaniment which involves contrasts (slow-fast, light-heavy)				

Directions for scoring: Note items in which the pupil has achieved, the items that need continued practice, and those that need to be introduced. Plan learning encounters in terms of analysis of achievement items. Ignore those items which do not apply.

The teacher studies carefully the data secured through the use of the checklist. Activities that will provide continued practice as well as introduce encounters for new learnings are planned. She reassesses the progress of the children periodically to assist her in further planning. However, she is constantly aware that to achieve, all children need to feel secure and loved, to be free from fear, and to have recognition as they participate in a variety of learning episodes.

PLANNING LEARNING ENCOUNTERS

As she plans opportunities for experiences and activities for and with the children, the teacher takes into consideration their individual and group likes, needs, and abilities, as well as the child's home life and experiential background. With these factors in mind, the teacher will plan so that the children may:

1. Plan together—for the day, for the period, and for special events.
2. Make decisions—as to work, play, rest, and behavior.

3. Learn new skills—as an individual child and as a group.
4. Expand interests—in special areas or in new areas.
5. Have balance—between active and quiet activities and between indoor and outdoor play.
6. Have opportunities—to laugh together, to console one another, to help one another.
7. Have opportunities to work alone—to browse among materials or to think and muse quietly.
8. Visit places—within the school, at home, an interesting place in the community, or have a person from outside the school visit them.
9. Establish routines—of physical habits, work habits, discipline, or self-direction and self-control.
10. Develop social values—following through activity and receiving group acceptance, developing a balance between independence or initiation and consideration or aggression, developing pride in ownership yet willingness to share, acquiring a feeling of security for self but also a sense of responsibility to the group.
11. Develop readiness—in reading, speech, mathematics, writing, according to child's maturity.
12. Grow—through creative self-expression in music, rhythm, dramatic play, art activities, games.
13. Explore natural environment—through observing, investigating, experimenting, experiencing.

As the teacher considers these points, she knows that she will not place emphasis on all of them each day, yet all are so interrelated that many of them will appear daily in some form. Certainly a group would not take a trip each day nor would someone from outside the school visit the group very often.

Teaching Strategies

How, then, does the teacher plan and teach in order to achieve the desired results? What are some of the strategies that she may use? Descriptions of a few teaching strategies follow. These are applicable to any subject area. Examples of use in various subject fields such as science and social studies are included in chapters dealing with the subjects.

Reinforcing, Clarifying, Explaining, and Discussing Incidents That Affect Children During the School Day. Often opportunities for reinforcing, clarifying, explaining, and discussing incidents that affect children during the school day are lost. However, a comment by the teacher at the right moment can be most effective in utilizing both in- and out-of-school experiences that children mention in their conversation. In the following example, two four-year-olds complain to Miss D., "We don't like Steve. He knocks our blocks down."

Miss D.: Why do you think he knocks them down?
Hal: He's just mean.
Joe (thoughtfully): He doesn't know how to play with other children.

MISS D.: Why do you think he doesn't know how?
JOE: He just came to nursery school.
MISS D.: How could we help him?

In response to the question, two suggestions were made.

1. "We could say 'Please don't knock down the blocks. We don't do that at nursery school.'"
2. "We could ask him to play with us."

These four-year-olds were being helped to understand that rules can help us live happily together.

COOPERATIVE PLANNING.   Cooperative planning means that the teacher and children plan together, examine alternatives, and make decisions that are appropriate for consideration by the child. They can participate in planning for many different activities such as field trips, cooking, a visit by a resource person or what to do in the classroom. For example, the teacher says, "This is a rainy day. We can't go out on the playground. What could we do inside?" The teacher and children discuss the possibilities available, make choices, and plan for their use.

Cooperative planning does not mean that the teacher already has the plan in mind and is trying to have the children guess what it is or to manipulate them into making correct choices. As one example of such manipulation, conscious or unconscious, one teacher said, "I let the children plan the lunch menu every day." When asked how it was possible to do this, she said, "Oh, I have the meal already planned and partially prepared. But I ask the children what they want for lunch. If they don't name what I have planned, I say, 'Oh, let's not have that today. What about fish? Tuna fish? You know how good that is.' And they agree."

COOKING.   Activities related to cooking are of interest to both nursery school and kindergarten children. Not only are these experiences enjoyable but they also provide opportunities for discussing and planning, taking turns, following directions, learning quantitative measurement, using desirable health habits, developing scientific concepts, and beginning reading experiences.

Gelatin desserts can be made by children. Water is heated by the teacher, but the measuring and stirring are done by the children. Cake mixes can be used for making cupcakes for a birthday party. A simple butter icing may be used to decorate the cake. Ice cream can be mixed and frozen in the classroom.

If a stove is not available in the classroom, an electric hotplate may be used or the food may be cooked in the school cafeteria. The refrigerator in the cafeteria may also be used if one is not available in the classroom.

In guiding cooking activities, the teacher should keep in mind the following suggestions:

Use "no-fail recipes."

Maintain constant, alert, adult supervision.

Exercise care in the use of the stove and hot liquids.

Discuss the safety rules.

Practice desirable health habits. Be sure that hands are washed and utensils are clean.

Relate cooking to various phases of the school program such as health, science, social studies, and holiday celebrations.

Picture the ingredients to be used on a chart as a reference for the children.

Experiment with using various measures, such as one tablespoon or one-half cup, before the cooking activity.

Keep the project simple enough so that the children will have a successful and happy experience.

Allow time for children to do the work.

The entire group need not "cook" at the same time.

A cooking activity can contribute to learning in the various areas of the curriculum.[1] For example:

1. Language Arts
   a. Discussing plans.
   b. Listening to and following directions.
   c. Learning new words.
   d. Reading plans and recipes.
2. Social Studies
   a. Learning about home activities.
   b. Working as a member of a group.
   c. Learning where foods come from and how they are transported.
   d. Understanding about division of labor.
3. Science
   a. Learning how foods grow.
   b. Understanding how matter changes form.
4. Mathematics
   a. Measuring ingredients.
   b. Understanding quantities.
   c. Learning how foods are sold; measuring; weighing.
5. Health and Safety
   a. Developing the concept that many foods help us grow strong.
   b. Practicing reasonable cautions—"cooking can be done safely."
   c. Practicing desirable health habits, such as handwashing.
   d. Helping improve self-image, because child is really doing something worthwhile.

FIELD TRIPS.   Visits may be made to spots within walking distance of the

[1]Tricia Godshall, "Discover Cooking With Preschoolers" (mimeographed), Project Florida Head Start, University of Miami, Coral Gables, n.d.

school, or sites farther away which necessitate transportation. In either case one should use the following checklist in preparing for the trip:

1. Formulate purpose of trip. Too many trips are taken merely because they are novel or unusual and provide an activity for the group. Trips should be made only after the teacher has clearly in mind her reasons for taking the trip, and feels that the trip offers the most effective method of helping the children to develop certain understandings and appreciations and to acquire certain knowledge and facts. In deciding whether the trip is the most effective method to use, it is important that the teacher consider such factors as the following:
   a. Length of time required for transportation and the visit. Considering the age of the children, is it too long? Will they become too tired? Will it interfere with the routines for eating and resting?
   b. Complexity of the concepts and difficulty of the facts to be gained. Are they appropriate for the maturity of the children? Could they be acquired more effectively when the child is older?
   c. Experience background of the children. Have the children had, or are they likely to have, this experience with their parents?
   d. Security of the child. Is the security of the child threatened by leaving school with "a stranger," an adult who is helping with the trip?
2. Obtain administrative permission. Investigate school policies covering field trips and observe these in planning for the trip.
3. Obtain written permission of the parents. The following is a sample form that may be used and covers trips for the entire school year:

. . . . has my permission to go on
          (Child's Name)
excursions away from Nursery School. I understand that these excursions will be planned and adequately supervised.

. . . .
           (Parent's Signature)

It is important, however, to notify parents of each trip away from school. Such notice helps parents to understand the value of the trip and to know the details involved that may influence the clothing the child wears that day, and the schedule for bringing and picking up the child.

4. Visit site before taking children. This is essential in order to determine whether or not the site is appropriate and can fulfill the purposes of the trip. Safety hazards should be noted. Talk with adults who will serve as guides and talk with the children.
5. Arrange transportation. When private cars are used, be sure that the parent has adequate liability insurance. Two adults should be in the car, one in the back seat. The number of children per car should be limited so that there is room for each child to sit down. If the group is walking, the number of adults will vary with the age of the children. With three-year-olds there should be at least one adult for every two children. For four- or five-year-olds, there should be at least two adults for every five or six children.
6. Invite parents to assist. Select parents whose presence in the school situation does

not overstimulate their own child. In order to help the adult "keep up" with the children assigned to her, each child might have a name tag, the color of the children's tags matching the color of the tag worn by the adult. Discuss with the parents the purposes of the trip. To provide consistent guidance, talk with them regarding the standards of behavior that have been developed for the trip.

7. Plan with the children. Talk about what we hope to see, to observe, to learn. Be sure that they know why they are taking the trip. Discuss reasons for standards of behavior, such as listen to the adult who is with you; sit down in the car; and when you get out of the car, wait for the group and the adult. Count the children before leaving school and frequently during the trip.

8. Evaluate the experience. Variety is needed here. Too often the group only discusses the trip or paints pictures about it. On one field trip a child was overheard to say, "Don't look 'cause when we get back we'll have to read and write." Although preschool children do not read or write about the trip, the comment reflects the child's reaction to the exclusive use of one type of evaluation. Children's comments, conversation, and dramatic play all can be used to determine whether or not the purposes of the trip have been fulfilled.

ORGANIZATION AND USE OF CENTERS OF INTEREST AND LEARNING CENTERS. The terms *learning center* or *station* are often used and the question arises as to the difference between them and the term *centers of interest* as used in programs for young children. A center of interest is just what the name implies— a place in the nursery, kindergarten, or child development center in which the child can engage in activities related to one of his various interests. These centers provide interrelated experiences that may be adapted to the child's interests, maturity, and experiential background. Through such experiences the child can grow in appreciation of his world, relationships, and roles. In such a center the child can manipulate objects, build, and engage in conversation and role-playing, and can learn each at his own level. The use of blocks may range from manipulation by some children to the building of a structure related to a topic of interest. One child may rock the doll as she or he plays alone, while three others may engage in cooperative play and role-playing.

The learning center has evolved as an attempt to individualize instruction for more effective education of children. Perhaps the main distinction lies in the fact that the learning center emphasizes cognitive growth and provides for self-evaluation. In a center of interest the child can manipulate and play with blocks. Opportunities for practicing physical and social skills as well as cognitive development are available. Some children, however, do not utilize them. In a learning center the cognitive aspects are pinpointed. Exploring behavior by itself is not considered to be learning, and provision must be made for opportunities by which the child's mind can be stretched.[2] There are certain tasks to be performed such as "Find 4 blocks that are just alike." Self-evalua-

---

[2]D. E. Day and D. W. Allen, "Organization for Individual Work," *Learning Centers: Children on Their Own* (Washington, D.C. ACEI, 1970), p. 31.

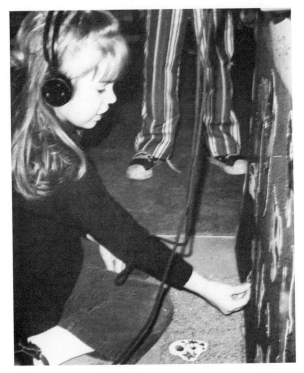

Figure 12. The learning center has evolved as an attempt to individualize instruction. The learning center emphasizes cognitive growth and provides for self-evaluation. This girl is listening and responding as she places shapes on the board.

tion can take place as the child puts the blocks in a frame or storage shelf to test for size.

In using centers with young children, whether called *Interest* or *Learning*, it is important that the intellectual growth of the child not be affected adversely—activities should not be boring and dull on the one hand, or too structured and demanding on the other.[3]

The role of the teacher in planning for and supervising the centers is an important one. Suggestions for the teacher in planning and organizing centers follow:

1. Select centers that are appropriate to the child's level of development and interests and vary these from time to time. Be sure that the centers are attractive, inviting, uncluttered, and safe. Enough equipment should be available so that the child does not have to wait too long for a turn. Some centers, such as block building and the doll corner are available each day. Variety may be provided by the addition of different materials on certain days. For example, toys related to transportation— trucks, trains, and airplanes—may be placed in the block-building area. Conversation may be encouraged by including toy telephones in the doll corner. Specific learning tasks may be added. The materials and/or tasks selected will vary with the emphasis that the teacher considers to be important at the time.

   Other centers of interest may be set up for a few days only. Such centers may

[3]Ibid. p. 32.

relate to a holiday or to the unit of study (see pp. 272–78, 310–14) that is in progress at the time.

2. Arrange for several centers of interest to be available each day and to be set up before the child arrives at school. The child's attention span is short and he may participate in several centers of interest during the morning. A wide variety of activities should be available to him. The following list of centers suggests the types that the teacher might set up for one day:

> Housekeeping Center or Doll House. Activities related to the home, kinds of homes, members of the family. A learning task may be planned to involve classification. For example, "Hang the clothing here. Put the cooking utensils on the table."
>
> Block Building. Construction of houses, trains, identification of community helpers who work on the train. Provide caps for conductor and engineer.
>
> Puzzle Table. (See p. 346 for suggestions as to use of puzzles.)
>
> Library Table. (See pp. 217–20 for suggestions as to use of books.) Books displayed for the day may relate to the unit which is under way.
>
> Sound Center. During a unit on *Sounds,* the center might include musical instruments, rubber bands, sandpaper, and blocks with which the child could experiment in making sounds.
>
> Art Center. The easel, the clay or dough table, scraps of paper for tearing and pasting may be available also.
>
> Mathematics Center. Scales for balancing, containers for measurement, and felt figures for comparing can be utilized. A suggested task might be, "How many nuts balance one apple?"

3. Set up centers around the room in order to utilize space and minimize conflicts. For example, use blocks in an area which is not in the direct line of traffic.

   Related centers should be near each other. Maintain a balance between quiet and noisy centers and between those that accommodate a group or an individual.

4. Maintain a classroom atmosphere that is conducive to effective use of the centers and one in which the child is free to move from one activity to another. Sufficient time is needed for the child to engage in the activity and to move around without being hurried or pushed. In supervising the centers of interest, the teacher observes the responses of children in the situation. She may find the following questions helpful:

   > What is the relation of the child to others in the situation? Does the child engage in solitary play, parallel play, cooperative play, share toys, take turns?
   >
   > How does the child use materials? Does the child show evidence of good coordination, a willingness to experiment with new media? Does he or she organize well?
   >
   > What is indicated about the experiential background of the child? Are there limited experiences, good vocabulary, secure home relationships?
   >
   > What concepts need to be clarified?

5. Guide the children's activities so that the experience may be satisfying and valuable. For example, the teacher may help each child find some activity, help a child get into a group, help in quarrel situations, raise questions which may clarify the situation, assist in problem-solving situations, and clarify use of materials.

6. Watch for indications of leads into future activities.

UNITS OF WORK. The term *unit* has a variety of meanings. Jarolimek points out that the main purpose of unit planning is to relate learnings to one another and to avoid a highly fragmented program.[4] The important characteristics of a unit plan include a series of learning opportunities that help the child understand the interrelatedness of various aspects of his social and physical environment, and also opportunities to engage in thought processes involved in meeting new learning situations.[5]

As defined by Jarolimek, the unit is a means of organizing materials for instructional purposes around some broad topic. The unit includes significant subject-matter content, involves children in learning activities through active participation both intellectually and physically, and modifies the child's behavior to the extent that he is able to cope with new problems and situations more competently and to achieve the goals thought to be important. As here used, *unit* refers to a way of organizing materials and activities for instructional purposes.

The choice of a unit is not based exclusively upon the interests of the child, nor is it entirely dependent upon the occurrence of some incident. The teacher utilizes both the child's interest and incidents within the framework of learnings to be taught.

Often the question is asked, "What can the children do tomorrow?" and the reply is in terms of activities in which the children may participate. The most important question, however, for the teacher to ask is, "What am I trying to help the children to learn, to understand, to experience?" When this has been answered, activities can be planned and incidents utilized.

The teacher should be more concerned about justifying some of the topics routinely used. She should ask herself frequently: What contribution will the study of this topic make toward helping this child become more competent for living in this modern world? Is this worthwhile? Why? What difference will this make in the life of the child? Honest answers to such questions can help to make the content and learnings more meaningful.

Once the learnings and the topic have been selected, the teacher will do further planning. The educational long-range goals have already been developed. These are reviewed frequently. Good planning for a unit involves the development of *resource units*, a *teaching unit*, and a *teaching plan*, each related to the goals the teacher hopes to achieve.

A *resource unit* is usually thought of as a collection of teaching materials and suggested activities organized around a topic such as "Our Homes," "Money Is Used for Many Things," or "Many People Help Us." These units will be developed well in advance by the teacher or a committee of teachers, as is done in some school systems. Such units do not necessarily limit the

---

[4]J. Jarolimek, *Social Studies in Elementary Education,* 4th ed. (New York: Macmillan Publishing Co., Inc., 1971), p. 62.

[5]Ibid., p. 72.

Figure 13. This learning episode involves a trip to see the fire engine, followed by dramatic play back at the center. Firemen's hats add interest.

teacher, because from these resources the teacher is free to develop a teaching unit which she plans for and with a specific group of children.

The *teaching unit* may be developed in several ways. The teacher will choose the plan most consistent with and appropriate to the background of experience and knowledge of the children of the group. Activities of varying types and levels of difficulty should be planned to meet the needs of each child. This is one way in which the teacher can provide for the children from differing socioeconomic backgrounds as well as differing levels of maturity and experience.

From the teaching unit, a *teaching plan* is developed. The teacher selects certain phases of the unit to emphasize for a day, or part of a day, and provides opportunities for experiences through which learning may take place.

Other terms are used to indicate related activities and learnings. Biber uses the term *episode* to describe a sequence of planned activities. The episode may consist of two or more parts.[6]

A unit of work may last for a part of a day, one day, or for several days, depending on the maturity and interest of the group. Whatever the length of time involved, whether it be a resource or teaching unit or a teaching plan, good planning includes (1) objectives or purposes; (2) activities or opportunities for learning experiences through which these objectives may be realized; (3) materials needed; and (4) plans for evaluating to determine whether or not the purposes have been achieved. Examples of units are included on pp. 272–78, 310–14.

INSTRUCTIONAL TECHNOLOGY

The use of instructional technology in children's centers has greatly increased in recent years. Educational media may be used to help children visualize and understand ideas more clearly.

Models, collections, and museums may be used for instructional purposes. Models and collections may belong to one of the parents, one of the children, or someone in the community. A file of such resources, identifying possible uses and values, can be most helpful. Expensive and rare collections which may be easily broken or damaged should not be brought to the nursery school or kindergarten. Museums, especially those for children, will often plan a special exhibit. Others have collections which may be borrowed by the teacher for use at school. For example, one Junior Museum has "Treasure Chests" for loan to schools and some are appropriate for the young child. The chests include pictures, books, filmstrips, and objects related to a specific topic.

Films, slides, filmstrips, and television programs can contribute to children's understandings when used for specific purposes. In using them, the teacher will find the following suggestions helpful:

---

[6]Barbara Biber et al., *Promoting Cognitive Growth: A Developmental Interaction Point of View* (Washington, D.C.: NAEYC, 1971), p. 47.

Always preview films, slides, and filmstrips and listen to recordings before using them with children. Judge their value and appropriateness in terms of length, difficulty, and number of concepts presented, vocabulary used, voice of the narrator, and relation to the teacher's purpose. Slides and filmstrips make questions and comments possible at the time each picture is shown. To use a film which shows only one scene directly related to the purpose and which contains many other concepts may be confusing to the child. One slide or a flat picture might be a better choice for effective teaching.

Clarify with the children the purpose or the reason for viewing the film, slide, or filmstrip. Relate the visual material to the problem or question with which the children are concerned. Use the visual materials more than once if possible. The second viewing often answers questions and clears up misunderstandings. Observe the behavior of the children, their attention, questions, and comments as indications of the value of the experience to them.

It is important that the teacher go with the child to books to "find out." The teacher may say, "I think I know where to find this." The teacher and child look at pictures together.

BULLETIN BOARDS. "Typically used for display purposes," says Jefferson, "the bulletin board's seasonal pictures and flat objects 'cutely' arranged prove meaningless to young children."[7] The most effective use occurs when the bulletin board reflects current interests of the group and when children are engaged in the activity. Such boards are called *involvement bulletin boards.*[8] Jefferson suggests the following as appropriate uses for the bulletin board with young children.[9]

1. Preparation for and summary of field trips.
2. Learning about current events and happenings.
3. Helping children learn colors and distinguish shapes.
4. Special projects.

PACKAGED MATERIALS. Commercially prepared materials are now available in many areas such as concept development, auditory and visual perception, and language. The *package*, however, is different from such materials. The package is an entire program and the primary purpose is to create a curriculum along with the necessary accessories,[10] a system of instructional media and materials along with a plan for their use. Some plans are very flexible while others are quite restrictive.

The packages have usually been field tested before general distribution. If a teacher is considering the use of packaged materials, it may be well to

[7]Ruth Jefferson, "Bulletin Boards for Young Children," *Involvement Bulletin Boards* (Washington, D.C.: ACEI, 1970), p. 60.

[8]Ibid.

[9]Ibid., pp. 60–62.

[10]Carolyn Wakefield, *Evaluation of Packaged Materials for Young Children,* Unpublished Graduate Paper, University of Maryland, College Park, 1971.

examine the objectives and how these are to be accomplished; the background research; opportunities for active participation by the children, and creative use by the children and teacher; initial cost and cost of replacement of parts; necessity for teacher training; and the relationship to other courses and activities in the school or center.[11]

RESOURCE PERSONS. Resource persons may be invited to talk with the children, to show pictures, materials or other items, or to share a skill such as singing, playing a musical instrument, or cooking. Such persons may be the parents or family members of a child in the group, some person in the community, or another teacher. If the person is to talk with the children, the teacher needs to be sure that he can talk with them in a manner they can understand. Don't ask someone to come and talk about a general topic such as "rocks." Before the visit be sure that he understands the questions raised by the children and the length of time he is to talk.

In summary the words of Murphy are appropriate.[12]

"Gimmicks for learning are a dime a dozen and there is a new bandwagon every year! . . . Not that all old methods are bad or that all new methods are good. Rather, we need to choose carefully and combine wisely the methods that will help children to become intelligent members of a democracy. To do this, we need to learn what each approach can offer and what are its hazards.

SCHEDULING THE DAY

Scheduling is only important as it assists the teacher to develop an effective educational program. The day's schedule, while it may vary in length, is much the same in a school or a day care center because each is based on what is good for children. There are conditions, however, which affect the teacher's plans. These include:

1. The chronological age, developmental level and experiential backgrounds of the children.
2. The length of the allotted school day.
3. Weather conditions
4. Bus schedules, car-pools, transportation variations.
5. Space and physical facilities, location of bathroom and playground.
6. Class enrollment
7. The ratio of adult leadership to the number of children.[13]

---

[11]Ibid., pp. 6–7.

[12]Lois B. Murphy, "Multiple Factors in Learning in the Day Care Center," *Child. Educ.*, 45:6 (1969), p. 311.

[13]*A Guide: Early Childhood Education in Florida Schools,* Bull. 76 (Tallahassee: Florida State Department of Education, 1969), p. 41.

A good day begins with a friendly informal exchange of greetings followed by some activity that has concern for the health of the child. Some schools require that the parent wait until this has been given the necessary attention before leaving the child at school. The daily school period varies according to the situation and purpose. The length of the day is not significant, provided there is proper balance between rest and play, with attention to indoor-outdoor play, and active and quiet activities. The general plan may vary from day to day; however, some orderly planning is important to the security of the child and the teacher. The schedule should not be so inflexible that special events and unexpected happenings cannot be a part of the program.

Some teachers find it desirable to develop a form to be used in planning and recording the activities for the day and for the week. Whatever the form used, it should allow space for specific notes to serve as reminders as the day develops and to record points to remember in future planning. Such forms provide space to list:

1. Large blocks of time with listing of activities for that period and the supplies and preparation needed for the activity (included in this will be notes for special activities or assistance for individual children or small groups needing attention).
2. Plans for routines—toileting, handwashing, lunch, and rest.
3. Duties for each of several adults working with the group.
4. Listing of any special notices to be duplicated for distribution to parents or specific directions to be given to children.

An example of a framework that includes blocks of activities follows:

1. Arrival. (Approximately 15 minutes.)
2. A period in which the children decide what they want to do and move freely from one activity to another. (For many children, toileting should be the first activity; this is especially true for the very young child.) The teacher plans and prepares for this period in advance. She provides for many and varied activities and uses many materials in these activities. Block building, painting at the easel, dramatic play, drawing with large crayons and chalk, looking at books on library table, working with clay, and many other indoor or outdoor activities are planned for each day and varied from day to day. (Approximately 60 minutes.)
3. A period for routines of toileting, eating, and resting or relaxing. The rest period may be a story hour or quiet music. Some children may go to sleep during this period. If this is habitual, the rest habits at home need checking. Freedom from glare and bright lights is important. The teacher is alert to notice that the lights appear different at her eye level and she checks light in terms of the child's eye level. The teacher should remain quiet and as a rule seated during this period. After the child relaxes, he may get up quietly and prepare for the next activity. Rest should be pleasant and happy and not regarded as punishment. (Approximately 20 minutes.)
4. A period of total group activity that may involve singing, experimenting with rhythm instruments, listening to records or a story (if not used in 2), or dramatization of a story read.
5. Outdoor play (if not in first period and weather permits). Activities with large-

muscle equipment, wheel toys, construction, balls, and ropes. All of the work-play periods are closely supervised and the activities are guided by the teacher. (Approximately 60 minutes.)

6. Evaluating and planning for the next day. Through these activities the teacher receives suggestions for the next steps, and the child leaves with a feeling of accomplishment and anticipation for returning the next day, which holds new challenges for him. The child gets ready to go home. (Approximately 20 minutes.)

7. Dismissal.

Teachers in centers that operate a morning session or an afternoon session, or both, find that they can adapt this schedule to suit the local situation. In schools that operate on a full day, the schedule will need to be adapted to include a 30 to 45 minute lunch period at school. This period will be followed by an afternoon session that includes a nap period of approximately 1½ hours and a period of outdoor play of approximately the same length.

Using the general framework for scheduling, the teacher makes a daily plan and schedule. The daily plan should include the following:

1. Purpose—a good reason related to broad purpose for each activity.
2. Flexibility—in terms of needed changes and alternate plans for inclement weather.
3. Areas of emphasis or units—short term and more than one a day, with several developed concurrently and others extending over several days with daily sub-units or focus.
4. Differentiation—special plans for children in terms of problems faced by each child.
5. Balance—vigorous activities followed by quiet activities and not too-long periods of time without a meal.
6. Materials—what is needed, what is new, what needs to be secured, what needs to be put out, what books are needed, and what books should be removed.
7. Routines—indoors and outdoors—rules, help from others, types of materials.
8. Evaluation—record of achievement, difficulties encountered, plans for the next lesson based on today's experience, handling of special children.
9. Activities—equipment needed.
10. Activities related to purpose for group, for individual child—finger plays, games, poetry, counting, and so on.
11. Duties of each adult involved in the situation.

Two examples of a daily schedule and plan follow. One schedule, for a center that operates all day, can be adjusted for sessions of varying lengths (note suggested dismissal times) and may be adapted and used in day care centers, Head Start Programs, kindergarten or nursery groups. The second schedule is for a group of three-year-old children in a half day program.

TABLE 10-2. DAILY SCHEDULE

8:30–9:00	Children enter center. Informal health check. Free play with materials such as puzzles, table toys, crayons, blocks. Outdoor play if weather permits. This is a good time to give special attention to individual children.

9:00–9:15	Clean up. Put materials in order for later morning work time. (Some materials might be left so that play can resume after breakfast or juice time.) Each day a few children with one adult help set up for breakfast or juice.
9:15–9:30	Breakfast or juice and crackers. Clean up.
9:30–9:45	Short discussion of day's plans, what was done the previous day, or other topics of interest to children. Include some music and physical activities.
9:45–10:30 indoors and/or outdoors	Work time. Housekeeping and dramatic play, carpentry and woodworking, water play, table games and toys, sharing and caring for pets, blocks, art activities such as finger painting, easel painting, wood collage, crayons, clay, play dough.
10:30–10:50	Clean up. Adults work with children.
10:50–11:00	Bathroom. If center set-up permits, children go to bathroom on their own as the need arises. If children must go at a specific time with adult supervision, it is possible to go in small groups.
11:00–11:30	Outdoor activities. If adults are available, stagger coming inside so that not all children arrive indoors at one time.
11:30–12:00	Clean up and getting ready for lunch. Quiet activity—story or rest. Getting ready for dismissal for those leaving before lunch.
12:00–12:45	Lunch. If possible children should be able to leave table when they are finished. They may participate in a quiet activity until the bus or car arrives or begin rest time if the program continues into the afternoon.
12:45–1:00	Getting ready for dismissal for those leaving at this point. Getting hats, coats, and art work. Listening to story or records.
12:45–2:00	Rest time. Children should *not have* to go to sleep. They should rest on mats or cots quietly. If possible they should rest in small groups or the room should be divided so that there are just a few children in each area. Provision should be made both for those children who wake up early and for those who sleep longer. An adult can take those waking early outside or to another area for quiet activities. One adult should stay with the sleepers.
2:00–2:15	Afternoon snack.
2:15–2:45	This time can be used in a very flexible way. Be sure to provide for individual needs. Some children need physical activity, others need quiet kinds of involvement. Outdoor time if weather permits: Activities such as water play, hiking, digging, science activities.
For indoors:	Table activities, manipulative materials, science activities, music, rhythms, stories, film strips, movies.
2:45–3:00	Dismissal for those leaving at this point. Some changes will be necessary if there is more than one class per center. Plans need to be made for the staggered use of the bathroom and playground so that facilities are used by only one class at a time.

Adapted from Sample Schedule distributed by the Head Start Regional Training Officer, Nancy Goldsmith, University of Maryland, 1970. (Mimeographed.)

Alternate Afternoon Plan For Children Remaining at the Center Until 5:30 or 6:00 P.M.	
2:00–2:30	Toileting, dressing, looking at books, playing with puzzles until all resters are awake.
2:30–2:50	Afternoon snack, table conversation, clean up.
2:50–3:20	Music, rhythms, singing, playing instruments, dancing, listening to records.
3:20	Outdoor play or special activity such as cooking, digging, and planting gardens, experimentation with science aspects of the environment.
4:20	Story, film-strips, movies, slides. Quiet games, review of the day, plans for next day.
5:00	Dismissal for some.
5:15	Light evening snack. Quiet games, songs, individual time with the teacher until picked up to go home.

Florida State Department of Education, op. cit., p. 45.

Half Day (Three-year-old children)	
9:00–9:45	Dramatic play, blockbuilding, easel painting, science (feeding fish, turtle, etc.), puppets, stories, singing.
9:45–10:00	Clean up, handwashing, toileting.
10:00–10:15	Snack or juice
10:15–10:40	Rest on mats
10:40–11:00	Put away mats, story, singing, rhythms.
11:00–12:00	Outside play, short trips.

Ibid., p. 44.

EVALUATING DAILY PLANNING

The teacher uses the following criteria to check activities and to determine how effective the plans were as developed and adapted with the children:

1. Was there a balance of activities as to type and place? Were these activities planned in terms of weather, space, length of session, and maturity of each member in the group?
2. Was provision made for each child to have time of his own to do as he chose? Were the periods kept short where the child was expected to sit in one place?
3. Was there a balance between large group, small group, and individual work-play?
4. Were there new materials, new activities, and new situations for learning provided for each child according to his interest and growth pattern? Were these paced to his need?
5. Was enough of the familiar included in the day in terms of routine, activity, and learnings to give the child security?
6. Did the children have freedom to create, to explore, to experiment? If so, what happened—how did each child use this time?
7. Were the activities and experiences goal-centered and so planned that the at-

titudes and feelings, the skills and information were satisfactorily developed? Were the desired results obtained or were the activities a form of busy work?

8. Was time provided for necessary routines so that no child became tense or frustrated?

9. Was special consideration given to planning for certain individual children with special needs?

10. Was the planning based on large blocks of time which could be used flexibly so that the day flowed through from activity to activity without any feelings of a break or tensions? Were the rest periods adequate?

11. Was the planning for this day a part of the over-all plan for the week and the year, and yet were they plans that suited this particular day for this particular group? Was this over-all plan used to provide an overview and a frame of reference for the planning for the day? Was this overview considered and replanned in terms of the group and the developmental pattern of each child in the group?

12. Were the plans considered as tentative and used as a guide to depart from and to return to as the group planned, lived, and learned together?

A plan for the next day should include an evaluation of the day's work in terms of the activities of each child. The teacher may make a list of needs which have been observed similar to the following.

Shaw did easel painting today and wants to paint tomorrow.

Karen and Kirsten chose table activities but needed adult attention to get started; introduce a new activity and let them continue without assistance.

Lisa was concerned about getting out to meet her mother; see that she is ready when her mother comes.

Gloria needs social development; encourage her to go in the doll corner.

Jennie needs to develop muscular coordination; guide her to play with wheel toys.

The finger painting was not well directed as children did not use it wisely or clean up well; postpone this activity until a later date.

The walk to the Post Office was very successful; plan another experience soon and check on safety learnings gained on this trip.

Counting of cups, napkins, and plates was very successful; continue and build on previous understandings.

Thus the teacher selected, planned, and organized centers of learning, introduced learning tasks, and helped the learner to interpret his experiences. She responded to evidences of learning, taking into account age, sex, patterns of physical growth, interests related to success, each child's emotional organization and learning process, as well as his relationships to others and his special talents, limitations, and/or disabilities. She did not begin with developing the skill but allowed each child to discover need and then develop skill and concepts in an atmosphere of the excitement and the joy of participating in the activity. There was an absence of pressure, but each child was challenged according to his potential on that day. The teacher was aware and mindful in her planning that as the child enjoys, explores, appreciates, and feels, she needs to plan so that method and content go hand in hand.

PLANNING FOR THE CHILD'S FIRST DAY

As a child leaves home and enters an organized group for the first time, whether it be his first experience of this nature or entry into a new school group, the teacher is concerned as to what will be expected of him in the daily program. She considers what she can do to assist him in making the transition with security, yet with anticipation, curiosity, and challenge from the unknown, the untried, the inexperienced.

Most schools find it better to induct the children on a staggered basis; that is, some on Monday and Wednesday, others on Tuesday and Thursday, and all on Friday. Other schools take two weeks to induct all of the children. In one kindergarten the following schedule was used:

Monday	—Group 1 (12 children)	9:00–11:00 A.M.
Tuesday	—Group 2 (13 children)	9:00–11:00 A.M.
Wednesday	—Group 1	8:30–12:00 noon
Thursday	—Group 2	8:30–12:00 noon
Friday	—Total Group	8:30–12:30 P.M.

Children need to be a part of a group but what happens to them as they enter the group for the first time has significance for their feeling of belonging to the group. It is the responsibility of the teacher to plan for this induction into the group so that the child comes to feel a part of a happy working situation. He can learn this only if he experiences it to be true.

Even though the daily planning is flexible throughout the year, the first day of the school (and also the first day for the child who enters later) demands even greater flexibility in planning. It is important that this day be a happy one for the child, the parent, and the teacher so that they may continue to "live and learn together" happily. On the first day, the regular routine can be observed, but much more time and individualized attention will need to be given in greeting the children and parents, for helping children to place their wraps and possessions in lockers, and for gaining security in the setting. Even though each child and his parent have visited the school previously, this time and attention is important on the first day. Name tags for children, parents, and teacher help to give security and assist the teacher in getting acquainted. An inspection tour of the room will orient and interest the child. Outdoor orientation will include instruction and guidance for the children in use of equipment.

After routines of toileting and handwashing, the children have a brief period of outdoor play. The bathroom routines will need guidance as to place and procedure. However, no child should be coerced to use the bathroom. He will develop proper habits as he gains security in his environment. The same is true of outdoor play. It may be that the children will feel more secure in the room. If so, all should remain unless there are two people to supervise, one indoors and the other outside.

Following the getting-acquainted period for each child, the children will need time to look, to handle, and to explore interesting materials and equipment. Provision should be made for centers of interest that will encourage manipulating, creating, building, exploring, and experimenting. Some will begin free play, others will move from activity to activity. This freedom of movement is important for release of tension and gaining security. After a majority of the children are actively interested in some center, the teacher will call them together. She may strike a gong, triangle, or a note on a piano, or sing a quiet call to come and sit down together. This then becomes a period for talking, sharing, listening, finger plays, singing, or storytelling. As a rule, midmorning lunch and rest are omitted the first day as the children are too excited to make these events practical. Therefore, the quiet period needs to be a time for relaxation.

The dismissal should be a happy time with discussion of plans for tomorrow, such as feeding the fish, building a train, or riding a tricycle. Care should be taken that each child leaves with his parent or the person designated in writing by the parent. Kindergarten children who live in the immediate vicinity can go home on their own, provided the school is in an uncongested traffic area and parents have given their permission.

By allowing the child's day to gradually be increased in length, time is granted for him to become adjusted to his new environment and to the change in his pattern of living which results from attending school.

Working Policies and Plans

Much of the planning for the year takes place before the school opens. Plans for the physical facilities, the necessary equipment, and basic supplies are related to the broader plans involving policies related to the number and type of children to be accepted. Policies will need to be developed and plans made regarding the following:

1. Registration—procedures, amount, and plan for payment of fees, scholarships, insurance and medical costs, and refund, if necessary, of fees paid.
2. Composition of Group—balance between boys and girls, limiting size of group to facilities and personnel, age range of group as related to staff and space.
3. Operation—the school day (hours and days), vacations, holidays, opening and closing dates, induction of children, provision for children who arrive early and for those who leave later, getting acquainted with children before entering school, lunch (if provided), and midmorning snack. The staggered entrance schedule can be a factor in helping the child make a satisfactory adjustment to school; this plan provides for the teacher to have a smaller number of children to orient to the new situation and, more important, the child has a smaller group to which he must adjust. Parent contacts and visits help the child and the teacher as well as the parents to plan for the child's adjustment in the school situation.
4. Health and Safety—health examination and inoculations before entering school, securing child's health history, daily health inspection and teacher observation

of health, provision for isolation or transportation home if needed, and information relative to contacting parents and preferred physician if needed. (See pp. 324–25.)

5. Transportation of Pupils—how provided, cost, regulations, provision for safe drivers, insurance coverage, and plans for emergencies. (See page 325.)

6. Working with Parents—initial interview, parents' stay at school during orientation and induction, mutual agreements and acceptance of responsibility between parents and teachers, reports to be made to and from school, scheduled parent conferences and informal contacts, parent observation and participation, follow-up at home of school activities, contact and work with parents who cannot or do not visit school, and provision for parent meetings and study groups.

7. Cooperation—with other schools in community, with community agencies, and institutions; coordination of school calendar and records with community calendar; provision for satisfactory transfer or transition to another school.

8. Interpreting the School Program—to parents, to general public, to other school groups.

9. Staff Responsibilities—working hours, provision for health examination and insurance, sick leave, substitutes.

10. Consultant Service—for child problems, for staff problems, for professional growth of staff.

SUMMARY

Good planning provides for desirable learning experiences that are educationally significant. It provides for continuity and balance day by day, but it also provides for relating the experiences so that the teaching objectives, the ideas, the teaching procedures or activities, the materials and resources are so organized that the insight and understanding of the child is continually deepened and broadened. For some children, the depth and breadth may be less deep and narrow, for others it will be deep and broad and for others, deeper and broader. To plan and to guide the learning encounters so that this will occur is the challenge of teaching.

Suggested Activities

1. Observe groups of three-, four-, and five-year-olds. How do their interests and maturity levels differ? What are the implications of these differences for planning for different age groups?

2. Observe the same groups and identify differing interests and maturity levels among the children of the same age groups. What does this imply to the teacher for her planning?

3. Plan a day's tentative activities for three-year-olds, for four-year-olds, for five-year-olds. Include goals. List materials needed, and teacher preparation required.

4. Indicate how the plan might be modified for a full day program.

5. Assess achievement of at least two children using Achievement Checklist on pages 147–150. Make plans for each child in terms of the data secured.

6. Select one teaching strategy. Plan for and use it with a group of three-, four-, or five-year-olds. Evaluate the effectiveness of your teaching. Make follow-up plans.

Related Readings

Association for Childhood Education International. *Migrant Children: Their Education*. Washington, D.C.: ACEI, 1971.

Barth, R. S. "On Selecting Materials for the Classroom," *Child. Educ.*, 47:6 (1971), pp. 311–314.

Bryan, D. M. "Education for the Culturally Deprived: Building on Pupil Experience," *Social Educ.*, 31:2 (1967), pp. 117–118.

Cannon, Gwendolyn M. "Kindergarten Class Size—A Study," *Child. Educ.*, 42:1 (1966), pp. 9–13.

Carlson, Ruth K. "Raising Self-Concepts of Disadvantaged Children Through Puppetry," *Elem. English*, 47:3 (1970), pp. 349–355.

Cohen, Shirley. "Planning Trips for Vulnerable Children," *Child. Educ.*, 48:4 (1972), pp. 192–196.

Education USA. *Preschool Breakthrough: What Works in Early Childhood Education*. Washington, D.C.: School Public Relations Association, NEA, 1970.

Elkind, D. "The Case for the Academic Preschool: Fact or Fiction?" *Young Children*, 25:3 (1970), pp. 132–141.

Elliott, B., and Mary Jo Woodfin. "Evaluating and Recording Children's Activities: Diagnosing Educational Need," *Learning Centers—Children on Their Own*. Washington, D.C.: ACEI, 1970.

Fennel, Margaret, and Elizabeth Kelly. "Children on Their Own—Centers and Stations for Learning," *Learning Centers—Children on Their Own*. Washington, D.C.: ACEI, 1970.

Katz, Lillian G. "Children and Teachers in Two Types of Head Start Classes," *Young Children*, 24:6 (1969), pp. 342–349.

Keliher, Alice V. "Effective Learning and Teacher-Pupil Ratio," *Child. Educ.*, 43:1 (1966), pp. 3–6.

Kohlberg, L. "Early Education: A Cognitive-Developmental View," *Child Development*, 39:4 (1968), pp. 1013–1062.

Kohn, S. *The Early Learning Center*. New York: Educ. Facilities Laboratory, 1970.

Mendelson, Anna. "Picture That," *Early Years*, 2:5 (1972), pp. 20–23.

Mukerji, Rose, and Helen F. Robison. "Teaching Strategies for Disadvantaged Kindergarten Children," *Young Children*, 21:4 (1966), pp. 195–199.

Rand, Helene. "Experimental Learning Reevaluated," *Young Children*, 25:6 (1970), pp. 363–366.

Rogers, V. R. "Open Schools on the British Model," *Educ. Leadership*, 29:5 (1972), pp. 401–402.

Sears, Pauline S., and Edith M. Dowley. "Research on Teaching in the Nursery School," *Handbook of Research and Teaching*, Chicago: Rand McNally and Co., 1963, pp. 814–864.

Seifert, K. "Comparison of Verbal Interaction in Two Preschool Programs," *Young Children*, 24:6 (1969), pp. 350–355.

Waynant, Louise. *A Learning Center Handbook* (Mimeographed). College Park, Md.: Reading Center, University of Maryland, 1970.

Young, B. B. "Checklist of Things to Do on the First Day of Kindergarten," *Grade Teacher*, 83:1 (1965), p. 153.

The Language Arts

The language arts are a part of daily living and are functional in every activity and experience. Speaking, listening, reading, and writing are interrelated and the skills are developed as the child participates in many varied activities throughout the day—at home as well as at school. Crosby says,

> Research in human growth and development and in learning reveals that for most physically and emotionally normal human beings, learning to communicate beyond the stage of crying or random babbling involves learning to listen, to speak, and to write, in the order listed. Listening and speaking serve as a base for reading and writing and, if rooted in experience, furnish a rich background of meaning for written and printed symbols.[1]

[1]Muriel Crosby, "Identifying Oral Language Relationships," *Children and Oral Language* (Washington, D.C.: ASCD, 1964), p. 9.

Each aspect of the language arts, however, is discussed separately in order to identify the trends, research, and the developmental sequence of skills in each area. The activities involving children are included to illustrate the contribution of the activity to the development of the skills. Questions that may arise as the teacher analyzes the value of the activity are identified and discussed.

SPEAKING

Great sums of money have been spent to support research and federal programs for children from low-income families. One aspect of this effort that has received much attention is the language used by these children as language usage skills are considered a prerequisite for school success. Spoken language, according to Anderson, is widely used and basic to all communication.[2]

Various aspects of speaking are discussed here. Earlier and more recent research and opinion are included. In considering speaking as one of the language arts, the speech and language of the child immediately come to mind.

Growth in Vocabulary

Growth in the vocabulary of the young child has been studied by a number of investigators whose reports indicate discrepancies in the estimated size of children's vocabularies. These differences may be due to the type of vocabulary test used, the definition of "word" adopted, and whether both the use and recognition vocabularies were studied.

One of the early vocabulary studies was done by Madorah Smith in 1926. Her estimates of the size of the vocabulary of young children have been widely utilized. She found the vocabulary to consist of 896 words at three years, 1,540 at four, 2,072 at five and 2,562 at six.[3] In the 1950's Loban found that at kindergarten level, subjects varied in vocabulary from 180 to about 5,000 words with 3,000 words as the average.[4] Since Smith's study, changes may have occurred in the speech of young children as a result of increased TV viewing, number of experiences, and changes in child-rearing practices.

An extensive study of language skills in children was completed by Mildred Templin in 1957. In comparing her work with earlier studies, she reports, "In the areas of articulation and vocabulary, one is impressed with the stability of results over a period of time among studies using comparable methods, but carried on with different samples and by different investigators. . . . Differences occur, however, in the increased loquacity of children in child-

---

[2]P. S. Anderson, *Language Skills in Elementary Education*, 2nd ed. (New York: Macmillan, Inc., 1972), p. 6.

[3]Madorah E. Smith, "An Investigation of the Development of the Sentence and the Extent of Vocabulary in Young Children," *University Iowa Studies Child Welf.*, 3:5 (1926), p. 54.

[4]W. Loban, *The Language of Elementary School Children* (Champaign, Ill.: NCTE, 1963), p. 37.

adult situations and in a tendency for children of the same age to use more mature language than they did twenty-five years ago."[5] More mature speech is interpreted as the use of fewer one-word remarks and simple and incomplete sentences and the use of more complex sentences and adverbial clauses.

By the age of three a child's articulation improves and becomes fairly clear. There is a sequence in the child's ability to pronounce the consonant sounds, and an understanding of this may be of help to parents and teachers. Ages at which 7 per cent of the subjects correctly produced specific consonant sounds in the Templin study are listed.[6]

3 years: m, n, ng, p, f, h, w
3.5 years: y
4 years: k, b, d, g, r
4.5 years: s, sh, ch
6 years: t, th, v, l
7 years: z, zh, j

Before entering school, children have had tremendous practice with spoken language. Estimates of the number of words spoken per day by the child range from 7,500 at three years to 10,500 at five.[7] The child has thus developed much of his skill in speaking before he receives any formal instruction. Noel states that by the time the child arrives at school age, he has already learned to speak with whatever sound system, grammar, and vocabulary he has heard most often at home or in his neighborhood.[8] Other studies by Loban and Strickland[9] confirm the fact that the language patterns of children are largely set by the time they reach school. Some children have had a lush environment and many experiences while others have had a meager background. Some have talked primarily with adults in a grown-up manner while others have been indulged with baby talk. The teacher may expect, then, to find some children entering nursery school or kindergarten able to speak fluently and distinctly while others know and use few words. The size of the vocabulary and the ability to articulate sounds vary from child to child.

Loban, in a longitudinal study of kindergarten children, used a random sample as well as a special subgroup of those ranking very high in language proficiency and one of those ranking very low. The high group of children

[5]Mildred C. Templin, *Certain Language Skills in Children,* Institute Child Welf. Monogr. Series XXVI (Minneapolis: Univ. Minn. Press, 1957), p. 150.

[6]Ibid., p. 53.

[7]Dora V. Smith, "Growth in Language Power as Related to Child Development," *Teaching Language in the Elementary School,* (Chicago: NSSE, 1944), 43rd Yearbook, Part II, pp. 52–97.

[8]Doris I. Noel, "A Comparative Study of the Relationship Between the Quality of a Child's Language Usage and the Quality and Types of Language Used in the Home," *J. Educ. Res., 47*:3 (1953), pp. 161–167.

[9]Ruth G. Strickland, *The Language of Elementary School Children: Its Relationship to the Language of Reading Textbooks and the Quality of Reading of Selected Children* (Bloomington, Ind.: School of Education, Indiana Univ., 1962).

Figure 14. Opportunities for verbal interaction are numerous in children's centers. The mother here talks with the child alone and encourages her to talk about her play. The telephone conversation involves communication with language—listening to others and expressing one's own ideas.

had a larger, more varied, and more readily accessible vocabulary. They used more words and communication units than did the low group and continued to maintain initial superiority. The low group, he found, "says less, has more difficulty saying it, and has less vocabulary with which to express what it says."[10]

Language in Early Childhood

From the birth cry to mature language, verbal development follows a definite pattern. According to Lenneberg, "it is only under conditions of intellectual or environmental deprivation that this pattern varies."[11]

During his early years, the child's language development reflects his mental processes, his interests, and relationships with his world. The use of the pronoun "I," which begins at about two years of age, reflects his interest in himself. As the child advances in age, there is an increase in the number of other pronouns used such as *he, we, you,* and *they,* and a trend toward more socialized speech in which children speak and respond to one another.

[10]Loban, op. cit., p. 43.

[11]E. L. Robbins, "Language Development Research," *Interpreting Language Arts Research for the Teacher* (Washington, D.C.: ASCD, 1970), p. 5.

At about age five or six the language abilities have developed so that children can usually handle language situations in an almost adult manner.[12] However, as the five-year-old encounters new experiences in kindergarten and makes the necessary adjustments, pressures may be reflected in his speech. He may temporarily revert to patterns of speech practiced at an earlier age.

Despite these common characteristics, the skill with which children use oral language when they enter school will vary markedly from child to child. Certain factors that influence language growth have been identified. The children referred to in the following discussion are those described in Chapter 9.

ENVIRONMENTAL INFLUENCES.   Robbins reports many studies supporting the notion that there are influences in the child's environment that interfere with his language development.[13] As reported by Robbins, research done by Hess and Shipman, Jensen, May, Olem and Reissman indicates "a direct relationship between the quality of the child's environmental circumstances and his language facility.[14]

It has been found that the speech patterns of the child from the less-favored economic or cultural environment are different from and often conflict with the language used in the school. Crosby says, "the child's natural language, often dynamic, descriptive and forceful is frequently not the language of acceptability in the school. Aware of the rejection of his natural language, the child is nevertheless unskilled and inexperienced in using the standard, informal English of the school."[15]

Recent studies have compared the language abilities of children from upper and lower socioeconomic levels on elements other than those found in standard English. Robbins says, "Their findings support the view that there are no significant differences between the language abilities of low and high socioeconomic children when nonstandard language criteria are used."[16]

The problem, then, becomes one of *different* language usage, and is treated in much the same manner as teaching another language to a young child.

Intervention programs have been developed to counteract the influence of the environment on the child's language development. Butler reports that these programs range from those in which the child is encouraged to express himself to those in which the child is "bombarded with language."[17] The program for disadvantaged Mexican-American children at the University of Arizona is one in which opportunities for wide experiences, language lessons, and teacher models are all included. Children engage in activities—field trips, cooking,

[12]A. T. Jersild, *Child Psychology,* 6th ed. (Englewood Cliffs, N.J.: Prentice-Hall, Inc., 1968), pp. 424–425.

[13]Robbins, op. cit., p. 8.

[14]Ibid., p. 11.

[15]Crosby, op. cit., p. 5.

[16]Robbins, op. cit., p. 11.

[17]Annie L. Butler, *Current Research in Early Childhood Education: A Compilation and Analysis for Program Planners* (Washington, D.C.: EKNE, 1970), p. 135.

art, construction—which stimulate conversation. Modeling of language is considered important and teachers use complex sentences when appropriate to lift the child's language. Lessons help the children understand the position of words in language learning.[18]

The quality and type of the teacher's interaction with the child are very important. Katz, after studying children and teachers in two types of Head Start classes concluded that perhaps teacher style was a more important factor than the method. She observed that the teachers in this study did not follow through on the specified teacher behavior. They tended to neglect the praise and supportive aspects of their role and the behaviors that seemed to interfere with the learning of children were increased.[19]

Grotberg, after reviewing the Head Start studies on language, says:[20]

> The studies on language of disadvantaged children suggest that their language development is generally below that of middle class children. Environmental factors seem to account for a large portion of the difference; . . . Further, the language behavior of the parents is a more reliable predictor of children's language behavior than socioeconomic factors. . . .

Whether the children come from middle class or disadvantaged homes the skill with which they use oral language will vary from child to child. Certain environmental factors that influence language are discussed here.

Family. The child's family is also an important consideration. An only child or a singleton seems to have the advantage probably because of the greater opportunity for association with adults. The number of children in the family affects the growth of vocabulary. At five and one-half years of age, the singleton uses 94 words, the twin 89 words, and the only child 104 words in 50 remarks.[21]

Considerable evidence in the literature cited earlier tends to indicate that there exists a marked relationship between socioeconomic status of family and the child's linguistic development. Children from more favored environments use more words meaningfully at earlier ages. In a more recent study, Templin found consistent differences in the language performance of children from upper and lower socioeconomic levels. Differences in the linguistic environment provided by homes of the two levels were recognized.[22]

Regarding the low group in his study, Loban points out that it is entirely possible that language proficiency may be culturally determined. If children at the least-favored socioeconomic levels experience a restricted language en-

[18]Ibid., pp. 133–134.

[19]Ibid., p. 39.

[20]Ibid., p. 135.

[21]Edith A. Davis, *The Development of Linguistic Skill in Twins, Singletons with Siblings, and Only Children from Age Five to Ten Years*, Institute Child Welf. Monogr. Series 14 (Minneapolis: Univ. Minn. Press, 1937), p. 114.

[22]Templin, op. cit., p. 147.

vironment that stresses only limited features of their language potential, they might be at a disadvantage in school and in the world beyond school.[23]

Shaw, one of the children described earlier, has these benefits, Roger, while coming from a wealthy home, lacks family contacts and experience. So do Jennie and Jan. The research of Milner regarding patterns of parent-child interaction seems important here.[24] Striking differences were found in the patterns of family life between first-grade children scoring high and low on language tests. Families of high "scorers" usually had breakfast together, engaged in conversation with the children at mealtime and before school. These children also received more overt affection from significant adults in the home. Milner's study points up the fact that parental attitudes toward children and habits of family life are the really significant factors for language development and they may vary with socioeconomic status.

In an effort to describe how mothers influence language development, Hess and Shipman studied parent teaching styles and found social class differences.[25] Lower-class mothers who had the lowest IQ's and who were poorly educated were the least effective in teaching their children.

What can the school do for Gloria, Roger, and Jennie who lack the intimate parent-child interaction growing out of shared experiences? Certainly the school cannot and should not replace the home. The teacher can, however, provide opportunities for these children to talk with her, and for her to show an interest in their conversation. She must help each child feel that he is important as an individual and that he can make a contribution to the group. Her task includes helping children to appreciate the speech of others, and providing opportunities to handle materials, to talk about them, to listen to the comments of other children, to ask questions, and to express feelings—all a part of learning.

Another Language [*Bilingualism*]. The bilingual child comes from a home in which two languages are spoken or in which the language spoken is different from the language spoken at school. According to this definition, the child from a home in which nonstandard English is spoken may be considered as bilingual. Karen and Kirsten of the group described are not only twins but also come from a home in which another language is spoken. In general the findings indicate that twins lag behind single-born children in language development.[26] To this expected lag in language development of twins must

[23]Loban, op. cit., p. 89.

[24]Esther Milner, "A Study of the Relationships Between Reading Readiness in Grade One School Children and Patterns of Parent-Child Interaction," *Child Develpm.*, 22:2 (1951), pp. 95–112.

[25]R. Hess and Virginia Shipman, "Parents as Teachers," in Celia S. Lavatelli, *Piaget's Theory Applied to an Early Childhood Curriculum* (Boston: American Science and Engineering, Inc., 1970), pp. 59–61.

[26]Ella Day, "The Development of Language in Twins: (I) A Comparison of Twins and Single Children," *Child Develpm.*, 3:3 (1932), pp. 179–190.

be added the complication of an additional language. Danish is spoken in the home along with English. After spending one summer in Denmark, the twins returned to school speaking very little English.

Although few studies have been concerned with the effect of bilingualism on the child's language development, there are examples of confusion that such children experience. Smith reported no delay in the first use of words by eight children in a bilingual environment, but confusion and uncertainty did seem to appear at a later age.[27] Darcey reports that as bilingualism occurs among children of immigrants or other minority groups, it often tends to reduce proficiency in both languages.[28] Hughes and Sanchez call attention to the fact that bilingualism is to be prized rather than decried.[29] The problem is created when the child has a *dual language handicap*. He cannot learn the second language well because he does not know the first language well. There is often the lack of clear concepts to which language symbols may be attached. This lack may probably be a product of a deprived environment.

There are those who recommend patterned drill as the most effective procedure for helping bilingual children. Others favor the "natural" method and hold that young children can acquire the structure of the language with sufficient exposure to a rich vocabulary and interactions with adults that include a complex syntactical model. Lavatelli recommends that a model for language training should incorporate the following features.[30]

1. Provision should be made for some language training in small group sessions in order to facilitate two-way communication between teacher and child.
2. The speech of the teacher should serve as a model in the sessions. Children should be encouraged to use the sentence structures which she is modeling.
3. The process of modeling should be carried on in a "natural conversational manner" during free play activities as well as in small group sessions.
4. The teacher should keep in mind the child's level of linguistic development as well as "the possible contribution of the structure to logical thinking."
5. The environment should be warm, friendly, and supportive.

Travel Experiences. The development of concepts to which symbols of communication can be attached is important in the language development of the young child. For him, this development of concepts is largely one of direct, personal experience. Bean reported that travel and events which broaden the

---

[27]Madorah E. Smith, "A Study of the Speech of Eight Bilingual Children of the Same Family," *Child Develpm.*, 6:1 (1935), pp. 19–25.

[28]Natalie T. Darcey, "A Review of the Literature on the Effects of Bilingualism upon the Measurement of Intelligence," *J. Genet. Psychol.*, 82:1 (1953), pp. 21–57.

[29]Marie Hughes and G. I. Sanchez, *Learning a New Language*, (Washington, D.C.: ACEI, 1958), p. 27.

[30]Celia S. Lavatelli, *Piaget's Theory Applied to an Early Childhood Curriculum* (Boston: American Science and Engineering, Inc., 1970), pp. 77–78.

Figure 15. At the dairy the child sees the cows and watches as they are milked. A friendly adult encourages him to reach out and to talk about what he sees. Field trips have been effective in encouraging language development.

child's experiences are accompanied or followed by increases in vocabulary.[31] While the kindergarten teacher cannot force the growth of language, she can provide experiences and events through which the children can increase their vocabularies. The trips around the neighborhood, to the train, to the fire station, and to the farm; picture books for the child and story books to be read to him; films, filmstrips, and recordings can be provided. For example, referring to the children in Chapter 9, Shaw has frequent trips to the beach and mountains, and hunts and fishes with his father. The twins, Karen and Kirsten, as well as Lisa and Gloria, have few trips in the community.

Olson and Larson report field trips as the most frequently used activity in an experimental curriculum for culturally deprived kindergarten children.

[31]C. H. Bean, "An Unusual Opportunity to Investigate the Psychology of Language," *J. Genet. Psychol.*, 40:2 (1932), pp. 181–202.

"Trips were assumed to be valuable in eliciting linguistic responses from children; language output could not be expected without provision for input. The planning and evaluation experiences relating to field trips provided opportunities for the growth of language facility."[32]

PERSONAL FACTORS. In addition to the environmental factors, there are personal factors which have an influence on the child's language development.

Intelligence. Differences in language development are closely related to the differences that have been found to exist in intellectual development. In the groups described on p. 141, there is the possibility of a wide variation in speech development. Shaw has been identified as a gifted child and Gloria as a superior one. These two seemingly have the ability to learn from their environment and to communicate to others what they have learned.

It is important to remember the limitations regarding intellectual measurement. Growth in language depends also upon other factors in addition to those discussed in this chapter. Children from deprived backgrounds may not have had the opportunities for developing their intellectual potential. According to Almy:[33]

> It may well be that interactions between perceptual and verbal experience, in the period when concepts are being formed, have considerable to do with the kind of general intellective ability the child displays later on. Further evidence on this may come from studies of enrichment of culturally deprived children whose general intellective ability is so often extremely low. These youngsters at preschool level do not appear so much to lack perceptual experience as verbal labels to apply to it.

Studies have shown that intelligence tests may not accurately reveal the potential of the highly creative individual. Getzels and Jackson suggest that the term *giftedness* should be used to include other potentially creative groups besides the children of high IQ.[34]

Sex. In nearly all aspects of language development that have been studied, there seems to be a slight difference in favor of girls. Olson, in comparing the growth curves in language for boys and girls from the same family, found that, age for age, the girls regularly exceeded the boys. He further states that many of the differences may be due to maturity rather than sex.[35] Boys at a given age attain achievements and behavior at about the same rate as somewhat younger

---

[32]J. L. Olson and R. G. Larson, "An Experimental Curriculum for Culturally Deprived Kindergarten Children," *Educ. Leadership*, 22:7 (1965), pp. 557.

[33]Millie Almy, "New Views on Intellectual Development in Early Childhood Education," *Intellectual Development: Another Look* (Washington, D.C.: ASCD, 1964), p. 21.

[34]J. W. Getzels and P. W. Jackson, "Giftedness and Creativity," *Newsletter* (Chicago: University of Chicago, November 1960), pp. 5–6.

[35]W. C. Olson, *Child Development*, 2nd ed. (Boston: D.C. Heath, 1959), p. 155.

girls. Young found sex differences in language development more marked among children of lower socioeconomic levels than among those from superior homes.[36] Templin found differences between the sexes less pronounced.[37] Many believe today that the differences are not due to sex or maturity but to environmental influences.

Health.   Loban found a low but positive correlation between health and language proficiency. He pointed out that the health measures which he used were crude and that the correlation might well be higher.[38]

EDUCATIONAL FACTORS.   If the educational influences can help to make the child's association with language pleasant he will be more likely than otherwise to have a positive attitude toward language.

Effects of Situation.   It was found by Van Alstyne that over half the time preschool children tended not to talk to other children while using certain play materials.[39] Some materials seemed to be more conducive to conversation than others. Play with dolls, blocks, crayons, and clay was accompanied by conversation for a high percentage of the time; painting, using scissors, and looking at books were low in conversation value. McCarthy in reporting this study comments:[40]

> It is interesting, in view of the sex differences previously shown, that the doll-corner activities and dishes, which are typical girl activities, were among the highest in conversation value. It might be concluded that certain differences in language are due to the situation, but it must also be remembered that certain situations may attract children of different levels of language development.

More recently, Crowe recorded the conversation of kindergarten children in nine activities.[41] She found that housekeeping play and group discussion held the greatest potential for language use, in both the amount and maturity of speech. Block play, dancing, and woodworking held least. Crowe suggests that adult participation, a concrete topic of conversation, physical arrangements, and noise seem to influence speech.

THE LANGUAGE PROGRAM.   Some of the characteristics of the spoken language of young children and the factors which influence it have been identi-

[36]F. M. Young, "An Analysis of Certain Variables in a Developmental Study of Language," *Genet. Physchol. Monogr.*, 23:1 (1941), pp. 3–141.

[37]Templin, op. cit., p. 147.

[38]Loban, op. cit., p. 87.

[39]Dorothy Van Alstyne, *Play Behavior and Choice of Play Materials of Preschool Children* (Chicago: Univ. of Chicago Press, 1932).

[40]Dorothea McCarthy, "Language Development in Children," *Manual of Child Psychology*, 2nd ed. (New York: John Wiley and Sons, 1954), p. 595.

[41]E. G. Crowe, "A Study of Kindergarten Activities for Language Development," C. B. Cazden, "The Neglected Situation in Child Language Research and Education," in F. Williams, ed., *Language and Poverty* (Chicago: Markham Publishing Company, 1970).

fied. With an awareness of these, the program can be planned to facilitate the language growth of children. Important elements include the teacher, the climate, and the goals.

Hess and Croft report that children seem to acquire vocabulary and pronunciation of words by imitation and repetition while the grammar seems to be acquired on their own as they learn to speak.[42] It is important then to provide opportunities for children to have much verbal interaction with one another and with adults on a one-to-one basis. The teacher can provide such opportunities as she elaborates and qualifies her answers to childrens' questions. She can read aloud from a variety of materials and make tapes, records, books and pictures available. It is important, however, that the teacher provide time for the child to talk about what he hears and sees.

The Teacher. It is important that the teacher take time to listen to the child. If preparations for the day have been made in advance, the teacher can be free to greet each child as he arrives. Here is an opportunity to practice the social courtesies of greeting, such as, "Good morning" or "Hello." The child, fresh from home, often has news to share. It can be fun for the child to talk to the teacher. It can be frustrating, too, trying to tell the teacher something very important while she is stirring paint, or cutting paper without even a glance in the child's direction, and making only a noncommittal, uninterested reply of "Yes" or "Oh." Perhaps the teacher is busy and doesn't have time at that moment to listen. If so, then she may say to the child, "I am busy, but I will talk with you as soon as I have finished." And she must be very sure to remember her promise and not keep the child waiting too long.

Speech instruction, according to Anderson, begins with the teacher's voice. The tone of her voice, her manner of speaking, and the vocabulary she uses all have an influence on the quality of instruction.[43] Her voice can invite conversation, or discourage it. A harsh, loud voice can irritate and embarrass while a soft, well-modulated voice can help one to be relaxed and comfortable.

The teacher's speech should set a good example in enunciation and pronunciation. It is easy to fall into habits of slovenly speech. The teacher should use the tape recorder and listen to her own speech.

The Climate. The atmosphere of the kindergarten, nursery school, or child development center reflects the attitude of the teacher. The atmosphere should be supportive, one in which a child is free to converse, to enjoy experiences, to use language, to make mistakes, and to correct them.

Lavatelli says that "the child should hear directed at him a wide variety of well formed utterances to which he must make a response."[44] She also suggests that for disadvantaged children there should be some time during the

---

[42]R. D. Hess and Doreen J. Croft, *Teachers of Young Children* (Boston: Houghton Mifflin Company, 1972), pp. 182–184.

[43]P. S. Anderson, op. cit., p. 83.

[44]Butler, op. cit., p. 133.

day when a child can be part of a small group, under the guidance of the teacher, and have an opportunity to listen, to respond and be responded to.[45]

As the teacher works in a relaxed, happy school atmosphere, she keeps in mind certain objectives of the language program for children.

The Goals.   As the teacher works with children she will help each child to accomplish the following:[46]

1. Develop fluency and naturalness in expression. Opportunities for many experiences will introduce new words and provide the child with something to talk about. These, together with the stimulation of an understanding teacher, can help the child gain desired fluency and spontaneity and build a functional vocabulary.

2. Develop the ability to speak distinctly in a pleasant voice with good control both as to volume and tone—a voice free of baby talk and incomplete enunciation, not too high, too loud, or too soft. The teacher may give guidance by such comments as, "I'm sorry, I didn't hear what you said. Tell me again and speak just a little louder, please." Such guidance helps the child realize that "too soft" voices can't be understood and the child is helped to feel adequate and secure enough to speak louder.

3. Form habits of correct usage. Constant criticism can interfere with the fluency and spontaneity of expression. Constructive helpfulness, gauged to the needs of the individual child, is essential. A child, enthusiastically telling about a trip may say, "Jim *had came* to my house." He may be helped by the teacher who listens to the comment, smiles, and repeats, "Jim *had come* to my house."

4. Use language as a social tool. "It is the task of the kindergarten teacher . . . to guide pupils in learning to talk freely and easily, to listen courteously to others, and to acquire habits of using socially accepted phrases such as 'thank you' and 'excuse me.'"[47] The school in which children are helped to develop an awareness of and concern for others offers opportunities for practice. If the teacher sincerely uses the accepted terms in her speech and actions, the children in this environment will use them also. Use of such words without an appreciation of their meaning is futile. The teacher may also use comments such as, "Voices that are too loud bother others. There are voices for the playground and voices for the kindergarten room. We are inside now."

5. Develop the ability to name, describe, and classify objects common in his environment. The teacher may talk with one child alone and give him the opportunity to name what he sees, feels, hears, or smells. Different children may be asked to categorize objects on one, two, or three dimensions: for example, find two green objects, two green circles, two large green circles.[48]

6. Develop the ability to communicate with others. This skill involves not only expressing one's ideas, but understanding what has been said; being able to repeat in one's own words what another has said and being able to respond appropri-

[45]Ibid.

[46]H. A. Greene and W. T. Petty, *Developing Language Skills in the Elementary School*, 2nd ed. (Boston: Allyn and Bacon, 1963), pp. 71–72.

[47]Ibid., p. 67.

[48]Louise M. Berman, ed. *Toward New Programs for Young Children* (College Park, Md.: University of Maryland, 1970), pp. 16–17.

ately to the meaning of another person's statement. The teacher may give directions such as "Lucy, please put the cups on the table."[49] The child may also
be helped in this regard by having the opportunity for retelling a story in his own
words after he has heard it read.

7. Organize his ideas in expression. Often, as he speaks, the child's mind races
ahead and the result is a disorganized comment or story. For example, listen as
Joe was telling about a hunting trip. "We got up early. We ate breakfast—and,
oh! We got dressed in our hunting clothes—and, oh! My mother bought me a new
rain coat and boots." At this point the teacher may say, "You were telling us
about your hunting trip," helping him to get back on the track, to organize his
ideas, and to relate his experiences in proper sequence.

8. Learn about the language. Strickland has identified elements in the field of linguistics which appear highly valuable for younger children and proposes that
development of concepts about language begin in kindergarten. While the concepts may seem formal and meaningless for the kindergarten child, the examples
indicate many opportunities for learning in relation to daily activities. Some of
the concepts and examples, as adapted, follow:[50]

> Language is a system of sounds.
> The patterns of sound convey meaning to those who know the language. (Learn
>   familiar words in another language—e.g., "Thank you.")
> Pitch, stress, and juncture are a part of the sound system of the language and
>   help to convey meaning.
>   (Use same words to convey different messages—e.g., *When* do you expect
>   him? When do you expect *him*?)
> The sounds convey meaning only when put together in patterns of words and
>   sentences.
>   (Help child speak in sentences. Note how meaning and emphasis are in-
>   fluenced by position of words in sentence—e.g., The boy in the yard ate his
>   lunch. The boy ate his lunch in the yard.)
> A language changes; old words may be given new meanings and new uses.
>   Likewise, old words are dropped and new words are coined of old parts to
>   represent new meanings or modifications of old ones.
>   (Note old words in Mother Goose Rhymes—"*fetch* a pail of water."
>   What does it mean today?
>   Note new words, "telstar," "supersonic."
>   Note new meanings for old words, "capsule.")

READING AND THE YOUNG CHILD

As the importance of early learning opportunities to a child's development
has been recognized, interest in early reading has become apparent. There are
those who believe that teaching reading to young children will give them academic advantage in later grades. Austin reports that approximately one fourth

[49]Ibid., pp. 17–20.

[50]Ruth G. Strickland, *The Contribution of Structural Linguistics to the Teaching of Reading, Writing,
and Grammar in the Elementary School* (Bloomington: School of Education, Indiana University, 1963),
pp. 7–9.

Figure 16. Listening to and enjoying stories, handling, using, and loving books can help the child to become interested in learning to read and to know that reading can be fun.

of the school systems maintaining kindergartens offer reading instruction at that level. Half of these systems offered the instruction for selected small groups of children, but one third of these systems taught reading to all of the children in the class.[51]

It is important to examine the proposals for early reading and the effects on children. Doman describes a plan for parents to use in teaching their baby to read, a plan which grew out of his work with brain-injured children. In recommending that the age of two years is the best time to begin and that any parent, willing to go to a "little trouble," can achieve results, Doman overlooks individual differences in both babies and parents.[52] Moore recommends the use of specially designed typewriters in teaching two- to five-year-olds to read.[53]

The Denver Study, a five-year research project, focused on making a comparison of the effectiveness of beginning reading instruction in kindergarten with beginning reading instruction in the first grade. Some conclusions of the researchers follow.[54]

> Beginning reading skills can be taught quite effectively to large numbers of typical kindergarten pupils. . . . The permanence of gains made as a result of being taught beginning reading in the kindergarten depended upon subsequent instruction; . . . and that the early reading program presented no blocks, physical or emotional, to later reading.

Nila B. Smith expresses the point of view of those who do not advocate early formal reading instruction:[55]

> Many studies have been directed toward the proper age for beginning instruction. Whether or not to teach reading to the preschool child is the question in the minds of many people at present. Can preschool children learn to read? Is it desirable for them to do so?
>
> Of course they can learn to read. Both Dr. Durkin and Dr. Almy found that many children read before they come to school. Back in 1926 Terman in his study of gifted children found that over 1 percent of his subjects learned to read before they were 3 years old, and that 2½ percent read before they were 5.
>
> We have plenty of evidence that young children can learn to read. All of us know preschool children who are reading. There is no question in regard to whether or not they *can* read; the main consideration is whether they should be *taught* to read at an early age.

[51]Mary C. Austin, "Current Reading Practices," *Teaching Young Children to Read* (U.S. Office of Education) (Washington, D.C.: U.S. Government Printing Office, 1964), pp. 16–20.

[52]G. Doman, *How to Teach Your Baby to Read* (New York: Random House, 1964).

[53]Maya Pines, "How Three-Year-Olds Teach Themselves to Read and Love It," *Harper's Magazine*, 226:1356 (1963), pp. 58–64.

[54]P. McKee and J. E. Brzeinski, *The Effectiveness of Teaching Reading in Kindergarten,* Cooperative Research Project No. 5-0371 (Denver: Denver Public Schools and the Colorado State Department of Education, 1966), pp. 80–86.

[55]Nila B. Smith, "Trends in Beginning Reading Since 1900," *Teaching Young Children to Read* (United States Office of Education) (Washington, D.C.: U.S. Government Printing Office, 1964), pp. 14–15.

Smith maintains that young children in kindergarten who want to read and are ready to read should be given the help they request. This procedure is quite different from introducing formal reading instruction to all kindergarten children. Smith reports that between 1915 and 1935, investigators found that from 20 to 24 per cent of first grade children were failing because of inability to read.[56] If such large numbers of children failed when taught reading at the age of six years, Smith questions, what would happen if formal reading were taught to all kindergarten pupils today.

Smith has identified certain misconceptions, as adapted below, which are held by those who advocate formal reading instruction for young children:[57]

1. They seem to consider reading as a growth separate and apart from all other growth, a phase of learning that can be worked on whenever the adult is ready. They overlook the fact that reading is an integral part of the total growth and development of the child.
2. They seem to hold an oversimplified concept of the reading process, thinking that when a child can pronounce a printed word he is reading. They forget that pronouncing words is not reading. There are important meanings to be gained from the words.
3. They seem to believe that all children are alike, disregarding individual differences. Some threes, some fours, and some fives can learn to read, but not all of them can. There are differences in ability as well as home environment and experiences— all of which influence a child's readiness for reading.

As one of the areas of the controversy relates to the permanence of early reading gains, it is well to examine the results of some research studies regarding the effect of early instruction on later school achievement.

Keister found that while five-year-olds could acquire reading skills at a normal rate and maintain them through the first grade, the skills seemed to lack permanence, tended to disappear between first and second grades, and the loss was not made up in the following years.[58]

After reviewing research in early reading, Mason and Prater made preliminary conclusions that include the following.[59]

1. When exposed to the same program, younger children make less progress than older ones with similar levels of intelligence.
2. The control of attention is likely to be difficult for young children, and attempts to force learning may lead to emotional reaction.

[56] Nila B. Smith, "Early Reading: Viewpoints," *Child. Educ.*, 42:4 (1965), p. 231.

[57] Ibid., p. 230.

[58] B. U. Keister, "Reading Skills Acquired by Five-Year-Old Children," *Elem. Sch. J.*, 41:8 (1941), pp. 587–596.

[59] G. Mason and Norma Jean Prater, "Early Reading and Reading Instruction," *Elem. English*, 43:5 (1966), pp. 483–488.

As the result of two longitudinal studies, Durkin reports that for the children who were early readers (because of help given at home) the average reading achievement was significantly higher, over as many as six school years, than that of equally bright schoolmates who did not begin reading until they entered first grade.[60] She emphasized, however, that the preschool readers did not always receive appropriate reading instruction once they entered first grade. Findings of the Denver Study indicated that the permanence of early reading gains was dependent upon subsequent reading instruction.

In analyzing the controversy regarding early reading, it is important to distinguish between prereading activities and formal reading instruction. It is also important to note whether formal reading instruction is intended for all children or whether it is recommended for those children who are ready for or are already reading. The evidence seems to indicate that instruction for all five-year-olds on a wholesale basis is questionable and may well be harmful for some children.

Other issues involved in the controversy relate to the nature of reading readiness, the question of when to begin the teaching of reading, and the meaning of the term *formal reading instruction*.

Prereading and Readiness Experiences

Perhaps there is no one educational term more discussed and less understood than *reading readiness*. According to Almy, *readiness* is no longer a fashionable term. Rather, "a concern for the cognitive or, as it is often phrased, with concept development, is widely manifest these days."[61] This statement may well be a correct assessment of the times but the terms *readiness* and *concept development* are not synonymous.

"Readiness," as Krogman explains, "implies a best-time for initiating a specific task situation."[62] Readiness for reading, then, has to do with the "best-time" for beginning reading instruction. Reading instruction, however, involves many tasks or learning situations of varying difficulty. The focus, then, is upon the relationship between the child's particular abilities and the learning opportunities available to him. Durkin says that readiness is still considered as a product of maturation, but a product in relation to a given set of circumstances.[63]

Theories of cognitive development have to do with how the child learns and what the teacher can do to facilitate such learning. There are some who feel that concern with cognitive or intellectual development means a disregard

---

[60]Dolores Durkin, *Teaching Them to Read* (Boston: Allyn and Bacon, Inc., 1970), pp. 71–72.

[61]Almy, op. cit., p. 12.

[62]W. M. Krogman, "Physical Growth as a Factor in the Behavioral Development of the Child," *New Dimensions in Learning* (Washington, D.C.: ASCD, 1963), pp. 15,21.

[63]Durkin, op. cit., p. 38.

for readiness and an acceptance of the practice of pushing the child, thus causing irreparable damage. Hunt says,

> Inasmuch as the optimum rate of intellectual development would mean also self-directing interest and curiosity and genuine pleasure in intellectual activity, promoting intellectual development properly need imply nothing like the grim urgency which has been associated with "pushing" children.[64]

As interpreted by Almy,[65]

> Intelligence, rather than being fixed by genetic factors at birth, emerges as it is nurtured. Each stage of development carries with it possibilities for the acquisition of new abilities, new ways of processing information. Unless each of these abilities is sufficiently exercised as it emerges, it will not develop fully and it will contribute little if at all to the demands of the next stage.

The prereading stage of development, then, carries with it possibilities for the acquisition of new abilities and the processing of new information. The child, having reached a certain stage in his development now has the opportunity to acquire certain visual skills such as looking at the page from left to right, top to bottom, to see likenesses and differences in letters. As he uses books, listens to stories, and helps to dictate stories to the teacher, he is processing information, is learning that printed words have meaning, that they say something. He is attaching the label of reading to the experiences he is having. He matches these experiences to those of having his mother read to him. He is forming a concept of reading. Interpreted this way, there is no conflict between the readiness concept and concern for cognitive development.

Some kindergarten teachers, even today, say they offer a reading readiness program, as if a child could be readied for the process of reading. There are others who believe that reading readiness cannot be developed by means of a program but depends entirely upon maturity. A hands-off policy is advocated, and they believe that aside from attempting to maintain sound healthy bodies, there is little that the teacher or parents can do for the child. These two extremes point up the argument of nature versus nurture, or maturity versus training.

An examination of what is meant by the term *reading readiness* may help the reader understand the distinctions made in this text. A child is ready for reading when his capacities are mature or adequate in relation to the requirements of a specific learning situation, in this instance, learning to read.

In relation to beginning reading there is a sequence of learning situations. For example, in relation to visual discrimination a child may be able to match

[64]J. McV. Hunt, *Intelligence and Experience* (New York: Ronald Press, 1961), p. 363.
[65]Almy, op. cit., p. 13.

colors, without concern for shape or size and is ready to engage in activities involving this ability. This does not necessarily mean, however, that he is ready for the more difficult discrimination required in seeing likenesses and differences in words.

This explanation implies that readiness for reading depends upon both nature and nurture, maturity, and training. Olson uses the equation, "Maturation × Nurture = Development," which may well be applied to readiness for reading.

There are some factors involved in readiness which are wholly dependent on maturation. The teacher cannot say to a child, "focus your eyes" or "coordinate your muscles" and expect such a response. That is impossible. Such development depends upon maturity. When this has been achieved, appropriate experiences may be supplied and the child learns happily and successfully. Olson states, "Synchronization between maturity and opportunity seems to be the safest guide to educational practice."[66]

Durkin reports that "a child's readiness to learn to read . . . is the product of maturation (nature) and of environmental factors (nurture).[67]

It is difficult, if not impossible, to isolate single factors involved in readiness, because of their interrelationship. A child with superior mental ability, rich experiential background, and good language development may not learn to read because of visual difficulties. On the other hand, adequate vision alone cannot insure success in reading. Such physical factors as age, vision, hearing, eye-hand coordination, and general health are considered important. Likewise, a child's concept of his ability to learn to read and his interest in reading affect the progress he will make. The quality of instruction that the child receives is also very important.

A look at these factors seems important here.

AGE. Chronological age has not been found to be a realistic index to readiness. Some children will begin reading at about six years of age. Some children, however, will be ready earlier; some not until later. Durkin reminds us that beginning reading in the first grade, at the age of six, is a product of convention, not of evidence that six years of age is an especially good time to begin reading.

VISION. The young child is usually far-sighted and only gradually do his eyes mature sufficiently for him to maintain them in focus at the distance required for reading. He may be able to see distant objects clearly, but the same object becomes blurred when examined closely at near vision. A child may look at a picture in a book on the table, seeing it clearly, and still have difficulty in looking at the small letters involved in a word.

---

[66]W. C. Olson, op. cit., p. 17, p. 14.

[67]Durkin, op. cit., p. 38.

According to Gesell, a child of five may have trouble in adapting to the blackboard and in making adjustments from far to near and near to far.[68]

Park and Burri found that the percentage of children with vision below 20-20 declined from approximately 50 per cent in the prereading stages to 20 to 35 per cent in the early elementary and junior high school period.[69] Good fusion, stereopsis, and the power to maintain binocular single vision also improve during this period.

One concern in relation to preschool reading has been the harmful effect upon a child's vision. Durkin points out, however, that these early concerns were not supported by research data and were not stated by medical personnel. And the lack of adequate research is still evident. Durkin recommends that until research on this question is available, caution should be exercised. She says that young children who show an interest in reading are probably visually ready for reading. When young children are not interested in reading, one "ought to keep in mind the dearth of facts about the effect of early reading on vision and be cautious."[70]

The kindergarten setting offers many opportunities for experiences that provide visual discrimination and training. Many such activities are used daily, but the teacher is often unaware of their value in readiness for reading. The child's response to these activities suggests his readiness for more complex situations or his need for some less difficult. A few activities are identified here to illustrate the opportunities available as the child plays, uses tools, paints, or looks at books. Note the progression from the simple to the more complex. From such a sequence, the teacher who is alert to the child's needs can select appropriate materials for learning encounters appropriate for each child.

Visual Perception. Choosing colors for painting; choosing colored paper for mounting or cutting; and commenting on clothes children are wearing are activities usually included in centers for young children. These offer opportunities for making gross discriminations.

The teacher may say, "Jane has a new *blue* sweater. It is just like Helen's. I have a blue bracelet. Everybody who is wearing something blue, stand up."

Games may be used in which matching involves only one color. Each child may be given a scrap of red paper (block, ball) and asked to find one other thing that is the same color as his paper and bring it to the teacher.

Objects may be matched according to two or three attributes. The teacher may say, "Find a red ball." "Find a little red ball."

Pictures, flannel figures, or shapes may be used. Place a triangle on the flannel board. From several shapes given to him, ask the child to find the shape,

---

[68]A. Gesell, Frances Ilg, and G. E. Bullis, *Vision: Its Development in Infant and Child* (New York: Paul B. Hoeber, 1948), p. 289.

[69]G. E. Park and Clara Burri, "Eye Maturation and Reading Difficulties," *J. Educ. Psychol.,* 34:9 (1943), pp. 535–546.

[70]Durkin, op. cit., pp. 50–51.

Figure 17. The kindergarten setting offers many opportunities for visual discrimination, training in visual perception, and the development of eye-hand coordination—all important skills in learning to read.

a triangle, just like the one on the board, and put his beside it. Other attributes such as size and color may be introduced with comments such as, "Find the largest red circle."

Activities involving letters and words may begin with showing the child his name on his locker or painting and later matching it with his name on an experience chart; or noting words that begin alike in the recipe for making apple sauce.

Visual Recall. Looking at pictures accompanying a story, remembering what was seen, and talking about the picture often occur in situations with children. The teacher may use question such as: "Look and see what else we need to make the cookies." She may use the simple game of "hide and seek" in the circle. The children close their eyes while the teacher indicates the child who is to leave the circle and hide. Children open their eyes and the teacher says, "Who is missing?"

The same game may be used with cards on which the children's names have been written.

Eye-Hand Coordination. Working with puzzles; rolling, throwing, catching balls; manipulating clay; painting; and hammering nails into wood offer opportunities in developing eye-hand coordination. The child can be helped to acquire other visual skills, such as looking at the picture book from front to back and top to bottom and the pictures from left to right across the page. Such skills can be acquired most effectively as the child examines picture books and observes the book as stories are read to him. Experience charts, records of trips, lists of committee responsibilities all may be used in developing the left to right eye-movement.

One child in first grade had developed the habit of looking at words from right to left. This was observed in the following situation: The sentence—"Here is the dog"—was on the board. The teacher gave the pointer to Herb and asked him to read it. He moved the pointer from *dog* to *Here* as he read the sentence. When asked to find the word *dog*, he pointed to *Here*; and to *dog* when asked to find *Here*. Visual examinations by competent specialists failed to reveal any difficulty. The doctors reported that the child had learned to look from right to left. A parent conference revealed that in kindergarten Herb had done many exercises for visual discrimination. Evidently these had not been closely supervised and he had found the picture that was different by beginning at the right side of the page. Well-meaning teachers who use formal readiness material without proper supervision may be encouraging the development of harmful habits.

In addition to the incidental situations in the kindergarten, which may be utilized by the teacher, various training programs have been designed to develop perceptual abilities.[71,72]

[71]Marianne Frostig, *Frostig Program for the Development of Vision Perception* (Chicago: Follett Publishing Co., 1964).

[72]*Fostering Growth in Perceptual Skills,* (Darien, Conn.: 1970). CCM Threshold Learning, Inc.

HEARING.   As children live the first five years of their lives, they hear many sounds about them, but by the time they enter kindergarten there are wide differences in their experiences with sounds and their awareness of sounds. Some children have listened to frogs croak, cows moo, sheep bleat, and dogs bark; others recognize the sounds of planes, trains, and trucks. For some there have been poetry, stories, and music. Others have had no one to share with them the fun of hearing different sounds or noises.

Some children are handicapped by faulty hearing, while others have normal hearing acuity but have not learned to discriminate differences in sounds. In either case, this deficiency in auditory acuity can be responsible for continued baby talk or faulty pronunciation. If a child does not hear the difference between two words, it will be difficult for him to distinguish between their printed symbols. The teacher should be alert to detect hearing difficulties, make adjustments for the child, and recommend correction to the parents.

Before learning to read, the majority of children will profit from learning about sounds with special reference to language. This should not be interpreted to mean formal phonetic drill but rather opportunities for experiences by which children become aware of sounds, and the ways in which sounds differ and are alike, and become able to discriminate, identify, and match sounds. Such experiences can offer beginning instruction in phonics. For example:

Sounds can be loud or soft—"Turn up the record player so that the record will be a little louder. I can't hear it." Or, "How do you feel when you hear this music?" "It is very soft and slow. I feel sleepy." Or, "Talk softly. The baby [doll] is asleep."

Sounds can be high or low. Match tones in music. The teacher strikes a note on the piano. She says to the child, "Find a sound that is low," or vice versa. In singing, call attention to the way in which the song goes up and down.

Sounds can be made by people, animals, and things. Ask the children to close their eyes, listen, and name the sounds they hear. Make a recording of the children's voices. Ask them to listen and identify the voices. Make a recording of sounds heard on the playground. Ask children to identify a sound and decide if it was made by a person, animal, or thing. Show pictures of animals and ask children to make a sound appropriate for each. Ask children to find a person, animal, or thing in the classroom that can make a sound. Listen to the sounds of each.

Sounds can be the same. Use poetry containing words that rhyme; stories with initial consonant sounds, such as choo choo, chug chug. The teacher may say, "milk," and ask the child, "Can you think of a word that begins with the same sound as milk?" Play a musical pattern on the piano or bells, such as *do do sol*. This may be done by child or teacher and the child repeats it.

OTHER PHYSICAL FACTORS.   The general health of the child and his nutritional status influence his energy level. A child who has frequent colds and is absent often must continually make adjustments to school. He may get settled and begin to feel comfortable with the group, then he is ill and out of school for four days. Upon his return he finds that the group is not as familiar as it was last week. Two days after his return he feels secure again. This happy state lasts only a few days and the child is out again and the process must be repeated.

Muscular control and development affects what the child can do. Jennie, you recall, has "jerky" muscular movements and is afraid to climb the jungle gym. This inability to climb successfully further limits her social contacts with other children.

EMOTIONAL-SOCIAL FACTORS. It is easier for a child who is emotionally secure in the school situation to learn to read. He is free to devote his attention to the job at hand. Jean, a six-year-old, returning home from her first day in first grade expressed this truth. Bounding through the front door, she called, "Mommie, a little girl cried at school today." For Jean, who had been so eager to go to school, the little girl's tears had evidently been quite a surprise. Her mother asked, "Why did the little girl cry?" Jean thought for a moment, then replied, "I guess she hadn't been to kindergarten. She didn't know her mother would come at 12 o'clock and everything would be all right."

The nursery school, kindergarten, or children's center can make a great contribution to the social and emotional adjustment of the child. He can learn to feel secure in a situation away from home with adults other than his parents. He can learn that the teacher is friendly, that everything is all right. The child can learn that groups can be friendly too—he can be a member and speak, sing, listen, or sit in the group! He can begin to direct his own behavior, to follow directions, to select and use materials, to assume responsibility for jobs in the room. A child lacking in this confidence and security is seldom ready for reading. It is difficult, if not impossible, to teach a crying child, or a child on the verge of tears, to learn to read.

Of the children described in the kindergarten, remember Jennie, who is not permitted to cry at home but cries often at kindergarten; Gloria who needs adult attention; the twins, who have each other; and Shaw, who continues to try, even in difficult situations. Who can doubt that emotional-social factors are involved here, as in every group of five-year-olds?

No book can tell you specifically what to do for these children. Perhaps for a time Jennie needs the opportunity to cry, to experience this natural outlet for her feelings. But since crying is not accepted at home, she needs to learn other outlets. Because she has good ability she may be helped to use words: "Please don't do that"; "I don't like it." When she can't have her way, she can be helped to find a substitute. The teacher can, while providing individual activities, also arrange for her to play and become friendly with one child, and gradually increase the size of the group to help her overcome her fear of children. This last suggestion may also prove one way of helping Gloria and the twins to include other children in their lives—not forcing them immediately into the total group but gradually building readiness for group activities, increasing slowly the number of children with whom they become involved.

Mental and Intellectual Factors.   Learning to read involves the ability to see and hear and other factors which have been identified, but it is more than these. It involves learning to associate meaning with symbols and to interpret what is read. Such skill requires the intellectual capacity and the mental maturity necessary to reason, to form meaningful associations, and to remember word forms. In one of the earlier studies, Morphett and Washburne found that among the first grade children studied, those with mental ages between 6.5 and 7.0 years profited most from the initial reading instruction.[73] The degree of mental maturity required for success in beginning reading depends to some extent on the way in which beginning reading is taught, the materials used and the child's interest in learning to read. Gates and Bond, however, report a low correlation of mental age with reading achievement. They conclude that the optimum time for beginning reading depends not entirely upon the child but also on the reading instruction he receives. They indicate that the general and social returns to the child from learning to read are important also.[74]

There appears to be a positive relationship between mental development and language development. Factors involved in the development of speech were discussed earlier in this chapter. Language is mentioned here to indicate the relationship to reading. It is oral language that relates the child's experience to the abstract word symbols. Language development is also related to home and experiential background. The child who has trips and visits in the community, associations with people, and knowledge of things around him will probably have more words in his vocabulary and more things to talk about. Almy found a significant, positive relationship between success in beginning reading and the child's experiences in kindergarten, in play, and with adults which involved being read to and looking at books, papers, and magazines.[75]

The child's capacity for learning to read is also influenced by his own concept of his ability, which is influenced by his previous experiences. Some present views of intellectual development assume that the position a child has reached indicates the intellectual progress he has already made, but the prediction of future development depends on knowledge of the experiences in store for the child.[76]

Attention Span.   In learning to read the child needs to be able to focus his attention on the specific instructional task.

A student in recording an anecdotal record wrote, "tension span," rather than "attention span." Perhaps in reality this was not an error. Tensions do build up and the span indicates the length of time before they interfere with the

---

[73]Mabel V. Morphett and C. Washburne, "When Should Children Begin to Read?" *Elem. Sch. J.,* 31:7 (1931). pp. 496–503.

[74]A. I. Gates and G. L. Bond, "Reading Readiness: A Study of Factors Determining Success and Failure in Beginning Reading," *Teach. Coll. Rec.,* 37:8 (1936), pp. 679–685.

[75]Millie C. Almy, *Children's Experiences Prior to First Grade and Success in Beginning Reading* (New York: Teachers College, Columbia University, 1949).

[76]Almy, *Intellectual Development: Another Look,* p. 13.

child's ability to attend. The attention span indicates the length of time for which a child can focus his thoughts on, listen to, or concentrate on a given topic. Olson states that it has been difficult to determine the attention span of children at different ages, but there is rather general agreement that the attention span of children for toys and play materials increases with age. The range from 7 to 20 minutes has been identified for the preschool period. Individual differences are great and the time seems to vary with the appropriateness of the material for the age.[77]

Again there is the relationship between maturity and experience. The kindergarten can provide opportunities for the child to focus his attention on a topic. It is important, however, that the content and length of time expected be appropriate for the maturity and the interests of the child.

In summary the following statements regarding readiness are important.

1. Readiness refers to a combination of abilities and understandings. It is not a single package consisting of specific abilities in specified quantities.
2. Readiness can not be determined by "a single-factor criterion."[78] There is a very close relationship between getting ready to read and reading.
3. Readiness indicates "a relationship between the abilities and understandings of a child and the type and quality of reading instruction that will be offered."[79] Both nature and nurture are involved.

Teaching Reading

One of the questions often raised in regard to teaching reading is when the instruction should begin. Durkin points out that there is no single, unequivocal answer.[80] There are many differences among children of the same chronological age and these must be considered in planning for reading instruction.

The time for beginning reading depends upon both the child's capacities and interest, and the type of reading instruction available. Rather than concern for the time to begin reading, the problem becomes one of assessing readiness and providing instructional opportunities that "provide the best match for the capacities and interests of the children to be taught."[81] More time needs to be spent considering "how to begin" rather than arguing about when the instruction should begin.

The term *reading instruction* does not necessarily mean formal instruction—a situation in which all the children are taught the same prescribed material

---

[77]W. C. Olson, op. cit., p. 95.

[78]Durkin, op. cit., p. 69.

[79]Ibid.

[80]Ibid., p. 58.

[81]Ibid., p. 43.

> or crayon. Often the announcement is made while the child's effort is expended
> in balancing the block rather than listening.
>
> d. Give explanations simply and in well-organized sequence.

4. Set a good example of attention. A teacher who is preoccupied with her own problems, such as writing a note or getting a drink of water while a recording is being played, does not emphasize the importance of listening. "A teacher who looks attentively into the face of the child who is talking, listens closely to what he is saying, tries to understand his exact meaning, however poorly phrased, and gives him the most thoughtful reply she is capable of, will hold that child's attention better than any device that can be suggested."[89]

5. Create a relaxed, happy atmosphere and relationship among the children and between them and yourself. (See pp. 57–81.) A child who is relaxed and free from emotional strain can listen more easily than the child who is uneasy, hostile, or afraid.

6. Help the child to develop an awareness of sounds, the sounds he hears every day. The teacher may begin by calling attention to types of sounds such as those of nature, or the traffic, or human sounds. She may say to the children, "Close your eyes. Listen carefully and tell me what you hear." They may identify the sounds and describe them as loud, soft, close, far away, sharp, and so on.

7. Provide many opportunities for a wide variety of meaningful listening experiences. There should be listening for pleasure, appreciation, and information. The teacher may use stories, poetry, records, directions, tapes, musical instruments, television, radio, and conversation with adults and other children.

8. Arrange opportunities for children to listen for certain purposes such as answering questions, solving riddles, completing rhymes, putting ideas in sequence, identifying words which do not rhyme, and detecting irrelevant sentences.[90]

WRITING

A nursery school teacher exclaimed in shocked tones, "Writing! Why the nursery school has nothing to do with writing!" Perhaps she was thinking in terms of formal instruction in writing, or perhaps she did not recognize the opportunities available for developing an awareness of writing and its values.

Before discussing when writing begins and the opportunities for beginning, it is important to emphasize the why of writing. The purpose of writing is to communicate or to express an idea. This purpose is so often lost in the beginning stages of practice. Handwriting is a tool, a means to an end. With this purpose in mind, one may examine the beginnings of writing, which occur long before the child takes pencil in hand to write.

The child scribbles and draws pictures. He can deliver or receive simple notes, invitations, or letters. He may dictate individually or participate as the group dictates and the teacher writes captions for pictures, experience charts,

---

[89]Monroe, op. cit., p. 178.

[90]P. C. Burns, Betty L. Broman, and Alberta L. Lowe, *The Language Arts in Childhood Education*, 2nd ed. (Chicago: Rand McNally and Company, 1971), pp. 71–73.

Figure 20. Manuscript writing is recommended for use with young children. Individual guidance in writing is given the child at the time he asks and is ready for it. The amount of actual writing will depend upon the child's experiences and interest, his intellectual, physical, and emotional maturity.

plans, invitations, thank-you notes, charts about pets, experiments, or some other phase of group interest.

At home the child has had the fun of receiving a letter addressed to him. In reply he has scribbled a note to Grandmother, often talking as he writes. The teacher offered to write the name for four-year-old Mary on her letter. The child replied, "You don't need to write it. I can do it. Here it is." (She pointed to a penciled scribble.) That signature sufficed for a while, but there came a time in nursery school when the scribble wasn't sufficient. Another child claimed Mary's picture, the one she had painted at the easel. The teacher said, "Next time, I'll write your name on the picture. Then we will know it is yours." Writing was important now—to communicate to others her name.

For a time Mary made no attempt to write her own name, but each time she asked the teacher to do it for her. She became aware that her name was written in other places too—her locker, her books, her sweater, and that there were other names that belonged to other children. *Such awareness also contributes to readiness for reading.* She learned that when the teacher wanted to tell Mother about a trip or something else at nursery school, sometimes she used the telephone, but sometimes she wrote her a note, either by hand or on the typewriter. The teacher said, "This is a message I have written to your mother."

Along with the experiences which helped to establish a need for writing, the child used clay, finger paint, easel paints and brushes, blocks, crayons, hammers and nails, puzzles, paste, and many other media. Through these experiences she was doing exercises that involved arm and finger movement, eye-hand coordination, and muscular control, all of which are essential to learning to write. Mary had these experiences in nursery school. For some children, these experiences with writing do not come in the nursery school or Head Start but are delayed until kindergarten or even first grade.

Anderson has identified three kinds of experiences that contribute to writing readiness.[91]

1. Manipulative experiences are planned to strengthen the muscles used in writing and to gain control over the writing tools.
2. Many activities are planned to increase the child's vocabulary.
3. Practice activities are related to the basic movements of writing, usually beginning at the chalkboard.

The amount of actual writing will depend on the child's experiences and interest, his intellectual, physical, and emotional maturity. Actual writing begins with attempts at writing letters, usually the letters in the child's name. The letters written with pencil, crayon, chalk, or paint will probably be of varying size, scattered over the page with little evidence of fine motor control. As this control develops the child can use smaller spaces and letters.

Formal writing instruction is not included in nursery school and is not usually undertaken in kindergarten. Individual guidance is given the child at the time he asks and is ready for it. His purposes will suggest the content. Following are some suggestions for guiding children who indicate readiness.

Materials

Provide large sheets (preferably 18 × 24) of unlined paper, such as newsprint, for the child to use. He may write with crayons, chalk, or pencil. If pencils are used it is easier for most children to use pencils with large, soft leads. As the child shows evidence of maturity and increased muscular control, fold the paper once in the middle for a crease, then smooth it out. He may write his name in the top and the bottom. Later, he may use the crease as the line on which to write the letters. After the child manages this easily, the paper may be folded into quarters.

Type of Writing

Manuscript writing (sometimes called print-script[92]) is recommended for use with young children because

1. Letter forms are based largely on circles and straight lines which require only simple strokes. This makes writing easier for the child who is just gaining skill

---

[91]Anderson, op. cit., pp. 178–179.
[92]Ibid., p. 176.

in the use of the small finger muscles and he is soon able to use writing for communicative purposes.

2. Letter forms more closely resemble printed forms than do the cursive script letters.
   The writing helps to encourage and reinforce beginning reading and the child is
   not confused by two types of writing.

Manuscript writing should be distinguished from the other types of writing
in use. It is often referred to as printing. While some of the letter forms are the
same as printing, others are different. Below are listed samples of writing. Note
differences in a, g, t, y.

Manuscript **and get yes**

Print   **and get yes**

All capitals **AND GET YES**

Cursive script *and get yes*

In writing children's names, capital letters are used by many kindergarten
teachers because they are all one size, as **TOM**. The child does not have to make
the adjustment in writing between upper and lower case letters. First grade
teachers sometimes complain because children coming from kindergarten use
the capital letters only, and it is necessary for them to change to the manuscript forms. One teacher tried using the manuscript forms with kindergarten
children. Lockers and other labels were done in manuscript. When a child
asked for help with his name or a word, it was written in manuscript. The
teacher used upper and lower case letters, but no attempt was made to have the
child use them. Some children were able to use "tall and small letters," such as
the name **Jack**. On the other hand, a child might write **JACK**, making no
difference in the height of the letters but using the manuscript forms. As the
child gained in muscular control, he began to use both sizes of letters and
gradually reduced their sizes.

Sometimes there was the comment, "That's not the way my mother writes
my name." The teacher replied, "There are different ways to write. This is the
writing we use in kindergarten." Some children, however, had not been taught
to write with only capital letters, and for them to begin with the manuscript
forms eliminated one type of writing.

Explain to parents the writing forms that are used. It may be a good idea to
provide a manuscript alphabet for them. If letter samples are displayed for reference by the children, they should be placed conveniently in the room at the
child's eye level.

Reversals

As the young child writes, one often notices that letters or numbers are
reversed, as **Ƨ** or **S**. The letters in a word may be written correctly but in a
reversed sequence, such as **nhoJ** for **John**. Such errors are common and are
often indicative of inexperience in writing from left to right, limited visual

memory as to how the number, letter, or word should look, and lack of mature eye-hand coordination. Watch the child as he writes. The right-handed child who has not yet learned to begin at the left side of the paper may put his pencil down at the extreme right side of the paper. There is no room to go to the right, so he writes to the left and as a result, **nhoↃ** . This is not strange, nor necessarily indicative of visual difficulty. It does indicate, however, that he needs guidance in establishing the left to right sequence.

As children practice and use writing, with proper guidance, such reversals usually disappear. If they persist, it may be advisable for the child to be referred for a visual examination.

Handedness

Theories regarding handedness appear to be conflicting and this confusion is reflected in practice. One theory holds that handedness is determined by cerebral dominance inherent in the child, while another takes the position that the child is born with no preference but learns to favor one hand over the other. If one accepts the first theory, then the teacher would not interfere with the child's hand preference. According to the second theory, the child can be taught to use his right hand without strain but this should be done before habits are formed that must be broken at a later time.

Olson states that "Perhaps the teaching profession has been oversold through an earlier literature which often painted the dire effects of handedness on speech and emotion."[93] Consequently, the child has been allowed to select the hand which he prefers to use. According to present thinking, this is probably wise.

The teacher, however, may sometimes permit the child to become left-handed accidentally. Some children, upon entering nursery school or kindergarten have not yet developed a hand preference, and as they begin to work with materials, may inadvertently use the left hand. The teacher can suggest, "Try using the scissors in your right hand." If the child makes the transfer easily, well and good. If he persists in using his left hand, it is probably wise not to insist that he change.

By writing the child's name in the left hand corner of the paper instead of the right the teacher can give the child a clue as to where to begin to write. Such procedure can also help the child in developing the "left to right" skill needed in reading.

If the child shows a decided preference for his left hand, the teacher needs to help him make necessary adjustments in the position of the paper and pencil or crayon. It is not necessary for the left-handed child to write in a cramped position with pencil pointing toward the right. The paper should be in front of the child, parallel to the edge of the table but slightly to the left of the center of his body. The pencil, crayon, or chalk should point in the direction opposite that of the right-handed child.

[93]W. C. Olson, op. cit., p. 88.

Most children, by the end of kindergarten, will regard writing as a means of communication and will be able to write their names.[94] There will be wide variations, however, as with all skills, because of the quality of the program and the teacher, as well as the child and his background.

TEACHER INVENTORY

The confident teacher of young children possesses certain information important to the child's development in the language arts. Anderson has developed a self-evaluation form for language teachers, a partial inventory that may be used in directing efforts toward improving one's understanding, knowledge, and skills. An adaptation of the form follows.[95]

Do I know
how children master language before coming to school?
how language instruction fits into the school day?
books that should be read to children?
how to share a picture book with little children?
how to direct children in a simple verse choir?
how to help a left-handed child learn to write well?
why I teach handwriting as I do?
why it is important to listen to children?

Can I
select and purchase books intelligently for a center for young children?
hold children's attention as I read or tell a story?
involve children in dramatic play and creative dramatics?
teach a finger play to a child and explain its importance to his parents?
read poetry well?
use manuscript (print-script) writing?
write legibly so as not to be embarrassed when writing a note to a parent?

If some of the answers are "no," it is suggested that you read carefully the discussion and practice the suggestions found in Chapters 11 and 12.

FOREIGN LANGUAGES

Americans are becoming increasingly aware of the importance of languages in communication and understanding between nations in the world today. Recognition of these facts has resulted in a heightened interest in teaching foreign languages to young children. To achieve this end a native, English-speaking child is given instruction in a foreign language for short periods of time spaced throughout the school week. Questions relating to the teaching of foreign languages include the query related to *when* the instruction begins. Carroll reports that research does not clearly indicate exactly when instruction

---

[94]Anderson, op. cit., pp. 173–174.
[95]Ibid., pp. 8–9.

in a foreign language should begin.[96] Penfield, a neurologist, states, "The time to begin what might be called a general schooling in secondary languages, in accordance with the demands of brain physiology, is between the ages of 4 and 10."[97] According to his statement, then, the language might be introduced as early as nursery school and as late as perhaps the fifth grade.

The time to begin language instruction depends also upon the goals of the language program. The early years can be important ones in developing an appreciation for and desirable attitudes toward other people, which can be accomplished in a variety of ways. If organized instruction is contemplated one should raise questions regarding the use of time and funds. "Skill in the English language is more important for American pupils than skill in a foreign language. . . . A foreign language program is not justified in the elementary school if it encroaches on pupil progress in the areas of the school's basic responsibilities."[98]

If, after reviewing the evidence, the decision is made to teach a foreign language to young children, there are other important questions yet to be answered.

Andersson lists criteria to be considered in selecting a teacher of foreign languages for young children.

1. The teacher should be well acquainted with the prevailing philosophy of and practice in the education of young children. She must be genuinely fond of and effective in working with children.
2. The teacher should possess a thorough knowledge of and enthusiasm for the language. Young children learn so easily by imitation, it is important that they have a good model to imitate.[99]

Another issue to be faced is that of making a choice among the many languages as to the one to be taught. In locations near the borders and adjacent to countries where other languages are spoken, the decision is not difficult. Where no such need is apparent, the choice may be influenced by other factors such as the availability of teachers, the social and economic need and cultural development.[100]

If another language is introduced in the kindergarten, then it is important to consider how the language should be taught.

Penfield recommends "the mother's method," the direct method of teaching language which is employed in the home. There, language for the child is

---

[96]J. B. Carroll, "Foreign Languages for Children—What Research Says," *Nat. Elem. Prin.,* 39:6 (1960), pp. 12–15.

[97]W. Penfield and L. Roberts, *Speech and Brain-Mechanisms* (Princeton, N.J.: Princeton Univ. Press, 1959), p. 255.

[98]The Educational Policies Commission, *Contemporary Issues in Elementary Education* (Washington, D.C.: NEA, 1960), p. 13.

[99]T. Andersson, *The Teaching of Foreign Languages in the Elementary School* (Boston: D. C. Heath, 1953), p. 43.

[100]Elizabeth Henson, "What About Teaching a Second Language to Elementary School Children?" *Child. Educ.,* 34:8 (1958), pp. 367–370.

only a means to an end, not an end in itself. "When he learns about words he is learning about life, learning to get what he wants, learning to share his own exciting ideas with others, learning to understand wonderful fairy tales and exciting facts about trains and trucks and animals and dolls."[101]

According to this point of view, then, there should be no question of teaching the child of this age to read or write in the foreign language. The oral-aural method of instruction is encouraged. A child first learns a foreign language orally as he does his own language.[102]

Some suggestions for teaching a foreign language to young children include the following:

1. The language experiences should be those which can be used in daily living. Translate as much as possible of the new language into action. Greetings, dramatizations, songs, nursery rhymes, role playing, and games may all be used effectively. The use of familiar experiences and everyday activities for games and dramatizations help to make them more meaningful. Avoid having children answer questions or recite in chorus since it is difficult to hear whether or not individual children are pronouncing words correctly.
2. Keep vocabulary of foreign language in relation to the spoken English of the child. A word should not be introduced in the foreign language until it is first a part of the child's vocabulary.
3. Create visual impressions of how the person who speaks the foreign language acts or behaves. Suggestions include the following:
   a. Invite a native speaker to visit class.
   b. Visit a home or center where the language is spoken natively.
   c. Use films.
4. Create a "climate of sound" in which the child hears foreign words spoken correctly. It is important that children use their learnings throughout the day.

Research findings can be used by groups in deciding whether or not to introduce foreign language instruction in the kindergarten. However, it should not be undertaken unless there is reasonable certainty that the teaching can be effective as evaluated by the criteria described.

The importance of the language arts and the communicative skills of speaking, listening, reading, and writing throughout the formative preschool period have been discussed. It is during these years that the child is rapidly learning the foundations of the communicative skills which are so crucial to later development in the language arts. Suggested language arts activities, materials, and content suitable for inclusion in the curriculum of good schools for young children are presented in Chapter 12.

Suggested Activities

1. Listen to and record the speech of three four-year-old children for a period of fifteen minutes each. Compare as to the total number of words spoken, the number of

[101]Penfield, op. cit., p. 254.

[102]O. E. Perez, *Spanish in Florida Elementary Schools* (Tallahassee: Florida State Department of Education, 1960), pp. i–iii.

different words spoken, the length of the sentences used, the interests revealed, and consonant sounds which were mispronounced. Identify possible reasons for similarities or differences. Do the same for three disadvantaged children of the same age. Compare findings.

2. On the basis of your observation of the children's speech, plan a language learning activity for one of the children. Use the activity with the child. Evaluate.

3. Observe in a kindergarten. Note activities and experiences used to help the child understand that "writing is communicating."

4. Observe a kindergarten teacher and note the ways by which she gained the attention of the group of children.

5. Observe a total group situation in the kindergarten. Identify children who had difficulty in listening. Discuss possible causes of the difficulty.

6. Practice manuscript writing. Write a note to a friend using this type of writing.

7. Record an experience story dictated by a child. Transfer the story to chart paper.

Related Readings

Anderson, P. S. "Speech and Listening," *Language Skills in Elementary Education*, 2nd ed. New York: Macmillan, Inc., 1972, pp. 57–118.

Becenti, Mabeth. "Children Who Speak Navajo," *Young Children*, 25:3 (1970), pp. 141–142.

Broman, Betty L. "The Spanish-Speaking Five-Year-Old," *Child. Educ.*, 48:7 (1972), pp. 362–364.

Brzeinski, J. E., and Howard, W. "Early Reading—How, Not When!" *Reading Teacher*, 25:3 (1972), pp. 239–242.

Cazden, C. B. "Studies of Early Language Acquisition," *Child. Educ.*, 46:3 (1969), pp. 127–131.

Childhood Education. "Valuing Diversity in Language," *Child. Educ.*, 46:3 (1969), entire issue.

Connell, Donna. "Auditory and Visual Discrimination in Kindergarten," *Elem. English*, 45:1 (1968), pp. 51–54.

Cowe, Eileen. "The Beginnings of Writing as an Extension of Thinking and Talking," *Elem. English*, 49:1 (1972), pp. 68–69.

Cratty, B. J. *Perceptual and Motor Development in Infants and Children*. New York: Macmillan, Inc., 1973.

DeHart, Ellen. "What's Involved in Being Able to Read?" *Young Children*, 23:4 (1968), pp. 202–210.

Deutsch, M. "The Role of Social Class in Language Development and Cognition," H. Passow, ed. *Education of the Disadvantaged*. New York: Holt, Rinehart and Winston, 1965.

Durkin, Dolores. *Teaching Young Children to Read*. Boston: Allyn and Bacon, 1972.

———. "A Language Arts Program for Pre-First Grade Children: Two-year Achievement Report," *Reading Research Quarterly*, 5 (Summer 1970), pp. 534–565.

Eisenson, Jon, and Mardel Ogilvie. *Speech Correction in the Schools*, 3rd ed. New York: Macmillan, Inc., 1971

Enstrom, E. A., and Doris Enstrom. "Signs of Readiness," *Elem. English*, 48:2 (1971), pp. 215–220.

————. "In Print Handwriting: Preventing and Solving Reversal Problems," *Elem. English*, 46:6 (1969), pp. 759–764.

Englehardt, Elizabeth. "A Pre-Reading Program," *Reading Teacher*, 23:6 (1970), pp. 535–538.

Enzmann, A. M. "A Look at Early Reading," *Reading Teacher*, 24:7 (1971), pp. 616–620.

Freshour, F. W. "Beginning Reading: Parents Can Help," *Reading Teacher*, 25:6 (1972), pp. 513–516.

Gamsky, N. R., and Faye W. Lloyd. "A Longitudinal Study of Visual Perceptual Training and Reading Achievement," *J. Educ. Research*, 64:10 (1971), pp. 451–454.

Ilg, Frances L. "The Child from Three to Eight with Implications for Reading," Belen C. Mills. *Understanding the Young Child and His Curriculum*. New York: Macmillan, Inc., 1972, pp. 315–323.

Jersild, A. T. "Handedness," *Child Psychology*, 6th ed. Englewood Cliffs, N.J.: Prentice-Hall, Inc., 1968, pp. 156–160.

————. "Language Development, Perceptual Development," *Child Psychology*, 6th ed. Englewood Cliffs, N.J.: Prentice-Hall, Inc., 1968, pp. 414–442.

Keislar, E. R., and J. D. McNeil. "Oral and Non-Oral Methods of Teaching Reading," *Educ. Leadership*, 25:8 (1968), pp. 761–764.

Kelley, Marjorie, and M. D. Chen. "An Experimental Study of Formal Reading Instruction at the Kindergarten Level," *J. of Educ. Research*, 60:5 (1967), pp. 224–229.

Landry, D. L. "The Neglect of Listening," *Elem. English*, 46:5 (1969), pp. 599–605.

Laurita, R. E. "Reversals: A Response to Frustrations," Reading Teacher, 25:1 (1971), pp. 45–51.

LaConte, Christine. "Reading in the Kindergarten: Fact or Fantasy?" *Elem. English*, 47:3 (1970) pp. 382–385.

Mood, Darlene. "Reading in the Kindergarten? A Critique of the Denver Study," *Educ. Leadership*, 24:5 (1967), pp. 339–403.

Moroney, Anne S., J. M. Wepman, and Sarah K. Hass. "Developmental Speech Inaccuracy and Speech Therapy in the Early School Years," *Elem. School J.*, 70:4 (1970), pp. 219–224.

Smith, Dora V. "Trends in Elementary School Language Arts Today," *Elem. English*, 49:3 (1972), pp. 326–334.

Smith, Mildred B. "Reading for the Culturally Disadvantaged," *Educ. Leadership*, 22:6 (1965), pp. 398–403. Also in Belen C. Mills. *Understanding the Young Child and His Curriculum*. New York: Macmillan, Inc., 1972, pp. 323–331.

Vernon, J. J. "Effects of Childhood Bilingualism," Part 1, *Elem. English*, 39:2 (1962), pp. 132–143; Part 2, *Elem. English*, 39:4 (1962), pp. 358–366.

Verdun, Trione. "Children Bring a Language to School," *Instructor*, 81:7 (1972), pp. 52–53.

Vukelich, Carol, and I. Beattie. "Teaching Reading in the Kindergarten: A Review of Recent Studies," *Child. Educ.* 48:6 (1972), pp. 327–329.

Wanat, S. F. "Language Acquisition: Basic Issues," *Reading Teacher*, 25:2 (1972), pp. 142–147.

Weiser, Margaret. "Awareness—One Key to Reading Readiness," *Young Children*, 25:6 (1970), pp. 340–344.

Growth Through Language Activities

Chapter 12

The child develops skill in the language arts as he participates in various experiences and activities. One activity can contribute to growth in several of the arts and, for that reason, activities have not been labeled as appropriate for reading, speaking, listening, or writing. Rather, the activities of storytelling, using poetry, sharing, and dramatizing are discussed and the ways in which each contributes to growth in the language arts noted. Certain activities have not been labeled for child development center, nursery school, or kindergarten because of the wide range of individual differences from group to group. Using information pertaining to development and experience of the children in her class, the teacher can select and adapt the activity most appropriate for them.

In working with children from less-privileged backgrounds, the teacher will find the language arts activities essential. It is especially important, however, that the teacher utilize the information pertaining to the maturity and experiential background of the children in the selection of the story, poem, book, or materials for dramatic play.

Although activities discussed in this chapter are labeled language arts activities, it is emphasized that these activities are applicable and usable in many different learning situations. Poetry may be read and stories told which relate to social studies, mathematics, and the other subject areas. Books with science content may be read to the children. Role-playing and dramatization are techniques useful in a variety of learning encounters.

STORYTELLING

Young children today enjoy a good story just as children always have. Although the content of the story may vary from generation to generation, the use of storytelling to entertain, to teach, and to develop appreciation of literature continues to be an important art.

While many other values are recognized, the discussion in this chapter will relate primarily to storytelling as an activity that offers opportunities for developing skills in the language arts. Specifically, the child may learn to listen and have experience in speaking as he talks about the story or as he tells stories himself. He may learn to keep in mind a sequence of ideas, increase his vocabulary, and enlarge the background of his experiences. These points are emphasized, not to limit the creative possibilities of storytelling nor to formalize the art, but rather to indicate ways in which this creative activity can make a contribution—a fact often overlooked.

Teachers without training in speech or dramatics may hesitate to undertake telling stories to children. Others have questions regarding the selection and use of stories. Rather than use a general discussion for guidance, questions that are often asked in regard to storytelling have been identified and suggested procedures have been discussed.

Selecting an Appropriate Story for Young Children

A checklist that may be used by the teacher in the selection of stories includes the following criteria:

1. A simple, well-developed plot, centered in one main sequence of events, structured so that a child can anticipate to some degree the outcome of events, with action predominant. A slight surprise element which makes the children wonder what will happen next can add much to the story.
2. A large amount of direct conversation.
3. Use of repetition, rhyme, and catch phrases that the child memorizes quickly and easily.
4. Use of carefully chosen, colorful language.
5. Situations involving familiar happenings. The new, unusual, and different may be included, but there must be enough of the familiar with which the child can identify. The "familiar happenings" will not be the same for all children. Children

Figure 21. An interesting story and a good storyteller encourage children to listen.

from less-privileged homes have often had different experiences. In selecting stories for them, their experiential background should be considered.
6. Simple and satisfying climax.
7. One main character with whom the child can easily identify. Too many characters can be confusing.
8. A variety of ethnic, cultural, and racial backgrounds. Such stories should present realistic pictures, not ridiculous sterotypes of racial or ethnic groups.

Deciding Whether to Tell or to Read a Story

The question is often asked as to whether a story should be read or told to the child. Examining the values involved, there appears to be a place for both telling and reading. Telling the story enables the teacher to establish and maintain eye contact with the children and thus encourage listening. Since no script is involved, she can easily make explanations or adaptations in length or vocabulary for the children. The story that is told seems more direct, informal, and intimate than one that is read. Reading the story, however, has the advantage of the example of the teacher reading from the book, helping the child to recognize that reading can be fun and to associate pleasure with reading. It is important that the teacher set a good example in holding the book and turning the pages, seated so that the book is at the eye-level of the children. She should be familiar enough with the story to be able to read it well. The book should not be a crutch to avoid the effort of learning the story.

Preparing and Telling a Story

Some teachers say that it is hard for them to learn to tell a story. Often the person thinks that she should memorize a story, word for word. There is no one way to tell a story, but the following suggestions for preparing and telling the story may be helpful:

1. Picture the story to yourself since the story should be learned as a series of pictures. Read the story slowly, forming a picture in your mind of each character and event. Close the book and think through the story in terms of the pictures you have made. Read the story again for language. The words fit themselves to the pictures and the story takes form.[1]
2. Use direct quotations when a character speaks.
3. Plan a good beginning to gain the attention of the audience. Avoid unnecessary descriptions and explanations.
4. Use a conversational tone of voice, speaking slowly and distinctly. Avoid excessive use of "and," "er." Avoid a sing-song uneven tone and a voice pitch which is too high.
5. Look directly at the children. Include all members of the group, not just those directly in front of you.
6. Sit on a low chair.
7. Use timing effectively, vary the tempo. As action increases and things begin to happen, hurry the tempo. Before a moment of question, surprise, or awe, a pause can be most effective.
8. Keep the story, or the listening period, within the limits of the child's attention span. The range from 7 to 20 minutes has been identified for the preschool period (see pages 197–198).
9. Following the story the children may have a few questions or comments. Take time for these, but do not force discussion by use of questions. This procedure often detracts from the child's enjoyment of the story. If, during the story, a child interrupts to relate an incident, one should encourage him to keep it until the story is finished. Occasionally such a contribution is valuable and should be allowed, but many such interruptions can spoil the story.

Helping Children Listen to the Story

Often the children want to crowd around the teacher to see the pictures as she reads or tells the story. She is concerned with getting them to sit down and listen. Before beginning the story, arrange for the children to sit in comfortable positions, in a group or in a semicircle, in front of the storyteller. Be sure they can hear and see easily. They may be seated either on the floor, on a rug, or in chairs.

Give the children an opportunity to see and enjoy the illustrations as the story is being told. This may be done in several ways. In telling a story, the teacher can hold the book in front and slightly to the side, always at the eye-

---

[1]Ruth Sawyer, *The Way of the Story Teller* (New York: Viking Press, 1962), pp. 131–148.

level of the children. Using the book in this way enables the child to see the pictures while the story is being told and helps to hold his attention.

The teacher may not find it necessary to show the pictures throughout the story. She can show the picture and say, "See the picture. Now I will tell you the story," or, "Just as soon as I tell you a part of the story I will show you the picture." She then pauses briefly at the appropriate time to share the picture. The teacher who forgets to show the picture invites trouble. The child who crowds up may be reminded quietly to sit down so that everyone can see.

When reading the story the teacher may also hold the book to the side to show the pictures to the children. If this practice is followed, the teacher will need to group the children so that all may see and so that it will not be necessary to turn her face and voice away from them. As the children become able to listen to the longer story with more plot, the teacher may not find it necessary to show the pictures while reading.

Using Aids in Storytelling

Aids can be used to make the story more effective and to offer variety. Figures or dolls representing the characters may be used by the teacher during the story or placed on the library table along with the book. The latter enables the child to handle the figures as he looks at the book. If dolls representing the characters are not available, pictures of the characters can be cut, mounted, and placed in small stands or racks. A flannel board is effective also, since figures cut from felt or flannel can be used on the board. Pictures made by the teacher or children can be prepared by gluing strips of sandpaper to the back of the picture. The story "The Peddler and His Caps" is appropriate for such use. It is important, however, that the aids be manipulated in such a way as not to distract the child's attention from the story.

Use of Books

Not by accident does a child develop a love for books, a feeling that books can be friends and companions, an awareness of the fun and enjoyment that can come from books, an appreciation of good literature, the knowledge that books can be sources of information, and an interest in caring for books. All of these attitudes, which it is hoped the young child will develop, evolve as the child has many pleasurable experiences with books both at home and at school.

Opportunities for the child to listen to and enjoy stories, read and told, to handle, use, and love books can help him to learn that reading can be fun and to become interested in learning to read. In selecting a book, the contents, illustrations, and physical make-up are important items to be considered.

Contents

Books of poetry, information, nature, holiday fun, folk stories, everyday experiences, inspiration, and those that stimulate creative expression, are essential.

As a rule the traditional fairy tales with cruel witches and stepmothers, kings, and queens are not used with young children. The child is not yet able to distinguish easily between fact and fancy, and the gruesome details, easily accepted later as "make believe," often trouble the young child. This does not mean, however, that fanciful tales are to be omitted. Some stories relate imaginative experiences of children. In other stories that are children's favorites, one will find animals speaking. Children often talk with animals or toys, and conversation of this type is within their range of experiences. Most fables are not suitable to use with young children. However, in some instances, if the moralizing is omitted, the storytelling value is high.

Arbuthnot suggests the following questions, which have been adapted, to help in evaluating a book:[2]

1. Does the book help the child to gain some insight into his own personal life or the lives of other people?
2. Does the plot or action of the story hold the child's interest?
3. Does the content add to the child's joy in living and his feeling that life is good?
4. Are the characters honest, well described, unforgettable?
5. Does the story include humor, dramatic elements, and beauty of language that are appropriate for the child and the story?
6. Is the information accurate? Will the information help to expand the child's experiential background?

   These questions should be considered as generalizations and not applied too rigidly. There may be books which do not measure up in every detail, yet may be good for a special child or occasion. Criteria suggested on pages 214–215 for selecting a story are also applicable to the contents of a book.

Illustrations

Attention should be given to the illustrations, remembering that young children usually read their books via pictures. The artist is really the co-storyteller and his work complements rather than supplements that of the author.[3] The content, mood, and feeling of the illustrations should match the plot and tone of the story. Just as the story's text includes things familiar to the young child with few details yet plenty of action, so should the illustrations. This is especially true of books for young children since they are largely picture books without text or with a very simple story.

Format

Book bindings should be sturdy and firmly stitched. The covers should be attractive in order to encourage the child to care for them. A binding that comes

[2]May Hill Arbuthnot, *Children and Books*, 3rd ed. (Glenview, Ill.: Scott, Foresman, 1964), p. 19.

[3]V. E. Herrick and L. B. Jacobs, *Children and the Language Arts* (Englewood Cliffs, N.J.: Prentice-Hall, 1955), p. 199.

off the book at the first careless handling can be most discouraging for the child.

Among the collection of books are those for holidays and special occasions that will not be used as often as some of the others. These books may be purchased in the less expensive editions, but the same criteria for content and illustrations apply. For the favorites that are used day in and day out, a good binding is an economy. The pages should be of strong, heavy paper to prevent their tearing easily as the child turns them.

Most of the books should be light enough and of a size that is easy for the child to handle. Some large books may be included for occasional use and enjoyment on the rug or the table.

Using Book Collections

The well-selected collection of books is not enough. To be effective in the lives of children, it must be well used. All of the books need not be displayed all the time. Change the books on the library table and in the library corner often. Unless this is done, the child may become so accustomed to seeing the book that it becomes a fixture rather than an exciting adventure. Display books attractively on a table or on a low shelf. Flowers, a plant, or cut-outs of characters in the story may be used to advantage.

Plan ahead so that the time spent in looking at or using books becomes important. Avoid using books when there is nothing else to do or just to "fill in." For example, the child may say to the teacher, "I've finished. I don't know what to do." Too often, an indifferent reply is made, "Go and get a book," and the child responds in the same indifferent manner.

Arrange for children to borrow a favorite book to take home and share with their families. In one kindergarten, choosing a book is a part of getting ready to go home. If the child wants a book, he brings it to the teacher and together they write his name on the book list. The list is posted, and when the book is returned the child checks his name off the list. Such a procedure helps children to develop responsibility in using and caring for books. Children may be encouraged to bring books from home to share with the group. A visit to a library can help to develop an interest in books and an understanding of how books are cared for.

The teacher, then, must not only select a good collection of books but must use them effectively with children. Her own interest in and knowledge of the classics as well as current books, her skill in using books with and reading them to children, and her own appreciation and enjoyment of books determine in a large measure the extent to which children gain the values which may be derived from books.

In selecting books for the collection, there are several sources which the teacher may consult:

1. Published book lists and catalogues. One that is inexpensive and revised fre-

quently is *A Bibliography of Books for Children*.[4] A list of inexpensive books, *Good and Inexpensive Books for Children*,[5] is revised every three years and is also available from the same source.

2. Reviews of books for children published in professional periodicals. The teacher may supplement the nursery school or kindergarten collection by borrowing books reviewed from a library. In some cities a teacher may borrow as many as twenty books for a two-week period. When these are returned, others can be selected.

POETRY

Experiences with poetry can be happy and spontaneous ones for children. They enjoy the sounds around them, create sounds, laugh at unusual combinations of words, sense the rhythm of running, skipping, and speaking. The spontaneous language of children is often poetic in nature. Dorothy, telling about the little bird that had fallen out of the nest, said, "The little bird was shivering with scaredness." Poetry, if well-selected and correctly used, can help the child to listen carefully; to learn new words and ways of expressing one's feelings; to develop increased auditory awareness or acuity; to improve the quality of his own voice; and to feel secure in the group as he participates in saying poetry with the group. Poetry can bring laughter and happiness to the child.

The success of the teacher in presenting poetry to children depends upon several factors: (1) the selection of verses which are appropriate for the age of the child and for use in a wide variety of situations; (2) the teacher and her appreciation of poetry and the manner in which she shares poetry with the children; and (3) the extent to which poetry is used.

Selecting Poetry for Use with Children

Children enjoy a wide variety of poems including those about the here and now; situations familiar to the child—playmates, clothing, and pets; poems about nature—the seasons, the wind, the falling leaves or signs of spring; poems that are fanciful and imaginative; holiday poems; humorous verses, and those filled with the repetition of unusual sounds with a singing quality. One should use poems related to the experience at hand, but it is undesirable to force correlations which do not fit.

The content of the poem should be sufficiently related to the child's experiences that he can understand something of the meaning expressed by the words.[6] How many children today are likely to understand Stevenson's likening the sound of the wind to the passing of "ladies skirts across the grass?" Jacobs says:

[4]*A Bibliography of Books for Children* (Washington, D.C.: ACEI, 1972).
[5]*Good and Inexpensive Books for Children* (Washington, D.C.: ACEI, 1972).
[6]Arbuthnot, op. cit., p. 195.

Children enjoy good poetry that:
   Gives them an exhilirating sense of melodious movement.
   Makes the everyday experiences of life vibrant.
   Tells wonderful stories.
   Releases health-giving laughter.
   Carries them into extravagant or fanciful situations.
   Extends their appreciation of their natural world.
   Creates memorable personages or characters.
   Sings its way into their minds and memories.[7]

Sharing Poetry with Children

First of all, if the child is to appreciate and enjoy poetry, it is imperative that the teacher appreciate poetry and share her enjoyment as she presents the poem to them. Arbuthnot suggests that in exploring a new poem, the teacher read it aloud first in order to become familiar with the words, mood, and tempo.[8] Unless this is done, she may not find the sound pattern or rhythm of the poem and as a result her reading will be dull and meaningless.

She may either read the poem or share it from memory. The teacher who knows a number of poems can share them informally with a small group or even with one child on the playground, while taking a walk, observing a pet, or whenever there is an opportunity. But no one teacher can memorize all the poems that will be needed. If she is familiar with children's poetry and knows where to find it, then she can share the poem at a later time, merely recalling the incident or mood to which it refers. However, not all poetry should be related to some thing or incident. Sometimes it is shared just for fun or pleasure.

Memorizing Poetry

Forced memorization of poems has turned many children away from poetry.[9] A teacher who often reads well-selected poetry to children in a simple, natural, and an appreciative manner will soon find that the children will "say" the poem with her. Many children will learn poems in this manner without the pressure to memorize.

Choral speaking (or a verse choir) for young children is largely speaking poetry in unison. Children may experiment with different ways of saying a verse, once it has been learned in the manner suggested above. For instance, the boys may say the verse, then the girls. Use questions such as, "How does it sound?" If questions or conversation are used, as in the verse "Sing-Song" by Christina Rossetti, try having one child speak those lines and the entire group the remaining lines. Some poems may be broken up and each child say a line or two. Mother Goose rhymes such as "Pease Porridge Hot" or "This Little Pig" are examples.

[7]L. B. Jacobs, "Enjoying Poetry with Children," in *Literature with Children* (Washington, D.C.: ACEI, 1972), pp. 33–34.

[8]Arbuthnot, op. cit., p. 205.

[9]Herrick and Jacobs, op. cit., pp. 211–217.

SHARING TIME AND GROUP DISCUSSION

The word *sharing* is often used in nursery school and kindergarten with reference to the use of toys and materials. It implies the willingness to "take turns" or to "let Jane have some clay." Sharing may also refer to communicating—between children or between teacher and child. For the child who is beginning nursery school, this communication may involve only a few words accompanied by a facial expression that emphasizes the thought. On the first cool morning, Mary arrived dressed in a new blue sweater. "Look," she said as she displayed the sweater, her eyes sparkling and her face alight with an expression of joy and well-being. As this informal communicating and sharing continues, the child uses more words to express her thoughts. As children become more secure in a group situation, they want and need to talk together, and a time in the school day for planning and sharing may be designated. This activity is usually considered appropriate for kindergarten groups, although some more mature nursery classes may begin such a period. The time for beginning such a group activity, however, will depend upon the children involved—their interests, attention span, and readiness to participate in a group situation.

This period for sharing is often known by the name of "Show and Tell," which has been somewhat discredited. Such a name implies an activity in which the child shows some object and tells about it. There are those who claim that it is an artificial situation and becomes a monotonous routine, thus losing its language value. Sharing time implies communication. Objects may be shown and talked about, but plans, incidents, and news may be discussed too by the teacher as well as by the children.

Discussion time, however, with teacher and children, is usually problem-centered. Plans may be made for a trip or a special project for the morning. The choice of activities may be discussed. This type of sharing time and discussion can be rich in opportunities for developing skills in the language arts. The child can learn to:

1. Speak distinctly and clearly.
2. Speak in front of a group.
3. Tell an incident in sequence.
4. Listen politely.
5. Take turns in speaking.
6. Speak in complete sentences.

Encouraging Children to Participate

Some children never speak in the group, and the question is often asked, "How may they be encouraged to participate?"

First, it is important to determine why the child does not participate. Is he afraid of a group situation? Could it be that he has nothing to share? Is he bored, uninterested? Not knowing the other children well, might he feel no need to communicate with them? The answers will depend upon the reason.

Only gradually does a child come to feel secure in a group situation. Both

Jennie and Gloria seemed to remain on the fringes. Fear of the group will not be overcome by forcing participation. Rather, the teacher may encourage sharing with her at times other than the organized period. Gradually, one or two children may be included by comments such as, "That is a beautiful book. Let's show it to Joe," or "Such good news! Tell Bob." The number of individuals may be expanded to form small groups, gradually increasing the size. One must remember that sharing does not always mean speaking. First attempts may involve showing a book or toy without a comment. With maturity and security, speaking will come later.

For a child who has nothing to share, the teacher may be alert during the day to help the child identify something worthy of sharing with the group. For example, as the child arrives in the morning, he tells the teacher that on his way to school he watched a squirrel scampering up a tree. A few questions such as "What was he carrying in his mouth?" may help the child clarify and identify the details of the incident. She may say, "That is a very interesting story. Please tell the other children at sharing time."

A child may become bored or lose interest because he does not have an opportunity to speak. This can happen when a few children are permitted to dominate the situation, speaking loudly and often. The teacher can help these children learn to take turns. A reminder, "You had a turn, Joe," may help. Consistently, the teacher must remind the children of those who have shared and those who still need a turn. A child with several items to share may need to be reminded, "You have told us about one thing. The other children need a turn before you tell us more."

Encouraging Good Habits of Listening

The teacher may refer to the suggestions pp. 200–203 regarding listening. In addition, it is important to help children learn what is involved in good listening. She may say to the child who is ready to share, "Look around the circle. See if everyone is ready to listen before you begin to speak."

DRAMATIZATION

The word *creativity* is often used only in connection with the arts. The discussions on using books, poetry, storytelling (pp. 214–221), and the creative arts, art and music (pp. 351–385), present creativity as related to these areas. Many activities considered simple and unimaginative may offer opportunities for creative expression. What is meant by creative expression? Greene and Petty state that for language expression to be creative, it must be:[10]

1. Original—based upon thoughts and ideas which are the child's own.
2. Based on a real desire of the child to express himself.
3. Different from the commonplace and unimaginative.

[10]H. A. Greene and W. T. Petty, *Developing Language Skills in the Elementary School* (Boston: Allyn and Bacon, 1959), p. 349.

Figure 22. In dramatic play children may try living as an adult and find out how it feels to have certain responsibilities. In this instance, Cynthia is the doctor.

According to this definition, conversation can be creative—as children talk at the lunch table, or as they watch together while the rabbits nibble their food. There are, however, other activities which are considered more conducive to creative expression.

Dramatization may take many forms, including dramatic play, creative dramatics, using puppets, and role-playing. While there is no clear-cut distinction between them, each does have a unique characteristic. The relationships and differences are shown in the definitions below:

Dramatic Play

Dramatic play is spontaneous and free of teacher direction or control. "In dramatic play, children identify themselves with persons or things with which they have had firsthand contact or about which they have learned vicariously."[11] Such play grows out of the experiences of the child.

Dramatic play among children from less-privileged areas may be expected to differ from that of children from more favored environments. The firsthand contacts and learnings are usually different. One group of children considered

[11]*Teachers Guide to Education in Early Childhood* (Sacramento: California State Department of Education, 1956), p. 209.

the policeman as a threat, a mean man, while others considered him to be a friend or helper. Such concepts influence the role-playing done by the children.

This type of play is one in which the child may try living life as an adult; find out how it feels to have certain responsibilities such as feeding the baby or cooking dinner; clarify concepts regarding the role of mother, the fireman, or the doctor; and practice certain basic language skills such as speaking, using conversation, listening, learning new words, clarifying the meaning of words, and social amenities. Dramatic play has other important values. In this section the aspects of dramatic play related to the language arts are included.

To a large extent the teacher determines if the values of dramatic play are realized. She needs to be sensitive to the individual child, have insight into the basic processes of living, and possess skill in group management.[12]

The teacher's responsibility includes providing many interesting opportunities for the children since the child's creative efforts are limited to his experience—trips, contacts with various people, recordings, books, pictures, and films; and proving space, materials, and time for the activity. Once this has been done, usually nothing more is required. If a child does not participate readily, the teacher may help the child enter the group by suggesting some role the child can assume.

The teacher does not direct the activity. The children do this. She seeks to guide the dramatic play so that the experience is satisfying to the children. This means that she may need to help in the settlement of a dispute and solving problems that arise. Timing of teacher help is very important, lest the play become disrupted and the children discouraged. The teacher also observes possible leads for further study and notes concepts which may need to be clarified.

John, Lisa, and Myron, who were building a train of large blocks, were engaged in a heated argument as to the location of the engine. John, the engineer, insisted that it was first, but Myron and Lisa were certain that it should be after the coaches. In talking with the children, it became evident that they did not know the purpose or the names of the various cars on the train or the people who work on the train. Here was a lead. A trip, a film, pictures, stories, models were all used to clarify the concept.

Puppets

Puppets are often used by children in dramatic play or dramatizations. The child who hesitates to speak with others or before the group may express himself freely through a puppet. With young children the puppets are generally used informally without screens or stories. Usually the conversation is supplied by the individual child or perhaps two children. Puppets are made available and the child chooses to use them as he wishes or needs to do so.

[12]Ruth Hartley, L. K. Frank, and R. M. Goldenson, *Understanding Children's Play*, (New York: Columbia University Press, 1952), p. 98.

Figure 23.   Puppets are generally used informally by young children without screen or stories. Conversation may be supplied by the individual child or perhaps by two children.

Puppets for the young are kept simple. Pictures of people or animals glued on sticks, sacks filled with air and with ends twisted to make a handle, or commercial hand puppets are all useful.

Role-Playing

More direct guidance is required on the part of the teacher in defining the roles and the situations than in dramatic play where the roles are selected by the children. In this activity the child plays the role or the situation as he chooses. The teacher must refrain from approving or disapproving of any part of the action or discussion, stating conclusions, or moralizing in order to insure freedom of expression. The teacher must accept the things the children say and do and maintain a permissive accepting attitude.

This does not mean, however, that anything goes and the teacher keeps "hands off" entirely. The scene may be stopped by the teacher saying, "We see how these people did it. Who has another way?" Or, "Thank you. Who has thought of something else one might do?" It may be decided that certain scenes are not appropriate and these will not be repeated.[13] In terms of language arts, role-playing can help the child feel a part of the group and to speak in the group, both in the role and in the discussion.

Suggestions for beginning and developing role-playing are presented in

[13]H. Nichols and Lois Williams, *Role-Playing for Children and Teachers* (Washington, D.C.: ACEI, 1960), p. 9.

the ACEI bulletin on role-playing. Those considered appropriate for kindergarten children are as follows:[14]

1. Begin with pantomime, using the game "Guess what I am doing." Repeat for
   several days until most of the children have taken part.
2. Next, use familiar scenes. For instance, the teacher might tell the children, "Show
   what might happen at home in the morning." The teacher could then say, "Who
   is in the home?" Characters are identified and the scene played several times with
   different children portraying the roles.
       Follow with a discussion of the scenes beginning with identification of things
   that were liked about the characters and moving on to feelings of the characters.
   Use questions, such as, "How did you feel when mother said, 'Come to breakfast'
   or 'Get dressed for school'?"
3. After spending considerable time in familiar situations, problems may be introduced into role-playing—problems related to playground conflicts, a birthday
   party, or other school scenes.
4. Use unfinished stories. A short story may be found which may be read in about
   two minutes or one may be created for the group of about the same length. Children assume roles of the various characters and complete the story.[15]

Creative Dramatics

In this group activity, an experience is acted out by the children as they are
guided in thinking, feeling, and creating their own dialogue and action. There
are no lines to be memorized, no formal audience, no costumes, or technical
aids. The dramatization may be original as to the idea or it may be based on a
poem or story written by someone else. Siks lists the four basic requirements:
(1) a group of children, (2) a leader or teacher, (3) space large enough for children
to move freely, and (4) an idea from which to create.[16]

Creative dramatics contributes to language arts skills as children speak,
communicate, and listen. Auditory discrimination may also be built. According
to Siks, "A child's ability to discriminate grows through such satisfying experiences as becoming a train engine that moves fast or slow; a train with a
light load or a heavy load . . . a train that is near or far away."[17] As children
play out appropriate stories and verses, they enjoy and learn to appreciate good
literature.

Lease and Siks offer suggestions for introducing creative dramatics to young
children.[18] They suggest that the teacher begin with

1. Rhythmic movement. Create the mood by several statements before asking the

[14]Ibid., p. 5.

[15]Ibid., pp. 5–25.

[16]Geraldine B. Siks, *Creative Dramatics, An Art for Children* (New York: Harper & Row, 1958),
p. 21.

[17]Ibid., p. 280.

[18]Ruth G. Lease and Geralding B. Siks, *Creative Dramatics in Home, School, and Community*
(New York: Harper & Row, 1952), p. 37.

question. "Let's pretend that we are going outside to pick up nuts. Let's see how many nuts we can find. What is one way you can look for the nuts?" Some may crawl on hands and knees, others walk slowly looking down on the ground, some skip, others run.

The children may also do characterizations in rhythmic movements. For instance, they may characterize animals by the way they walk and sound, the weather, the wind blowing, rain falling.

2. Songs. Many children's songs suggest action, pantomime, or characterizations. The teacher may sing while the children do the actions. She may use a recording to which the children respond or let one group of children sing while the remainder pantomime. Singing games offer opportunities for beginning experiences in this area also.

3. Finger plays. As children participate in finger plays, vivid pictures may be formed in their minds and they may be guided to feel and act as characters felt in the finger play.

4. Dramatic play, as discussed on page 224.

5. Pantomime poetry or verse. Nursery rhymes, Mother Goose, and other poems that are short, the characterizations limited, and the action direct, are appropriate.

After children have had considerable experience in the activities already described, they are ready to play the role of an individual character. The teacher selects a verse already familiar to the group, for instance, "The Caterpillar," and says it to the children.

> Fuzzy wuzzy, creepy crawly
> Caterpillar funny,
> You will be a butterfly
> When the days are sunny.
>
> Winging, flinging, dancing, springing
> Butterfly so yellow,
> You were once a caterpillar,
> Wiggly, wiggly fellow.[19]

Then she may say something like this, "Here is some nice green grass. Let's all be caterpillars crawling on the grass." After the children have enjoyed being caterpillars, she may say, "What creepy, crawly caterpillars. Now you have become a butterfly. How do you think the butterfly feels? Let's all be butterflies here on the grass." The questions will lead to lively discussion and creative thinking. It is important, however, that the teacher not spend too long in talking and planning with little children. They are eager to *do*, to play the role. The teacher, in talking about the characters, will do well to discuss how the butterfly feels, rather than what it says or does. As Lease and Siks say, "When children are thinking and feeling in character, the action will be spontaneous."[20]

Following group participation in the roles of the different characters, one

[19]Lillian Schulz, "The Caterpillar," in ACEI, *Sung Under the Silver Umbrella* (New York: Macmillan Publishing Co., 1962), p. 77.

[20]Lease and Siks, op. cit., p. 39.

child will be chosen to be the butterfly and one to be the caterpillar. This may be repeated several times with different children playing the different characters.

6. Dramatize or play a story. Folk tales provide stories which are short and in which the actions and feelings of the characters are easily identified. Suggestions pertaining to pantomime are relevant here. Once the children are familiar with the story, the teacher may plan briefly with the children for one scene of the story. Do not try to plan for the entire story at one time. Characters are identified and children asked to play the different roles. They may be helped to assume roles of the different characters by questions directed to the entire group. For instance, if the story were *Three Billy Goats Gruff*, comments such as the following might be used. "What kind of goat was the first billy goat? How did he feel when he heard the Old Troll? Tell us about the Old Troll. What kind of creature was he?"

Emphasis is not placed on remembering what the character says. Once the child has a feeling for the character and senses how he feels, then the child's speech as well as his actions will be spontaneous. The child may easily forget *what* he is to say if he has been taught only the words. If he is playing the *role*, then there are several different ways he may express the character's feelings and he is seldom at a loss for words.

SUMMARY

Pressures to begin formal instruction earlier are beginning to be felt at the preschool level. This is especially true in the kindergarten where the insistence on "getting ready for first grade reading" has resulted in some practices that are undesirable from the standpoint of the growth and development of the child.

Teachers who have used activities such as stories, poetry, and dramatic play without analyzing, understanding, and noting ways in which they contribute to growth in the language arts may not be articulate in resisting questionable practices. The chart on page 230 summarizes the contributions of each activity included in the chapter, not to prove the academic value of the activities described, but to emphasize the fact that creative, spontaneous language experiences can also contribute to foundation learnings.

Suggested Activities

1. Select, prepare, and tell a story appropriate for a four- or five-year-old group of children. Evaluate your performance in terms of the criteria presented on page 216. Select another story and prepare figures for use on a flannel board to accompany it.

2. Begin to keep a poetry file. Choose three topics appropriate for the young child, such as Play, Bed-Time, Holidays, Minorities. For each topic, select and record several poems.

3. Examine a collection of books for young children. Select and evaluate three each of picture books, and books that deal with concept development, holidays, and minority groups, in terms of criteria presented on page 218.

4. Visit a center for young children and become acquainted with several of the chil-

TABLE 12-1
CONTRIBUTIONS OF LANGUAGE ART ACTIVITIES

	Reading Readiness	Listening	Speaking	Writing
1. Dramatization	Visual and auditory discrimination, enriched vocabulary; clarification of concepts; interest in books and reading.	Appreciation and enjoyment of good literature; listening while others speak.	Discussion and planning, speaking in front of group, taking turns in speaking; feeling secure and a member of the group.	Recognition of value of writing; list of characters on chart.
2. Poetry	Auditory acuity; hear likenesses and differences in sounds.	Appreciation and enjoyment of poetry.	Encourages distinct speech; encourages speaking before the group; choral reading may help him feel a part of the group.	Use of writing to record one's ideas.
3. Storytelling	Experience in listening; enriched vocabulary; clarification of concepts; interest in books and reading.	Appreciation and enjoyment of good literature.	Conversation about the story.	Recognizing that a story is recorded for others to share at a later date.
4. Sharing	Enriches vocabulary; clarifies concepts; listens; keeps in mind a sequence of ideas.	Experience in listening to other children.	Takes turns in speaking; speaks distinctly and clearly; tells an incident in sequence; speaks in front of group; speaks in complete sentences; develops a sentence sense; takes part in group planning; asks questions.	Awareness of importance of writing through dictating plans or invitations.

dren. For the group, select a story and read it to them. On another occasion, select a poem and say or share it with the group. Evaluate.

5. Visit a center for young children and observe them engaged in dramatic play. Note the roles that the children seem to be assuming and the topics for play. Compare your observations with those of others in your class. How do you account for differences?

6. Visit a materials center or a distributor's display. Examine current kits and packaged materials for young children in reading, writing, speaking, and language development. Evaluate in terms of the goals of your center.

Related Readings

Anderson, P. S. "Rediscovering Children's Literature," *Language Skills in Elementary Education,* 2nd ed. New York: Macmillan Publishing Co., 1972, pp. 121–168.

Batinich, Mary. "Language Experience Activities," *Reading Teacher,* 23:6 (1970), pp. 539–546.

Beyer, Evelyn. "Language Learning—Fresh, Vivid and Their Own," *Child. Educ.,* 48:1 (1971), pp. 21–24.

Burns, P. C., Betty L. Broman, Alberta L. Lowe. *The Language Arts in Childhood Education,* 2nd ed. Chicago: Rand McNally and Company, 1971.

Chambers, D. W. "Children's Literature and the Allied Arts," *Elem. English,* 48:6 (1971), pp. 622–627.

Cohen, Dorothy H. "Word Meaning and the Literacy Experience in Early Childhood," *Elem. English,* 46:7 (1969), pp. 914–925.

Cohen, M. D., ed. *Literature with Children.* Washington, D.C.: ACEI, 1972.

Cowe, Eileen. "Showing and Sharing in the Kindergarten," *Child. Educ.,* 47:6, (1971), pp. 300–302.

DuBois, Eloise B. "Values and Techniques of Creative Dramatics," *Child. Educ., 47:7* (1971), pp. 368–370.

Fitzgerald, Alice Irene. "Literature Approved by Today's Kindergarten Children," *Elem. English,* 48:8 (1971), pp. 953–959.

Gilpatric, Naomi. "Power of Picture Books to Change Child's Self-Image," *Elem. English,* 46:5 (1969), pp. 570–574.

Hall, Mary Anne. *Teaching Reading as a Language Experience.* Columbus, Ohio: Charles E. Merrill Publishing Company, 1970.

Hawkins, Roberta. "Nursery Rhymes: Mirrors of a Culture," *Elem. English,* 48:6 (1971), pp. 617–621.

Hayes, Eloise. "Expanding the Child's World Through Drama and Movement," *Child. Educ.,* 47:7 (1971), pp. 360–367.

Herrick, V. E., and Marcella Nervobig. *Using Experience Charts with Children.* Columbus Ohio: Charles E. Merrill Books, 1964.

Huber, Marian B. *Story and Verse for Children,* 3rd ed. New York: Macmillan, Inc., 1965.

Jacobs, L. B. and Others. *Using Literature with Young Children.,* New York: Teachers College Press, Columbia University, 1965.

Kindergarten Bilingual Resource Handbook. 6745A Calmont St., Ft. Worth, Texas 76116; The National Consortia for Bilingual Education, 1971.

Lavatelli, Celia Stendler. "An Approach to Language Learning," *Young Children,* 24:6 (1969), pp. 368–376.

Lee, Dorris M., and R. V. Allen. *Learning to Read Through Experience,* 2nd ed. New York: Appleton-Century-Crofts, 1963.

McCaslin, Nellie. *Creative Dramatics in the Classroom.* New York: David McKay Company, Inc., 1968.

Monroe, Marion, and Bernice Rogers. *Foundations for Reading: Informal Pre-Reading Procedures.* Chicago: Scott, Foresman, 1964.

National Institute of Neurological Diseases and Stroke, National Institutes of Health. *Learning to Talk—Speech, Hearing and Language Problems of the Pre-School Child.* Washington, D.C.: U.S. Government Printing Office, 1970.

Perryman, Lucile. *Guide to Children's Magazines, Newspapers, Reference Books.* Washington, D.C.: ACEI, 1972.

Swift, M. S., Mary Uelli, Tracey Warner, and D. Klein. "Preschool Books and Mother-Child Communication," *Reading Teacher,* 25:3 (1971), pp. 236–238.

Tanyzer, H., and Jean Karl, eds. *Reading, Children's Books, and Our Pluralistic Society.* Newark, Del.: International Reading Association, 1972.

The World in Children's Picture Books. Washington, D.C.: ACEI, 1968.

Tidyman, W. F., Charlene W. Smith, and Marguerite Butterfield. "Children's Literature," *Teaching the Language Arts,* 3rd ed. New York: McGraw-Hill Book Company, 1969, pp. 181–209.

White, Doris, Compiler. *Multi-ethnic Books for Head Start Children, Part I: Black and Integrated Literature.* Urbana, Ill.: ERIC Clearinghouse on Early Childhood Education and National Laboratory on Early Childhood Education.

Chapter 13

Mathematics

Long before a child enters the nursery school or kindergarten, the beginnings of mathematical skills and understandings are being established. He makes judgments—the beginnings of the reasoning process—as he gauges the space he needs to get his tricycle through the door, as he estimates how high to raise his foot to climb on the jungle gym, as he counts his cookies, or as he decides who has the most ice cream. He estimates the size of the block he needs to fill a space, or decides the position in which to place a toy to make it balance. He establishes the beginning of concepts of money and money values as he inserts a penny or a nickel in the machine to purchase a piece of gum or candy. He uses a dime or a nickel to ride on the pony, in the airplane or boat placed on the sidewalk in front of a store. He selects coins to take to Sunday School.

The young child loves to chant; as he chants "one, two, three," he is using numbers, but he is not really counting. The words "one, two, three" do not have number meaning for him until he uses this counting to solve a problem.

Since these experiences are a part of his life and living, they have not been planned and organized to insure that the young child is developing all the desired mathematical concepts. However, the perceptions developed in babyhood make a great contribution later to understandings and skills in quantitative thinking.

THE MATHEMATICS CURRICULUM

Changes in the teaching of mathematics are taking place rapidly as the findings of research and of curriculum development groups are being translated into the curriculum. Hence, new content and new methods in mathematics are gradually becoming a part of the school experience of the young child.

As educators and scholars in mathematics have worked cooperatively in redesigning the instructional program from kindergarten through high school, they have applied two results of recent research: (1) children can deal with mathematical concepts at an earlier age than previously thought; and (2) children can and will discover mathematics for themselves if the appropriate situations are provided. They have recognized that children will enjoy mathematics when they are led to discover the contribution of mathematics to their lives.

The concern is with the development of concepts. Almy points out that it takes well-informed teachers who understand much about ways children think as well as the subjects which they teach. In experimentation there is a trend to revive such earlier systems of instruction as the Montessori materials. There is also a trend toward making an analysis of the cognitive elements of curriculum. Another trend is the attempt to break specific disciplines into their component parts and to match the learning of these to the intellectual abilities of the children. The mathematics curriculum devised by Dienes in England in which the children teach themselves is an example. The program requires a teacher who not only knows how children think but who also can provide an environment in which the child can make his own discoveries and correct his own mistakes. Children's understanding in a particular subject area can be considerably accelerated through concept formation and their ability to use vocabulary appropriately. Consideration should be given as to how much benefit to later intellectual development can come to children from early childhood education programs designed primarily for acceleration in a given area.[1]

According to Almy, "New views on the nature of intellectual development open up new possibilities for influencing children's thinking, for guiding their encounter with the world in ways that will give them an increasingly better command of it."[2] Teaching the child to form mathematical concepts will need

---

[1] Millie Almy, "New Views on Intellectual Development in Early Childhood Education," in *Intellectual Development, Another Look* (Washington, D.C.: ASCD, 1964), pp. 12–25.

[2] Ibid., p. 25.

Figure 24. As children use blocks they compare and name shapes and sizes and identify likenesses and differences.

to be based upon understanding the child and his thinking so that "he may not only be *free to develop his intellect* but also *free to be a more effective person*."[3]

Swenson points out that "life is a search for meaning" and that "the young child, in a peculiar sense, spends his waking hours trying to find out meanings."[4] This search for meaning motivates him to question, to investigate, to try and try again a given task.

The teacher utilizes the young child's innate search for meaning as she provides situations in his environment that will challenge him and will also provide many and varied experiences by which he can develop mathematical concepts and skills. Meanings can best be developed by the child through his own experiences. The younger the child, the more necessary it becomes that opportunities for real experiences be provided. The teacher knows that provision for the concept to be used in varied contexts is important to the development of meaning. She plans for new situations that will involve the same skills yet contribute to a broader understanding. She is consistently building a foundation for the development of meaning as related to the mathematical processes and their use to achieve a desired goal. The child builds understandings as he adds, subtracts, multiplies, or divides in his play and work activities. These concepts and processes, introduced and used in their simplest

[3]Ibid., p. 26.

[4]Esther J. Swenson, *Making Primary Arithmetic Meaningful to Children* (Washington, D.C.: Department of Kindergarten-Primary Education, NEA, 1961), p. 3.

form, are identified as mathematical processes. Thus the child begins to understand the purpose for which the process is used.

As the teacher guides the child's activities and provides varied experiences, the child comes to understand the relationship between the different processes—how they are alike and how they differ. As he counts, works in groups, uses money, plays alone or with a group, he enlarges his understanding and extends his mathematical concepts until they have meaning for him whenever they occur.

According to Deans, number language emerges as the child becomes aware of numbers as a part of his world. She states that "home experiences involving numbers become more vital as they find their way in the classroom and become a part of the child's school arithmetic."[5]

Pitcher points out that "Academic learnings, even more than any other content at the pre-school level, must be 'tailor made' for the particular child; and we must bear in mind his degree of readiness and his immediate and long-term needs. Always the learnings must flow from the actual experiences the child has had with objects and events."[6] As the teacher observes each child, she helps him move at his own pace from the stages of "doing" to the stage of "thinking as he does" and to drawing conclusions. Thus, she guides him as he learns such complex concepts as groups and sets, comparison and order. These school experiences of the child need to be varied, not alone for content but according to the maturity level of the child.

According to Olson's studies, "size, shape, strength, appearance, and the timing of growth help to determine the situations in which children find themselves. Thus the uniqueness of the pattern for an individual has meanings which are different from meanings running through a group of individuals."[7]

From his summary of the research related to planning mathematical experiences for children, Russell suggests that certain mathematical concepts may not be expected to develop up to seven or eight years of age. Various studies indicate that maturity factors must be considered in planning mathematical experiences for children. Some children exhibit mature mathematical readiness when they arrive at school; others require a long period of time and participation in many well-planned activities before this same stage of readiness can be observed.[8] These initial experiences should contribute to the child's level of thinking; however, they should have game-like qualities as well as provide manipulative experiences with concrete materials. Other studies have ignored maturational factors in planning mathematical activities.

Piaget points out that older children not only know more but they do dif-

---

[5]Edwina Deans, *Arithmetic: Children Use It* (Washington, D.C.: ACEI, 1954), p. 56.

[6]Evelyn Goodenough Pitcher, et al., *Helping Children Learn* (Columbus, Ohio: Charles E. Merrill Books, 1966), p. 95.

[7]W. C. Olson, *Child Development*, 2nd ed. (Boston: D. C. Heath, 1959), pp. 220–221.

[8]D. Russell, *Children's Thinking* (Boston; Ginn & Co., 1956), pp. 126–128.

ferent things with what they learn; their thinking becomes more logical; they can solve problems and all parts need not be included to make up a whole. By adroit questioning the teacher can discover what a child knows and how he acquired this knowledge. As the child matures he learns to classify objects in several different classes at the same time.

Because children vary in intelligence in terms of rate of growth and ability, any mathematical program will need to be varied and to differ in terms of the preschool group. As the child explores and manipulates, he discovers; hence, the role of the teacher is to guide and stimulate the child. Freedom to play is an important part of the child's intellectual and mathematical development.[9]

From the work of Piaget and others came the belief that part of a preschool day should be planned for concept teaching and the other part of the day should be less directed and used for the teacher to observe the children and the gains made by them in the more structured situation.[10]

Objectives of the Mathematics Program

There may not be common agreement about specific objectives and ways of implementing these objectives. However, each teacher must accept the responsibility for attaining the following general objectives: (1) an understanding of mathematical ideas; (2) the ability to solve problems; (3) techniques and skills of computation; (4) an atmosphere for creative thinking; and (5) a differentiated program for individual differences.[11]

It is important in achieving these objectives that (1) the concepts are built up gradually; (2) the ideas are developed to the point of real understanding before attaching technical terminology and symbols; (3) the ideas are associated with environmental situations; (4) the introduction of new material is governed by concepts already acquired; and (5) the instructional mathematics program is developed as an integral part of the total curriculum.

The New Mathematics Program

Many parents and teachers claim that the so-called "New Math" is the same old primary arithmetic dressed up in a new form. It is true that with the introduction of curriculum changes some may consider modern mathematics as using sets; others may think of it as using number bases or number lines, number properties or inequalities. Each of these concepts does reflect the nature of modern mathematics in part. But to see modern mathematics only in terms of its parts can only result in false impressions and misconceptions of its scope and purpose.

[9]Celia Stendler Lavatelli. *Piaget's Theory Applied to an Early Childhood Curriculum* (Cambridge, Mass.: American Science and Engineering, Inc., 1970), pp. 27–44.

[10]Ibid., pp. 5–24.

[11]*New Directions in Mathematics* (Washington, D.C.: ACEI, 1965), p. 21.

The modern mathematics program needs to be based on the nature of the child and the nature of learning. The program places emphasis on developing concepts instead of mainly computational skills. Mathematics is presented as a system of thinking built on a structure of principles and relationships. Previous experience forms the base for new learning and mathematical insight. It includes new ways of working with children and provides for use of many and varied experiences with a variety of materials.

The growth of mathematical concepts is an important part of the preschool child's learnings. To guide this growth satisfactorily the teacher works informally with the children. As new concepts emerge the child is led to tell the complete number story in sentences as opposed to answering questions with a number or a phrase. Problem solving is not confined to problems related to arithmetic but the process is used to solve whatever problem the individual meets. The child is encouraged to discover for himself new relationships through multiple approaches as means to understanding.

Alpenfels warns against pressure on children and states that "a child needs to dream as well as to master the 'new arithmetic.' . . . It is very easy to tell teachers to do this. But it is not so easy to add new insights and new techniques."[12]

Heimer points out that parents need to become acquainted with and to understand some of the mathematics that has been created during the last century. Thus, the child is freed from the anxieties of parent misunderstandings and ensuing conflicts between the parents and school.[13]

In the "New Math" curriculum in schools for young children emphasis is placed upon the following aspects:[14]

1. Groups or sets (collections) in terms of one-to-one relationship, correspondence and matching, classification of sets, equal (identical) and equivalent, abstracting idea of number from equivalent sets, properties of set operations, commutativity of equal sets, equivalent sets of objects and pictures of objects, and sets and subsets, empty sets, set union and separation as they occur in the on-going experiences of the children.

2. Numbers through abstracting the idea of cardinal number from equivalent sets, understanding sets of numbers, counting one through 10 or 12, ordinal numbers from first through third and some through four or five, and counting by saying number names and recognizing that the last number named is the cardinal number of the set.

3. Numeration system through recognizing that a number has many names, and number-numeral distinction without written work.

4. Addition and subtraction through inverse relations in experiences involving set unions and set operations.

[12]Ethel J. Alpenfels, "Conformity, Censors, Sensitivity," *Child. Educ.*, 41:4 (1964), p. 169.

[13]Ralph T. Heimer and Miriam S. Newman, *The New Mathematics for Parents* (New York: Holt, Rinehart and Winston, 1965), pp. 11, 108.

[14]*Implementing Mathematics Programs in California*, A Guide K-8 (Menlo Park, Calif.: Pacific Coast Publishers, 1965), pp. 18–45.

5. Properties of the mathematical operation such as commutativity explained through union of sets or groups (collections).

6. Order, relations, and mathematical sentences as concepts of one more, one less, taller than, shorter than, larger than, and so on, are developed.

7. Problem solving in informal situations through answering such questions as "What do we know?" and "What do we wish to find out?"; analyzing procedures and techniques used, solving problems without numbers as well as one with numbers, and recognizing that there are many ways to solve a problem.

8. Measurement through use of vocabulary of comparison of objects with each other and through use of nonstandard units as well as measurement of liquids and money.

9. Geometry through acquaintance with geometric shapes in environment and through geometric designs in puzzles and other objects in the life of the child; recognition of two-dimensional shapes as squares, circles, triangles, and rectangles as they appear in meaningful activities; and comparison of sizes, shapes, and distance as there is a need in life situations.

10. Graphing and statistics through use of tally marks, simple charts for record keeping, comparison of objects, and so on, that have functional use in activities of the child.

Through varied experiences with many types of materials, children are guided to begin looking at number properties through such activities as the following:[15]

1. Identifying "sets" (well-defined collections, groups) of objects such as sets of dishes, sets of blocks, etc., deciding whether certain objects such as sets of cups and saucers can be divided into a sub-set of cups and a sub-set of saucers.

2. Identifying a missing member of a "set" such as a missing cup or crayon, and so on.

3. Dividing "sets" into "sub-sets" of items that are equal but not identical.

4. Locating "empty" situations, as flowers in a vase.

5. Discovering through arrangements of objects or children how "sets" may be manipulated by "partition" or "union" or "sub-sets."

6. Building the mathematical vocabulary and refining mathematical generalizations through exploratory experiences.

A child may be able to count by rote to 100 and yet not have a clear understanding of the meaning involved in such numerals as 5 or 7. Through counting objects in various sets the cardinal meaning of numerals can be developed. He learns that a "set" is a well-defined collection of objects that is either a perception of objects or a mental pattern of thinking. By matching sets of the same value a feeling of "twoness," "fiveness," and so on, is developed. As children compare sets, the results may be recorded by the teacher to show that some sets have more objects than others; this is the time to introduce the symbol > for greater than or the symbol = for equal.

According to Piaget, the child's conception of numbers takes place in terms of three stages: (1) perception which is coordination only within the field of

---

[15]Heimer, op. cit., p. 11.

perception; (2) operations which go beyond field of perception; and (3) transition from perception to deduction, progressive coordination of operations and gradual development reversibility.[16] Cardinal number is a class whose elements are conceived as "units" that are equivalent and distinct so that they can be seriated. Ordinal numbers are a series whose terms follow one another according to relations of order and determine the position; they are also units that are equivalent and therefore can be grouped in a class.[17] He also points out that there is a mutual relationship between classes and relations and that class and number are mutually dependent.[18]

He states that a child first guesses at the correspondence or order of one of a series and then makes a guess as to correspondence of one to another. Later he uses cardination but ignores ordination; then he makes use of ordination but ignores cardination. Then the child uses ordination and cardination but does not coordinate position. These stages first require provoked correspondence, which develops into spontaneous correspondence.[19]

DEVELOPMENT OF MATHEMATICAL CONCEPTS, UNDERSTANDINGS, AND ABILITIES

Many preschools do not have a special period for mathematics. This does not mean that the teacher has not planned for each child. The teacher may give individual help in small groups of children. She may work with a larger group in which each child contributes according to his maturity. Accurate records are kept so as not to leave gaps in learning. The teacher keeps a record of how each child uses what is taught as he participates in other activities and in his free play. Teachers need to recognize that children must participate in learning activities so that they have both correct and incorrect answers derived from a number of experiences. The experiences and activities are so planned and organized that the teaching is developed through *incidental* and *not accidental* experiences which provide opportunities for learning. Olson states that "The great hazard to the growth process is now commonly recognized as deprivation, whether it be of food, of experience, or of affection. The easiest things to discover and to appraise in the study of the curriculum are the areas where there is presence or absence of experience."[20] To avoid deprivation in certain areas of number experiences, it is essential then, in using the incidental method of teaching, that the teacher give attention to the laws or conditions of learning as related to arithmetic, to questions related to planning for and organizing

---

[16]Jean Piaget, *The Child's Conception of Numbers* (New York: Humanities Press, 1952); and *The Child's Concept of Geometry* (New York: Basic Books, 1960).

[17]Ibid., p. 157.

[18]Ibid., p. 147.

[19]Ibid., p. 47.

[20]Olson, op. cit., p. 380.

Figure 25. In dramatic play Wanda and Billy use the vocabulary related to money. They have opportunities to recognize and understand the relative value of coins and bills.

experiences, and to the developmental sequence of arithmetical skills. Children may be deprived of the opportunities they need for full maturation if the teacher does not understand the significance of the activities provided and also does not have the insight and skills essential to planning and developing these experiences.

Conditions for Learning

In planning for functional settings for the beginnings of mathematical concepts and skills, it is important to consider the conditions which make for effective learning. Barnes points out, (1) "we learn what we select to learn"; (2) "skills are not ends in themselves"; and (3) "the philosophy of the school should be such that each child is allowed to develop his own skill pattern."[21] This applies to the selection and development of the experiences while maintaining a permissive situation.

The teacher, then, needs to:

1. Recognize that learning is continuous and developmental; that is, each stage is dependent upon successive developments that preceded it.
2. Understand that the rate of introduction of new concepts is significant to the learning and that this rate differs for each child.

[21]Marcillene Barnes, "Skills with Style," *Child. Educ., 37*:6 (1961), p. 259.

3. Provide for development of understanding before acquisition of skill. Recall based upon understanding is more accurate and builds greater security. This method also provides for longer retention than mere memorization of facts.
4. Recognize that the number concept to be developed determines the method and organization. For example, the development of understanding of measures does necessarily follow the same sequence as for building understandings in counting.
5. Provide for repetition of and reuse in a different situation the concepts previously presented and partially learned. These experiences in number situations should be those that would normally confront the young child and that would involve him in the manipulative *use* of numbers and in *quantitative* thinking, including building, dramatic play, cooking, taking attendance, and so on.
6. Recognize that number language emerges from experience, however, the activities and situations for helping the child to acquire this language need to be consciously planned for each child as well as for the group.
7. Recognize that the child's interest and his ability are inseparable and interrelated factors as to what and how fast a child can and will develop the number concepts. That is, any plan for teaching must be based upon a careful study of each child in the group. The experiences must be selected, organized, and developed so that each child is provided learning opportunities according to his previous experiences and his learning potential.
8. Make the purpose clear and the questions intelligent and meaningful for the child.

Analyzing Mathematical Learnings

The teacher recognizes that the children are ready for experiences that build on and extend previous experiences; these experiences are limited but bear repetition in different settings. He counts spoons, children, and napkins. This change in the setting is important so that the concept and not the setting can be learned. Therefore, the skillful teacher utilizes all the natural settings that occur in the daily life of the school as she uses the quantitative words correctly in situations. For example, she says: "It is 10 o'clock—time for our lunch," or "It is 12 o'clock—the time your mother will meet you," or "In 10 minutes your father will come."

When going on excursions, the teacher may use a compass with the children to guide their directions or to determine the direction an airplane is flying. She is careful to use such words as *high, low, higher than, lower than, slow, fast, faster, far away, near.* On a trip children observe street signs pointing directions and listing distances. As the child plays he estimates, then measures, and compares distances that he jumps or runs.

Often the large thermometer in the room is read and recorded on the large calendar as the changes in weather are noted or the date is discussed.

Count-down for games and division of materials for work and play become opportunities for developing number learnings if the teacher is alert and plans the activities in terms of the readiness of the children. Selected songs, games, and finger plays develop interest in and provide for motivated repetition of concepts presented.

Concepts of quantity and of contrasting sizes and shapes are introduced and used informally; however, provisions for these activities are consciously planned by the teacher. Guided observations and discussions assist the children to know many quantitative words and to apply them in meaningful situations. Through this procedure the teacher guides the children to make contrasts and to select and use the proper word to express this contrast quantitatively.

Planning and Organizing Experiences

Only through listing the attitudes, skills, and understandings desired, can a teacher select and plan wisely for the continuous sequential development of number concepts. She must plan in terms of the development of individuals and small groups of children as well as for the larger group. The teacher will find questions such as the following useful in planning:

1. What seems important and desirable to teach, and why?
2. What is there in the child's or children's experience, at home or at school, on which this understanding or skill may be built?
3. What stimulation, explanation, adaptations, and directions are likely to be needed?
4. What must be prepared before the children arrive?
5. How can the purposes and the questions be made clear to the child?
6. What types of activities and experiences will be most purposeful and meaningful to the child as he uses and applies this skill or concept?
7. What kinds of materials will be needed and are they suitable, available, and accessible?
8. What should be observed in order to determine next steps in pre-planning for the following day?

As activities are planned, the teacher records and analyzes the types of home and school experiences that have contributed to the child's number readiness. She builds on and supplements these experiences; she also plans with the parents so that additional opportunities may be provided in the home for the child to apply and to reuse what he has learned at school.

In one kindergarten, a list of five names written under the word "thermometer" was observed on the teacher's desk. Upon inquiry the teacher explained that as the result of a recent activity, she had found that these five children did not know how to measure the temperature in the classroom. She had listed these children as those who would need special activities and guidance in the use of the thermometer.

In this same room was another list of children's names written under the figure "25¢." Explanation of this list indicated that these children should be included in activities related to the trip to the store, and that guided experiences should be provided for them to use 25¢ in *real* money (as a quarter, five nickels, or two dimes and a nickel) in functional situations.

All planning for experiences should be flexible, yet should make provision for situations that will require use of mathematics and quantitative thinking in a broad program. This program must be comprehensive yet balanced.

Developmental Sequence of Mathematical Skills

The teacher is so familiar with the curriculum and the developmental sequence of arithmetical skills that she takes advantage of each experience as it occurs. In addition, she projects and develops many creative situations through which the desired mathematical learnings are functionally introduced, used, reused, and evaluated. These meaningful experiences offer opportunities for the child to develop simple understandings that later unfold as he meets more and more difficult situations. Therefore, the teacher needs to make a careful listing of abilities, the developmental sequence required for learning skills, possible teaching experiences and procedures, plans for parent cooperation at school and at home, and ways of evaluating the progress for each child and for groups of children.

Such a list of the concepts, abilities, and understandings to be used as a frame of reference or as a basis for planning, and for analyzing the present development and the progress of young children in arithmetical skills and understanding, may be found in the following chart. Emphasis is placed upon simple beginnings in nursery school and expansion of the skills and understandings according to the developmental pace of each child. No attempt is made to force the child to acquire skills; these result as he understands and finds use for them in his daily living. Hence, no designation is made as to specific experiences for nursery school and for the kindergarten.

Figure 26. A graph of birthdays offers opportunities for counting, comparing, discussing, and reading.

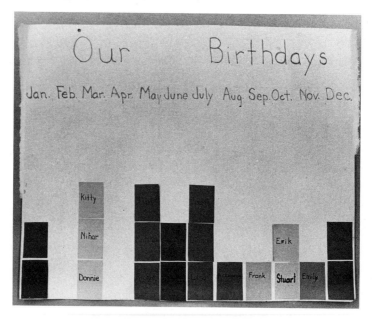

Abilities	Possible Teaching Procedures and Situations
I. Vocabulary	
To use number words that at first have no numerical significance.	Place emphasis upon experiences that will demand number judgments in routines such as resting, toileting, cleaning up, convening into a group, planning for better ways of work, engaging in dramatic play or block building, playing store, measuring height and weight.
To understand and use meaningful vocabulary with reference to numbers.	
To acquire vocabulary of number names: understand and use such quantitative words as *all, big, bunch, group, many, more, most, once, small, together, heavy, light, tall, short.*	
II. Counting	
To establish one-to-one relationship.	Count by rote which may or may not have meaning for the child.
To recognize small groups without counting, such as groups of two, groups of three, groups of four.	Do not mistake counting by rote as evidence of readiness to work with numerals.
To develop feelings of oneness, twoness, threeness, fourness.	Begin with child touching each object as he counts. Repeat this in various experiences until this need to touch or to point to objects is no longer necessary.
	Use rhyming words, finger plays, singing games.
	Recognize pairs, two's as in shoes, mittens, bicycles.
	Extend to three's as in tricycle or in games.
	Provide for many manipulative counting situations with beads, buttons, cookies, napkins, children, chairs. Match beads, blocks, and so on.
	Construct houses, trucks, wagons and compare size and shape needed.
	Play games that require selection in terms of comparison.
To compare through noting changes in size and form.	Compare and contrast blocks as to shape and size.
	Arrange groups of blocks, as to purpose and discuss size and shape.
To extend counting concept to "how many," "how many more," and later to "how many less" or "how many fewer" through six as it appears in the environment; the more mature children may extend these concepts through ten.	Determine number of places, quantity of milk, silverware, napkins, and so on, needed at table.
	Estimate "how many," or "how much," or "how long," then weigh or measure to verify.

Abilities	Possible Teaching Procedures and Situations
	Play games involving "more" or "less."
To extend counting through use of ordinals and acquiring additional vocabulary such as *first, second, next, last, pair, partner.*	Provide experiences for taking turns and situations requiring recording of events.
To recognize the printed symbol of numbers (this will interest the more mature child).	Read (and probably place) numbers in charts.
To observe figures and develop readiness for writing.	Identify numbers on the television.
	Observe figures on a page.
	Dial telephone numbers.
	Play with number cut-outs.
	Write home address.
	Provide for play with figure cut-outs.
	Make certain no pressure is exerted on the child to attempt to write figures before his small muscles are coordinated and he can perceive relationships.
	Call figures by name; do not refer to them as numbers.
	(*Note:* Writing numbers is not taught except when child requests help in writing. Reversal tendencies are a warning to the teacher that the child may not be ready to write.)

III. Fractions

Abilities	Possible Teaching Procedures and Situations
To begin knowledge of simple fractions usually at about six years of age.	Provide for sharing in terms of "half an apple," "a whole cookie," "half a sandwich."
To extend whole concept into use of parts and acquisition of vocabulary suited to this concept.	
To understand and use vocabulary to express parts of a whole, such as: $1/2$, $1/2$ *cup, cup; both, divide, piece, middle, double, alike.*	Plan situations requiring use of half a sheet of paper.
	Use vocabulary in comparing blocks and other objects as to size as "half as big" and so on.
	Prepare cocoa, jello, or cookies using measuring spoons and cups.
	Weigh objects with balancing scales.
	Measure height and weight using scale and discussing fractional parts.

Abilities	Possible Teaching Procedures and Situations
	Measure milk or fruit juice from quarts to fractional part in cups or glasses for lunch.

IV. Shape

Abilities	Possible Teaching Procedures and Situations
To understand and note shape and size of objects and places in environment, especially circle, square, triangle.	Observe and discuss objects and places in environment.
	Read and discuss stories involving number concepts, such as *The Three Bears,* or Ethel Berkley, *The Size of It.* (See list on pp. 252–253.)
To understand and use vocabulary to express size and shape such as *big, little, middle-sized, tall, thin, fat, tiny, wee.*	Discuss shape and size of small musical instruments.
	Discuss shape and size of containers, wheels, balls, and so on, for different purposes in terms of use.
To understand and use relationship words such as *large—small, full—empty, short—long, near—far, round—square.*	Provide opportunities to select container in terms of purpose.
To recognize that certain shapes are useful for a given purpose and that types of containers have different capacities.	Estimate and verify validity of selection.
	Build with blocks, put away toys, and so on, and discuss shape and size in terms of use.
To acquire such vocabulary as *quart, pint, cup, empty, full.*	
To recognize and understand size and shapes as related to construction.	

V. Measurement

Abilities	Possible Teaching Procedures and Situations
Space:	Ask questions about size.
To acquire and use vocabulary related to shape, size, capacity, and distance, such as *measure, big, fat, wee, tiny, short, wide, deep, low, high, hole, pound, ruler, teaspoon, tablespoon, cup, quart, pint, speedometer, round, circle, square, cube, cone, triangle.*	Discuss paper, pencils, rulers, yardsticks, and so on, in terms of shape, size, and purpose.
	Use ruler and yardstick in woodworking activities.
	Estimate how many small glasses in a quart, cookies in a box.
	Emphasize vocabulary as trips and excursions are planned and taken, or in giving directions or playing games.
	Listen to children talk to determine if their vocabulary is growing.
To extend concept of round to circle, circle from round to round and flat, and then to round and flat and with a center.	Find objects of different shapes in room, as a part of toys.

Abilities	Possible Teaching Procedures and Situations
V. Measurement	

Gingerbread Boys
1 Stick margarine
1 cup brown sugar
1 egg
Mix
Add 2 boxes Gingerbread Mix
1 cup flour
Mix
Bake 350°
12-15 minutes

Figure 27. The recipe for "Gingerbread Boys" is available for reference as the children work. This activity can involve use of measurement, simple fractions, counting, and reading.

Discuss how different shapes are useful for different purposes.

Experiment with filling different type containers.

Use much water play and sand activities involving weighing and measuring capacity.

To understand and use vocabulary related to distance, direction, and location, such as: *indoors, outdoors, front, back, top, bottom, beside.*

Measure distance child runs, jumps, or throws a ball.

Let child give directions to children.

Distinguish between right and left hand.

Discuss direction as to where one is when on tours.

Abilities	Possible Teaching Procedures and Situations
Temperature:	
To begin development of understanding and awareness of variations in temperature and adjustments made accordingly.	Post a large thermometer and call children's attention to it.
To acquire and use vocabulary related to temperature such as: *hot, cool, cold, warm, freeze, summer, spring, fall, winter, thermometer.*	Check temperature and record on calendar periodically but not necessarily daily. Summarize findings.
	Discuss various ways of telling temperature. Observe and discuss habits of people, animals, trees, and so on, according to changes in temperature.
	Discuss school nurse taking temperature.
	Post pictures of cool things, warm things, and discuss.
Time:	
To begin to understand duration of time and time sequence.	Respond to different ryhthmic time patterns.
To acquire and use vocabulary related to time such as: *now, soon, night, day, week, days of week, hour, minute, sometime.*	Discuss why certain things take longer to do than others.
	Discuss events that precede or follow other events.
To begin in understanding and using clock as a means of measuring time.	Use clock to determine actions.
To begin to understand calendar for measuring and recording time.	Call attention to clock in relation to jobs as discussed.
	Ask questions requiring clock—use words *hour, minute,* and so on.
	Raise such questions as "What time for lunch, to go swimming, how long until lunch?"
	Read and discuss books such as *All Kinds of Time* by Harry Behn or *Mike Mulligan and His Steam Shovel* by Virginia Lee Burton. However, this discussion should not destroy the enjoyment of the story by overemphasizing the number words and concepts.
	Post an attractive calendar.
	Fill in days and dates on calendar on bulletin board.
	Discuss days, dates, and special events.
	Note special days for celebrations.
Weight:	
To begin to develop concept of weight.	Lift different objects.

Abilities	Possible Teaching Procedures and Situations
V. Measurement	
Simple understandings related to balancing objects (like or unlike weights).	Discuss why some are heavier than others although smaller.
To begin to understand use of lever.	Weigh on scales, balancing scales.
To acquire and use vocabulary related to weight such as *pounds, ounces, scales, balance, lift, float, heavier, even, light, weigh, weight.*	Use wheel or slanted board to raise objects.
	Weigh and record child's weight.
	Weight other objects.
	Read labels giving weight.
VI. Money and Money Values	
To understand and use vocabulary related to money as a measure of value and as a means of use, such as: *buy, sell, trade, money, nickel, five cents, penny, dime, quarter, dollar, coin, change, pay, cost.*	Provide frequent opportunities to discuss with child and group value of coins, cost of toys or gifts, and counting.
To recognize and begin to understand relative value of coins and their use.	Identify in terms of purpose, penny, nickel, dime, quarter, half-dollar, and dollar (silver and paper).
	Buy supplies at room or school store.
These money experiences are provided as they become functional according to the child's maturity and purpose.	Pay for lunch.
	Pay for transportation.

TEACHING MATERIALS AND RESOURCES

Grossnickle states that there are four kinds of instructional materials: (1) real experiences; (2) manipulative materials; (3) pictorial materials and (4) symbolic materials.[22] In selecting materials, the teacher utilizes those that are available and functional in the life of the child at home and at school. The clock, the calendar, lunch money, the toy store, the thermometer, the thermostat, the barometer, the scales, the yardstick, the ruler, the drink and cookies for the midmorning snack, the chairs, and the tables may be used as a teaching resource.

Manipulative materials used within the home can be collected and used in the classroom—egg cartons, empty berry boxes, bottle tops, small and large boxes, buttons, and empty spools. Children's socks, shoes, gloves also provide valuable resources. Other manipulative materials such as the following need to be readily available in the classroom:

[22]F. E. Grossnickle, et al., "Instructional Materials for Teaching Arithmetic," *The Teaching of Arithmetic* (50th Yearbook), Part II (NSSE) (Chicago: University of Chicago Press, 1951), pp. 155–185.

Manipulative Materials

Empty spools, enameled in red, blue, or green.
Straws and tooth picks of various colors.
Balls of several sizes.
Large wooden beads of many colors.
Blocks of varied size and shape.
Empty milk or fruit cartons in quarts, pints, half pints.
Measuring cups marked into thirds, fourths, and halves.
Separate measuring cups holding $1/3$, $1/2$, and $1/4$ cups.
Measuring spoons.
Bottle caps, aluminum washers, colored plastic clothespins.
Toy money in coins and paper dollars.
Scraps of lumber.
Nails of several sizes.
Simple tools as hammer, saws.
Scraps of cloth of varied sizes, colors, shapes, and materials.
Paper bags of many sizes.
Cardboard clock.
Stop watch.
Clock with alarm.
Clock with second hand.
Timers for stove and for egg.
Sundial.
Scales of several types—balance, kitchen, bathroom, postal.
Cubes of soap.
Cake pans of various sizes and shapes, and muffin tins.
Peg boards, flannel boards with toys and figures.
Magnetic board.
Toy telephones, cash registers, adding machines.
Various types of dials—TV, washing machine, and radio.
Puzzles with geometric designs.
Calendar.
Thermometer.

The mathematical materials that have been provided and distributed by publishers of professional materials may be added if funds are available.

Pictorial materials have a place and a carefully selected picture file is of great value in illustrating the use of arithmetic in daily life. A collection of books, stories, finger plays, and poems that expand arithmetical concepts is a valuable resource for the teacher to read and for the children to look at or to take home to be shared. Such materials need to be selected carefully as to relationship with and treatment of the concepts to be developed, and the maturity of the child. This material should be artistic both in content and in the method of presentation. The mathematical problem should be involved in the story, and the content and use should be essential to the solution of the problem in the story. Through use of these materials the child acquires facility in use of vocabulary and builds understanding for use in more complex situations.

Books

Some books that teachers have found of value are listed below.

Asbjornsen, P. C., and J. E. Moe. *The Three Billy Goats Gruff*. Harcourt, Brace & World, 1957.

Auerbach, Marjorie. *Seven Uncles Come to Dinner*. Alfred A. Knopf, 1963.

Barr, Katherine. *Seven Chicks Missing*. Henry L. Walch, 1962.

Barum, Arline. *One Bright Monday Morning*. Random House, 1962.

Behn, Harry. *All Kinds of Time*. Harcourt, Brace & World, 1959.

Beim, Jerrold. *The Smallest Boy in the Class*. William R. Morrow, 1959.

Beim, L. *Two Is a Team*. Harcourt, Brace and World, 1966.

Berkley, Ethel S. *The Size of It and Ups and Downs*. E. M. Hale and Co., 1960.

———. *Big and Little, Up and Down, Early Concepts of Size and Direction*. William R. Scott, 1960.

Bishop, Claire. *Twenty-Two Bears*. Viking Press, 1964.

Bishop, Claire H., and Kurt Wiese. *The Five Chinese Brothers*. E. M. Hale and Co., 1958.

Branley, Franklyn. *Big Tracks, Little Tracks*. Crowell-Collier, 1960.

Budley, Blossom, and Vladimir Bobri. *A Cat Can't Count*. Lothrop, Lee, and Shepard Co., 1962.

Campbell, Alice B., et al. *Poems for Counting*. Holt, Rinehart and Winston, 1963.

Colman, Hilda. *Watch That Watch*. William R. Morrow, 1962.

Elkin, B. *Six Foolish Fishermen*. E. M. Hale and Co., 1963.

Fedenico, Helen. *Numbers*. Golden Press, 1963.

Fisher, Margery M. *One and One*. Dial Press, 1963.

Friskey, Margaret. *Seven Diving Ducks*. David McKay Co., 1960.

Grayson, Marion F. *Let's Do Fingerplays*. Robert Luce, 1962.

Haley, Gail. *One, Two, Buckle My Shoe*. Doubleday & Co., 1961.

Hughes, Peter. *The Emperor's Oblong Pancake*. Abelard Schuman, 1962.

Jacobs, Joseph. *The Three Wishes*. Whittlesly Howe, 1961.

Jerichin, Cecile. *Hello! Do You Know My Name?* G. P. Putnam's Sons, 1963.

Keyes, Juliet. *Two Little Birds and Three*. Houghton Mifflin, 1960.

Kessler, Leonard. *I Made a Line*. Grosset and Dunlap, 1962.

———. *The Worm, The Bird and You*. Dodd, Mead & Co., 1962.

Kohn, Bernice. *Everything Has a Shape*. Prentice-Hall, 1964.

———. *Everything Has a Size*. Prentice-Hall, 1964.

Lathan, Jean L., and Bee Lewi. *The Cuckoo That Couldn't Count*. Macmillan, Inc., 1961.

Leodhas, Sorche Mic. *All in the Morning Early*. Holt, Rinehart and Winston, 1963.

Le Sieg, Theo. *Ten Apples Up on Top*. Random House, 1961.

Rand, Ann and Paul. *Little I*. Harcourt, Brace & World, 1962.

Rolf, Myller. *How Big Is a Foot*. Atheneum Bess, 1962.

Schlein, Miriam. *Shapes*. E. M. Hale and Co., 1952.

Schott, Andrew F. *The Littlest One*. Tools for Education, Inc. 1961.

Scott, Binder, and J. S. Thompson. *Rhymes for Fingers and Flannel Boards*. Webster Publishing Co., 1960

Sendak, Maurice. *One Way Johnny*. Harper & Row, 1962.

Shuman, Diane. *My Counting Book*. Rand McNally, 1963.

Slobodkina, Esphyr. *The Clock*. E. M. Hale and Co., 1961.
Steiner, Charlotte. *Ten in a Family*. Alfred A. Knopf, 1960.
Stobbs, William, illustrator. *The Story of the Three Bears*. McGraw-Hill Book Co., 1965.
Sullivan, Joan. *Round is a Pancake*. Holt, Rinehart and Winston, 1963.
True, Louise. *Number Men*. Children's Press, 1962.

Evaluating Mathematical Learnings

Evaluation is an essential part of any school program but it becomes increasingly important in a program based largely on incidental teaching. Since the experiences are a part of the child's life and living, it is necessary to check to see whether he is making progress in all the areas of the number program. Suppes points out that the emphasis should be placed on *understanding* concepts as opposed to perfection of *rote skills*. He states that "no one seems to be very clear about the exact specification of the behavior required to exhibit understanding."[23]

The teacher will do a better job of guiding mathematical learnings if she makes the following evaluations:

The Program

1. Has provision been made for experiences involving all abilities listed on page 245, counting, measurement, vocabulary, and so on? It is easy to have had many experiences in one area and comparatively few or even none in another area.
2. Is the teaching in terms of the readiness of the children? According to Swenson, "The attainment of readiness is a continuing process of becoming more ready than one was previously. Adults will understand the learning of children much better if they will think in terms of their being more or less ready rather than ready or unready."[24] No two children will be at the same level of readiness; even if two appear to give the same response, one may have a more complete understanding.
3. Has there been practice in the repetition of a skill in a functional setting? Brownell and Henrickson state that "The fundamental method of teaching some factual material, most symbols, and arbitrary associations in general remains, as always, the administration of repetitive practice. The statement holds true regardless of the way in which children *learn* these materials."[25] Therefore, the teacher checks to see if this repetition is found throughout the day as the children work and play together.
4. Is there a variety of materials and methods designed to develop the desired number concepts? Consider, for example, the use of rhymes or finger plays in counting.

[23]P. Suppes, "The Formation of Mathematical Concepts in Primary Children," *Intellectual Development: Another Look* (Washington, D.C.: ASCD, 1964), p. 99.

[24]Esther J. Swenson, "Arithmetic for Pre-School and Primary-Grade Children," *The Teaching of Arithmetic* (50th Yearbook), Part II (NSSE) (Chicago: University of Chicago Press, 1951), p. 55.

[25]W. A. Brownell and G. Henrickson, "How Children Learn Information, Concepts, and Generalizations," in *Learning and Instruction* (49th Yearbook), Part I (NSSE) (Chicago: University of Chicago Press, 1950), pp. 92–128.

Figure 28. In the Mathematics Center Marsha places the correct card on the horses. "Yes, there are seven horses."

Wheat states that rhymes and other activities often called rote-counting have little value except for the memorization of number names and that counting always involves the projected purpose of finding out "how many." This does not imply that these activities have no place in the development of the number program. It does mean that they should be used in terms of what they can contribute, namely, *memorization of number names in order.*[26] It will be necessary for the teacher to check and see whether or not other activities are provided to develop further skill in counting.

Analyzing the Progress of the Individual Child

The teacher observes the child in his activities to determine the degree to which he has acquired mathematical skill and understanding. She evaluates progress as she notes for each child his ability (1) to match objects, (2) to determine if he has enough, too many, or too few, (3) to count without skipping but using number names in correct order, (4) to match number names with objects or to give a correct number of objects for a number name, and (5) as he strings beads, to count them by one's or in groups of two's or three's.

Ilg and Ames point out that "The writing of numbers is often easier to evaluate than the writing of letters with their upper and lower case forms. Much can be learned from the child's writing of numbers up to 20 or as far

[26]H. G. Wheat, *How to Teach Arithmetic* (Evanston, Ill.: Row, Peterson, 1961), pp. 22–23.

toward 20 as he can go."[27] They found that observation of the child as he writes numbers provides an excellent opportunity to study the child in terms of use of the nondominant hand, placement of numbers on paper, organization of lines, breaking points in number, size and shape of numbers, reversals, and so on. For example, at the age of five a given child's ability may be spotty but before he reaches five and one half years this ability may be greatly improved.[28]

As the teacher evaluates, she records her findings. She keeps a record for each child which she summarizes frequently in order to secure valuable aid for her planning and to guide her as she works with him. This record of the child includes analyses of the following:

1. Concepts of words having to do with size, shape, spatial relationship, time, temperature, and money.
2. Ability to secure necessary information by counting.
3. Ability to distinguish shapes.
4. Understanding of fractional parts.
5. Understanding of spatial relationships.
6. Knowledge that relates to the clock as it measures time and the calendar's use to record days, weeks, and months.
7. Ability to discriminate simple measurements in quantitative terms.
8. Familiarity with money values and use of money coins.

The teacher checks to see if the children learn easily, use their own words or words they have heard, remember what they have heard, use ideas in a new setting, and can apply the idea to a new learning. If any of these are unsatisfactory, she again presents the idea but in a new activity of experience. (See pages 245–250.)

As the year progresses, the teacher periodically summarizes her work, the progress of the children, checks against the list prepared to serve as a guide, and adjusts her plans for teaching as well as provides new experiences for the children as the evaluation indicates. She confers and plans with the parent in order that the number experiences at school and at home may supplement and complement each other.

Olson points out that, "It is important that persons charged with nurturing the early learning of a child should agree on the kinds of things to be learned. Otherwise, the child may be subjected to opposing objectives and methods."[29]

Thus, each child is guided and assisted to progress at his own rate and in his own developmental pattern as he acquires a number vocabulary and mathematical skills based on understanding through use in a functional setting. He learns to put together carefully these beginnings of number language to express his purposes as he discovers their meaning and use in solving a

---

[27]Frances L. Ilg and Louise Bates Ames, *School Readiness* (New York: Harper & Row, 1965), pp. 54–55.

[28]Ibid.

[29]Olson, op. cit., p. 381.

personal problem. He develops independence in use of these understandings and skills when he attacks new problems. As he matures, he gains self-confidence in his ability to figure out ways to solve problems intelligently and creatively.

Suggested Activities

1. Contact a group of children in the neighborhood, in the home, and/or in an organized group. Talk with them informally and jot down examples of number vocabulary used. Note their ability to count, to recognize common coins, and to select coins in terms of relative values. Note differences among three-, four-, five-, and six-year-olds and differences among children of the same age group.

2. Observe a group of three-, four-, and five-year-olds in nursery school or kindergarten. List the vocabulary used by the group in terms of size and weight, distance, time, temperature, and shape.

3. List some suggested activities suitable for two- or three-year-old children at varying stages in the development of mathematical concepts.

4. Discuss the differences among the relative value of the incidental, the social, the drill, and the meaningful approach in the development of mathematical concepts and abilities and understandings. Justify your statements as to relative values of these approaches.

5. Observe in a school for three-, four-, and/or five-year-olds. List materials available for the children and how these materials were utilized in the development of mathematical abilities and understandings.

   Describe the method and organization used by the teacher to guide the children in their selection and use of these materials.

   Note provision made by the teacher to involve the children in a different situation through use of concepts previously presented and partially learned.

   Describe how the number language emerged from the experience.

6. Discuss the importance of planning, readapting plans, and continuing evaluation in providing experiences for the development of mathematical skills and concepts. List ways in which the teacher can do this effectively.

Related Readings

Ashlock, R. "What Math for Fours and Fives?" *Child. Educ.*, 43:7 (1967), pp. 469–473.

Copeland, R. W. *How Children Learn Mathematics: Teaching Implications of Piaget's Research,* 2nd ed. New York: Macmillan, Inc., 1974.

Davis, R. B. *The Changing Curriculum: Mathematics.* Washington, D.C.: ASCD, 1967.

Deutsch, M., and associates. *The Disadvantaged Child.* New York: Basic Books, 1967.

Glennon, V. J., and L. G. Callahan. *Elementary School Mathematics: A Guide to Current Research*, 3rd ed. Washington, D.C.: ASCD, 1968.

Heard, I. M. "Mathematical Concepts and Abilities Possessed by Kindergarten Entrants," *Arithmetic Teacher*, 17:4 (1970), pp. 340–341.

Inhelder, B., and J. Piaget. *The Early Growth of Logic in the Child.* New York: Harper & Row, 1969.

Intellectual Development: Another Look. Washington, D.C.: ASCD, 1964.

Kean, J. M. "Research—The Impact of Head Start. An Evaluation of the Effects of Head Start on Children's Cognitive and Affective Development," *Child. Educ., 46*:9 (1970), pp. 449–453.

Kohlberg, L. "Early Education, A Cognitive Developmental View," *Child. Develpm., 39*:4 (1968), pp. 1013–1062.

McClentie, J. "Unit of Measure," *Arithmetic Teacher, 13*:7 (1966), pp. 385–386.

Montague, D. O. "Arithmetic Concepts of Kindergarten Children in Contrasting Socio-economic Areas," *Elem. Sch. J., 64*:7 (1964), pp. 393–397.

New Directions in Mathematics. Washington, D.C.: ACEI, 1965.

Pollach, S., and Juliena Gensley. "When Do They Learn Geometry?" *Young Children, 20*:1 (1964), pp. 52–55.

Rea, R. E., and R. E. Reys. "Mathematics Competence of Entering Kindergartners," *Arithmetic Teacher, 17*:1 (1970), pp. 63–74.

Schlinsog, G. W. "More About Mathematics in the Kindergarten," *Arithmetic Teacher, 13*:8 (1968), pp. 701–705.

Smith, I. D. "The Effect of Training Procedures upon the Acquisition of Conservation of Weight," *Child Develpm., 39*:2 (1968), pp. 515–526.

Suydam, Marilyn N., and C. A. Riedesel. "An Interpretive Study of Research and Development in Elementary School Mathematics," *Child. Educ., 47*:4 (1971), pp. 221–226.

Swenson, Esther S. *Teaching Mathematics to Children,* 2nd ed. New York: Macmillan, Inc., 1973.

The Social Studies

Strikes, riots, pollution, rapid change, unemployment, moon landings, assassinations, and violence—all these are realities of the present-day world that intrude even into centers for young children.

Education for facing such social problems cannot be delayed until the children are older. The early years are very important and instruction must begin during these years. Hess and Easton attempted to discover the concepts, attitudes, and values held by children about the political world. Data collected seem to indicate that the child's political world begins to take shape before he enters elementary school and is subject to rapid change. Many basic political attitudes and values are firmly established by the end of elementary school.[1]

Lambert and Klineberg reported views which children hold of their own and foreign peoples. Such findings seem to imply the necessity of early concern

[1]R. Hess and D. Easton, "The Role of the Elementary School in Political Socialization," *The School Review*, 70:3 (1962), pp. 257–265.

Figure 29. Realities of the present-day world are evident in children's centers. Dennis has assumed the role of an astronaut.

for the development of international views and attitudes essential to inter-cultural and international understanding. For example, by age six children stressed differences rather than similarities of people from other countries.[2] Goodman reported that the onset of bigotry and racially related value systems is to be found in children as young as four years.[3] Findings such as these should influence both the content and the techniques of social studies for young children and emphasize the importance of social studies in the child develop-ment center, the nursery school, and the kindergarten.

Social studies education, says Jarolimek, has the task of helping the young to grow in their understanding of and sensitivity to the physical and social forces at work around them so that they may shape their lives in harmony

[2]W. E. Lambert and O. Klineberg, *Children's Views of Foreign Peoples.* (New York: Appleton-Century-Crofts, Inc., 1967).

[3]Mary Ellen Goodman, *Race Awareness in Young Children,* rev. ed. (New York: Macmillan, Inc., 1964).

with those forces. Such education must help children generate hope in the future and confidence in their ability to solve social problems.[4]

In order to accomplish the task the teachers of young children need help with questions such as the following:

1. Why are social studies included in the program for young children?
2. What is taught in social studies in the nursery school and kindergarten?
3. What are some common fallacies about social learnings for young children?
4. How does the teacher plan and organize her work for teaching in this area?
5. What learning situations—teaching strategies, activities, and experiences—are best for children of these age groups?

Why Teach Social Studies?

Through content and experiences, the social studies are designed to develop intelligent, responsible, self-directing individuals who can function as members of groups—family, community, world—with which they become identified.

The aims and objectives of the social studies program can be stated as follows:

1. Develop understandings of cooperative group living with an awareness of and appreciation for the rights of others, personal property, honesty, courtesy, responsibility.
2. Broaden the child's social environment through guided opportunities to live, play, work, and meet with other children and adults of various backgrounds, religions, and races.
3. Explore the child's here-and-now interests in his environment, focusing on home, school, and neighborhood; stress the interdependence of man in neighborhood and community.
4. Aid the child's understanding of his dependence upon parents, older siblings, teachers, school personnel, neighborhood and community helpers, and how he can help others.
5. Stretch the child's horizon to include new understandings relating to children in other countries of the world and their ways of living.[5]

Social studies are concerned, then, with behavior, goals, values, skills, and knowledge. The objectives may be classified in three categories: understandings, which deal with knowledge and knowing; attitudes, which deal with values, appreciations, ideals, and feelings; and skills, which deal with using and applying learnings.[6]

Concepts, skills, and behavior are all interrelated. In guiding behavior, it

---

[4] J. Jarolimek, *Social Studies in Elementary Education*, 4th ed. (New York: Macmillan, Inc., 1971), pp. 1–2.

[5] *A Guide: Early Childhood Education in Florida Schools*, Bull. 76 (Tallahassee: Florida State Department of Education, 1969), p. 23.

[6] Jarolimek, op. cit., p. 10.

is necessary to consider the feelings and needs as well as the ideas, attitudes, and skills of the child. As Ojemann pointed out, if a child is in a position where his security, self-respect, or activity is seriously threatened, it will be difficult for him to cooperate with others.[7]

In setting up learning situations and planning teaching strategies, the teacher must make sure that each child has opportunities to gain some measure of self-respect, satisfaction, assurance, and emotional security through the desired behavior. This is easier said than done. To indicate something of the difficulty involved, it is important to examine some of the fallacies to which teachers are prone.

The first fallacy is *to view beliefs and social action as separate*. The tendency has been to act and teach as if the child will behave as he is told, not as he observes others behaving. The admonition, "Do as I say, not as I do," is perhaps a futile one. It is from his environment that the child learns of people and things.

What a child comes to recognize as important usually depends on what values are set on the event by his parents, teachers, and other adults. Rasey and Menge state, "Children see their world as through a glass, darkly or brightly, as their adults reflect or transmit it to them." Speaking of the teacher, they point out:[8]

> Whether he wants the responsibility or not, the fact remains that our own choices and preferences are themselves contagious, and ways of life of young humans always have a considerable admixture of the choices and preferences of those in their human environment.

Research in this area tends to support the statements made by Rasey and Menge that the values and attitudes of children reflect those of parents, teachers, and other adults in the community. Hill questioned urban children as to their ideals and found that 30 per cent of the seven-year-olds named fathers and mothers as their ideals.[9] Havighurst asked children to respond to the topic, "The Person I Would Like To Be When I Grow Up." Concepts as to the ideal self in early childhood tended to represent an identification with one or both parents.[10]

According to Trager, the Philadelphia studies have shown that if the culture practices and condones rejection, children tend to behave and think in terms

---

[7]R. Ojemann, "Social Studies in Light of Knowledge about Children," *Social Studies in the Elementary School* (56th Yearbook NSSE), (Chicago: University of Chicago Press, 1957), p. 78.

[8]Marie Rasey and J. W. Menge, *What We Learn from Children* (New York: Harper & Row, 1956), p. 39.

[9]D. S. Hill, "Personification of Ideals by Urban Children," *J. Soc. Psychol.*, 1:2 (1930), pp. 379–392.

[10]R. J. Havighurst, Myra Z. Robinson, and Mildred Dorr, "The Development of the Ideal Self in Childhood and Adolescence," *J. Educ. Res.*, 40:4 (1946), pp. 241–257.

Figure 30. Early contact with children from other countries can contribute to the development of intercultural and international understandings.

of rejection.[11] Even in kindergarten, children accepted adult concepts and attitudes toward racial and religious groups. "One of the most socially wasteful learnings children get from their schooling is the habit of viewing beliefs and social action as separated one from the other."[12]

Harris, Gough, and Martin found a direct relationship between the attitudes of parents and children. Parents who are accepting of themselves, their children, and other people have a positive influence on their children while those with negative attitudes have a negative influence.[13]

One who teaches young children needs to be reminded of the implications of the old saying, "What you are speaks so loud I can't hear what you say." The school situation must be planned so as to help children to observe and practice behavior consistent with the beliefs and values which it is hoped they will choose.

Another common fallacy is *to assume that all children are at the same stage of maturity and have had the same experiences.* In planning teaching strategies in the social studies, the question is frequently asked as to when the child

[11]Helen G. Trager and Marian R. Yarrow, *They Learn What They Live: Prejudice in Young Children* (New York: Harper & Row, 1952), p. 392.

[12]Alice Miel and Peggy Brogan, *More Than Social Studies* (Englewood Cliffs, N.J.: Prentice-Hall, 1957), p. 133.

[13]Reported in Celia Stendler and W. Martin, *Intergroup Education in Kindergarten-Primary Grades,* (New York: Macmillan Publishing Co., 1953), p. 11.

should begin the study of history or geography. The reply is often made in terms of age or grade levels. The answer, however, should be when concepts of time, geographical location, and distance are sufficiently developed so that he can profit from such studies. Since the development of such concepts depends on both the nature of the child and the experiences he has had, the time will not be the same for all children of a given age. However, the experiences provided in early childhood contribute to the development of the concepts essential to the study of history, geography, and other social studies.

Life experiences which have an influence on achievement include[14] patterns of physical growth, development of interests, child's emotional organization, quality of child's relations with others, social class, national background, family, and family values.

Backgrounds of children vary widely. Lacey studied 125 social concepts of children in grades one through three. She found that the differences in concept development within a grade group seemed to be of more importance than the differences between grades.[15] Harrison used fifty common terms relating to time and found that children of high intelligence in the kindergarten scored almost as many correct responses as children of lower intelligence in the third grade.[16]

The third fallacy is *to assume that when a child uses labels or words he understands the meaning of the word or concept.* Since there is no inevitable connection between the meaning of a concept and the word that stands for it, it is quite possible for a child to use the word with little understanding of the meaning or even the wrong meaning. For example, a "train-bearer" to a four-year-old meant a little boy carrying a "choo-choo" train. One group of five-year-olds talked about being kind to one another. That they did not understand the meaning of kindness was evidenced by the fact that immediately following the discussion, these same children forced another child out of the playhouse.

Another fallacy is *to assume that the values that adults hold for the child are the same as the child's values.* The question, then, becomes one of asking how the child learns what he ought to do. Just because the child knows the desired response does not mean that he will behave in that way. The child may answer as he thinks adults want him to answer. Fite and Jersild found that during an interview a three- or four-year-old may say that fighting is bad, yet actually engage in fighting.[17] Combs says that "Our greatest failures are those connected

[14]Sybil K. Richardson and Faith W. Smitter, "The Learner," *Learning and the Teacher,* 1959 Yearbook (Washington, D.C.: ASCD, 1959), pp. 29–34.

[15]Joy M. Lacey, *Social Studies Concepts of Children in the First Three Grades* (New York: Teachers College, Columbia University, 1932).

[16]M. Lucile Harrison, "The Nature and Development of Concepts of Time Among Young Children," *Elem. Sch. J.,* 34:7 (1934), pp. 507–514.

[17]M. D. Fite and A. T. Jersild, "Agressive Behavior in Young Children and Children's Attitudes Toward Aggression," *Genet. Psychol. Monogr.,* 22:2 (1940), pp. 151–319.

with the problem of helping people to behave differently as a result of the information we have provided them."[18]

Children need opportunities to discover the personal value and usefulness of the concept. Until the child finds that he can solve his problems satisfactorily, get a turn at the slide, or use the blocks without fighting, he will probably continue to hit, grab, and push. He needs help in finding different ways of solving a problem and of evaluating the various methods.

To correct these fallacies and to plan effectively for learning situations through which the objectives of the social studies may be realized, it is essential to observe the following basic principles:

1. Children must have an opportunity to clarify what they say and to relate this to what they do; to live what they learn; to experience and to practice kindness, courtesy, sharing; and to make choices. Verbalization alone is not adequate.
2. Meaningful experiences closely related to the activities of the child and behavioral goals are essential. The child must find in the desired behavior some satisfaction, some enhancement of his self-respect, security, and personal worth.
3. Standards, teaching strategies, and learning activities must be adapted to the differences prevalent in the group. Each child needs the opportunity to participate in challenging activities, to make choices, and assume responsibilities suited to his background.

What to Teach: Content

Social studies in nursery school and kindergarten focus on the immediate environment and experiences of the child. The use of themes to indicate areas of study for different age levels has been widely practiced. Themes for young children have been related to the child's experiences in the here and now. "Living Together in Home and School" is typical of the themes selected for kindergarten and first grade. "Community Helpers" is often the topic for the second grade. At successive grade levels the child studies about the state, the nation, and the world, both historically and geographically.

Such an organization has value as revealed by the research related to the development of time and space concepts in children. Ames found that while four-year-olds can indicate that an event took place before or after a meal, he cannot tell the time of day or the day of the week.[19] Oakden and Sturt found that not until age eleven are concepts of historical time sufficiently developed to place historical characters in chronological order.[20]

Dunfee, however, reports that

[18]A. W. Combs, "Personality Theory and Its Implications for Curriculum Development," *Learning More About Learning* (Washington, D.C.: ASCD, 1959), p. 9.

[19]Louise B. Ames, "The Development of the Sense of Time in the Young Child," *J. Genet. Psychol.*, 68:1 (1946), pp. 97–125.

[20]E. C. Oakden and M. Sturt, "Development of Knowledge of Time in Children," *Brit. J. Psychol.*, 12:4 (1922), pp. 309–336.

a review of the studies of time concepts seems to indicate that children may be able to understand time and chronology concepts at an earlier age than previously predicted and that many children are receptive to planned instruction in these relationships.[21]

The authors recognize the limitations of the child's concept of time and his experiential background. They are aware, however, of the impossibility of limiting the child's learnings to those of the home and school. Many children, by the age of five, have lived in other countries or have some member of their family living abroad. By means of television the child becomes aware of holidays and hears something of their historical significance. Few, if any, children move sequentially from home to school, to community, state, nation, and the world in their experiences. Fraser states:

> The principle of selecting and arranging learning experiences in terms of children's experiential backgrounds remains valid. Implementation of the principle requires a realistic appraisal of the experiences and needs of today's children.[22]

An appraisal was made by Wann who, with a group of teachers, studied three-, four-, and five-year-old children in their own classrooms over a period of five years. He reported

> The readiness of young children for challenging intellectual experiences was evident throughout the study. The young children were eager to gather information to apply to their conversations and their play situations. They were attempting to see relationships, to make generalizations, to discriminate, to classify. They were curious and concerned about the daily occurrences of group living, about friendship and family, neighbor and neighborhood. They were interested in the faraway in time and space. . . . They were trying to interpret and have interpreted for them the many facets of the world around them. Not all children were at the same point of intellectual development. Some had more information on a greater variety of topics, others had less.[23]

The store of information young children have today, their continual quest for knowledge, and their struggle to organize information into a meaningful conceptual framework have significant implications for school programs. It is apparent that teachers of young children must support their efforts to acquire information and to organize it.

Not only do most children have wider knowledge today, but it has been found that they can learn more than was formerly expected. Almy points to the

---

[21]Maxine Dunfee, *Elementary Social Studies: A Guide to Current Research* (Washington, D.C.: ASCD, 1970), p. 29.

[22]Dorothy M. Fraser, "The Organization of the Elementary School Social Studies Curriculum," *Social Studies in the Elementary School*, Part II (NSSE) (Chicago: University of Chicago Press, 1957), p. 141.

[23]K. D. Wann, Miriam S. Dorn, and Elizabeth A. Liddle, *Fostering Intellectual Development in Young Children* (New York: Teachers College, Columbia University, 1962), p. 98.

Figure 31. Concepts in the areas of economics, conservation, geography, and civics can be developed as children engage in this learning episode or unit. Cooperative planning, a trip to the grocery store, preparing vegetables and cooking soup, and dramatic play are among the teaching strategies used.

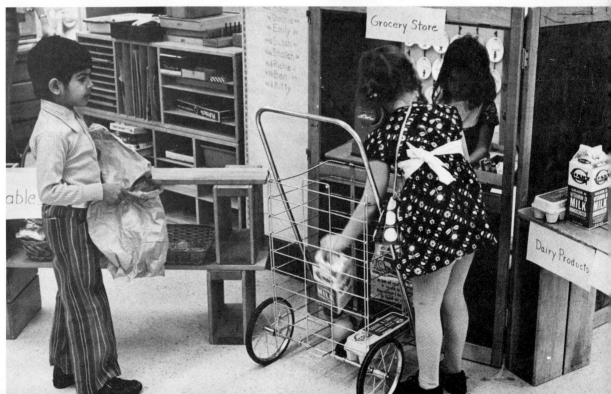

possibility that some degree of acceleration in the rate of intellectual development in young children can be achieved.[24] Combs explains that human capacities for behavior depend upon perception and therefore are more open to change than has been thought.[25]

In view of the changing experiences and concepts of children, it appears wise to enlarge the scope of the social studies for young children to include understandings from all the major areas of social studies and provide for the growth of children through constantly enlarging experiences. Simple ideas introduced in the nursery school and kindergarten will lay a foundation for understanding more complex ones in later grades. Such a "spiral approach" introduces concepts to the young child and provides for reteaching these concepts in a more complex situation at a later date. According to Brunner, in the spiral curriculum "ideas are first presented in a form and language, honest though imprecise, which can be grasped by the child, ideas which can be revisited later with greater precision and power until finally, the student has received the reward of mastery."[26]

As an example of this approach, certain areas of the social studies are listed. For each area some of the concepts appropriate for the child development center, the nursery school, and the kindergarten are listed, along with suggested opportunities for experiences that can contribute to the development of concepts, understandings, values, and skills:

TABLE 14-1
LEARNINGS IN SOCIAL STUDIES

Area	Examples of Concepts To Be Learned	Some Learning Encounters and Activities That Can Contribute to Concept Development
1. Citizenship education.	Each person has worth and dignity. We are not all alike.	Introduce each child in class. Talk about how children are alike and yet different. Use books, songs, pictures, discussion.
2. Civics.	Rules can help us live happily together (respect for rules and regulations).	Participate in discussion of "limits" or "rules" for the slide. Make plans for taking a walk. Note "how we cross the street," "why we walk on the sidewalk." Accept "limits" set by group.
3. Conservation.	Money is used to buy food, clothing, and school supplies. They can be used freely but without waste (respect for personal and public property).	Take care of one's own possessions. Hang coat in locker, wear apron while painting. Use paper towels as needed. Help clean up after work period.

[24]Millie Almy, "New Views in Intellectual Development in Early Childhood Education," *Intellectual Development: Another Look* (Washington D.C.: ASCD, 1964), p. 21.

[25]Combs, *Learning More About Learning*, op. cit., p. 13.

[26]J. S. Bruner, *On Knowing* (Cambridge, Mass.: Harvard University Press, 1962), p. 62.

Area	Examples of Concepts To Be Learned	Some Learning Encounters and Activities That Can Contribute to Concept Development
4. Economics.	Understanding that people do different types of work (appreciation of contribution of others). People live in different types of homes (understanding of how others live).	Learn about the work that parents do, use stories, pictures, trips, visitors, and discussion. Learn about homes in which the children live; trailer, apartment, one-story houses. Use pictures, art products, trips, stories, discussion.
5. History— American heritage.	Understanding that great men had great ideas. They were honest, brave, kind (historical understanding). An event is a part of a chronological series. Simple time relationships exist. Our society changes.	Celebrate holidays. Emphasize historic significance. Use stories, films, trips, role-playing, music, bulletin-board displays. Discuss and clarify meaning of honest, brave, kind. Learn how time is measured. Use clock and calendar. Discuss important events in lives of the children. Observe changes in neighborhood or town. Discuss reasons for change.
6. Geography— where we live. Relationship of scientific and social change.	Understanding that people travel in different ways. Messages are sent in different ways. Weather affects the way we dress and where we play (readiness for geography).	Learn about the ways people travel. Take a bus or train ride. Visit the airport. Send messages—use telephone, mail a letter. Observe evidence of seasonal changes.
7. International understandings.	An awareness of other people in other countries. Children live and play in other countries. (Recognition that people are different—not necessarily that one is better than another.)	Learn games and songs of children in other lands. Compare them with games and songs of the kindergarten children. Invite persons from other lands to talk with children.
8. Anthropology.	People live according to certain values, skills, and traditions.	Talk about how each family celebrates birthdays. Role play social skills. Make choices and examine alternatives. Consider what each child values most. Examine behavior of group.
9. Sociology.	The family is the basic social unit in our society.	Learn about members of the family. Play roles of family members. Use pictures, books, and songs.
10. Environmental education— ecology.	Water and air can be polluted. Many familiar sounds cause noise pollution. Waste disposal is a severe problem.	Observe effects of air pollution on one's eyes and breathing. Note effects of water pollution on where children can swim. Identify sounds which contribute to noise pollution. Plan to reduce noise at school and home. Plan for cleaning room. Observe disposal of school waste.

PLANNING AND TEACHING

A teacher, aware of the major areas of the social studies and concepts appropriate for nursery school and kindergarten, will find many opportunities for helping the child to develop desirable habits, attitudes, and skills and to gain useful information.

Suggested strategies for planning and teaching are discussed on pages 151–162, and the reader is urged to refer to this section for a more detailed treatment. Certain strategies are illustrated here with examples from the social studies.

REINFORCING, CLARIFYING, EXPLAINING, AND DISCUSSING INCIDENTS THAT AFFECT CHILDREN DURING THE SCHOOL DAY. For example, one Monday morning the kindergarten children were telling about what they had done over the weekend.

> Jack: "I went to Sunday School. I go to the Presbyterian Sunday School."
> Joseph: "I don't. We go to the Episcopal Church."
> Several children joined in, identifying the church that they attended. Then Edith spoke. "I don't go to Sunday School. My mother doesn't take me." The teacher replied, "On Sunday, Jack and Joseph went to church with their parents. Edith stayed at home. We can do that because we live in our country, the United States. In our country, mothers and fathers can choose whether or not they want to go to church. They can choose the church, too."
> While children at this age do not understand the term "religious freedom," a discussion such as this can provide the experience on which generalizations can be developed later. This opportunity for children to talk about different religions can contribute to fulfilling the second objective on page 61.

COOPERATIVE PLANNING. An example of cooperative planning follows: The kindergarten children had been given a collie puppy. It was their very own puppy, and it must have a name. The teacher and children sat down together.

> Teacher: "Several of you have already suggested names for the puppy. Hugh wants 'Candy.' Glenn wants 'Collie'; Joan wants 'Spot.' How shall we decide?"
> Glenn: "We could vote."
> Teacher: "Yes, we can vote. That means I will write down each name: Candy, Collie, and Spot. Then I will ask each of you to tell me the name you like best. We will count to see how many children like each name. The name that the most of you like will be the name of our puppy. Do you want to do it that way?"
> Children: "Yes."
> Teacher: "Think for a moment about the names: Candy, Collie, and Spot. Decide on the one you want."
> Each name was written on a piece of newsprint. As each child's name was called, the teacher made a mark by his choice. Together they counted the marks:

Candy—20.
Spot—3.
Collie—2.

Teacher: "Candy has 20 votes. That is more votes than for the other two. So Candy will be our puppy's name."

Glenn, who wanted "Collie," angrily stamped his foot and said, "Why vote, if you can't get what you want?

Teacher: "Glenn, we vote to give everyone a chance to say what he wants. You didn't get your choice this time. We will vote again some other time on another idea. Maybe you will win then."

This learning encounter can help the children develop understandings of cooperative group living and an appreciation for the rights of others, the first objective on page 61.

FIELD TRIPS. The use of field trips is discussed on pages 153–155. The suggestions for planning and evaluating are also applicable to the social studies.

Trips may be made in connection with the study of a variety of topics in the community. Trips may be made to centers such as the library, the fire station, or the post office; sources of food supply such as the farm, the orchard or grove, the dairy, the supermarket; transportation to locations such as the airport, the railroad terminal, bus station, a street or highway; the home, which could include a look at the various types of homes and the actual construction of a building.

INSTRUCTIONAL TECHNOLOGY. See pages 160–161 for detailed discussion relating to the use of instructional technology.

RESOURCE PERSONS. In the following examples, parents and members of the family served as resource persons. The teacher said, "Stephen's grandfather is visiting us today. He doesn't speak English but he will play his violin for us."

At another time she said, "Mrs. Olson is Swedish and in her family they make a gingerbread house every year at Christmas time. She is here today to help us make one."

CENTERS OF INTEREST AND LEARNING CENTERS. See pages 155–157. As children participate in the centers, there is opportunity for them to gain the following values related to social studies:

Sharing materials, toys, and turns.
Using materials freely but without waste.
Respecting the rights and feelings of others.
Understanding their own rights and how to stand up for them.
Respecting limits or rules which have been made for the good of the group.
Learning and following everyday routines.
Learning about the physical and social environment.
Communicating with others.
Making choices and decisions.
Cooperating with others.
Formulating and clarifying ideas.

UNITS OF WORK. Resource units, teaching units, and teaching plans are discussed on pages 158–160. In selecting the topic for study, a balance among various areas of the social studies is desirable. It is possible for an undue proportion of time to be spent in activities that contribute most directly to one area. For example, geographic understandings may be emphasized to the extent that the child may have few learning encounters in other areas of social studies. Children need contact with history and anthropology too.

Examining the background of the children can give leads to topics. McAulay found in interviewing 70 second-graders that 63 of the children could name at least two duties of the policeman and 65 at least one duty of the fireman. Units had been planned on both topics.[27] The same situation exists in many kindergartens and other children's centers.

The teacher should not be upset by the fact that children already have some information about a topic selected for study. She needs to find out what the children already know and make plans for the educational needs of individual children. There is so much to learn and know that children should not be bored with the repetition of information already familiar to them. The unit type of organization offers flexibility and makes possible a variety of learning opportunities that can be adapted to individual needs and interests.

A plan for organizing a unit of work, and a unit developed according to the plan, are described. The unit selected relates to "Feelings." At the beginning of the school year there is the opportunity to utilize the interests of children in getting acquainted with one another. The teacher can help them develop beginning learnings in the area of citizenship education, to learn that each person has feelings, and that feelings affect behavior.

A RESOURCE UNIT

Unit Outline	Unit—Feelings: How Do I Feel? How Do Others Feel? For Five-Year-Olds—Early in the Year
1. *Purposes*: These give direction to the unit. Here the expected outcomes are stated. Simply state the purpose or task "What am I trying to do? What do I hope to accomplish?	a. *Purposes of This Unit*. To help the child achieve beginnings of self-understanding; to develop the ability to identify and express his feelings or emotions; to become aware of the feelings of others; and to begin to understand how feelings influence behavior.
	b. *Concepts to Be Developed*. I have feelings. I can be happy, thankful, angry, afraid. Other children have feelings too. They can be happy, etc. The way we feel affects how we act. If I am happy I may be kind. If a child is angry he may cry, hit, snatch. The way I treat other children affects how they feel.
2. *Initiating the Unit*: Plan to initiate the study of the unit in such a way as to arouse the curiosity and interest of the children. Regardless of the	

[27]J. D. McAulay, "Social Studies in the Primary Grades," *Social Educ.*, 18:8 (1954), pp. 357–358.

A Resource Unit (Cont.)

Unit Outline	Unit—Feelings: How Do I Feel? How Do Others Feel? For Five-Year-Olds—Early in the Year

plan for beginning the unit, children should be involved in the planning. Several means of initiating units are listed:

a. Teacher Suggestion. The teacher may propose certain questions about the topic, leave questions unanswered, provoke some discussion, and then say that the answers to the questions will be found during the study of the topic.

When the children come together for a group session, the teacher can introduce each child individually. She might ask, "What were you like when you were a baby?" "How much have you grown since you were born?" "What does it mean to grow?" "How do you feel now that you are five years old?" "How did you feel when you came to school?"

The teacher may use a story, such as *The Growing Story*, following it with questions such as those above.

Questions such as "How do you feel?" may need to be followed by words such as *afraid? happy? lonely?* Thus the teacher can help the child find the meaning for these terms and also for his feelings.

b. Incidents. Some incident or happening in the life of a child or in the local community, state, nation, or world might be the means of creating interest in a particular topic. For example, a good time to have a unit on the circus is when the circus comes to town. Holidays, festivals, and seasons of the year also offer leads.

The incident—It is the first day the children are together. As the teacher greets each child, she pins a name tag on him and says, "This is your name." She may ask, "What do you like about your name?"

c. Audiovisual Materials. Use of any of the following: motion pictures, filmstrips, slides, flat pictures, recordings, radio, field trips, TV, or resource persons.

d. On-Going Experience. A preceding unit may lead directly into a second unit. If interest in the preceding unit was high, it should be sufficient to carry over into a second unit.

e. Arranged Environment. Arrange a display of some type in which books, objects, pictures draw attention to a particular topic. For example, if the unit to be studied is on "Our Homes," the teacher would arrange books, pictures, and models of different types of homes on a table or bulletin board. The arrangement should be set up the day before and children should be permitted

Polaroid pictures could be taken of each child and mounted on the bulletin board. Actions in pictures could be labeled in connection with teacher questions such as "What were you doing there?" "How did you feel doing that?"

A RESOURCE UNIT (Cont.)

Unit Outline	Unit—Feelings: How Do I Feel? How Do Others Feel? For Five-Year-Olds—Early in the Year

some time to view the display, to talk freely about the things they see. They may identify the specific questions and topics to be considered.

3. *Learning Opportunities*: There must be a relationship between the learning opportunities and the purposes. It is through the activities that the purposes set up at the beginning of the unit are attained. Learning activities should be numerous and varied so that individual differences can be met. The following is a list of possible activities. They are not listed in order of importance. One unit may not include all of them. Activities are classified according to subject areas to illustrate how a topic such as *Feelings* can offer opportunities for academic learnings in the various subject areas. It is important to remember that one activity can contribute to learnings in several areas.

a. Language Activities. Discussion, dramatization, conversation, telling stories, listening to stories and poems, and writing letters and stories (dictated to the teacher), looking at books.

Make a tape recording of children's voices. Ask children to listen and each identify his own voice. The teacher may ask, "How did you feel when you heard your voice? How did your voice sound?"

Listen to stories, poems, recordings about a child or children.

Look at books about a child or children. Books such as *What Mary Jo Wanted* and *Will I Have a Friend?* could provide identity figures for the children and encourage them to express their feelings about characters in the stories and their own personal wants and attitudes. Possible teacher questions might include "Why do you think Mary Jo wanted a puppy?" "What does it mean to share ?" "What is a friend?" "How do we make friends?" "How do friends feel about each other?"

Role playing could emphasize the feelings of children and how these feelings influence their behavior. Pictures can provide a good beginning. Possible questions include "What do you think is happening here?" "How do you think the children feel?" "Why?" "What do you think the children might do next?" "Show us." The *Let's Start Collection* can be helpful.

Feelie Boxes can be fun. Objects of different

A Resource Unit (Cont.)

Unit Outline	Unit—Feelings: How Do I Feel? How Do Others Feel? For Five-Year-Olds—Early in the Year
	shapes are included. The child is asked to reach into the box and respond to the questions "How does it feel?" "What shape do you think it is?" "Is it a happy shape?" "How do you know?" Make picture books using titles such as "How I Feel Today," or "My Friends." Pictures may come from magazines or they may be drawn or painted. Create poems or stories (dictated to teacher). Note children's names under photographs. Play games: Identify child by his voice. "Who am I?" Practice use of courteous terms such as "thank you" and "excuse me." Discuss meanings of terms and relate them to how one feels. Develop meanings for vocabulary words such as happy, thankful, angry, lonely, *friend, enemy, afraid, hope.*
b. Community Resources. Field trips to places of interest such as city hall, library, post office, airport, bakery, grocery, and farm. The immediate school environment is a laboratory in itself. Many individuals in the community can be brought into the class-room as resource persons. Don't overlook parents as resource people; they have much to offer.	Dramatize while others identify the feeling.
c. Audiovisual Experiences. Films, filmstrips, slides, radio, recordings, television, models, charts, graphs, flat pictures, dioramas, wall murals.	View films and filmstrips. *The Joy of Being You* and *All Kinds of Feelings* are filmstrips that can be used to introduce children to their own feelings, how they may be expressed, and the meaning of feelings such as joy or loneliness. Listen to and respond to recordings. The song *Growing* (album by Hap Palmer) encourages children to feel what it is like to grow.
d. Handicrafts and Arts. Painting, clay model-ing, paper mache modeling, and construc-tion out of paper or wood.	Paint and draw pictures of self and others. Children can trace around each other on large sheets of paper placed on the floor. Details may be filled in later. Teacher questions might include "Is your face happy?" "How do you think your friend feels in his picture?" Use finger paint. Questions that may be asked include "How does the paint feel on your hands?"

A Resource Unit (Cont.)

Unit Outline	Unit—Feelings: How Do I Feel? How Do Others Feel? For Five-Year-Olds—Early in the Year
	View reproductions of famous paintings. Ask questions that relate to how the painter might have felt when painting the picture and how the people in the picture feel.
	Make paper bag puppets. Faces could be happy, sad, or lonely.
	Make a picture time line of growth from babyhood to the age of five years.
	Make a silhouette of each child and label with child's name.
e. Music and Physical Activities. Songs, rhythms, games, listening to records, playing instruments.	Play musical selections on piano or record player. Ask children to listen to and respond to questions such as "How does the music make you feel?" "Sleepy?" "Lazy?" "Happy?" "If you feel like that music how would you act? Show us."
	Sing songs about self and other children. Songs such as "If You're Happy and You Know It" can be used for encouraging responses. Feelings such as *sleepy* or *hungry* can also be used.
	Use an adaptation of the game "Simon Says." Ask a small group of children to face a mirror and to make facial expressions to match certain feelings. For example, "Simon says to make a happy face (or to make a frown or to be afraid)."
f. Number Activities. Opportunities for counting, measuring, weighing, development of concepts and vocabulary.	Weigh and measure children. Chart differences over time period. Involve children. Make a time line, using pictures of the children from birth to time of school entrance.
	Make cookies for someone to make him happy.
g. Growth in Social Skills and Attitudes. Opportunities for leadership, cooperation, a dramatization, a film, or a discussion period may be used.	Make choices.
	Share materials and equipment.
	Take turns. Discuss how one feels when he shares or takes turns, and how the other child feels. Avoid moralizing.
	Cooperate in clean-up.
	Learn other children's names.
	Practice courtesy in asking for and receiving materials, turns, etc. Relate to feelings.
4. *Evaluation*: Ask the question "How can I know whether or not the purposes stated in the beginning have been realized?"	See evidences of desired behavior on p. 272.

A RESOURCE UNIT (Cont.)

Unit Outline	Unit—Feelings: How Do I Feel? How Do Others Feel? For Five-Year-Olds—Early in the Year
	Observe dramatic play. Note conversations and comments of children for indications of self and others that have developed.
	Observe children's behavior for evidences of planning, sharing, assuming responsibility, using courteous forms of speech.
	Observe children's art products. See pp. 370–373.
5. *List of Materials*: List the materials needed to teach the unit. The materials should be accessible and ready to use when needed.	Use anecdotal records. See pp. 412–413.

BOOKS

Anglund, Joan W. *A Friend Is Someone Who Likes You*. New York: Harcourt Brace Jovanovich, 1958.

Beim, Jerrold and Lorraine Beim. *Two Is a Team*. New York: Harcourt Brace Jovanovich, 1945.

Bromhall, Winifred. *Peter's Three Friends*. New York: Knopf, 1964.

Bryant, Bernice. *Let's Be Friends*. Chicago; Children's Press, 1954.

Cole, William. *Frances Face-Maker*. New York: World, 1963.

Cohen, Miriam. *Will I Have a Friend?* New York: Macmillan, Inc., 1967.

Ets, Marie H. *Just Me*. New York: Viking Press, 1965.

Evans, Eva K. *People Are Important*. New York: Capitol, 1957.

Green, Mary M. *Is It Hard? Is It Easy?* New York: Scott, 1960.

Guilfoile, Elizabeth. *Nobody Listens to Andrew*. Chicago: Follett, 1957.

Keats, E. J. *The Snowy Day*. New York: Viking, 1962.

———. *Whistle for Willie*. New York: Viking, 1964.

Keesler, L. and Ethel Keesler. *Kim and Me*. New York: Doubleday, 1960.

Kushin, Karla. *Just Like Everybody Else*. New York: Harper & Row, 1959.

Krauss, Ruth. *The Growing Story*. New York: Harper & Row, 1947.

Ness, Evaline. *Exactly Alike*. New York: Scribners, 1964.

Udry, Janice May. *Let's Be Enemies*. New York: Harper & Row, 1961.

———. *What Mary Jo Shared*. Chicago: Whitman, 1966.

———. *What Mary Jo Wanted*. Chicago: Whitman, 1968.

Vreeken, Elizabeth. *The Little Boy Who Would Not Say His Name*. Chicago: Follett, 1959.

Williams, Gweneive. *Timid Timothy*. Eau Claire, Wis.: E. M. Hale, 1940.

Yashima, Taro. *Youngest One*. New York: Viking, 1959.

FILMSTRIPS

The Joy of Being You. (6970), Scholastic Kindle Filmstrips, 902 Sylvan Avenue, Englewood Cliffs, New Jersey 07632.

All Kinds of Feelings. (6968), Scholastic Kindle Filmstrips, 902 Sylvan Avenue, Englewood Cliffs, New Jersey 07632.

RECORDS

Learning Basic Skills Through Music. Vol. I, Educational Activities, Inc., Box 392, Freeport, New York 11520.

POETRY

Aldis, Dorothy. *All Together.* New York: Putnam, 1952.
Frank, Josetts, ed. *Poems to Read to the Very Young.* New York: Random House, 1961.
Hopkins, Lee Bennett, ed. *Me: A Book of Poems.* New York: Seabury Press, 1970.
Jacobs, Leland B., *Alphabet for Girls.* New York: Holt, Rinehart and Winston, 1969.
Livingston, Myra C. *Whispers and Other Poems.* New York: Harcourt Brace Jovanovich, 1957.
Untermeyer, Louis, ed. *The Golden Treasury of Poetry.* New York: Holden, 1959.

PICTURE SETS

Let's Start Picture Collection: School Experiences: Urban Environment. Scholastic Magazine, 902 Sylvan Avenue, Englewood Cliffs, New Jersey 07632.
Role Playing Photo-Problems for Young Children. Holt, Rinehart and Winston, New York, New York 10017.

SONGS

McCall, Adeline. *This Is Music.* Boston: Allyn and Bacon, 1966.
Nelson, Mary J., and Gladys Tipton. *Music for Early Childhood.* New York: Silver Burdett Co., 1952.
Pitts, Lilla Belle et al. *The Kindergarten Book.* Boston: Ginn Co., 1949.
Seeger, Ruth Crawford. *American Folk Songs for Children.* New York: Doubleday & Co., 1948.
Winn, Marie, ed. *Children's Songs.* New York: Simon & Schuster, 1966.
Zetlin, Patty. *Castle in My City—Songs for Young Children.* San Carlos, Calif.: Golden Gate Junior Books, 1966.

Suggestions for parts of the unit adapted from C. K. Ducolon, *Loving: A Process Approach,* unpublished graduate paper, University of Maryland, College Park, May 1971.

The *teaching unit* may be developed from the resource unit, after the teacher becomes acquainted with the children. Looking at the unit, "Feelings" the teacher may decide to use the concepts, "I have feelings," "Other children have feelings." Selections which are appropriate may be selected from the resource unit.

The *daily teaching plan* is developed from the teaching unit and includes detailed plans for the day. For example:

Albert enters kindergarten a few days after the other children. The teacher decides to use this incident in developing beginning understandings of the concept, "I have feelings. Other children have feelings too." The plan for this part of the day might include the following:

1. Purposes: To help each child achieve beginning understandings of his feelings and feelings of the other children, as evidenced by such statements as
   "I didn't know anybody when I came to kindergarten. I was lonesome. Now I am glad."
   "Albert has some friends now. He likes to play with me."
2. Initiating the plan: When Albert came to kindergarten he was introduced individually to the children. Later in the morning as the children come together for a group session the teacher might say,
   "Albert came to kindergarten today for the first time. How did you feel when you came to school? Happy? Afraid? Lonely? How do you think Albert felt? Why?"
3. Learning Opportunities: Discuss questions. Discuss ways to help children feel happy at kindergarten. Jot down children's comments. Make into experience chart later. Summarize suggestions. Read story, *Will I Have A Friend?*
4. Materials:
   Book: Cohen, Miriam. *Will I Have a Friend?* New York: Macmillan, Inc., 1967.
   Paper and marker for experience chart.
5. Evaluation: Observe children's behavior for evidences of concern for the feelings of others. Note conversations and comments of children.

At other times, on other days, the teacher may continue to provide opportunities for experiences through which the children may learn about feelings. The teacher may select other concepts and provide appropriate learning opportunities. Little by little, experience by experience, the understandings, attitudes, and skills are learned. As one teacher was told, she must "just keep on keeping on."

Suggested Activities

1. Select one concept to be developed in nursery school or kindergarten from the areas listed on pages 268–269. Plan a resource unit for developing this concept, using the suggested outline found on pages 272–278. Indicate the age level for which the unit is planned. Select another concept. Plan a series of learning encounters for developing this concept.
2. Observe in a children's center. Describe ways in which the teacher is helping the children or a child develop an understanding and acceptance of others, how they live and feel.
3. Note the ways in which the backgrounds of children in a group that you visited differ. Describe ways in which the teacher is making provision for the variety.
4. Discuss in class the time concepts of young children. How do these concepts affect teaching strategies and learning encounters planned for the young child?
5. Select a site that you consider to be appropriate for a field trip for young children. Visit the site and evaluate it in terms of the checklist on pp. 153–155.

6. Visit a center for young children and observe dramatic play. Note the role of the teacher in the situation. List possible values of this experience for the children.
7. Select one holiday that comes during the school year. Plan and describe three activities related to this holiday that you consider appropriate for kindergarten children. Indicate social studies concepts that may be developed through the activities.

Related Readings

Abrahams, R. "Cultural Differences and the Melting Pot Ideology," *Educ. Leadership*, 29:2 (1971), pp. 118–121.

Buschoff, Lottie K. "Going on a Trip?" *Young Children*, 26:4 (1971), pp. 224–232.

Clark, Kenneth B. *Prejudice and Your Child*. Boston: Beacon Press, 1963.

Cohen, M. D., ed. *Learning to Live as Neighbors*. Washington, D.C.: ACEI, 1972.

DeSart, Helen, and Unabelle Trytten. "Geographic Readiness in the Kindergarten," *J. Geography*, 60:7 (1961), pp. 331–335.

Endsley, R. C., and Keith Osborn, "Children's Reactions to TV Violence: A Review of Research," *Young Children*, 26:1 (1970), pp. 4–11.

Estvan, F. J. "Social Perception of Nursery-School Children," *Elem. Sch. J.*, 66:7 (1966), pp. 377–385.

————. "Studies in Social Perception: Objectivity," *J. Educ. Res.*, 59:7 (1966), pp. 320–326.

Gabaldon, A. "A Rebirth of Interest in Heritage Identity," *Educ. Leadership*, 29:2 (1971), pp. 122–124.

Goodman, Mary Ellen. *The Culture of Childhood*. New York: Teachers College Press, Columbia University, 1970.

Herman, W. L., Jr. *Current Research in Elementary School Social Studies*. New York: Macmillan, Inc., 1969.

Kerchoff, R. K., and Sherry G. Trella. "Teaching Race Relations in the Nursery School," *Young Children*, 27:4 (1972), pp. 240–248.

Lane, Mary B., F. F. Elzey, and Mary Leivos. *Nurseries in Cross-Cultural Education*. San Francisco: San Francisco State College, 1971.

Likover, Belle. "The Effect of Black History," *Children*, 17:5 (1970), pp. 177–182.

Moyer, Joan E. *Bases for World Understanding and Cooperation—Suggestions for Teaching the Young Child*. Washington, D.C.: ASCD, 1970.

Preston, R. C. "What Social Studies Content for Primary Grades?" *Social Educ.*, 29:3 (1965), pp. 147–148.

Redl, Fritz. "The Nature and Nurture of Prejudice," *Child. Educ.*, 45:5 (1969), pp. 254–257.

Renaud, Mary, ed. *Bringing the World into Your Classroom*. Washington, D.C.: NSSE, 1968, pp. 3–11.

Rosenhan, D. "The Kindness of Children," *Young Children*, 25:1 (1969), pp. 30–34.

Rueff, J. "Political Science in Elementary Social Studies," *Instructor*, (1966), pp. 52–53.

Shaftel, Fannie P., and G. Shaftel. *Role-Playing for Social Values: Decision Making in the Social Studies*. Englewood Cliffs, N.J.: Prentice-Hall, Inc., 1967, pp. 129–148; 183–188.

Spodek, B. "Social Studies Programs in the Kindergarten," *Young Children*, 20:5 (1965), pp. 284–289.

Sunderlin, Sylvia, ed. *Migrant Children: Their Education.* Washington, D.C.: ACEI, 1971.

Weaver, V. P. "Social Concepts for Early Childhood Education," *Educ. Leadership*, 22:5 (1965), pp. 296–299, 343.

World Traveler. (Published by the Alexander Graham Bell Assoc. for the Deaf, Inc., 1537 35th St. NW, Washington, D.C. 20007), 2:4 and 3:2.

Children and Values

Educating for values is no simple task. The responsibility for value development is shared by the school, the home, organized religion, and various agencies of the community. This does not however, lessen the task of the school, for value development is an integral part of the learning process.[1]

Berman writes,

> Most persons responsible for inducting the young into the culture are concerned that they learn what the culture prizes. Through exhortation, but more frequently through example, the young become dimly aware of the most pervasive values peculiar to a given group of people.[2]

[1]ASCD, *Toward Better Teaching*, 1949 Yearbook. (Washington, D.C.: ASCD, 1949), pp. 154–155.

[2]Louise M. Berman, *New Priorities in the Curriculum* (Columbus, Ohio: Charles E. Merrill Publishers, 1968), p. 155.

Such learning, however, is complicated by the very nature of American society. There are groups differing as to race, national origin, religious beliefs, and social and economic levels.

Many persons believe that the family plays a crucial role for children in the development of values and awareness. Raths points out, however, that the changes in the family are dramatic, if not frightening. The consequence, he says, has been a growing confusion and conflict in relation to values.[3]

What Are Values?

Values form the basis for inner direction by the individual. They have been defined by many authorities in many ways. Several definitions follow.

> A value is the comparative weight, esteem, or price attached by the individual to a given idea, person, or object.[4]
> Values are standards applied to thought or action, principles, preferences on a scale of priorities, or commitments to what one feels is desirable.[5]
> Our values show what we tend to do with our limited time and energy.[6]

Values, says Raths, are based on the three processes of choosing, prizing, and acting. He has identified criteria, all of which must be met if something is to be called a value. One must choose freely from alternatives, after considering the consequences of each alternative. One cherishes his values and is willing to affirm them publicly. One acts upon his values, and repeats them. They are incorporated into his behavior and tend to persist.[7]

VALUES GROW OUT OF AND CHANGE WITH EXPERIENCE. For children, values build up as the result of their many experiences both in and out of school. For example:

> It was May. Jane was sharing with the teacher some feelings about nursery school. She said, "You know, when I first came to nursery school I didn't hang up my sweater. I didn't play with the other children. I hit them. Now I put things in my locker and I like to play with Mary and Brenda." The teacher replied, "You have learned many things in nursery school. You have learned to care for your belongings. You have learned to play with Mary, Brenda, and the others."

THE IMPORTANCE OF AN EXPERIENCE IN RELATION TO VALUE BUILDING VARIES ACCORDING TO THE INDIVIDUAL CHILD, HIS MATURITY, FAMILY, FRIENDS, AND

---

[3]L. E. Raths, M. Harmin, S. B. Simon, *Values and Teaching: Working with Values in the Classroom* (Columbus, Ohio: Charles E. Merrill Publishers, 1966), pp. 15–20.

[4]ASCD, op. cit., p. 154.

[5]*Report to the President*, (Washington, D.C.: The White House Conference on Children, 1970), p. 63.

[6]Raths, op. cit., p. 27.

[7]Ibid., pp. 28–30.

BACKGROUND OF EXPERIENCES. A situation may be helpful to one child in formulating his values but it may not have the same results for another child. For example:

> One morning the five-year-olds were moving with music. Maria skipped gracefully and Rose said, "Maria can skip. She's good. Look at Albert. He's so funny." This situation, including Rose's remark, offered Maria an opportunity for building a positive self-concept while for Albert the effect was probably negative.

SOME OF THE VALUES AN INDIVIDUAL HOLDS AND EXHIBITS MAY CONFLICT WITH ONE ANOTHER. The child may value friendship and want very much to play with other children. He may not recognize that his aggressive behavior patterns stand in the way. For example:

> Ted wanted to play with Robert and Juan, two five-year-old boys who were using the blocks. Ted picked up a ball and threw it at the block structure. When talking with the teacher he asked, "What else could I do? I wanted to play with them."

In considering values it is important to remember that, "the formative school years present a challenge to the educator to contribute to the development of values desirable in a democracy. This whole area of appreciations, interests and goals, character and morality, social and spiritual values is basic to the entire educational process."[8]

WHICH VALUES TO TEACH?

"In a pluralistic society, diversity is an important value that our educational institutions should express."[9] Fantini's statement describes, however, the dilemma faced by the teachers of young children. When values are divergent and in conflict, what can the teacher do? The following quotations offer criteria for the selection of values to be taught.

> For a pluralistic society to survive, certain common values must be accepted, such as mutual respect and concern for the welfare of others. These common values take precedence over the freedom to be different. Pluralism is not a justification for polarization and estrangement.[10]

> In this society with its many values, some confused and conflicting, two values are basic: a belief in the potential worth of each individual, and reliance upon the method of individual and group intelligence in the solution of problems. When either of these basic values is challenged, democracy is threatened. The teacher, as the agent of a

[8]ASCD, op. cit., p. 9.

[9]M. D. Fantini, "Public Schools of Choice and the Plurality of Publics," *Educ. Leadership*, 28:6 (1971), p. 585.

[10]*Report to the President*, White House Conference, op. cit., p. 64.

democratic state, has a responsibility to help students develop attitudes and beliefs that are consistent with these fundamentals of democracy.[11]

Pressure to have the teacher of young children work for acceptance of values held by the majority violates one of the democratic values—reliance on intelligence, which involves examining different points of view and evolving one's own values.

Recent efforts on the part of some persons interested in respecting a diversity of values have apparently gone to the extreme of accepting any behavior that is different by reason of racial, class, or ethnic origin as "good." Prejudice or violence or aggressive behavior, for example, may be strong in certain situations. In relation to this, Forum 3 of the White House Conference on Children reported,

> Any manifestation of pluralism, cultural identity, or individuality becomes invalid when it contradicts or conflicts with the "inalienable rights" and "privileges of others." This basic American understanding is crucial to any consideration of values and must be a fundamental lesson in value learning for every American child.[12]

There has been a tendency to consider middle-class values as those of children in suburbia and lower-class values as belonging to children of the inner city. Such a tendency not only overlooks migrant and rural children but those of differing social, ethnic, and minority groups as well. The tendency implies a stereotype, assuming that all persons of the same class have the same values. To the contrary, values that are held by the family and that affect the child may differ greatly from the stereotype. Families in the inner city as well as those in suburbia and rural areas may value cleanliness and good health for their children. Families in the inner city may not have the resources necessary to maintain cleanliness and good health but that does not mean that these qualities are not valued.

However, beliefs and feelings about what children should be and do differ widely. The teacher needs to know the behavior patterns expected of each child and the cultural beliefs about what he should do and be. Such knowledge can help the teacher in dealing with value conflicts between the home and the school.

As the teacher placed her hand on Jimmy's shoulder, he yelled, "Take your hand off my shoulder." The teacher's gesture of affection was interpreted by the child as an agressive act.

Aggressive behavior may be valued in each of two homes, yet the value may be expressed in different behavior patterns. In one home the child shows aggression verbally, talks loudly, and perhaps ignores others who want a

[11]ASCD, op. cit., p. 155.

[12]*Report to the President*, White House Conference, op. cit., p. 64.

chance to speak. In another home the child may be encouraged to hit and fight in order to "get along." The difference may be in the behavior manifestations rather than in the value itself.

The teacher must begin with the children where they are and must use the resources of each child and his cultural background in order to help him identify and clarify his values.

The values common in our democracy need to be considered, because these are the values that the schools hope to develop. One such statement was made by the Educational Policies Commission.[13] The values listed in this report are used here as the basis for developing a statement appropriate for young children. It is important not only that the values be known but that the teacher recognize behavior, comments, and attitudes of children that are conducive to the realization of the values. A statement of values, including teacher goals expressed in terms of children's behavior, attitudes, and comments, follows.

HUMAN PERSONALITY

Teacher's goal: Help each child—

1. To have a sense of personal worth and to know that:
   "My Daddy and Mother love me.
   My teacher loves me too.
   I can climb high on the jungle gym.
   I am Ann's friend."

2. To feel secure in the nursery or kindergarten and to feel that:
   "I belong to this group.
   The children like to play with me.
   The children miss me when I am not here.
   The teacher misses me when I am absent.
   The children are glad to see me when I come in the morning.
   Ann is my friend."

3. To develop self-understanding as expressed through:
   "I like to play with Sue.
   Sometimes, when children won't let me play with their toys, I get mad and hit them.
   I can talk with Jim, instead of hitting him.
   Children don't like for me to hit them."

4. To gain insight into the behavior of others and to understand that:
   "Jim can't fix the block house. It is going to fall. I will help him.
   Tom is crying. He fell and cut his foot.
   Joe hasn't been to school before. He doesn't know how we play."

[13]National Education Association and American Association of School Administrators, Educational Policies Commission, *Moral and Spiritual Values in Public Schools* (Washington, D.C., 1951).

(Courtesy of Head Start)

Figure 32. Frances is gaining some insight into the behavior of others. She understands that Tracey is crying because he fell and hurt his hand.

MORAL RESPONSIBILITY

Teacher's goal: Help each child—

1. To develop a willingness to try new activities and experiences as evidenced by such statements as:
   "I don't know how to paint on the easel, but I can try.
   I haven't been to the airport. I might be afraid. But Miss Jones will go with us—mother, too. I can have fun."
2. To recognize ownership and understand that:
   "Some things belong to me. Some things belong to others. Some things are for all of us to use.
   I will share only the things that belong to me or that are for all of us to use.
   I will ask if I may use something that belongs to somebody else.
   I will use materials carefully."
3. To develop consideration for the welfare and convenience of others. For example:
   "Miss Jones is reading a story. The children want to hear. I will not play the record player now.

It is lunch time. I will come to the table. I will not keep the other children waiting."
4. To develop a willingness to let others have turns and practice such behavior as evidenced in:
   "Here is a ball. You can play with it.
   Jim, you can ride the tractor now."
5. To gain an understanding of what it means to do a job. For example:
   "I will get the things I need to work with. I'm going to paint. I need an apron.
   I will finish my job.
   I will put materials away."

INSTITUTIONS AS THE SERVANTS OF MEN

Teacher's goal: Help each child—
1. To develop an understanding that each person has a job to do. For example:
   "There are many jobs to be done at school.
   The teachers teach children. They read stories to us. They watch us when we play.
   The janitor cleans our room. He sweeps the floor. He washes the windows."
2. To understand that some jobs help all of us. For example:
   "The policeman helps us cross the street. He reminds the cars to drive slowly in front of our school.
   Mrs. Brown cooks the food for our lunch at school."

COMMON CONSENT

Teacher's goal: Help each child—
1. To develop the willingness to talk things over. For example:
   "If I talk to somebody, I don't have to hit him, or snatch his toy."
2. To gain an appreciation of the value of planning together. For example:
   "We all have good ideas.
   Now we all know what we are going to do."
3. To develop an understanding of how we plan together. For example:
   "We can talk about what we want to do. We can ask questions.
   We talk about what we can do.
   We decide what we will do.
   There are different ways to do things."
4. To gain an understanding of the individual's responsibility for following a plan. For example:
   "We made a plan. I helped.
   I will do what we decided.
   Jim forgot. He came down the slide 'head first.' What did we decide to do?"

DEVOTION TO TRUTH

Teacher's goal: Help each child—
1. To learn that some things are true and some things are not true, and to understand that:

"Some children tease just for fun.
Some stories are make-believe and I enjoy them.
Sometimes I can pretend or make-believe.
Sometimes children do not understand what their mother said and tell something that is not true.
Sometimes children 'make up' a story just to get others to listen.
Sometimes children are afraid to tell what really happened."
2. To learn how we can find out the truth. For example:
"We can go and see for ourselves.
We can look at pictures.
We can look at movies.
We can ask grown-ups.
We can listen while grown-ups read to us."
3. To develop understanding of what it means to be honest. For example:
"I will try to remember what happened.
I won't blame Jim when he didn't hit me. I will remember that I was angry and I pushed Jim.
Jane didn't make me fall and skin my knee. I wasn't looking where I was going. I tripped and fell.
I will try to find right answers.
When I am asked a question, I will tell the truth.
I can ask myself if this is the best I can do."

Respect for Excellence

Teacher's goal: Help each child—
1. To learn to do one thing well, such as walk straight, rest comfortably, drive a nail all the way into the board.
2. To come to recognize his best effort, as evidenced by such statements as:
"I can do it better now. Watch me.
I will try.
I don't like this picture. I tore it.
I'm tired now. I'll make another boat tomorrow."
3. To appreciate the achievements of others, as evidenced by the following statements:
"Jan built a big block house.
Look, Joe can skip.
I like your picture. That's good."
4. To set standards for himself. For example:
"I want to tie my shoe. Please help me."
5. To enjoy learning, as evidenced by such statements as:
"It is fun to say new words.
I have learned a poem. I can say it."

Brotherhood

Teacher's goal: Help each child—
1. To develop an understanding that children are different, yet alike. For example:

"We are different in the way we talk, look, dress, worship, the food we eat, the games we play, and the homes we live in.
But we do talk, eat, wear clothing, worship, play, and live in homes.
I live in a brick house. Joe lives in an apartment. I am happy in my home. He is happy in his.
Jane's hair is curly and blond. Tina's hair is straight and black."

2. To develop a willingness to treat other children as he wants to be treated. For example:
"I will take turns.
I will share my toys."

SPIRITUAL ENRICHMENT

Teacher's goal: Help each child—
1. To develop sensitivity to and appreciation for beauty. For example:
"The bird is hopping on the grass.
The sun is so gold and shiny.
Oh, look. See the little new leaf."
2. To engage in creative activities, with resulting comments such as:
"I know what we can do. I thought about it. [creative thinking]
The little bird was shivering with scaredness. [creative language]
The music makes me want to dance and dance."
3. To experience successful achievement. For example:
"You were a good helper, Joe. You put the blocks away.
I did it! I did it! I did it! I painted a house."
4. To develop an understanding that there is law and order in our natural world which we can regard with reverence and wonder. For example:
"There are seasons. It is spring. The flowers are blooming.
The sun sets in the evening. The sun rises in the morning."
5. To develop an appreciation of kindness, friendliness, cooperation, and loyalty in others. For example:
"When I was lonesome, Pam played with me.
Miss Helms helped me fix my truck.
Sam let me look at his book. He was kind to me."
6. To learn that God is very great. He created beauty for us to enjoy. One child said:
"See the little new moon. God made it. I wish the sky was full of little new moons."

Many early childhood experiences can build spiritual values if the teacher is consciously working toward that end. Her role is an important one.

DEVELOPING VALUES

According to Havighurst, "Moral character is learned and therefore is a proper object of education. It is learned, however, in various ways and at various levels of complexity."[14] This concern for the development of moral

---

[14]R. J. Havighurst, "Moral Character and Religious Education," *Relig. Educ.*, 51:3 (1956), pp. 165–167.

values, beliefs, and character among the young is not new. Through the years various methods have been used in teaching morals. "In colonial times great reliance was placed upon reading, memorizing, and repeating religious material such as the Lord's Prayer, the Creed, the Ten Commandments, and a catechism."[15] The earliest textbooks were filled with selections which presented moral precepts designed to be memorized.

Later, plans for systematic instruction in such areas as morals, manners, patriotism, and citizenship were developed and used. Grades were given in desirable character traits—reliability, judgment, and industry. Organizations sponsored contests to prepare the best theme or to deliver the best address on a patriotic topic.

The Character Education Inquiry, begun in 1924, raised questions regarding the methods of character education which were then in use. Hartshorne and May reported that "the main attention of educators should be placed not so much on devices for teaching honesty or any other 'trait' as on the reconstruction of school practices in such a way as to provide not occasional but consistent and regular opportunities for the successful use by both teachers and pupils of such forms of conduct as make for the common good."[16] Kohlberg says that the findings of recent research support these conclusions.[17]

According to Miel and Brogan, in the early 'thirties, as schools participated in the "activity movement," attempts were made to plan enterprises that would build character. During the 'forties, educators concerned themselves with ways of helping children develop moral and spiritual values. "More attention was given to children's ability to identify with storybook characters, and there was keen interest in promoting good human relations through intercultural or intergroup education."[18]

One of the forums of the 1960 White House Conference on Children and Youth considered the topic, Beliefs—Religions, spiritual and secular beliefs and personal codes of conduct which affect the development of the young. "The Forum affirmed 'the importance of personal faith in God, the strengthening of moral and religious values, and the necessity for a continuing re-examination of personal conduct in order that the Nation's children may realize their full potential for a creative life in freedom and dignity.' The ethical principles to be set before our young people 'have as their ultimate source the belief that man is created by God and is therefore possessed of dignity as an individual.' Churches, synagogues, character-building agencies, and all citizens were called

[15]Alice Miel and Peggy Brogan, *More Than Social Studies* (Englewood Cliffs, N.J.: Prentice-Hall, 1957), p. 122.

[16]H. Hartshorne and M. A. May, *Studies in Deceit* (New York: Macmillan Publishing Co., 1928), p. 414.

[17]L. Kohlberg, "Development of Moral Character and Ideology," in M. L. Hoffman and Lois W. Hoffman, *Review of Child Development Research*, Volume one (New York: Russell Sage Foundation, 1964), p. 426.

[18]Miel and Brogan, op. cit., p. 126.

upon to cooperate in encouraging moral and religious training, values, and beliefs among our children and youth."[19]

Throughout the years along with the concern for the development of moral and spiritual values, there has been the concern for the role of the public school in this area of instruction.

Schools for young children are operated under various auspices. Some are public schools while others are private or church-related. Still others are sponsored by an organization or community agency. Centers supported by public funds, in keeping with the ideas that have been expressed, avoid sectarian emphasis. The church-related and private centers, however, may present spiritual and moral values from their denominational point of view. Regardless, however, of the sponsorship of the school, certain principles are basic to the development of these values in young children.

Jones points out that the capacity to grow spiritually must be nourished just as the capacity to grow physically. The nourishment, however, must be provided in terms of the needs and capacities of a child of a given age. "Over-stimulation may be as detrimental to the child's development as is malnutrition."[20] It is important then to provide the needed spiritual nourishment to each child at each stage in his growth.

By the age of four the child is becoming assertive. He has a lively mind and asks many questions, some of which relate to God, the universe, and who made it. Gesell says that, "the vast intangible creative force called God is often grasped rather well by the mind of the four-year-old."[21] He is beginning to understand relationships, and he needs help in comprehending the difference between the activity of God and the work of man. A child, for example, is told that "God gives us food." He should, however, be helped to see that man, using the sun, rain, and soil provided by God, can grow plants or fruit which can be used as food. Man may work with God.

At this age the child often shows a marked interest in death but has little understanding of its meaning. His comments, however, may sound plausible because his vocabulary exceeds his experiences. The finality of death is not yet understood. By five years of age, the child has the tendency to bring God within the scope of his everyday world. The age of six is described as the peak period of the child's interest in a creative power to which he can relate himself. He thinks of God in terms of creation. Prayers are becoming important to him.[22]

Some children think of God as kind and loving, while others think of Him as stern, terrifying, and awe-inspiring. Jersild points out that a child's concept

---

[19]*Conference Proceedings* (Washington, D.C.: The Golden Anniversary White House Conference on Children and Youth, Inc., 1960), p. 192.

[20]Mary Alice Jones, *Guiding Children in Christian Growth* (Nashville, Tenn.: Abingdon Press, 1949), p. 11.

[21]A. Gesell and Frances Ilg, *Child Development, II* (New York: Harper & Row, 1949), p. 86.

[22]Ibid., I, p. 128.

of God as father will be influenced by his experience with his own father or others in a paternal role. His concepts of sin and forgiveness will be influenced by the ways he has been treated when he misbehaved.[23]

Harms reported that, regardless of different backgrounds and experiences, children show a similar pattern of development in their religious concepts.[24]

"The growth in understanding right and wrong is a slow process, dependent upon a growing ability to think, to reason, to make comparisons, to foresee consequences."[25] By the age of three, the child usually knows that some behavior is considered good and some bad by adults he knows. At five years the child is able to make some generalizations when the situations are similar. The child up to seven or eight years of age usually accepts, almost entirely, the values of his parents and family. Young children coming from different homes bring with them the values of their parents.

COGNITIVE DEVELOPMENTAL APPROACH. Piaget is the principal exponent of the cognitive-developmental approach to moral development. This approach involves analysis of the thought structures which underlie the moral concepts of persons at different age levels. Such analysis is used to define a general development.[26] Piaget has evolved two broad stages of moral development which include the following:[27]

1. "Moral realism, morality of constraint or heteronomous morality." In this stage the child feels that he must comply with rules because they are "sacred and unalterable." Behaviors are viewed by the child as totally right or wrong and he thinks that others view them the same way. The rightness or wrongness of an act is judged on the basis of the consequence or punishment. For example, severe punishment may be interpreted to mean that the deed was very wrong. Violations of rules are followed by accidents or misfortunes.

2. "Autonomous morality, morality of cooperation or reciprocity." In this stage rules are not viewed as unchangeable but as established and maintained through mutual agreement and thus subject to modification in response to the situation. In determining right or wrong, one considers the role of "intention." "Did he mean to do it? or was it an accident?" Now the child is more likely to consider the welfare of others and considers punishment as related to a consequence of an act. For example, an act that causes much damage may deserve more punishment. In making the transition from one stage to the next, Piaget holds that both maturation and experience are involved.[28]

Kohlberg has developed levels of moral orientation and stages within each

[23]A. T. Jersild, *Child Psychology*, 6th ed. (Englewood Cliffs, N.J.: Prentice-Hall, Inc., (1968), p. 520.

[24]E. Harms, "The Development of Religious Experience in Children," *Am. J. Sociol., 50*:2 (1944), pp. 112–122.

[25]Jones, op. cit., p. 29.

[26]M. L. Hoffman, "Moral Development," in P. H. Mussen, ed., *Carmichael's Manual of Child Psychology*, 3rd ed. (New York: John Wiley and Sons, Inc., 1970), p. 264.

[27]Ibid., pp. 256–266.

[28]Ibid., p. 266.

level.[29] The levels include the premoral level, the morality of conventional role-conformity, and the morality of self-accepted moral principles.

CLARIFYING STRATEGIES. Raths identifies four basic approaches to the development of values current in schools today: the lecture method, use of peer group pressure, finding or setting examples for children to respect and emulate, and a reward and punishment rationale.[30] Raths contends that these methods are rather ineffective, "partially because they are based on the assumption that the knowledge of moral and ethical choices necessarily leads to ethical conduct."[31] Such an assumption, he holds, seems to have little basis in fact. Raths recommends the use of clarification procedures by which the teacher strives to (a) establish a climate of psychological safety, and (b) apply clarifying strategies.[32]

In establishing a climate of psychological safety, the following procedures are suggested:

1. Express nonjudgmental attitudes. In order to provide an atmosphere in which children are free to express themselves without threat of disapproval or ridicule teachers should refrain from using expressions such as "That's poor." "Can't you do better than that?" "That's good." Rather use comments such as "You've finished the picture." "You climbed on the jungle gym."
2. Manifest concerns. The teacher should be concerned with the ideas the child expresses. This may be done by listening to the child and remembering what he has said. If the teacher shows no interest in listening, the child is not likely to be interested in sharing his thoughts.
3. Provide opportunities for the sharing of ideas. Children need to be able to express their opinions, feelings, beliefs about moral issues significant to the young child. Such issues might include "taking care of our things" or "taking turns."

Two clarifying strategies, with examples pertinent to young children, follow:

1. Asking questions. The teacher may try to clarify the ideas or feelings expressed by the children by asking questions. For example: Leroy was feeding the rabbit. Douglas pushed him away and stuck the carrot into the hutch. Leroy yelled, "I hate you." "I hate the rabbit." "I hate nursery school." The teacher, using the clarifying strategy might say, "You don't like for Douglas to take the carrot away from you and feed the rabbit. Is that what you mean?" or "You don't like to come to nursery school. Is that what you mean?"
   The five-year-olds were planning a trip to the apple orchard. Sandra exclaims, "I have a good idea. We can get the school bus to take us." The teacher may say, "In what way is that a good idea?"
2. Acceptance without judgment. The purpose of an exchange of ideas between teacher and child is to clarify children's ideas. It is important that the teacher

[29]Ibid., pp. 276–277.

[30]J. D. Raths, "A Strategy for Developing Values," *Educ. Leadership, 21*:8 (1964), pp. 509–514.
[31]Ibid., p. 511.
[32]Ibid., pp. 512–514.

find a way to accept these ideas without communicating agreement or praise of them, except in cases where the health or safety of the group is involved. For example: Nancy, with her sandy hair cut very short, was gently stroking Mary's long dark hair. She said, "It's so soft. It's so long. I wish I had long hair like Mary's." The teacher might reply, "I can see how you would feel that way."

Instant changes and miracles are not likely, according to Raths. He says, "It may take a long sustained effort to help children develop serious purposes and aspirations through the clarifying process. For a free society, opportunities to clarify and to choose must be created again and again."[33]

PROCESS SKILLS. Berman suggests that one way to create values is to provide the time, setting, and encouragement for children to reflect upon life, its meaning and what the child can, wishes, or ought to do.[34] "Loving" has been identified as one of the process skills that should help the young child handle himself and his world more effectively and to gain a better understanding of others.

If teachers want children to become loving individuals, opportunities must be provided for them to learn what it means to love and be loved. See p. 274 for suggested learning opportunities. Leiserson has developed suggestions for creating a loving environment for young children.[35] These suggestions may be familiar. They are used in this context, however, to indicate how the creating of a loving environment can be related to guiding the behavior of children, or teaching social studies, music, or any phase of the curriculum. Loving is a vital part of the curriculum. An adaptation of her suggestions follows:

In a loving environment the teacher:
1. Looks at each child as a unique person and gives the child opportunities to develop a positive self-concept. She may say, for example, "Erik's feeling very grown-up. His new shirt is size 5."[36]
2. Helps each child feel accepted and that he belongs to the group. She learns the children's names quickly, is courteous, and shows the children that she is happy to see them. For example, she may say, "I'm glad that you are feeling better. We missed you yesterday."[37]
3. Gives support and assurance to the child and lets him know her expectations in regard to the school environment. For example, she may say, "It isn't safe to climb on top of the brick wall. There's concrete below if you should fall."[38]
4. Lets children learn by experience, sometimes through mistakes and at other times

[33]Raths, op. cit., p. 514.

[34]Berman, op. cit., p. 173.

[35]Marion L. Leiserson, *Creating a "Loving" Environment for Young Children* (College Park, Md.: University of Maryland, 1971), pp. 3–12.

[36]Ibid., p. 3.

[37]Ibid., p. 5.

[38]Ibid.

Figure 33. The teacher works to develop a willingness on the part of the boys to let others have a turn. She may need to give assurance when a child wants to ask for a turn.

through successes. The child may say, "My caterpillar crawled out because I didn't have the top on the jar."[39]

5. Helps the child understand that he creates his own emotional environment. She helps him see the effect of his actions on others. The teacher said, "She was knocked down when you bumped her. Is there something you could do to make her feel better?"[40]

6. Listens to children. What the child has to say is important and his comments indicate concepts that he has developed. After the child tore the paper cover of a book the teacher explained, "After the story you can help me mend the cover."
   Child: "What does *mend* mean?"
   Teacher: "It means to fix or repair it."
   Child: "Okay, but can I sit on your lap now and hear the story? Then I can be quiet."[41]

[39]Ibid.

[40]Ibid., p. 8.

[41]Ibid., p. 9.

7. Helps the children to assume responsibilities. She may say, "Do you remember what our plants need to grow? Could you take care of them today?"[42]

8. Appears relaxed, pleasant, and in control of the classroom. She lets the children know that she is available if help is needed. She might say, "Sometimes boots are tight. I'm here if you need help with them."[43]

SCHOOL PRACTICES.   As one consciously works to build values, questions often arise regarding practices. Practices in public schools must be in accordance with the legal interpretation regarding religious instruction. If certain practices are contrary, they should be omitted. Some of these questions are identified and discussed here:

1. Shall we say "Grace" at mealtime if there are children of different faiths in the group?

   Grace at mealtime is one way of helping children to develop a spirit of appreciation and thankfulness. If Grace is used, however, it is important that the teacher keep in mind the following:

   a. Grace, if it is to develop the value of appreciation, should be said happily and reverently. Take time for the children to be seated, relaxed, and ready. Avoid statements such as "Hurry and be quiet so we can say Grace and you can have your juice." Such comments emphasize not the purpose of the Grace, but characterize it as something "to get through with" in order to be able to eat.

   b. If the Grace is to be said by all the children, select a form which is acceptable to all faiths. To thank God is usually acceptable to both Christian and Jewish parents. If there are children in the group who come from homes without affiliation, it may be well to use a statement such as "We are thankful for our food" or "We are glad that we have food to eat."

   c. Grace is only one way of expressing appreciation. There are many other opportunities throughout the day.

   The children may learn a poem to use as a prayer, or sing a song which expresses thanks. On other days, each child may say his own "thank you," whispered quietly, or a child may volunteer to say Grace for the group, expressing thanks in his own words.

2. Should a special time each day be set aside for a "devotional" or "worship" period?

   Heinz has said that "Worship has a very special place in the kindergarten. . . . Worship can come from a fleeting moment of wonder, as when it was discovered that a moth had emerged from the cocoon."[44]

   There are times, however, when a teacher makes definite plans for guiding children into worship. In making such plans, it is well to remember that worship cannot be forced. Music, pictures, stories, poetry, and Bible selections can be used as aids in creating an atmosphere and helping children worship. The suggestions made in regard to planning other group situations, and the selection of materials are appropriate here.

---

[42]Ibid., p. 10.

[43]Ibid., p. 11.

[44]Mamie W. Heinz, *Growing and Learning in the Kindergarten* (Richmond, Va.: John Knox Press, 1959), p. 122.

3. How may selections from the Bible be used with young children?

Much of the language in the Bible is difficult for the children to understand. In choosing selections from the Bible to be used with young children, Heinz formulated questions which may be of help to the teacher. Does the selection—

a. Help the child to grow in appreciation and understanding of God?

b. Add to his feeling of security and love, or does it promote fear?

c. Create a feeling of wonder and beauty for the child?[45]

Jones suggests the following verses from the Bible as appropriate for the young child:[46]

> He has made everything beautiful in its time.
> A child is known by his doings.
> God is Love.
> Love one another.

The way in which these verses are used is very important. They may be used many times, not for memorization, but as they relate to the experience which the children are having. A verse thus used can help a child to express his thoughts of God.

4. How can differences in the religious backgrounds of children be respected in celebrating religious holidays such as Christmas?

Celebration of religious holidays should be planned in such a way as to respect the worth and dignity of each child and not to threaten his security or place in the group. If children have been helped to become aware of the differences among the children in the group and to know that they are all accepted, this awareness can be used as an approach to understanding different religious beliefs and the way in which people in other lands celebrate Christmas. If children from Christian and Jewish homes are in the group, both may have an opportunity to share their beliefs. A Jewish child and his mother can tell the others about Hanukkah, while another child and his mother may share a crèche and tell of the birth of Jesus. In both celebrations, gifts are given even though the origin of the gift giving is different. It is suggested that the interpretation of a religious belief be given by a person of that faith in order that the interpretation be accurate. In this way each child can accept his own religious beliefs and yet understand those of others, thus furthering intercultural understanding among young children.

Mary, relating her Christian activities, said, "I mailed Christmas cards to everybody in my kindergarten but three." The adult to whom she was talking asked, "Why didn't you mail cards to the three children?" Mary replied, "They are Jewish. They don't believe in Christmas as we do. They have Hanukkah. I didn't want to hurt their feelings."

If society is to survive, there must be values in which the majority of citizens believe. Kagan states "That too many Americans have lost the feeling that what they do has lasting importance at all has become the focus of attention of the

---

[45]Ibid., p. 128.

[46]Jones, op. cit., p. 100.

honest critics of our day. . . . These critics plead for more "inner directed persons interested in the independent thinking a democracy requires."[47]

Values form the basis for this inner-direction by the individual. It is in the early years that the foundation for moral and spiritual values is laid. "So far as we can tell," say Sears, Maccoby, and Levin, "there is a learning of internal control that goes on mainly in the years before puberty, perhaps chiefly in the first six to ten years, determining the extent to which conscience will operate throughout the rest of life."[48]

According to Dewey: "A child's moral upbringing has an affect upon him which will remain largely untouched by anything that happens to him thereafter. If he has had a stable upbringing, whether on good principles or on bad ones, it will be extremely difficult for him to abandon those principles in later life—difficult but not impossible."[49]

Suggested Activities

1. Reread the description of the broad stages of moral development evolved by Piaget, pages 293–294. Visit a center for young children and describe situations in which a child's or children's behavior illustrate the first stage.

2. Arrange for a panel to discuss in class the role of the public school in developing values and moral conduct.

3. Visit a center for young children. Look for situations in which the teacher uses a clarifying strategy, as described by Raths, pp. 294–295, in developing values. Share your observations with the class.

4. Reread the section, "What Are Values?", pp. 283–284. Visit a children's center and describe situations which illustrate the characteristics of operational values with children. Share your observations with the class.

5. Conduct a class discussion on the topic, "Which Values to Teach Young Children."

6. Visit a kindergarten and note the ways in which the teacher seeks to develop "a climate of psychological safety."

7. Identify values that you have chosen, cherish, and affirm. What do you believe to be the source of these values?

8. Visit a center for young children. Observe how the teacher tries to create a "loving" environment. How do her techniques compare with those presented on p. 295?

[47]H. E. Kagan, "Teaching Values to Our Children," *Children and Youth in the 1960's* (Washington, D.C.: White House Conference on Children and Youth, Inc., 1960), p. 57.

[48]R. R. Sears, E. E. Maccoby, and H. Levin, *Patterns of Child Rearing* (Evanston, Ill.: Row Peterson, 1957), pp. 367–368.

[49]R. E. Dewey, F. W. Gramlich, and D. Loftsgordon, *Problems of Ethics* (New York: Macmillan, Inc., 1961), p. 480.

Related Readings

Association for Childhood Education International. *Children and Today's World*. Washington, D.C.: ACEI, 1967.

Banks, J. A. "Teaching Ethnic Minority Studies with a Focus on Culture," *Educ. Leadership*, 29:2 (1971), pp. 113–117.

Berkowitz, L. *The Development of Motives and Values in the Child*. New York: Basic Books, 1964.

Brown, Ina Corinne. "What Is Valued in Different Cultures," *Educ. Leadership*, 27:2 (1969), 151–154.

Combs, A. W., Chm. "Convictions, Beliefs and Values," *Perceiving, Behaving, Becoming*. Washington, D.C.: ASCD, 1962, pp. 198–212.

Committee on Religion and Education. *The Function of the Public Schools in Dealing with Religion*. Washington, D.C.: The American Council on Education, 1953.

Engbertson, W.C. "Values of Children—How They Are Developed," *Child. Educ.*, 35:6 (1961), pp. 259–264.

Jersild, A. T. "Moral Development and Religion." in *Child Psychology*, 6th ed. Englewood Cliffs, N.J.: Prentice-Hall, Inc., 1968, pp. 506–524.

Jones, Jessie Orton. *Small Rain*. New York: Viking Press, 1943.

––––––. *This Is the Way*. New York: Viking Press, 1951.

Kohlberg, L. "Moral Development and Identification," in *Child Psychology*: The Sixty-second Yearbook of NSSE. Chicago: University of Chicago Press, 1963, pp. 277–332.

––––––. "Development of Moral Character and Moral Ideology," *Review of Child Development Research*, Vol 1. New York: Russell Sage Foundation, 1964, pp. 283–332.

––––––. "The Child as a Moral Philosopher," *Psychology Today*, 2:4 (1968), pp. 24–31.

Lang, M. "Value Development in the Classroom," *Child. Educ.*, 41:3 (1964), pp. 123–126.

Leeper, R. R., ed. "Values: The Challenge, The Dilemma," *Curricular Concerns in a Revolutionary Era*. Washington, D.C.: ASCD, 1971, pp. 2–26.

Metcalf, L. E., ed. *Values Education* (1971 Yearbook, NCSS) Washington, D.C.: NCSS, 1971.

National Institute of Child Health and Human Development. *The Acquisition and Development of Values: Perspectives on Research*. Washington, D.C.: United States Government Printing Office, 1969.

Piaget, J. *The Moral Judgment of the Child*. New York: Free Press, 1965.

Rains, S., and Ruby Morris. "The Role of the Primary Teacher in Character Education," *Young Children*, 25:2 (1969), pp. 105–108.

Religion and the Schools: From Prayer to Public Aid. Washington, D.C.: National School Public Relations, NEA, 1970.

Redbird-Selam, Helen Marie, and L. B. Selam. "Cultural Conflict in the Classroom," *Social Educ.*, 36:5 (1972), pp. 513–519.

Tanyzer, H., and Jean Karl, eds. *Reading, Children's Books and Our Pluralistic Society*. Newark, Del.: International Reading Association, 1972.

Chapter **16**

Science

The young child and science seem to go together. The child is active, he is curious, and he likes to manipulate and experiment with objects. He asks many questions about how, why, where, and when. He possesses those characteristics that are important to the study of science.

Have you observed a young child watching intently as the squirrel nibbles the acorn held tightly in his paws, or as the jet streaks across the sky? Have you heard a young child ask, "Why does it rain? How does it work?" Have you listened as he mused, "Don't be afraid. I love you. Pretty little white chicken!" or perhaps chanted, "The sun is shining! The sun is shining! It is hot, hot, hot!" As the young child watches, wonders, studies, and questions, he is experiencing science as a part of his everyday living. Such experiences can help the child to gain an appreciation of the world around him; to keep alive the sense of wonder; to understand the orderliness of the universe; to develop a method of thinking and finding answers to questions.

Figure 34. These boys participate in the processes of science. They are also developing skills of observation and description.

In science education today the processes of learning are emphasized. The "process approach" offers opportunities for the child to participate in the processes of science as inquiry, as exploration, and as discovery, and to begin development of skills in observation, description, problem solving, classification, seeing relationships, logical reasoning, and inferring. Each child should progress, at his own rate, from concrete learnings (facts) through conceptual images (concepts) to more abstract generalizations. For example, a child experiences daily changes in the weather, in night and day, in plants and animals and from such concrete facts develop a concept of change. This concept can serve as a basis for future understanding of the generalization that living things and the environment change all the time.[1]

In teaching children who live in the inner city it is especially important that the science program be based on the child's environment. Skeel reminds the teacher that the environment of the inner city is not one of "butterflies and fishes." These may become a part of it but are not the most effective topics for beginning. Begin with questions important to the child, such as, "What happens to the garbage?" or "Why does it rain?" From these topics the child's environment may be extended in many of the ways discussed in this chapter.[2]

[1]*A Guide: Early Childhood Education in Florida Schools,* Bull. 76 (Tallahassee: Florida State Department of Education, 1969), p. 24.

[2]Dorothy J. Skeel, *Children of the Street, Teaching in the Inner-City* (Pacific Palisades, Cal.: Goodyear Publishing Company, Inc., 1971), pp. 71–72.

SOME GOALS IN TEACHING SCIENCE

Blough holds that the major objectives for teaching science are essentially the same at every level of learning. "They vary only to the degree that they are attainable at a given level."[3] The teacher needs to be aware of them even though she may make only a small step toward achieving them. She must understand the ultimate purpose if she is to make an effective beginning.

Four generally recognized goals are presented in the following outline, with suggestions for realizing them.[4]

1. To develop in children the ability to solve problems through the use of methods of science. To help children begin to become problem solvers and achieve these skills the teacher may do the following:
   a. Make as much use as possible of the natural curiosity of children and of their many questions.
   b. Help children say exactly what they want to find out. The statement of the questions or problems is important.
   c. Help children grow in suggesting ways to find out. Call these ways by names: looking, experimenting (or trying out), and listening.
   d. Keep trying things together. For example: "Remember what we did the other day to find out? Could we try it again?"
   e. Label these experiences *science.*
   f. Remember that the process of discovery is as important as what is discovered.
   g. Guide discovery by suggesting processes without telling the answer.
2. To develop in children an attitude—commonly called a scientific attitude. Elements of such an attitude are: Don't jump to conclusions, look at a matter from all sides, evaluate sources of information, be open-minded, don't be superstitious. To help the very young to take the beginning step in the direction of developing this attitude the teacher may use comments and questions such as the following:
   a. "Do you think that was a true story?"
   b. "Let's measure and find out."
   c. "Shall we try it *again* and see what happens?"
   d. "Let's *look at more* pictures and books."
   e. "Let's each take a turn at looking and see if we all see the same thing." (Observe carefully and often.)
   f. "How much does it weigh?"
   g. "What can we find out by looking?"
   h. "What can we do to be sure?"
   i. "Wonder who said that."
   j. "Let's see who wrote the book?"
3. To help children gain scientific knowledge and information. Subject matter can

---

[3]G. O. Blough, "Content and Process in the Kindergarten," address to New England Kindergarten Conference, November 1966 (Mimeographed).

[4]Ibid.

be over-emphasized but it can also be neglected. It should be selected from the environment of the children. Since process and content are so closely related, the following suggestions are similar to those for problem solving.

  a. Keep the learning of information at the children's level but *don't underestimate* children's abilities and interests.
  b. *Intend* to have children begin to learn some science ideas.
  c. Help children put ideas together. Recall related information and help children go as far as they can in seeing relationships.
  d. Keep a record of some of the things children have learned. They can't read it. They don't need to, but they can listen to it.

4. To develop in children an interest and appreciation in the science around them. To help in developing this interest and appreciation, suggestions for the teacher follow:

  a. Keep the interest children have, add to it, and broaden it.
  b. Try for satisfying experiences so that interest will grow.
  c. Urge children to show and discuss, to listen and to think, to manipulate, and to wonder.
  d. Present materials and problems that will open new interests children have not thought about.
  e. Remember you cannot help another person get interested in or have an appreciation for science unless you yourself are interested.

CHARACTERISTICS OF AN ADEQUATE SCIENCE PROGRAM

Evidences of science can be found in almost every center for young children. This does not mean, however, that one can find a well-balanced science program in all schools for young children. Science to many teachers has meant only a haphazard approach to nature study. This approach has been based on the incidental method and has utilized the casual consideration of some object: a leaf, a pet, or a rock brought into school by one of the children. This procedure is often justified because the child brings to school that which is of interest to him and the child's interests form a reliable basis for the science curriculum. Interests are important in program planning but dependence on them for the total program often results in gaps in content. Some areas receive overemphasis while others are untouched. Furthermore, children's interests are limited by experience. A child may not bring a certain object to kindergarten or discuss a specific topic when he knows nothing about it. He might become very interested if he had the opportunity to become acquainted with the topic.

Blough and Schwartz make the following statement regarding the incidental approach:[5]

[5]G. O. Blough and J. Schwartz, *Elementary School Science and How to Teach It* (New York: Holt, Rinehart and Winston, 1964), p. 41.

The so-called "incidental" interests of children cannot be ignored, for if they are, we miss some excellent learning opportunities. Neither can they form the chief basis for our courses. If they do, we leave out valuable material and have a hodgepodge curriculum.

How then can teachers utilize the incidents and yet provide a well-balanced science program that is flexible and adaptable to the needs and interests of children? It is important first to consider the requirements for an adequate science program for young children. These include:

1. *Planning which is both definite and flexible.* It is important that planning be both definite and flexible. This does not mean a detailed outline of specific learnings to be followed rigidly. Rather, there is a framework which is flexible enough for children and teachers to plan cooperatively for experiences that meet their particular needs. Such a framework often helps the teacher to utilize incidents more effectively because she sees in the situation possibilities for developing certain concepts. Without such planning many incidents may not be utilized or too many incidents of a similar nature may be emphasized; thereby the science program may tend to be limited in scope.
2. *Understandings from all major areas of science.* These understandings include all major areas of science, the earth and universe, living things and their activities, man and his environment, and matter and energy. Children are interested in all of these areas. Simple ideas which are introduced in a children's center lay a foundation for understanding more complex ones later as children grow through constantly enlarging experiences. At one time the belief that science for children should deal primarily with biological concepts was prevalent. Investigators have found that children are also interested in the physical sciences.[6] They have found, too, that young children are able to generalize to some extent. This skill is not one that appears suddenly but one that develops steadily with maturation and experience.[7]

    Some of the areas and some generalizations appropriate for young children are listed. Some suggested activities, through which the learnings may be achieved are also included. For each episode the teacher will develop goals, concepts, and vocabulary to be utilized for the children with whom she is working.

[6]H. Mutsfeld, "Science Experiences Afford Opportunity for Experimentation," *Child. Educ.*, 29:2 (1952), p. 81.

[7]J. G. Navarra, *The Development of Scientific Concepts in a Young Child* (New York: Teachers College, Columbia University, 1955).

Area	Examples of Facts and Concepts To Be Learned	Some Activities and Learning Encounters That Can Contribute to Concept Development
Matter and Energy	Air is around us. Air fills space. Wind moves many things. Heat changes some things. We breathe air. Fire needs air to burn. Air has water in it. Substances can change form (water is found in more than one form). Electricity makes light. A magnet will pull some things but will not pull other things. Sounds travel a long distance. Many things make sound. Machines do work for us. Some machines burn fuel; some use electricity; some are run by the wind.	Churn milk. Make butter. Cook different foods and observe changes. Observe ice or snow melt. Observe things that are being moved by the wind. Blow up toy balloons. Experiment with magnets. Visit a building under construction. Collect pictures of machines used to help man.
Living Things and Their Activities	Living things need air, water, warmth, and food. Animals eat different foods. Animals move about in different ways. Some plants grow on land; some plants grow in water. Some plants grow from seeds; some plants grow from bulbs. Some trees lose their leaves in winter; some do not. Animals and plants make adaptations to changes in seasons. All animals have young animals. Some young animals need care; some do not. Some animals migrate in winter.	Hatch chicken eggs. Visit a zoo and observe different animals. Plant a garden. Care for plants. Construct a bird feeder. Observe birds. Collect different seeds. Dramatize and compare ways in which various animals move. Collect examples of homes of various animals.
Our Earth and the Universe	The moon, sun, and other stars are in the sky. Man has put satellites in orbit around the earth. Man has traveled in rockets into outer space. Stars move in the sky. The sun gives light and heat. The earth is composed of water and soil. Air is around the earth. There are different kinds of soils.	Observe and measure shadows at different times of the day. Engage in shadow plays.

Area	Examples of Facts and Concepts To Be Learned	Some Activities and Learning Encounters That Can Contribute to Concept Development
Man and His Environment	Man uses plants and animals for food, clothing, and shelter. Animals help man work. Man uses animals for pleasure. Man can travel in many ways. Man uses and controls light. Man uses and controls heat. Living things are dependent on one another. Man can help to keep the earth clean. Litter pollutes the environment.	Collect samples of different soils. Make a trip to the store. Note vegetables (plants) used for food. Note meats (animals) used for food. Pick up and put away toys on the playground. Clean up the classroom. Visit a farm. Observe and note foods grown. Make an exhibit of ways man lights his home. Collect pictures of where heat comes from. Place trash cans on the playground. Have an anti-litter campaign. Collect pictures of ways water is used in the home.

3. *Integration of science learnings with other experiences of the young child.* In studying "living things and their activities," the science learnings may be closely related to health and social studies. With the change in weather, living things make adaptations to the cold or heat. Children may discuss the relation of proper clothing to health status. The ways in which clothing is secured relate to social learnings. Experiences are needed that help the child see how science is related to his own life; for example, electricity for light, cooking, cooling, and heating. The social implications of science in relation to community activities help children to understand why transportation is important and why the city provides water.

4. *Variety and balance in the activities in which children participate.* Field trips, experiments, instructional media, observations, learning centers, and resource people afford opportunities for a wide variety of science experiences. This does not mean that every science experience will include a field trip or an experiment. The teacher will choose carefully the activities most appropriate for developing the basic generalization under study.

How to Teach Science to Young Children

A variety of teaching strategies are described on pages 151–162. Refer to these in planning learning strategies for science. Examples of some of these strategies as applied to science follow.

Figure 35. Caring for pets affords opportunities to broaden the experiential learnings. Questions may be used to sharpen or focus observation. How does the animal eat its food? Where does it sleep in the cage?

1. Clarifying, explaining, reinforcing, and discussing comments made by children and sharing ideas and things brought to school by them are valuable techniques. Jane entered the kindergarten wearing a new red jacket. She greeted the teacher and said, "I wore my coat because it is cold. It is very cold—almost to freezing." The teacher said, "Yes, it is cold. How do you know it is freezing outside?"

   Jane: "The weatherman said so on TV."

   Teacher: "How does the weatherman know it is freezing?"

   Jane: "Because he is a weatherman."

   Teacher: "He reads the thermometer and finds out how cold it is. There is a thermometer in our room. Let's put it outside and see what happens." The teacher and Jane cross the room together.

2. The science center is a part of the room that reflects what children are doing in science. The pets or animals may be kept here. There may be an aquarium or a terrarium. Books with pictures that answer children's questions can be displayed. Materials for manipulation and experimentation are placed there. These may include magnets, dry cells, a magnifying glass, and a tuning fork.

3. The Learning Center. See pp. 155–157.

4. Caring for living things affords opportunities for children to broaden the experiental learnings they have developed regarding both plants and animals. Animals and plants can be compared, differences and likenesses noted. An awareness of the many kinds of plants and animals and an understanding of what is involved in the care of living things can be fostered.

Caterpillars, guinea pigs, hamsters, birds, dogs, chickens, mice, fish, tadpoles, cats, and even goats have been cared for at school, either in the classroom or outside near the building. It is important that cages be kept clean and proper food and water be provided. Arrangements for care over the weekend should be made. Often arrangements can be made with parents for a child to take one of the pets home with him.

When using animals with young children the teacher may need to be responsible for their handling, encouraging but not forcing the children to observe and to "pet" them. A child, not knowing how to handle the pet, usually squeezes it, causing the animal to react by biting or scratching. Then the child may become frightened or hurt and as a result the desired learnings are not accomplished. Also, the animal may be injured.

5. Observations may be closely related to any of the activities for science experiences that have been described. Observations, however, may be planned as an activity for the nursery school or kindergarten room. Children will watch birds, fish, bees, ants, rabbits, turtles, or rats intently, sometimes talking to one another, but often looking and musing alone.

   Listen to three-year-old Ann as she watches the white rats:
   "Long tails, long tails, long tails!"
   Questions may be used to sharpen or focus the observation. For example: "How does the animal eat its food? How does it move? What does it eat? Where does it sleep in the cage?"

6. Resource persons who are invited to talk with the children about some aspect of science may be parents of a child in the group, another teacher, or some other person in the community. In selecting such a person, the teacher needs to be sure that he can talk with the children in a manner they can understand. Don't ask someone to come and talk about a general topic such as "rocks." Before the visit be sure that he understands the questions raised by the children and the length of time he is to talk.

7. Experiments are planned to test, to try out ideas, and to help the child to come to accurate conclusions. They are not arranged to provide a display of magic and arouse fears and doubts in the child's mind. If there is a problem to be solved, children may be helped to use an experiment in finding the solution. The following steps may be used:
   a. State the problem of the experiment in order that children know what they are trying to find out.
   b. Decide on what is to be done to solve the problem or answer the question.
   c. Get the materials needed.
   d. Do the activities agreed upon.
   e. Observe carefully what happens.
   f. Answer the question.

The following example is used to illustrate these steps. With young children, the problem of the experiment often grows out of their questions. The teacher, rather than answering the question with a "yes" or "no," sees in the question an opportunity for experimentation and problem solving. For example:

Jim is showing Sam how his magnet will attract and pull nails to it. He comments, "My magnet will pull anything."

Sam replies, "Oh no, it won't. I know."

"Miss W., will this magnet pull anything?"

Miss W. answers, "Let's see. Will a magnet pull iron nails?"

"Yes," the boys reply.

"Iron tacks?" "Yes."

"A pencil?" Sam is not sure, though Jim is confident.

Miss W. asks, "How can we find out if a magnet will pull a pencil?"

"We can try it and see," said Sam.

"Yes," said Miss W. "Are there other things you would like to try?"

"Oh yes." Looking around the room the boys name blocks, iron screws, chalk, crayons, and scissors. "Let's see if the magnet pulls them."

The boys take the magnet from one object to another and test the pull. Miss W. asked, "Did the magnet pull the blocks?" "No."

"The iron screws?" "Yes." "Chalk?" "No." "Crayons?" "No." "Scissors?" "Yes."

"Your magnet won't pull everything. It won't pull chalk, crayons, or blocks," concluded Sam.

Jim looked down at the floor, crestfallen that his magnet had let him down. Miss W. said, "That's right, the magnet won't pull everything. But, Jim, your magnet will pull some things. What kind of things will it pull?"

Jim's face brightened as he said, "My magnet won't pull everything, but it will pull some things. It will pull iron and steel things."

The teacher should encourage the child to tell what he finds out. She encourages him to speak in sentences and explain his findings clearly. For example, "Can you explain it better?" "Begin, 'I found out. . . .'"

8. The unit, as a means of organizing materials, is discussed on pp. 271–279 in relation to social studies. The unit plan may also be used as a means of organizing science materials. As an example, a unit related to ecology is presented below. One value of the unit plan for organizing is that materials and activities are included to provide for a range in ability, maturity, and interests appropriate for a group of children, whether they be three, four, or five years of age, or whether they live in the city or the suburb.

A RESOURCE UNIT

Generalizations from the area, *Man and His Environment,* have been developed into the following resource unit. One concept may be selected and developed in a learning episode or a series of encounters. Appropriate activities and materials may be selected and utilized.

Figure 36. Science affords meaningful encounters with the environment. The praying mantis eats a grasshopper. "What did the grasshopper eat? How can you find out?"

ENCOUNTERS WITH THE ENVIRONMENT

1. *Purposes*: To help the children begin to:
   a. Develop an awareness of, and an appreciation for the environment as evidenced by statements such as:
      "See the tiny green leaves. Spring must be here."
      "This yard is a mess. There is paper all over it."
   b. Know that living things and the environment change all the time. Some changes are caused by nature, some by man. For example:
      "Look at the crack in the walk. It is getting bigger."
      "The rain washed the sand out of the box."
   c. Understand that living things depend upon one another and upon their environment. For example:
      "The plant grows toward the sun."
      "We picked oranges from the tree."
2. *Initiating the unit*: Leads into *Encounters with the Environment* may come from:
   a. Incidents. For example, a child's comment, "There is so much junk here I can't work." The teacher may say, "You can't work at the table. Why?" During the conversation other children may be involved and questions raised. "Where do the books belong? Where are the puzzles kept? How can we have space to work and play?" Follow with discussion and planning.
   b. Teacher suggestion. Arrange for a walk. Questions may be raised: "What happened to the sand in the box? Why did the leaves fall from the tree? Why did the sidewalk crack? What changes have people made?" Follow with discussion and planning.

3. *Learning opportunities*: Take a walk or a field trip. On various trips ask children to observe: (1) evidences of change on the playground, (2) evidences of beauty in the environment, (3) things that make them feel happy, and (4) evidences that living things depend upon one another and their environment.

    a. Develop meanings for such words as *environment, living things, waste, change, depend.*

    b. Rake leaves. Make a compost heap or observe what happens to leaves left in the gutter or a corner of the yard.

    c. Plant a garden. If possible, pick and cook vegetables.

    d. Visit an orchard. Pick apples. See how many ways the children can use the apples.

    e. Visit a farm. Pick vegetables. Gather eggs. Watch as cows are milked.

    f. Pull up a weed by the roots. Observe how it looks next day.

    g. Ask children to identify natural things by touch: grass, water, leaf, peach, each other.

       by smell: flower, grass, soil, leaf, apple.

       by taste: apple, orange, banana.[8]

    h. Record natural sounds such as a bird singing or fussing, wind blowing, cricket chirping, leaves rustling. Play recording. Listen carefully and identify sounds.[9]

    i. Make gifts for parents using "recoverables from the recycling heap." Examples: Make paper weights. Children collect smooth, clean rocks and decorate with poster paint. Make wall plaques (piece of plywood and shellac) or a pencil holder (tin-can base). Children collect scraps of string, yarn, cord. Cover wood or can with glue. Pull, wind, twist pieces of string, etc., into design.[10]

    j. Make miniature trash receptacles. Decorate milk cartons, coffee cans, paper bags. Use at home, at school, or in the car. Involve parents.

    k. Collect samples of soil from different places (around the building if possible). Compare as to color, moisture, temperature. "How do they feel? How are they different?" Spread out samples of soil on the paper. Pick out animals (earthworms, crickets, etc.) and put them in a jar. Ask questions such as "How many different kinds of animals did you find? Were there the same number in each kind of soil?"[11]

    l. Take a trip to the zoo. Focus on foods of animals. Find out the native foods of animals and the food given them in the zoo. Ask where the zoo foods come from. Ask children to name foods which they give their pets. Ask them to find out where the foods come from.[12]

    m. If changes are taking place near the children's center (buildings being torn down, highways being built, construction) ask children to observe changes. Take photographs.[13] Ask questions such as, Are there as many homes now?

---

[8]R. Caras, "Time to Join the World," *Early Years*, 2:9 (1972), p. 36.

[9]Ibid.

[10]Maija Kaljo, "Love, Nature and the Recycling Heap," *Early Years*, 2:9 (1972), pp. 38–39.

[11]Beth Schultz, "Your Town: A Biotic Community with People," *Environmental Education in the Elementary School* (Washington, D.C.: NSTA, 1972), p. 35.

[12]Ibid.

[13]Ibid., p. 34.

Stores? Plants? Trees? Animals?" Observe how tools and power help men work.

   n. Observe birds and try to find out what they are eating. "Are they eating seeds? Insects? Berries?"

   o. Collect leaves that have been damaged by insects. "Why did the insect damage the leaf?"[14]

   p. Dig up a plant from hard, dry soil. Plant it in loose, fertile soil and keep it watered. Observe what happens. Discuss reasons.[15]

   q. Turn the hose on the playground on hard soil and again on soft, loose soil. Observe the running water and the materials it carries away. Discuss meaning of *erosion*. After a rain, collect muddy water from the street or yard. Observe sediment that settles to the bottom. "What is it? Where did it come from?"

   r. Observe that the praying mantis eats a grasshopper. "What did the grasshopper eat? How can you find out?"[16]

   s. Plant bean seeds. Expose some seedlings to more light than others. "What are the differences? Why?"

  4. *Evaluation*: Observe dramatic play. Note comments and conversations of children for awareness of interdependence, environment, change.

Observe children's behavior for evidences of assuming responsibility, caring for materials.

Observe children's art products.

  5. *List of Materials*:

Books

Alexander, Anne. *Noise in the Night*. Chicago: Rand McNally, 1966.

Atwood, Ann. *The Wild Young Desert*. New York: Scribners, 1970.

Borten, Helen. *Do You Hear What I Hear?* Eau Claire, Wis.: E. M. Hale, 1966.

Busch, Phyllis S. *Puddles and Ponds: Living Things in Watery Places*. New York: World, 1969.

———. *At Home in Its Habitat: Animal Neighborhoods*. New York: World, 1970.

———. *Swamp Spring*. New York: Macmillan, Inc., 1969.

Dayton, Mona. *Earth and Sky*. New York: Harper & Row, 1969.

Hawes, Judy. *What I Like About Toads*. New York: Crowell, 1969.

Hazen, Barbara S. *Where Do Bears Sleep?* Reading, Mass.: Addison-Wesley, 1970.

Hurs, Edith Thacher. *Wilson's World*. New York: Harper & Row, 1971.

May, J. *Alligator Hole*. Chicago: Follett, 1969.

———. *Blue River*. New York: Holiday House, 1971.

Merz, R. *The Mockingbird Book*. New York: Harper & Row, 1962.

Miles, Miska. *Apricot ABC*. Boston: Little Brown, 1969.

Peet, B. *The Wump World*. Boston: Houghton Mifflin, 1970.

Pelgreen, J. *Backyard Safari*. New York: Doubleday, 1971.

Podendorf, Illa. *Everyday Is Earth Day*. Children's Press, 1971.

---

[14]Ibid., p. 35.

[15]Ibid., p. 36.

[16]Beth Schultz, "Ecology for the Child," *Environmental Education in the Elementary School* (Washington, D.C.: NSTA, 1972), p. 14.

Pringle, Laurence P., ed. *Discovering the Outdoors*. Garden City, N.Y.: The Natural History Press, 1969.

Pringle, Laurence P. *From Field to Forest: How Plants and Animals Change the Land*. New York: World, 1970.

Seuss, Dr. *The Lorax*. New York: Random House, 1971.

Showers, Paul. *Listening Walk*. New York: Macmillan, Inc., 1961.

Shulevitz, Uri. *Rain Rain Rivers*. New York: Farrar, 1969.

Tresslet, Alvin. *The Beaver Pond*. New York: Lothrop, 1970.

———. *It's Time Now!*. New York: Lothrop, 1969.

Van Leeuwen, Jean. *One Day in Summer*. New York: Random House, 1969.

Filmstrips

Plant and Animal Relationships: The Forest, The Pond, The Desert, The Swamp, The Seashore, The Grasslands. Encyclopedia Britannica Films, Inc., 1150 Wilmette Ave., Wilmette, Ill.

Discovering Life Around Us Series: A Visit to the: Seashore, Farm, Garden, Weeds, Pond. Encyclopedia Britannica Films, Inc. 1150 Wilmette Avenue., Wilmette, Ill.

Poetry

Association for Childhood Education International. *Sung Under the Silver Umbrella*. New York: Macmillan, Inc., 1952.

Arbuthnot, May Hill, ed. *Time for Poetry*. Chicago: Scott, Foresman, 1961.

Behn, Harry, translated by. *Cricket Songs*. New York: Harcourt, 1964.

Bramblett, Ella. *Sheets of Green*. New York: Crowell, 1968.

Fischer, Aileen. *In the Middle of the Night*. New York: Crowell, 1965.

———. *In the Woods, in the Meadow, in the Sky*. New York: Scribners, 1965.

Ferris, Helen, ed. *Favorite Poems Old and New*. New York: Doubleday, 1957.

Stevenson, R. L. *A Child's Garden of Verses*. New York: Watts, 1966.

Songs

McCall, Adeline. *This Is Music*. Boston: Allyn and Bacon, 1966.

Nelson, Mary J., and Gladys Tipton. *Music for Early Childhood*. New York: Silver Burdett Co., 1952.

Pitts, Lilla Belle, et al. *The Kindergarten Book*. Boston; Ginn Co., 1949.

Winn, Marie, ed. *Children's Songs*. New York: Simon & Schuster, 1966.

Zeitlin, Patty. *Castle in My City—Songs for Young Children*. San Carlos, Calif.: Golden Gate Junior Books, 1966.

Suggested Activities

1. Select one generalization to be developed with young children from the areas listed on pages 306–307. Plan a resource unit for developing this generalization, using the suggested outlines found on pages 271–279 and 310–314.

2. Select a site which you think might possibly be appropriate for a field trip by a four-year-old group. Visit the site and evaluate it. Share your conclusions with the class.

3. Visit a kindergarten. Observe and list evidences of science activities. Identify the areas, listed on pages 305–307, to which the activities contribute. Note the generalizations which are being developed. Share your findings with the class.

4. In your class conduct an experiment that you consider to be appropriate for young children, using the steps listed on p. 309.

5. Select an activity or learning encounter listed on pp. 306–307. Plan and develop it with young children. Evaluate.

6. Listen to and evaluate five recordings with science content for use with young children.

7. Visit a library or a center with a collection of children's books. Select and evaluate five books with science content for use with young children. Indicate the areas of science (pp. 305–307) in which the books may be used.

8. View and evaluate filmstrips for use with children. Describe how you might use the filmstrips.

9. Make a collection of flat pictures for use in science with the young child.

Related Readings

ACEI. "The World's Bounty," *Child. Educ.*, 40:8 (1964), entire issue.

———. "Outdoor Education," *Child. Educ.*, 44:2 (1967), entire issue.

———. "The Living World," *Child. Educ.*, 47:4 (1971), entire issue.

Beadle, Pat. "Science Everyday: The Inquiry Approach," *Instructor*, 81:9 (1972), p. 47.

Bennett, L. M., and Gloria Bassett. "Games and Things for Preschool Science," *Science and Children*, 9:5 (1972), pp. 25–27.

Bennett, L. M., Rose F. Spicola, and Marcia Vogelsang. "Pre-School Children Learn Science," *Science and Children*, 7:8 (1970), pp. 10–11.

Blough, Glenn O. "Some How's and Why's of Teaching Elementary Science," *Keeping Up With Elementary Education*, 17:1 (1971), pp. 9–12.

Buschoff, Lottie K. "Going on a Trip?" *Young Children*, 26:4 (1971), pp. 224–232.

Bybee, R. W. "Earth Science with a Focus on the Child's Environment," *Science and Children*, 9:1 (1971), pp. 11–14.

Bybee, R. W., and Alan McCormack, "Applying Piaget's Theory," *Science and Children*, 8:4 (1970), pp. 14–17.

Chittenden, E. A. "Piaget and Elementary Science," *Science and Children*, 8:4 (1970), pp. 9–15.

Cordier, Mary H. "Young Children's Attitudes About Environment," *Science and Children*, 7:7 (1969), pp. 19–21. Also in *Environmental Education in the Elementary School*. Washington, D.C.: NSTA, 1972, pp. 5–7.

Gratz, Pauline. "Maintaining a Supportive Physical Environment for Man," *Educ. Leadership*, 27:2 (1969), pp. 173–175. Also in *Curricular Concerns in a Revolutionary Era*. Washington, D.C.: ASCD, 1971, pp. 261–263.

Haughton, Rosemary. "The Forgotten Garden of Childhood," *Réalitiés*, 258 (May 1972), pp. 42–47.

Hill, Katherine B. "Science for Children—Why?" *Science and Children*, 3:8 (1966), pp. 11–12.

Hungerford, H. "Science Everyday: The Incidental Approach," *Instructor*, 81:9 (1972), p. 46.

Hymes, J. L., Jr. "Fives as Scientists," *Grade Teacher*, 81:8 (1964), p. 15.

Inbody, D. "Kindergarten and First Grade Science," *Science and Children*, 1:4 (1963), pp. 26–28.

————. "Children's Understandings of Natural Phenomena," *Science Educ.*, 47:3, pp. 270–278.

Kluge, Jean. "What the World Needs Now: Environmental Education for Young Children," *Young Children*, 26:5 (1971), pp. 260–263.

Knapp, C. E. "Conducting a Field Trip: Organizational Patterns for Instruction," *Science and Children*, 8:1 (1970), pp. 26–28.

Kolson, C. J., G. C. Jeffers, and P. H. Lamb. "Oral Science Vocabulary of Kindergarten Children," *Science Educ.*, 47:4 (1963), pp. 408–415. Also in Mills, Belen C. *Understanding the Young Child and His Curriculum*. New York: Macmillan, Inc., 1972.

Newman, D. "Sciencing for Young Children," *Young Children*, 27:4 (1972), pp. 215–226.

Pennington, G. "The Word Is Adventure," *Instructor*, 81:7 (1972), pp. 74–76.

Pratt, Grace K. "Developing Concepts About Science in Young Children," *Science and Children*, 1:4 (1963), pp. 21–22.

Stant, Margaret A. *The Young Child, His Activities and Materials*. Englewood Cliffs, N.J.: Prentice-Hall, Inc., 1972, pp. 95–105.

Williams, D. L., and W. L. Herman, Jr. *Current Research in Elementary School Science*. New York: Macmillan, Inc., 1971.

Young Children and Science. Washington, D.C.: ACEI, 1964.

Health and Safety

The health of young children has been identified as an area of special concern in Project Head Start because, "a child who is in poor health will function at a level considerably lower than that of a well child."[1] The comprehensive goals of Project Head Start are planned to bring high quality health services to poor children. These include finding and remedying any existing health defects; ensuring a child's future health by providing preventive services (such as immunization, health education); and improving the health of all members of the child's family and of the community.[2] Such goals, however, are appropriate for all children. Such a statement is not intended to minimize the importance of these goals for the poor but to emphasize their significance for all. The

---

[1]Project Head Start, *Head Start, A Child Development Program* (Washington, D.C.: U.S. Government Printing Office, 1970), p. 2.

[2]Project Head Start, *Project Head Start, Health Services—A Guide for Project Directors and Health Personnel* (Washington, D.C.: U.S. Government Printing Office, 1969), p. 5.

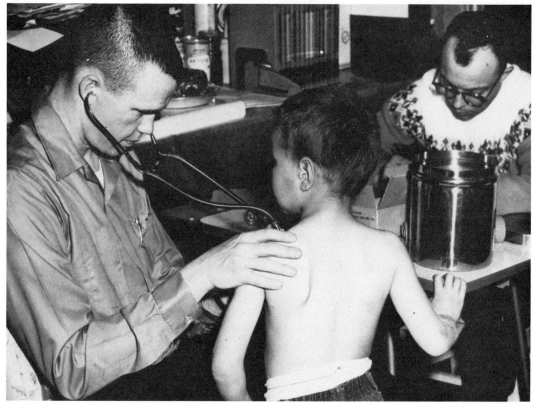

Figure 37.   The early school years are fraught with health and safety hazards. Thorough examinations are important in the early detection of illness and of existing health defects.

health services may come from different sources but they are important to all young children.

A broader and deeper concept of health has emerged, as evidenced by the following definition.

> Health is a state of physical, mental, and social well being and depends upon the interaction of these dimensions. Health is dynamic, in that it is ever changing.
>
> Health is influenced by the interaction of many hereditary and environmental factors and conditions over which the individual may exercise varying amounts of control. Some aspects of everyone's health can be improved.[3]

According to this definition, "health" in any center for young children is

[3]Joint Committee on Health Problems in Education of the NEA and AMA, *Why Health Education* (Chicago: AMA, 1965), pp. 2–3.

most effective if it is incorporated into all of the activities of the center. Health education cannot be limited to such activities as "daily inspections," "hand-washing," "special demonstrations," and "play in the out-of-doors."

The definition includes these aspects, of course, but also emphasizes the importance of a healthful environment that offers opportunities to practice and acquire desirable information, habits, and attitudes and to participate in activities that contribute to healthful living. These are broad inclusive terms that must be analyzed and the implications for teachers of young children noted. Health and safety are considered together because of the interrelationships involved.

A HEALTHFUL ENVIRONMENT

The school environment determines to a considerable extent the quality of healthful living possible in the situation. Too often emphasis has been placed upon the physical aspects of the environment, assuming that adequate space, toilet facilities, and appropriate equipment assured healthful living. There is increased recognition, however, that the best physical environment can be wasted unless the teacher is alert to its utilization and opportunities for learning. The sunshine may be glorious, but if the teacher plans no time in the out-of-doors the children cannot experience its values. Playground equipment that offers opportunities for exercise and muscular growth will be useless if the children are kept inside. Well-planned bathrooms with wash basins and toilets, exactly the right size, may not contribute to the development of desirable habits and attitudes if they are not kept clean and pleasant.

The recognition of each child and his parents as persons of worth, the provision for each child of an educational program appropriate to his developmental level, and the maintenance of a warm and accepting human environment all contribute to the positive mental health of each child. The total program of an adequate center for children can be considered as a mental health service and a significant part of a healthful environment.[4]

Effective use of an adequate environment can benefit the young child greatly. It is essential that attention be given not alone to the adequacy of the environment but to the effective use of it in developing physical, mental, and social health. This concept of a healthful environment maintains that children will learn when they are involved in situations concerning health and safety and are then helped to practice consistently what they have learned. The effectiveness of this approach depends on such factors as the school personnel, the emotional tone of the situation, physical facilities, policies, and program.

[4]*Project Head Start, Health Services,* op. cit., p. 48.

SCHOOL PERSONNEL

According to Rasey, children learn from people and things and of the two, human beings appear to be more crucial. What a child considers important usually depends upon the values placed on the event by the people with whom he comes in contact. "Children see their world as through a glass, darkly or brightly, as their adults reflect or transmit it to them."[5]

All adults in the school situation are important to children. School personnel includes all persons who have any responsibility for the school or a part of the program. Their responsibilities include maintaining and utilizing a healthful environment as well as good personal health.

The teacher, however, is the key person in the situation. It is essential that the teacher be in good physical health. Energy and vigor are prerequisites for alert, active, yet intelligent, patient, and sympathetic guidance of children. Regular physical examinations, an adequate diet, sufficient rest, appropriate recreation, and comfortable clothing are as important for the teacher as for the child. Yet these alone are not enough. The teacher's mental health is most important. Jersild points out that for a teacher to know those whom he teaches, he must know himself.[6]

Witherspoon has formulated the following questions that may be used by the teacher for self-examination:[7]

Do I see children as they really are? Or, are my concepts clouded by my own experiences as a child?

Can I show kindness and affection toward others? Or, do I feel that this is unnecessary?

Do my actions and deeds reflect confidence and integrity? Or, are they merely an attempt to "save face" in order to protect me from myself?

Recognizing that how I feel about my life and my environment is the only frame of reference that enables me to evaluate my actions, am I happy with my lot in life? Or, do I feel that this life has been unkind to me?

Do I view myself as physically healthy, ambitious, and enthusiastic? Or, do I see myself as tired all the time even though I am healthy in the physical sense?

Do I usually finish each day with a feeling of pride of accomplishment? Or, do I go home merely feeling that I have done my duty whether anything was accomplished or not?

Is working with young children what I most like to do? Or, do I see teaching as a job?

[5]Marie I. Rasey and J. W. Menge, *What We Learn from Children* (New York: Harper & Row, 1956), p. 39.

[6]A. T. Jersild, *When Teachers Face Themselves* (New York: Teachers College, Columbia University, 1955), p. 26.

[7]R. L. Witherspoon, "Teacher, Know Thyself," *Child. Educ.*, 35:2 (1958), p. 56.

Am I sure that others think of me as their friend? Or, do I feel that I am not quite sure
whether I have any friends at all?

Do I face crises calmly and confidently so that I can face reality whatever it may be?
Or, do serious "accidents" always happen to me?

Do I recognize when I need help? Or, am I afraid of what others will think of me if
I seek assistance?

If the teacher can answer "yes" to the first part of these questions, the
children in her classroom have a person who can help them to become confident, alert, and imaginative. If the teacher truthfully has to answer "yes" to
some (or all) of the last parts of these questions, there is need for her to evaluate
herself carefully and resolve to do something about it. The self-concept of the
teacher is as important as that of each child she teaches.

The teacher's knowledge of the growth and development of children influences her expectations of them. What the teacher expects has a great effect
on the mental health of the child and the emotional tone of the classroom. Expressing undue concern when a three-year-old has an accident and wets his
pants, insisting upon the use of "good adult manners" by the four-year-olds,
or expecting each five-year-old to cut out an object evenly and smoothly along
a line can result in anxieties and negative attitudes, neither of which are
conducive to positive mental health. A teacher who understands three's, four's
and five's does not indulge them, but paces expectations and activities to their
developmental level.

Alert supervision by the teacher is imperative in order to safeguard the
health and safety of the children. This means careful observation of the child
for signs of illness such as flushed face, paleness, listlessness, irritability,
coughing, sneezing, running nose; adjusting wraps to changes of temperature
or activity; closing or opening windows to prevent drafts or improve ventilation; raising or lowering shades for proper lighting; seeing that cups, spoons,
and other eating utensils are not used in common; removing safety hazards;
paying close attention to children who are climbing in high places or to children
using such tools as hammers, saws, hoes, or shovels. As Read says, "the skillful teacher never relaxes her watchfulness."[8]

The teacher's attitude can greatly facilitate or hinder the team approach to
health. Such an approach makes it possible to utilize the contributions of the
parents, the physician, the nurse, and the psychologist, as well as the teacher.
No one person can do the job adequately alone. The teacher needs to know the
resources available within the community and understand how they may be
used for children. She recognizes that she cannot do everything herself and
that it is a sign of strength, not weakness, to ask for help. Through this approach, common understandings regarding the goals of the health program and
the role of each member of the team can be developed.

[8]Katherine H. Read, *The Nursery School* (Philadelphia: W. B. Saunders, 1960), p. 88.

PHYSICAL FACILITIES

Physical facilities, equipment, and grounds are discussed on pages 418–437. In this section the emphasis is placed on the use of the facilities to promote health and safety.

Facilities for Rest

Facilities for resting in all-day schools include cots, sheets, and blankets. Spacing of the cots is important (approximately 3 ft. apart) so that children will not lie with faces too close together. Shades should be drawn to facilitate rest. Quiet music is sometimes played during the rest period.

In schools not operating an all-day program, rugs and towels are often used for a midmorning rest. Such practice may be questioned on two important points:

1. If the floor is not warm and free from drafts, the rug or towel may not provide adequate protection for the child. Pads, from $1/2$ to 1 inch thick, are now being used in some schools. These are not as expensive as cots and yet provide more adequate protection from the cold floor. The pads may be made of foam rubber or cotton, with a washable cover. A plastic cover can be easily cleaned, whereas a cotton slip must be laundered frequently.
2. If rugs or towels are stacked together, the side of the rug next to the floor may be placed in contact with the "face" side of the next rug. This hazard can be minimized by having the floor side clearly marked, folded to the outside, and stored in each individual's locker. In order to prevent the "head part" from being folded to the "foot part," teach the child to first fold the rug lengthwise. If mats are used, the floor side should be marked also. Sheets can be used and stored in each child's locker. Children should be involved in the process of getting out and storing cots or mats.

Drinking Fountains

Drinking fountains, if used, should be low enough for the child to reach easily. It is important that the child be taught to drink so as not to put his mouth on the fountain. This is not easy for the child and supervision is necessary. For these reasons, individual paper cups are used in some schools.

Lockers

It is recommended that each child have his own locker in which to keep clothing and supplies. Individual lockers are of value in helping the child establish proper habits of caring for clothing and supplies. Moreover, there is less danger of spreading contagious diseases when children's wraps are kept separate in individual lockers. It is often desirable to provide some lockers or storage cabinets on casters for use in partitioning off areas and for increased flexibility of activities in the room.

Figure 38. A warm and accepting human environment contributes to the positive mental health of each child. This girl in an all-day center sleeps peacefully while her mother is at work.

Furniture

Furniture should be of appropriate size for each child. This means that not all furniture within the classroom will be the same size. As children differ in height, so should the tables and chairs. It is important that tables and chairs be matched and that a high chair not be used at a low table. Help the child to decide whether or not he has the right chair by using such questions as:

1. Can your feet reach the floor?
2. Is there room for your knees under the table?
3. Are you comfortable?

Play Equipment

Play equipment and toys that are sources of danger should be repaired or removed. Broken toys with sharp edges and protruding nails, unsteady ladders, splintery boards and blocks are examples. Loose gravel, sticks, or stones on the playground as well as roots, stumps, and holes can be safety hazards. Constant vigilance is essential.

Temperature, Ventilation, and Lighting

Temperature, ventilation, and lighting are important factors to consider in helping the child acquire desirable habits and attitudes. Although maintaining proper temperature, lighting, and ventilation is the responsibility of the teacher, it is important that opportunities for learning by the children be utilized. Comments and the activities which follow illustrate the teaching opportunities. For example, the comment, "John, I feel too warm—let's check the thermometer," helps John learn the following:

1. The thermometer is used to measure temperature.
2. The correct temperature for the room.
3. To become aware of feeling uncomfortable when one is too warm.
4. Some things to do when one is too warm.

In schools where the temperature is regulated by an engineer at a central control, the teacher assumes responsibility for reporting undesirable temperatures.

Another example involves Jane who is looking at a book in the bright sunlight. The teacher may adjust the shade while the child is unaware of what she has done. Or the teacher may say "Jane, your book is in the sunshine. The glare makes you squint your eyes. Let's fix the shade"; or, "Move your chair over here, out of the sun." This situation can help Jane to learn the following:

1. Looking at or reading books in direct sunlight is not a desirable health practice.
2. Why she squints and how the eyes feel in such a situation.
3. Some things to do to correct the situation.

POLICIES

Policies relating to health and safety should be formulated, made available to parents and all personnel involved, and consistently enforced. Policies are needed in the following areas:

Physical Examinations for Children, Teachers, Aides, and Other School Personnel

Such examinations should be made within one month prior to the date the child enters school or the adult begins work at the school. Forms for recording the results of the examination may be secured from the local health authority or developed by the school. Records should be filed so as to be easily accessible.

Immunizations

Those required should be specified by a health authority. Records of immunizations should be kept up to date.

Communicable Diseases

Policies should cover procedure when a child or adult has been exposed, the length of time a child should stay out of school when he has a communicable disease, and on what authority he is readmitted to school. Usually it is wise to follow the policies set by the local health authority.

Accidents and Sudden Illness at School

Such policies should include the procedure for contacting parents or a person designated by the parents (if they cannot be reached), and for contacting the child's physician, or providing the authority to use another physician if the child's cannot be reached. The extent of the school's liability and insurance coverage in such situations should be clearly defined and made known to the parents.

Health Information

Policies are needed regarding procedures for informing parents of defects observed by the teacher or the nurse, results of screening tests, information regarding height and weight, and of the incidence of a contagious disease in the group.

Morning Inspection

The routine for morning inspection (by teacher or nurse) needs to be understood by parents and children. Such a policy will probably state that the parent or adult bringing the child to school must wait until the child has been checked and admitted to the group.

Transportation

If transportation to and from school is provided by the school, then a policy is needed as to the number of children transported in each car, the responsibility of the driver for the conduct of the children, the conduct expected of the children in the car, and the procedure for having a child delivered to someone or at someplace other than home. If parents and their cars are used for field trips, policies are needed to ascertain the amount of liability insurance the driver of the car should carry, number of children and adults per car, and the conduct expected of the children.

PRACTICES AND PROGRAM

Direct instruction in health is not usually undertaken with very young children. Rather, teaching is done in connection with the daily school activities and routines.

This does not mean that all teaching is incidental and that no planning is necessary. To illustrate how goals in health and safety can be identified and opportunities used to achieve these goals, instructional areas are suggested.[9]

For each of the areas there are listed concepts, beginning understandings, and learnings that it is hoped the child will achieve. Activities and learning encounters through which these may be realized are also listed. From these concepts and activities the teacher can select those that are appropriate for the group of children she is teaching. At regular intervals the teacher should review the activities in which the children have participated, note areas in which there has been little or no activity, evaluate progress toward goals, and plan for additional activities and learning encounters in needed areas.

Area	Examples of Concepts To Be Learned	Some Learning Encounters and Activities That Can Contribute to Concept Development
The Body and Its Care	Children grow at different rates. The nose is an organ for breathing and smelling.	Weigh and measure children. Discuss sizes of children in group. Talk about different sizes in plants and animals. Identify some things by smell. Talk about keeping objects out of the nose.
Family Health and Living	Families are different in size, ages of the members, and in their customs. Growth and reproduction are common to all living things.	Talk about how birthdays and other holidays are celebrated in each child's family. Make family pictures. Invite family members to visit the school or center. Show pictures of mothers and babies. Show pictures of mother animals and their babies. Learn names for mother animals and their babies.
Food and Nutrition	Good foods help children grow. We eat food for growth, energy, and enjoyment. Foods come from plants and animals.	Plant a vegetable garden. Prepare, serve, and eat a variety of foods and beverages, such as fruit, fruit juices, and raw vegetables. Visit a farm, a dairy, a grocery store, or supermarket.
Environmental and Community Health	Children can help to keep the community clean. There are doctors, nurses, and dentists who help us keep well.	Engage in cooperative planning by teacher and children for care of center, playground, and equipment. Engage in dramatic play.

[9]*A Guide: Early Childhood Education in Florida Schools,* Bull. 76 (Tallahassee: Florida State Department of Education, 1969), pp. 37-38.

Area	Examples of Concepts To Be Learned	Some Learning Encounters and Activities That Can Contribute to Concept Development
	Hospitals are built to care for people who need special care.	Arrange for a visit by a public health nurse. Visit the school clinic.
Safety	Getting in and out of a car safely helps to prevent accidents. One must not tease pets or play with strange animals.	Talk about safe ways to get in and out of cars. Dramatize getting in and out of cars safely. Demonstrate getting in and out of cars safely. Care for pets.
Mental Health and Human Relations	Each child is alike and different from all other children. Kindness, thoughtfulness, and courtesy help us live together happily. Young children, as well as adults, have responsibilities.	Talk about ways in which children are alike and different. Share toys and materials. Talk about treatment of classmates. Send letters, dictated to the teacher, of thanks and appreciation. List jobs to be done in relation to a certain activity. Choose jobs to do.

Areas of concern for the health and safety of young children in the various types of centers include the school environment, physical facilities, practices, and the program, all of which are interrelated. As the child experiences a healthful school environment, uses desirable health and safety practices, as he participates in a school program appropriate to his needs and maturity, he has the opportunity to develop into an individual who experiences physical, mental, and social well-being.

Suggested Activities

1. Visit the local health unit. Secure a copy of regulations and policies pertaining to communicable diseases. Discuss in class.
2. Identify agencies or organizations in the community that may serve as health resources; for example, the county or city health unit, the speech and hearing clinic, mental health clinic. For each one determine the services available, the cost, and referral procedures.
3. Visit a playground for young children. Identify any possible safety hazards.
4. Select one concept to be developed from the areas listed on pages 326–327. Plan a learning encounter appropriate for developing this concept and utilize your plan with a group of young children. Evaluate the activity.

5. Reread the material relating to policies. Visit a center for children and talk with the teacher regarding the center's policies on the topics listed on pp. 324–325.

Related Readings

Aaron, J. E., F. Bridges, and D. O. Ritzel. *First Aid and Emergency Care*. New York: Macmillan, Inc., 1972.

Bell, J. E., and Elisabeth A. Bell, "Family Participation in Hospital Care for Children," *Children*, 17:4 (1970), pp. 154–157.

Birch, H. G., and J. D. Gussow. *Disadvantaged Children: Health, Nutrition, and School Failure*. New York: Harcourt Brace Jovanovich, 1970.

Brooks, Mary M. "Play for Hospitalized Children," *Young Children*, 24:4 (1969), pp. 219–224.

Calderone, M. S. "Sex Education and the Very Young Child," *PTA Magazine*, 61:2 (1966), pp. 16–18.

Cohen, M. D., ed. *Children and Drugs*. Washington, D.C.: ACEI, 1972.

Dayton, D. H. "Early Malnutrition and Human Development," *Children*, 16:6 (1969), pp. 210–217.

Foster, Florence P. "Nutrition and Educational Experience: Interrelated Variables in Children's Learning," *Young Children*, 27:5 (1972), pp. 284–287.

Hunter, Gertrude T. "Health Care Through Head Start," *Children*, 17:4 (1970), pp. 149–153.

Lin-Fu, Jane S. "Childhood Lead Poisoning . . . An Eradicable Disease," *Children*, 17:1 (1970), pp. 3–9.

Millar, T. P. "The Hospital and the Preschool Child," *Children*, 17:5 (1970), pp. 171–176.

Nolte, Ann E., W. A. Stebbins, V. E. Bowers, and Barbara Fossett. "Health Values for Young Children," *Instructor*, 81:1 (1971), pp. 47–54.

Nutrition and Intellectual Growth in Children. Washington, D.C.: ACEI, 1968.

Scrimshaw, N. S., and J. E. Gordon, eds. *Malnutrition, Learning, and Behavior*. Cambridge, Mass.: The MIT Press, 1968.

Wallace, Helen M. "Some Thoughts on Planning Health Care for Children and Youth," *Children*, 18:3 (1971), pp. 95–100.

Waetjen, W. B., and R. R. Leeper, eds. *Learning and Mental Health in the School*. Washington, D.C.: ASCD, 1966.

Play Activities

Chapter 18

"The Educational Role of Play in Early Childhood" was the theme of the XIIIth World Assembly of OMEP.[1] The selection of this topic indicates something of the current concern and controversy regarding the value of play in programs for young children. As Butler says,

> Almost without exception programs in early childhood education include an element of play, but there are vast differences in what is meant by play and what is believed to be its relative value.[2]

[1]World Organization for Early Childhood Education, XIIIth World Assembly, held in Bonn, Germany, August 5–11, 1971.

[2]Annie L. Butler, *Current Research in Early Childhood Education: A Compilation and Analysis for Program Planners* (American Association of Elementary-Kindergarten-Nursery Educators, 1970), p. 13.

In the direct-instruction type of program, play usually involves use of equipment to teach specific concepts and teacher-directed games to stimulate language and thought. Play is directed by the nature of the equipment. Spontaneous play is usually limited to short periods of outdoor activity that is not considered to make any significant contribution to learning. In what are termed the *more open* centers, "self-initiated play is the major vehicle for learning."[3]

Some of the conflict relates to what is considered good education for the young—the emphasis on cognitive learning as opposed to a more broadly based curriculum.

Almy says that psychoanalytic theory has long regarded spontaneous play as a reflection not only of the child's emotional needs but also of his developing intellectual competence.[4] There are teachers, however, who are so preoccupied with the emotional aspects of play that they neglect its intellectual connotations. Utilizing the cognitive values of spontaneous play does not necessarily mean pushing or pressuring the child but rather nurturing basic abilities as they develop. The teacher needs to diagnose cognitive functioning as revealed in play. With evidence regarding the child's curiosity, his interest in investigation, in problem solving, and in mastery, the teacher can give guidance in play and in other curricular areas.

Herron and Sutton-Smith report that children in Head Start Programs do not always evidence the same kind of capacity in make-believe as do some children in other middle class centers. Neither do they seem to show as much interest in make-believe stories or show the same capacity for thinking about things that are remote in time and place.[5] They raise the question as to whether the middle-class parent, by playing with his children, reading and talking to them, and providing play equipment, is actually encouraging the development of representative capacity and critical thinking.

Often inner city children have inadequate space or materials at home for physical movement and play activities. It is especially important that these children have opportunities for play.[6]

PLAY OF THE YOUNG CHILD

Part of the confusion regarding the value of play, says Frank, "arises from the old distinction between work and play, with the feeling that, while work is good, play is somewhat questionable, if not bad or sinful."[7]

---

[3]Ibid., p. 14.

[4]Millie Almy, "Spontaneous Play: An Avenue for Intellectual Development," *Young Children*, 22:5 (1967), pp. 265–277.

[5]R. E. Herron and B. Sutton-Smith, *Child's Play* (New York: John Wiley and Sons, Inc., 1971), p. 2.

[6]Dorothy J. Skeel, *Children of the Street: Teaching in the Inner City* (Pacific Palisades, California: Goodyear Publishing Company, Inc., 1971), pp. 80–81.

[7]L. K. Frank, "Introduction," in Ruth E. Hartley and R. M. Goldenson, *The Complete Book of Children's Play* (New York: Thomas Y. Crowell, 1957), p. viii.

Figure 39. It has been said that play is a child's work. The young child often plays alone. Austin creates his work as he "paints" with water.

In order to clarify the meaning of play, one should examine the research and theories regarding its nature and function.

In reviewing the research on the behavior development of children, Butler reports very little investigation related to play during the past ten years.[8] Earlier research may be helpful. Olson describes three theories regarding play.

The *recapitulation* theory states that the individual in his play development passes through stages that are typical of those through which the race has passed. When applied on the playground, this theory resulted in somewhat arbitrary division of ages and the experiences appropriate for them. Investigations, however, have shown that children of a given age differ widely in the development of their play interests and that there is much overlapping between age groups. According to another theory, not all the energy produced by the child is needed for growth, and play is the result of an accumulation of surplus energy. The *recreation* theory maintains that through play, tensions may be released and relaxed. The *anticipatory* or *preparatory* theory "considers play as primarily a preparation for future life and work; in make-believe, children are practicing for future roles."[9] Each theory presents an aspect of the truth regarding play. Hurlock reported earlier experimental studies of children's play by Bott, Arlitt, Van Alstyne, Parten and others.[10] A brief summary of the review follows.

[8]Annie L. Butler, "Areas of Recent Research in Early Childhood Education," *Child. Educ.,* 48:3 (1971), p. 146.

[9]W. C. Olson, *Child Development,* 2nd ed. (Boston: D.C. Heath, 1959), p. 94.

[10]Elizabeth B. Hurlock, "Experimental Investigations of Children's Play," R. E. Herron and B. Sutton-Smith, *Child's Play* (New York: John Wiley and Sons, Inc., 1971), pp. 51–70.

The child at three usually enjoys an activity as an end in itself, but by five shows interest in the end result. Imaginative play reaches its peak between five and eight years of age. The dramatic play of fours centered around living conditions, animals, and family relations.

Play that involves skilled muscular movement is very popular during childhood. The young child likes to test his powers of muscular control by such activities as hopping on one foot or walking along the edge of a curb.

An important element in children's play is construction and building. The young child begins to save and collect things.

The average attention span for the eight most popular play materials was 7.0 minutes for two years, 8.9 for three, 12.3 for four, and 13.6 for five years.

No definite preference was shown for playmates of the same or the opposite sex. Apparent sex differences in play are due to training.

Among three- and four-year-old children raw material such as sand and blocks were ranked as first choice. Dolls representing children were favored by the five-year-old children.

Frank expresses the point of view held today by many of those who work with young children: "Play is the way the child learns what none can teach him. It is the way he explores and orients himself to the actual world of space and time, of things, animals, structures and people. . . . Play is the child's work."[11] Play can be satisfying and pleasurable and these are good values for young children.

From his observation of children, Piaget states that games (synonymous with play) "reproduce what has struck the child or evoke what has pleased him or enabled him to be more fully part of his environment."[12]

Scarfe considers play to be an educational process:[13]

A child's play is his way of exploring and experimenting while he builds up relations with the world and with himself. In play he is learning to learn. He is also discovering how to come to terms with the world, to cope with life's tasks, to master skills. In particular he is learning how to gain confidence. In play a child is continually discovering himself anew.

Jersild identifies characteristics and purposes of a child's play. Apart from being a self-chosen activity, any new play experience often involves an element of risk.[14] This is true when a child seeks to climb, build, ride a bicycle, use a hammer or saw, or even paint on an easel. One five-year-old expressed it this way: "I don't know how, but I guess I can try."

[11]Frank, op. cit., pp. vii, viii.

[12]J. Piaget, *Play, Dreams and Imitation in Childhood*, trans. Gattengo and Hodgson (New York: W. W. Norton, 1962), p. 155.

[13]N. V. Scarfe, "Play Is Education," in *Readings from Childhood Education* (Washington, D.C.: ACEI, 1966), p. 357.

[14]A. T. Jersild, *Child Psychology*, 5th ed. (Englewood Cliffs, N.J.: Prentice-Hall, 1960), pp. 424–425.

Repetition is also an important aspect of children's play. Through repetition the child can consolidate his skills and, as he becomes more expert he begins to experiment on his own. The child learns to ride a tricycle and is content to ride it up and down the sidewalk or porch, repeating the skill he has learned. Soon, however, he experiments as he backs up, turns around, rides fast and slow. In a short time the tricycle becomes a part of dramatic play. A traffic sign and a policeman are added.

Play may serve as a means of helping the child solve a problem. A child may select a toy that represents an object he fears or one toward which he has resentment. Play serves as a means of self-assertion through which a child can declare his needs. If he wants affection he can be the "baby" in the dramatic play. In this role he can receive attention and affection as he is fed, rocked, or put to bed.

Closely related to this is the role of play in self-revealment. Observing a child at play one may note his joys, fears, or hopes revealed. Although this is the basis for play therapy, even the teacher who is not a trained therapist can learn much from watching the child as he plays.

Through play a child learns many things. He is helped to develop social relationships and skills. He learns to use play materials and equipment with others; to take turns; to lead and to follow; to ask for what he wants or needs; to understand the role of mother, baby, father, or the doctor. As children climb, walk, skip, and jump, they are exercising muscles and gaining in physical fitness. Contact with other children and the need to communicate with them help to stimulate language growth. The following incidents illustrate some of the values of play:

Dan opened the door of the storage room and rolled the wagon in. Quickly he loaded it with blocks, just as many as he could pile on the wagon. As he pulled the wagon through the door, blocks fell in every direction. Without annoyance or concern he pushed the wagon in again and repeated the process. But this time, with an empty wagon, he stopped and looked. He rolled the empty wagon in and out the door. No difficulty. Then he rolled the wagon back in again and loaded it carefully. Not one block extended beyond the edge of the wagon. He pulled the wagon safely out into the yard without losing a single block. Dan had encountered a problem and worked out a solution, all in play.

An elaborate train had been built from blocks and Jane, Pete, Joe, and Charles were ready to "play train." Roles were assigned and the conductor and passengers took their places. The engineer, however, went to the back of the train. As the teacher watched, the train was ready to pull out of the station. She said to Joe, "You are the engineer. What is your job?" Joe replied, "Oh, I'm just the engineer." Pete added, "He drives the train." Teacher, "If the engineer drives the train, where does he need to be?" The light dawned. Joe crawled onto the engine.

Observation of these children at play helped the teacher to know that Joe and perhaps Jane and Charles did not know the role of the engineer. This evaluation of their knowledge of trains indicated to the teacher the need for pictures, stories, and perhaps a field trip in order to clarify their understanding. Interest and curiosity are aroused and questions raised which result in increased vocabulary and clarification of concepts. Play can serve as a means of helping the teacher to evaluate the learning, attitudes, and understandings of the child.

THE DEVELOPMENTAL SEQUENCES OF PLAY ACTIVITIES

How then can play be planned in order to achieve these values for children? Jersild says, "Generally speaking, the younger the child is, the more will the things he chooses to do give an indication of what he can do or can learn to like to do in the selection of equipment, materials, and supplies."[15] The teacher then needs to know the developmental sequences of play activities and how to use the information in the selection of activities and equipment. Strang says that "the play life of a child is an index of his social maturity and reveals his personality more clearly than any activity."[16] This is illustrated in the following incident:

> On a warm, sunny fall day, the four-year-olds were busy in the nursery school yard. Three had climbed up into the tree house. Others were at the jungle gym and the tire swing. Some were running around on the grass and some were building with blocks. A student observer remarked, "I'm going to teach four-year-olds," When asked the reason for her choice, she replied, "Oh, they are so easy to work with. Just look. Everybody is busy and happy." The instructor sitting beside her asked, "What do you think would happen if the teacher suddenly called the children together to play a game of baseball?" In amazement the student replied, "Why, she wouldn't do that!" "But if she did? Would they be playing as happily or contentedly?" For a moment she was puzzled, but then she smiled slowly as she asked the instructor, "Are you saying to me that the four-year-olds are playing this way because the teacher has structured the situation and planned it according to what the children can do?" The student answered her own question. "That's it," she said, "Fours aren't just naturally good. They are playing this way because of the way the teacher plans for and guides their play."

And so it is! The teacher needs to know the developmental sequence of play and to recognize the variations in maturity and interests that will be found among individual children.

Parten classified children's play behavior into six categories: unoccupied, solitary, onlooker, parallel, associative, and cooperative. The sequence includes ages three through five years.[17] Although ages are identified in relation to the

---

[15]Ibid., p. 424.

[16]Ruth Strang, *An Introduction to Child Study* (New York: Macmillan Publishing Co., 1951), p. 495.

[17]Mildred Parten, "Social Participation Among Pre-School Children," *J. Abnorm. and Soc. Psychol.*, 27:3 (1932), pp. 243–269.

developmental sequence of play, the teacher who understands children knows that each child progresses at his own rate. Some fives are not ready for cooperative play, while some fours cooperate easily and well.

As the child begins to play, he first plays alone and engages in solitary play. As an "onlooker" he watches as the others play. In parallel play he plays alongside another child and usually enjoys being with him but is primarily interested in his own activity. Associative play is characterized by an increased interest in playing with other children. Two or three may play together in a group but both the group and activity change constantly. Dramatization and imagination are beginning to enter into play. The child is willing to wait his turn and, with supervision, will put his toys away. His block play is concerned largely with manipulation, rather than building any one thing.

As the child continues to grow and play he may choose a friend of the same sex for a specific play activity. A marked increase is noted in the constructive use of materials. He uses blocks to build something. In the dramatization of play, he likes to dress up and finds props such as a cowboy hat, nurse's cap, or doctor's bag important. He may suggest turns but is often bossy in directing others. He is not yet ready to make the social adjustment necessary for participation in group games.

The five-year-old usually can engage in cooperative play, the size of the group ranging from two to five children. Piaget believes that really cooperative play does not develop until after the age of seven or eight.[18] There is a definite interest in finishing an undertaking, even though it may need to be carried over from one day to the next. The request, "May I leave my block house and fort up? I haven't finished. Do I have to put the blocks away now?" is familiar to the kindergarten teacher. Dramatic play can be creative, both in actions and costumes which may be created from materials at hand. By this age there is usually fairly good control of body movement. The five-year-olds like climbing and other activities involving the large muscles. As a rule they are not ready for organized group games.

The first dramatic play of the young child usually centers around the situation most familiar and important to him, but the situation may vary according to the background of the child. For many children the situation will be the home. From this, he branches to individuals important to his immediate world—the doctor, the grocer, and the policeman. Other roles are added as experiences with books, stories, and television reveal cowboys, spaceships, boats, and airplanes. The characteristics of play that have been described can be used by the teacher as guides in the selection of equipment, materials, and activities.

Hartley, Frank and Goldenson report, from records of children three to five and a half years old, eight functions that dramatic play serves in usual group

---

[18]Susanna Millar, *The Psychology of Play* (Baltimore, Md.: Penguin Books, 1968), p. 178.

situations of preschool centers. Through dramatic play the child has the opportunity

"(1) to imitate adults; (2) to play out real life roles in an intense way; (3) to reflect relationships and experiences; (4) to express passing needs; (5) to release unacceptable impulses; (6) to reverse roles usually taken; (7) to mirror growth; and (8) to work out problems and experiment with solutions."[19]

Matterson describes three categories of children's play.[20] *Creative play* is encouraged by providing raw materials of all kinds such as sand, paint, and scraps. In *imaginative play* a child can create situations for himself and work out reactions and solutions. Dress-up clothes encourage this type of play. *Adventure play* involves overcoming obstacles, gaining new skills through exercising and using the coordination that exists.

SELECTION OF EQUIPMENT AND SUPPLIES

The activity planned for the child indicates the basis for the selection of appropriate equipment and materials. In a good school or center, a variety of materials are provided. These are the media through which children develop physical strength and motor coordination, dramatic play, creative activities, and social skills. Materials should be available for both indoor and outdoor activities; apparatus for climbing, balancing, and building; materials with which to create, manipulate, and dramatize. Not only should materials be available in variety and abundance but they should be used creatively. Equipment and supplies need not be expensive. An ingenious teacher with imagination can improvise and collect materials that children greatly enjoy. Toys, especially wagons and tricycles in good repair and outgrown by older children, may be donated to the school. Parents handy with tools can contribute equipment.

However, there are equipment and supplies that must be purchased. Other materials, such as art supplies, should be included in the yearly budget. Items to be bought as a part of a long-time purchasing plan include wheel toys, blocks, puzzles, equipment for dramatic play, musical instruments, and stationary outdoor equipment such as the jungle gym. The stationary equipment is expensive and should be selected carefully in terms of the total amount of money available.

Criteria for selection and purchase are needed. Questions that may be asked

---

[19]Ruth Hartley, L. K. Frank, and R. M. Goldenson, *Understanding Children's Play*, (New York: Columbia University Press, 1952), pp. 27–28.

[20]E. M. Matterson, *Play and Playthings for the Preschool Child* (Baltimore, Md.: Penguin Books, 1967), pp. 5–8.

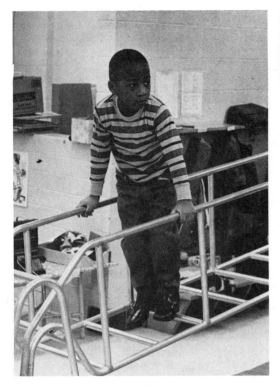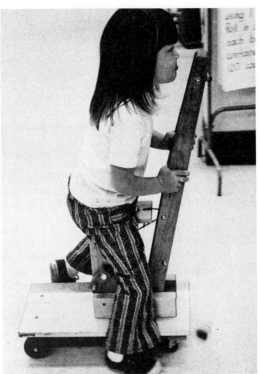

Figure 40. Adventure play involves overcoming obstacles, and gaining new skills through exercising and using the coordination that exists.

in evaluating materials have been adapted from the ACEI criteria used for testing equipment and supplies:[21]

> For what age levels is the item most suitable?
> Is the material of which it is made suitable?
> Is the size correct?
> Is the form suitable for its use?
> Is the color pleasing?
> Is the surface easily cleaned?
> Is the surface durable?
> Is the article strong enough?
> Are edges rounded, not sharp?
> Is paint nonpoisonous?
> Is the article noninflammable?
> Will the article withstand weather conditions? Hard usage?

[21]*Equipment and Supplies* (Washington, D.C.: ACEI, 1968), p. 4.

Can the article be used for more than one purpose? By more than one child?

Does the article stimulate in children curiosity, interest, manipulation, initiative, resourcefulness, problem-solving, imagination, creativity?

Does it develop muscular coordination, freedom of movement, manual skills?

Does it develop techniques in reading, writing, numbers?

Does it promote growth toward independence, exploration, group activity, social relationships, international relationships?

In planning for and guiding activities and in selecting equipment and materials, there is need to utilize the understandings regarding the nature and the developmental sequence of play. In the discussion of both indoor and outdoor play activities, space, and equipment, the recommendations are based on an understanding of the child and his play.

Outdoor Play

Outdoor play can help to lessen the pressures on children which often result from living under crowded conditions. "Healthy children," says Baker, "are likely to be those who spend a great deal of time outdoors where they can play actively and imaginatively.[22] "Baker continues,[23]

> For a child, time spent watching clouds in the sky or the patterns of light and shadow through trees or discovering some of the many objects to be found outdoors are experiences of wonder. They feed the eager curiosity of childhood, which is the basis for learning.

The outdoor environment offers many opportunities for physical activity, for exploring, discovering and learning. To made adequate provision for outdoor play, consideration of several factors is necessary.

Space

Children need playgrounds that are accessible, large enough, interesting, and safe. In 1954, the Association for Childhood Education International stated that research in this area was lacking but recommended a minimum of 75 to 100 square feet of play area per child. If several groups of children use the area and the space is limited, a schedule for using the yard should be provided so that all children are not outdoors at one time.[24]

Bengtsson points out, however, the importance of the playground itself and suggests that consideration be given to the proportions of the area.[25] There may

---

[22]Katherine Read Baker, "Extending the Indoors Outside," *Housing for Early Childhood Education* (Washington, D.C.: ACEI, 1968), p. 59.

[23]Ibid.

[24]*Plan of Action for Children 1953–55* (Washington, D.C.: ACEI, 1953).

[25]A. Bengtsson, *Environmental Planning for Children's Play* (New York: Praeger Publishers, 1970), 154.

Figure 41. The outdoor environment offers many opportunities for physical activity. Outdoor play can help to lessen pressures on children.

be need for some type of enclosing wall, screen, or shrubs to create some secluded areas and give a feeling of security and intimacy. A clear view for supervision is important but at times children like to carry on play free from interruption. The smaller units within the area can provide shelter from the wind and the sun.

Features such as slopes and mounds or even an undulating asphalt surface provide variety and help to make the area more interesting. For the safety of children a fence with adequate fastenings on the gate is essential.

Baker suggests that the area be located on the south side of the building where there will be sun and light throughout the day.[26]

The play area should include:

1. a balance of space in the sun and shade.
2. a hard surface area where wheel toys can be used, balls bounced, and block structures built.
3. a balance of open and secluded areas.
4. a grassy plot for playing, running, and romping.
5. a spot for pets, gardens, and digging.

[26]Baker, op. cit., p. 60.

6. an area for sand play and manipulative activities.
7. a space for water play.

This outdoor space should be used as an integral part of the school.

Equipment and Supplies

In selecting appropriate equipment and supplies the maturity level of the child furnishes one fundamental criterion. As a child matures he may continue to use familiar materials but in a different manner.

In order, however, to challenge his improved skills, new, fresh materials and more complex equipment are also needed.[27]

Stone observed children at play in a variety of parks and playgrounds in the United States and reported that the many ways in which children actually use play equipment are sometimes quite different from what the designers had in mind.[28]

The young child likes to work and rework materials. The observations seem to suggest that the provision of simple, manipulable, and imaginative materials is important.

Stationary equipment should be placed and installed around the outer edge of the yard so that supervision is easy and each separate piece is far enough apart to prevent accidents. The equipment must be carefully and safely installed and maintained in good repair. Sand, sawdust, or tanbark should be placed under all climbing and swinging apparatus in order to break falls.

Because of the expense and space involved, few play yards can include all items listed here or available on the market today. Those chosen should be carefully selected in terms of the criteria listed on page 337 and the total budget. Apparatus that encourages large muscle development and is usually included on the play area is listed below:

1. The Jungle Gym. The jungle gym is an arrangement of strong metal pipes or wooden rungs. For outdoor use a metal gym is recommended; a wooden structure may be used indoors. The distance between rungs of the gym should be such that it can be managed by the children using the gym. Also useful are modifications of the gym—the climbing frame and a rope with knots tied about 18 in. apart suspended from a well-braced frame.

2. The Sand Area. The sandbox should be large enough for children to get into. A minimum of 50 to 60 square feet of space is desirable. A ledge or shelf around the edge helps to keep the sand contained and may be used as a seat or walking board. The sandbox must be covered when not in use in order to keep dirt, refuse, and animals out of the sand. In constructing a sandbox it is recommended that the floor be covered with brick or about 4 in. of gravel to facilitate drainage and then filled with from 18 to 24 in. of sand. The outdoor sandbox should be located so as to be in the sun for a part of the day. Utensils for sand play, such as shovels,

[27]ACEI, *Equipment and Supplies*, op. cit.

[28]Jeanette Galambos Stone, *Play and Playgrounds* (Washington, D.C.: NAEYC, 1970), pp. 15–63.

pails, and small dishes are needed. Inspect these utensils frequently and discard broken or rusty toys.

3. Swings. Some teachers prefer not to include swings because of the safety hazards involved. As the younger child jumps from the swing, he may fall and be struck by the seat of the swing. Even a five-year-old is likely to forget and run in front of the swing. A safer type of swing for the younger child has a canvas strip for the seat. For the four- or five-year-old a swing may be made by attaching an old tire (with holes punched to prevent accumulation of water), to the end of a strong rope, suspended from well-braced frames. On the playground, swings should be placed so as not to be in line of traffic as the children run from one piece of equipment to another. It is important to arrange for a protective barrier to prevent a child from accidentally running in front of the moving swings. Bengtsson recommends a deep layer of soft sand under the swings.[29] The sand, he says, should extend well to the front and rear of the swings.

4. Slide. A standard slide that is metal and rust-proof with a safe climbing ladder is recommended. The height of the ladder and slide should be in relation to the age of the children. The slide should be placed so that it can be easily supervised, yet not in line of traffic to and from other equipment. A slide may be constructed as a part of a play platform.

   Bengtsson suggests a slide of generous width that does not require as much courage to climb and can be used in a variety of ways.[30] He says that it is wise to arrange a slide so that a ladder is not needed, maybe bedded in a natural slope of the ground.

5. Platforms. A play platform with a railing and fence around the top offers possibilities for dramatic play. Suggested measurements are: height, 5 to 7 ft.; platform, 4 by 6 ft. The steps may be from 20 to 36 in. wide, and the risers should be of appropriate height for the children using them—approximately 3 to 6 inches. Ladders are often used in place of steps.

6. Merry-Go-Round. Although this piece of equipment is popular with the children, it is one that requires very close and careful supervision to assure safety for those using it. The apparatus offers opportunity for pushing and running at the kindergarten level. Most younger children do not have the muscular control and coordination required.

7. Miscellaneous. For example, a large sewer pipe, set lengthwise and firmly in cement affords opportunities for climbing over and through it. A tree trunk can be used for the same purpose. Old tires may be used to make units to crawl and climb in, to roll, to lift, or to carry. Stone suggests that old equipment such as cars or boats, can stimulate eager minds and bodies.[31]

MOVABLE EQUIPMENT FOR THE PLAYGROUND INCLUDES THE FOLLOWING:

1. Walking Boards. Cleats should be bolted to the bottom of the plank about 6 in. from the end to keep the plank from slipping when placed on boxes or sawhorses.

[29]Bengtsson, op. cit., pp. 203–205.

[30]Ibid., p. 200.

[31]Stone, op. cit., p. 63.

It is suggested that planks be of varying lengths, ranging from 4 ft. to 6 ft. long, 1 in. thick, and from 8 in. to 10 in. wide. From 8 to 12 planks are needed for each group.

2. Sawhorses. A suggested size is from 1 ft. 6 in. to 3 ft. high and of varying widths, from 18 to 36 in. These may be used with ladders for climbing and with cleated boards for walking. From 4 to 6 sawhorses are recommended for each group.

3. Ladders. These may be metal, rope, or wood but should be light and sturdy enough to be moved or dragged around easily by children. Cleats or hooks should be attached to each end. Recommended sizes include 3-, 4-, or 5-ft. lengths by 14-in. width.

4. Balls. Lightweight balls in both medium and large sizes are recommended. Include rubber balls 8 to 24 in. in diameter. Beanbags may also be used for throwing and catching.

5. Jump Ropes. Include both long ones to be turned by an adult and short ones for individual children. For younger children not able to jump the rope, lengths of rope of various sizes have many play uses.

6. Wheel Toys. The wagon and tricycle (12 in. and 16 in. ball-bearing wheels) and a wheel-barrow may be used both indoors and outdoors.

7. Tools for Gardening. Include items such as shovels, rakes, watering cans, trowels, and hoes. These items should be durable and child-size.

8. Miscellaneous. Such items include kegs, packing boxes, drag boxes, boats, car or jeep bodies, a large airplane or truck tire or tube. All such equipment should be safe for use—free of nails, splinters, glass, rough and broken edges, and rusted edges. Inspect often and discard equipment no longer safe for children to use. Adequate provision needs to be made for storage of outdoor equipment when not in use. The storage area should be adjacent to the play area.

9. Building blocks and tools for woodworking may be used out-of-doors also. See pages 345 and 347 for recommendations.

Games

Nursery school children are usually not ready for organized games and only very simple games are appropriate for the kindergarten. Games suggested for use in the kindergarten include those that require little group cooperation, have few rules or directions, and do not include the competitive element or refined coordinated movements not yet developed by the child. Choose games in which many children can participate at the same time rather than those in which most children are inactive while only a few are active. Tag, Loobey Loo, Here We Go Round the Mulberry Bush, and Musical Chairs are examples of games that involve all children and are loosely organized. Imitative games such as Follow the Leader and Simon Says are also appropriate.

As the teacher begins using games, the directions should be given one at a time, followed by the activity. For example, the first direction may be, "Take hands and make a circle." The teacher then moves among the group helping each child as needed. This is done before the next direction is given. In games which involve choices, some children may not be chosen. In order that all children may have a chance to play the game, ask those who have not had a turn to raise their hands. Ask the child who is making the choice to select a child whose hand is raised.

Activities

Water play is enjoyed by children in whatever form it may be available. Hartley, Frank, and Goldenson say that water play offers more varied experience and keener pleasure to the development of sensation and feeling than any other material except finger-paint.[32] Water play offers opportunities for flexibility, experimentation, and exploration. Materials such as a spray, small buckets and pans, a water hose, are inexpensive and contribute much to the activity.

Many indoor activities can be moved outdoors or to an open porch or patio, such as the following.

Using books and telling stories are discussed on pages 214–220. A table with books may be set up in a quiet, shaded spot. Small rugs or mats may be used for the children to sit on during a group story period.

Imitative activities include the imitation of actions or movements of another child or person, an animal, or a machine. The child gives his interpretation of the way another person or thing moves or acts. The teacher may name the activity by saying, "Show me how you would fly if you were a bird," and the child creates his own response. The child, however, may imitate a person, animal, or thing and ask others to name or identify it.

Story plays usually involve a series of bodily movements based on a story or a plot.[33] They are generally a sequence of events created by the teacher with the help of the children. All of the participants do all of the actions together as the story is told. Story plays are related to the experiences of the children, have a simple plot, and include activities that promote the use of large muscles. Story plays may be developed on topics such as playing on the beach or playing in the leaves.

Musical and rhythmical activities are presented on pages 374–385, art activities on pages 369–374, and dramatic play on pages 224–225. Suggestions made in those sections are applicable for the outdoor play area.

Picnics and snacks may be enjoyed on the playground also.

Supervision

Children should be supervised on the playground at all times. The teacher must be alert to the entire situation. Even when talking or occupied with one child she does not turn her back on or forget the group. Remove objects that

[32]Hartley, Frank, and Goldenson, op. cit., p. 185.

[33]Clarice D. Wills and Lucile Lindberg, *Kindergarten for Today's Children* (Chicago: Follett Pub. Co., 1967), pp. 243–245.

might cause a child to trip and fall. Definite limits relating to the use of apparatus must be set and consistently maintained. For example:

1. We run on the grass, not in front of the swings.
2. We need both our hands for climbing on the jungle gym. We leave blocks, boards, and dolls on the ground.
3. We slide down the slide. We climb up the ladder.

Evaluation

Questions that may be used in evaluating outdoor activities include the following:

1. Are the equipment and space adequate for the development of motor skills and muscular coordination?
2. Is the equipment placed so as to facilitate supervision and minimize the possibility of accidents?
3. Is there a variety of play equipment available—both stationary and movable? Is it varied in size and complexity to challenge children and lead to the development of new skills?
4. Does the teacher's supervision and guidance of the activities result in the continued physical, social, emotional, and intellectual growth of the child?

Indoor Play

Adequate provision for indoor play requires consideration of such factors as the following:

Space

Indoor space required for good school living varies in each situation. For example, in warmer climates more time can be spent out-of-doors and it is possible to place all climbing apparatus outside and to use porches and patios. Less indoor space may be necessary. Arrangement of furniture and equipment also affects the space available. It is important, however, that the space be adequate to provide for a variety of equipment and activities and to enable children to move about freely without feeling cramped or crowded.

According to Jefferson, authorities differ as to recommendations for indoor floor space, "but the range from 35 to 60 square feet per child will provide a fair-sized room for a group of from 15 to 25 children."[34]

Equipment, Supplies, and Activities

CLIMBING APPARATUS. In sections where weather conditions necessitate children remaining indoors for a considerable part of the time, indoor apparatus should be provided. Hardwood, movable apparatus, such as a jungle gym or slide, may be used. Walking boards can be used indoors as well.

[34]Ruth E. Jefferson, "Indoor Facilities," *Housing for Early Childhood Education* (Washington: ACEI, 1968), p. 41.

BLOCKS. Blocks are one of the basic play materials for children of nursery school-kindergarten age that "are now recognized as the number-one raw material for play."[35] As children begin to use blocks, they are largely concerned with manipulating them—stacking, pushing, carrying, and lifting. After a time, this manipulation begins to be meaningful. A long row of blocks, carefully arranged on the floor, becomes a road; and a toy car, or even another block, is driven over the road. Gradually the child begins to plan his structures and to test his own ideas. "Look, I'm going to build a tall bridge."

Play with blocks can provide opportunities for the following:

1. Physical release and the development of muscular coordination through lifting, carrying, and piling.
2. Emotional release through dramatic play. The child may express feelings of aggression, hostility, satisfaction of achievement, or fear.
3. Creative expression and the development of a sense of design and form.
4. Cognitive growth through the development of concepts and language opportunities.
5. Development of concepts of size, shape, and number values.
6. Development of readiness for reading through conversation, observation of size and shapes, and the need for additional information from books for his dramatic play.

In the guidance of block play, the teacher has an opportunity to observe what the child has absorbed of life going on around him as to ideas, information, relationships, and possible confusions. Rather than criticize or correct his errors, the teacher has the responsibility of creating a situation in which the child can learn and enrich his experiences. The child, however, does need to be held to the highest standards that he is able to attain. The teacher may use questions to help the child evaluate his structure. For example, "How do people get into your house?" Franklin suggests that if a child is careless in leaving unused blocks around, the teacher may offer to help him put away the blocks he does not need.[36] Indoors, blocks should be stored on open shelves near the floor area where they are used. Provide ample floor space and adequate time for block play.

In selecting blocks, it is recommended that they be hollow and large enough to make structures that children can actually use. Suggested numbers and sizes include:[37]

36 hollow blocks, 12 in. by 12 in. by 6 in., with hand holes or rope handles.
12 hollow blocks, 24 in. by 12 in. by 6 in.
12 hollow blocks, half units, triangles.

In addition to the hollow blocks the following are suggested:

[35]Rowenna M. Shoemaker, *All in Play* (New York: Play Schools Association, 1958), p. 17.

[36]Adele Franklin, "Blocks—A Tool of Learning," *Child. Educ.*, 26:5 (1950), pp. 209–213.

[37]*Equipment and Supplies*, op. cit., pp. 8, 10.

1 set building blocks, straight cuts, 500 or more, various sizes.

8 boards, 6 in. by 3 ft. long.

1 set of blocks which fasten together to make permanent structures large enough to accommodate children.

1 or 2 sets "stay-put" blocks fastening together with snaps, bolts, or pegs.

A waterproof finish will make the blocks suitable for outdoor use as well. Small trains, cars, farm animals, and people may be included in the block building area.

A good set of blocks represents a considerable financial investment but will last for many years. Cardboard blocks, which are much less expensive, are available and may be assembled for use. These are lighter in weight and do not provide the same experience in lifting as the heavier wooden blocks. There is one advantage, however; less noise is involved when they fall. A collection of wooden boxes can be assembled and used out-of-doors for building and construction.

Accessories for block building can contribute to the dramatic play in which the child may engage. These may include miniature family figures, community helpers, zoo and farm animals, transportation toys, and other materials such as baskets, boxes, or crates.[38]

PUZZLES.   The wooden jig-saw puzzle, framed or interlocked, is preferred. For the youngest nursery school child, the puzzle may consist of two or three pieces, such as of an animal, to be fitted into a frame. The number of pieces increases with age and the fours can handle from five to eight pieces in the frame. Framed puzzles are still preferred for the fives but some children of this age can handle puzzles of the interlocking type.

A frame into which the puzzle can be slipped for storage is recommended. Put the same color on the backs of all pieces of one puzzle. This helps in identifying the parts of one puzzle and minimizes confusion when several children are using puzzles at the same table. Values of puzzles include opportunities for eye-hand coordination, use of small muscles, recognition of shape and color, and use of visual memory.

EQUIPMENT FOR DRAMATIC PLAY.   The teacher's role in guiding dramatic play has been presented on pages 224–225. At this point, the emphasis is placed on materials and equipment conducive to dramatic play. Among the most important materials are blocks, mentioned above. Equipment conducive to dramatic play is not listed. Rather, suggestions are made to indicate the types of materials that may be used creatively. Equipment related to family living and housekeeping usually includes dolls and accessories. The dolls should be unbreakable and washable, both boys and girls, and representative of different races and occupations. Clothing for the dolls as well as a bed (large and sturdy), a bathinette, and a carriage are all appropriate. Clothes for dressing up (includ-

---

[38]*A Guide for Early Childhood Education in Florida Schools* (Bull. 76) (Tallahassee: Florida State Department of Education, 1969), pp. 61–62.

ing hats, gloves, pocket books, ties, and gloves) help children to assume various roles.

Materials for housekeeping include a variety of furniture, the amount depending on the space available. Children often find uses for a table, chairs (including a rocker), dishes, a sink, a stove and cooking utensils, and a broom and other cleaning supplies. The toy telephone encourages conversation and language development.

Games and toys may be used separately or in relation to block play or other types of dramatic play. A cash register may be used at "the store." A set of family dolls and toy animals is frequently used. Accessories such as a fireman's hat, a conductor's or a painter's cap, or an astronaut's helmet contribute to the play of children. Wooden animals, people, airplanes, trucks, trains and boats can be stimulating too. Color cones, peg boards, dominoes (picture or large size with regular dots), pounding peg boards, picture lotto games, and wooden beads for stringing are only a few of the games and activities that can be provided.

The teacher's imagination and ingenuity offer many leads for creative materials. Although some equipment may be purchased, much can be improvised. Parent involvement can be especially helpful in this area.

WORKBENCH AND TOOLS.   "Most children have a natural interest in working with wood and tools. It is one area of play content that most children do not have to be urged to try."[39] Early attempts at woodworking are largely manipulative. Have you observed a child drive one nail after another into a soft piece of wood or saw a board, just to be sawing? As in other activities, the manipulation begins to have meaning and the child realizes that the board he has sawed looks like a boat. Then he usually begins to have ideas that he wants to test. The results may be crude and show little similarity to the finished product they represent, but the value of the activity does not lie in the finished product. Woodworking provides opportunities for eye-hand coordination; use of large muscles; emotional and physical release; social growth through sharing, taking turns, working together, caring for tools; and experimentation.

Suggestions for the use of tools include the following:

1. Have an adult supervise the workbench at all times when it is in use by the children.
2. Arrange plenty of space for the child who is working.
3. Limit number of hammers and saws in use at one time.
4. Store tools in a safe place. A tool board (a peg board) may be mounted on the wall or on the inside of a door and serve as a convenient and safe way to care for tools. The shapes of tools may be outlined on the board in order to make storage easier. Hooks for tools should be strong.

In selecting tools for use by young children, it is important to remember

---

[39]Shoemaker, op. cit., p. 29.

that they should be of excellent quality. Questions that may be used as criteria for the selection of tools are listed below:[40]

1. Are the tools suitable for the age and interests of the child using them? Consider the child's stage of motor control and muscular strength. Do they serve the number of children involved?
2. Are the tools of good quality, adequate for long and hard use? Can they be re-sharpened, reconditioned, and broken parts replaced?
3. Will they build a child's respect for tools as a functional means to an end, stimulate interest, and encourage a wide variety of experiences?
4. Do they afford the means for developing in children appreciation for fine furniture and construction, in wood, in many forms?

Tools and supplies suggested for woodworking include the following:

Hammers (claw), 6 oz. to 10 oz. in weight for nursery school; 13 oz. to 16 oz. for kindergarten.
Saws (crosscut) 12 in. and 16 in.
Screwdrivers.
Clamps.
Workbench—the bench should be the correct height for the children. If a carpenter's workbench is not available, use sturdy wooden worktables or low broad-topped sawhorses with vises.
Pliers, screwdriver, ruler, yardstick.
Hand drill and bits.
Soft wood.
Dowel rods, different sizes.
Nails—large heads, assorted sizes.

GAMES. The comments and suggestions for outdoor games, pages 342–343, are also applicable for indoor use.

COOKING. See pages 152–153.

Evaluation

Questions that may be used in evaluating indoor play activities include the following:

1. Are materials and equipment conducive to dramatic play? Are they arranged in such a way as to be available to the children? Is there enough space for several groups or centers of interest to be active at the same time?
2. Is there time for individual and small group play, or is the time so tightly scheduled that there is little opportunity for participation in play activities.
3. Is there a variety of play equipment available—wheel toys, blocks, games, dolls, housekeeping equipment? Is it varied enough in complexity to challenge children and lead to new skills?
4. Does the teacher's guidance of the activities result in the continued physical, social, emotional, and intellectual growth of the child? For example, the children

---

[40]*Creating with Materials for Work and Play*, Leaflet 5 (Washington, D.C.: ACEI, 1957), p. 3.

used blocks, barrels, and boxes in building a train. Are they encouraged to explore this interest in trains and gain more information? Are accessories added? Are pictures made available?

5. Are the experiences that children are having sufficiently rich and varied to provide a background for creative play? Are pictures and books available to help children recall and relive experiences?

The understanding of the importance of play in a child's life is closely related to the concern for the healthy development of all children. Play activities should be appropriate to the developmental level of the children in the group and a balanced program provided. Equipment should be carefully selected.

Although play is fun for the children, it is also work for them. They need resourceful, creative guidance, adequate space, materials, and equipment.

Suggested Activities

1. Discuss in class the values of play for young children. Observe young children at play and note the values that you think they may be gaining.
2. Visit a center for young children and observe the children at play. Note examples of basic intellectual skills being used, such as investigation, or classification. Share your findings with the class. Note factors in the situation that you think may influence the achievement of cognitive values of play.
3. Visit a nursery school and kindergarten. Observe and describe situations which are examples of parallel play and cooperative play.
4. Visit a local toy store. Select and evaluate five toys in terms of the criteria presented on pages 337–338. Share your findings with the class.
5. Construct a game or piece of equipment that may be used in dramatic play of a young child.
6. Observe and describe examples of creative, imaginative, and adventure play as described by Matterson, p. 336.
7. Visit a playground for young children and do the following:
   a. Evaluate the play area in terms of comments on p. 339.
   b. Note any safety hazards.
   c. Describe any play materials or equipment that seem to be unusual or especially creative.
8. Reread the opportunities for learning through block play, pp. 345–346. Observe children involved in block play. Describe and give examples of learning that the children seem to be achieving.

Related Readings

Almy, Millie. *Spontaneous Play—An Avenue of Intellectual Development.* New York: Bulletin of the Institute of Child Study, 28:2 (1966).

Andrews, Gladys (Fleming). "Movement—A Way of Learning," *Physical Education for Children's Healthful Living.* Washington, D.C.: ACEI, 1968, pp. 37–47.

Aaron, D., and Bonnie P. Winawer. *Child's Play, A Creative Approach to Playspaces for Today's Children.* New York: Harper & Row, 1965.

Bower, E. M. "Play's the Thing," *Today's Education*, 57:6 (1968), pp. 10–13. Also in *Elementary Education Today: Its Impact on Children*. Washington, D.C.: EKNE, 1971, pp. 36–40.

Dennis, L. "Play in Dewey's Theory of Education," *Young Children*, 25:4 (1970), pp. 230–235.

D'heurle, Adma, and J. N. Fiemer. "On Play," *Elem. Sch. J.*, 72:5 (1971), pp. 118–123.

Dimondstein, Geraldine. *Children Dance in the Classroom*. New York: Macmillan Publishing Co., 1972.

Ebbeck, F. N. "Learning from Play in Other Cultures," *Child. Educ.*, 48:2 (1971), pp. 68–74.

Etkes, A. B. "Where the Play's the Thing," *Early Years*, 2:9, (1972), pp. 46–49.

Friedberg, M. P. *Playgrounds for City Children*. Washington, D.C.: ACEI, 1969.

Hartley, Ruth E. "Play, The Essential Ingredient," *Child. Educ.*, 48:2 (1971), pp. 80–84.

Hurlock, Elizabeth B. "Experimental Investigations of Childhood Play," *Mental Hygiene*, 52:3 (1968).

Kritchevsky, Sybil, Elizabeth Prescott, and Lee Walling. *Planning Environments for Young Children: Physical Space*. Washington, D.C.: NAEYC, 1969.

Matterson, Elizabeth. *Games for the Very Young*. New York: Heritage Press, 1971.

Rasmus, Carolyn J. "A Formula for Play: Child + Space + Imagination," *Physical Education for Children's Healthful Living*. Washington, D.C.: ACEI, 1968, pp. 27–36.

Rasmussen, Margaret, ed. *Play—Children's Business*. Washington, D.C.: ACEI, 1963.

Rosecrans, C. J. "Play—The Language of Children," *Mental Hygiene*, 52:3 (1968), pp. 367–373.

Smilansky, S. *The Effects of Socio-dramatic Play of Disadvantaged Children*. New York: John Wiley and Sons, 1968.

Starks, Ester B. *Block Building*. Washington, D.C. EKNE, 1965.

Stern, V. *A Pilot Study of the Cognitive Aspects of Young Children's Play*. New York: Bank Street College of Education Early Childhood Center, 1970 (Mimeographed).

Sutton-Smith, B. "Child's Play—Very Serious Business," *Psychology Today*, 5:7 (1971), pp. 66–69, 87.

Stone, Jeannette G. *Play and Play Grounds*. Washington, D.C.: NAEYC, 1970.

Van Camp, Sarah S. "How Free Is Free Play?" *Young Children*, 27:4 (1972), pp. 205–208.

The Creative Arts:
Art and Music
Chapter 19

Creativity is a complex process that usually involves a range of qualities including awareness, originality, fluency, flexibility, commitment, and complexity.[1] The creative product may be something tangible, such as a poem; or it may be intangible, such as a new way of attacking problems.[2]

Too often creativity is considered to be solely in the province of the fine arts. Recent findings in creativity, however, indicate that many aspects of the school program can be learned more effectively in creative ways.[3] Although creativity is discussed in connection with art and music, this is not intended to imply that the creative process is limited to these two areas of the

[1]Louise M. Berman, ed., *Toward New Programs for Young Children* (College Park, Md.: University of Maryland, 1970), pp. 45–52.

[2]Louise M. Berman, *New Priorities in the Curriculum* (Columbus, Ohio: Charles E. Merrill Publishing Company, 1968), pp. 139–140.

[3]E. P. Torrance, "Adventuring in Creativity," *Child. Educ.*, 40:2 (1963), p. 79.

Figure 42. In any group of children aged three to five years, all three stages of development in art are likely to be represented. One easel painting is largely the result of manipulating the brush and making strokes with little or no use of concepts or percepts. In the others, the child has painted forms with some relationship to reality and beginning concern for organization.

curriculum. Creativity in the language arts was presented on pages 223–229. A look at creativity and the principles underlying its development indicates that whatever the curriculum area there is opportunity for creative teaching and learning.

The young child, if encouraged to do so, approaches all experiences creatively.

On a warm, spring day, brushes and pails of water were available in the yard for water painting. Sam painted the box industriously. Turning, he said, "I'm painting Mr. Nobody." As he moved his brush up and down in the air, he sang

$$\text{I'm} \uparrow \overset{\text{painting}}{} \downarrow \text{Mr.} \uparrow \overset{\text{no}}{} \downarrow \text{body:}$$

The teacher reinforced his rhythm by singing

$$\text{Sam} \uparrow \overset{\text{made}}{a} \downarrow \uparrow \overset{\text{happy}}{} \downarrow \text{song.}$$

Mike and Peter were talking about their birthdays coming up next week.

PETER: I'll be five years old.
MIKE: That's nothing. I'll be five years old too.
PETER: But I'm taller than you and I'm bigger too.
MIKE: I'm just as tall as you are. See.

The boys backed up against each other, each trying to prove his point. The teacher walked over and said, "Boys, if you want to know how tall you are, you can use the yardstick." She demonstrated its use and left Mike and Peter to figure out their problems—a creative experience in measurement.

FOSTERING CREATIVITY

According to Torrance:[4]

From the best research evidence available and the observations of many investigators, creative imagination during early childhood seems to reach a peak between four- and four-and-a-half years, and is followed by a drop at about age five when the child enters school for the first time. This drop has generally been regarded as the inevitable phenomenon in nature. There are now indications, however, that this drop in five-year-olds is a man-made rather than a natural phenomenon.

It seems urgent, then, that school experiences and opportunities of young children be examined. What happens to discourage creativity?

[4]Ibid., p. 83.

Obstacles to Creative Thinking

Hendrickson and Torrance have identified several cultural obstacles to creative thinking. These and some of the authors' examples follow:[5]

PEER PRESSURES FOR CONFORMITY. Children exert a powerful influence on one another, even at an early age. This influence may affect choice of activity, clothing, or actions. One four-year-old wore cowboy boots to nursery school and soon "everybody" was wearing boots—even though they were hot and unsuitable for climbing and rhythmic activities. Parents reported pressure at home from their child to buy the boots and to wear them. Not until the teacher worked with the parents was it possible to relieve this pressure.

PRESSURES AGAINST QUESTIONING AND EXPLORATION. Even though the questioning stage is a phase of the young child's development, attempts are often made to squelch the asking of "What, why, and when." Rather, the emphasis is all too often on listening to and following directions. Have you heard an adult say, "Don't ask me why. Just do as I say"? Listening to and following directions are important skills but so is questioning. Instead of discouraging the child from asking questions, the teacher should help him learn how to ask the right questions. Closely allied with this obstacle is the tendency to equate questioning with misbehavior. The child who asks the question is often considered impudent or impolite.

EMPHASIS ON SEX-ROLE DIFFERENCES. In our culture certain traits and activities have been associated with masculinity or femininity. Comments such as, "The girls may play in the doll house. The boys may use the blocks," or "Girls don't work with tools," tend to limit opportunities for exploration and discovery. Some children have sacrificed their creativity in order to maintain expected sex roles.

A SUCCESS-ORIENTED CULTURE THAT MAKES ERRORS FATAL AND MAKES CHILDREN AFRAID TO TAKE A CHANCE ON TRYING A NEW APPROACH. One five-year-old had encountered this obstacle early. Each day he chose to play with blocks but consistently avoided the easel. After much encouragement to Joel to try the easel, the teacher said to him, "Today you are going to paint on the easel." In dismay Joel replied, "I can't. I don't know how. I might make a mistake." The teacher reassured him, "It's all right if you make a mistake. Go ahead and try." With relief in his voice, Joel said, "Okay. I don't know how, but I guess I can learn." Joel had older brothers who adored him but who teased him when he made a mistake. Joel soon learned to avoid the teasing by doing the things he could do well and without a mistake.

WORK-PLAY DICHOTOMY. In an austere, no-fun, all-business atmosphere,

---

[5]P. R. Hendrickson and E. P. Torrance, "Some Implications for Art Education from the Minnesota Studies of Creative Thinking," *Creativity and Art Education* (Washington, D.C.: National Art Education Association, 1963), pp. 20–25.

there is evidence that creative thinking abilities are usually least used. The philosophy of the old adage, "Work while you work and play while you play," seems to prevail still with many persons rather than a recognition that play can be the child's work.

How can the curriculum and methods be planned in order to overcome these obstacles?

Planning for Creativity

The teacher herself is the first concern. To foster creativity in children, the teacher must be an adequate, fully functioning person. According to Combs, such persons have the following characteristics: "(a) a positive view of self, (b) identification with others, (c) openness to experience and acceptance, and (d) a rich and available perceptual field."[6] Acquiring these characteristics requires that "we all do more efficiently and effectively what some of us now do only sometimes and haphazardly."[7]

Carlson suggests that the teacher's inner resources can be developed through:[8]

1. Eliminating negative, hostile thoughts, fears, and feelings.
2. Building more positive satisfactions through undertaking new experiences.
3. Participating in original thinking processes.
4. Developing a more active *awareness* of environmental learning experiences.
5. Discovering new dimensions of learning.

Next, the methods of the teacher, her ways of working with children, and the school program should be examined. Suggestions for change follow:[9]

1. Discard regimented routines, such as following directions for drawing or using patterns or models to be imitated.
2. Identify points in one's practice that are examples of stereotyped, habit-bound teaching performance. Project an alternative that is less rigid, more flexible.
3. Be attentive to the unusual questions children ask.
4. Respect the unusual ideas of children.
5. Show children that their ideas have value.
6. Give credit for self-initiated learning.
7. Provide chances for learning and discovery without threats of immediate evaluation.
8. Encourage aspects of behavior often attributed to the creative process. An adaptation from *Toward New Programs for Young Children* follows.[10]

[6]A. W. Combs, "A Perceptual View of the Adequate Personality," *Perceiving, Behaving, Becoming* (1962 Yearbook) (Washington, D.C.: ASCD, 1962), p. 51.

[7]Ibid., p. 62.

[8]Ruth K. Carlson, "Emergence of Creative Personality," *Child. Educ.*, 36:9 (1960), p. 404.

[9]E. P. Torrance, "Conditions for Creative Learning," *Child. Educ.*, 39:8 (1963), pp. 369–370; Laura Zirbes, "What Creative Teaching Means," *Child. Educ.*, 33:2 (1956), pp. 53–54; and Carlson, op. cit., p. 403.

[10]Berman, *Toward New Programs for Young Children*, op. cit., pp. 43–50.

Awareness—of the five senses, detail, perceptions, alternatives. Suggestions follow.

Provide a wide range of environmental stimuli such as trips, walks, and opportunities for touching, smelling, hearing, tasting, and seeing. Show a "surprise box" that contains an object. Ask questions such as "Can you tell what is in the box? How can you tell without looking?" Use questions about materials which children are using, such as, "How does it feel? How does it taste?" Sensitize child to feelings of others. Use comments such as "Mary fell down. How do you think she feels?"

Originality—in manipulating constructive materials, in questioning and wondering, in using new and novel responses. Suggestions follow.

Make a collage tray available. Include materials such as leather, styrofoam, feathers, fabrics, cotton, and wood scraps. The teacher may say, "The materials are for you to use. See what you can make."

Fluency—in the production of ideas and possible solutions to a problem. Suggestions follow.

Give the child a box of objects and say, "What can you do with these? Observe number of ideas and time required for expression. Encourage verbalization of problem for clarification. The teacher may say, "Tell me what the trouble is. Why do you think the bridge fell?"

Flexibility—in using information in a variety of ways, developing and using a flexible schedule. Suggestions follow.

Provide opportunities for the child to experiment with many types of materials to see how many ways he can use one material. Help the child expand verbally his experiences by comments such as "Why were you surprised?" "What else did it remind you of?"

Involve child in planning a change of schedule.

9. Release the child's fears, hostilities, aggressions, and substitute a feeling of confidence, security, and satisfaction with his school activities.

The creative being does not emerge suddenly. He develops gradually and grows as he faces problems and situations, recognizes them, and is able to solve or face them successfully. Experiences in art and music as well as other activities in children's centers can contribute to the development of a creative individual.

ART ACTIVITIES

There are evidences of art activities in almost every child development center, nursery school, and kindergarten. In some situations one can see children working individually or in small groups, moving about freely, engaging in a variety of creative activities. In other rooms, however, one can find all the children seated, quietly engaged in the same activity, coloring pictures, all very much alike. These two extremes indicate that even though there are art activities in almost every center, children are having quite different experiences and are acquiring quite different values and attitudes.

Art activities are considered an important part of any program for young children. Most children enjoy art activities, but there are also other reasons for including them.

Values of Art Activities

Art for the young child is a means of self-expression. He uses art to express what he does, sees, feels, thinks, and talks about. Art activities provide him with opportunities to explore and experiment, to express ideas and feelings about himself and the world around him. They strengthen his ability to imagine and to observe, and increase his sensitiveness to himself and to others. As he works with materials he assumes responsibility for choosing and shaping them, uses judgment and control, and gains success experiences that aid in establishing a self-concept of worth as an individual.

Art experiences have therapeutic values. Through art materials the child can express feelings that are otherwise unacceptable and can learn to handle such feelings in an acceptable manner. Since the young child's speech is limited, he can often express his strong feelings through art experiences which involve psychomotor activity. Materials such as clay for pounding, paper for tearing, and nails for hammering offer opportunities for handling negative feelings through positive action.

John, who pounds the clay with such vehemence, has learned that this is an acceptable way to work off the anger he feels toward the child who has the train he wanted to run. As he pounds and squeezes, he drains off his angry feelings to make them more manageable.

Helping a child to turn his feelings into creative channels gives him an outlet he can use throughout his life. To offer him patterns or models could block this means of expression and prevent future growth; asking him what he has drawn or telling him how to do it might be just as detrimental. By leaving him free to use materials in his own way, the teacher can sometimes gain insight into a child's private world by observing how he uses such materials, the results he obtains, and the way he feels about these results.

Children grow socially through art experiences. As they participate in self-chosen activities, groups form easily from common interests. They learn to share materials, tools, and ideas, to make decisions, and to experience the give and take of group living. They learn to respect the rights, property, opinions, and feelings of others. As individuals interact with each other, group leadership qualities develop and children become aware of the importance of cooperation and self-control. These values are derived when children are free to choose materials and use them in their own way.

Intellectual growth takes place through art activities as the child invents new ways of using materials and refines methods he has previously used. As he becomes absorbed in his work, he finds a need for more mature speech in order to talk about it, to explain, or to inquire. Concepts are developed as the child explores the properties of materials such as clay or paint, and learns such terms as *slick, pliable, soft,* and *hard.* The child can develop an art vocabulary, using words such as *artist, texture, color,* and *space*. The greater the variety of materials with which he works, the greater his confidence in his ability to express himself. As he grows in ability to define problems and seek solutions, he grows in creative ability.

Opportunities for physical growth, exercise, and motor coordination are also available. As the child uses his fingers in painting or drawing with crayons and in manipulating clay, he is developing muscular control that he will use later in handwriting. Selecting shapes, choosing colors, and determining sizes offer opportunities for visual discrimination.

Environment for Growth

The role of the teacher in art activities is to create an environment that fosters optimum growth, a setting that is challenging and stimulating, and that gives opportunities for the beginnings of aesthetic appreciation. Following are suggestions for the teacher in creating such an environment.

INDIVIDUAL ATTENTION.   Children grow in depth and quality of ideas, in spontaneity and clarity of expression when they are accepted as individuals. The teacher helps each child to experience some success every day, to develop a healthy attitude toward mistakes, and gradually to assume responsibilities in the care of materials. She guides, supports, and extends his thinking. She must create a feeling of security that leaves the child free to think, imagine, select, and make decisions.

The teacher offers help when needed, raises questions to stimulate thought, and gives her wholehearted approval of the child's honest attempts. Through her wise guidance, the child is increasingly able to take part in planning activities and in assuming more and more responsibility for maintaining the orderliness and attractiveness of the room. This requires time and planning so that the child will know where materials are kept, can take these out as needed and can return them when finished. This also requires a teacher who is friendly, sincere, and understanding. Suggestions for becoming a more creative teacher are found on pages 356–357.

PROVISION OF ADEQUATE SPACE, TIME, AND MATERIALS.   Space is needed to enable children to move freely, to work alone or in small groups, at tables, easels, or on the floor, inside and out-of-doors; to permit children to obtain, arrange, and care for equipment and materials easily. The teacher must provide time for unhurried, satisfying explorations, time to make and carry out plans, time for each child to work at his own rate, and to clean up when he has finished. The teacher must also provide a variety of materials from which the child may choose. These materials are discussed on pages 370–374.

To meet the needs of all the children, the teacher makes allowance for their short attention span by offering them a choice of several activities. She provides large sheets of paper, large brushes, chalks, and wax crayons, and generous amounts of clay and dough, scissors, woodworking and scrap materials because she recognizes their limited eye-hand coordination and muscular development.

√Because taste and feel are so important to young children, she makes certain that materials are safe and washable. She provides many kinds of kinesthetic experiences with ample opportunity to indulge in tactile explorations where the child uses his hands for a tool. She recognizes her own limitations by offering one "messy" or new medium requiring close supervision with several familiar media which the children can handle by themselves.

In making a selection of the types of materials for the day's use, the teacher may choose the scrap material and puzzles because they are familiar to the children and can be handled by them with few demands on her time and energy. She can then give her time and attention to the finger painting which does require supervision. Had she wanted to introduce a new material, she would have handled it in the same manner. The doll corner, blocks, and easel painting are available every day. The children are permitted to move freely from one activity to the other, which encourages them to make choices and to assume the responsibility of finding something to do.

The art area should be accessible to water needed for mixing paint and cleaning up, should have adequate light, and should afford space away from the classroom traffic. Cleaning materials and space for drying paintings are also needed.[11]

CREATIVE EXPRESSION.   Children need rich experiences to stimulate creative expression. This should begin with their everyday living and their love of play. Through discussions of what they have seen or felt, or by talking with them about their play, the teacher can help them to vividly recall happenings they had only vaguely noticed before. (See pages 356–357.) They should be encouraged to talk about themselves and their feelings toward others, and to dramatize these feelings. Through bodily action, children often are stimulated to express themselves in other media. By providing a variety of materials, the teacher enables them to select the media best suited to their individual need.

Planned trips are another means of stimulating creative expression. The teacher must not only plan these excursions, but later help the children to relive and recall them more fully through discussions and questions. The wise teacher does not necessarily expect to see these experiences depicted in the child's art. She has given him ideas for creative thinking. He must have freedom to choose what he wishes to express. As the children work following a trip, the teacher observes their behavior and seeks ways of helping them change habits and attitudes and to deepen their awareness of their environment. She can call attention to flowers, trees, birds, asking, "Are the two the same shape, color? Tell me how they are different." She recognizes that their creations indicate their frustrations and problems as well as their ideas of themselves and their surroundings.

PARENTAL ATTITUDES TOWARD THE CHILD'S CREATIVE EXPRESSION.   The

---

[11]*A Guide: Early Childhood Education in Florida Schools,* Bull. 76 (Tallahassee: Florida State Department of Education, 1969), p. 35.

teacher must also act as interpreter of the child's work to his parents who often mistakenly stifle creative growth through imposing adult standards and ideas on him. The understanding teacher helps parents to appreciate the art qualities of children's drawings and to be familiar with the developmental stages the child goes through In this way they may savor and enjoy each succeeding phase as well as provide a home atmosphere conducive to such wholesome growth. She can suggest suitable materials and ways of presenting them to the child at home. A suggestion that space be provided for the child to display his artistic endeavor often opens new avenues of enjoyment for both parent and child. One parent of a nursery school child kept his paintings on the kitchen bulletin board where all might enjoy and discuss them.

Some inner city parents, as well as some in suburbia, show little, if any, appreciation of their children's art and often little, if any, space is made available for displaying what the child brings home. Consequently many children are not encouraged by the home and may become downhearted and disinterested.

As parents become involved in school activities, serving as aides or attending meetings at school, the teacher has the opportunity to show them their children's art. She can express her appreciation of the child's work as well as explain something of how the child is expressing his growth and ideas. As she talks with the parents, she can suggest comments and questions that might be used with the child, emphasizing the importance of conversation for language development. A decorated folder may be given to the parent for keeping samples of the child's work.

The teacher should talk with parents about the use of coloring books. Parents sometimes need help in seeing the poor art qualities present in coloring books as well as the physical inability of the small child to stay within lines. They need to realize that patterns may rob the child of self-confidence and deaden imagination and spontaneity so important to all learning. Models can sometimes rob children of the opportunity for self-expression. Telling children how to paint can keep them from using their own ideas and initiative.

CONSIDERATION OF DEVELOPMENTAL LEVEL. The teacher should know the characteristic stages of growth in children's art and the developmental levels through which such growth evolves. (See pages 362–364.) It is important that the teacher know and use the findings of research related to children and art. It has been found, for example, that middle-class children, using finger paints, evidence more anxiety about getting dirty, staying dirty, and show less interest in the products they produce while dirty than do lower-class children.[12] Such findings can give clues to the teacher for working more effectively and understandingly with children of differing home backgrounds.

There is a pattern of developmental levels through which a child's artistic

[12]Thelma G. Alper, H. T. Blane, and Barbara K. Abrams, "Reaction of Middle and Lower Class Children to Fingerpaints as a Function of Class Differences in Child-Training Practices," *J. Abnorm. and Soc. Psychol.*, 51:3 (1955), pp. 439–448.

Figure 43. This girl is manipulating the hammer and pounding nails. As she gains skill in using materials and equipment she attains feelings of success which contribute to a positive self-concept.

expression evolves. These levels of maturation determine the selection of media, the size of paper and tools, and the kinds of experiences that will prove most effective for stimulating future growth. Through the years efforts have been made to relate developmental aspects of children's drawing with chronological age. As early as 1895, Sully attempted to classify stages of development from aimless scribbling at age two to a more sophisticated treatment of the human figure at six years.[13] The extensive studies by Gesell and his associates, establishing norms for behavior, have influenced theories of the developmental stages of art. Lowenfeld identified these stages as scribbling, presymbolic, and symbolic. He emphasized that exceptions with regard to the period over which any stage is extended are quite frequent.[14]

[13]J. Sully, *Studies of Childhood* (New York: Appleton-Century-Crofts, 1895), pp. 331–398.

[14]V. Lowenfeld and W. L. Brittain, *Creative and Mental Growth*, 5th ed. (New York: Macmillan Inc., 1970). pp. 64–97.

McFee reviewed the study of Sontag, Baker, and Nelson, as well as the work of Bayley, and summarized their findings by concluding that, "growth is more organismic than linear, and that at any given time all the variables of growth in a given child need to be considered."[15] She also points out that the findings of the study of children's art made at the Cleveland Museum suggest that even "Lowenfeld's levels of development are too narrow in range and do not include all the dimensions of art behavior."[16]

The stages, as identified by Lowenfeld, are described here in order to picture the sequence of development. Although each child progresses through these stages, he does so at his own rate. In a group, ages three to five years, there are likely to be children in all three stages of development. Activities geared to only one of these would limit children who happen to be in other stages. The same child may not develop in all media at the same rate, owing to experience with and interest in the media. It is important for the teacher not only to understand the general stages of growth in art but also the development levels in each medium.

The scribbling stage begins when the child is first introduced to pencil, crayons, clay, or other media and usually extends to about the fourth year. The first efforts of the child are exploratory and largely muscular activity. He is interested in the tool or material and what it can do. If using a crayon, he swings his arm and watches the resulting marks on the paper and soon becomes aware that he can control them by lifting the crayon up or repeatedly drawing lines consciously up and down and across the paper. Tasting is as important as feeling at this stage, so precautions must be taken to see that the materials are safe.

From uncontrolled muscular activity the child gradually develops the ability to make circular patterns. The development of motor control and muscular coordination is the major growth at this age level. To be able to hold a tool and make it go in the direction he desires is a step in development. Until this level is reached, the child is not ready or able to perform other tasks requiring coordination such as eating and dressing. When he begins to name his scribbles or tell stories about them, he has taken still another step in development. He is no longer thinking in terms of physical action but in terms of images and symbols. These symbols hold meaning for the child if not for the adult, so confidence and encouragement must be given. A simple "Tell me about your picture" gives the child a feeling of pride in his work and encourages him to imagine and to verbalize.

Between the ages of four and seven, a different mode of painting begins in which the child consciously creates forms. He continuously tries out new concepts in an effort to establish his own individual pattern or symbol. This stage, known as the presymbolic, is characterized by his constantly changing

[15]June King McFee, *Preparation for Art,* 2nd ed. (Belmont, Calif: Wadsworth, 1970), p. 220.
[16]Ibid., p. 238.

symbols. This presymbolic stage begins as the child strives for a relationship with reality in his drawings. A circle for a head with lines representing arms or legs gives a resemblance to a man. As the child becomes more aware of his relationship to his environment he feels a need to enrich his new-found symbol and he produces a large variety of symbols for the same object. This shows flexibility and ability to adjust. Because the child is most flexible at this time, it is important that the teacher stimulate and increase his awareness through individual experiences. He is not aware of himself as part of the environment. When he sees himself as part of the environment, he places everything on the base line.

McFee has identified three stages in the child's development in art.[17] The first stage is largely manipulation with little or no use of concepts or percepts. McFee does not suggest ages for this stage because she holds that the time at which it begins or ends depends on the opportunities the children have. She quotes Dubin's study, which indicates that young children can change their level of graphic representation by being encouraged to conceptualize about what they are doing.[18]

McFee's second stage covers the time when the child symbolizes his experiences. The third stage relates to realism, the time when the child is concerned with styles of design, and organization.

McFee says that a teacher should consider the individual and environmental influences on the child, as well as his physical and psychological growth.[19]

Providing Opportunities in Art

Authorities advocate the use of a creative approach as the most appropriate method for working with young children. The teacher who uses a creative approach encourages the child to choose his art activity, the way in which he will express or do it, and the way in which he will organize his ideas or materials. This does not mean that the child proceeds without guidance; it does mean that he makes his own decisions and choices.

There are times when it may seem wise for all the children to use the same topic, which may be selected by either the children or the teacher. This may sound rather formal; however, each child is free to choose how he will develop and organize the topic. As time for the Easter egg hung approached, the children needed baskets for their eggs. They made their baskets, but what a variety of baskets! Some were very intricate, made by cutting and folding paper. Others were oatmeal boxes, gay with fingerpainting papers glued on. Other oatmeal boxes were painted with tempera paints. Berry baskets were painted and handles attached. Each child made his basket according to the level of

[17]Ibid., pp. 240–241.
[18]Ibid., p. 240.
[19]Ibid., p. 220.

Figure 44. A creative teacher can provide unlimited opportunities for art activities: modeling, cutting, pasting and tearing, using chalk and crayons, and painting.

his ability and perception. How did the teacher manage this with so many children and only one adult to help?

The teacher and the children talked about the many possibilities for making baskets. She secured the materials and arranged them in areas around the room. One table had scissors, colored sheets of construction paper, rulers, and paste. On another table there were boxes, paint, heavy cord for handles, scissors, colored paper, fingerpaintings, magazine pictures, and paste. Berry baskets, paint, cord, and scissors were in another work area. The teacher also set up blocks, puzzles, and easels. These activities were familiar to the children and required a minimum amount of supervision.

Not every child could work on baskets at the same time, because space and teacher help were not sufficient for this. The teacher and children discussed the materials available and the children went to work in the area where the materials they needed were available. Some worked on baskets. As one child finished his basket another child took his place. A part of the group worked with blocks, puzzles, and at the easel. After experimenting, each child was free to move to another center if he wished. The teacher observed as she moved about the room. She was available as needed.

Contrast this situation with a directed lesson in which every child not only made a basket but made the same kind. The teacher gave directions, step by step. When each child finished the step, he had to wait until directions were given for the next step. Sue and Jim finished quickly and found it difficult to wait while the teacher helped Jerry. Jerry knew that "he was holding everybody up," and he felt inept and embarrassed.

In both situations the children had experience in following directions and using art media. The creative situation, in addition, offered an opportunity for choices and decision-making, working at one's own pace, expressing one's own ideas, assuming responsibility, and building confidence in one's self.

There are those who reject the creative method for such reasons as these: "The child must learn to follow directions"; "The child must learn to color within the lines"; "With only one teacher it is impossible to let children do whatever they choose. One teacher can't supervise all of them"; "Parents expect their child to make what the other children make." Such statements indicate a mistaken concept of the creative approach as being one of "confused pandemonium."

Two mothers were observing in a kindergarten as the children were preparing for the work period, or as some call it, "the art activity period." The teacher and children talked together about activities available for the day. The teacher turned to John and asked, "What do you plan to do?" To another child she said, "What do you want to do?" Then she said, "Those who have made a choice may go to work. If you have not decided, wait just a minute and I will help you."

The mothers were aghast. "Does she let them do just what they want to do?"

"No," was the reply. "The child chooses within the limits of the activities available. The teacher has selected those which she considers appropriate for the day. But the child does make a choice and the ability to make a decision is an important skill. Note that all children have not yet acquired this skill. The teacher must help them."

As the mothers watched, they saw children assume responsibility for getting the materials they needed, using them, and putting them away. As a child finished one job, he was free to move to another. Jim finished a picture at the easel and went to play with three other boys in the block corner. Children shared materials and took turns. Some had to wait for their turns at the fingerpainting table or wait to use the dry cell batteries in the electricity center. The teacher moved quietly among the children, reminding a child to put on his apron before painting and talking with another about his work.

At the close of the period, the mothers realized that what had looked like an unplanned, do-as-you-please period had been a time of meaningful experiencing and learning. In making choices, children had followed directions. They were free to choose, to move about, to be self-directive, and to explore to the extent that their freedom did not interfere with that of others or did not damage property.

Evaluation

To know if the children are achieving the values and skills it is hoped they will derive through art activities, the teacher has to collect evidence for the purpose of evaluation. Techniques which may be used follow:

SAMPLES OF CHILDREN'S WORK. Samples of work can be used to observe progress as the child moves through the developmental sequence from scribbling to forms which he consciously creates. A folder of the child's paintings and drawings and samples of other work, such as clay and wood, may be used for this purpose. It is important to date each product. Such samples may be helpful to the teacher in talking with parents.

CONVERSATION. Informal conversation often takes place while the child works. This gives clues as to the child's ideas and how he feels about himself, his work, and others. For example:

> One of the children stops her painting long enough to ask for more red paint. The teacher puts a spoonful on her paper and the child moves the red paint into a yellow area. She looks up with a smile of wonder and pride and says, "Did you know I could make orange? I put red and yellow together and made orange."

There may be other conversation between the teacher and the child regarding the child's work. Questions such as, "What is it?" may be asking the child to identify an object when he had no object in mind. Perhaps he was only manipulating and using materials. Comments such as, "I like your car," may indicate to the child that the teacher has not recognized the object he has made. Use comments that do not put the child in an embarrassing position. "Tell me about your picture," or "You have used such pretty, bright colors—I like the red," are much more appropriate for the young child.

Jefferson points out that it is not necessary to discuss everything that children produce in art. Children may be apprehensive if they know everything they produce will be discussed.[20] Negative comments during a discussion may be embarrassing for a child. He may lose feelings of confidence as well as his enjoyment of art.

In considering a discussion of art products, it is well to remember that the young child may not appreciate pictures made by other children. According to Munro, research and experience indicate that while children make schematic

[20]Blanche Jefferson, *Teaching Art to Children* (Boston: Allyn and Bacon, 1959), pp. 88–89.

pictures, they tend to prefer more realistic ones. This means that they do not prefer to look at the type of pictures they make themselves.[21]

ANECDOTAL RECORDS. Children's reactions during art experiences constitute a significant part of the child's behavior at school and serve as a source for understanding him. Anecdotal records of this behavior can be helpful. Their uses are discussed in Chapter 21.

RECORDS OF WORK CHOICES. A record of choices of activities which the children make from day to day can help to identify the child who uses only one or a limited number of media; the child who skips from one material to another, not following through with the selected task; the child who uses a variety of materials freely and wisely. Such evidence can be used in helping the child. An example follows:

TABLE 19-1
WORK CHOICES

Date	Blocks	Easel	Puzzles	Clay	Tools
12-9-73	Tom Bill	Ruth Jane Hal	Ruth Jane Hal	Ruth Jane	Tom Joe

List activities for the day across the top of the sheet. Write the child's name under one or more activities in which the child participates.

TEACHER'S EVALUATION. A weekly summary for each child can include the teachers reactions to the child and his art activities, such as "Free in movement, Restricted in movement. Dependent. Experimental."

INTERPRETATION OF CHILDREN'S ART PRODUCTS. The psychological interpretation of children's paintings or drawings is wisely referred to the psychologist. There are, however, studies and scales which may be used to help the teacher gain greater insight into the children's products.[22]

---

[21]T. Munro, "Children's Art Abilities: Studies at the Cleveland Museum of Art," E. W. Eisner and D. W. Ecker, *Readings in Art Education* (Waltham, Mass.: Blaisdell Publishing Company, 1966), pp. 179–180.

[22]Florence L. Goodenough, *Children's Drawings: A Handbook of Child Psychology* (Worcester, Mass.: Clark University Press, 1931); D. B. Harris, *Children's Drawings as Measures of Intellectual Maturity (A Revision and Extension of Goodenough Draw-A-Man Test)* (New York: Harcourt Brace Jovanovich, 1963); Rhoda Kellog, *What Children Scribble and Why* (San Francisco: San Francisco Golden Gate Nursery, 1955); and Beatrice Lantz, *Easel Age Scale* (Los Angeles: California Test Bureau, 1955).

Types of Activities

Through a variety of well-planned activities in an environment where the child is free to explore and experiment, he progressively becomes aware of his environment and is better able to communicate this awareness to others. Moving at his own pace, he develops and refines the large muscles, strengthens the smaller ones, increases eye-hand coordination, and gains shape and color concepts which build toward reading readiness. He develops socially through sharing materials, taking turns, and assuming increasing responsibilities for using these materials and cleaning up afterward. Three-year-old Jane at the dough table showed this social growth when she said "I want to share with you." Tom, in the block corner also evidenced it when he told the teacher, "Look at my house. It has room for some more people." As he works and plays with paints, clay, blocks, and tools, he is building perceptual and thinking abilities as a basis for further learning. As he gains skill in using materials, he grows in self-confidence.

Materials for art activities are unlimited. A creative teacher can provide for art activities even with a limited budget. She sees possibilities in materials around her, such as cloth, straw, boxes, gift wrappings, and feathers. It is important to help children see beauty and value in the world around them— in seedpods, leaves, grasses, and sand. Such materials may be called "junk" by some but to the creative teacher they offer opportunities for enriching experiences for boys and girls. The use of such materials is limited only by the vision of the teacher. The creative teacher experiments with new ways of presenting them and evaluates their true worth to the children using them. There was no doubt in the teacher's mind about the feeling of achievement Jerry experienced when he confronted the powdered tempera in small dishes with a jar of water and brushes nearby. He wet his brush, dipped it into the dry paint and then applied it to the paper. With shining eyes he exclaimed, "I made paint." She also shared Judy's delight in the kinesthetic sensation of finger paint that equaled her enchantment with the color as she sang, "Purple hands, purple hands, look at my purple hands."

The following chart (on pages 370–374), gives some of the basic materials for optimum creative growth. The chart also presents types of activities and attempts to suggest developmental levels in each type of media. It also lists the important values of each activity and suggests some of the responsibilities of the teacher in making the art experiences meaningful to the child. Following the chart are recipes for some of the materials that are suggested for use with the young child. It is hoped that these will encourage the teacher to experiment with ways of using these and other materials.

Art experiences for the young child are basic to developing a happy, whole-some, and creative personality. Through these early experiences in art he develops the ability to imagine, feel, explore, and express ideas. He learns to

MODELING
(CLAY, DOUGH, SAWDUST AND WHEAT PASTE, SALT CERAMIC)

Characteristics of Work	Values Derived	Teacher Techniques
Beats and pounds followed by breaking and rolling (consciously controlled).	Develops large and small muscles and eye-hand co-ordination. Provides direct sensory experiences deeply satisfying to children.	Provide frequent opportunities to explore material. Encourage feeling, handling, and verbalizing.
Names product.		
Begins to pull out or add on details such as nose, ears, arms, legs.	Stimulates different kind of thinking, builds concepts of form, allows changing of these concepts.	Do not model or show how to make something.
Product has meaning for adult.	Provides another outlet for emotional release and aggressive impulses.	Keep materials soft and pliable by storing properly.

PASTING AND USING SCRAPS

Characteristics of Work	Values Derived	Teacher Techniques
Child feels, manipulates, and explores. He uses paste lavishly showing little interest in its purpose. Uses with other materials such as scraps and sand.	Provides tactile experience and opportunities for manipulation and co-ordination. Offers emotional release and opportunity to acquire motor skill.	Furnish enough to allow child freedom to explore its uses and experiment. Help child find its use as a tool for creative expression. Use with scraps, sand, paper, crayons, cotton, cloth, styrofoam, and feathers.

CUTTING AND TEARING

Characteristics of Work	Values Derived	Teacher Techniques
Child cuts and tears aimlessly exploring possibilities of material.	Builds muscle control, eye-hand coordination.	Provide scissors when child can handle them; be sure they will cut.
He practices for skill trying to control scissors and direction of tearing.	Provides another means of self-expression.	Teach the child proper safety rules.
He names his forms.	Offers opportunities to grow creatively and in awareness of form concepts.	Help child to discover the possibilities of tearing.
They have meaning for adult.	Provides another means for release of tensions.	Provide variety of colors and textures of paper, fabrics, and materials.
He combines colors and textures.		

FINGER PAINTING

Characteristics of Work	Values Derived	Teacher Techniques
Child feels and experiments with paints. He uses fingers, hands, and arms, overlays and mixes all colors. Exploration is long accompanied by smearing and finally frenzied smearing. He experiments with patterns. He develops an appreciation for form and color.	Allows release from home pressures to keep clean by offering an acceptable means just to mess. Frees inhibited children for greater spontaneity. Provides social growth and openness to contact. It provides kinesthetic and tactual sensation and opportunity for large muscle activity. It encourages creative expression through its direct contact between child and product and a chance for self-discovery.	Provide free choice of paper, or oilcloth. Allow child freedom to experiment. Encourage this freedom by painting to music, talking about swing of body. Allow time to continue as long as interest is sustained. Allow child to mix the paints. Provide several choices of colors. Encourage children to clean up themselves.

PAINTING
(WORKING WITH PAINT, STRING, SOAP, SAND, CHALK, CRAYON)

Characteristics of Work	Values Derived	Teacher Techniques
Child uses it to explore, to spread and overlay. Lines and circles appear, then form, using squares and blocks of color. Child names his painting, the adult sees meaning. Beginning evidence of relating objects.	Allows the child opportunity to work alone. Offers opportunity to experiment, explore, and express feelings which the young child finds difficult to put into words. Provides a means for motor expression. Helps the withdrawn child to give form to his feelings and accept help. Permits messing in a controlled form and helps the too-neat child ease into finger paint and clay.	Furnish large sheets of paper, large brushes, and a choice of rich bright colors including red, yellow, and blue. Easel of suitable height, away from traffic, should be available at all times so that children can paint satisfying experiences or frustrations as they feel the need. Locate activity in area that cannot be harmed by paint. Use linoleum or plastic on floor. Provide opportunities for painting on tables, the floor, and outdoors. Include variations such as *spatter painting* (Hold wire screen over paper. Dip toothbrush in paint and rub over screen.); *straw painting* (Put blob of paint on paper. Blow through straw on the paint to create designs.);

PAINTING (Cont.)
(WORKING WITH PAINT, STRING, SOAP, SAND, CHALK, CRAYON)

Characteristics of Work	Values Derived	Teacher Techniques
		string painting (Dip string into paint. Drop string on paper. Pull around to make designs.); *printing* (Use objects such as paper cups, pencil erasers, cut vegetables, ends of tubes or straws, cookie cutters. Dip into paint and print on paper. Add a few drops of glycerin or oil of wintergreen to paint mixture to keep it from becoming smelly).

USING BLOCKS

Characteristics of Work	Values Derived	Teacher Techniques
Child plays with single blocks.	Their flexibility and ease of handling make an excellent first medium for the child.	Provide ample space and materials.
He stacks them.		Allow opportunity to leave structure up when desired.
He creates a building and then names it.	Their cleanness and sturdiness are nonthreatening to children from homes with parents' admonitions against dirt and breaking.	Warn children ahead of time to clean up.
He states kind of building and then builds it.		Watch for ways of helping timid child to participate.
He uses knowledge he has gained in dramatic play.[23]	They offer opportunities for playing alone, parallel to, or in cooperation with others.	Offer help when needed to prevent frustration.
	Offer sense of achievement and power to cope with physical world.	Avoid setting patterns.
	Offer emotional release through tearing down or dramatic play.	Listen to and observe child while building to gain insights into behavior and growth.
	Offer physical release through lifting, carrying, and piling.	

[23]Frances M. Guanella, "Block Building Activities of Young Children," *Arch. Psychol.* 26:174 (1934), p. 92, cited by D. H. Russell, *Children's Thinking* (Boston: Ginn Co., 1956).

Characteristics of Work	Values Derived	Teacher Techniques
	Cultivate creative expression and a sense of design.	
	Offer opportunities for problem solving, growth in number concepts, and language.	

RECIPES

Fixative

For chalk:
1. Glue thinned with water to the consistency of milk.
2. One part shellac. Two parts denatured alcohol.

For chalk, pastello, and charcoal:
1. Gum arabic, thin with water until consistency of thin mucilage. Spray—repeat twice.
2. Spray powdered milk mixed with water.

Colored Dough

3 cups flour
$3/4$ cup salt
dry paint or 2 tsp. food coloring
$1/2$ cup water

Sift flour and salt together into a pan. Mix coloring with water and add gradually to flour and salt mixture. Knead as you would bread dough until the mixture is smooth and easy to handle. The more the mixture is kneaded, the smoother it becomes. If mixture becomes sticky add more flour. When not in use, place in plastic bag and keep in a cool place. (Should last at least two weeks.)

Sawdust	Wheat-paste Mixture
4 cups sawdust 2 cups wheat flour 1 cup water	2 cups wheat flour $3 1/2$ cups cold water

Produces a very pliable media—used like dough but not as firm a consistency. (Liquid starch —mixed with sawdust and powdered paint or with tissue paper.)

Paste

1 tbsp. powdered alum
1 cup flour
$1 1/2$ pts. boiling water
Few drops oil of cloves

Mix flour and alum in cold water. Add boiling water and cook for two minutes. Add a few drops of oil of cloves.

Finger Paint

$1/2$ cup dry starch
$1 1/3$ cups boiling water
$1/2$ cup soap flakes
Vegetable coloring, show card or poster paint
1 tbsp. glycerin

Mix the starch with enough cold water to make a smooth paste. Add boiling water and cook the paste until glossy. Stir in the dry soap flakes while the mixture is still warm. Cool. Add glycerin and pour the mixture into jars. The mixture can be kept for a week if it is covered with a damp cloth or a tight lid. Add color later.

Two or three tablespoons of liquid starch may be poured on the wet paper, one-half teaspoon powdered paint added and mixed as the child paints with it.

Sand Painting

Add ¼ part paint powder to 1 part sand and combine in large shakers. Use extra container to empty excess sand. Children shake on paper they have covered with paste. This is also excellent outside on the bare ground.

Soap Painting

Fill small dishes with soap powder. Add a little powdered paint and water. Mix thoroughly until it has a medium texture (not too stiff nor too soft). Children apply to various kinds of paper with fingers or brushes.

share materials, to cooperate, assume responsibility, and to grow in awareness of himself as an individual and of his relation to those around him. He becomes involved in making choices, judging outcomes, and solving problems. As he works with materials he develops his sense of feeling and perception and becomes sensitive to his needs and the needs of others. As he gains skill in using materials, he attains feelings of success that help to establish a self-concept of worth as an individual and as a member of the group. His finished creations reflect his unique personality and insights.

Music Activities

The child's world is filled with music. On the TV he hears the musical accompaniment for the commercials. The country singer plays his guitar and the cowboy picks his banjo as he sings his plaintive folk song. On the radio one record after another is played. Some children have their own record players and a collection of recordings. Even with so much music of varying types in the lives of children, Smith says that the child's musical tastes are not fixed and definite when he comes to school.[24] It becomes increasingly important to consider the role of music in all centers for young children.

Music experiences are an integral part of the child's school day, a part of many activities and learnings. Music can contribute to the development of each child, according to his individual pattern of growth and development. Smith reminds teachers, however, that some experiences that a child may have with music may hinder his aesthetic growth.[25]

Music helped Matt to grow socially. He was a very aggressive five-year-old, eager for attention regardless of how it was gained. He swaggered up to Miss S. who was standing near the piano. "I'll bet you don't know 'Ten Little Indians,'"

[24]R. B. Smith, *Music in the Child's Education* (New York: The Ronald Press, 1970), p. 4.
[25]Ibid., pp. 4–5.

he boasted. The teacher smiled, sat down, and played the song. "Is that the song you mean?" Matt nodded. She replied, "Sing it with me." Together they sang several songs. Matt not only enjoyed singing but found in singing an acceptable form of recognition.

Jim gained in physical development as he galloped across the playground, sometimes alone, sometimes with other "horses," and often with the teacher. Jane became aware of the quality of sounds and gained in auditory acuity as she experimented with instruments. The drum, the bells, and the sticks all sounded different, and she learned to distinguish among them. Lois remembered the words of the song she sang as she rocked the doll. Ann listened at nursery school and sang the songs at home. Sam created his own song.

Music can contribute in many ways by offering opportunities for listening, creating, singing, rhythmic responses, and playing instruments. Through these activities, the child experiences pleasure, joy, and creative expression; develops listening skills and auditory discrimination; gains in physical development and use of his body; and increases the range and flexibility of his voice. The child grows in his appreciation of music and can learn to be discriminating in his choices.

Shull states, "Many educators are apparently unaware of vocal music by many distinguished composers written especially for children to sing."[26] Shull found a considerable body of songs and music of distinguished composers appropriate for use with young children.

The first responses of the young child to music may appear awkward and uncertain, but as he grows physically and socially as well as in the enjoyment and understanding of music, his responses are gradually refined. A variety of free and pleasurable experiences in music invite participation by the child. To provide a balance, activities should include singing, creating, listening, and experiences with rhythms and instruments. For each activity there is a sequence of development from the first simple responses to those which are more complicated and refined. Knowledge and understanding of this sequence can enable the teacher to pace experiences to the level of the child's development.

For example, because the child is not ready to participate in one activity, the teacher may decide he should not be forced and leave him alone. True, he should not be forced, but activities can be paced to his development, and he can be helped to take the next step. "Not forcing" does not necessarily mean leaving the child alone, unchallenged, and untouched for weeks or months. For example, a four-year-old, unable to skip, should not be subjected to drill in the practice of skipping each day. It does not mean, however, that nothing is done. Rather, the teacher who understands the growth and development of the child, as well as the stages of development of the skill of skipping, can arrange many worthwhile experiences. There will be opportunities to climb,

---

[26]C. N. Shull, *A Study of Children's Vocal Literature Written by Selected Distinguished Composers,* Unpublished Dissertation, Florida State University, Tallahassee, June 1961.

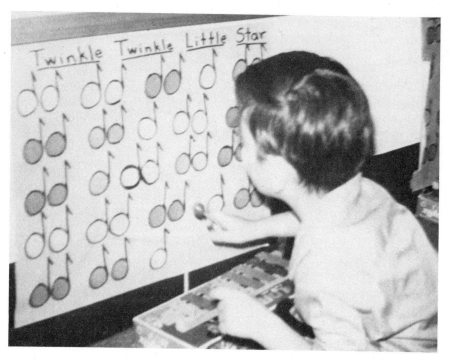

Figure 45. Donald uses the xylophone in the music center. Tuned bells and the auto-harp are also effective instruments for exploring music.

and run, and jump, all of which can help the child to gain control of the large muscles. As he experiments with bodily movements, he will set his own tempo which the teacher can emphasize. He listens to music, he responds, and his rhythmic response is accepted. Gradually, in keeping with the child's rate of maturity, he reaches the point where skipping is possible.

Nye and Nye make suggestions for helping the disadvantaged child musically.[27] In reality the suggestions are applicable to all children.

1. Examine and analyze a child's background. Involve him in planning and exploring songs he would like to sing or know; instruments and rhythmic movements he might use with a song.
2. Provide opportunities for the child to use divergent and creative ways of interpretation.
3. Find out and understand conditions in which the child may live. There may be complete indifference to musical values and experiences.
4. Involve parents in music activities at school. Help them to know of musical programs and experiences available to them in the community and of appropriate programs for viewing on TV.

[27]R. E. Nye and Vernice T. Nye, *Music in the Elementary School*, 3rd ed. (Englewood Cliffs, N.J.: Prentice-Hall, Inc., 1970), pp. 558–571.

5. Encourage the child in self evaluation. Evaluate the child's progress in order to meet his needs.

Developmental Sequence of Music Activities

The description of the developmental sequence presented here attempts to give a picture of the stages through which each child passes at his own rate, and to help identify the next step that he is able to take. Such a sequence can prove helpful in making plans for a variety of individuals and situations. Wide differences among the group should not lead the teacher to the conclusion that some children can benefit from musical activities and others not. Smith says, ''all young children have musical capacities, and all should have the opportunity to develop this potential.''[28]

SINGING

Developmental Sequence	Suggestions to the Teacher
The Child: 1. Enjoys listening to song sung by another; sings spontaneously as he plays.	1. Children are at differing levels in the developmental sequence.
2. Responds with actions to song sung by another.	Don't expect same response of all children. Give each child an opportunity to participate at his level.
3. Joins in with an occasional word or phrase as another sings.	a. Some will listen as they are in block corner while others come to piano for a song. Accept child in doll corner at
4. Sings with an adult or group but not always in time with them (may be a measure behind and may not use the same words).	his level, but don't leave him there all year. Work to help him take the next step and the next. Perhaps sing a song (lullaby or one appropriate to the activity) for him in the doll corner. He
5. Sings along with adult or group, able to match tones.	can rock the doll as you sing.
6. Sings alone.	b. Some learn words easily and sing with teacher, accept this along with the
7. Selects and requests favorite songs.	response of an occasional word and a
8. Recognizes songs sung or played by others.	happy, eager expression. Avoid such statements as:
9. The child's voice range centers around G above middle C, but the voice he uses often varies with the activity and the purpose for his singing.[29] Smith reports a range from middle C to G above.[30]	''Now let's *all* sing.'' ''Jane knows *all* the words. Jane, sing them for us. Now listen so you can learn the words too.''
10. Acquires a repertoire of songs.	Jane can sing alone for the group, yes —but not as a model which may discourage others.

[28]Smith, op. cit., p. 9.

[29]A. T. Jersild and Sylvia F. Beinstock, ''A Study of the Development of Children's Ability to Sing,'' *J. Educ. Psychol.*, 25:10 (1939), p. 491.

[30]Smith, op. cit., p. 17.

Singing (Cont.)

Developmental Sequence	Suggestions to the Teacher
11. Sings tunefully.	2. Include songs of varying length, tonal range, and content.
	3. Provide many opportunities for singing throughout the day. Avoid "sing-song-ing" every comment to the child, but chanting some comments offers opportunities for individual and group responses.

"Mary has a new doll.
Who gave it to you?"

—

      —

          —

 —

  —

    —

      —

Ma-ry
   has a
      new doll.
Who
  gave
   it
    to
     you?

4. Limit length of group musical experiences, taking into account the attention span of the group. A few songs, well-selected, sung happily, and enjoyed can be of much more value than a longer period in which children may lose interest.

5. Select songs within the expected voice range of the young child. Many songs are written too high for the majority of kindergarten children. The range within the song should not extend beyond three to four adjacent notes. A little more difficult songs vary in total range but a limited-range pattern should be repeated several times.[31]

6. Include songs

   a. of a variety of types—patriotic songs, religious songs and hymns, songs about holidays, the here and now, everyday

[31]Ibid., p. 18.

SINGING (Cont.)

Developmental Sequence	Suggestions to the Teacher
	experiences, counting, folk songs, familiar songs.
	b. of a pleasing melody and musical appeal.
	c. that are brief, simple, and repeat certain phrases.
	d. containing words that are easily sung.

LISTENING

Developmental Sequence	Suggestions to the Teacher
The child:	1. Include a variety of musical listening experiences.
1. Is engrossed in one activity but listens just enough to be aware of what is being sung or played.	a. Different purposes: Mood—fast, slow, happy, sad, rhythmic response. Stories in music. Sounds.
2. Enjoys a short song, a recording, or an instrument, alone or with an adult (range of attention span varies from 2 to 20 minutes).	b. Different types: Recordings—vocal and instrumental. Instruments—teacher plays piano, a father plays a horn, another child plays with a rhythm stick.
3. Enjoys a short song, recording, or an instrument along with a few other children —gradually the size of the group expands to include the entire nursery or kindergarten group.	

Figure 46. Kim and Stanley choose a record for use in their dramatic and rhythmic activity. They have learned to use the record player and handle records carefully.

LISTENING (Cont.)

Developmental Sequence	Suggestions to the Teacher
4. Listens and analyzes what he hears. He can distinguish between loud and soft or happy and sad music. He can listen for details and for answers to questions. He can listen to his own singing and playing in order to correct or to match tones. He can listen to accompaniment for rhythmic responses.	Singing—teacher sings, mother sings, another child sings. c. Individual and in a group. d. Resource people—sing or play an instrument. 2. Watch child who spends too much time listening. He may be using this as an escape from group adjustment—may need help getting into the group. The suggestions listed for language arts (p. 200), are applicable in listening to music.

RHYTHMIC EXPERIENCES

Developmental Sequence	Suggestions to the Teacher
The child expresses rhythm through: 1. Making random movements, using large muscles. 2. Moving rhythmically in his own way for short periods of time. 3. Moving rhythmically in his own way, he responds when teacher emphasizes his movement with an accompaniment. 4. Moving at fast tempo before he conforms to slower tempos. 5. Adjusting bodily movements to accompaniment of regular beat. Can "keep time." 6. Listening before participating. 7. Adjusting bodily movements to accompaniment which involves contrasts (slow and fast, light and heavy). 8. Acquiring musical concepts of terms— high-low, short-long, fast-slow, and expressing them through movement.	1. Provide space and opportunity for movement. 2. Observe child's movements and his tempo. Accompany him with piano, percussion instrument, or by clapping in his own tempo. He sets the pace. Avoid accompaniments that include melodic and harmonic elements.[32] 3. Help child with transition from moving rhythmically in his own tempo to moving to an accompaniment. For example, the teacher might say, "Tim, I've been beating the drum as you walk. I will do it again and beat every time you take a step. Then I am going to beat differently—maybe faster or maybe slower. Listen and see if you can walk when I beat the drum." 4. Provide accompaniments in faster tempos, using those that invite the slower more deliberate movements at a later time. Vary soft and loud tones. 5. Use even foot patterns such as walking, marching, running before the uneven patterns like galloping and skipping.[33]

[32]A. T. Jersild and Sylvia F. Beinstock, *Development of Rhythm in Young Children* (New York: Teachers College, Columbia University, 1937), p. 96.

[33]Ibid., p. 71.

RHYTHMIC EXPERIENCES (Cont.)

Developmental Sequence	Suggestions to the Teacher
	6. Play accompaniments to which child can respond. Be sure that rhythm is regular and easily detected. Ask child to listen first and then respond to the music. Avoid getting children on floor and saying, "Do what the music says" without first giving them an opportunity to listen. Avoid saying, "I am going to play some skipping music" (or galloping music). Children may respond to the music by walking, running, whirling, skipping, galloping, or in many other ways. Let the child choose his response to the music.
	7. Play very high and very low tones. Ask the child to show where each tone is by raising or lowering his arms. After listening, ask the child where he heard light, heavy, loud tones.
	8. Do not expect same response of all children.
	a. Some will respond individually or in small groups—not even all kindergarteners are ready to participate in a large group.
	b. Skipping requires greater skill in muscular control than some of the other activities such as walking or running. Not all fours or even fives can skip. This is another reason for letting a child choose his own response rather than asking everyone to skip.

PLAYING INSTRUMENTS

Developmental Sequence	Suggestions to the Teacher
The Child:	
1. Manipulates and experiments with instruments; becomes aware of differences in sounds in relation to ways in which the instruments are played; comes to recognize sounds of various instruments.	1. Place instruments so they are available to children. Provide opportunity for children to experiment freely. Expect "noise" at first. Use instruments both inside and out of doors. Avoid showing child "how to hold instrument." Help him evaluate sound in relation to way he holds tambourine or triangle. "Which way sounds better?"
2. Uses instrument as accompaniment to his movements—beats rhythm sticks as he marches, but not necessarily in time with his steps.	Help him discover how to hold an instrument in order to get the best tone.
3. Listens to music and is able to identify the instrument that makes the appropriate sound.	Help child discover tonal qualities of instrument. Which instrument has the

PLAYING INSTRUMENTS (Cont.)

Developmental Sequence	Suggestions to the Teacher
4. Plays instrument and responds accurately to tempo of a recording or another instrument.	highest sound? the lowest? Play the drum with hand, a wooden mallet, a yarn mallet. How does it sound?
5. Plays instrument along with a small group of other children.	2. Play music and ask child to listen and to decide which instrument will be appropriate. Play music again and child accompanies with his instrument. Let child choose instrument appropriate for a certain rhythm, such as a rain dance or a Funny Clown, or one that has a certain tone color such as one that sounds like an airplane or the wind. Avoid such statements as, "All drums play," or "All together, play." Listening and responding creatively help the child to develop sensitivity to mood, and good listening habits as well as auditory acuity and discrimination.
6. Is interested in and curious about instruments that adults play.	
7. Learns names of several of the better known instruments, such as the violin or trumpet.	
8. Listens and identifies sound of different instruments. Knows when certain instruments are playing in a musical selection.	
	Such procedure is followed first for individual children and later for the group.

Figure 47. The piano is available to the children. This girl is experimenting with the keys of the piano. She finds that there are high sounds and low sounds.

PLAYING INSTRUMENTS

Developmental Sequence	Suggestions to the Teacher
	The formal rhythm band often requires strict conformity and adherence to the pattern designed by the teacher which may tend to discourage creative listening and responses.
	3. Bring real instruments to school for children to see and touch. Invite an adult or a youth to play for the children. Children may visit an orchestra rehearsal.
	4. Provide recordings of instrumental music.
	5. Tuned bells and the autoharp are effective instruments for exploring music.

CREATING

Developmental Sequence	Suggestions to the Teacher
The child:	
1. Chants as he swings, piles blocks, or pulls his wagon. This may be a play on words, experimenting with sounds.	1. While suggestions here are limited largely to singing, this is not intended to imply that this is the only musical experience which lends itself to the creative approach. Other suggestions were made specifically for rhythmic experiences, page 380.
2. Experiments with instruments and sounds.	
3. Suggests a new word for a song; for example, in the song "Do you know what says, Quack! Quack!?" Child may substitute "bow-wow," or "mew, mew," etc.[34]	2. Create a permissive atmosphere in which the child feels free to chant and sing as he works and plays.
4. Makes up extra verses for a song.	3. Select songs containing words and phrases for which other words may be substituted.
5. Chooses an appropriate instrument and accompanies a song or a recording.	4. Sing animal song to child. Then ask a question such as "Can you think of another animal which makes a sound? Sing it."
6. Interprets the mood of music in rhythmic movement. Moves expressively.	5. Permit child to listen to song or recording and then select instrument for accompaniment.
7. Dramatizes a song.	
8. Makes up a song cooperatively and later individually. Sings the words in developing tune.	6. Play recordings characterized by a mood or moods. Let child listen and respond. Properties such as scarves or flags may be helpful in interpreting the mood.
9. Creates an original melody or tune.	7. Use songs with words that give clues to movement, or singing games. For example, in the song "This Old Man" children may choose to have the old man come "hop-

[34]Mary J. Nelson and Gladys Tipton, *Music for Early Childhood* (New York: Silver Burdett, 1952), p. 16.

CREATING (Cont.)

Developmental Sequence	Suggestions to the Teacher
	ping" or "skipping" home.[35] Another example might be "Community Helpers."[36]
	8. Creating a song may be a group activity. Joe brought a "possum" to the kindergarten. As the group gathered around the piano he asked Miss T., "Do you know a song about a possum?" Miss T.: "No, Joe, I don't, but perhaps we could make up a song about the possum."
	To the group Miss T. said, "Let's see if we can make a song about the possum."
	What would you want to sing first?"
	Sally: "We could tell his name."
	Miss T.: "Yes, we could. Sing it for us Sally."
	Sally sang, "Pete the Possum."
	Miss T. repeated Sally's phrase. This procedure was continued until the following song was completed.
	Pete the Possum, in a cage, His tail is long, His nose is sharp.
	Miss T. played the tune on the piano and recorded the notes. If she had not been able to play the tune she could have sung it several times in order to remember the tune.

As the child progresses through the developmental sequences described for singing, listening, rhythmic experiences, and creating, musical experiences can help him to develop in many ways. For certain children music has special advantages. The overactive, aggressive child can be helped to become relaxed and less tense; the shy, timid child can be helped to become involved in group experience. For each child music can:

1. Promote appreciation and enjoyment.
2. Encourage discrimination in the choice of music and other aesthetic experiences.
3. Develop an awareness of and sensitivity to sounds as well as auditory acuity.
4. Develop and extend voice range.
5. Provide experiences in listening.

[35]Ibid., p. 43.
[36]Ibid., p. 19.

6. Promote growth in motor control.
7. Develop intellectual and emotional capacities.

Suggested Activities

1. Visit a nursery school, kindergarten and a child development center. Observe children engaged in art activities. Describe the activity and indicate the stage of art development in which several children seem to be.

2. Use one of the recipes, pp. 373–374, and prepare a medium for use by children. Experiment with ways of using the medium. Name the values that you feel the children gained from participating in this activity.

3. Examine one of the scales or studies listed on page 368. Use the information in relation to drawings of several children. How do you feel the scale helped you gain insight into the child's product?

4. Observe a group of young children and note any peer pressures that seem to affect a child's choice of activity or his actions. How do you feel such conformity may influence a child's creative activities? What do you feel is the teacher's role in such situations?

5. Visit a center for young children and describe the approach to art or the philosophy of the teacher regarding the art of the young child. What evidence do you see that the philosophy and practices are consistent? What is your philosophy? Discuss your observations with your class.

6. Make a list of art supplies and materials that you might order for your classroom. Compile a list of sources of art supplies. List materials that may be made by the teacher and/or parents.

7. Observe a child's movements and his tempo. Accompany him with a percussion instrument, or by clapping hands. Follow his tempo.

8. Listen to and evaluate five recordings for use with young children.

9. Learn five songs appropriate for use with young children. Teach them to members of the class and to young children.

10. Reread the suggestions for "creating" in music on pp. 383–384. Select one suggestion and use it with a small group of young children. Do you feel that you accomplished your goals? What changes might you make when you use this activity again?

Related Readings

Andrews, Gladys. *Creative Rhythmic Movement for Children*. Englewood Cliffs, N.J.: Prentice-Hall, Inc., 1954.

Aronoff, Frances Webber. *Music and Young Children*. New York: Holt, Rinehart and Winston, 1969.

Art Guide—Let's Create a Form and *Let's Make a Picture*. Washington, D.C.: ACEI, 1969.

Biacini, Americole, Ronald Thomas, and Lenore Pogonowski. *M.M.C.P. Interaction-Early Childhood Music Curriculum*, 2nd ed. Bardonia, N.Y. 10954: Media Materials, Inc. No date.

Bits and Pieces. *Imaginative Uses for Children's Learning*. Washington, D.C.: ACEI, 1967.

Brandhofer, Marijane. "Carpentry for Young Children," *Young Children, 27*:1 (1971), pp. 17–23.

Cherry, Clare. *Creative Movement for the Developing Child, A Nursery School Handbook for Non-Musicians,* Rev. ed. Belmont, Calif.: Fearon Publishers, 1971.

Cornelius, Ruth. "Rhythm Is Everywhere," *Early Years, 2*:5 (1972), pp. 32–35.

Doll, Edna, and Mary Jarman Nelson. *Rhythms Today.* Morristown, N.J.: Silver Burdett Company, 1965.

Dubin, Elizabeth Ruth. "The Effect of Training on the Tempo of Development of Graphic Representation in Preschool Children," *J. of Experimental Educ., 15* (1946), pp. 163–173.

Foster, F. P. "Song Within: Music and the Disadvantaged Preschool Child," *Young Children, 20*:6 (1965), pp. 373–376.

Hattwick, Melvin S. "The Role of Pitch Level and Range in Singing of Preschool, First Grade and Second Grade Children," *Child Develpm., 4*:4 (1933), pp. 281–291.

Jersild, A. T., and Sylvia F. Beinstock. "The Influence of Training on the Vocal Ability of Three-Year-Old Children," *Child Develpm., 11*:4 (1931), pp. 272–291.

Johnson, Pauline. "Art for the Young Child," *Art Education* (64th Yearbook, Part II), University of Chicago Press: NSSE, 1965, pp. 51–85.

Kellog, Rhoda. *Analyzing Children's Art.* Palo Alto, Calif.: National Press Books, 1969.

Kellog, Rhoda, with S. O'Dell. *The Psychology of Children's Art.* New York: Random House, 1967.

Marantz, K. *A Bibliography of Children's Art Literature.* Washington, D.C.: NAEA, 1965.

Moffitt, Mary W. *Woodworking for Children.* 196 Bleecker St., New York: Early Childhood Education of New York, 1972.

McLeod, Catherine. "Growing Up With Music," *Réalitiés, 259* (June 1972), pp. 72–79.

Myerson, Edith S. "Listen to What I Made! From Musical Theory to Usable Instrument," *Young Children, 26*:2 (1970), pp. 90–92.

Nixon, Arne J. *A Child's Right to the Expressive Arts.* Washington, D.C.: ACEI, 1969.

Schwartz, Julia B., and Nancy J. Douglas. *Increasing the Awareness of Art Ideas of Culturally Deprived Kindergarten Children Through Experience with Ceramics.* (Project No. 6-8647, Office of Education, U.S. Dept. of Health, Education, and Welfare) Tallahassee, Florida: Florida State University, 1967.

————. *The Effects of Teacher In-Service Education on the Development of Art Ideas with Six-Year-Old Culturally Deprived Children.* Tallahassee, Fla.: Southeastern Educational Laboratory, 1967.

Silverman, R. H. "Art for the Disadvantaged," *NEA J, 55*:4 (1966), pp. 29–31.

Williams, F. E. "Teaching for Creativity," *Instructor, 81*:4, 1971, pp. 42–44.

Organizing
Centers for
Young
Children

Part III

Figure 48. (OVERLEAF) Home visits are valuable for the parent and the teacher to become acquainted before the child enters school. They help the teacher learn about the child's background.

Involving Parents as Partners

Chapter 20

Since the last revision of this text there have been important developments regarding the role of parents in the education of their young children. Perhaps the most important factor was political in nature resulting in a demand, growing out of the civil rights movement, on the part of low-income and minority groups that control of the education of their children be returned to them. This demand resulted from the fact that the public schools had failed to enable children of such groups to succeed in school and at the same time allow time to retain pride in their respective cultural heritage. A second factor was the mounting research evidence pointing to the importance of parent-child interactions in bringing about conditions, the exact variables of which are not yet clearly understood, that are necessary for the stimulation of early cognitive development. Theoretically, at least, such stimulation is necessary if children are to be able to cope with the expectations of the public schools.

So great was the conviction of the importance of the above factors that federally sponsored programs such as Head Start, Follow Through, and Parent

Child Center programs, mandated parent involvement. The implementation of these mandates varied from complete control, including conducting the instructional program itself, to more or less superficial participation in occasional meetings, invited classroom visits, and field trips. As a further safeguard to be sure parents were involved, half of the members of Advisory Councils or Committees had to be parents of the children served. In theory, these groups had considerable power in making decisions regarding staffing, the nature of the program, and influence on administrative and supervisory matters. In practice, these groups often participated only to the extent of approving what those in charge wished them to approve. As time went on, with encouragement from consultative services provided to the programs, poor people were, for the first time, learning to have a part in the destiny of their children.

Although parent involvement certainly is educational in nature for parents, a clear distinction should be made between parent education and parent involvement, as the concept of parent education appears in much of the earlier educational literature. The term *parent education* connotes that the parents are learners being "taught." *Parent involvement* places stress on parents as teachers of their children and having a decision-making role in what should be taught and by whom. Implicit was the argument that children disadvantaged by racial discrimination and poverty have a cumulative deficit of early home and community experiences seemingly necessary for later academic success in the public schools. Hence the need arises for involvement of parents in the early and/or compensatory education of their children. However, there may be an "inherent contradiction between the arguments that have to do with cumulative deficit and those which support ethnic pride and self-determination for ghetto communities."[1] If the goal of later success in public school is to be reached, then parents must acquire the skills and strategies necessary to be the teachers of their young children. Accordingly, parent education and parent involvement cannot be independent of each other. This complex problem calls for innovation and change never before demanded of education.

Both the home and the school have important functions to serve in educating the child. Neither can work effectively without the understanding, support, and assistance of the other. Guiding the development of the child is a cooperative endeavor. The parent and the teacher need to see the whole child, as he reacts in his life at school and at home, in order to provide a complete program for him. The quality of the teacher-parent relationships during this early period will have an influence upon the child throughout his formative years.

The seeds of the point of view described at the beginning of this chapter had appeared in earlier educational literature. However, the present concept of involvement, giving the parent a major role, had not evolved until recently.

---

[1]Robert D. Hess, et al., "Parent Involvement in Early Education", *Day Care: Resources for Decisions*, Edith H. Grotberg, ed., (Washington D.C.: Office of Economic Opportunity, 1971), p. 267.

During the past two decades, recognition of the importance of the changing role of parents in their relationships to the school has been pointed out by many educators. For example, in 1953 Hymes[2] stated,

Home-school relations have two broad goals:

To bring about a better understanding, between parents and leaders, of what children are like; and

To bring about a better understanding, between teachers and parents, of good education.

He further states:[3]

When these goals are achieved, parents and teachers work together as a united team, and youngsters gain in two ways:

They have a richer, fuller, more nourishing life, in school and out, than otherwise would be open to them; and

They have more consistent guidance in school and out; they stand a better chance of living up to the peak of their powers.

Parents and Teachers Work Together

Contact between parents and teacher should be a two-way process, from home to school and from school to home. In schools or centers where parent involvement is not required parents often feel the school should contact them and many times the teacher wishes the parents would invite her into the child's home for a friendly visit. Some teachers are hesitant to call the parents' attention to this need for partnership in working with the child, either because the teacher herself is rather inexperienced or the parent has given a false impression of dominance or lack of interest in discussing the child's development. The teacher may have given parents this false impression by being too impersonal, distant, or hurried. Some parents do not understand that the teacher is interested in the child's home life from the time he leaves school until his return, because it will assist her in working with the child at school. As late as 1959 the concept that parents could have "correct" educational goals for their children seemed remote as indicated by the following quotation from Brim:

The educator must know and state his own values, work with parents to do the same with theirs, assist in the achievement of those which are agreed upon, seek democratically to win the parent to his point of view, where they disagree, by rational persuasion, and, finally, withdraw and refuse to help where the parent insists on the pursuit of goals which the educator believes to be evil.[4]

[2]J. L. Hymes, Jr., *Effective Home-School Relations* (Englewood Cliffs, N.J.: Prentice-Hall, 1953), p. 9.

[3]Ibid.

[4]O. G. Brim, Jr., *Education for Child Rearing* (New York: Russell Sage Foundation, 1959), p. 90.

Inadequate communication between school and home pertaining to aims or goals may hinder the continuous progress of the child.[5]

According to Leonard, Vandeman, and Miles, "When school and home enjoy understanding it is comparatively easy for one to approach the other in any individual or group situation that may exist. When teachers and parents discover ways of accomplishing common goals, and when their common activities are an essential part of the school, some sort of teacher-parent counseling system is already in operation."[6]

Parents and teachers can offer invaluable assistance to each other in their efforts to understand the child. Too often parents feel the nursery school teacher is the person who knows "all about children." The teacher may try to discover more about the child through his parents but doesn't quite know how to do this. Thus, each adult is seeking to know the other, but doesn't seem able to reach the other. Differences in educational, social, and economic levels may cause some parents and teachers to feel insecure in the presence of each other.

What appears to be parental indifference is often in reality insecurity and low self esteem. Thus, reaching and knowing such a parent may become a challenge to the teacher. Providing transportation, arranging meeting times suitable to the parents, avoiding formal meetings, and encouraging participation may be ways to involve such parents. The parents need to know the daily and weekly happenings that involve their child so that they may supplement and extend at home the experiences the child has at school. Most schools use a variety of procedures for the teacher and the parent to work together and to keep the parent informed as to the activities planned for the year, as well as changes occurring in the weekly schedule.

In many centers these experiences are maximized when the parent has a part in the actual planning of the program. In others, parents work with the children as aides or volunteers. In some instances parents assume major instructional responsibilities after having served as aides and participated in "on the job" training. Many experimental and pilot projects, described elsewhere, have been developed with the principal goal being to assist parents to serve in the role of teacher of their own children. While the Cooperative preschool movement has flourished for several decades, one of its major goals was to provide preschool experiences for children at a modest cost to parents.

When parents are not familiar with the purpose and plan for the activities of the school, they may be suspicious of the total program. Since the parents will feel more comfortable if they know what is expected of them, the teacher finds many ways to keep them informed. Bulletin board displays are placed so as to be easily observed when the parent brings or comes for the child.

[5]Grace Langdon and I. W. Stout, *Teacher-Parent Interviews* (Englewood Cliffs, N.J.: Prentice-Hall, 1954).

[6]Edith M. Leonard, Dorothy D. Vandeman, and Lillian E. Miles, *Counseling with Parents in Early Childhood Education* (New York: Macmillan, Inc., 1954), p. 2.

Notices of meetings, lists of children for various group activities, menus for the day, special notices, displays of children's work, and interesting material for parents are posted and changed frequently so that the parent is challenged to stop, look, and read. Some teachers send short notes home with the children. These notes assist in keeping all parents informed of special events and unusual happenings; the note may even be on some particular item of interest related specifically to their child's activities.

Even though all parents are different, they are alike in their desire to secure the best education for their child. They may also share the fear that their child is not like other children. Many parents are concerned that they are not providing adequately for their child. They need assistance and guidance in understanding what to provide and what not to provide. The wise teacher utilizes these concerns and builds upon the similarity of parents as she plans for parent meetings and group study. Since the school program needs to be concerned about differing social status, it provides an excellent opportunity for parents and children to have social experiences that will make it possible for the children to learn to live and work together with people from different backgrounds.

Regardless of the type and goals of the center or school, its program will be greatly enhanced by maximum parent involvement and participation. The strategies suggested in the following several pages have been useful in many different types of situations in an attempt to improve parent-teacher-child understandings and relationships.

TEACHERS AND PARENTS COMMUNICATE

Sheehy states that, "Person-to-person and day-by-day relationships are important, not only in their immediate results, but they affect the entire school and community. Organizations are important and necessary but, as long as teachers continue to 'speak' to parents and parents to teachers, there will be no gaps to bridge between the school and the community."[7]

Teachers and parents communicate in many ways including the following:

Home Visits

Too often plans are made for the parents to come to the school for a visit and yet no recognition is given to the need for the teacher to become acquainted with the child in his own home. A family interview, in order to fill out a child's history, is a helpful way to learn the home surroundings. The child becomes better acquainted with the teacher by actually seeing her visit in his home. The parent is more at ease in his own surroundings and more apt to verbalize problems or questions. The teacher gains much through actually seeing how the family lives and how they feel about sending the child to school. Insight into

[7]Emma D. Sheehy, *The Fives and Sixes Go to School* (New York: Holt, Rinehart and Winston, 1954), p. 356.

feelings between family members may result from such a home visit. Teachers usually find a home visit will be more profitable if (a) the visit is arranged at the convenience of the parents, (b) there is adequate time for both teacher and parent to talk uninterruptedly, and (c) the child is playing nearby where he can be observed yet not always within hearing distance of the adults' discussion.

Home visits before the child enters school are valuable for the teacher and the parent in becoming acquainted and in giving insight into the background of the child. A friendly social visit will make the child, as well as the parent, more comfortable on the first day at school. The visit will make the child feel important in the eyes of the teacher, and it will help him to feel secure as he enlarges his circle of peers at school.

Today, thousands of children have had one, two, or more years of preschool group experience before entering public kindergarten or first grade. In Home Start, Head Start, Parent Child Centers, and similar type programs, much of the instructional program will have been carried out in the home by the staff members as well as by the parents themselves. Wise public school leadership will find ways to continue this close working relationship with parents. Otherwise, there is a real danger of alienating parents to the extent that children accustomed to having their parents as partners in their education may well lose some of the gains made earlier.

School Visits

The parent, accompanied by the child, needs to visit the school before the child enters to become acquainted with the facilities and to encourage the child to anticipate entering school. These visits also make it possible for the parent to learn about the program and to assist the teacher in orienting the child to his first days at school.

Communication between parents and teacher needs to be encouraged when the parent brings the child to school each morning. Some teachers give parents the impression that it is not necessary or desirable for the parent to remain at school. Thus, the parent gradually builds up the feeling that it is not good for him to linger or to spend a part of a day in the school. When this results, communication has broken down between teacher and parent. The parent should be encouraged to stay long enough to see that the child is engaged in an activity, then leave.

Too often the school personnel give the impression that they feel parents are prying into their activities. Not only do the parents have the right, but they also have the responsibility to know what the school is doing for the child and how the school plans to develop its program. Both the teacher and the parent may gain further insight into the child's behavior through a conference held soon after a visit or planned observation. Scheduling the visits so that only one child's parents observe and visit the school on a given day will be more profitable and less disturbing to the children and the activities under the teacher's direction, than if several parents visit on the same day. The teacher needs to (a) develop an understanding of the place for and the importance of a planned visit to the school, (b) plan ahead, setting the actual time and date of the visit, (c) plan the procedures for the visit with both the child and the parent, and (d) provide for free time to discuss the child's activities as the parent observes the child in relation to the school itself, or at an early time shortly after the visit. If a simple observation guide in the form of suggestions for the visit is provided, the parent will feel more comfortable and the first observations may be more profitable. Soon parents will feel less dependent on an extrinsic factor. However, these written suggestions may be profitable at each visit, if they are planned to point out certain phases and aspects of the program or to assist the parents in gaining deeper insight into their child's development as he works, plays, and lives in a school situation. Some teachers do not find it desirable to prepare an observation guide; they prefer to make accessible pad and pencil so that the parents may jot down questions or comments to be discussed later in the follow-up conference.

For example, one teacher planned for parent observations to follow a group meeting that was devoted to the specific topic, "The Child's Adjustment at School." Following a discussion of the topic, the teacher talked with the parents about planned observations at school and distributed "guides" pointing out various aspects of adjustment to be observed. A school visit was then scheduled for each parent, to be followed by an individual conference.

Telephone Conversations

Frequently a telephone conversation is thought to substitute for a scheduled conference. Like casual visits, these conversations make a definite contribution and have a place in communicating with parents. Minor routine situations, unexpected developments such as illness or a visit to the doctor, or some item which the teacher does not wish to discuss before the child may be discussed on the telephone. Scheduled conferences can be confirmed by the teacher with the parent in a telephone conversation, especially if the parent does not have the opportunity or does not avail himself of the privilege of casual contacts.

Casual Visits

Parents communicate much information to the teacher and to other parents as they bring children to school or call for them later. The teacher can secure many cues as to a child's behavior and parent's attitude through analyzing remarks made in these casual contacts. It is necessary for the teacher to be alert to these cues because they may aid in gaining insight into how to work most profitably with the child during the day. The parent who states "We are running late this morning, we all overslept as we had unexpected relatives arrive late last night," may be giving many hints of how this will affect her child's day at school. These contacts also give the teacher an opportunity to comment to the parent about the child. For example, she may say, "Janie seemed tired today. Did she watch television after her bedtime last night?" or, "Jimmy sang alone in music today."

The value of casual contacts should not be underestimated; they make a significant contribution to the parent-teacher relationship by establishing rapport, paving the way and providing a means for scheduling the planned conference at a later date. Through these contacts, the teacher, the parent, and the child share moments of unified interest and learn to talk freely, one with the other.

Planned Conferences

Through these frequent, casual contacts, many so-called conferences are held by parents and teacher. However, they should not replace the scheduled conference. Sometimes teachers feel that it is not necessary to hold regularly scheduled conferences if they know the family and can develop an understanding of the child's home background through these informal discussions. Too often the true feelings of the parent, or the teacher, or the child, may not be revealed in a casual visit; the problems needing discussion may be of the nature that the parent and the teacher do not wish those nearby to overhear. In addition, the teacher has not had time to study the child's record and to prepare for the conference, and the time is too limited to discuss problems, plans, purposes, procedures, progress, and follow-up activities. Many more areas can be discussed, recorded information studied, and feelings communicated in a planned conference.

The teacher needs to build an understanding of the need for and the purpose of a regular conference with the parent, whether it be held only once during the school year or more often. Each child as an individual needs to be carefully considered and some tentative plans made by the teacher prior to the conference in order to discuss progress with the parents. Types of records are discussed in detail in Chapter 21, "Recording the Development of Children." An individual folder for each child is recommended in which the teacher may insert short notes from time to time. Many teachers keep a written account of a child's reactions, achievements, and problems during the day; these are added to the collection in the folder. By reviewing each child's folder frequently, a teacher can discover children for whom she has accumulated valuable materials and those for whom she has little information. For the latter, the teacher needs to plan for closer observation and recording of information so that a conference about such a child may have more meaning. The teacher may have recorded little about some children because she has been so absorbed in helping a difficult child or one who is more interesting to her. Through analyzing the children's records, she can plan to balance her time and attention to record activities of all children.

The planned conference should be a two-way affair in which the parent may not only learn of the child's progress, but may also have an opportunity to discuss differences of beliefs and procedures relative to working with the child. In many instances the child may not have made much progress or change.

Although the teacher recognizes the child as a growing, maturing individual, there are times when there appears to be little or no growth or change. The parent may not understand that this is satisfactory progress for the child at this time. The teacher needs to interpret what the behavior in the school situation means to the total growth of children.

Many teachers ask how they can actually communicate with a parent in a conference. A teacher needs to:

Recognize that each parent is an individual with his own needs, attitudes, values, and beliefs and accept him as a person even though differing with his beliefs.

Accept her responsibility to plan and prepare for the conference by organizing thoughts and materials prior to the conference.

Arrange for a place for the conference where there will be no interruptions.

Provide uninterrupted time and give the impression of being unhurried and interested in the child and the parent and of being informed as to goals for the progress of the child.

Be warmly accepting of what the parent has to contribute.

Be honest and truthful; keep personal feelings, facial expressions out of the situation and avoid appearing shocked.

Listen and find out why the parent feels or thinks as he does.

Encourage the parent to work out possible ways of meeting problems.

Avoid destructive criticism.

Allow time for changed thinking, do not force thinking or advice on parent.

Remember that the conference should be kept strictly confidential and treat a parental or child problem in confidence.

Conclude the conference on a helpful and professional basis, by questioning what suggestions the parent has for follow-through or further work with the child at school, as well as planning with the parent for home activities and for future conferences.

Reassure the parent that the teacher and the parent are partners in planning for and working with the child at all times.

The teacher can communicate by means of such phrases as "Have you noticed how well Susan can walk the planks now?" or "I have been so proud of Harold lately, he is beginning to share the tricycle more readily." The way a teacher phrases her statements and the tone of her voice will assist her in talking easily and profitably with any parent, and especially with one who may be on the defensive worrying over what problems the teacher has encountered with his child.

Since communication between teachers and parents is a two-way process, the following positive suggestions may assist adults in gaining insight into relationships with each other:

Show genuine interest in the child.

Avoid being authoritative or too "teaching."

Avoid arguments, becoming defensive over the way activities are carried through at school.

Listen for small cues about the child, then ask for clarification of certain points.

Avoid labeling or jumping to conclusions too quickly.

Offer several suggestions as to action rather than just telling what to do.

Attempt to arrive at some conclusions or points to be carried through by all concerned.

Observation Form for Parent

A short observation form may be helpful to both the teacher and the parent to use as a guide in a conference after the parent has observed the children in a group situation. A tentative form that could be useful follows.

AIMS OF THE PARENT OBSERVATION

1. To understand what children are like who are the same age as your child.
2. To know the daily schedule and the why's of various activities.
3. To learn how the teacher guides each child.
4. To attain insights as your child relates to the other children.

As you observe, try to be objective and avoid seeking out your child. Instead observe as many children as you can. Think of this experience as a learning one, stay in the background, write down questions or points as they occur. A planned conference will follow your observation.

POINTS TO OBSERVE

1. Observe the teacher in a variety of activities.
   a. Note her answers to children's questions.
   b. Watch how she relates to each child, what she says and does.
   c. How is she alert to any and all situations?
   d. How does she guide the group smoothly into other activities?
   e. How does she handle difficult situations?
2. Would you have handled activities in the same way or what would you have done differently? Why?
3. Observe certain children other than your own.
   Note the following:
   a. How they respond to other children. Examples of sharing, trying to join a group, difficult behavior.
   b. How independent are they in activities?
   c. Are there special abilities shown by certain children in art, music?
   d. Use of language, number of questions.
   e. Length of time the child stays with an activity.

Study Groups

A group of parents and teachers may wish to plan a few short discussion groups whereby all may study various aspects of child development or behavior. These groups may meet weekly or monthly, usually in a series consisting of planned meetings. One of the teachers who has been successful with group discussions may wish to begin the planning, leading, and organizing of such a group.

A few parents think that they or their child are the only ones who have a certain problem. Parents often find it very reassuring to discuss common problems. Most study groups have difficulty in finding a suitable meeting time because today's parents are so involved with many outside activities. The success of such a series of discussions comes from finding out ahead of time when the majority who are interested in a given problem can meet. Good leadership is very important. Interesting topics for discussion that will appeal to all attending will avoid turning the discussion into an information type of service. Adults benefit more from study through discussion groups because they have actually participated and voiced opinions, as well as shared experiences.

The Planned Parent Meeting

Many teachers plan meetings regularly to bring parents and teachers together. Some of these parent meetings are planned according to the recommendation of the National Congress of Parents and Teachers; whereas others are initiated only by the teacher. The purpose of a meeting may be to communicate school policies to parents, to let adults know what the daily program may be or what types of activities or seasonal events are planned, to view a good film, or to hear an authority on some phase of child development.

To hold the continued interest of the parent who previously has had children in school can be a challenge to teachers. If meetings become repetitious with little attention paid to the needs of parents, low attendance can be expected. Few fathers can attend parent meetings if they are at inconvenient times. A short social period designed to see that all parents become acquainted will help provide more and better meetings.

Some teachers may feel it is only necessary to have a meeting of parents at the beginning of the year to "inform the parents" of various school policies and another meeting at the end of the school year as a demonstration ceremony "to show the parents" how the child can perform. Such demonstrations may be overstimulating to children and really serve little purpose. Graduation ceremonies for young children may have meaning to adults but hold no place in the program of good schools.

The most successful meetings are ones in which parents help plan and actually participate in the meeting itself. A questionnaire sent home to parents with a list of topics as an "interest finder" may provide helpful information for a parent committee in organizing these meetings. It is important that all the members have an opportunity at the first meeting to list problems according to interests and to plan an agenda of topics. Usually a series of five or six discussion or study meetings will hold the interest better than a large number. Some topics that might lead to continuing group discussion are: Helping Children Learn to Share; How to Prepare the Preschool Child for the Arrival of a New Baby; The Grandparents' Role in the Child's Home; Facing Crises in the Home. The presentation of mental health plays related to one of these topics adds interest and variety.

To provide good group discussion, it may be advisable to utilize additional human or material resources. Advance planning with members to bring in pertinent material or information about a topic, circulating reading material ahead of time, using bulletin board displays prior to the day of the meeting of the study group, are essential activities for the leader's preparation to produce a good flow of discussion from all members.

Parent Participation

There are innumerable areas in the school's activities in which the parents can enrich the curriculum. Some parent participation will extend and enrich the school experiences; however, the type and the amount of the participation should be carefully considered so that the amount of the parent activity does not usurp the authority or the leadership of the teacher. Areas in which parent participation is particularly helpful include story-telling, music and art activities, field trips, group parties and picnics, library activities, celebration of special events or holidays, and parent work-parties. Or a parent could be a resource person in a specialized area or activity. As the parents work and talk together with the teacher and the children, they develop a greater interest in and a deeper understanding of the program. In each group of children there will be some parents who have special talents or hobbies and who have the time and facilities to profitably enrich the lives of all the children through use of this talent. Opportunities for all parents to contribute in a variety of activities will build pride in the child's heritage and appreciation of the worth and dignity of all occupations.

In the parent-cooperative school it is expected that each parent will participate at specific times during the week as an assistant teacher. In all the participation of adults in programs for young children, a plan of weekly discussions between the directing teacher and the parents is essential for good management.

Disadvantaged Parents

Parents may feel inferior to their child's teacher. The teacher may need to involve the parents in certain ways in order to know them better and to help them feel more at ease. Learning the skills and abilities of the parents can be a beginning in knowing the parents. A parent who plays a musical instrument or who has a special talent as well as the one who is willing to give a little of himself in other ways may feel more needed. A broader concept of parent involvement has evolved with Head Start. Parents participate not only as helpers and in parent meetings, but also in decision-making that involves certain policies and that concerns the program as related to their own children. Included is the parents' responsibility for carrying out the program both at home and school so that each supplements and supports the other. Additional suggestions may be found in Chapters 7 and 8.

In some regions, non-English speaking parents may need interpretation through a teacher skilled in their language. Also, adult classes in English may have to be arranged. A number of programs for parents that have been success-ful are described by several supervisors of parent education in certain Cali-fornia schools.[8]

Materials for Parents

A special room for parents at the school where they may spend time looking over books or other materials is important as a parent center for many occasions. In such a room several parents may visit together or a parent conference can be held. Children's art work or other creative achievements can be displayed, or a lending library of materials for parents can be arranged. Not all schools can provide a room for this purpose; however, it is important that some place be made available and reserved even though it be a corner in a room or the end of a hall.

Newsletters

Some schools send out weekly or monthly newsletters to parents; others distribute letters semiannually. As teachers and parents work together on this project, they will find that sharing experiences is most meaningful.

Brochures and bulletins as well as the informal newsletter have an important place in keeping parents informed and assisting them to understand and as-sume responsibility for extending the child's school experiences so that there is no conflict of goal or method between the home and the school. Through these brochures, parents learn about school policies related to school entrance, size of groups, purposes, special services, fees, health provisions, school cal-endar and plans for parent contacts, participation and visits, as well as of special activities scheduled throughout the year. Printed or mimeographed bulletins assist in interpreting the school program and in building understanding of the purpose and plan for the activities in the school year. Special bulletins can be prepared as new developments indicate a need; for example, during an epidemic a bulletin might give information and policies relating to school attendance or it might serve the purpose of informing the parents that their child had been exposed to a certain disease and indicate procedures to be observed in safeguarding the child and other children.

Bulletins and handbooks for parents should be carefully planned and pre-pared. Much of the content in these bulletins and brochures should be devoted to giving the parent information relative to the school's preparation for the child.

SUMMARY

The happiest and most successful teacher is the one who regards parents as partners and friends in the program of educating the child. Many feel this goal can best be met by insuring parents a larger role in determining and

---

[8]Milton Babitz, "Serving Families of the Underprivileged," *Calif. Educ.,* 11:3 (1964), pp. 17–19.

Figure 49. Parent participation can enrich and extend the school's activities.

carrying out the educational experiences of their young children. Parents have become active partners with schools and centers in the early education of their children. Instructional materials and strategies designed to be carried out in the home, or begun in the center or school and continued in the home, have become a major influence in early education. Parents working with professionals on advisory committees, or as aides, volunteers, or teachers have become a vital force in early childhood education. These innovations, resulting mainly from research findings indicating parent-child interaction as an essential ingredient of early foundation cognitive development, and the desire of minority group parents to have more control of their children's educational opportunities have placed new and major responsibilities on families, particularly on the parents of low-income families. In turn, the need for further education of the parents themselves has increased. Child development centers and schools for young children are becoming true partnership ventures with parents sharing equal responsibilities with staff personnel.

As children enter the traditional public kindergartens and first grades it is important that these responsibilities continue to be shared. Some of the ways to enhance this sharing are home visits, school visits, establishment of parent advisory committees, telephone conversations, casual visits, planned conferences, study groups and parent meetings, parent participation in the classroom, sharing of materials designed for parents, and periodic newsletters and other evaluative materials.

The outcome of early education may well rest primarily on the success or failure of parent involvement in the programs. Every good teacher hopes to help each child with whom she works and to challenge him to learn and to prepare for more complex tasks. These desires are fundamentally the same as those of the parents. The task of the school is one of finding ways through which the drive to reach the goals of both groups may be integrated into a common endeavor.

Suggested Activities

1. Interview a Child Development Center, nursery school, or kindergarten teacher as to the procedure used in making home visits or holding parent conferences. Determine the frequency of such visits, the attitude of the teacher concerning them. From this interview, evaluate your own feelings in regard to the necessity of holding these visits or conferences.

2. Attend a parent meeting held by a Child Development Center, nursery school, or kindergarten. Observe the reactions of parents and note types of questions asked by parents. Determine frequency of meetings and types of usual programs. Evaluate these meetings.

3. Observe the teacher-parent contacts when children are brought to the Center, nursery school, or kindergarten or when children are called for at the close of the school session. Note types of information obtained through such contacts for further insight into children's actions at school.

4. Study the parent bulletin board and parent bookshelf provided in a school for young children and make a report of your findings to the group.
5. Attend a Child Development Center, nursery school, or kindergarten Parent Advisory Council meeting. Determine the degree to which parents are involved in the control of their children's education.

Related Readings

Bossard, J. H. S., and E. S. Boll. *The Sociology of Child Development,* 4th ed. New York: Harper & Row, 1960.

Furman, R. A. "Experiences in Nursery School Consultations," *Young Children,* 22:2 (1966), pp. 84–95.

Fusco, Gene. *School-Home Parentship.* Department of Health, Education and Welfare. Washington, D.C.: U.S. Government Printing Office, 1964.

Ginott, H. G. *Between Parent and Child.* New York: Macmillan, Inc., 1965.

Hess, R. D., and Roberta Meyer Bear. *Early Education.* Chicago: Aldine Publishing Company, 1968, Chapter 8.

Hess, R. D., and Doreen J. Croft. *Teachers of Young Children.* Boston: Houghton Mifflin, 1972, Chapter 3.

Medinnus, Gene R. *Readings in The Psychology of Parent-Child Relations.* New York: John Wiley & Sons, 1967.

Points for Parents, No. 10. Washington, D.C.: Office of Economic Opportunity, 1966.

Parents Are Needed—Suggestions on Parent Participation in Child Development Centers, No. 6. Washington, D.C.: Office of Economic Opportunity, 1965.

Strang, Ruth. *Helping Your Child Develop His Potentialities.* New York: E. P. Dutton, 1965.

Willmon, Betty Jean. *The Influence of Parent Participation and Involvement on the Achievement of Pupils Attending Leon County Head Start Program as Measured by a Reading Readiness Test.* Unpublished Doctor's Dissertation, Florida State University 1967.

Wolman, T. G. "A Preschool Program for Disadvantaged Children—The New Rochelle Story," *Young Children,* 21:2 (1965).

Recording
the Development
of Children

The best possible time to obtain accurate information, not only concerning a child, but also concerning his family background, is during the preschool years. Teacher and parent feel a close bond of responsibility for a young child. Never again will the parent so freely express personal feelings, family problems, or concerns. A careful record, not in scores or numbers alone, but in accurate descriptive anecdotes, accounts of actual happenings, and of what is observed or said will provide the basis for each child's cumulative school file. Such records have proved of inestimable value to the child's teachers during later school years. Teachers of young children should be skilled in record keeping and in the ability to share the child's strengths, weaknesses, and needs with parents.

Consistent with changing points of view, what is considered as the most important information to know about a child's development has changed drastically during the past decade. Not only has new terminology come into the picture, but new concepts of evaluation have evolved. The use of tests and direct measurement continues, and searches for more meaningful ways of determining behavioral and growth changes are emerging. The search goes on because the traditional IQ and achievement test scores, although valuable, inadequately furnish information needed to justify the cost of intervention or early start programs. As in all phases of business and industry, such concepts as cost analysis and accountability have found their way into the educational world. With early education a high priority area of education, early childhood education has not escaped the demands of lawmakers and parents for account-ability. Early attempts using test results have failed to meet the critieria for success needed for continued support of early education programs. After a review of commonly accepted educational rationale for record keeping, the above concepts and their implementation will be treated in more detail later in this chapter.

Many teachers feel that permanent records should not be kept, especially if behavior of a personal nature is recorded. They argue that anyone reading these records later will likely be biased by them and thus actual harm to the child involved might result. Yet no one argues in this manner when physicians record events of a personal nature. The medical profession has long recognized the value of the developmental medical record. Child development specialists, too, know their value. The crux of the matter is that teachers who are truly professional know the importance of the past behavioral development of the children they teach. A child with special problems, even if these are no longer present, may need certain kinds of treatment if the problems are not to recur. Sound curriculum development is always based on the variation present in the needs of each group of children involved. Without a record of what has taken place in the past, the teacher is at a distinct disadvantage. The necessity of accuracy in recording thus becomes evident.

Because development and developmental changes occur so rapidly during the early childhood years, a carefully kept developmental record is essential in planning and providing the best possible activities, learning experiences, and opportunities for the health, safety, and well-being of each child. A teacher, knowing that a child walked a little later, or learned to talk somewhat slower than most children his age, will not have as high expectations for him in ac-tivities involving fine muscular control or language fluency as she will have for certain other children. In discussing problems of this type with parents, the teacher probably will learn of the parent's concern and be able to suggest ways in which the parent can be more accepting, thus reducing obstacles to the child's healthy personal or self-development.

The importance of parent-teacher conferences has been recognized and is discussed in Chapter 20. However, the value of a written record of the con-ference is often overlooked. While teachers find it difficult at times, it is desir-able to send to the parents by first-class mail a summary report of periodic parent-teacher conferences. Such letters may, of necessity, omit certain confidential information. Parents find this procedure very helpful and the school copy becomes a valuable part of the child's record.[1] Copies of these letters; health reports including immunization, illnesses, and annual physical examination results; family background file; and the informal type of observations mentioned earlier provide the best possible type of record keeping during the early childhood years. Formal or uniform printed report cards, though often used, probably have little or no place in the nursery school or kindergarten program.

The Space Age has already had its impact on early childhood education. There are those who believe that education, particularly reading, should be formalized as early as two or three years of age (see p. 185). Advocates cite the urgency of the times as necessitating immediate and large-scale action in which expediency sometimes takes priority. Only a careful evaluation of each child's abilities and developmental status can provide an adequate basis on which the teacher can judge when children possess a sufficient readiness for specific experiences such as beginning reading. The harmful effects, from a mental health point of view, of forcing learning experiences too early have long been known. Because readiness is related to maturation and development rather than chronological age, some children can benefit from certain experiences long before the majority of children of the same age. Guidance, based on observed facts, is as important during the early years as later; thus evaluation based on careful study and records of such evaluation becomes an important responsibility of the teacher of young children. The teacher must now become aware, more than ever before, of the importance of child study as a branch of science and the contributions that have and can be made.

Why Records Are Necessary

Innovation in program development often brings about changes in procedures, materials used, and teaching strategies employed. Furthermore, all of the above are apt to change from time to time as programmers discover "what is working" or "what is not working." This fact mandates careful recording at all times for more or less continuous decision making.

Studying Young Children

Present-day educational philosophy and practice stress the importance of providing a curriculum, not only in keeping with the goals and purposes of the school, but also in keeping with the ability, growth, and development of the children involved. This implies that the teacher must, at all times, know

[1] LaMittice Pearson, "Reaction of Teachers and Parents to the Letter-Summary Method Used for Reporting Parent-Teacher Conferences at the Florida State University Nursery School," unpublished Seminar Study, The Florida State University Institute of Human Development, Tallahassee, 1956.

a great deal about, and understand the motivations of the children she teaches. This is particularly true of teachers of young children, for important changes occur rapidly at this age. Following the work of Freud, "the present century has witnessed a shift to intensive investigations of early childhood from many theoretical points of view because of a realization of the importance of this period to later development and behavior."[2]

Colleges and universities were quick to see the value of having organized educational programs with young children for research purposes as well as for teacher education purposes. These laboratory and research programs necessitated extensive record keeping, often burdening teachers and students with the task of recording "everything observable."

Today, records are kept for specific purposes. The teacher in a nonresearch school must ask, "What is it that should be known about each child and why? What should be known about a child's family, his neighborhood, his health history, his personal characteristics, or his playmates?" Such questions must be answered and interpreted in terms of the school's purposes and goals. When this procedure is followed, it is likely that no two schools will keep identical records. While records of young children will have much in common, more extensive recording will be required for some children than for others. Although a school may wish to use a standard form for common information about all its children, it must also provide the necessary flexibility in record keeping to enable planning for maximum opportunities for each individual child. Overstandardization of records is probably as undesirable as standard reporting forms in child development centers, nursery schools, and kindergartens. In no way should this "be construed as an effort to depreciate the value of good records and reports. In fact, it may necessitate a new look at how and what to record."[3]

Murphy and research collaborators at Sarah Lawrence College presented a detailed study of one child as a sample of normal childhood.[4] This is an excellent example of the difficulty and complexity of the task of assessing and understanding personality development. Study of such materials will enable teachers to appreciate not only the importance of but also the care that should be exercised in gathering and recording information that will be of value in understanding children. A conscientious and continuous effort on the part of the teacher to learn more about each child in the group is essential to a good educational program for young children. Because memory cannot always be relied on to produce accurate recall of important events or the recurrence of significant behavioral incidents, a recording system is necessary. As previously pointed out, such a system must have flexibility to be effective.

[2]R. L. Witherspoon, "Studying Young Children," *Nursery School Portfolio*, Leaflet 9 (Washington, D.C.: ACEI, 1961), p. 1.

[3]Ibid.

[4]Lois Barclay Murphy, *Personality in Young Children*, Vol. II (New York: Basic Books, 1956).

What to Record

Obviously, everything that happens cannot be recorded. What is recorded, in addition to basic identification information and objective data such as height, weight, health immunizations, and similar materials, will be determined largely by the purpose of the school. Each item recorded should include the date, time, and place, and the name of the person recording. If the school is one of the usual university or college laboratory schools, the information will be organized in keeping with the needs of observing and participating students. The teacher should plan with the students' instructors so that the records will serve a useful purpose in the college classes as well as assist the teacher in an understanding of each child and his needs.

If the school serves as a research laboratory, the records will be kept to satisfy the demands of the particular research being undertaken at the time. Witherspoon indicates that:[5]

> An understanding of approaches used will make the research process more intelligent and provide better results. . . . An experiment may seek only a single, often minute, clue which when fitted into existing or proposed theories may set off a chain reaction of efforts needed in understanding children. A teacher or parent cannot usually be expected to do research, but cooperation with those who are trained to and whose work it is to do research can benefit all concerned.

Summarizing observations of children playing with miniature life toys, Hartley, Frank, and Goldenson have concluded:[6]

> These detailed records have unique value for studying the child at leisure, for checking impressionistic opinions against factual data, and for focusing several minds on a single problem without subjecting the child to intolerable scrutiny.

Many approaches to studying children have been proposed, each demanding different information and different types of records. Witherspoon states the present trend as follows:[7]

> Many students and teachers are finding a problem approach to child study more challenging and profitable than the traditional directed observation, case studies, cumulative records and testing "programs." New insights into individual children and individual parent or teacher motivations will be discovered when a group of teachers undertakes, for example, a study of the development of responsibility in children.

[5]Witherspoon, op. cit., p. 3.

[6]Ruth E. Hartley, L. K. Frank, and R. M. Goldenson, *New Play Experiences for Children* (New York: Columbia University Press, 1952), p. 49.

[7]Witherspoon, op. cit., p. 2.

When teachers and parents respond to a questionnaire prepared cooperatively and dealing with what they expect of children, they may be surprised to find that they are not in agreement. When children are asked to answer the same questions in relation to the expectations of home and school, more surprises may be expected. Such evidence provides excellent information for individual teacher-parent conferences, parent group discussions, and individual stock-taking by teachers. Getting ready to read, eating patterns, using free time, learning to be friends, what school life is like, leadership and later underachieving, and homework are only a few problems which make interesting "springboards" for studying young children.

The instructional process in the various areas of the curriculum is facilitated by a continuous record of the activities each child engages in. In order to insure a balance among the activities in which each child participates, the teacher keeps a record of his choices. A duplicated summary form containing the names of children and activities usually available provides a simple procedure for checking each child's participation. Samples of each child's paintings, crayon drawings, and so on, and teacher-made sketches of the results of participation in construction activities, along with dates and teacher comments, become a valuable part of the child's cumulative file.

Currently, in some situations stress is placed on the prior development of behavioral objectives. This simply means that if the teacher or the research staff is to be able to assess the effectiveness of the program efforts, the teacher must know prior to instruction what the end result of that instruction is expected to be. She must be able to observe, or otherwise be able to show, the degree to which each objective has been achieved. For example, if the stated objective is for each child to be able to recognize his name in print by the middle of the kindergarten year, the teacher (or test examiner) can arrange situations at mid-year that will indicate whether each child recognizes his name.

Starting with a set of generalized goals such as ability to classify objects by size, color, and form, the teacher then determines which specific concepts— like big, little, red, blue, round, square, and so on—the child must know in order to achieve the larger goal. Once these specific objectives are spelled out and placed in order of difficulty, teaching strategies and materials are devised to enable the child to experience and thus learn each of the specific concepts necessary to the achievement of the larger goal.

It is necessary, at any point in time during the above process, to assess where each child is if instruction is to be meaningful and efficient. As the rate of achievement will vary from child to child, it is essential that daily records be kept. If the objectives have been clearly defined, arranged in a sequence to fit the planned strategies, and available in multiple copies (one for each child), record keeping is greatly simplified. All the teacher has to do is enter the date after each item when it is achieved by each particular child. This is a type of "formative" evaluation and eventually becomes a record of "summative" evaluation. Formative evaluation takes place "while the course or instructional program is in progress, whereas 'summative' evaluation occurs at . . . the end of the instructional program."[8]

Of course it is impossible to foresee all events and their expected end results. Nevertheless, it is invaluable both from the standpoint of accountability and for planning teaching and learning situations to have an attainable plan for the group and for each individual child. The latter is essential to the success of an individually prescribed instruction program. Fitting expectancies to attained levels of development has long been a goal of education. Careful, accurate, continuous records for each child go a long way toward making this goal attainable.

Recording Observations

Most authorities agree that planned observation for a specific purpose and a more or less informal type of recording best serve the purposes for which most teachers of young children need records. It is desirable to begin records as early as possible: "Young children are honest and frank; they usually express their feelings freely in action and word. Teachers and parents let a golden opportunity pass when they learn to ignore the continuous activities, imaginations, and antics of the children in their presence. They tend to arrive at this conclusion: 'I just don't understand Mary. I guess she never will grow up and get out of my hair.' "[9]

However, although the above is essential for obtaining and maintaining an on-going global picture of each child's stream of development, such records are insufficient to meet today's accountability standards. Such concepts as cognitive stimulation, intervention, and compensatory education all imply that something is being interjected into the path that the child's development is taking to change its course. School lunch programs have been developed to assure proper nutrition for the growing child. Infant stimulation programs for babies and young children from deprived homes are designed to head off the cumulative learning deficit so commonly found among children from such homes. Remedial reading, for example, strives to help the child make up for missed experiences to enable him to read on a level with his more fortunate peers. It is no longer sufficient to assume that these and similar programs will produce the desired results or that IQ changes and test scores are the relevant criteria of measurement.

The first rule of good record keeping is to know what it is that should be recorded and why. Short and long term goals defined in attainable and observable objectives enable the teacher "to know" which behaviors and achievements to look for as a result of her instructional activities. Take time to stop, look, and listen. Be perceptive of the child's feelings whether they be those

---

[8]Daniel Tanner, *Using Behavioral Objectives in the Classroom* (New York: Macmillan, Inc., 1972), p. 5.

[9]Witherspoon, op. cit., p. 2.

of elation or those of fear and insecurity. Once the teacher learns how to be observant and to share in understanding the child's reactions at all times, it becomes easier "to accept a child for what he is and to include in his record significant events and signs of progress or retardation in his developmental pattern."[10]

A second rule is to recognize the importance of making and recording observations over a period of time. Young children grow and change rapidly and this pattern of change or lack of change should be clearly evident in the record. Many teachers have a pencil and pad handy at all times in order to briefly note situations or events that are expanded into a full account at the close of the day. Anecdotal records and behavior journals provide a convenient method of systematizing records.[11]

Recording of any kind requires objectivity. However, sensitivity to the meaning of what is observed is necessary if a desirable course of action is to be pursued. In the words of Lee and Lee:[12]

We must try as well as we can to "see" through his [the child's] perceptions—first, the situation he is in and, second, what his present actions may accomplish for him. We must put aside for the moment the situation as it is and try only to see it as he feels it. We must not consider the actions that he really might take in it, but rather we must only consider the actions that he, for many reasons, sees himself as able to make.

Many forms, record books, and manuals for recording the behavior of children have been published. Suchman has prepared one of the most extensive guides.[13]

THE CASE STUDY. Perhaps the most frequently used technique for studying children is the case study, which serves as a means of bringing together in an organized fashion all the information that can be learned about an individual child. Case studies probably serve their purpose best when made for particular children who do not seem to be getting along well academically or socially. The careful collection of accurate information about such a child will usually enable the teacher to evaluate the difficulty. Witherspoon points out that:[14]

If the child is to be helped, the teacher must know his unique characteristics and needs and have some knowledge of underlying developmental trends and an understanding of their causes. Because the case study entails a history of what has occurred, it can

[10]Witherspoon, op. cit., p. 2.

[11]For a detailed manual for use of the behavior journal see W. C. Olson, *Child Development*, 2nd ed. (Boston: D. C. Heath, 1959), pp. 467–473.

[12]J. M. Lee and Dorris M. Lee, *The Child and His Development* (New York: Appleton-Century-Crofts, 1958), p. 291.

[13]J. Richard Suchman, *Observation and Analysis in Child Development: A Laboratory Manual* (New York: Harcourt Brace Jovanovich, 1959).

[14]Witherspoon, op. cit., p. 3.

be very helpful in providing useful insights and at the same time point the way for future development. The case study should not be considered as merely a diagnostic tool but should spell out the direction of events and provide useful suggestions and recommendations for the future.

Most teachers have had adequate training that enables them to experiment with the use of case materials. At first, teachers tend to put emphasis on academic matters and their case studies tend to be heavily weighted with this type of information. Unfortunately, few school records contain even the most elementary knowledge of the home and family situations from which the children come. Undesirable behavior may be noted without reference to personal or social factors that may be the cause of the behavior described. It is easy for the teacher to interpret findings superficially on the basis of incomplete information and thus confirm earlier suspicions, preconceptions and prejudices. The writing of objective records requires skill and an open mind in order to see the deeper underlying emotional stresses and conflicts. At times it is desirable to call in the school psychologist or other specialist to assist with interpretation. Yet "Despite these shortcomings, the case study approach offers the teacher a challenging opportunity to study objectively certain youngsters and certain problems encountered."[15]

Case studies usually include detailed information organized under such broad categories as developmental history of the child, family characteristics and history, socioeconomic status and community relationships, behavior descriptions, and appraisal and recommendations. A recent manual providing a guide for the preparation of case studies has been prepared by Garrison, Kingston, and Dekle.[16]

THE BEHAVIOR JOURNAL. Many teachers find the behavior journal, referred to earlier, a convenient and valuable way to keep a continuous developmental record of children. Uses of the behavior journal as summarized by Olson are characteristic of the practical value of other observational techniques. His summary follows:[17]

1. In schools where the report to the parents is of the letter type, the recorded incidents furnish a useful basis for the behavioral aspects of the letter.
2. The journal reveals points of strength and weakness in the public relations program.
3. The recurring problems indicate points at which parent education is needed.
4. The records reveal gaps in curriculum planning.
5. Specific entries provide useful supplementary data for personal, educational, and vocational counseling.
6. The incidents may be used in instruction to illustrate principles of child development.

[15]Ibid., p. 4.

[16]K. C. Garrison, A. Kingston, and O. T. Dekle, *Students' Workbook for the Psychology of Childhood* (New York: Charles Scribner's Sons, 1967).

[17]Olson, op. cit., p. 471.

7. The making of the record stimulates teachers to the consideration of the problems of individual children.
8. The accumulation and persistence of unusual behavior items assists in locating children who require special diagnostic study and treatment.
9. The journal gives the specialist to whom the child is referred additional data for diagnostic purposes.
10. The record points to the incipience and development of special talents.
11. The journal furnishes material for appraisal and research. It may assist in locating significant research issues and in setting the conditions for objective and controlled studies.

TESTS.   In an educational world where precision and objective measurement are held in high esteem, it is only natural that an effort would be made to apply the same procedures to young children. Consistent with the testing movement in general, early efforts were made to develop tests to measure the intelligence of infants and young children. Typical of these efforts were the *Minnesota Pre-School Scale,*[18] *Cattell Intelligence Scale for Young Children,*[19] *Merrill-Palmer Scale,*[20] and *The California First Year and Pre-School Scales.*[21] The pioneering work of Gesell has provided a wealth of information about the growth and development of children.[22]

Currently, because of the need to measure results of programs for disadvantaged children, many new preschool tests are being developed although long-range values have not yet been established. It is likely that many valuable tests will emerge as a result of the Head Start research program of the Office of Child Development. (Tests being widely used are the *Peabody Vocabulary Test, The Illinois Test of Psycholinguistic Abilities* (ITPA), *The Revised Stanford Binet,* and the *Bayley Scales of Infant Development*). Test results used in the context of the purpose for which the test was intended can be invaluable to the teacher in her day-to-day planning as well as providing an index of progress over time. However, using tests to predict later aptitudes can be very hazardous. Preschool tests of intelligence, for example, have been repeatedly shown to be poor predicators of later intelligence test scores.[23] Preschool tests require special training and skills not commonly acquired in testing courses. Tests should not be administered to preschool children unless the examiner is thoroughly familiar with the characteristics of the age of the child being tested if the results are to be valid and useful.

[18]Florence L. Goodenough and M. J. Van Wagenen, *Minnesota Preschool Scales—Forms A and B,* rev. ed. (Minneapolis: Educational Test Bureau, 1940).

[19]Psyche Cattell, *The Measurement of Intelligence of Infants and Young Children* (New York: Psychological Corporation, 1940).

[20]Rachel Stutsman, *Mental Measurement of Preschool Children with a Guide for the Administration of the Merrill-Palmer Scale of Mental Tests* (Yonkers, N.Y.: World Book, 1931).

[21]Nancy Bayley, "On the Growth of Intelligence," *Amer. Psychol.,* 10:12 (1955), pp. 805–818.

[22]Arnold Gesell and C. S. Amatruda, *Development Diagnosis,* 2nd ed. (New York: Paul B. Hoeber, 1947).

[23]Ibid.

SUMMARY

With the advent of programs for young children based on such concepts as "intervention," "cognitive stimulation," and "compensatory education" as opposed to programs based on more or less fixed inherent and maturational influences, new dimensions have been added to evaluation and record keeping. Of necessity, programs designed to achieve specific goals and desired end results require a new look at the importance of records of children's development. In addition, these programs require careful recording of instructional and teaching strategies employed as well as a continuous assessment of progress. If properly done these records will be an invaluable adjunct to the "child study" type records so long in use. Together such records should help "fit" instructional practices to child needs.

The keeping of developmental records, if they are used later, is one of the most important tasks of the teacher of young children. Adequate records compiled during the early years provide the foundation of, and point the direction for, each child's cumulative school file. They are an invaluable adjunct when reporting to parents whether verbally or in writing. Copies of letters to parents summarizing conferences add valuable understandings to the cumulative file.

Recording skill requires objectivity and a perceptive awareness of the meaning underlying behavior and events. To be of greatest value, records must be kept continuously and maintain flexibility in terms of procedures adopted and the end results desired. Of the many possible study and reporting procedures used today, records of formative and summative evaluation objectively recorded, well-planned observational techniques, purposeful case studies, and concientiously kept behavior journals are among the most promising and challenging. Results of standardized tests when used for the purposes intended provide an invaluable guide to curriculum planning and evaluation. Frequent analyses of the information thus secured and recorded in each child's cumulative file provides one of the most useful means that the teacher has at her disposal to assist in understanding and guiding the growth, development, and behavior of young children.

Suggested Activities

1. Visit the centers or schools for young children in your community and determine the methods used in each for reporting to parents. Summarize your findings and make recommendations for changes or improvement in these practices.

2. Write to public schools having kindergartens and ask for an explanation of the methods used for reporting pupil progress to parents. Request samples if formal report cards or printed evaluation forms are used. Evaluate your findings in light of the material in this chapter.

3. While visiting schools for young children in your community, ask about the type

and number of records kept. Are these records sent to the school when the child enters first grade? Do they become a part of the school's cumulative record for each child?

4. Ask first grade teachers what information they would like to have on each entering child. From these suggestions, formulate a possible record plan for obtaining the necessary information.

5. Discuss the pros and cons of using formal report cards in nursery schools and kindergartens.

6. Review several recent research reports to find out what tests and techniques are currently being used with young children.

Related Readings

Bayley, Nancy. "On the Growth of Intelligence," *Am. Psychol.*, 10:12 (1955), pp. 805–818.

Buros, O. K., ed. *The Fifth Mental Measurements Yearbook*. Highland Park, N.J.: Gryphon Press, 1959.

Cattell, Psyche. *The Measurement of Intelligence of Infants and Young Children*. New York: Psychological Corporation, 1940.

Garrison, K. C., A. J. Kingston, and O. T. Dekle. *Students' Workbook for the Psychology of Children*. New York: Charles Scribner's Sons, 1967.

Gesell, A., and C. S. Amatruda. *Development Diagnosis*, 2nd ed. New York: Paul B. Hoeber, 1947.

Goodenough, Florence L., and M. J. Van Wagener. *Minnesota Preschool Scales—Forms A and B*, rev. ed. Minneapolis: Educ. Test Bureau, 1940.

Guilford, J. P. "Intelligence: 1965 Model," *Am. Psychol.*, 21:1 (1966), pp. 20–26.

Langdon, Grace, and Irving W. Stout. *Teaching in the Primary Grades*. New York: Macmillan, Inc., 1964, Chapter 20.

Lessinger, Leon M. *Every Kid a Winner: Accountability in Education*. New York: Simon & Schuster, 1970.

Mager, R. F. *Preparing Instructional Objectives*. Palo Alto, Calif.: Fearon Publishers, 1962.

Olson, W. C. *Child Development*. Boston: D. C. Heath, 1959, Chapter 11, Appendix D, E.

Peterson, Dorothy G., and Velma D. Hayden. *Teaching and Learning in the Elementary School*. New York: Appleton-Century-Crofts, 1961, Chapter 15.

Stutsman, Rachel. *Mental Measurement of Preschool Children with a Guide for the Administration of the Merrill-Palmer Scale of Mental Tests*. Yonkers-on-Hudson, N. Y.: World Book Co., 1931.

Suchman, J. F. *Observation and Analysis on Child Development: A Laboratory Manual*. New York: Harcourt Brace Jovanovich, 1959.

Tanner, D. *Using Behavioral Objectives in the Classroom*. New York: Macmillan, Inc., 1972.

Thomas, A., et al. *Behavioral Development in Early Childhood*. New York: New York University Press, 1963.

Physical Facilities, Equipment, and Materials

Chapter **22**

In planning for and selecting the physical facilities, equipment, and materials for any age group, consideration must be given to what the child is like, his nature and needs, and how he learns. Recognition must be given to the fact that *children are alike yet different.*

The design of a center should fit the goals for the center. Provision should be made for physical facilities in five general areas: (1) a place for the less mature child to play with blocks or crafts, housekeeping facilities, and manipulative toys; (2) a room or an area for the more mature group which has books, typewriter, audio-visual toys and equipment, science projects, a display space for exhibits, and a tutoring area; (3) an administrative area; (4) a testing center and, if observation is a part of the program, an observation booth; and (5) an outdoor area which extends the indoor area and which has rebuildable structures, water and sand areas, and animals for children to feed, and, if small, to hold. Good lighting is necessary whether the center is a new or a remodeled building.

Hymes points out that "since young children are constantly active they need two kinds of classrooms: simple space indoors and more generous space outdoors."[1] While physical facilities do not determine the environment, satisfactory facilities greatly assist in developing a challenging and satisfactory learning situation. Either the absence of adequate facilities and materials, or the provision of quantities of inappropriate materials may curtail the effectiveness of the learning.

An analysis of pages 26–46 shows that the young child is active and vigorous, curious about his environment, learns from his peers, and learns through concrete rather than abstract experiences. Therefore, the physical facilities and equipment provided for this age group should be functional for the development of children at this maturity level and should be selected to allow for a wide range of abilities and growth patterns.

Jenkins, Schacter, and Bauer point out that although many environmental factors influence emotional growth,[2] "any assessment of social growth is relative because it may change according to the situation in which the child finds himself." The most vital and unchanging need in a good environment for children is good people. Parents are most important and the wise teacher draws the parents into the classroom to observe, to assist, to aid, to share, and to cook.

A good teacher is relaxed and pleasant, likes people, is sensitive to needs and values, is friendly yet firm, gives affection without involvement, has a sense of humor and is always a learner. The teacher starts the year armed with facts; thus, she is able to interpret and justify the plan for each child because she knows what she is doing and why as she selects and uses the facilities to further the development of the children.

Among other important adults who shape the preschool child's environment are the doctor, the nurse, the social worker, the secretary, the custodian, the nutritionist, the aide, and the volunteers. When all become an effective working team with mutual respect and understanding of children, they become a vital part of the child's learning environment.

Simple and safe facilities, equipment, and furnishings permit freedom of activity and provide for creativity on the part of the child. The selection of the site, the arrangement of the classroom, and the plantings in the outdoor area stimulate learning and interest the child in the natural environment as well as encourage him to contact his physical world.

In one definition, "the learning environment is the atmosphere one senses as he approaches a school or looks in the door of a classroom. . . . The best learning environment is one which stimulates the individual to reach constantly for new horizons, new understandings, new experiences, to ask questions as

[1] J. L. Hymes, Jr., *Teaching the Young Child.* (Columbus, Ohio: Charles E. Merrill Company, 1968), p. 92.

[2] Gladys G. Jenkins, Helen Schacter, and W. W. Bauer, *These Are Your Children* (Chicago: Scott, Foresman, 1953), p. 13.

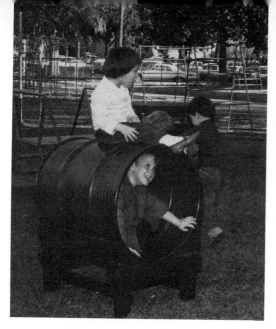

Figure 50. A large pipe set lengthwise and firmly in a base affords opportunities for children to climb over and through it. A tree trunk can be used for climbing too. Old equipment, such as cars or boats, stimulates eager minds and bodies.

eagerly at forty as at four."[3] It is true also that, "A child responds to the places in which he finds himself and the things which surround him as well as the people. Places can be frightening or friendly."[4] This concept of the learning environment makes it essential that all physical facilities, equipment, and materials be considered carefully in their relationship to the total learning situation and that they be selected and used in accordance with basic principles of child growth.

According to Coble, the ratio between adults and students determines the room arrangement and choice of activities. The planning for and arrangement of facilities should take into account interrelated activities and housekeeping responsibilities so as to make for smooth operation of the child's day of play and work times, transition times, and eating and resting periods. Some simple reminders listed were (1) Equipment and materials requiring close eyework should be in the best light; (2) creative work, block building, and so on, need protection from traffic; (3) space for quiet activities should be provided together, and space for noisy activities should be together and removed from quiet areas; and (4) all equipment and material should be appropriate and in good condition.[5]

Hochman states that, "A room efficiently organized in terms of space, orderliness, comfort, and convenience gives the children better opportunity for

[3]R. R. Leeper, ed., *Creating a Good Environment for Learning* (1954 Yearbook, ASCD) (Washington, D.C.: ASCD, 1954), p. 3.

[4]Ibid., p. 8.

[5]Clara Coble, "Teacher—Planner of the Nursery School," *Space Arrangement Beauty in School* (Washington, D.C.: ACEI, 1958), p. 6.

working effectively and creatively."[6] Even though kindergartens may meet basic requirements of space, movable furniture, varied material, and generous storage space, they may still need reorganization in light of newer program concepts.

Berson says that before determining the kinds of physical facilities needed, "first outline the characteristics, aims, objectives and purposes of the program and then determine exactly how many pupils, teachers, aides, parents, and others are to be accommodated."[7] Dinkmeyer states that "the most significant factors in environment appear to be those which promote an atmosphere of security, of basic trust, whether it be between parent and child or teacher and child."[8]

Environmental factors can operate to facilitate or inhibit intellectual development. There is also considerable evidence to show that the early years of a child's life are the most critical period of perception and intellectual development. Therefore, the classroom environment should provide challenges and should lead to definite goals.

The attitudes and feelings of the young child in his first educational adventure are extremely important to him at this age and to his continued school experiences. The school environment should invite the child to participate in activities and to have experiences through which he may learn the joy of discovering, of exploring, of creating, of experimenting and of observing. This requires many types of materials and equipment in a suitable space; however, the amounts, the variety, and the timing for use should not be such that they overpower the child. The skillful teacher retains some materials and draws upon them throughout the year in order to provide new, richer, and more challenging experiences. She continues the use of many materials over an extended period and adds others as situations and timing make it advisable.

Space is an important factor in providing a rich environment for learning, but it is only significant to the degree that it assists in providing a suitable climate for learning. The environment should include equipment and materials that are functional for the development of the desired learnings, appear beautiful and comfortable from the child's point of view, and challenge the child to develop emotionally and socially as well as mentally and physically.

Since the classroom is for the child, it needs to reflect children's tastes, interests, and activities. Brightness and balance in tone, beauty and hygiene, friendliness and warmth, freedom for movement, places to be alone, arrangements for small cluster groups and for the total group to work, are requisites. The wise teacher includes the challenge of color in a room that by shape and

[6]Vivienne Hochman, "Kindergarten-Primary Rooms Reflect Interests," *Space Arrangement Beauty in School* (Washington, D.C.: ACEI, 1958), p. 7.

[7]Minnie P. Berson and William H. Chase, "Planning Preschool Facilities," *Amer. Educ.*, 2:10 (1966), pp. 7–11.

[8]Don C. Dinkmeyer, *Child Development, The Emerging Self* (Englewood Cliffs, N.J.: Prentice-Hall, 1965), p. 81.

layout makes provision for exploration, play, and rest, as well as crannies and nooks for quiet thinking and work.

According to Berson, "Even a community well able to afford extravagance today prefers schoolrooms of simple, free flowing lines, natural materials, and an absence of ostentation."[9] Converted buildings, including warehouses and fire stations are being used in many programs. Quonset huts, churches, and many types of mobile units serve as a basis for a broader type of service which contacts children and families who were not reached before.

Olson points out that "Health, comfort and safety are the primary concern" in planning the environment for children and youth.[10] Clean air, adequate lighting, temperature within a satisfactory range for child adjustment without strain, a sound level that does not demand competition from external or internal noises, and convenient movable furniture are major specifications for the physical environment.

During World War II the importance of suitable housing for schools for young children was brought sharply into focus. However, prior to that date leaders in programs for young children had placed much emphasis upon developing understanding among architects and persons planning school buildings as to what was required to insure facilities functional in terms of the projected curriculum. The architect, today, has this concept of planning rooms that will stimulate the child's imagination rather than providing a room of beauty that may be static forever. Varied floor levels and ceilings relieve monotony and a more friendly atmosphere is created by lower ceilings. However, some ceilings need to be higher to accommodate some types of play apparatus and equipment that is used indoors.

In planning for space, consideration must be given to the provision for adequate amounts of indoor and outdoor areas according to location, situation, and climate. The proportionate relationship between indoor and outdoor space will differ also in terms of the program to be developed. The location should be accessible to the children and on a site that is drained satisfactorily, is away from distracting noises, and is removed from people who will be annoyed by the children's voices while at play. Adequate and safe parking while vehicles take on and discharge children is essential. The outdoor area needs to be regular in outline so that outdoor play can be supervised satisfactorily. The number of children that should be enrolled depends on the amount of space that can be provided in relation to the number of qualified personnel employed.

The classroom building needs to be adaptable for use, properly insulated against heat and cold, fireproofed and soundproofed, built close to the ground, free from exposed wires, and accessible for delivery of supplies as well as for garbage pick-up and disposal.

Suitable light, both artificial and natural, is required for program development, but it should be used wisely in order to safeguard the child's eyesight.

[9]Minnie P. Berson, *Kindergarten, Your Child's Big Step* (New York: E. P. Dutton, 1959), p. 81.

[10]W. C. Olson, *Child Development*, 2nd ed. (Boston: D. C. Heath, 1959), p. 67.

Figure 51. Blocks are essential in good centers for young children. They should be sturdy, of hardwood, free of splinters, and sanded smooth. In addition to providing for large muscle activity, blocks provide endless opportunities for the creation of shapes and forms. They are practical, too, in that they can be used for the basic structure of many activities.

Room arrangements that make satisfactory use of available light are especially important for activities requiring concentration, such as painting and looking at books. Adequate space will make this possible.

Heat and ventilation, sanitary facilities including drinking fountains, lockers, storage for children's wraps and possessions, the walls, the floors, furniture and equipment, dining facilities, space for isolation of a sick child including toilet facilities, storage space for teacher use, space for conferences —all require careful consideration and planning as the provision for space is made.

CRITERIA FOR SELECTION OF FACILITIES

It is generally accepted that the physical facilities in schools for young children should be checked according to the following criteria.[11]

---

[11]Address by Dr. Hazel Gabbard, reprinted in *Good Schools for Children Under Six in Florida*, Florida State University, Tallahassee, 1955, pp. 29–30.

1. Is the indoor and outdoor space large enough to permit each child to investigate, explore, and experiment?
2. Does the room arrangement provide for a traffic pattern that permits children to move about with freedom and safety?
3. Is there a sufficient variety of equipment and materials so that some children may play alone, some engage in parallel play and others in groups?
4. Are there materials and equipment for active work and play as well as for quiet work and play?
5. Is each article adaptable to many uses or limited to one? For example, a climbing tower can be used for several purposes, a slide for only one.
6. Is the article so finished and constructed that it will withstand vigorous use by many young children?
7. Must the article be permanently placed or can it be removed when the children have lost interest in it or need stimulation? Is there adequate storage space for such articles when not in use?
8. If adequate equipment and material cannot be supplied, what makeshift article has the teacher provided which will insure a well-rounded kindergarten program? (If only temporary storage space is possible, what improvised arrangements have been made to help children develop desirable work habits and orderliness?)
9. Does each article of material and equipment have a specific educational objective appropriate to the development and needs of kindergarten children?

INDOOR SPACE

The schoolroom should be large enough for children to live and work together without being regimented. The inside work space should be adaptable, flexible, livable, and homelike. The shape and layout are significant. A rectangular room may lend itself more readily to activities than a square one. The room should be on the ground floor and have no hidden areas so that it can be easily supervised. It should also be adjacent to toilet facilities. The entrance should be near the street level. The amount of space should be adequate for the children to move about easily so they may use large muscles; approximately 40 to 60 square feet per child is recommended. If there is no space to grow plants outdoors, opportunities for this activity should be provided indoors.

Acoustics

Recent information concerning the effect of noise on man both physically and psychologically has pointed to the need for providing satisfactory acoustics in schools for young children. Provision for appropriate communication is difficult when noises from air conditioning and other mechanical equipment, as well as noise of cars and other unwanted sounds, come into the classroom. To eliminate some of the sound, draperies, carpets on floors, and soft materials on walls and ceilings may be added.

Acoustical absorption underfoot appears to be more efficient per dollar

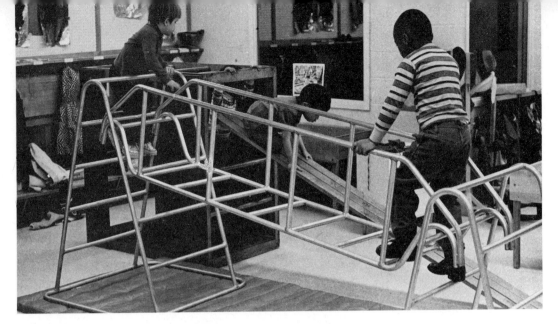

Figure 52. Movable equipment for climbing can be used indoors on cold and rainy days. Open shelves are needed for storage.

invested than materials placed overhead. A carpeted floor is attractive and easy to maintain. It provides a comfortable surface on which the child may work. (However, there should be a hard, uncarpeted surface for art work.) This area needs to be cleaned daily with water and after any spill during the day. Using carpet of different colors helps to separate the areas of work and provides a pleasing appearance.

Noise from tables and chairs may be reduced by padding with pieces of carpeting on furniture legs. Tablecloths on luncheon tables to reduce clatter, area rugs, a padding on furniture legs, removable pads on surface of tables used for pounding and hammering, and a door or movable screen to keep out kitchen noises are some inexpensive ways to eliminate unnecessary sounds. Some suggested acoustical principles include provision of fewer and movable walls, acoustical flooring, a luminous ceiling, semi-insulation to soften the most fundamental sound reflecting surfaces, satisfactory room arrangements, and isolation of plumbing piping.[12]

Acoustical ceilings ranging from 10 to 11 feet high are desirable to relieve noise and to provide for a feeling of freedom.

Walls

The wall space should be usable and employed to further on-going activities and not to exhibit the best work of a few children. An abundance of "pinning space" at the eye level of the child is desirable.

The arrangement of windows and doors should allow large spaces for

[12]D. W. Rapp, *Noise in the Nursery School*, An unpublished paper, Human Development Institute, Florida State University, 1966.

425

bulletin boards, for attaching things to pull on, and for a small amount of chalkboard. However, portable chalkboards are generally considered preferable to those fastened to the wall because they can be used more functionally. If movable, they may also serve as room dividers or screens. Green chalkboards are more aesthetic and generally considered to be better for the eyes.

The walls may be a type of vinyl porous material, soft pine, or of some material that will deaden the noise and can be used for bulletin space. Walls that are washable, especially to the height of the child, are recommended. Shifting inside walls provide for a wider variety of activities and a greater use of space. According to type, the walls, floor, and ceiling will either subdue or add to the noise and thereby contribute to or detract from the provision for a classroom climate suitable for work and play. Carefully selected colors can add to the light available in the room.

Rooms with walls in a variety of colors provide beauty and challenge as well as add to the feeling of spaciousness. This challenge of color and space is a requisite in the well-planned schoolroom. Upon entering the room, the child, the parent, and the teacher should have a feeling of relaxation as well as challenge; however, the primary colors and challenging situations should be so skillfully used that they do not overstimulate the child. Primary colors, which children like, need to be carefully selected and utilized for toys and equipment to add brightness and to provide accent in an environment of the more subdued tones of the walls and the plain floors.

Floors

The floors should be sanitary and of a material that can easily be kept clean. Flooring material needs to deaden sound and be suited to hard wear. Because, in schools for young children, much of the child's activity is on the floor, provision for warmth and freedom from drafts is a necessity. No bare concrete flooring should be allowed in the floor space. Popular floor coverings include linoleum, a variety of woods, and rubber or plastic tiles.

The dining area may also be the playroom. The floors in this dining space, the tables, and the chairs should be of materials that can be easily cleaned and the space should be adequately ventilated. All food preparation and serving centers should conform to the standards established by the local and state boards of health.

Windows and Doors

The exits and windows are an important part of the learning environment. Therefore, their placement and type need careful consideration. The windows should be low enough so that a child can see out. They should be fitted with shades or blinds. Translucent shades or Venetian blinds assist in regulating the light; however, care must be exercised in adjusting Venetian blinds in order to avoid bands of bright light or direct sunlight. An overhanging roof and/or awnings help to regulate the glare. All windows need to be fitted with guards, screens, or both. The windows in the area used for dining must be screened. If any of the windows look out on a brick wall or unsightly area this space may be covered and used advantageously for classroom displays.

All outside doors should be light in weight so that the children can handle them easily. They should be hung so as to open out of the building. Double doors leading to the playground are desirable. The doorknobs should be low enough to be in easy reach of the child and of the type that he can readily turn. No self-locking or swinging doors should be included.

Ventilation, Heat, Light, and Drinking Fountains

Draft-free cross ventilation by open windows is desirable. However, climatic conditions in given areas need to be considered. The windows should be easily operated and screened with the screens hooked beyond the child's reach. Humidity should range between 50 per cent and 65 per cent and the temperature maintained evenly throughout the room between 68° and 72° F. The use of radiant heat has become more widespread even in climates that require little heat. Thermostats and thermometers should be located at the child's eye level or breathing level when seated. These are not for child use, however; therefore, provision should be made to protect them. This will make it possible for them to also be used as a functional part of the curriculum. All heaters, registers, and fans should be provided with a heavy safety guard. Electric outlets are needed every 10 to 12 feet. They should be covered and above the reach of the child. The fuse box should be convenient to the teacher but beyond the child's reach.

Although specialists plan the lighting, the teacher should be alert to the need for control of light in terms of changing conditions throughout the day. Plans must be made for light control in order to insure ample quantity of good light evenly distributed over the room. Too bright a light is distracting and frustrating to the child. Skillful use of paint may assist in making dark areas brighter and to control the areas which are too bright.[13] Skylights and transluscent walls help to maintain an effective light situation. Natural light is better for displays of work.

Rest or Sleeping Facilities

Provision for rest is recognized as important in schools for young children; hence, rest facilities are considered essential. All schools should make some provision for relaxation or rest periods. If the length of the day requires that sleeping arrangements be provided, they should include removable washable covers for cots, portable screens, and storage space for sleeping facilities. Cots, pads, mats, butcher paper, small rugs, or blankets are frequently used for the rest period. Sanitation and laundering may present a problem. Cor-

---

[13]N. L. Engelhardt, N. L. Engelhardt, Jr., and S. Leggett, *Planning Elementary School Buildings* (New York: F. W. Dodge Corp., 1953).

rugated paper cut in proper lengths and bound at ends has been used satisfactorily. This type of paper mat may be discarded and replaced frequently as
it becomes worn or soiled. The economy of this type of pad makes it practical,
for all mats may be destroyed in the event of an epidemic. It should not be
necessary to move furniture in the room in order to put cots in place for sleeping. The cots may range in size from 27 by 48 inches for four-year-olds, 27 by
52 inches for four- to five-year-olds, to 27 by 54 inches for children of five to
seven years of age.

Sanitary Facilities

Running water and sinks are essentials in preparing for and cleaning up
after activities in the school. The toilet and handwashing facilities should be
adjacent to or easily accessible both to the outdoor and the indoor space. One
large or two smaller rooms are needed. One for boys and one for girls are provided in some localities; in other localities a large one is used by both groups.
Exhaust fans in toilet facilities and an outside window are requisites. The toilet
floor should be of ceramic or washable tile. One lavatory and one toilet for every
ten children is essential but a ratio of one toilet for five children is preferred.
Toilet fixtures with seats varying from 10 to 13 inches from the floor and
lavatories 23 to 24 inches from the floor are desirable if four- and five-year-
olds are included. The sizes will vary according to the sizes of the children who
will use them, However, steps can be used for the smaller children to adjust
the higher fixtures for their use. Provision for the fixture of suitable size assists in the development of routines and also promotes a feeling of self-confidence and independence within the child. The lavatory should be placed
near the door as a reminder to the child to use it after toileting. The sink in
the bathroom and playroom should be large, have automatic tepid water—
no hot water—and be equipped with a disposal drain to catch clay, sand, and
so on, before draining into the regular disposal unit.

Lockers and Storage Space

Well-planned storage space assists the child in learning to accept responsibility for caring for floor equipment. Each child needs a place of his own to
store his wraps and personal belongings. Locker space may take many forms
but all types should provide for easy usability by the child. Usually 10 to 15
inches is adequate for depth and 10 to 12 inches for width. The height may
total 35 inches with rod or hooks for clothing and include a shelf 7 inches from
top and a rack for shoes 10 inches from the floor. The actual space for hanging
coats must be adequate for the child who uses the locker. If the coats and rest
pads are stored in the individual lockers, the space should be increased in
height and width accordingly. Many nursery schools and kindergartens provide special coat facilities.

The necessary supply cabinets may need to have doors; however, many
cupboards and shelves can be built in sections and can be easily moved to

Figure 53. Running water and sinks are essentials in preparing for and cleaning up after activities. Fixtures of suitable size assist in the development of self-confidence and independence.

make work centers or for use as screens. These will need to be equipped with casters, drawers, and trays, as well as open shelves, according to plans for use. Storage space should be provided for large toys, large paper, blocks, and supplies as well as for the smaller articles. All storage space should be well ventilated.

There must be storage space for art materials. Arrangements should be made for both large and standard sized materials. Smaller materials, such as scissors and paints, need separate storage space.

The adults need storage space too. This should include storage space for wraps; space for a lavatory, commode, and possibly a shower; a table or desk; a comfortable chair and something to "stretch out" on. The space should allow for privacy for the adult and also for conferences with child, parent, or fellow workers.

A tutoring booth is essential so that the child may be free from his peers and devote all his time to his special work while he is working with teacher or consultant. This area also can be used for testing of individual children or a small group. The space may also be used for small group or individual activities. This area may be arranged by the use of bookcases and dividers on casters; however, the walls should be transparent or low enough for supervision if there is only one teacher for the center.

Figure 54. Each child needs a place of his own to hang up his wraps and store his boots and other personal belongings.

OUTDOOR PLAY SPACE

Children need to play outdoors. The children who live in apartments or crowded housing units especially need to have opportunities for outdoor play; they need to feel the wind on their faces or hair, to see blossoms floating by, to watch things grow as they feel the grass under their feet and even between their toes.

Outdoor space should be so arranged and equipped that it provides opportunities for enriching experiences rather than restricting activities. If the outdoor space is adjacent to indoor play space, much of the equipment can be used in either indoor or outdoor activities.

From 75 to 200 square feet per child under seven years of age should be provided for outdoor play space depending on location and program. This should be adjacent to the playroom and located on one side of the building so as to be easily supervised. The covering of outdoor space may vary and include both grass and paved surfaces. All play space should be durable and easily cleaned, be able to shed water and dry quickly, be free from safety or fire hazards, and be made of resilient surface so it will not injure a child if he falls upon it. Shade is essential, and a balance between sun and shade should be established. Trees are valuable for shade, light, and sound control. A covered terrace or porch should be approached by a ramp (no steps) located near the playroom and entered through double doors off the playroom.

The outdoor space should provide for a variety of activities such as climbing, using wheel toys, gardening, water play, and for cages for outdoor animals used as pets or for observation. Water for plant care and water play should be available. However, sanitary provision for the water and water drainage is essential. Outdoor storage space for large toys and equipment and materials for outdoor play should be located near the playground and easily accessible by a ramp rather than steps. The ceiling should be high enough for an adult to stand. Safety and fire precautions must be observed and the surface should be waterproofed.

In hot, extremely cold, and rainy climates it is well to have a part of the space covered. Shelters from prevailing winds can be provided. The play areas should provide both for sunny and for shady spaces.

Outdoor space should be securely fenced with a nonsplintering material and kept in good repair. The construction should be such that it will have child-proof exits. It needs to be sufficiently high and constructed that it will not invite climbing. A gate that can be locked should be provided. The space should be landscaped for privacy. The use of border plants will make for a spacious park-like atmosphere as well as provide protection from prevailing winds. All play space should be free from rocks and glass. All sandboxes or places reserved for digging need to be protected from animals and covered when not in use. Concrete sandboxes which may be emptied and covered when not in use are cheaper if used over a long period of time. However, this type of sandbox should have adequate drainage before pouring. A digging area that is not part of the formal garden provides freedom for use and yet protects the child.

Landscaping is particularly important for the young child. He needs to have corners for play, secret places for being alone and for small group activities but not away from the watchful eyes of the teacher. Hardy plants that bloom at different seasons provide a pleasing effect but they should be placed so as not to interfere with the child's play. Adequate landscaping helps to provide for protection from the weather.

The surface of the outdoor play area is particularly important. Grass is the best possible surface and some grassy surface should be provided for all centers. A part of the area may be sloping, but all areas should be well drained. Surfaces for wheel toys, which are important to the child's development, need a hard base.

EQUIPMENT AND MATERIALS

There should be a close relationship between the equipment and materials provided and the curriculum objectives of the school. The purposes and goals of the program give direction to the use of the equipment and materials. In the chapters on "Play Activities" and "Health and Safety," the selection and use of equipment and materials have been presented as they would be used in the development of that phase of the program. Likewise, as each curriculum area was presented, the equipment and materials needed and their use were discussed.

The placement of equipment stimulates play but may also create a problem if not carefully situated so that children can move from one piece of equipment to an adjacent play center without meeting a safety hazard.

Throughout the day and during the entire school year, each child needs equipment to climb on, to hang from, to stretch to and from, and to balance on; materials and equipment for dramatic play, for rhythms, for creative expression through art experiences, for constructing and building. That is, he needs equipment and materials that demand that he do something as contrasted with equipment and materials that are finished products to admire and to use.

Boxes, barrels, ramps, wagons, pull toys, shovels and hoes, parts of old automobiles, rubber tubes, kegs with rubber tops for drums, live animals, large and small blocks, and rafts and pools for water play are essential to a creative enriching play area. Children need sinks, running water, sand, art media, musical instruments with which to experiment; materials to observe and feel; and materials to create. They need books, outdoor and indoor science materials through which they can discover and explore.

More than all this, they need space and freedom to use these materials under wise guidance as opposed to a teacher-dominated and -directed program. Kits and packages of equipment and supplies designed to meet the total needs of a preschool program should be carefully analyzed as they may not provide for the range of individual differences within groups and particular localities.

A wide range of materials is important to give sufficient variety to the children's activities. As each piece of equipment is selected, three questions should be used as criteria: Is it suitable for this age group? What can the child do with it that will further his learning? Will it encourage him to do something based upon use of his own ideas rather than just watch it operate?

Outdoor play is not always vigorous. Provision should be made for outdoor play that involves musical instruments, easel painting, clay modeling, or even following a slow moving animal. Boxes and crates are simple outdoor equipment that provide a challenge and an opportunity for the young child to imagine, to recreate, and to enjoy the land of make believe.

The selection of suitable equipment and supplies depends on the age and maturity of children, the program planned, and the number of children to be included in the group. The physical facilities—indoor and outdoor space— will affect the type and amount of equipment to be supplied. Teacher interest and preference is a factor to be considered. However, teacher interest should not limit the program; there are certain basic pieces of equipment and consumable supplies that appear to be needed by all groups.

Sources for securing these supplies and recommended listings of the equipment and supplies needed according to the size of the group may be found in *Equipment and Supplies* published by the Association for Childhood Education International.[14] The criteria used for testing the items listed include suitability for age level, safety features, sanitary and health provisions, favorable price range, and appropriateness for use in school and at home. A classified list of equipment and supplies and a directory of the manufacturer or distributor are included. Many of the items listed may be secured locally and some items are marked with an asterisk (*) to indicate that they may be bought safely at a local store or made by a local carpenter.

Supplies and Equipment

Some of the equipment and materials usually found in schools for young children are included in the following listing. It should be noted that one or more of each type will be found in most schools but not all that are listed may be found in any given school. In addition, many others are available. This is a general list and no item should be included unless it is functional to the program. The amount and quality will vary with the size and type of group and with teachers. The list includes the following:

Art Materials and Supplies. Brushes varying in size and length of handle, easels, clay, crayons, powder paint, finger paint; muslin, oilcloth, paper for finger painting and crayons, newsprint, tagboard; paste and brush, blunt scissors; yarn, sewing basket with varying sizes of thread, and large-eyed needles.

Woodworking. Claw hammers, nails of assorted sizes, files and cards for cleaning files, scraps of soft wood and beaver board, saws, screwdrivers and screws of assorted size, workbench with clamps, yardstick and rulers, hand-drill, monkey wrench, planes, sandpaper, dowel rods, screw eyes, pliers, paint, varnish, shellac, brushes, linseed oil, and paint remover.

Science. Aquarium and herbarium with cover (material for making), barometer, thermometer, compass, cage for pets, magnifying glass and access to microscope, horseshoes, glass jars with lids, preserving fluid for specimens, tuning fork, prisms, collection of various types of magnets, iron filings, blotters, seeds, gardening tools, watering cans, weathervane and weather glass, measuring vessels, and spoons.

Musical Instruments. Autoharp, drum, rhythm sticks, songbells, tuned time bells, tom-tom, triangle, tone blocks, xylophone, piano and bench, phonograph and recordings; also radio and television available for special purposes and for special occasions.

Water Play. A wading pool, hoses, a tube, a table with metal or plastic pans, and a place to wash doll clothes.

Toys. Playhouse toys, water play equipment, puzzles of varying types and difficulty, games, transportation toys of all types, building blocks, and other manipulative construction toys.

[14]*Equipment and Supplies* (Washington, D.C.: ACEI, 1968).

Wheel Toys. Wagons, tricycles, "kiddie-kar," wheelbarrow, trucks, tractors, boards equipped with large casters.

Stationary Play Equipment. Jungle gym, climbers of different varieties, slides, swings, bridges, ladders, boards, mazes, gangplanks, pools, sandbox, platforms.

Sandbox. See "Outdoor Play Space."

Numbers. Dominoes, calendar, measuring cups, containers, measuring spoons, play money, scales, rulers, yardstick, tape measure, peg boards, games, abacus, collection of articles for counting such as beads, buttons, sticks.

Audiovisual Facilities. United States flag, films and filmstrips; record player and recordings; globe, maps, pictures, picture books, costumes, magazines and catalogs, puppets, and access to projectors, screen, and tape recorder.

Animals. See pp. 308–309.

Housekeeping Equipment and Supplies. Suitable and in sufficient quantity—stove and refrigerator may be on casters. If stove not available, a hot plate can be substituted. Equipment for cleaning up "spills" and for child care of room; tissues, paper towels, and roll of brown paper.

Storage. Discussed under physical facilities.

First Aid and Safety. Large Red Cross first-aid kit for emergency, and smaller kit for daily use. Fire extinguisher easily accessible and in good condition at all times.

Miscellaneous Supplies. The teacher will need forms for admitting child, for recording progress and personal data, and for transmitting child's record. She will also need a pencil for china marking, twine, pencils, paste, and pastebrushes, boxes for storing, beads and beadlaces, chart rack, large scissors, colored and white tissue, colored construction paper, cleaning tissue, paper towels; roll of 36-inch brown paper, materials for making finger paint and other art media; adhesive and mending tape, scotch tape, masking tape, chalk, erasers, stationery and envelopes, stamps, a marking pad and pencil, erasers, paper clips, large crayons of black and primary colors, pencil sharpener, pen holder and assorted sizes of lettering pens, India ink, felt marking pen, pins (straight and safety), stapler and staples, eyelet punch and eyelets, reinforcements, and rubber bands. She will need access to a primer sized typewriter, typewriter ribbons, paper and carbons, and to a duplicator, carbon, and paper for duplicating.

Furniture

The furniture should be movable, durable, comfortable, attractive, child-sized, storable, and easy to clean. Single purpose furniture restricts the child and takes up needed play space.

Tables. These should be varied as to height, ranging from 15 to 22 inches high to fit the sizes of the children. Differing shapes provide for a variety of uses.

Chairs. They should be stackable, light enough for children to handle, movable without undue noise. Chairs should be in varied sizes, from 14 to 20 inches high, depending on ages and sizes of children. Check by placing hand, palm down, between front of chair seat and upper part of child's leg; space will not be adequate for adult hand if height is correct. Larger chairs for teacher and other adults are needed.

Display Racks and Bookshelves. Preferably movable on casters—shelves easily accessible to child.

Clock. Large face with arabic numerals, preferably black hands on white face.

Easels. Easily adjustable to child's size (so that elbows are even with bottom of paper), portable with washable surface; include trays to hold cans of paint and provide clips to hold paper.

For equipment to make its contribution to child development, it must be educationally sound. For example, the tone quality of the piano must be good, the books suitably illustrated, and the tools usable (not toy saws and hammer). All equipment and materials have many uses: therefore, no definite plan for exclusive use to develop a single concept or skill is planned by the teacher. Dangerous swinging objects, apparatus that requires taking turns, and single use equipment restrict a child's ability to create his own play or to work creatively in a group.

As the teacher offers opportunities for more complex intellectual experiences, she selects the materials and equipment that will be needed. As the child uses these materials in his work-play activities, he makes the equipment or material into whatever he perceives them to be. Through observation of the child at this work-play, the teacher gains greater insight for further planning of his activities and for determining what additional materials will be desirable. She can also decide what materials are not suitable for this child at this time.

The alert teacher is constantly searching for new equipment and materials that are challenging to children. She keeps informed as to what is available locally and also what is being placed on the market. However, she is careful to select each item in terms of its suitability for the school situation. Many of the recently developed types of equipment have functional qualities, provide for multi-use, and are designed in accordance with sound educational theory. These she provides in terms of a balanced program and adequacy of the budget. When choices are made it is important to consider whether or not the material, good though it may be, makes wisest use of the funds.

Parents and children benefit from building or preparing equipment and facilities. For example, pens, cages, and aquariums are essential equipment for a school. They may be purchased; however, there are values to be obtained from building them cooperatively or from sharing one that is brought from a home.

Criteria for Selecting Equipment

In selecting the basic equipment and materials for a school for a young child, the teacher needs to consider:

1. The ages and maturity of the children.
2. The size of the group.
3. The available budget.
4. The type of housing—size, architecture, space for equipment and its storage.
5. Suitability of equipment to program planned and to the children.
6. The provision for balance of types and varieties for each curriculum area.

7. The safety, adaptability, and suitability to local situations in terms of climate, economic conditions, and child needs.
8. The potential of the material to encourage and stimulate learning.

Use and Care of Equipment

The children need to learn to use and to care for the equipment and materials. Therefore, establishing routines and procedures for use and storing will assist the child and the teacher as they develop such helpful patterns of behavior as:

1. Wearing aprons or coveralls when painting.
2. Returning all tools, scissors, crayons, blocks, toys to designated storage space when not in use. (Cleaning all paint brushes and modeling boards before storing.)
3. Cleaning up all spilled paint, shellac, or varnish immediately. Learning what to use for each. For example, cold water for water paint, turpentine for varnish or paint, and alcohol for shellac.
4. Storing oily rags or cloths with shellac on them in metal containers away from heat or papers.
5. Repairing toys or equipment that need mending immediately. They should not be used until this repair is completed.
6. Cleaning and picking up in the play space after activity.
7. Storing hats and coats in a definite place and in an orderly manner.

THE ROLE OF THE TEACHER

Some activities require the teacher to participate, others require the teacher to observe, and others may be initiated by the child. The teacher must be able to see the children as they use equipment. The placement and arrangement of equipment contribute greatly to its use. Accessibility and easy use in an uncluttered environment is the goal of each teacher. Neatness can be a virtue, but also it can detract from the use of equipment. A certain amount of orderliness is required or the environment will be confusing to the child. The children soon learn the places for things and enjoy using them and replacing them. Frequently, teachers rearrange the equipment; the children will need reorientation to this change unless the teacher and the children together planned and made the change.

Many teachers find it desirable to use a limited amount of movable equipment at one time and add to it as the weeks go by. They and the children plan together for the use, the placing, and the care of this additional material. This type of planning provides for new and challenging experiences with the added equipment and permits the child to have a part in the plans for arrangement. Thus, the classroom truly becomes the children's and the teacher's work-play space.

Regardless of the type and amount of physical facilities, equipment, and materials available and used, the teacher—her resourcefulness, vision, initiative, creativity—is the most important learning material in any classroom. The resourceful teacher knows that it is the use of the space, equipment, and materials that determines the teaching effectiveness. She recognizes that responsibility and ingenuity are developed through the functional use of buildings, equipment, and materials as she and the children discover better ways of arranging and using them for a given purpose. The teacher provides many opportunities for new learnings as she and the children explore together. The curriculum of the school then challenges and guides the use of materials and resources; it does not limit or curtail the learning activities; neither are materials and resources permitted to limit or to warp the curriculum.

Suggested Activities

1. Observe in a center for young children and describe how the physical environment seems to affect the development of the children, the activities planned, and the use of equipment.

2. List and describe the ways in which teachers, parents, and interested community persons can work cooperatively to provide adequate physical facilities for schools for young children. Discuss the relative value of this cooperative effort.

3. Discuss how the environment contributes to the provision for individual differences among young children.

4. Make a list of equipment and supplies essential to the development of a good school for three-, four-, and five-year-olds. Describe how these may be provided. Check local stores and recent catalogs, compare prices and make a purchase order.

5. Draw a diagram of two classrooms and two playgrounds for young children, showing how learning opportunities may be provided in different settings.

6. Examine packaged learning materials. Evaluate these in terms of criteria on pages 161–162.

7. Visit a playground. Note the location of equipment and discuss advantages and disadvantages.

8. Visit a playground and note improvised, creative, and unusual equipment.

Related Readings

Baker, Katherine Read. *Let's Play Outdoors*. Washington, D.C.: NAEYC, 1966.

Dattner, R. *Design for Play*. New York: N.Y.: Van Nostrand Reinhold Co., 1969.

Deutsch, M., et al. *Memorandum on Facilities for Early Childhood Education*. New York: Educational Facilities Laboratories, Inc., 1970.

Educational Facilities Laboratories, Inc. *Schools Without Walls*. New York: 1965.

Gross, R., and Judith Murphy. *Educational Change and Architectural Consequences*. New York: Educational Facilities Laboratories, Inc., 1968.

Haase, R. W. *Designing the Child Development Center*. Washington, D.C.: Project Head Start Community Action Program, Office of Economic Opportunity, U.S. Department of Health, Education, and Welfare, 1968.

Kohn, S. *The Early Learning Center*. New York: Educational Facilities Laboratories, Inc., 1970.

Kritchevsky, Sybil, and Elizabeth Prescott. *Planning Environments for Young Children —Physical Space*. Washington, D.C.: NAEYC, 1969.

Lipson, Rosella. "A Mobile Preschool," *Young Children*, 24:3 (1969).

Loeffler, Margaret. *The Prepared Environment*. New York: Trustees of Canady School, 1967.

Matterson, E. M. *Play and Playthings for the Preschool Child*. Baltimore, Md.: Penguin Books, Inc., 1967.

Osmon, F. L. *Child Care Centers for Migrant Farm Labor Camps*. San Francisco: Rosenburg Foundation, 1966.

Planning and Development of Facilities for Pre-Primary Education. Athens, Georgia: University of Georgia, Bureau of Education Studies and Field Services, 1969.

Roepere, Annemarie. *Preliminary Outline of Life in the Domes*. Bloomfield Hills, Mich.: Roeper City and Country Schools, Inc., 1969.

Sunderlin, Sylvia, ed. *Equipment and Supplies Tested and Approved for Preschool/Home/School*. Washington, D.C.: ACEI, 1968.

The Threshold Program and Materials for Early Learning Centers. Chicago: CCM School Materials, Inc., 1969.

Todd, Vivian Edmiston. *The Years Before School: Guiding Preschool Children*. 2nd ed. New York: Macmillan, Inc., 1970.

Tonigan, R., et al. *Child Care and Development Centers, Model Neighborhoods, Albuquerque, New Mexico, or Mr. Architect, This Is How We Want Our Centers to Perform*. Albuquerque, N.M.: University of New Mexico, Institute for Social Research and Development, 1970.

Providing for Children Who Need Uniquely Different Services

Chapter **23**

The Exceptional Child—including the gifted, those having learning disabilities, the physically handicapped, the maladjusted, the disadvantaged, or culturally deprived—requires uniquely different services. The preschool years are the most critical for a child's future development. The lack of attention to a child's handicap during the preschool years may lead to deterioration of his potential to lead a normal life.

Every child is exceptional in that he is unique. Children differ in degree. According to Dunn, "equality of educational opportunity . . . is achieved through enabling each pupil to develop at his own pace, and, as nearly as possible, to the maximum of his potentialities. Therefore, the true meaning of equality of opportunity lies in diversified rather than similar school programs."[1]

[1]L. M. Dunn, ed., *Exceptional Children in the Schools* (New York: Holt, Rinehart and Winston, 1963), p. 5.

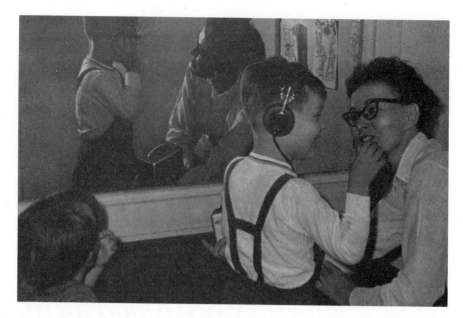

Figure 55. It is important that exceptional children find a secure relationship with and acceptance by others in their early years. Here a hard-of-hearing boy explores his world through senses supplementary to auditory and with the assistance of an understanding and professionally trained adult.

There are many programs and projects, with and without grants, that have unusual facets for working with children who are uniquely different.[2]

A description of the program planned and financed through state departments of education is included in Public Law 91-230, Part C, Title VI. This program provides for (1) participation of parents, (2) training of personnel, (3) evaluation, (4) dissemination of information, (5) coordination with other agencies, (6) special activities, and (7) appropriations. Grants have been awarded to the Division of Training Programs, Bureau of Education for Handicapped in the University of Texas; to the University of Southern California; and to the American Speech and Hearing Association project to disseminate information on speech and language development, and the communication needs and problems of young children to teachers, leaders, and parents of young children in preschools throughout the United States.[3]

Weber lists centers that are established to study certain aspects of education of the disadvantaged child. They include (1) A Parent Education Project in

[2]*The Report to the President: White House Conference on Children* (Washington, D.C.: Superintendent of Documents, U.S. Government Printing Office, 1970), pp. 197–206.

[3]*Program Description, Handicapped Children's Early Education Program* (Program Development Branch, Division of Educational Services, Bureau of Education for the Handicapped, U.S. Office of Education, October 25, 1971.)

Gainesville, Florida; (2) Frank Porter Graham Child Development Center in Chapel Hill, North Carolina; (3) Nurseries in Cross Cultural Education in San Francisco, California; (4) Bank Street Early Childhood Center in New York City; (5) A Piaget Derived Curriculum in Ypsilanti, Michigan; (6) an integrated nursery school in Wayne State University; (7) Parent Participation Nursery Schools and Children's Centers in Berkeley, California; (8) University of Chicago Laboratory Nursery School in Chicago, Illinois; (9) Pre-Kindergarten Demonstration Center in Rochester, New York; and (10) Early Childhood Education Study in Newton, Massachusetts.[4]

MEETING THE NEEDS OF THE EXCEPTIONAL CHILD

Many exceptional children can profit more by being a part of a regular group. For some children the extent of being exceptional is such that it is necessary to make special educational provisions for them. As different expectancies are set for children in terms of their capacities, varied teaching procedures, materials, and facilities are provided. These are selected in terms of the level of capacity, the limitations, and the characteristics of the individual child.

It is never too early for the exceptional child to have opportunities to become friends and to play with other children. All children learn from each other how to give and to take, the rules to follow, and to share and to have things shared with them. The physically handicapped, the intellectually handicapped, the maladjusted, and the gifted child need to, and should wish to, be treated as other children and to share in those tasks in which he can participate. He needs these opportunities for participation provided in terms of what he is able to do. He also needs special opportunities provided for him to develop the skills and to have experiences adapted to his special abilities and needs.

The teacher is always the primary factor in the learning situation in any classroom. Recognition of this fact becomes increasingly important when the teacher is expected to meet the demands of one or more children who need something different from or in addition to the planned program for the usual group. Additional qualifications and specialized training are essential for the teacher required to guide the deviations. Because of the specialized demands of working with these children, teachers and leaders in schools for young children find it desirable to establish some criteria to assist in determining how many and which atypical children can be included satisfactorily within the group.

In admitting exceptional children, as with all children, the needs of the child and the school's ability to serve them are the primary factors in determining whether the child can be accepted in a group.

In establishing policies and planning for admission of an exceptional child,

[4]Evelyn Weber, *Early Childhood Education: Perspectives on Change* (Worthington, Ohio: Charles A. Jones Publishing Co., 1970), pp. 71–95.

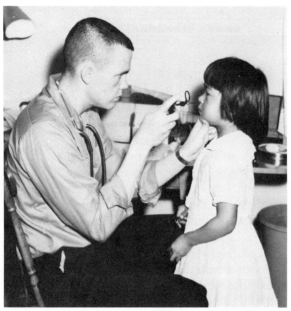

(Courtesy of Head Start)

Figure 56. It is important that a child's *exception* be found in his early years and that a plan be made for his particular educational needs.

consideration is given to such problems as: What special demands will be made on the teacher? Are there other children now in the group who require special attention? Will the demands of this child require an undue proportion of the teacher's time and energy, thus curtailing the work with the other members of the group? Are the necessary materials and facilities available to provide for the best development of this child? Most important, is the teacher qualified personally and does she have the professional competence essential for the development of the program required by this particular child?

All teachers of young children have the responsibility of identifying the child within the group who needs special assistance and guidance over and beyond what she can provide. Through early identification, diagnosis, and treatment, many deviations can be corrected or adjustments can be made which are difficult if not impossible to make at a later date. Through counsel with the parents, plans can be developed to provide for the special needs of the exceptional child. In the classroom the special differences within the individuals can be identified and the decision made as to the best school situation for the child's guidance.

According to Olson, "It has become less and less customary to isolate exceptional children, and the tendency is to provide opportunities for work and play among children of all types so they can profit by such association. There is no fixed pattern and there probably should be none at our present state of knowledge. . . . A lush environment has in it both the qualitative and quantitative opportunities for the learning and growth of the least and the most able in any type of activity."[5]

Whenever appropriate, handicapped children should live with, play with, and go to school with "normal" children.[6] The arguments concern whether it is in the best interests for the gifted and for the intellectually handicapped to remain in the regular classroom. The relative values of the provision for the growth of these children within the regular school and within a special school are constantly under study. Research today indicates the acceptance by the normal group of the mentally or physically handicapped child. However, it appears that the mentally retarded child often has difficulty in adjusting to the regular classroom and also in securing acceptance. The physically handicapped usually encounters neither of these problems to a great degree. The demands of the child on the teacher because of the physical handicap will need to be carefully studied and measures provided to relieve the extra demand so that her services to the total group are not curtailed. The following is an examination of the different types of the exceptional encountered in children and the provisions made for them.

THE GIFTED CHILD

When the gifted are segregated, their achievements may be spectacular in special areas. However, there appears to be no real evidence that they have gained materially over what they would have acquired in a heterogeneous group working in a rich environment under capable guidance. There is always the problem of what would have occurred if the gifted child had been or had not been accelerated. Any good program for children allows and provides for differences, and the curriculum is developed to meet the needs of the gifted as well as the average and the retarded. The needs of these individuals are identified and planned for in such a way that each child becomes an accepted, contributing member of the group.

All children have gifts. The task of the teacher is to identify and to provide a suitable climate for their growth. As special abilities of children are noticed, records are made so that they may continue to receive guidance in terms of their special gift, whether the child be intellectually gifted or specially talented. In identifying these children, the teacher does not place total dependence upon her own observation and test data but seeks counsel and assistance from other professional sources.

According to Passow, "There are no unique methods for teaching gifted children. In some ways, the apparent differences stem not so much from what the teacher does as from what the gifted child brings to the situation. His

---

[5]W. C. Olson, *Child Development*, 2nd ed. (Boston: D. C. Heath, 1959), p. 434.

[6]*Report to the President*, op. cit., pp. 199–206.

ability to think, understand, create, initiate, relate, and imagine gives a qualitative dimension to the teaching-learning situation which may contrast visibly with the classroom environment of the average student."[7]

These gifted children have needs common to all children, including the development of the beginnings of basic concepts in all areas. They need provision for many stimulating and varied opportunities that develop initiative; to have the range and scope of their knowledge increased; to develop the power of working independently; to avoid the danger of becoming "one-sided" or interested in only a limited area; to have the acceptance of their peers even though they have superior ability in one or more areas; to overcome emotional stress in a socially acceptable manner and not to seek refuge in day-dreaming. With these children the teacher places stress on independent thinking and action, and building relationships and concepts as opposed to learning multiple facts. Challenging situations are provided to develop critical thinking.

It is generally agreed that enrichment is the best method of working with these children. The teacher will find it helpful to utilize the many community resources—physical and human—to aid and to supplement her teaching. This she plans and develops as she works with the child's parents. She knows that the child may lose the genuine respect of his peers if she permits him to "always know the answers," to dictate what needs to be done, to be impatient with slower learners, or to draw attention constantly to self. The teacher herself may contribute to the antisocial attitude by always holding the child up as an example. Therefore, she is ever mindful that the child may become a "mental giant yet be a moral dwarf" and thereby not be capable as a mature person to make a real contribution to society. A good school for young children will provide adequate challenge for the superior child without "special" consideration and at the same time use these provisions for the enrichment of the educational experiences of the other children.

Children with Mental Retardation

In working with the child who has a learning disability, the teacher needs insight into how to help him discover his strengths as well as to assist him with his liabilities; she needs to accept him as a person as well as a child to be taught. It is important that this child's exception be noted in his early years and that a plan be made for his particular educational needs.

The degree of retardation is a significant factor in determining the placement of the intellectually handicapped child. If the retarded child is retained in a regular group, his progress will be slower than that of the other members of the group; he will need more praise and extrinsic rewards for his successes;

---

[7]A. H. Passow, "Enrichment of Education for the Gifted," *Education for the Gifted* (57th Yearbook, Part II, NSSE) (Chicago: University of Chicago Press, 1958), p. 198.

Figure 57.   In working with the child who has a learning disability, the teacher needs insight into how to discover his strengths, as well as how to assist him with his liabilities.

his tasks will need to be briefer, less complex, and more routine with greater repetition—this repetition may and should be in varied situations. Many more and different concrete materials and experiences are required for this child. It will take him longer to succeed; he will need more time to make his adjustments socially and emotionally. Serenity, happiness, and acceptance are essential to him; these he secures from the attitudes and feelings of those around him as well as from the climate of the classroom.

In the life of every parent of a retarded child there comes a time when plans must be made for schooling. "Mental retardation is a very complex problem, and many of these complexities make a difference in how the retarded child is educated."[8] These retarded children have special educational needs in terms of understanding, specially prepared and skilled teachers, and a specially developed curriculum. Because of their difficulty in learning, they need and learn best by special methods. Avery found that benefits from

[8]H. M. Williams, *The Retarded Child Goes to School* (No. 123) (Washington, D.C.: U.S. Dept. of Health, Education, and Welfare, 1960), p. 1.

attendance at preschool would seem to indicate that a good preschool is worth a trial even though some people question whether young children of this type suffer by separation from home.[9]

Going to school is a time of many adjustments for all children and it is more complicated for the mentally retarded. Safety, conformity to routines, languages and social readiness, ability in self-help activities, and stability and emotional adaptability need to be considered carefully. It is important to plan for admission of a mentally retarded child and to determine whether his best interests as well as those of the other children in the group are to be served. Kirk suggests that certain educable children should be placed in a special preschool program at as early an age as possible.[10]

Because it is difficult to predict how well a retarded child will fit into a group, many schools accept these children on a trial basis. The parents will need guidance as to further school plans if the child cannot be retained in the school. Most states have some provision for the child whose retardation is such that he cannot be absorbed within a group. Some communities have a school program for the children who are capable of instruction but not with the regular group. Materials on these programs and suggestions for guidance of schools in counseling parents of retarded children may be secured from The National Association for Retarded Children, 420 Lexington Avenue, New York, N.Y. Private residential schools have been available for retarded children for many years. A listing of these schools is published annually by the American Association on Mental Deficiency, 5201 Connecticut Ave. N.W., Washington, D.C. 20015.

Early Congressional Acts have given impetus to work with mental retardation and have provided opportunities for assistance to the preschool teacher of the mentally retarded child. Public Law 88-164, the Mental Retardation Facilities and Community Health Centers Construction Act passed by the 88th Congress and signed by President Kennedy, October 31, 1963, provided for: (1) research centers, grants for the construction of university affiliated facilities and for the construction of state centers maintained by the state; (2) the construction of community health centers; and (3) the training of teachers of the mentally retarded and other handicapped children as well as for research and demonstration projects in the education of the handicapped child. Public Law 88-156, the Maternal Health and Mental Retardation Amendments of 1963, provides an increase in child health and crippled children's services.[11]

The President's Panel on Mental Retardation in 1962 reported that the symptoms of the mentally retarded child are not always obvious but that early

[9]Charlotte B. Avery, "Social Competence of Pre-School, Acoustically Handicapped Children," *Exceptional Child*, 15 (1948), pp. 71–73, 88.

[10]S. A. Kirk, *Early Education of Mentally Retarded: An Experimental Study* (Urbana, Ill.: University of Illinois Press, 1958), pp. 121–122.

[11]*Mental Retardation, Plans and Programs* (Washington, D.C.: Department of Health, Education, and Welfare, June 1965).

recognition and treatment offer the best prognosis. About 85 per cent of the retarded children can benefit from special education. Many children who are considered retarded are later found to be emotionally disturbed rather than having a mental defect existing from birth. To assist in identifying the retarded child, the teacher needs (1) A record of age of development of such skills as creeping, crawling, standing, and talking; (2) an analysis of motor coordination of the child; (3) a record of vocabulary, interest in books, speech habits or impediments, memory span, ability to generalize, perceptual difficulties; (4) a history of physical difficulties, illnesses; and (5) a record of his ability to socialize; acceptance and rejection by peers.

When the retarded child is located the teacher works with the parents and with agencies who are skilled in diagnosing such problems. The ratio of pupil to teacher needs to be reduced to provide time for individual guidance; extra space is needed to avoid pushing or crowding and to provide for greater opportunities for creative play.

THE PHYSICALLY HANDICAPPED CHILD

Educational services to handicapped children who are under 21 years of age are provided through federal programs. Services are made available to children who have been identified by state educational agencies as being mentally retarded, visually impaired, deaf, hard of hearing, speech impaired, seriously emotionally disturbed, learning disabled, or other wise have health impairments to the extent that they can not benefit from the regular educational program. Included in such programs are (1) aid for handicapped in state supported and operated schools, (2) special education and related services, (3) programs to advance creativity in the schools, and (4) vocational education for handicapped children.[12]

The orthopedically handicapped child is the least difficult to absorb within a regular group. However, the crippling defect must be minor or special provision must be made for handling the child. Overprotectiveness on the part of the children, teacher, or other adults is one of the problems encountered in working with this type of child. The greatest problem may be the overprotectiveness of the parents. Even though at times it is difficult to enforce, the child must become independent through use of his own resources.

The type and degree of the handicap determines the program. Some of these children were born with a handicap; others have acquired it after birth. Some of these handicaps may be fully corrected; however, many children with severe handicaps need to be provided with special kinds of educational services. It is extremely important that handicapped children receive help before starting regular school. If successfully helped at an early age, the problems for

---

[12]*Four Programs for Educational Services to Handicapped Children.* (Washington, D.C.: U.S. Department of Health, Education, and Welfare, October 1971.), Item 2, Part C, Title II.

the parent as well as for the child are lessened and the opportunities for the child are expanded because of early acceptance of the handicap and participation in a planned educational program to utilize all of the child's assets. Because of the flexibility and work with individuals in schools for young children, an excellent opportunity for such growth is available. Parents of these children increase their ability to help their child by assisting, observing, and working with the teacher. Through conferences, teachers and parents may give each other ideas that will be helpful in working with the child.

Defective Vision

The blind or partially seeing child will need to learn through his other senses; however, he must learn to do all things that he can do for himself safely and successfully. Children with partial sight need different books, periods of frequent rest for their eyes, and a greater provision for safety. They also need encouragement and a sense of belonging. Often they can excel in games requiring auditory acuity. Many opportunities should be provided for them to develop and use this skill, thereby securing recognition and experiencing success within their peer group.

Figure 58.   Glasses have opened a new world for this girl.

Children who are having difficulty with vision may rub their eyes frequently or blink when attempting to see objects; they frequently sit in a tense position or make facial expressions indicating intense effort to see. Children exhibiting these characteristics should be referred for testing by competent individuals. In the classroom they should have frequent rest periods and protection from glare or from work requiring close vision.

Defective Hearing

The child with defective hearing will need help according to the type of hearing impairment. The deaf child who has never heard has a greater problem than one who has lost his hearing after acquiring speech. Both of these groups have greater needs than the partially deaf or hard-of-hearing child. The young child needs his hearing tested frequently; often correction can be made if defects are discovered soon enough. The child with defective hearing should at all times be seated so as to see the teacher's lips. Careful observation of his participation with the group will avoid his forming habits of withdrawal because of his inability to hear.

A program for deaf and hard-of-hearing children was developed at The Florida State University Institute of Human Development in cooperation with personnel from the Department of Education Services for Exceptional Children, and the Speech and Hearing Clinic. Aware of the importance of an early educational start for these children (otherwise the deaf or near-deaf child will not learn language or achieve social and personal skills possessed by other children of this age), it was decided to place one such child in each of the Institute's preschool age groups. A teacher with specialized training in the field devoted half her time to the four children and also served as a consultant to the regular teachers. One of the major problems faced by atypical children is the difficulty of achieving group acceptance. How this was accomplished for one totally deaf child is described:

> Larry did not enter the group without considerable thought and preparation. Since each group of children in the school was to have a deaf or near-deaf child, decisions had to be made as to the group in which each child should be placed. This decision fell to the speech and hearing therapist who had worked closely with the children and their parents. Armed with the information and insights she had gained plus extensive clinical findings, she visited each group to see which group of children and teacher might offer the best school environment for each child. Larry, age four, who is totally deaf, was placed in the four-year-old group.

> The week before Larry was to join the group was a busy one for teacher and children. The teacher felt that the children should have some sense of the world, different from their own, in which Larry lived. They also needed to understand that he had not had the 4½ months of playing together which they had shared so he would be lacking in the degree of social living they had obtained. It was decided that an approach to sounds around them might be an opening wedge in evolving this awareness. The children listened to the sounds around them during sharing period. They talked about what they heard. Stories were read, like "Muffin" the little black dog who got a cinder

Figure 59.   This boy can hear the other children better now that he is wearing an "aid" and has become an accepted member of the group.

in his eye and couldn't see, but could hear. When the children's interest was high, the teacher asked the children to tell her what they heard when they put their hands over their ears tightly. In unison they replied, "Nothing."

Then the teacher told them about Larry who couldn't hear yet wanted to come to school. She asked them how they could talk to him if he couldn't hear. Don said, "We could show him," and began to point directions. The children eagerly took up the suggestion and began to communicate with each other by gestures.

Larry entered school, a welcome addition to the group. His welcome was short-lived, however. He was not accustomed to such social acceptance and before long was entering each group like a friendly puppy, knocking down block houses with a wide friendly grin or grabbing a doll from the doll house and running to the far end of the yard. The warm acceptance changed to resentment and isolation for Larry by the group.

A week later at discussion time, while Larry was attending speech class, the teacher asked them what they thought of Larry. "We don't like him," came the reply. "Why?" asked the teacher. "He knocks down our blocks," was a quick response. "Why do you suppose he does that?" she asked them. For a minute there was silence and then Susan said, "Maybe he doesn't know how to play with us. Tom used to knock them down too." The rest of the group agreed. The conversation turned to what they could do to help him. "We could tell him not to knock down our blocks by shaking our heads," Tom suggested. This was tried but Larry thought the children were playing again. The children smiled as they shook their heads. Another discussion brought out the need for a serious face as the negative head shake was given.

Despite these initial difficulties, after four months in nursery school, Larry is an accepted member of the group, with no more than the usual four-year-old setbacks for outbursts of destruction. The warmth of acceptance permeates the group. This warmth was shown one day as Larry entered the door of the nursery school and met Tom coming out. Impulsively Tom threw his arms around Larry and kissed him on the cheek. Larry smiled in happy surprise and both boys went their individual ways.

Each of the deaf and hard-of-hearing children has made a surprisingly good adjustment to his group and, as a result of intensive therapy, is attaining language facility. It is likely that these children will experience much less retardation during later school years than is common for children with severe or total hearing handicaps. Hamilton states that "The responsibility of the teacher in charge, in adapting to the needs of these children, is to provide constant language stimulation—sometimes referred to as auditory bombardment."[13] Through the use of a wide variety of art materials, dramatic play, structured music experiences, story sharing, and an assortment of toys, expressive outlets are provided for the frustrations experienced by the child. Hamilton's study examined the values derived from children being in a normal group with at least a year in a nursery school with "like" children. The need for planning with parents to understand and to accept adapted programs became evident. The study revealed that the "possibilities for children with limited hearing are exciting and hopeful."[14]

Impaired Speech

The majority of cases of impaired speech involve faulty articulation. Most of these articulatory speech difficulties occur at an early age. Stuttering and nonfluency rate are other commonly found forms of speech impairment. Suggestions for working with children's speech development are discussed in Chapter 11. The teacher needs to distinguish between actual speech impairment and speech difficulties that are a normal part of the child's developmental sequence. The child with impaired speech will need special help apart from the group even though he benefits from participating with the regular group.

[13]Alicia Hamilton, "A Preschool Program for Children with Limited Hearing," *Young Children*, 21:5 (1966), p. 267.

[14]Ibid., pp. 269–271.

Physical defects such as cleft palate and harelip will need medical attention and correction.

Whatever the speech problem, the teacher should identify the children who need help; secure counsel and assistance as she provides special help to the child to the degree that her training, experience, and teaching load permit; and work with parents and other agencies in providing for the total needs of the child.

A calm, helpful, and accepting manner in a relaxed climate is an effective method of work with children with speech difficulties. The teacher must be careful not to embarrass the child. In a classroom where a free, spontaneous atmosphere prevails, where tension is dispelled with a friendly remark or humorous situation, the speech of many children will improve.[15] However, there are special skills and procedures for which the teacher must have training. If the teacher does not have this competency, she may secure assistance from individuals with special training.

The teacher is ever alert to insure that problems of these children are not being developed in the other members of the group. For example, the attention and help on a speech problem with one child may encourage imitation on the part of another child in order to secure the desired attention.

The Maladjusted Child

The child who experiences social and emotional conflict situations often has problems of personal and group adjustment. All children have conflicts, but most children develop the ability to resolve these conflicts through socially approved activities and procedures. The release of tensions through dramatics, play experiences, or creative activities has been discussed in previous chapters. A few children need help from adults to release their tensions and to resolve their conflicts. Careful guidance by the teacher may be all that is required. However, if these problems continue and are serious, the teacher and the parents need and should have the help of a specially trained person. The teacher identifies these children and refers them to the proper agencies. The teacher then cooperates in working out a satisfactory solution. In working with these children who can be retrained in the group, the teacher will find helpful suggestions in the material in Chapter 5.

The Culturally Deprived Child

Thousands of children each year enter school with severe educational disadvantages. Prior to 1960 the focus of education for the disadvantaged was on programs for dropouts, and remedial work in the slums. By 1960, it had become evident that such programs come too late in the child's life and that

---

[15]W. Johnson, et al., *Speech Handicapped School Children* (New York: Harper & Row, 1956).

preprimary education programs for culturally deprived children are essential. (See Chapter 6, pp. 86–90.)

The early years are particularly important for the culturally deprived child. During this period he explores his physical world, becomes sensitive to his environment, has opportunity for action responses, reproduces and symbolizes his experiences, and uses language to follow through his concepts. The child who is deprived may not have opportunity to talk in standard English, to share, and to have close relationships. Educational practices should be adjusted to meet these needs.

The problems of the culturally deprived are many and complex. In planning programs, it is essential to consider what changes and what additional provisions are required for these children and how these may be achieved. Recognition of the problems of these children has rapidly led to a preschool movement inasmuch as the deprivation starts to build up at an early age. Such deprivation progressively limits the child as he attempts to fit into schools with children who have had parental teaching, care, and value development. The program for these children must provide a balance between order and freedom that is a steady routine but with freedom to explore, ask questions, and to expect and receive answers from adults. This type of program needs to be continued without interruption. The parents of these children should be actively involved in the program to provide for this continuity in the child's home environment. Because the development of the child's self concept takes place along with the development of language it is important that the program for these children begin at an early age.

In working with the disadvantaged young child, the teacher's plans are based upon the recognition that disadvantaged children are not dull children. The plan should include ways of helping enrich the child's environment; provision for helping the child to master language related to specific situations; opportunities for helping mothers develop the cognitive facilities needed by their children; provision for differentiated instruction; utilization of informal language; and gradual development of a more formal mode of communication.

OTHER CHILDREN NEEDING UNIQUE SERVICES

Children of Working Mothers

Although many women who work place their children in preschool programs, there are many more who do not, either because of short hours, the cost, or for other reasons.[16]

Employment of women is increasing at a rapid rate. A survey made in 1965 revealed that only 5 per cent of the children under five years were cared

[16]S. Low and Pearl G. Spindler, *Child Care Arrangements of Working Mothers in the United States* (Washington, D.C.: U.S. Department of Health, Education, and Welfare and U.S. Department of Labor, 1967), pp. 3–9.

for in day care centers; the others were cared for by relatives, or in other homes. Many parents do not recognize the importance of the early years and think that a child of this age needs only custodial care.

A program of care involves physical safety and development, nutritional needs, health needs, and educational activities under guidance. The environment is important, but the greatest need is the presence of a warm, loving adult who takes time to listen, is sympathetic and encouraging but also assists the child in selecting activities to help him grow and become independent. Some type of parental involvement is necessary; however, it is more difficult to schedule especially if the mother works long hours.[17]

The Migrant Child

Providing preschool experiences for the children of migrant families presents difficulties because of the pattern of work—moving from place to place as the need for labor arises. In addition, the migrant families have their own values in terms of speech, honesty, and love. They give their children a sense of belonging to the family but not to the larger group.

There are, however, significant developments in migrant education that include aide training, use of consultants, continuous progress plans, demonstration schools, evaluation, health and nutrition, home and family education, interagency involvement, interstate cooperation, instructional packages, migrant centers, mobile units, parent involvement, preschool programs, six-month extended day programs, programs for Spanish speaking children, student and volunteer involvement, teacher education, uniform migrant transfer record forms. There are also plans for computerized services.[18, 19] Florida, Idaho, New York, and Oregon have developed educational programs for migrant children. The programs involve the use of teacher aides and volunteer services. Special teacher education projects and in-service education programs have also been developed. Except during school hours, no law protects the children, and facilities vary from community to community.

GUIDELINES FOR TEACHERS

Following are some guidelines for teachers working with exceptional children in regular school groups:

1. Determine if the school program and the teacher are suitable for the child.
2. Study the child; keep records of the child for guidance in teaching and for use by others who work with the child.

[17]Annie L. Butler, *The Child's Right to Quality Day Care* (Washington, D.C.: ACEI, 1970).

[18]Sylvia Sunderlin, ed., *Migrant Children: Their Education* (Washington, D.C.: ACEI, 1971), pp. 3–6, 35–61.

[19]H. A. Curtis and J. A. Klock, *Florida Prekindergarten Migrant Compensatory Program: An Evaluation.* Florida State University, Tallahassee, Florida, 1972. (Mimeographed.)

3. Work in close cooperation with the parents in planning programs and activities for the child.
4. Refer for further testing and evaluation all children whose behavior indicates that they are exceptional.
5. Secure guidance and assistance from trained personnel in terms of specific needs of the child.
6. Recognize personal limitations and attempt only those specialized techniques that are justified through personal training and experience.
7. Transfer out of the school those children whose deviation creates too great a demand or who cannot benefit from the program. Counsel with parents as to procedures for planning further placement or services for the child.

All good teachers realize the importance of identifying the special needs and helping each child within the group. The exceptional child has specific needs and the teacher understands how to help him profit from the school activities as well as how to plan specific activities for him. By identifying these special needs and assisting him to profit from his experiences in an environment free from pressure, many emotional and social problems for the child can be prevented. As the child grows in group participation and becomes involved in goal identification, he is growing in responsibility and leadership. As parents and teachers work cooperatively, each child is guided toward the beginnings of educational fulfillment.

All agencies, public and private, should recognize the need to communicate, cooperate, and coordinate their activities to achieve a healthy environment in the interest of children.

Suggested Activities

1. Observe a group of children. List ways the teacher adjusts activities for exceptional children. List activities in which exceptional children participate as regular members of the group. Discuss the value of both types of activities.
2. Read and discuss in class references available in your library that are related to work with children who are uniquely different in their early years.
3. Make a list of special services available for assisting the teacher as she works with children who are uniquely different as members of a regular group. Describe how these are selected, contacted, and used with special children. Indicate how this special assistance is valuable.
4. List guides for the teachers in schools for young children in identifying and working with exceptional children—the gifted, the emotionally disturbed, the mentally retarded, the hard of hearing, the partially sighted, the speech defective, the physically handicapped, and the culturally deprived.
5. Determine the provisions made for children who are uniquely different in your community.
6. Visit such a center and describe how the program is adjusted to the level of each of the differences observed.

Related Readings

Biber, Barbara. *Young Deprived Children and Their Educational Needs.* Washington, D.C.: ACEI, 1967.

Boguslawski, Dorothy Beers. *Guide for Establishing and Operating Day Care Centers for Young Children.* New York: Child Welfare League of America, Inc., 1966.

Bureau of Educational Research and Development. *Educating Disadvantaged Children Under Six.* Washington, D.C.: U.S. Government Printing Office, 1965.

Caldwell, B. M. "The Rationale of Early Intervention," *Exceptional Children, 36*:9 (1970), pp. 717–726.

Cohen, M. D., ed. *That All Children May Learn We Must Learn.* Washington, D.C.: ACEI, 1970.

Education for the Gifted. 57th Yearbook, Part II (NSSE). Chicago: University of Chicago Press, 1958, Chapter III, pp. 41–63.

Gorton, H. B., and R. L. Robinson. "For Better Results: A Full Day Kindergarten," *Educ., 89*:3 (1969), pp. 217–221.

Gray, Susan, R. A. Klaus, J. O. Miller, and Bettye S. Forrester. *Before First Grade: The Early Training Project.* New York: Teachers College, Columbia University, 1966.

Grotberg, Edith, ed. *Critical Issues in Research Related to Disadvantaged Children.* Princeton, N.J.: Educational Testing Service, 1969.

Hamlin, Ruth, Rose Mukerji, and Margaret Yonemura. *Schools for Young Disadvantaged Children.* New York: Teachers College Press, Teachers College, Columbia University, 1967.

Hartup, W., and Nancy Smothergill, eds. *The Young Child—Reviews of Research.* Washington, D.C.: NAEYC, 1970.

Hellmuth, J., ed. *Disadvantaged Child.* Vol. I. Seattle, Washington: Special Child Publication, 1967.

————. *Disadvantaged Child: Head Start and Early Intervention.* Vol. II. Seattle, Washington: Brunner Mazel, Inc., 1968.

Kunz, Jean, and Joan E. Moyer. "Comparison of Economically Disadvantaged and Economically Advantaged Kindergarten Children," *J. of Educ. Res., 62*:9 (1969), pp. 372–395.

Nimnicht, G., Oralee McAfee, and J. Meier. *The New Nursery School.* New York: General Learning Corporation, Early Learning Division, 1969.

Robison, Helen F. *Project Child: Evolution of a Curriculum to Heighten Intellectual and Language Development.* New York: Teachers College, Columbia University, 1969.

Ruderman, Florence. *Child Care and Working Mothers.* New York: Child Welfare League of America, Inc., 1968.

Specifications for Making Buildings and Facilities Accessible to and Usable by the Physically Handicapped. New York: U.S. American Standards Institute, 1961.

Teaching the Disadvantaged Young Child. Washington, D.C.: NAEYC, 1966.

Wallace, Helen M. "Day Care for Handicapped Children in the East Bay Area of California," *Young Children, 21*:3 (1966), pp. 151–161.

The Next Step

Chapter 24

Preparation for the *next step* from a children's center, a kindergarten, or a preschool into the first grade requires the help of the adults in the child's preschool life and the child's parents. The teacher in the school he will attend will also need the help of the parents and the previous responsible adults. The child will learn what he is ready to learn and it is important to recognize that each child is different from all other children and will need to learn at his own pace. He learns, thinks, and acts as an individual and will need help in continuing to be encouraged, to be made to feel secure, and to know that he has a guiding hand as he takes this big next step. The wise preschool teacher knows this and prepares the child to look forward to this next step with joy and anticipation. As his world gets larger and larger he needs to feel the security of a sound foundation based on his satisfactory experiences in accepting responsibility, planning and deciding wisely, completing tasks undertaken, meeting failure as well as success confidently.

Two factors are large contributors in determining the child's adjustment to the new environment; namely, his pattern of individual growth and his background of home experience. Many preschools provide opportunities for the children to visit the school nearby to talk to the teacher and children, to become familiar with the facilities, and to see the various fascinating materials they will use in their experiences the following year. Schools may vary in type and plan of organization but all will have common elements that will assist the children to continue in their growth. The children will have greater security if the preschool teacher as well as the parents show that they believe in the school and that it will be a happy place for them to continue their work.

A conference between the parents and the teacher in the first grade will help provide for satisfactory adjustment as well as promote parent interest in the school and provide a means of communication between parents and teacher. Transportation plans can be discussed as well as the child's previous experiences in preschool, his health records, and any special interests and problems. At the conference the concern is not for the child's future in terms of expectations but for the *now as it affects the future*. The preschool teacher is an effective contributor to the discussion. In addition to her experiences in working with the child she has records of activities and an assessment of his progress that will assist the new teacher to guide the child so that his growth will not be interrupted through frustration, repetition, overt demands, or fear. The teacher-to-be cannot know whether she can respond appropriately until she has developed the skills of teaching the individual child, but she can profit from the experiences of the previous teacher.

The wise teacher knows that to be successful the child needs to build on all that has gone before. The child enters school wanting to grow and does not need to be pushed or prodded into maturing. He enters as a whole human being and cannot be divided into parts. When he enters the first grade he may suffer from a variety of conceptual errors. It is pathetic for a child to get a feeling of inadequacy because the teacher does not recognize that it is a matter of slower maturity in earlier years. Failure in the beginning of his school career can be disastrous to his concept of himself as an adequate person.

It is important that the preschool have provided certain basic information to the school the child will enter. The preschool teacher knows this and will have prepared the child and his parents. She will have made available the records of the child to the school he will enter. The next step may be into another group within the same school environment or to a school within the immediate community, or even to a school in another community.

As the child takes the next step the teacher, child, and parents feel that he can:

1. Look at himself objectively for his age—determining his strengths and weaknesses.
2. Be self-directing as he makes new friends in the broader social and scientific world.
3. Make decisions after weighing the differing results of his choice.

4. Draw upon his rich background of experiences for thinking, feeling, and learning as he participates in new and broader activities.
5. Communicate with his peers and with adults as he lives in more complex situations.
6. Express his feelings in esthetic experiences.
7. Maintain his health as he grows physically.
8. Take his parents into partnership as he participates in larger activities because he has the security gained from his preschool experiences as his teacher and his parents worked cooperatively for his development.

Suggested Activities

1. Make a list of activities that may be provided to assist the preschool child to become oriented to the new school situations.
2. Plan an interview between parents and teacher in the new school. Collect records that will need to be given to the teacher of the child as he takes the next step. List activities of the preschool teacher to assist parents in preparing for interview.
3. List the type of environment and the plan for instruction that will be faced by the child as he enters the more formal school situations. State what the preschool can do to insure that the child meets these new experiences with trust, confidence, and a feeling of self-worth.

Related Readings

Bassett, G. W. *Innovations in Primary Education: A Study of Recent Developments in Primary Education in England and the U.S.A.* New York: Wiley Interservice, 1970.

Borton, T. *Reach, Touch and Teach.* New York: McGraw-Hill, 1970.

Bronfenbrenner, U. *Two Worlds of Childhood, U.S. & U.S.S.R.* New York: Russell Sage, 1970.

Burton, W. H. *The Guidance of Learning Activities.* New York: Appleton-Century-Crofts, 1962.

"Early Childhood Education Programs," *Education*, 91:2 (1970), pp. 107–109.

Engelmann, S. *Preventing Failure in the Primary Grades.* Chicago: Science Research Associates, 1969.

English, M. D. "Innovation: The Delicate Art in Teacher Education," *Educ. Leadership*, 28:7 (1971), pp. 704–706.

Feelings and Learning. Washington, D.C.: ACEI, 1963.

Frazier, A, ed. *The New Elementary School.* Washington, D.C.: ASCD, 1968.

Glasser, W. *Schools Without Failure.* New York: Harper & Row, 1969.

Hicks, V., et al. *The New Elementary School Curriculum.* New York: Van Nostrand Reinhold Co., 1970.

Hillson, M. *Elementary Education: Current Issues and Research.* New York: The Free Press, 1967.

Ilg, Frances L., and Louise Bates Ames. *School Readiness.* New York: Harper & Row, 1965.

Jenkins, Gladys Gardner, Helen S. Schacter, and W. W. Bauer. *These Are Your Children.* Chicago: Scott, Foresman, 1966.

Lee, J. M. *Elementary Education, Today and Tomorrow.* Boston: Allyn & Bacon, 1966.

Marsh, L. G. *Alongside the Child: Experiences in the English Primary School.* New York: Praeger Publishers, 1970.

Shuster, A. H., and M. E. Ploghoft. *The Emerging Elementary Curriculum: Methods and Procedures.* Columbus, Ohio: Charles E. Merrill Publishers, 1970.

Smart, Mollie S., and R. C. Smart. *Children: Development and Relationships,* 2nd ed. New York: Macmillan, Inc., 1972.

Smith, L. M., and Pat M. Keith. *Anatomy of Education Innovation: An Organizational Analysis of the Elementary School.* New York: John Wiley & Sons, 1971.

Stahl, Dona K., and Patricia Murphy Anzalone. *Individualized Teaching in the Elementary School.* West Nyack, N.Y.: Parker Publishing Co., 1970.

Weber, Evelyn. *Early Childhood Education. Perspectives on Change.* Worthington, Ohio: C. A. Jones Publishing Co., 1970.

"What Are the Sources of Early Childhood Education," *Young Children, 26:1* (1970), pp. 48–50.

Publications of Selected Organizations and Agencies Interested in Educational Programs for Young Children

American Association for Elementary-Kindergarten-Nursery Educators, 1201 16th Street, N.W., Washington, D.C. 20036. Publishes *Educating Children: Early and Middle Years*, four issues, a newsletter (three issues), bulletins, and a yearbook.

American Home Economics Association, 2010 Massachusetts Ave., N.W., Washington, D.C. 20036. Publishes *Journal of Home Economics* monthly.

Association for Childhood Education International, 3615 Wisconsin Avenue, N.W., Washington, D.C. 20016. Publishes *Childhood Education* eight times a year and bulletins, leaflets, and books pertaining to nursery schools, kindergartens, and elementary grades.

Child Study Association of America, 132 East 74th Street, New York, N.Y. 10021. Published *Child Study* quarterly. Ceased publication Summer 1960. Now publishes pamphlets periodically.

Child Welfare League of America, Inc., 44 East 23rd Street, New York, N.Y. 10010. Publishes *Child Welfare* monthly.

Council for Exceptional Children, 1411 Jefferson Davis Highway, Arlington, Va. 22202.

Day Care and Child Development Council of America, Inc., 1401 K Street, N.W., Washington, D.C. 20005.

National Association for the Education of Young Children, 1834 Connecticut Ave., N.W., Washington, D.C. 20009. Publishes *Young Children* (bimonthly), bulletins, and materials for persons concerned with the education of young children.

National Association for Mental Health, 10 Columbus Circle, New York, N.Y. 10019. Publishes *American Theater Wing Community Plays* and pamphlets for parents and teachers.

National Congress of Parents and Teachers, 700 North Rush Street, Chicago, Ill., 60511. Publishes *The National Parent-Teacher* and study guides for parent meetings and study groups.

National Council on Family Relations, 1219 University Avenue Southeast, Minneapolis, Minn. 55414. Publishes *Marriage and Family Living* quarterly.

National Council of Jewish Women, 1 West 47th Street, New York, N.Y. 10036.

Office of Child Development, U.S. Department of Health, Education, and Welfare, Washington, D.C. 20201.

Office of Economic Opportunity, U.S. Department of Health, Education, and Welfare, Washington, D.C. 20500 (1200 19th St., N.W.). Publishes materials and guides for Head Start programs.

Society for Research in Child Development, Inc., University of Chicago Press, Chicago, Ill. 60637. Publishes *Child Development* quarterly, *Child Development Abstracts*, and *Child Development Monographs*.

U.S. Department of Health, Education, and Welfare. Publishes bulletins pertaining to children. List of publications free from U.S. Government Printing Office, Supt. of Documents, Washington, D.C. 20402. Children's Bureau: Publishes *Children* six times a year.

Other Resources

American Public Welfare Association, Inc., 1313 East 60 Street, Chicago, Illinois 60637.

Bank Sheet College of Education, 69 Bank Street, New York, N.Y. 10011.

Black Child Development Educational Center, 1028 Connecticut Avenue, N.W., Suite 306, Washington, D.C. 20036.

ERIC/ECE, Educational Resources Information Center, Early Childhood Education, University of Illinois at Urbana, Champaign, 805 West Pennsylvania Avenue, Urbana, Illinois 61801.

National Advisory Council on the Education of Disadvantaged Children, 1717 H Street, N.W., Washington, D.C. 11003.

National Association of Social Workers, Inc., 2 Park Avenue, New York, N.Y. 12202.

National Committee on Education of Migrant Children, 145 E. 32nd Street, New York, N.Y. 10016.

UNESCO Publications Center, 317 East 34th Street, New York, N.Y. 10016.

United States National Committee for Early Childhood Education, Member of World Organization for Early Childhood Education (OMEP), Margaret Devine, Chairman, 81 Irving Place, New York, N.Y. 10003.

463

Sources for Films
on Early Childhood

It is suggested that contacts be made with media centers at the various state universities, state departments of education, and the National Audio-Visual Center, National Archives and Records Service, General Services Administration, Washington, D.C. 20409. Information regarding films may be secured from these sources.

References

See additional references at end of each chapter.

Articles

ACEI Teacher Education Committee. "Standards for Teachers in Early Childhood Education," *Child. Educ.*, 35:2 (1958), pp. 65–66.

Almy, Millie. "Spontaneous Play: An Avenue for Intellectual Development," *Young Children*, 22:5 (1967), pp. 265–277.

Alpenfels, Ethel S. "Conformity, Censors, Sensitivity," *Child. Educ.*, 41:4 (1964), p. 169.

———. "Foreword—Children at Work," *Child. Educ.*, 37:8 (1961), pp. 364–365.

Alper, Thelma G., H. T. Blane, and Barbara K. Abrams. "Reaction of Middle and Lower Class Children to Finger Paints as a Function of Class Differences in Child-Training Practices," *J. Abnorm. and Soc. Psychol.*, 51:3 (1955), pp. 439–448.

Ames, Louise B. "The Development of the Sense of Time in the Young Child," *J. Genet. Psychol.*, 68:1 (1946), pp. 97–125.

Anderson, J. E. "A Half Century of Learning About Children," *NEA J.*, 42:3 (1953), pp. 139–141.

Avery, Charlotte B. "Social Competence of Pre-School Acoustically Handicapped Children," *Except. Child., 15* (1948), pp. 71–73, 28.

Babitz, M. "Serving Families of the Underprivileged," *Calif. Educ., 11* (1964).

Bain, Katherine. "Commentary: The Physically Abused Child," *Pediatrics, 31*:6 (1963), pp. 895–897.

Barnes, Marcillene. "Skills with Style," *Child. Educ., 37*:6 (1961), pp. 259.

Bean, C. H. "An Unusual Opportunity to Investigate the Psychology of Language," *J. Genet. Psychol., 40*:2 (1932), pp. 181–202.

Berkman, D. "The Myth of Educational Technology," *Educ. Record, 36*:4 (1972), pp. 451–460.

Beyer, Evelyn. "Montessori in the Space Age?" *NEA J., 52*:9 (1963), pp. 35–36.

Bliss, Leora B. "Certification of Teachers in Nursery Schools and Day Care Centers," *Child. Educ., 34*:6 (1958), pp. 275–278.

Brieland, D. "Cultural and Social Change," *Young Children, 20*:4 (1965), pp. 223–229.

Brophy, Alice M. "Children's Centers—Three Decades of Progress," *J. of Nursery Educ., 19*:3 (1964), pp. 173–181.

Brunner, Catherine. "Deprivation—Its Effects, Its Remedies," *Educ. Leadership, 23*:2 (1965), pp. 103–107.

Burtt, Merilyn. "The Effect of a Man Teacher," *Young Children, 21*:2 (1965), pp. 92–98.

Butler, Annie L. "Areas of Recent Research in Early Childhood Education," *Child. Educ., 48*:3 (1971), pp. 143–147.

Caldwell, B. M. "The Rationale of Early Intervention," *Except. Children, 36*:9 (1970), pp. 717–726.

Calvin, A. D., et al. "Studies in Adult Learning Since 1930," *J. Educ. Res., 50*:4 (1956), pp. 273–285.

Caras, R. "Time to Join the World," *Early Years, 2*:9 (1972), pp. 36–37.

Carleton, Charles S. "Head Start or False Start," *Am. Educ., 2*:8 (1965), pp. 20–22.

Carlson, Ruth K. "Emergence of Creative Personality," *Child. Educ., 36*:9 (1960), pp. 402–404.

Carnegie Corporation of New York Quart., 9:2 (1961), pp. 3–4.

Carroll, J. B. "Foreign Languages for Children—What Research Says," *Nat. Elem. Prin., 39*:6 (1960), pp. 12–15.

Carroll, Marian. "Academic Achievement and Adjustment of Underage and Overage Third-graders," *J. Ed. Res., 50*:8 (1963), pp. 415–419.

Costin, Lela B. "Training Nonprofessionals for a Child Welfare Service," *Children, 13*:2 (1968), pp. 63–68.

Darcey, Natalie T. "A Review of the Literature on the Effects of Bilingualism upon the Measurement of Intelligence," *J. Genet. Psychol., 82*:1 (1953), pp. 21–57.

Darwin, C. "Biographical Sketch of an Infant," *Mind, 2* (1877), pp. 285–294

Day, Ella. "The Developement of Language in Twins: I. A Comparison of Twins and Single Children," *Child Develpm., 3*:3 (1932), pp. 179–190.

Denemark, G. W., and W. J. Matson. "Why Teach Children a Foreign Language?" *Nat. Elem. Prin., 39*:6 (1960), pp. 6–11.

Deutsch, M. "Facilitating Development in the Pre-School Child: Social and Psychological Perspectives," *Merrill-Palmer Quart., 10*:3 (1964), pp. 249–263.

"Early Childhood Education Programs," *Educ., 91*:2 (1970), pp. 107–109.

Engbertson, W. C. "Values of Children—How They Are Developed." *Child. Educ., 35*:6 (1961), pp. 259–264.

English, M. D. "Innovation: The Delicate Art in Teacher Education," *Educ. Leadership*, 28:7 (1971), pp. 704–706.

Fantini, M. D. "Public Schools of Choice and the Plurality of Publics," *Educ. Leadership*, 28:6 (1971), pp. 585–591.

Fauls, Lydia B., and W. D. Smith. "Sex-Role Learning of Five Year Olds," *J. Genet. Psychol.*, 89:2 (1956), pp. 105–117.

Fisher, M. F. "Language Patterns of Pre-School Children," *J. Exp. Educ.*, 1:1 (1932), pp. 70–74.

Fite, Mary D., and A. T. Jersild. "Aggressive Behavior in Young Children and Children's Attitudes Toward Aggression," *Genet. Psychol. Monogr.*, 22:2 (1940), pp. 151–319.

Foshay, A. W. "A Modest Proposal," *Educ. Leadership*, 18:8 (1961), pp. 506–516, 528.

Franklin, Adele. "Blocks—A Tool of Learning," *Child. Educ.*, 26:5 (1950), pp. 209–213.

Gates, A. I. and Bond, G. L. "Reading Readiness: A Study of Factors Determining Success and Failure in Beginning Reading," *Teach. Coll. Rec.*, 37:8 (1936), pp. 679–685.

Getzels J. W., and Jackson, P. W. "Giftedness and Creativity," *Newsletter*. Chicago: University of Chicago, November 1960.

Goldschmidt, M. L. "Early Cognitive Development and Preschool Education," *Internat. J. of Early Child. Educ.*, 3:1 (1971), pp. 1–7.

Gorton, H. B., and R. L. Robinson. "For Better Results: A Full Day Kindergarten," *Educ.*, 89:3 (1969), pp. 217–221.

Hall, G. S. "The Contents of Children's Minds," *Pedag. Sem.*, 1:2 (1891), pp. 139–173.

Halliwell, J. W., and Belle W. Stein. "Achievement of Early and Late School Starters," *Elem. English*, 41:6 (1964), pp. 631–639.

Hammond, Sarah Lou, et al. "Good Days for Children," *Child. Educ.*, 36:1 (1959), pp. 4–16.

Hampleman, R. S. "A Study of the Reading Achievement of Early and Late School Starters," *Elem. English*, 36:5 (1959), pp. 331–334.

Harms, E. "The Development of Religious Experience in Children," *Amer. J. Sociol.*, 50:2 (1944), pp. 112–122.

Harrison, M. Lucile. "The Nature and Development of Concepts of Time Among Young Children," *Elem. Sch. J.*, 34:7 (1934), pp. 507–514.

Havighurst, R. J. "Moral Character and Religious Education," *Relig. Educ.*, 51:3 (1956), pp. 163–169.

Havighurst, R. J., Myra Z. Robinson, and Mildred Dorr. "The Development of the Ideal Self in Childhood Adolescence," *J. Educ. Res.*, 40:4 (1946), pp. 241–257.

Headley, Neith. "The Kindergarten Comes of Age," *NEA J.*, 43:3 (1954), pp. 153–154.

Heard, I. M. "Mathematical Concepts and Abilities Possessed by Kindergarten Entrants," *Arithmetic Teacher*, 17:4 (1970), pp. 340–341.

Hendrickson, P. R., and E. P. Torrance. "Some Implications for Art Education from the Minnesota Studies of Creative Thinking," *Creativity in Art Education*. Washington, D.C.: NAEA, 1963, pp. 20–25.

Henson, Elizabeth. "What About Teaching A Second Language to Elementary School Children?" *Child. Educ.*, 34:8 (1958), pp. 367–370.

Hess, R., and D. Easton. "The Role of the Elementary School in Political Socialization," *The School Review*, 70:3 (1962), pp. 265–275.

Hess, R. D., et al., "Parent Involvement in Early Education," *Day Care: Resources for Decisions*, Grotberg, Edith H., ed., Washington, D.C.: Office of Economic Opportunity, (1971), pp. 265–285.

Hicks, J. A. "The Acquisition of Motor Skill in Young Children: A Study of the Effects of Practice in Throwing at a Moving Target," *Child. Develpm., 1*:2 (1930), pp. 379–392.

Hill, D. S. "Personification of Ideals by Urban Children," *J. Soc. Psychol., 1*:2 (1930), pp. 90–105.

Huey, Frances. "Learning Potential of the Young Child," *Educ. Leadership., 23*:2 (1965), pp. 119–120.

Hymes, J. L., Jr. "Montessori," *Educ. Leadership, 23*:2 (1965), pp. 127–131.

Ilgenfritz, M. P. "Mothers on Their Own—Widows and Divorcees," *Marr. and Fam. Liv., 23*:1 (1961), pp. 38–41.

Jersild, A. T., and Sylvia F. Beinstock. "A Study of the Development of Children's Ability to Sing," *J. Educ. Psychol., 25*:10 (1939), pp. 481–503.

Johnson, Marguerite W. "The Effect on the Behavior of Variation in the Amount of Play Equipment," *Child Develpm., 6*:1 (1935), pp. 56–68.

Kagan, H. E. "Teaching Values to Our Children," in *Children and Youth in the 1960's.* Washington, D.C.: White House Conference on Children and Youth, 1960, pp. 57–65.

Kaljo, Maija. "Love, Nature and the Recycling Heap," *Early Years, 2*:9 (1972), pp. 38–39.

Kamerman, Shelia B., A. J. Kahn, and Brenda G. McGowan. "Research and Advocacy," *Children Today, 1*:2 (1972), pp. 35–36.

Katz, Lillian G. "Stop, Look and Listen Before You Condition," *ERIC/ECE Newsletter, 5*:6 (1971), pp. 1–2.

Kean, J. M. "Research—The Impact of Head Start. An Evaluation of the Effects of Head Start on Children's Cognitive and Affective Development," *Child. Educ., 46*:9 (1970), pp. 449–453.

Keister, B. U. "Reading Skills Acquired by Five-Year-Old Children," *Elem. Sch. J., 41*:8 (1941), pp. 587–596.

"Kindergarten: Time to Read," *Washington Monitor*, Supplement to *Education U.S.A.* Washington, D.C.: NSPRA, September 29, 1966.

Klaus, R. A., and Susan W. Gray. "Murfreesboro Preschool Program for Culturally Deprived Children," *Child. Educ., 42*:2 (1965), pp. 92–97.

Klein, Jenny W. "Head Start: Intervention for What?" *Educ. Leadership, 29*:1 (1971), pp. 16–19.

Kohlberg, L. "Early Intervention, A Cognitive Developmental View," *Child Develpm., 39*:4 (1968), pp. 1013–1062.

Kunz, Jean, and Joan E. Moyer. "Comparison of Economically Disadvantaged and Economically Advantaged Kindergarten Children, *J. of Educ. Res., 62*:9 (1969), pp. 372–395.

Leeper, R. R. "A Time for Reevaluation," *Educ. Leadership, 29*:1 (1971), p. 3.

Lemkau, P. V. "A Psychiatrist's View of Housing," *Proceedings of Housing Conference*, Publication 180. Philadelphia: Pennsylvania State University, College of Home Economics. (Copyrighted Paper.)

Lessinger, L. M. "Teachers in the Age of Accountability," *Instructor, 80*:10 (1971), pp. 19–20.

Lipson, Rosella. "A Mobile Preschool," *Young Children, 24*:3 (1969), pp. 154–156.

Loving, A. D. "Intervention for What?" *Educ. Leadership, 29*:1 (1971), p. 7.

McAulay, J. D. "Social Studies in the Primary Grades," *Soc. Educ., 18*:8 (1954), pp. 357–358.

McClentie, J. "Unit of Measure," *Arithmetic Teacher, 13*:7 (1966), pp. 385–286.

McConkie, Gwen W., and Marie M. Hughes. "Quality of Classroom Living Related to Size of Kindergarten Group," *Child. Educ.*, 32:9 (1956), pp. 428–432.

Mackie, Romaine P. "Exceptional Years for Exceptional Children," *Sch. Life*, 40:4 (1958), pp. 8–10.

Mason, G., and Norma J. Prater. "Early Reading and Reading Instruction," *Elem. English*, 43:5 (1966), pp. 483–488.

Mills, W. H., and G. L. McDaniels. "Montessori, Yesterday and Today," *Young Children*, 21:3 (1966), pp. 137–141.

Milner, Esther. "Study of the Relationships Between Reading Readiness in Grade One School Children and Patterns of Parent-Child Interaction," *Child Develpm.*, 22:2 (1951), pp. 95–112.

Montague, D. O. "Arithmetic Concepts of Kindergarten Children in Contrasting Socio-economic Areas," *Elem. Sch. J.*, 64:7 (1964), pp. 393–397.

Morphett, Mabel V., and C. Washburne. "When Should Children Begin to Read?" *Elem. Sch. J.*, 31:7 (1931), pp. 496–503.

Mukerji, Rose. "Roots in Early Childhood for Continuous Learning," *Young Children*, 20:6 (1965), pp. 342–351.

Murchison, C., and S. Langer. "Tiedemann's Observations on the Development of the Mental Faculties of Children," *J. Genet. Psychol.*, 34:2 (1921), pp. 205–230.

Murphy, Lois B. "Multiple Factors in Learning in the Day Care Center," *Child. Educ.*, 45:6 (1969), pp. 311–320.

Mutsfield, H. "Science Experiences Afford Opportunity for Experimentation," *Child. Educ.*, 29:2 (1952), p. 81.

Newgarten, B. L., and K. Weinstein. "The Changing American Grandparents," in *Marr. and Fam. Liv.*, 16:1 (1964).

Noel, Doris I. "A Comparative Study of the Relationship Between the Quality of a Child's Language Usage and the Quality and Types of Language Used in the Home," *J. Educ. Res.*, 47:3 (1953), pp. 161–167.

Oakden, E. C., and M. Sturt. "Development of Knowledge of Time in Children," *Brit. J. Psychol.*, 12:4 (1922), pp. 309–336.

Ojemann, R., and K. Pritchett. "Piaget and the Role of Guided Experience in Human Development," *Perceptual and Motor Skills*, 17 (1963).

Olson, J. L., and R. G. Larson. "An Experimental Curriculum for Culturally Deprived Kindergarten Children," *Educ. Leadership*, 22:7 (1965), pp. 553–558.

Osborn, Keith. "Project Head Start—An Assessment," *Educ. Leadership*, 23 (1965), pp. 98–103.

Palmer, E. L. "Television Instruction and the Preschool Child," *J. of Early Child.*, 4:1 (1972), OMEP, Dublin, Ireland: Irish University Press, pp. 11–17.

Park, G. E., and Clara Burri. "Eye Maturation and Reading Difficulties," *J. Educ. Psychol.*, 34:9 (1943), pp. 535–546.

Parten, M. B. "Social Participation Among Pre-School Children," *J. Abnorm. Soc. Psychol.*, 27:3 (1932), pp. 243–269.

Paulsen, M. G. "Legal Protections Against Child Abuse," *Children*, 13:2 (1966), pp. 43–48.

Peet, Anne. "Why Not Enough Public School Kindergartens?" *Young Children*, 21:2 (1965), pp. 112–116.

Pines, Maya. "How Three Year Olds Teach Themselves to Read and Love It," *Harper's Magazine*, 226:1356 (1963), pp. 58–64.

Pollach, S., and Juliena Gensley. "When Do They Learn Geometry?" *Young Children,* 20:1 (1964), pp. 52–55.

"Project Head Start," *NEA J.*, 54:7 (1965), pp. 58–59.

Raths, J. D. "A Strategy for Developing Values," *Educ. Leadership*, 21:8 (1964), pp. 509–512.

Rea, R. E., and R. E. Reys. "Mathematics Competence of Entering Kindergarteners," *Arithmetic Teacher*, 17:1 (1970), pp. 63–74.

Ross, Irwin. "Head Start Is a Banner Project," *The PTA Magazine*, 60:7 (1965), pp. 20–23.

Russell, D. "Goals for American Education: The Individual Focus," *Educ. Leadership*, 28:6 (1971), pp. 592–594.

Sanger, Marjorie. "Journey in Search of Nursery Education," *J. of Nursery Educ.*, 18:4 (1963), pp. 253–262.

Schlinsog, G. W. "More About Mathematics in the Kindergarten," *Arithmetic Teacher*, 13:8 (1968), pp. 701–705.

Schuler, S. "Before Selecting a Nursery School, Stop, Look and Listen," *Ladies Home J.*, 80:8 (1963), pp. 60–62.

Senn, M. J. "Fads and Facts as the Bases of Child-Care Practices," *Children*, 4:2 (1957), pp. 43–47.

Shane, H. "Social Experiences and Selfhood," *Child. Educ.*, 33:7 (1957), pp. 297–303.

Smith, I. D. "The Effect of Training Procedures upon the Acquisition of Weight," *Child Develpm.*, 39:2 (1968), pp. 515–526.

Smith, Madorah E. "A Study of the Speech of Eight Bilingual Children of the Same Family," *Child Develpm.*, 6:1 (1935), pp. 19–25.

Smith, Mary K. "Measurement of the Size of General English Vocabulary Through the Elementary Grades and High School," *Genet. Psychol. Monogr.*, 24:2 (1941), pp. 311–345.

Smith, Nila B., "Early Reading: Viewpoints," *Child. Educ.*, 42:4 (1965), pp. 229–241.

Spodek, B. "Is Massive Intervention the Answer?" *Educ. Leadership.*, 23:2 (1965), pp. 108–112.

———. "Poverty, Education and the Young Child," *Young Children,* 21:1 (1965), pp. 2–9.

Steiner, A. K. "A Report of School Laws, Early Elementary Education," *Sch. Life*, 39:8 (1957), pp. 1–8.

"Systematic Observation," *J. of Res. and Develpm. in Educ.*, 4:1 (1970), Athens, Georgia: College of Education, University of Georgia.

Taine, H. "On the Acquisition of Language by Children," *Mind*, 2 (1877), pp. 252–259.

Torrance, E. P. "Adventuring in Creativity," *Child. Educ.*, 40:2 (1963), pp. 79–88.

———. "Conditions for Creative Learning," *Child. Educ.*, 39:8 (1963), pp. 367–370.

Van Til, W. "A Question of Values," *Educ. Leadership*, 18:8 (1961), pp. 478–479.

Wallace, Helen M. "Day Care for Handicapped Children," *Young Children*, 21:3 (1966), pp. 151–161.

Wann, K. D. "Children Want to Know," *Child. Educ.*, 37:1 (1960), pp. 8–12.

Ward, S. A. "Components of a Child Advocacy Program," *Children Today*, 1:2 (1972), pp. 38–40.

"What Are the Sources of Early Childhood Education," *Young Children*, 26:1 (1970), pp. 48–50.

Witherspoon, R. L. "Teacher, Know Thyself," *Child. Educ.*, 35:2 (1958), pp. 56–59.

———. "Studying Young Children," *Nursery School Portfolio*, Leaflet 9. Washington, D.C.: ACEI, (1961).

Wohlwile, J. F. "A Study of the Number Concepts by Scalogram Analysis," *J. Genet. Psychol.*, 97 (1960), pp. 345–347.

Wolman, Thelma G. "Preschool Program for Disadvantaged Children—The New Rochelle Story," *Young Children*, 21:2 (1965), pp. 98–111.

Young, F. M. "An Analysis of Certain Variables in a Developmental Study of Language," *Genet. Psychol. Monogr.*, 23:1 (1941), pp. 3–141.

Zirbes, Laura. "What Creative Teaching Means," *Child. Educ.*, 33:2 (1956), pp. 51–54.

Books

ACEI. *Sung Under The Silver Umbrella*. New York: Macmillan, Inc., 1962.

Almy, Millie C. *Children's Experiences Prior to First Grade and Success in Beginning Reading*. New York: Teachers College, Columbia University, 1949.

Anderson, P. S. *Language Skills in Elementary Education*, 2nd ed. New York: Macmillan, Inc., 1972.

Anderson, T. *The Teaching of Foreign Languages in the Elementary School*. Boston: D. C. Heath & Company, 1953.

Andrews, F. E. *Numbers Please*. Boston: Brown, Little, 1961.

Arbuthnot, May Hill. *Children and Books*, 3rd ed. Glenview, Ill.: Scott, Foresman, 1964.

Arbuthnot, May Hill. *Time for Poetry*. Chicago: Scott Foresman, 1951.

ASCD, *Toward Better Teaching*, 1949 Yearbook (ASCD). Washington, D.C.: ASCD, 1949.

Baldwin, Alfred L. *Theories of Child Development*. New York: John Wiley & Sons, Inc., 1968.

Barnett, G. E. "Looking for Spiritual Values: A Summary and Interpretation," in *Spiritual Values in the Elementary School*, 26th Yearbook. Washington, D.C.: NEA, 1947, pp. 243–251.

Bassett, G. W. *Innovations in Primary Education: A Study of Recent Developments in Primary Education in England and the U. S. A*. New York: Wiley Interservice, 1970.

Beadle, Muriel. *A Child's Mind*. Garden City, New York: Doubleday & Co., 1970.

Beatty, Walcott H., ed. *Improving Educational Assessment & An Inventory of Measures of Affective Behavior*. Washington, D.C.: ASCD, NEA, 1969.

Bengtsson, A. *Environmental Planning for Children's Play*. New York: Praeger Publishers, 1970.

Bereiter, C. and S. Englemann. *Teaching Disadvantaged Children in Preschool*. Englewood Cliffs, N. J.: Prentice-Hall, 1966.

Berman, Louise M. *New Priorities in the Curriculum*. Columbus, Ohio: Charles E. Merrill Publishing Co., 1968.

Berson, Minnie P. *Kindergarten, Your Child's Big Step*. New York: E. P. Dutton, 1959.

Beyer, Evelyn, et al., eds. *Montessori in Perspective*. Washington, D.C.: NAEYC, 1971.

Bissell, Joan S. *Implementation of Planned Variation in Head Start*, First Year Report, Review and Summary. Washington, D.C.: OCD, HEW, 1971.

Bloom, B. S. *Stability and Change in Human Characteristics*. New York: John Wiley and Sons, 1964.

Blough, G. O., and J. Schwartz. *Elementary School Science and How to Teach It*. New York: Holt, Rinehart & Winston, 1964.

Boguslawski, Dorothy B. *Guide for Establishing and Operating Day Care Centers for Young Children*. New York: Child Welfare League of America, Inc., 1966.

Borton, T. *Reach, Touch and Teach*. New York: McGraw-Hill, 1970.

Breckenridge, Marion E., and E. Lee Vincent. *Child Development*, 4th ed. Philadelphia: W. B. Saunders, 1960.

Brim, O. G., Jr. *Education for Child Rearing*. New York: Russell Sage Foundation, 1959.

Bronfenbrenner, U. *Two Worlds of Childhood, U.S. & U.S.S.R.* New York: Russell Sage Foundation, 1970.

Brownell, W. A., and G. Henrickson. "How Children Learn Information, Concepts and Generalizations," in *Learning and Instruction*, 49th Yearbook, Part I (NSSE). Chicago, University of Chicago Press, 1950, pp. 92–128.

Bruner, J. S. *On Knowing*. Cambridge, Mass.: Harvard University Press, 1962.

Bruner, J. S. *Toward a Theory of Instruction*. New York: W. W. Norton & Co., Inc., 1968.

Burns, P. C., Betty L. Broman, Alberta L. Lowe. *The Language Arts in Childhood Education*, 2nd ed. Chicago: Rand McNally and Co., 1971.

Burton, W. H. *The Guidance of Learning Activities*. New York: Appleton-Century-Crofts, 1962.

Butler, Annie L. *Current Research in Early Childhood Education: A Compilation and Analysis for Program Planners*. Washington, D.C.: EKNE, 1970.

Cazden, C. B. "The Neglected Situation in Child Language Research and Education," in F. Williams. *Language and Poverty*, Chicago: Markham Publishing Co., 1970, pp. 81–101.

Children in a Changing World. Washington, D.C.: The Golden Anniversary White House Conference on Children and Youth, Inc., 1960.

Chilman, C.S. *Growing Up Poor*. HEW, Welfare Administration, Division of Research, No. 13. Washington, D.C.: U.S. Government Printing Office.

Class, N. E. *Licensing of Child Care Facilities by State Welfare Departments*. HEW, Social and Rehabilitation Service, Children's Bureau, 1968.

Combs, A. W. "A Perceptual View of the Adequate Personality," in *Perceiving, Behaving, Becoming*, 1962 Yearbook. Washington, D.C.: ASCD, 1962, pp. 50–64.

Combs, A. W., Chm. *Perceiving, Behaving, Becoming*, 1962 Yearbook. Washington, D.C. ASCD, 1962.

Comenius, J. A. (Komensky). *The Great Didactic*. 1657.

———. *Orbis Pictus*. 1658.

Commission on the English Curriculum of the National Council of Teachers of English, Dora V. Smith, Ch. *Language Arts for Today's Children*. New York: Appleton-Century-Crofts, 1954.

Compilation of Legislation on Title I Financial Assistance to Local Educational Agencies for The Education of Children of Low Income Families. (Reflecting 1966, 1967, and 1970 Amendments). Washington, D.C.: HEW, July 1971.

Conference Proceedings. Washington, D.C.: Midcentury White House Conference on Children and Youth, 1950.

———. Washington, D.C.: The Golden Anniversary White House Conference on Children and Youth, 1960.

Copeland, R. W. *How Children Learn Mathematics: Teaching Implications of Piaget's Research*. New York: Macmillan, Inc., 1970.

Crary, R. W. *Humanizing The School*. New York: Alfred A. Knopf, 1969.

Curtis, H. A. and Joseph A. Block. *Florida Pre-kindergarten Migrant Compensatory Program: An Evaluation*. Tallahassee, Florida: The Florida State University (1972). Mimeographed.

Dalgliesh, Alice. *First Experiences with Literature.* New York: Charles Scribner's Sons, 1937.

Dattner, R. *Design for Play.* New York: Van Nostrand Reinhold Co., 1969.

Deese, J. "Comments and Conclusions," in U. Bellugi and R. Brown, *The Acquisition of Language, Monogr. Soc. Res. Child Develpm., 29*:1 (1964).

Deutsch, M., and Associates. *The Disadvantaged Child.* New York: Basic Books, 1967.

Dewey, R. E., F. W. Gramlich, and D. Loftsgordon. *Problems of Ethics.* New York: Macmillan, Inc., 1961.

Dittman, Laura, ed. *Early Child Care: The New Perspectives.* New York: Atherton Press, 1968.

Doman, G. *How to Teach Your Baby to Read.* New York: Random House, 1964.

Durkin, Dolores. *Teaching Them to Read.* Boston: Allyn and Bacon, Inc., 1970.

Education for the Gifted. 57th Yearbook, Part II (NSSE). Chicago: University of Chicago Press, 1958, pp. 41–63.

The Educational Policies Commission. *Contemporary Issues in Elementary Education.* Washington, D.C.: NEA, 1960.

Educational Policies Commission. *Moral and Spiritual Values in Public Schools.* Washington, D.C.: NEA and AASA, 1951.

Elyot, Sir Thomas. *The Boke Named the Governour,* 1531. London: J. M. Dent, 1907.

Engelhardt, N. L., N. L. Engelhardt, Jr., and S. Leggett. *Planning Elementary School Buildings.* New York: F. W. Dodge, 1953.

Englemann, S. *Preventing Failure in the Primary Grades.* Chicago: Science Research Associates, 1969.

Flavell, J. H. *The Developmental Psychology of Jean Piaget.* New York: Van Nostrand, 1964.

Focus on Children and Youth. Washington, D.C.: The Golden Anniversary White House Conference on Children and Youth, 1960.

Fraser, Dorothy M. "The Organization of the Elementary School Social Studies Curriculum," *Social Studies in the Elementary School,* 56th Yearbook, Part II (NSSE). Chicago: University of Chicago Press, 1957, pp. 129–162.

Frazier, A., ed. *The New Elementary School.* Washington, D.C.: ASCD, 1969.

Froebel, F. *The Education of Man.* New York: Appleton-Century-Crofts, 1903.

Frost, J. L. ed. *Early Childhood Education Rediscovered.* New York: Holt, Rinehart and Winston, Inc., 1968.

Gabbard, Hazel F. "Status and Trends in Early Childhood Education," in *Those First School Years,* 39th Yearbook. Washington, D.C.: NEA, pp. 219–239.

Galton, F. *Hereditary Genius,* 1869.

Garrison, K. C. *Growth and Development,* 2nd ed. New York: Longmans, Green, 1959.

Garrison, K. C. and Jones, F. R. *The Psychology of Human Development.* Scranton, Pa.: International Textbook Co., 1968.

Gesell, A., et al. *The First Five Years of Life.* New York: Harper & Row, 1940.

Gesell, A., and Frances Ilg. *Child Development.* New York: Harper & Row, 1949.

Gesell, A., Frances Ilg, and G. E. Bullis. *Vision, Its Development in Infant and Child.* New York: Paul B. Hoebner, 1948.

Ginzberg, E., ed. *The Nation's Children,* 3 vols. Washington, D.C.: The Golden Anniversary White House Conference on Children and Youth, 1960.

———, ed. *Children and Youth in the 1960's, Survey Papers.* Washington, D.C.: The Golden Anniversary White House Conference on Children and Youth, 1960.

Glasser, W. *Schools Without Failure*. New York: Harper & Row, 1969.

Goertzel, Mildred G., and V. Goertzel. *Cradles of Eminence*. New York: Little, Brown, 1962; previewed in *New York Herald Tribune*, April 21, 1961.

Goodenough, Florence L. "Anger in Young Children," *Univ. Minn. Inst. Child Welf. Monogr. Ser.*, No. 9, 1931.

———. "Children's Drawings," in *A Handbook of Child Psychology*. Worcester, Mass.: Clark University Press, 1931.

Goodman, Mary Ellen. *Race Awareness in Young Children*, rev. ed. New York: Crowell-Collier, 1964.

Goodykoontz, Bess, Mary Dabney Davis, and Hazel F. Gabbard. "Recent History and Present Status of Education for Young Children," in *Early Childhood Education*, 46th Yearbook, Part II (NSSE). Chicago: University of Chicago Press, 1947, pp. 44–69.

Gordon I. J., ed. *Early Childhood Education*, The 71st Yearbook (NSSE), Part II. Chicago: The University of Chicago Press, 1972.

Gray, Susan, et al. *Before First Grade: The Early Training Project*. New York: Teachers College, Columbia University, 1966.

Green, J. A., ed. *Life and Work of Pestalozzi*. London: W. B. Clive, 1913.

Greene, H. A., and W. T. Petty. *Developing Language Skills in the Elementary School*, 2nd ed. Boston: Allyn and Bacon, 1963.

Gross, R., and Judith Murphy. *Educational Change and Architectural Consequences*. New York: Educational Facilities Laboratories, Inc., 1968.

Grossnickle, F. E., et al. "Instructional Materials for Teaching Arithmetic," in *The Teaching of Arithmetic*, 50th Yearbook, Part II (NSSE). Chicago: University of Chicago Press, 1951, pp. 155–185.

Grotberg, Edith H., ed. *Critical Issues in Research Relating to Disadvantaged Children*. Princeton, N. J.: Educational Testing Service, 1969.

———. *Day Care: Resources for Decisions*. Washington, D.C.: OEO, 1971.

Hall, Mary Anne. *Teaching Reading as a Language Experience*. Columbus, Ohio: Charles E. Merrill Publishing Co., 1970.

Hamlin, Ruth, Rose Mukerji, and Margaret Yonemura. *Schools for Young Disadvantaged Children*. New York: Teachers College Press, Teachers College, Columbia University, 1967.

Harris, D. B. *Children's Drawings as Measures of Intellectual Maturity* (A revision and extention of Goodenough Draw-A-Man Test). New York: Harcourt, Brace, & World, 1963.

Hartley, Ruth E., and R. M. Goldenson. *The Complete Book of Children's Play*. New York: Crowell, 1957.

Hartley, Ruth E., L. K. Frank, and R. M. Goldenson. *New Play Experiences for Children*. New York: Columbia University Press, 1952.

Hartshorne, H., and M. A. May. *Studies in Deceit*. New York: Macmillan, Inc., 1928.

Hartup, W. ed. *The Young Child—Reviews of Research, Vol. II*. Washington, D.C.: NAEYC, 1972.

Hartup, W., and Nancy Smothergill, eds. *The Young Child—Reviews of Research, Vol. I*. Washington, D.C.: NAEYC, 1970.

Hechinger, F. M., ed. *Pre-School Education Today*. Garden City, N.Y.: Doubleday and Co., 1966.

Heimer, Ralph T., and Miriam S. Newman. *The New Mathematics for Parents*. New York: Holt, Rinehart and Winston, 1965.

Heinz, Mamie W. *Growing and Learning at the Kindergarten.* Richmond, Va.: John Knox, 1959.

Hellmuth, J., ed. *Disadvantaged Child: Head Start and Early Intervention.* Seattle, Wash.: Brunner Mazel, Inc., 1968.

Hellmuth, J., ed. *Disadvantaged Child, Vol I.* Seattle, Wash.: Special Child Publications, 1967.

Hendrickson, P. R., and E. P. Torrance. "Some Implications for Art Education from the Minnesota Studies of Creative Thinking," *Creativity in Art Education.* Washington, D.C.: NAEA, 1963, pp. 20–25.

Herrick, V. E., and L. B. Jacobs. *Children and the Language Arts.* Englewood Cliffs, N.J.: Prentice-Hall, 1951.

Herron, R. E., and B. Sutton-Smith. *Child's Play.* New York: John Wiley and Sons, 1971.

Hess, R. D., and Bear, Roberta M., eds. *Early Education.* Chicago: Aldine Publishing Co., 1968.

Hess, R. D. and Croft, Doreen J. *Teachers of Young Children.* Boston: Houghton Mifflin Co., 1972.

Hicks, V. et al. *The New Elementary School Curriculum.* New York: Van Nostrand Reinhold Co., 1970.

Hildreth, Gertrude. *Readiness for School Beginners.* Yonkers, N.Y.: World Book, 1950.

Hilgard, E. *Theories of Learning,* 2nd ed. New York: Appleton-Century-Crofts, 1956.

Hillson, M. *Elementary Education: Current Issues and Research.* New York: Free Press, 1967.

Hoffman, M. L. "Moral Development," in *Charmichael's Manual of Child Psychology.* New York: John Wiley and Sons, 1970, pp. 251–359.

Hollingshead, A. B., and F. C. Redlich. *Social Class and Mental Illness.* New York: John Wiley and Sons, 1958.

Hunt, J. McV. *Intelligence and Experience.* New York: Ronald Press, 1961.

Hurd, G. E. *Primary Enrollment.* Washington, D.C.: HEW 1969.

Hymes, J. L., Jr. *Behavior and Misbehavior.* Englewood Cliffs, N.J.: Prentice-Hall, Inc., 1955.

Hymes, J. L., Jr. *Effective Home-School Relations.* Englewood Cliffs, N.J.: Prentice-Hall, 1953.

Hymes, J. L., Jr. *Teaching the Young Child.* Columbus, Ohio: Charles E. Merrill Co., 1968.

Ilg, Frances L., and Louise Bates Ames. *School Readiness.* New York: Harper & Row, 1965.

Implementing Mathematics Programs in California, A Guide K-8. Menlo Park, Calif.: Pacific Coast Publishers, 1965.

Inhelder, B., and J. Piaget. *The Early Growth of Logic in the Child.* New York: Harper & Row, 1969.

Jarolimek, J. *Social Studies in Elementary Education.* 4th ed. New York: Macmillan, Inc., 1971.

Jefferson, Blanche. *Teaching Art to Children.* Boston: Allyn and Bacon, 1959.

Jenkins, Gladys G., Helen Schacter, and W. W. Bauer. *These Are Your Children,* 2nd ed. Chicago: Scott, Foresman, 1953.

Jersild, A. T. *Child Psychology,* Sixth edition, Englewood Cliffs, N.J.: Prentice Hall, 1968.

Jersild, A. T. *When Teachers Face Themselves.* New York: Teachers College, Columbia University, 1955.

————. *Child Psychology*, 5th ed. Englewood Cliffs, N.J.: Prentice-Hall, 1960.

Jersild, A. T., and Frances B. Holmes. "Children's Fears," *Child Develpm. Monogr.*, No. 20, 1935.

Jersild, A. T., and Sylvia Beinstock. *Development of Rhythm in Young Children*. New York: Bureau of Publications, Teachers College, Columbia University, 1937.

Johnson, O. G., and Bommarito, J. W. *Tests and Measurement in Child Development: A Handbook*. San Francisco: Jossey-Bass, Inc., 1971.

Johnson, W., et al. *Speech Handicapped School Children*. New York: Harper & Row, 1956.

Joint Committee on Health Problems in Education of the NEA and AMA. *Why Health Education?* Chicago: AMA, 1965.

Jones, Mary Alice. *Guiding Children in Christian Growth*. Nashville, Tenn.: Abingdon Press, 1949.

Jowett, B., trans. *Dialogues of Plato,* 2 vols. New York: Random House, 1937.

Kagan, H. E. "Teaching Values to Our Children," *Children and Youth in the 1960's*. Washington, D.C.: White House Conference on Children and Youth, 1960, pp. 57–65.

Kagan, J., and H. Moss. *Birth to Maturity*. New York: John Wiley and Sons, 1962.

Kahl, J. A. *The American Class Structure*. New York: Holt, Rinehart & Winston, 1959.

Kelley, E. C. "The Fully Functioning Self," *Perceiving, Behaving, Becoming*, 1962 Yearbook. Washington, D.C.: ASCD, 1962, pp. 9–20.

Kellog, Rhoda. *What Children Scribble And Why*. San Francisco: San Francisco Golden Gate Nursery, 1955.

Kirk, S. A. *Early Education of Mentally Retarded: An Experimental Study*. Urbana, Ill.: University of Illinois Press, 1958.

Kohl, Herbert R. *The Open Classroom*. New York: A New York Review Book Distributed by Random House, 1969.

Kohn, S. *The Early Learning Center* (Profiles of Significant Schools). New York: Educational Facilities Laboratories, Inc., 1970.

Kolberg, L. "Development of Moral Character and Ideology," in *Review of Child Development Research*, Vol. I. New York: Russell Sage Foundation, 1964, pp. 383–431.

Lacey, Joy M. *Social Studies Concepts of Children in the First Three Grades*. New York: Teachers College, Columbia University, 1932.

Lambert, Hazel M. *Early Childhood Education*. Boston: Allyn & Bacon, 1960.

Lambert, W. E. and O. Klineberg. *Children's Views of Foreign Peoples*. New York: Appleton-Century-Crofts, Inc., 1967.

Landreth, Catherine. *The Psychology of Early Childhood*. New York: Alfred A. Knopf, 1958.

Langdon, Grace, and I. W. Stout. *Teacher-Parent Interviews*. Englewood Cliffs, N.J.: Prentice-Hall, 1954.

Lavetelli, Celia S. *Piaget's Theory Applied to an Early Childhood Curriculum*. Boston: American Science and Engineering, Inc., 1970.

Lease, Ruth G., and Geraldine B. Siks. *Creative Dramatics in Home, School, and Community*. New York: Harper & Row, 1952.

Lee, J. H. *Elementary Education, Today and Tomorrow*. Boston: Allyn & Bacon, 1966.

Lee, J. M., and Dorris M. Lee. *The Child and His Development*. New York: Appleton-Century-Crofts, 1952.

Leeper, R. R., ed. *Creating a Good Environment for Learning*, 1954 Yearbook (ASCD). Washington, D.C.: ASCD, 1954.

Leonard, Edith M., Dorothy D. Vandeman, and Lillian E. Miles. *Counseling with Parents in Early Childhood Education.* New York: Macmillan, Inc., 1954.

Lessinger, L. M. *Every Kid A Winner: Accountability in Education.* New York: Simon & Schuster, 1970.

Locke, John. *An Essay Concerning Human Understanding,* Bk. 2, 1689.

Loeffler, Margaret. *The Prepared Environment.* New York: Trustees of Canady School, 1967.

Low, S., and Pearl G. Spindler, *Child Care Arrangements of Working Mothers in the United States.* Washington, D.C.: HEW and Department of Labor, Children's Bureau, 1968.

Lowenfeld, V., and W. L. Brittain, 5th ed. *Creative and Mental Growth.* New York: Macmillan, Inc., 1970.

Mager, Robert F. *Preparing Instructional Objectives.* Palo Alto, Calif.: Fearon Publishers, 1962.

Malone, Margaret. *Congressional Research Services, A Summary of Selected Proposals Related to Child Care.* Washington, D.C.: Library of Congress, June 24, 1971.

Marks, J. L., C. R. Purdy, and L. B. Kinney. *Teaching Arithmetic for Understanding.* New York: McGraw-Hill Book Co., 1958.

Marsh, L. G. *Alongside the Child: Experiences in the English Primary School.* New York: Praeger Publishers, 1970.

Matterson, E. M. *Play and Playthings for the Preschool Child.* Baltimore, Md.: Penguin Books, 1967.

McCarthy, Dorothea. "Language Development in Children," *Manual of Child Psychology,* ed. L. Carmichael, 2nd ed. New York: John Wiley and Sons, 1954, pp. 492–630.

McFee, June King. *Preparation for Art.* San Francisco: Wadsworth, 1961.

McFee, June King. *Preparation for Art,* 2nd ed. San Francisco: Wadsworth, 1970.

Mead, M., and M. Wolfenstein. *Childhood in Contemporary Cultures.* Chicago: University of Chicago Press, 1955.

Merrill-Palmer School, Sixteenth Report for the Years 1945–47. Detroit: Merrill-Palmer School, 1947.

Merry, Frieda K., and R. V. Merry. *The First Two Decades of Life,* 2nd ed. New York: Harper & Row, 1958.

Miel, Alice, and Peggy Brogan. *More Than Social Studies.* Englewood Cliffs, N.J.: Prentice-Hall, 1957.

Millar, Susanna. *The Psychology of Play.* Baltimore, Md.: Penguin Books, 1968.

Mills, Belen C., ed. *Understanding the Young Child and His Curriculum.* New York: Macmillan, Inc., 1972.

Mills, Belen C., and Mills, R. A., eds. *Designing Instructional Strategies for Young Children.* Dubuque, Iowa: Wm. C. Brown Co., 1972.

Monroe, Marion. *Growing into Reading.* Chicago: Scott, Foresman, 1951.

Monroe, W. S., ed. *Comenius' School of Infancy.* Boston: D. C. Heath, 1908.

Montessori, Maria. *The Montessori Method.* New York: Frederick A. Stokes, 1912.

Moss, Bernice R., W. H. Southworth, and J. L. Reichert, eds. *Health Education,* 5th ed. Washington, D.C.: NEA, 1961.

Munro, T. "Children's Art Abilities: Studies at the Cleveland Museum of Art," E. W. Eisner and D. W. Ecker, *Readings in Art Education.* Waltham, Mass.: Blaisnell Publishing Co., 1966, pp. 163–180.

Murphy, Lois Barclay. *Personality in Young Children*, Vol. II. New York: Basic Books, 1956.

———. *Social Behavior and Child Personality: An Exploratory Study of Some Roots of Sympathy*. New York: Columbia University Press, 1937.

Mussen, Paul H., ed. *Carmichael's Manual of Child Psychology*, Vol's I & II, 3rd ed. New York: John Wiley and Sons, Inc., 1970.

Mussen, P. H., J. J. Conger, and J. Kagen. *Readings in Child Development and Personality*. New York: Harper & Row, 1970.

Navarra, J. G. *The Development of Scientific Concepts in a Young Child*. New York: Teachers College, Columbia University, 1955.

Naylor, Naomi Le B., and Marguerite Bittner. *Curricular Development Program for Preschool Teacher Aides: Final Report*. Edwardsville, Ill.: Southern Illinois University, Center for the Study of Crime, Delinquency, and Correction, 1967.

Nelson, Mary J., and Gladys Tipton. *Music for Early Childhood*. New York: Silver Burdett, 1952.

Nimnicht, G., Oralee McAfee, and J. Meier. *The New Nursery School*. New York: General Learning Corporation, Early Learning Division, 1969.

Nye, F. I., and L. W. Hoffman. *The Employed Mother in America*. Chicago: Rand McNally, 1963.

Nye, R. E., and Vernice T. Nye. *Music in the Elementary School* 3rd ed. Englewood Cliffs, N.J.: Prentice-Hall, Inc., 1970.

Ojeman, R. *A Teaching Program On Human Behavior and Mental Health*. Iowa City: State University of Iowa, 1960.

———. "Social Studies in Light of Knowledge about Children," in *Social Studies in the Elementary School*, 56th Yearbook, Part II (NSSE). Chicago: University of Chicago Press, 1957, pp. 76–119.

Olson, W. C. *Child Development*, 2nd ed. Boston: D.C. Heath, 1959.

Orem, R. C. *A Montessori Handbook*. New York: Capricorn Books, 1966.

Passow, A. H. "Enrichment of Education for the Gifted," *Education for the Gifted*, 57th Yearbook, Part II (NSSE). Chicago: University of Chicago Press, 1958, pp. 198–221.

Penfield, W., and L. Roberts. *Speech and Brain Mechanisms*. Princeton, N.J.: Princeton University Press, 1959.

Pestalozzi, J. H. *How Gertrude Teaches Her Children*, 1898.

Phillips, J. L. *The Origins of Intellect*. San Francisco: W. H. Freeman & Co., 1969.

Piaget, J. *Play, Dreams and Imitation in Childhood*. Trans. Gattengo and Hodgson. New York: W. W. Norton, 1962.

Pitts, Lilla Belle. *The Kindergarten Book*. Boston: Ginn Co., 1949.

Planning and Development of Facilities for Pre-Primary Education, Athens, Ga.: University of Georgia, Bureau of Education Studies and Field Services, 1969.

Prescott, D. A. *The Child in the Educative Process*. New York: McGraw-Hill Book Co., 1957.

Preyer, W. *Die Seele des Kindes*, 2 vols., 1888.

Profiles of Children, White House Conference on Children, 1970. Washington, D.C.: U.S. Government Printing Office, 1970.

Rambusch, Nancy McCormick. *Learning How to Learn—An American Approach to Montessori*. Baltimore, Md.: Helicon Press, 1962.

Rapport, Virginia, and Mary N. S. W. Parker. *Learning Centers—Children on Their Own*. Washington, D.C.: ACEI, 1970.

Rasey, Marie, and J. W. Menge. *What We Learn from Children*. New York: Harper & Row, 1956.

Raths, L. E., M. Harmin, and, S. B. Simon. *Values and Teaching: Working With Values in the Classroom*. Columbus, Ohio: Charles E. Merrill Books, Inc., 1966.

Read, Katherine H. *The Nursery School*. Philadelphia: W. B. Saunders, 1960.

Report to the President, White House Conference on Children, 1970. Washington, D.C.: U.S. Government Printing Office, 1970.

Richardson, Sybil K., and Faith W. Smitter. "The Learner," in *Learning and the Teacher*, 1959 Yearbook (ASCD). Washington, D.C.: NEA, 1959, pp. 27–36.

Roepers, Annemarie. *Preliminary Outline of Life in the Domes*. Bloomfield Hills, Mich.: Roeper City and Country Schools, Inc., August 1969.

Rogers, V. R. *Teaching in the British Primary School*. New York: Macmillan, Inc., 1970.

Rousseau, Jean-Jacques. *Emile*, trans. Barbara Foxley. London: J. M. Dent, 1911.

Ruderman, Florence. *Child Care and Working Mothers*. New York: Child Welfare League of America, Inc., 1968.

Rusk, R. R. *The Doctrines of Great Educators*. London: Macmillan, Inc., 1926.

Russell, D. *Children's Thinking*. Waltham, Mass.: Blaisdell Publishing Company, 1956.

Sawyer, Ruth. *The Way of the Story Teller*. New York: Viking Press, 1962.

Scarfe, N. V. "Play Is Education," *Readings from Childhood Education*. Washington, D.C.: ACEI, 1966, pp. 356–361.

Schramm, L. J., and E. B. Parker. *Television in the Lives of Our Children*. Stanford, Calif.: Stanford University Press, 1961.

Schultz, Beth. "Ecology for the Child," *Environmental Education in the Elementary School*. Washington, D.C.: NSTA, 1972, pp. 14–15.

Schultz, Beth. "Your Town: A Biotic Community with People," *Environmental Education in the Elementary School*. Washington, D.C.: NSTA, 1972, pp. 33–35.

Schuster, A. H., and M. E. Ploghoft. *The Emerging Elementary Curriculum: Methods and Procedures*. Columbus, Ohio, Charles E. Merrill Publishing Co, 1970.

Sears, R., E. Maccoby, and H. Levin. *Patterns of Child Rearing*. Evanston, Ill.: Row, Peterson, 1957.

Sheehy, Emma E. *The Fives and Sixies Go to School*. New York: Holt, Rinehart and Winston, 1954.

Siks, Geraldine, B. *Creative Dramatics, An Art for Children*. New York: Harper & Row, 1958.

Skeel, Dorothy J. *Children of the Street: Teaching in the Inner City*. Pacific Palisades, Calif.:, Goodyear Publishing Co., Inc., 1971.

Skinner, B. F. *Walden Two*. New York: Macmillan, Inc., 1948.

Smart, Mollie S., and Smart, R. C. *Children—Development and Relationships*. 2nd ed. New York: Macmillan, Inc., 1972.

Smith, Dora V. "Growth in Language Power as Related to Child Development," *Teaching Language in the Elementary School*, 43rd Yearbook, Part II (NSSE). Chicago: University of Chicago Press, 1944, pp. 52–97.

Smith, L. M., and Pat M. Keith. *Anatomy of Education Innovation: An Organizational Analysis of the Elementary School*. New York: John Wiley and Sons, Inc., 1971.

Smith, R. B. *Music in the Child's Education*. New York: The Ronald Press, 1970.

Stagner, R. *Psychology of Personality*, 2nd ed. New York: McGraw-Hill Book Co., 1948.

Stahl, Dona K., and Patricia Murphy Anzalone. *Individualized Teaching in the Elementary School*. West Nyack, N.Y.: Parker Publishing Co., 1970.

Stant, Margaret A. *The Young Child: His Activities and Materials*. Englewood Cliffs, N.J.: Prentice-Hall, Inc., 1972.

The States Report on Children and Youth. Washington, D.C.: The Golden Anniversary White House Conference on Children and Youth, 1960.

Stendler, Celia B. *Children of Brasstown*. Urbana, Ill.: University of Illinois Press, 1949.

Stendler, Celia and W. Martin. *Intergroup Education in Kindergarten-Primary Grades*. New York: Macmillan, Inc., 1953.

Stone, L. J., and J. Church. *Childhood and Adolescence*, 2nd ed. New York: Random House, 1968.

Strang, Ruth. *An Introduction to Child Study*. New York: Macmillan, Inc., 1951.

Sully, J. *Studies of Childhood*. New York: Appleton-Century-Crofts, 1895.

Swenson, Esther J. "Arithmetic for Pre-School and Primary-Grade Children," *The Teaching of Arithmetic*, 50th Yearbook, Part II (NSSE). Chicago: University of Chicago Press, 1951, pp. 53–75.

Swenson, Esther J. *Teaching Mathematics to Children*, 2nd ed. New York: Macmillan, Inc., 1973.

Teachers Guide to Education in Early Childhood. Sacramento: California State Department of Educ., 1956.

Thompson, G. G. *Child Psychology: Growth Trends in Psychological Adjustment*. Boston: Houghton Mifflin, 1952.

Thorndike, E. L., et al. *Adult Learning*. New York: Macmillan, Inc., 1928.

Todd, Vivian E. *The Years Before School: Guiding Preschool Children*, 2nd ed. New York: Macmillan, Inc., 1970.

Tonigan, R., et al. *Child Care and Development Centers, Model Neighborhoods, Albuquerque, New Mexico, or Mr. Architect, This Is How We Want Our Centers to Perform*. Albuquerque, New Mexico: University of New Mexico, Institute for Social Research and Development, 1970.

Torrance, E. *Guiding Creative Talent*. New York: Ronald Press, 1960.

Trager, Helen G., and Marian R. Yarrow. *They Learn What They Live: Prejudice in Young Children*. New York: Harper & Row, 1952.

Tryon, Caroline, and J. W. Lilienthal. "Development Tasks: The Concept and Its Importance," *Fostering Mental Health in Our Schools*, 1950 Yearbook. Washington, D.C.: ASCD, 1950.

U.S. Bureau of the Census, *Statistical Abstracts of the United States*. Washington, D.C.: U.S. Government Printing Office, 1962, 1964, 1966.

U.S. Office of Education, Biennial Survey of Education in the U.S. *Statistics of State School Systems, 1949–50*. Washington, D.C.: U.S. Government Printing Office, 1952, Chap. IV.

Van Alstyne, Dorothy. *Play Behavior and Choice of Play Materials of Preschool Children*. Chicago: University of Chicago Press, 1932.

von Marenholz-Bülow, Baroness B. *Reminiscences of Frederick Froebel*, 1877.

Wadsworth, B. J. *Piaget's Theory of Cognitive Development*. New York: David McKay Co., Inc., 1971.

Wann, K. D., Miriam S. Darn, and Elizabeth A. Liddle. *Fostering Intellectual Development in Young Children*. New York: Teachers College, Columbia University, 1962.

Watson, R. I. *Psychology of the Child*. New York: John Wiley and Sons, 1959.

Weber, Evelyn. *Early Childhood Education: Perspectives on Change*. Worthington, Ohio: Charles A. Jones Publishing Co., 1970.

Weikart, D. P., et al. *The Cognitively Oriented Curriculum*. Washington, D.C.: NAEYC (ERIC & NAEYC Publication), 1971.

Wheat, H. G. *How To Teach Arithmetic*. Evanston, Ill.: Row, Peterson, 1961.

Willcockson, Mary, ed. *Social Education of Young Children*. Washington, D.C.: National Council for the Social Studies, 1950.

Williams, F., ed. *Language and Poverty*. Chicago: Markham Publishing Company, 1970.

Wills, Clarice D., and Lucile Lindberg. *Kindergarten for Today's Children*. Chicago: Follett Pub. Co., 1967.

Wills, Clarice D., and W. H. Stegeman. *Living in the Kindergarten*. Chicago: Follett, 1956.

Yamamoto, Kaoru, ed. *The Child and His Image*. Boston: Houghton-Mifflin Co., 1972.

Zaporozhets, A. V. "The Development of Perception in the Preschool Child," in *European Research in Cognitive Development, Monogr. Soc. Res. Child Develpm.*, 30:2 (1965), pp. 83–101.

Pamphlets

A Bibliography of Books for Children. Washington, D.C.: ACEI, 1972.

A Guide: Early Childhood Education in Florida Schools. Bulletin, 76. Tallahassee: Florida State Department of Education, 1969.

Almy, Millie. "New Views on Intellectual Development in Early Childhood Education," *Intellectual Development, Another Look*. Washington, D.C.: ASCD, 1964, pp. 12–25.

AASA. *Open Space Schools*. Washington, D.C.: AASA, 1971.

American Council on Education. *The Function of the Public Schools in Dealing with Religion*. A Report on the Exploratory Study made for the American Council on Education by the Committee on Religion and Education, 1953.

An Invitation to Help Head Start Developmental Programs. Washington, D.C.: Project Head Start, OEO, 1967.

Anderson, J. E. "Principles of Child Development," *Early Education*. Washington, D.C.: NEA, 1956, pp. 14–21.

Austin, Mary C. "Current Reading Practices," *Teaching Young Children to Read* (U.S. Office of Education). Washington, D.C.: U.S. Government Printing Office, 1964, pp. 16–20.

Baker, Katherine Read, "Extending the Indoors Outside," *Housing for Early Childhood Education*. Washington, D.C.: ACEI, 1968, pp. 59–66.

Baker, Katherine Read. *Let's Play Outdoors*. Washington, D.C.: NAEYC, 1966.

Becker, W. C., D. R. Thomas, and D. Carnine. *Reducing Behavior Problems: An Operant Conditioning Guide for Teachers*. Urbana, Ill.: ERIC Clearing House, University of Illinois, 1969.

Berman, Louise M., ed. *Decision Making in Young Children*. College Park, Md.: University of Maryland, 1971.

Berman, Louise M. *Toward New Programs for Young Children*. College Park, Md.: University of Maryland, 1970.

Better Health for Florida's Children (Bull. 4E) Tallahassee: Florida State Department of Education, 1957.

Biber, Barbara. *Young Deprived Children and Their Educational Needs.* Washington, D.C.: ACEI, 1967.

Biber, Barbara et al. *Promoting Cognitive Growth: A Developmental-Interaction Point of View.* Washington, D.C., 1971.

Bureau of Educational Research and Development. *Educating Disadvantaged Children Under Six.* Washington, D.C.: OEO, HEW, U.S. Government Printing Office, 1965.

Bureau of Educ. Res. and Develpm., *Enrollment of 3, 4, and 5 Year Olds in Nursery Schools and Kindergartens.* Washington, D.C.: U.S. Department of Health, Education and Welfare, June 1965, p. 10.

Burgess, Evangeline. *Values in Early Childhood Education.* Washington, D.C.: NEA, 1965.

Cemrel Newsletter. St. Ann, Missouri: CEMREL, 10646 St. Charles Road 63074.

"Child Care and Guidance: A Suggested Post High School *Curriculum.*" Washington, D.C.: OE, HEW, 1967.

Chilman, Catherine. "Child-Rearing and Family Relationship Patterns of the Very Poor," *Welfare in Review.* Washington, D.C.: U.S. Department of Health, Education and Welfare, January 1965.

Coble, Clara. "Teacher-Planner of the Nursery School," *Space Arrangement Beauty in School.* Washington, D.C.: ACEI, 1958, pp. 4-6.

Cohen, M. D., ed. *That All Children May Learn We Must Learn.* (Reprinted). Washington, D.C.: ACEI, 1970.

Combs, A. W. "Personality Theory and Its Implications for Curriculum Development," in *Learning More About Learning.* Washington, D.C.: ASCD, 1959, pp. 5-20.

Council of Chief State School Officers. *Responsibilities of State Department of Education for Nursery School and Kindergarten, A Policy Statement.* Washington, D.C.: NEA, 1961.

Creating with Materials for Work and Play, Leaflet 5. Washington, D.C.: ACEI, 1957.

Crosby, Muriel. "Identifying Oral Language Relationships," *Children and Oral Language.* Washington, D.C.: ASCD, 1964, pp. 3-9.

Cutts, W. G. *Teaching Young Children to Read* (U.S. Office of Education). Washington, D.C.: U.S. Government Printing Office, 1964.

Darney, Elizabeth Doak. *What Does the Nursery Teacher Teach?* Washington, D.C.: NAEYC, 1965.

Davis, Edith A. *The Development of Linguistic Skill in Twins, Singletons With Siblings, and Only Children From Age Five To Ten Years,* Institute Child Welf. Monogr. Series No. 14. Minneapolis: University of Minnesota Press, 1937.

Davis, Mary Dabney. *Nursery Schools, Their Development and Current Practices in the United States* (Bull. No. 9, U.S. Office of Education). Washington, D.C.: U.S. Government Printing Office, 1932.

Davis, R. B. *The Changing Curriculum: Mathematics.* Washington, D.C.: ASCD, 1967.

Dawson, Mildred. *Learning to Listen,* Language Arts Notes, No. 3. Yonkers-on-Hudson, N.Y.: World Book Company.

Day, D. E., and Allen, D. W. "Organization for Individual Work," *Learning Centers: Children on Their Own.* Washington, D.C.: ACEI, 1970, pp. 26-37.

Dean, S. E. *Elementary School Administration and Organization* (Bull. No. 11, U.S. Office of Education). Washington, D.C.: U.S. Government Printing Office, 1960.

Deans, Edwina. *Arithmetic, Children Use It.* Washington, D.C.: ACEI, 1954.

Deutsch, M., et al. *Memorandum on Facilities for Early Childhood Education.* New York: Educational Facilities Laboratories, Inc., 1970.

Dunfee, Maxine. *Elementary Social Studies: A Guide to Current Research*. Washington, D.C.: ASCD, 1970.

"Early Childhood Development: Alternatives for Program Implementation in the States." Denver: Education Commission of the States, 1971.

Educational Facilities Laboratory, Inc. *Schools Without Walls*. New York, 1965.

Educational Policies Commission. *Contemporary Issues in Elementary Education*. Washington, D.C.: NEA, 1960.

Equipment and Supplies. Washington, D.C.: ACEI, 1968.

Evans, Eleanor. "Vents for Children's Feelings," *Discipline*. Washington, D.C.: ACEI, 1957, pp. 25–31.

Experiencing the Language Arts, Bull. No. 34. Tallahassee: Florida State Department of Education, 1948.

Family Economics Review. U.S. Department of Agriculture, ARS 62-5, December 1966.

"Feelings and Learning." Washington, D.C.: ACEI, 1963.

Friedburg, M. P. *Playgrounds of City Children*, Washington, D.C.: ACEI, 1969.

Good and Inexpensive Books for Children. Washington, D.C.: ACEI, 1972.

Goodlad, J. I., M. Frances Klein, and Associates. *Behind the Classroom Door*. Worthington, Ohio: Charles A. Jones Publishing Co., 1970.

Goodlad, J. I., et al. *The Changing School Curriculum*. New York: The Fund for the Advancement of Education, 1966.

A Guide for Organizing and Developing a Kindergarten Program in Florida, Bull. No. 53A, rev. Tallahassee: Florida State Department of Education, 1955.

Haberman, M., and Blanche Persky, eds. *Preliminary Report of the Ad Hoc Joint Committee on the Preparation of Nursery and Kindergarten Teachers*. Washington, D.C.: NEA, National Commission on Teacher Education and Professional Standards., 1969.

Hease, R. W. *Designing the Child Development Center*. Washington, D.C.: Project Head Start Community Action Program. Washington, D.C.: OEO, HEW, 1968.

Hochman, Vivienne. "Kindergarten-Primary Rooms Reflect Interests," *Space Arrangement Beauty in School*. Washington, D.C.: ACEI, 1958, pp. 7–9.

Hoppock, Anne A. *All Children Have Gifts*. Washington, D.C.: ACEI, 1958.

Horowitz, Sandra B. *From Theory to Practice: A Personal Diary of a Teacher of Young Children*. College Park, Md.: University of Maryland, 1971.

Howard, A. E. *Characteristics of Early Childhood Teacher Education*. Washington, D.C.: ACEI, 1967.

Hughes, Marie, and G. I. Sanchez. *Learning a New Language*. Washington, D.C.: ACEI, 1958.

Hymes, J. "They Act Their Age," *Discipline*. Washington, D.C.: ACEI, 1957, pp. 18–25.

Implementing Mathematics Programs in California, A Guide K-8. Menlo Park, Calif., 1965.

Intellectual Development: Another Look. Washington, D.C.: ASCD, NEA, 1964.

Interim Policy Guide for the 4-C Program Pilot Phase. Washington, D.C.: OCD, HEW, 1969.

Jacobs, L. B. "Enjoying Poetry with Children," *Literature with Children*. Washington, D.C.: ACEI, 1972, pp. 32–35.

Jefferson, Ruth E. "Bulletin Boards for Young Children," *Involvement Bulletin Boards*. Washington, D.C.: ACEI, 1970, pp. 57–63.

Jefferson, Ruth E. "Indoor Facilities," *Housing for Early Childhood Education*. Washington, D.C.: ACEI, 1968, pp. 41–52.

Jersild, A. T. and F. V. Markey. "Conflicts Between Preschool Children," *Child Develpm. Monogr.*, No. 21, 1935.

Kritchevsky, Sybil, and Elizabeth Prescott. *Planning Environments for Young Children —Physical Space*. Washington, D.C.: NAEYC, 1969.

Krogman, W. M. "Physical Growth as a Factor in the Behavioral Development of the Child," *New Dimensions in Learning*. Washington, D.C.: ASCD, 1963, pp. 8–23.

Lantz, Beatrice. *Easel Age Scale*. Los Angeles: California Test Bureau, 1955.

Leiserson, Marion Lawrence. *Creating "Loving" Environment for Children*. College Park: University of Maryland, 1971.

Loban, W. *The Language of Elementary School Children*. Champaign, Ill.: NCTE, 1963.

Macdonald, J. "The Open School: Curriculum Concepts," in *Open Education*. Washington, D.C.: NAEYC, 1970, pp. 23–37.

McCartney, Johanna B. "A Good Day for the Twos and Threes," in *Nursery School Portfolio*, Leaflet No. 2. Washington, D.C.: ACEI, 1961.

McFarland, Margaret B. "A Good Day for the Fours," in *Nursery School Portfolio*, Leaflet No. 3. Washington, D.C.: ACEI, 1961.

McKee, P. and J. E. Brzeinski. *The Effectiveness of Teaching Reading in Kindergarten*. Cooperative Research Project No. 5-0371. Denver: Denver Public Schools and the Colorado State Department of Education, 1966.

Montessori in Perspective. National Association for the Education of Young Children, Publication #406, Washington, D.C., 1966.

Moustakas, C. E., and Minnie Berson. *A Directory of Nursery Schools and Child Care Centers in the United States*. Detroit, Mich.: The Merrill-Palmer School, 1951.

Moyer, Joan E. *Bases for World Understanding and Cooperation*. Washington, D.C.: ASCD, NEA, 1970.

National Commission on Teacher Education. *A Manual of Certification Requirements for School Personnel in the United States*. Washington, D.C.: NEA, 1970.

NEA Research Bulletin. Washington, D.C.: NEA, Research Division, Vol. 49, No. 3, October 1971.

New Directions in Mathematics. Washington, D.C.: ACEI, 1965.

Nichols, H., and Lois Williams. *Role-Playing for Children and Teachers*. Washington, D.C.: ACEI, 1960.

Osmon, F. L. *Child Care Centers for Migrant Farm Labor Camps*. San Francisco: Rosenburg Foundation, 1966.

Perez, O. E. *Spanish in Florida Elementary Schools*. Tallahassee: Florida State Department of Education, 1960.

Plan of Action for Children 1953–55. Washington, D.C.: ACEI, 1953.

Prelude to School, An Evaluation of an Inner-City Program. Report No. 3. Washington, D.C.: U.S. Department of Health, HEW, 1968.

Preparing for Employment in Child Care Services in Pensylvania Schools. Harrisburg, Pa.: State Department of Public Instruction, 1968.

Prescott, Elizabeth. *A Pilot Study of Day-Care Centers and Their Clientele*. Washington, D.C.: U.S. Government Printing Office, 1965.

Project Head Start. *Head Start—A Community Action Program*. Washington, D.C.: U.S. Government Printing Office, 1968.

Project Head Start. *Project Head Start, Health Services—A Guide for Project Directors and Health Personnel*. Washington, D.C.: U.S. Government Printing Office, 1969.

Project Head Start Statistical Fact Sheet Fiscal Year 1971. Washington, D.C.: OEO, HEW, 1971.

Research Relating to Children. ERIC Clearing House on Early Childhood Education. Washington, D.C.: Superintendent of Documents. U.S. Government Printing Office, Current.

Robbins, E. L. "Language Development Research," *Interpreting Language Arts Research for the Teacher.* Washington, D.C.: ASCD, 1970, pp. 3–12.

Robinson, Helen F. *Project Child: Evolution of a Curriculum to Heighten Intellectual and Language Development.* New York: Teachers College, Columbia University, 1969.

Schloss, Samuel. *Enrollment of 3-, 4-, and 5-Year Olds in Nursery Schools and Kindergartens.* Washington, D.C.: U.S. Department of Health, Education, and Welfare, 1965.

——. *Nursery-Kindergarten Enrollment of Children Under Six.* Washington, D.C.: U.S. Department of Health, Education, and Welfare, 1965.

Sherer, Lorraine. *How Good Is Our Kindergarten?* Washington, D.C.: ACEI, 1959.

Shoemaker, Rowena. *All in Play.* New York: Play Schools Association, Inc., 1958.

Smith, Madorah E. "An Investigation of the Development of the Sentence and the Extent of Vocabulary in Young Children," *Univ. Iowa Studies Child Welf.,* 3:5 (1926).

Smith, Nila B. "Trends in Beginning Reading Since 1900," in *Teaching Young Children to Read* (U.S. Office of Education). Washington, D.C.: U.S. Government Printing Office, 1964, pp. 5–15.

Specifications for Making Buildings and Facilities Accessible to, and Usable by, the Physically Handicapped. New York: U.S. American Standards Institute, 1961.

Spodek. "Introduction," in *Open Education.* Washington, D.C.: NAEYC, 1970, pp. 5–9.

Stone, Jeanette Galambos. *Play and Playgrounds.* Washington, D.C.: NAEYC, 1970.

Strickland, Ruth G. *The Contribution of Structural Linguistics to the Teaching of Reading, Writing, and Grammar in the Elementary School.* Bloomington: School of Education, Indiana University, 1963.

——. *The Language of Elementary School Children: Its Relationship to the Language of Reading Textbooks and the Quality of Reading of Selected Children.* Bloomington: School of Education, Indiana University, 1962.

Study of Selected Children in Head Start Planned Variations 1969–1970, 3 Case Studies of Children. Washington, D.C.: University of Maryland and OCD, HEW, October 1970.

Sunderlin, Sylvia, ed. *Aides to Teachers and Children.* Washington, D.C.: ACEI, 1967.

——. *Equipment and Supplies Tested and Approved for Preschool Home School.* Washington, D.C.: ACEI, 1967.

——. *Migrant Children: Their Education.* Washington, D.C.: ACEI, 1971.

Swenson, Esther J. *Making Primary Arithmetic Meaningful to Children.* Washington, D.C.: NEA, 1961.

Tanner, Daniel. *Using Behavioral Objectives in the Classroom.* New York: Macmillan, Inc., 1972.

Teacher Job Shortage. NEA Research Bulletin, 49:3, Washington, D.C., NEA, October 1971.

Teaching The Disadvantaged Young Child. Washington, D.C.: NAEYC, 1966.

Templin, Mildred C. *Certain Language Skills in Children,* Institute of Child Welf. Monogr. Series XXVI. Minneapolis: University of Minnesota Press, 1957.

Tentative Guide to Teaching Moral and Spiritual Foundation in American Democracy. Tallahassee: Florida State Department of Education, 1956.

Thompson, E. E., and A. E. Hamalainen. *Foreign Language Teaching in Elementary Schools.* Washington, D.C.: ASCD, 1958.

The Threshold Program and Materials for Early Learning Centers. Chicago: CCM School Materials, Inc., 1969.

U.S. Bureau of the Census. *Population Characteristics,* Series p-20, No. 156. Washington, D.C.: U.S. Government Printing Office, Dec., 1966.

U.S. Department of Labor, Women's Bureau, *Who Are the Working Mothers?* Leaflet No. 37. Washington, D.C.: U.S. Government Printing Office, April 1965.

Volunteers in the Child Development Program. Washington, D.C.: Project Head Start, OEO, 1968.

Weikart, D. P. *The Cognitively Oriented Curriculum.* Washington, D.C.: NAEYC, 1971.

Williams, H. M. *The Retarded Child Goes to School,* U.S. Dept. of Health, Education and Welfare, Pamphlet No. 123, Washington, D.C., 1960.

Witherspoon, R. L. "Studying Young Children," *Nursery School Portfolio,* Leaflet No. 9. Washington, D.C.: ACEI, 1961.

Unpublished Materials

Bliss, Leora B. "A Survey of State Regulations Relating to Certification of Teachers in Nursery Schools and Day Care Centers." Unpublished Master's Thesis, Oregon State College, 1957.

Blough, G. O. "Content and Process in Kindergarten," Address, New England Kindergarten Conference, November 1966.

Florida Council on Elementary Education. "A Study of the Optimum Entrance Age in Florida Schools." Committee Six, Tallahassee, 1957 (Mimeographed).

Forbes, Marcia Boyer. "Parental Selection of Schools for Pre-School Children." Unpublished Master's Thesis, Florida State University, 1960.

Gabbard, Dr. Hazel. Address, reproduced in *Good Schools for Children Under Six in Florida,* Florida State University, Tallahassee, 1955, pp. 29–32.

Godshall, Tricia. *Discover Cooking with Preschoolers.* Coral Gables, Fla.: Project Florida Head Start, University of Miami, no date (Mimeographed).

Lacayo, Maria. "Organizing a Foreign Language Program in a County." Address, National Convention of the American Association of Spanish and Portuguese, Chicago, December 30, 1961.

McKee, P., and J. E. Brezeinski. "The Effectiveness of Teaching Reading in the Kindergarten," *Cooperative Research Project No. 5-0371,* The Denver Public Schools and The Colorado State Department of Educ., Denver, 1966 (Mimeographed).

Pearson, LaMattice. "Reaction of Teachers and Parents to the Letter-Summary Method Used for Reporting Parent-Teacher Conferences at the Florida State University Nursery School." Unpublished Seminar Study, The Florida State University Institute of Human Development, Tallahassee, 1956.

The Preparation and Status of Preschool Teachers. Oslo, Norway: OMEP, July 1966 (Mimeographed).

Rapp, Don. "Noise in the Nursery School," an unpublished paper, Human Development Institute, Florida State University, 1966.

Recommendations of Study Groups at National Day Care Conference, Washington, D.C., November 18, 1960 (Mimeographed).

Rhodes, Frances. *A Study of the Effects of Various Types of Rest Periods in a Morning Kindergarten on the Behavior Characteristics of Five Year Olds.* Unpublished Graduate Paper, Florida State University, Tallahassee, 1954.

Shull, C. N. "A Study of Children's Vocal Literature Written by Selected Distinguished Composers." Unpublished Dissertation, Florida State University, Tallahassee, June 1961.

Some Suggestions for the Development of Sensory and Language Skills at the Kindergarten and Primary Level. Rockville, Md.: Montgomery County Public Schools, 1970 (Mimeographed).

Wakefield, Carolyn S. *Evaluation of Packaged Materials for Young Children.* Unpublished Graduate Paper, University of Maryland, College Park, 1971.

Index

489